The Cure FAQ

The Cure FAQ

All That's Left to Know About the Most Heartbreakingly Excellent Rock Band the World Has Ever Known

Christian Gerard

Guilford, Connecticut

Backbeat Books
An imprint of Globe Pequot, the trade division of
The Rowman & Littlefield Publishing Group, Inc.
4501 Forbes Blvd., Ste. 200
Lanham, MD 20706
www.rowman.com

Distributed by NATIONAL BOOK NETWORK

Copyright © 2021 by Christian Gerard

The FAQ series was conceived by Robert Rodriguez and developed with Stuart Shea.

Book design by Snow Creative Services

All rights reserved. No part of this book may be reproduced in any form or by any electronic or mechanical means, including information storage and retrieval systems, without written permission from the publisher, except by a reviewer who may quote passages in a review.

British Library Cataloguing in Publication Information available

Library of Congress Cataloging-in-Publication Data
Names: Gerard, Christian (Music journalist) author.
Title: The Cure FAQ : all that's left to know about the most heartbreakingly excellent rock band the world has ever known / Christian Gerard.
Description: Lanham : Backbeat, 2020. | Series: FAQ | Includes bibliographical references and index.
Identifiers: LCCN 2020003410 (print) | LCCN 2020003411 (ebook) | ISBN 9781617137075 (paperback) | ISBN 9781493053988 (epub)
Subjects: LCSH: Cure (Musical group) | Rock music—England—History and criticism. | Post-punk music—England—History and criticism. | Gothic rock music—England—History and criticism.
Classification: LCC ML421.C87 G47 2020 (print) | LCC ML421.C87 (ebook) | DDC 782.42166092/2 [B]—dc23
LC record available at https://lccn.loc.gov/2020003410
LC ebook record available at https://lccn.loc.gov/2020003411

♾™ The paper used in this publication meets the minimum requirements of American National Standard for Information Sciences—Permanence of Paper for Printed Library Materials, ANSI/NISO Z39.48-1992

To my beloved Mitchel Scot Judkins... you left us far too soon. I miss you more every day. I will never let go of you in my heart. Transformer man, my Gemini. I know you are at peace, and we shall be together. Love forever.

To my mother Linda, the kindest person I've ever known. Her love and support have meant everything. To my late father Sam, whose faith in me never wavered even when mine was gone completely.

Contents

Foreword: Wind on My Face, Sound in My Ears *by Mark Saunders* ix
Acknowledgments xv
Introduction: O Death ... Rock Me 1

1. Sordid Details Following: Robert Smith 9
2. So Close to Something Better Left Unknown: The Formative Years 19
3. Radio-Friendly Unit Shifters: Chris Parry and Fiction Records 27
4. Degenerate the Faithful: "Killing an Arab" 33
5. You Would Cry Too: *Three Imaginary Boys* 39
6. Ticking Away the Moments: *Seventeen Seconds* 53
7. Thunder in Our Hearts: Simon Gallup 63
8. The Ghosts of My Life: *Faith* 71
9. Bereft in Deathly Bloom: The Cure in Goth 83
10. Sex Is Violent: *Pornography* 91
11. Once Upon a Time in a Land Called Fantasy: The Pop Singles 101
12. Pictures Came and Broke Your Heart: The Cure in Video 111
13. Twisted Under Sideways Down: The Glove's *Blue Sunshine* 125
14. A Siren Singing You to Shipwreck: Robert Smith as a Banshee 133
15. Feed Your Head: *The Top* 139
16. Lost in Motion, Locked Together: The Extended Cure 149
17. Never Quite as It Seems: *The Head on the Door* 159
18. Hold on to These Moments as They Pass: The Cure Compiled 171
19. Started Out Down a Dirty Road: The Cure in Concert, Part 1 (1976–1986) 181
20. There's Fever in the Funk House, Now: *Kiss Me, Kiss Me, Kiss Me* 193
21. What You Had and What You Lost: *Disintegration* 205
22. Playing That Organ Must Count for Something: Laurence Tolhurst 219
23. Feel Like Swirling and Dancin': *Mixed Up, Torn Down,* and the Remixes 231
24. I Will Rise ... and You'll See Me Return: *Wish* 239
25. Reach Out and Touch the Flame: The Cure's Live Albums and DVDs 253
26. The Rhythm Has Control: The Drummers 263
27. Believe Me, I'm Going to Be Big: The Cure in Popular Culture 269
28. We've All Gone Crazy Lately: *Wild Mood Swings* 281

29	The Good Old Days May Not Return: The Cure in Concert, Part 2 (1987–1999)	295
30	Hello Darkness, My Old Friend: *Bloodflowers*	305
31	This and That, These and Those: The Cure's Hidden Gems	317
32	Just When You Think You've Got It Down: *The Cure*	327
33	Seemed So Very Real: *4:13 Dream*	337
34	I Guess I'll Know When I Get There: The Cure in Concert, Part 3 (2000–2019)	347
35	They Shine for You, They Burn for All to See: The Cure's Legacy	359

Selected Bibliography 369
Selected Index 373

Foreword: Wind on My Face, Sound in My Ears

by Mark Saunders

First, I have to admit to being late in discovering the Cure. I know, it's shocking. I'm sorry! But if it's any consolation, my first introduction to the band was pretty excellent!

In 1984, I got my first job as an assistant engineer (which is English for "tea boy"!) in West Side Studios in West London—owned by the successful production duo of Clive Langer and Alan Winstanley (Madness, Dexy's Midnight Runners, Teardrop Explodes, Elvis Costello and later on Bush). About a year later, the studio was booked for a day by Fiction Records, The Cure's record label, for a remix of The Cure's perfect pop song "Boys Don't Cry."

At the start of the session, legendary Cure producer Dave Allen handed me a tape box containing the precious twenty-four-track master of "Boys Don't Cry" and asked me to load it up on the tape machine. On opening the box I was met with a strong musty smell and saw that the tape appeared to be discolored and stained with mold. I turned around, with no doubt a shocked expression, to Dave, who said, "I know! It has supposedly been professionally cleaned!" The studio tech guy was very skeptical about playing this nasty-looking tape on his treasured Studer A800 tape machine, but he conceded, being as it belonged to the Cure.

After threading the tape on the machine, I tentatively pressed "play" and expected the sound to be anything but pristine—but to the surprise of all present, "Boys Don't Cry" popped out of the speakers, sounding none the worse for wear and eager to be remixed. It sounded amazing—especially those iconic clean rhythm guitars!

The reason for the tape's precarious state turned out to be a leaky washing machine in Chris Parry's basement. Chris was the somewhat relaxed boss of Fiction Records and the man who signed the Cure and helped them toward goth stardom.

Chris had great musical taste because he also signed Siouxsie and the Banshees and the Jam to Polydor Records before signing the Cure to Fiction after Polydor didn't share his enthusiasm for the young Robert Smith et al. Chris had apparently thought that keeping some of the band's precious multitrack tapes in the basement near his washing machine was just fine.

After the "Boys Don't Cry" remix, my next interaction with the Cure happened a couple years later when I'd graduated from making the tea to actually making records. In 1986, I'd worked with producer Dave Allen at West Side Studios as an engineer on three tracks for a newly signed band to Geffen Records (home to Guns N' Roses, Mötley Crüe, and Aerosmith). The Chameleons, from Manchester, were flown to Antigua to sign a massive deal with Geffen, who had great expectations for the band to be "the next U2." This they might have been, except they broke up before their first album for Geffen, *Strange Times*, got released!

Unfortunately (or fortunately in hindsight), in 1985, Dave Allen had persuaded me to leave West Side Studios to go freelance so I could engineer the Chameleons for him. It was a bit early in my engineering career to be waltzing off into the more precarious world of freelance engineering. At that time, I didn't have a big discography of hits that I'd worked on under my belt. So, very kindly, Dave asked the nice folks at Fiction if they could help me find some work, as I'd stuck my neck out on the line to do the Chameleons album with him. Fiction was already managing Dave as a producer, finding him other work in between Cure projects.

Chris Parry was yachting around the world at this point and would be for a couple more years, so it was a long time before I finally got to meet him. In the meantime, Fiction found me some cool work, and my career in the more pop/electronic field was flourishing. When Chris arrived back on dry land, I'd just finished Neneh Cherry's *Raw Like Sushi* album, and her biggest hit, "Buffalo Stance," had done very nicely in the charts—and it was my first coproduction.

When I met with Chris Parry for the first time, he'd just heard the finished Neneh Cherry album and liked it a lot—so much so that he managed to snag a share of the publishing on it! Chris said, "I've got to get you to meet Robert—maybe you guys could work together on something." This sounded like a pretty great idea to me!

My first meeting with Robert Smith was a little strange and intimidating to be honest. I seem to remember Robert sitting at ninety degrees to me and barely making eye contact. He talked mainly through Chris rather than directly to me. As weird as it was, the idea of my doing a radio-friendly mix of "Lullaby" came out of that first meeting.

Working on "Lullaby" was a big moment for me. Like the rest of *Disintegration*, it was beautifully recorded by Dave Allen and sonically gorgeous. I was nervous because I worked on the mix alone for a long time, and Robert came in to listen only at the end. When Robert came in, he was completely different than he had been at our first meeting—he was relaxed and perfectly communicative. He liked the mix, and I don't remember any drastic changes apart from his vocal levels. Robert loves his vocals to be loud!

I also made the extended version of "Lullaby" that would later appear on *Mixed Up* during the same studio session. When Robert listened to it for the first time, I was tense because I'd added a few little bubbly synthesizer lines, and I wasn't sure if this crossed some kind of delicate mixer/artist boundary. Would my trivial musical offerings be accepted or immediately trashed with a warning never to pollute a work of perfection that obviously needed not another note? It was a huge relief to see Robert's eyebrows lift, followed by a nod of approval my way at the moment my first synthesizer part crossed the tape's play head in the mix.

Mixing the single release of "Lovesong" was special for me. I remember Chris Parry calling me, saying that he wanted me to work on a more radio-friendly version of "Lovesong," but the sticky part was that the Cure was on tour, and he wanted Robert to check the mix before we called it a wrap. Fortunately, this meant we'd have to go to Paris because that was the only place the Cure would play for two nights on the tour, and Chris figured we might need two days to work on the song. The Cure was playing two sold-out nights at the Palais Omnisport de Paris-Bercy: about 16,000 people per night. They were huge in France at the time. and I was really excited at the prospect of getting to one of those gigs.

I forget the name of the studio in Paris, but it was a concrete underground bunker in the Pigalle district, the seedy red-light area of the city. The mix initially went pretty swiftly, but in the early evening when it was time to lay the mix to the half-inch tape machine and call it a day, the SSL mixing console started making awful thunder-like noises. We couldn't lay down the mix without weird rumbling noises ruining it.

When I asked if we could get a maintenance engineer ASAP, the French assistant, in typical French recording studio style, shrugged his shoulders and said, "I am very sorry, he is skiing, he always skis the whole of March." This wasn't what I wanted to hear. In London, a decent studio would almost always have a maintenance guy on duty or on call, especially if the client was someone as big as the Cure.

We resorted to laying down the mix to the half-inch until we'd hear the thunder, then wait for the noise to go away, and then lay down the next section until the next bout of thunder and so on. I then had to edit the pieces together to create the full-length mix. This was frustrating, as the mixing desk noises were getting more frequent, and I was quite expecting that it would die completely at any moment.

Finally, we had the whole master mix edited together, so Chris Parry and I jumped into a cab and headed to Bercy, arriving just in time to hear Robert yell, "Goodnight Paris!" and see the band wave and leave the stage for the night!

For my remixes of "A Forest," "The Walk," and "Let's Go to Bed" for the *Mixed Up* sessions, I got to play along, add parts galore, and manipulate and twist the original parts as much as I wanted, the ultimate creative license. Of course, Robert is the one who decides a mix's fate: to be used on the album or ditched. These remixes were immense fun, especially "A Forest," my favorite of all the Cure's songs.

Although most of my work with the Cure has been mixing or remixing, I recorded two songs with them from scratch: "Harold and Joe" and "Never Enough." They needed a new song for the *Mixed Up* album, and Robert booked a few days at a studio in Surrey whose name I can't recall. As I walked into the studio on the first day, I saw the longtime Cure roadie Perry Bamonte standing at a keyboard with a pair of headphones on, and he gave me a nervous little wave. I was informed that Robert had just fired Roger O'Donnell and had given Perry the promotion from roadie to keyboard player in the Cure—quite the step up! Perry was frantically learning the keyboard parts for an upcoming tour!

Robert told me that he wanted an electronic feel for the new song, so it ended up just the two of us in the control room working on what would become "Harold and Joe." Whenever we took a break to eat or I left the control room, I wasn't getting very good vibes from the band. I soon realized they were getting bored and pissed off that they weren't part of the recording process. Eventually, Simon, Porl, and Boris stormed into the live room and started jamming together while occasionally glaring at me through the glass—like it was my idea to go electronic!

In the live room, there was one microphone set up for Robert to sing into, a beautiful vintage Neumann U47. When Robert stepped out of the room to use the bathroom, I opened the channel on the mixing desk into which this U47 was plugged to hear what the rest of the band was playing. I was blown away— it sounded tough and understandably full of angst, but it was really exciting! When he reappeared, I said, "Robert, you have to hear this!" And a few seconds later, Robert was in the live room working on what would be "Never Enough." It all happened really fast. My assistant miked up the drums, bass, and guitar as the band worked out the song. In a very short space of time, they were ready to record the backing track.

When I mixed "Never Enough" at Master Rock studios in West London, I'd just got my first computer that could record audio onto a hard drive. It was the first piece of software that Digidesign (the makers of the industry-standard Pro Tools digital audio workstation) ever released, called Soundtools. It could only record two channels of audio, so it was quite limited, but it was brilliant for editing mixes and remixes.

No longer did I have to splice pieces of magnetic tape together with a piece of sticky tape. With magnetic tape, if an edit didn't work, I'd have to pick the sticky tape off with my fingernail, put in the piece of tape I took out, splice it all back together again, and start over. Now I could hit the "undo" button! For "Never Enough," I looped the opening lick of Porl's guitar riff because I think Porl played it in that particularly groovy way only once, and I wanted to hear it again and again. Without my new piece of software, this would have been much trickier.

When I went to see the Cure at a gig not long after that mix session, Porl came bounding up to me backstage to profusely thank me for the mix on "Never Enough." He said, "I've never been so heavily featured on a Cure song before!"

I recently saw the Cure headline a 2018 British Summertime Festival gig at Hyde Park in front of 50,000 people on a scorching hot day in July. As good as the other bands were, including Interpol, Editors, and Goldfrapp, it was amazing to me at what a higher level the Cure operated on that day. Forty years to the day from the band's first-ever gig, and they sounded incredibly youthful, urgent, intense, and energetic with Robert's voice sounding as good as it ever had. They played for more than two hours, and I was in awe by how many in the crowd could sing along with nearly every word to almost every song.

There's no doubting the brilliance of the Cure and Robert's genius songwriting, but it has always struck me as bizarre that Robert, the ultimate king of goth, could get away with flitting between releasing some of darkest riff-laden, not-for-the-fainthearted-listener works to writing some of the most fantastic, feel-good, soppy, romantic love songs ever!

Imagine you've discovered the Cure in the early days, and by the time *Pornography* comes out, you are fully gothed up. It takes hours of makeup and wardrobe work before you can ever leave the house, which, of course, would only be under the cover of darkness. Then skip ahead a year, and you rush to the record store, possibly even risking daylight exposure, to pick up your copy of *Japanese Whispers*.

You get home, and with trembling black-nailed hands, you place the record on the deck and put the needle down, only to be greeted by the positively chipper "Let's Go to Bed!" By the time you get to "The Lovecats," you're in a complete pop-induced tizzy. I'd have loved to have been a fly on the wall at that moment! You'd think there would have been a goth revolution with Cure records being smashed and burned in the streets.

But luckily for us all, Robert, God bless him, somehow brilliantly pulled off this musical dichotomy.

Mark Saunders is a veteran British producer/mixer/engineer with more than thirty years of music industry experience. In addition to his work with the Cure, Saunders has engineered and produced work for high-profile artists including David Bowie, Erasure, Neneh Cherry, Cyndi Lauper, a-ha, David Byrne, Tricky, Alison Moyet, Shiny Toy Guns, Lisa Stansfield, the Farm, and many others. Read more about Mark Saunders's career at www.marksaunders.com.

Acknowledgments

The research and writing of *The Cure FAQ* followed the tracks of an emotional roller coaster beyond imagining. This project, written mostly in Virginia, West Virginia, and Minnesota, helped keep me sane and provided an important sense of purpose during the three most tumultuous and difficult years of my life.

Love and thanks to my mother Linda and to my late father Sam for their guidance and unwavering support. They instilled in me a love for rock 'n' roll from a very young age, thanks in large part to their truly excellent record collection, but also an ambition and belief that I could accomplish anything I wanted. My mom is the greatest. She has stood by me through times great and terrible, always with a gentle smile and unyielding determination. Dad didn't think much of the Cure when I was a teenager. Whenever I played them, he turned a bit surly. His attitude changed when I told him about this project. He was incredibly proud, and it pains me that he isn't around to see the finished product in bookstores.

Special thanks to my beloved sister Gina for dragging me and this book across the finish line. This book would have died a thousand deaths, each more gruesome than the last, if not for her unfailing love and support. She kept me afloat in my life's darkest days, and I'll never forget it.

Love and thanks to Mitchel Scot Judkins, a kind and gentle soul, a kindred spirit and an invaluable boost during the manuscript's final stages. He was almost feverish in his determination to help me finish this book, and he did so in numerous ways. Mitchel knew more than anyone how important this project was for me, and that seeing it through would be an enormous positive victory after a year of nothing but one bitter defeat after another in various aspects of life. On November 26, 2019, I received an e-mail from the publisher basically telling me that "you can relax now, we'll take it from here." Mitchel died less than a week later, during the early morning hours of Monday, December 29, 2019. He was only 29. I thought I knew what pain was, but I never truly did until that morning, and it hasn't abated.

I am profoundly grateful for the time Mitchel and I had together, as short as it was, and for his eagerness to help with this project. When we first met, he knew nothing at all about the Cure, but that soon changed as he was exposed to more and more of the Cure's deep catalog, and he grew to admire them. "Pictures of You" was his favorite, which makes it very bittersweet for me to hear today. Some others he particularly liked were "Just Like Heaven," "A Strange Day," "In Between Days," "I Don't Know What's Going On," "Jupiter Crash," "Wrong Number," and "Where the Birds Always Sing."

That frantic final night, when the manuscript was finally being turned in, our respective anxieties fed off each other, bouncing and echoing even higher, until we were positively manic. But I finally hit the "send" button, we hugged, then let off some steam and celebrated. Later that morning, I noticed he had left a message in a blank word document and left it open on my computer monitor: "You are the best fella, I love my guy. Congrats!!"

I am grateful to Mitchel's family for their gracious support and kindness in the midst of such profound sorrow. To his mom Michelle, his dad Eric, Granny Vonnie, Grandad Ross, and his Aunt Sarah, in particular: it's easy to understand why Mitchel became such an extraordinary young man, such a light in the darkness.

I am so grateful for the trust that Robert Lecker of the Lecker Agency placed in me. Special thanks to Bernadette Malavarca for shepherding this project through its early stages. Enormous thanks to Rowman & Littlefield for their faith in me. John Cerullo, Carol Flannery, Barbara Claire, and Jessica Thwaite—thank you so much for your understanding, encouragement and support, patience beyond what anyone would have the right to expect, and all your hard work on this project.

Eternal gratitude to Sarah Zupko and Karen Zarker, the outstanding editors at *PopMatters*. Thank you to Todd Franson, the brilliant photographer who pointed the way on this journey. Thanks to all at *Metro Weekly* and the *Washington Blade*.

To Malcolm: so many things that we never will undo; I know you're sorry, I'm sorry too.

Special thanks Mark Saunders, a supremely talented producer, a kind and generous person, and a huge source of inspiration and support during this project. Thanks to Steve Lyon, another terrific producer and a wealth of information. Thanks to Ignasi, owner of the essential site www.thecurerecords.com, who worked very hard under tight time constraints to help with this project. The book's subtitle, "The Cure FAQ: All That's Left to Know About the Most Heartbreakingly Excellent Rock Band the World Has Ever Known," is borrowed from Trent Reznor's speech inducting the Cure into the Rock and Roll Hall of Fame.

Thanks to my friends and extended family in Virginia, West Virginia, North Carolina, the Twin Cities, the D.C. metro area, and elsewhere. Special thanks to Dan Jackson, Dottie Lanham, Leigh Ann McCulty, Jennifer Roberts, James Clarke, Rich Nagle, Heather Zaug, Jim Knaack, Tracie Dorfman, Travis Markley, Andy Tinker, Jesse Thomas, Dante Sapp, Omar Martinez, Juan Felipe Rincon, Johnny Indovina, Andi Harriman, Inez Rogatsky, Darren Guy, Benjamin Londa, José Ramón García Alvarez, and Regina Kalisz.

Special thanks to Jamie Conover Stewart for her tremendous encouragement, enthusiasm, and assistance. Thanks to Carlos & James, Sir Robert Kennedy, Shayla & P.J., Mein, Matthew Flores, Patricia Harmon, Christopher McKay, Darrin Reffitt, Chris Lacy, Ian Lekus, Melissa Billings, Sarah Richardson, Mark Stevens, Edward Colavito, Cle Acklin, Arusha Baker, Ray Garcia, Jaysen Kralovetz, John Sanders, the Crawley Museum, Tony Kimsal, Janet Holstrom, Michael Geddes, Jim Rocks, Sandy Bain, Richard C. Materna, Kieran Daly, Cary Perry, Terry Kelly, Becky Taylor Terry, and Fabian Doty. Thanks to Mobius Records in Fairfax, Virginia; Electric Fetus in Minneapolis; and Down in the Valley in Golden Valley, Minnesota.

Thanks to Mrs. Kathleen Lohmann for being the first outside of my parents to encourage me to write.

Most of all, thanks to Robert Smith, Simon Gallup, Roger O'Donnell, Pearl Thompson, Boris Williams, Jason Cooper, Laurence Tolhurst, Perry Bamonte, Michael Dempsey, Phil Thornalley, Matthieu Hartley, Reeves Gabrels, the late Andy Anderson, Chris Parry, and everyone else who has been a part of the Cure family over the years. Thanks to all the fans who've been supporting the Cure's strange musical fantasy for four decades. You made this all possible.

Introduction: O Death . . . Rock Me

O death! rock me asleep
Bring me on quiet rest;
Yet pass my guiltless ghost
Out of my careful breast:
Toll on the passing bell,
Ring out the doleful knell,
Let the sound of my death tell,
For I must die.
There is no remedy,
For now I die.

—Anne Boleyn, written in the last few days of her life while she was imprisoned in the Tower of London, awaiting her May 19, 1536, execution

It doesn't matter if we all die.

—Robert Smith, the Cure—"One Hundred Years," 1982

Henry VIII, by the grace of God, king of England, France, and Ireland, understood the divine right of kings. He was subject to no earthly authority, his mandate to rule ordained by the God who guided his every word and deed. The king tested this supremacy in pursuit of a young woman named Anne Boleyn, the consequences of which shook the foundations of power in Europe and changed history forever.

Anne's elegant beauty, provocative sensuality, and wit intoxicated a king already drunk by the power of his own dominion. In direct defiance of the pope, Henry sought to annul his marriage to Catherine of Aragon so that Anne Boleyn could become his queen. Aided by allies in the English Parliament, the king wrested control of the Church of England away from Rome, thereby severing all ties with the pope. He anointed himself Supreme Head of the Church and swiftly set aside his first wife in favor of Anne Boleyn.

Things started so well between Henry VIII and Anne Boleyn. Giddy over her swift ascension, Anne embraced her new role with extravagance and became a queen with taste expensive enough to match her husband's. Her keen intelligence and wicked sense of humor served her well, and she proved quite adept at helping the king maneuver through the many deep and treacherous political currents swirling around them. Unfortunately for Anne Boleyn, the good feelings wouldn't last.

The flirtatious audacity that thrilled Henry when he and Anne met as illicit lovers seemed unbecoming for a queen, and her flash-fire temper began to grate on him. Anne's political scheming created powerful enemies, some of whom were influential with the king.

Ultimately, it was Henry's obsessive need for a male heir that sealed her fate. Although Anne gave birth to the future Queen Elizabeth I, after a series of tragic miscarriages, she was thrown to the wolves. On May 2, 1536, Anne was arrested on charges of adultery, treason, and incest and imprisoned in the Tower of London. Less than two weeks later, she was convicted and sentenced to die.

In the early morning of Friday, May 19, 1536, the dark-haired beauty Anne Boleyn, twenty-nine years of age, was brought from her room of confinement in the Tower of London to the White Tower, where a scaffold awaited. Accompanied by two ladies-in-waiting, Anne was unbowed as she climbed onto the platform. She was lovely to the very end. A bright red petticoat peeked from under a smoky gray patterned gown lined with fur, around which draped a beautiful ermine mantle, fit for royalty.

Anne faced the crowd that had gathered to watch her die with the hint of an impish smile, as if she alone knew a secret joke that everyone else would discover soon enough. The crowd hushed, and she spoke briefly in a calm and confident voice.

She uttered not one negative word about the king, nor did she protest the absurd charges against her, saying only that, "according to the law, and by the law, I am judged to die, and therefore I will speak nothing against it." She finished with an expression of devotion: "O Lord have mercy on me, to God I commend my soul." Many of the spectators were in tears by the end of her remarks.

Anne's mantle and headdress were removed, and her long, dark hair was tucked under a cap to ensure that her neck was clearly visible to the expert French swordsman brought in by her husband just for the occasion. She bid good-bye to the ladies accompanying her, beseeching their prayers as they wept. She knelt, and a blindfold was placed over her eyes.

Thus in the darkness, kneeling, Anne whispered a mantra to herself, quickly, over and over again: "Jesu, receive my soul; O Lord, God have pity on my soul. Jesu, receive my soul; O Lord, God have pity on my soul. Jesu, receive my soul..."

In the end, for Anne Boleyn, there was nothing left but faith.

King Henry did not attend the beheading of his former wife. On May 30, 1536, a few days after the body of Anne Boleyn was unceremoniously dumped into an unmarked grave at the Chapel of St. Peter ad Vincula in the Tower of London, Henry married Jane Seymour in the Queen's Closet at Whitehall.

He reigned until his death eleven years later, having gone through six wives in all. Blighted by disease, the king endured long and painful months as a haunted shadow of his former self, unable to call on any power to return his youth, health, and glory. God evidently had stopped listening.

During those long and painful nights, when all the king could do was lie in bed and let his fever dreams and hazy, disease-ravaged memories stalk his mind like ghostly pantomimes, perhaps he heard Anne Boleyn's wicked laugh ring through the darkness to taunt him, a hallucination so vivid and troubling that he must have quailed in terror at this tormentor from beyond the grave. Perhaps he even felt guilt, although this seems out of character. Nor would Anne Boleyn have ever felt mirth at Henry's misfortune no matter how he had wronged her. That kind of cruelty and vengeance was not in her, something he might have known if he hadn't thrown her away.

Henry VIII died a broken man on January 28, 1547, at age fifty-five.

Also during that fateful year of 1536, King Henry created a private hunting reserve called Hyde Park. Located in the heart of London, it was carved from a vast expanse of land the king had seized from the monks at Westminster Abbey. Henry spent many hours there riding his horse and hunting deer. Hyde Park became the king's favorite refuge and perhaps ultimately his recompense.

Hyde Park outlived Henry VIII and survived the passage of many kings and queens, a site for both royalty and commoners, serving many purposes over the centuries but always as a refuge. Centuries have passed, and much of the world has changed beyond recognition, yet Hyde Park remains where Henry VIII left it.

In recent decades, Hyde Park has hosted a series of high-profile performances by some of the greatest artists in rock 'n' roll history, uniting millions of people from every conceivable walk of life in celebrations of music and dance, life and love, revelry and reflection, and anything under the sun that might fit the occasion. A veritable parade of rock royalty has sauntered, strolled, and strutted across the stage erected on Henry VIII's former hunting ground, starting in the 1960s with bands like Pink Floyd, Fleetwood Mac, Blind Faith, King Crimson, and the Rolling Stones.

London is one of those rare places in the world where the dim past and the modern day intertwine to the point that it becomes common. Given that they are from such different worlds, the notion of Henry VIII and Mick Jagger stalking the same territory is hard to fathom. Of course, Henry would be aghast if he saw the spectacle. Anne Boleyn, though—it's easy to imagine that she would fit right in with the crowd, singing, dancing and rocking out late into the night. Henry would have scowled in disapproval, which of course makes the prospect even more enticing to envision.

Anne surely would have been delighted by a band with a capacity for light and darkness as profound as her own. Perhaps she was there in spirit under the lights on July 7, 2018, as history caught up to the present and smiles of sorrow and tears of joy painted the faces of fans gathered to celebrate a band whose music captures their hearts and souls like no other.

That was the night when rock legend Robert Smith and his bandmates celebrated the fortieth anniversary of their first gig as the Cure by delivering a knockout performance and proving once again that they are one of the greatest rock bands of a generation. The special show constituted this year's British Summer Time Hyde Park, a yearly event presented by financial giant Barclays.

It was one of the hottest days of the London summer, and by the time the Cure took the stage, most of the crowd had been battered continuously by the sun for hours. The gates opened at 11:30 a.m., allowing those fans seeking to secure a prime spot near the stage ample opportunity to do so provided that they could withstand the scorching heat.

Hordes of fans arrived early, drawn by an absolutely killer lineup of openers that were handpicked by Robert Smith himself: the Twilight Sad, Slowdive, Ride, Editors, Goldfrapp, and Interpol, all artists deeply indebted to the Cure as they developed their own sound. It must have been a thrill for each of these great bands to share the stage with the Cure for such a momentous event.

Finally, as the clock ticked down to 8:08 p.m., softly tinkling bells chimed out into the night, stoking the crowd's restless anticipation higher with each passing second. Finally, the tension broke with a deafening roar of love and excitement erupting from the tightly-packed mass in tandem with a sudden majestic swoon of synths. Once again taking its familiar role as concert opener, "Plainsong" soared over and through the crowd, sparking flashbacks and more than a few tears. *This* is what the adoring faithful had been awaiting.

After a final fade of keyboards wrapped up the first track, lead vocalist Robert Smith, that most dour and unassuming of pop stars, turned to his familiar six-string bass for the second number, "Pictures of You." His voice thick with profound longing, Smith exposes the unending ache of absence which emerges when love's warm glow is frosted over by barren regret. Memories that were once joyous, photographs that sparked a quick flashing smile, are now steeped in sorrow, and the past is almost lost somehow. Smith and childhood friend, bassist Simon Gallup, wove through the intricate interplay that is the classic song's defining musical characteristic with precision, often grooving face to face in a mid-tempo dance they had performed hundreds of times before.

Despite the sweltering heat, the crowd showed no hesitation in drenching themselves with even greater slicks of sweat by dancing with joyful abandon to "High," the first of the Cure's upbeat pop tracks to make an appearance.

Robert Smith, dressed in his usual formless black shirt and slacks, said ruefully to the audience early on, "I can't really talk until the sun goes down. It's taking all my energy not to dissolve." By the time he had eased into the guitar introduction for the dramatic rocker "A Night Like This," Smith looked to be on the verge of melting into a pool of steaming black goo (with a smudge of indestructible red lipstick across the center) at any moment. The song reached a dramatic climax as ace guitarist Reeves Gabrels electrified the crowd with a blazing solo.

As the show progressed, the Cure mixed some of their biggest singles with a few select deep cuts that have become fan favorites over the years. Standards like "The Walk," "Lovesong," and "In Between Days" became buoyant sing-alongs, and "Just Like Heaven" was as transcendent as ever. "The End of the World," a quirky pop nugget from 2004 that in previous shows had often fit awkwardly alongside all those essential classics, finally seemed worthy of inclusion as The Cure delivered a confident performance superior to the studio recording.

As always, the audience sang along full throttle to the iconic keyboard riff on "Play for Today," a nearly forty-year-old song that was never a single but remains a fan favorite. The Cure closed the main set with a thunderous rally of six dramatic, guitar-heavy epics: "Shake Dog Shake," "Burn," "Fascination Street," "Never Enough," "From the Edge of the Deep Green Sea," and "Disintegration."

After a quick breather, the Cure sauntered back onstage for the first encore, and, with a flash of light, the stage was swathed by the image of a giant silvery spiderweb for their biggest U.K. single, "Lullaby." More hits followed in rapid succession, including the acid-folk sing-along "The Caterpillar" and a trio of certifiable pop classics: "Friday I'm in Love," "Close to Me," and "Why Can't I Be You?"

Robert Smith is notoriously bashful and doesn't speak much onstage, but on this night, he couldn't resist as he stood behind the microphone with a broad smile, clearly touched by the crowd's warm approval. He said, "I have to thank everyone that was here tonight, everyone that played today. And thank you all for coming! Of course, forty years ago this weekend it was the first time we played as the Cure in the Rocket in Crawley. And if you had asked me then, 'What do you think you'll be doing in forty years,' I think I would have been wrong in my answer. But it's thanks to everyone around me that I'm still here and to you as well. Thank you very much!"

To finish off the night, the Cure ripped through five of their key early numbers, some of which were played during that now-historic gig at the Rocket being celebrated by this event. "Boys Don't Cry," "Jumping Someone Else's Train," "Grinding Halt," and "10:15 Saturday Night" transported everyone back to a time when the Cure were a barely-known trio bashing out their tunes to tiny crowds in and around West Sussex, not all that far south of Hyde Park.

They ended with how it all started, with a savage rendition of "Killing an Arab," a song that Robert Smith, pushing sixty at the time of this show, wrote as a sixteen-year-old high school student. The Cure's debut single, "Killing an Arab," released in 1978, tied the threads of history into a knot that will never be unraveled. On a hot summer night in Hyde Park, a refuge for royalty, memories were made that nobody in the band or the crowd will ever forget. A year later, fans in major cities all over the world could watch the show on the big screen as the Cure's long-time video director Tim Pope turned the performance into an acclaimed concert film. In October 2019, fans would be able to purchase the show on DVD and audio CDs as part of superbly constructed box set.

And if from some eternal purgatory King Henry XIII watched all of this unfold with teeth clenched in helpless outrage, then that only makes it better.

The Cure in Brief

More than forty years after their formation, the Cure remains one of the most influential and beloved rock bands of their generation. Led by creative mastermind Robert Smith, with his signature black spiderweb hair, smudged lipstick, and swamp-water voice, the band has produced a staggering body of work despite a frequently shifting lineup. The Cure are among the architects of alternative rock, massively influential and commercially successful beyond their most fanciful imaginations. They've sold millions of albums, scored a string of classic singles, and have staged their epic concerts to adoring fans all over the globe.

The Cure began life in the late 1970s as a punk-inspired power-pop trio from Crawley, a gloomy working-class outer suburb of London. Their demo caught the attention of Chris Parry at Polydor Records, who signed them to his new subsidiary label Fiction and produced their debut album, *Three Imaginary Boys*, released in May 1979. As Robert Smith's confidence as a songwriter progressed, the band's sound shifted darker and more contemplative. Over the next three years, the Cure produced a trilogy of classics that are in turn stark, beautifully funereal, and bristling with rage: *Seventeen Seconds*, *Faith*, and *Pornography*.

Despite the increasingly difficult and uncompromising nature of the music and few pop hooks to be found, the Cure's popularity grew with each new album. They built their U.K. fan base steadily, toured in the United States for the first time, and became increasingly popular in France, Netherlands, Belgium, and Australia. Their music connected with countless fans on a deep emotional level as an authentic reflection of their own thoughts and feelings articulated with blazing intensity, honesty, and otherworldly beauty.

The dark cast of the music (which led to the Cure's being connected with the goth scene, whether they wished to or not), an almost nonstop schedule, and increasing substance abuse combined to shake the band to its foundations. The Cure fractured acrimoniously following their grueling 1982 tour in support of *Pornography*. Tensions were so fraught as the tour neared its close that Robert Smith and Simon Gallup got into a fistfight at a bar following a show in Austria, and they parted ways. At this point, the Cure had effectively ceased to exist as a functioning band, and their future seemed uncertain at best.

Robert Smith wasn't sure if the Cure should rise from the ashes given that it was just he and former drummer Lol Tolhurst, who would ostensibly switch to keyboards even though he had no ability to play them. Fiction Records boss Chris Parry urged Robert to write a frothy pop song to break the band's stereotypical image. Written by Robert Smith as a sardonic riposte at the usual fare heard on mainstream radio, the melodic synth pop of "Let's Go to Bed" shifted the trajectory of the band's career dramatically. Their sonic palate broadened considerably, and their first two big pop hits in the United Kingdom followed: "The Walk" and "The Lovecats."

The Cure's sharp left turn into more radio-friendly synth pop helped formulate the sound of their golden years. A series of landmark albums, including *The Head on the Door*, *Kiss Me Kiss Me Kiss Me*, *Disintegration*, and *Wish* meshed jubilant pop with searing epics of isolation, disillusionment, and heartbreak. They scored international hits with "Lovesong," "Friday I'm in Love," "In Between Days," "Just Like Heaven," "Close to Me," and "Pictures of You," to name just a few.

Few artists reflect the shifts and surges of our psyches in every direction imaginable like the Cure. Although their studio output has slowed in recent years, they still sell out major venues. On March 29, 2019, in New York City, the Cure's artistry and cultural importance were recognized and celebrated as they were inducted into the Rock and Roll Hall of Fame. They are now enshrined alongside other titans of rock, such as the Beatles, Jimi Hendrix, the Rolling Stones, Aretha Franklin, Bob Dylan, Madonna, Prince, and Robert Smith's hero David Bowie.

The Cure have delivered endless hours of entertainment, refuge, introspection, bewilderment, understanding, comfort, commiseration, freakishly uninhibited dancing, and, for many who have been lonely and outcast, a sense of belonging and a connection not only to the music but with like-minded fans around the world.

1

Sordid Details Following: Robert Smith

The iconic front man behind every vision of the Cure is a rock 'n' roll legend whether he likes it or not.

The Cure's music is everything and nothing, distinct yet undefinable, an ever-shifting galaxy of sound that begins and ends with Robert Smith. One cannot conjure the band's name without his image rising like a sacred demigod of melancholy, his face ghostly and pale beneath a shock of twisted black hair, his red-smeared mouth tempting our thoughts with endless possibility. His murky tenor is immediately recognizable, like everything else about him.

Robert Smith is the architect of this sonic bang. Who is he exactly? Smith's larger-than-life persona is so familiar that it seems like we've always known him. The truth is that we know very little about the man behind the makeup. The Robert Smith we hear on record or see onstage is a character much like David Bowie's doom-laden guitar hero Ziggy Stardust or his sleek and decadent Thin White Duke. Bowie's career was built on the expression of music through rapidly changing guises he invented. Robert Smith created only one character, a stage version of himself, that he's stuck with for nearly four decades.

He is imposing: over six feet tall in bulky boots and layered in various hues of black. Whenever he must interact with anyone outside his immediate comfort zone of friends and family, the hair and makeup become his armor. It just seems right—it's the way Robert Smith is supposed to look. Media observers have noted his razor-sharp intelligence, a self-deprecating wit, an encyclopedic knowledge of music, and a striking genuineness. He truly is Robert Smith, exactly as one would expect in every aspect.

As for the music, we are rarely offered so much as a glimpse of what's underneath his impenetrable mask. We may glean hints, but these are hard to decipher. Robert sometimes divulges the inspiration for a song, but the answers he gives are not always reliable. He makes contradictory statements or changes his story with each telling, and sometimes he invents things just for the fun of it. He delights in confounding.

Beyond that, we can only speculate what is real in a song and what is make-believe. He probably doesn't always know himself. Inspiration is mysterious and can be drawn from anywhere. We don't get to see Robert Smith's personal life because he doesn't expose it to the entire world.

And why should he? He presents Robert Smith of the Cure, the legend, the iconic rock 'n' roll superhero. The rest is none of our business apart from what he chooses to divulge. Part of it, surely, is mythmaking. Smith is shrewd enough to understand that some of his appeal comes with his mystery. Sometimes the magic is lost if you know too much about an illusion.

In a very real way, Robert Smith *is* the Cure, although he would reject this assertion. He was the spark that flared the band into existence. His vision, musical ingenuity, and determination elevated an awkward pop-punk trio of teenagers into one of the most successful and influential rock bands of a generation. Although other band members have certainly contributed, the Cure's music arises largely from Robert Smith's boundless talent. He is an intuitively gifted songwriter and musician with the self-confidence to trust his instincts in pursuit of whatever sound happens to be echoing around in his head. He also represents the band's image, which is every bit as recognizable as their music.

Robert James Smith was born on April 21, 1959, to James Alexander and Rita Mary of Blackpool, Lancashire. His brother Richard and sister Margaret were much older, so after Robert arrived, his parents decided he should have a sibling closer to his own age, and Janet was born on August 30, 1960.

In December 1962, James accepted a promotion and relocated the family to Horley in Surrey. It was there that Robert attended St. Francis Primary School and met a young lad named Laurence Tolhurst. Finally, in March 1966, the family migrated nine kilometers south to the larger town of Crawley, which became the birthplace of the Cure.

Robert's upbringing was upper middle class and might be described as almost idyllic if not for the angst endemic to those consigned to an adolescence in Crawley. Music was an enormous part of his life from an early age. His father was a talented singer, his mother was a pianist, and they often sang impromptu duets. Encouraged by their parents, both Robert and Janet started piano lessons around the same time. It soon became clear that Janet outclassed her big brother on the piano by a mile—by several miles.

Rather than compete with a child prodigy, Robert switched to guitar. He was seven when his brother Richard showed him basic chords. He made enough progress that, two years later, his parents signed him up for classical guitar lessons with one of virtuoso John Williams's students. The teacher didn't think much of the burgeoning guitarist's progress, and Robert quit after becoming frustrated with the constant non–rock 'n' roll rehearsing. At this point already, Robert was demonstrating his strong predilection for doing things his way or no way.

Amped in part by his school buds who'd also caught rock 'n' roll fever and helped along by his growing guitar skills, Robert's childhood love for music bloomed into a lifelong passion. He's always been first and foremost a consummate music fan, and it's his appreciation for music that has been the biggest driver of his own creativity. When Robert Smith was thirteen, a Starman electrified his soul with a jolt of red and blue lighting hurled down to earth from the outer realms. David Bowie's jaw-dropping 1972 appearance on *Top of the Pops* left an enormous impression on Robert and his friends, along with countless others all over Britain.

Bowie's *Ziggy Stardust* was the first album he ever bought, and suddenly *his* music was in focus. Robert credits the legend with being more influential over his own style than any other artist. Bowie's genre-bending fearlessness was something that Robert kept in mind while deliberately shifting styles for each new Cure album.

Robert's love for Bowie led him to another glam-rock obsession, the Sensational Alex Harvey Band, and others, such as Roxy Music, Sweet, Marc Bolan, Slade, and Gary Glitter, became a big part of his rotation. Robert even latched on to the genre's fashion sense to an extent. As a thirteen-year-old at St. Wilfred's, his long hair often trailed behind the collar of a full-length women's fur coat.

Although glam was a fixture, Robert habitually listened to an eclectic range of artists. He was a Jimi Hendrix devotee and became so enamored by "Purple Haze" during one stretch that he'd spin it at least a dozen times daily. He was a Thin Lizzy fanatic, and with the help of his brother and his ever-obliging parents, he'd travel to surrounding cities to see multiple shows whenever possible. He'd been a Beatles fan since early childhood, and he fell in love with the delicate folk pop of Nick Drake at age ten when his brother played him *Five Leaves Left*.

The rock 'n' roll universe quaked again in 1976 as punk crash-landed like a meteor, with bands like the Clash and the Sex Pistols shifting the trajectory of popular music forever. Robert loved both, but it was the melding of punk muscle with strong melody by the Buzzcocks and the Stranglers that excited him the most. This influx of energy spurred him and his friends, who'd already been jamming to the best of their rudimentary abilities, to new levels of urgency and ambition in their quest to catch the punk fueled train out of Crawley and into a bigger world.

Maybe it was Robert's long-held love for Jimi Hendrix that caused the wind to whisper her name. As thirteen turned to fourteen, music wasn't the only thing on his mind. Young love was in the air. Robert Smith and Mary Poole were students together at St. Wilfrid's when she accepted his nervous offer to partner with him for a drama class project. They soon became inseparable, bonding through a shared love for music and film, similarly dour worldviews, wicked senses of humor, and an appreciation for the absurdities in life. For their first movie date, the choice was *Texas Chainsaw Massacre*.

Those tentative first steps turned into one of rock 'n' roll's greatest love stories. Robert and Mary have remained together ever since those early days apart perhaps for a few rocky patches of separation. Mary's skepticism over Robert's long-term potential as a musician helped fuel his early ambition. Over the years, she's remained a trusted adviser and critical ear, never sugarcoating it when the Cure produces music she doesn't like.

Robert proposed to Mary in 1986 while they were in the south of France for the Cure's *Kiss Me, Kiss Me, Kiss Me* sessions. They married on August 13, 1988, at Worth Abbey, just a few miles from Crawley. Longtime Cure bassist Simon Gallup stood as best man, and the couple's first dance was Bowie's "Life on Mars?" Robert later said of the day, "It was perfect. Everyone shone and then fell over."

As Robert Smith's greatest muse, Mary (or "M") has long been the Cure's heart. In 1989, "Lovesong" brought the Cure to number two in the United States, their biggest pop hit by far. It seems obligatory for every writer who's ever penned a piece about the song to mention that Robert wrote the lyrics as a wedding gift for Mary. But, while it may be the most famous, "Lovesong" is just one of many Cure songs that were shaped by Robert's intensely strong thoughts and feelings about his wife.

Robert has kept his life outside of the Cure as private as possible, and Mary has studiously avoided the spotlight, although she did appear resplendently swaying and singing along as her husband performed at the Rock and Roll Hall of Fame induction ceremony in March 2019. In some ways, being in the Cure is something that Robert can turn on and off like a switch. The couple leads an ordinary life when the switch is off, staying close to family and lavishing love and attention on their many nieces and nephews.

Although he's fond of children, Robert has steadfastly insisted that he and Mary have never aspired to be parents themselves. His standard reply when the frequently asked question is posed yet again is a variation of the same refrain: "Life is pretty horrible. I would never impose it on anyone."

There's a touch of wry humor there, but he's also serious. For all the humor and whimsy that infuses a large portion of his work, most of Robert Smith's music with the Cure is shrouded by a haunted darkness that is real, not a goth illusion. There is a reason why many Cure fans tend to be loners, outsiders, and outcasts. Robert Smith doesn't shy away from the basest impulses of the human psyche. He has the keen ability to translate thoughts and feelings that course through us untamed, bubbling to surface in times of crisis, in a way that connects. He paints road maps to parts of ourselves that we may only barely grasp at the edges if at all.

There's an aspect of artifice to the Cure's pop side that's pure entertainment, but even at their campiest, the Cure's potency can be attributed to one aspect more than any other: it's genuine. In a 1988 fanzine interview, Robert Smith described his lyrics as a mixture of fear, fiction, and reality. He said, "I rarely know calm. In anything." In an interview format that often generates glib responses, Smith let slip an important nugget of truth that succinctly describes his vast library of song lyrics spanning decades.

Authenticity is vitally important to the Cure's ability to create and also for their ability to connect with fans as strongly as they do. Robert Smith has been a careful guardian of the Cure's name and legacy since the beginning, and he's been able to maintain the Cure's artistic integrity even when they've scored mainstream success.

Even as a studio novice barely out of his teens, Robert has demanded and received total creative control of the Cure's output. With very few exceptions, the Cure's music has remained unshackled from secondary considerations, such as commercial viability, a luxury that very few artists enjoy. Under Robert Smith's leadership, the Cure has rarely sold out or compromised. They don't follow trends or chase after obvious top-forty hits. When they have scored big on the pop charts, it's been the mainstream swerving erratically enough to swallow them up for a time, not a purposeful dash for the commercial promised land. They don't cater to a particular group or subset of listener. The Cure's music is for anyone who cares to listen with no limits or boundaries.

Robert Smith's unique voice is the most easily identifiable aspect of the Cure's music, and he uses it to maximum effect. It's hard to mistake him for anybody else. Smith is adept at using the right phrasing and tone to bring meaning and feel to a song: consider his fearful half whispers on "Lullaby" and "Fear of Ghosts," for example, or the mystery and tension he injects into "Like Cockatoos" or the weary resignation of "Out of This World." Early on, Smith's punkish vocals were short, clipped, and sometimes sneery. Around the time of *Faith*, he became more confident, stretching his murky tenor in ways he'd never before tried.

For 1984's *The Top*, he fearlessly explored the possibilities that his odd voice presented, daring off-kilter vocal theatrics that most singers would never attempt. He reined it in for the highly focused *Head on the Door* (1986), only to stretch it to the max on *Kiss Me, Kiss Me, Kiss Me* (1987). Robert's disciplined work on *Disintegration* (1989) may be the finest of his career.

Along with bassist Simon Gallup, Smith is also responsible for writing most of the Cure's music. His innovative melodic guitar technique is an essential part of their sound. He is by no means a virtuoso, nor does he pretend to be, but he knows how to capture a mood. Robert's sparse patterns and clean tones, usually detuned and often layered with chorus effects, are unique and notoriously difficult to replicate.

One of the Cure's signature sounds is generated from Robert's inventive use of the Bass VI. Prior to recording *Faith* in 1981, he acquired a vintage 1960s Fender Olympic White model from producer Mike Hedges and used it extensively on that album. It's been a fixture ever since, most notably on tracks like "Pictures of You," "High," "There Is No If . . . ," and many others.

Unlike a typical six-string bass, which yields a much lower tone and is tuned in straight fourths from a low B, the Bass VI is like a regular electric guitar, only tuned a full octave lower (to a natural E), the same as a standard four-string bass (although with much lighter strings). A Bass VI is short scale (typically thirty inches compared to the thirty-four to thirty-five inches for a six-string bass) and has tight string space like a normal electric guitar rather than the wider neck found on the six-string bass.

Robert Smith most often buys guitars based on appearance and then has them altered to meet his own peculiar requirements. In 2005, he partnered with the California-based manufacturer Schecter to create the UltraCure and the UltraCure VI, custom guitars designed to his specifications. Robert loves to tweak his sound with guitar pedals, and he has used many over the years. Some of his favorites to use with the Cure include the CH-1 Super Chorus, SD-1 Super Overdrive, BF-2 Flanger, PN-2 Tremolo/Pan, and the BD-2 Blues Driver, among others. Robert's guitar rig for touring is ultrasimple—just a basic Rowland practice amp and a pedal board with six BOSS pedals.

The songwriting process begins with an instrumental sketch, often by demoed by Robert but with frequent contributions by Simon Gallup and others. The band workup of a track usually begins with just a bass line and drum pattern, with words added once the demo is more fully developed. Unlike the music, which is often collaborative, the lyrics are almost entirely penned by Robert Smith.

As a lyricist, Robert draws heavily from his own life, delving into his thoughts, emotions, and experiences. He revisits certain thematic elements frequently, including substance use, the fear of lost love, and sexual obsession. Smith also colors his work with ideas drawn from film and literature, areas in which he truly seems insatiable and limitless. He is a voracious reader, with three books typically in the works at any given moment. Robert's fondness for cheesy B-movies and horror flicks is a frequent source of inspiration for some of his more nightmarish and psychedelic tracks.

Robert has hinted numerous times about the possibility of a solo album, which thus far has remained elusive. Several specific projects have been rumored, including an album of instrumentals and a potential film score project for video director Tim Pope. In 1991, Robert claimed in an interview that he'd been working on an acoustic solo album inspired by Nick Drake, with several songs reportedly completed: "Ariel," "The Four of Us," "In France," and "Melancholia." None of these or other rumored solo projects have emerged. He's released a handful of solo tracks consisting largely of soundtrack tunes and covers. In interviews after the Hall of Fame induction, Robert has mentioned in the press there are two new Cure albums essentially finished and one solo album that he describes as "noise." Only time will tell if this becomes reality.

A possible explanation for the ever-elusive solo album, mentions of which have become something of an in-joke, is that Robert is simply spinning tales. He's been known to invent stories for the media over the years, sometimes giving contradictory explanations for song meanings or providing multiple different versions of events. Robert Smith is gifted at creative mythmaking when it suits him, and he's employed it frequently over the years with great success. Although sometimes he's just having a laugh, often there is a more serious goal with these ploys. He's been able to carefully shape the media narrative and conventional wisdom in various ways to the Cure's benefit.

The Cure's most widely revered album, *Disintegration*, has risen in stature over the years thanks in part to how Robert has been able to frame it. He wasted no time claiming that the Cure's tour in support of the album would be their last. He was miserably depressed and was binging on alcohol and hallucinogenic drugs and not shy in disclosing these facts. He claims he was overcome with thoughts of mortality because he would be turning thirty, and it troubled him to no end that he had not yet recorded a masterpiece.

His pop popularity was a dreadful thing; he absolutely hated the Cure's being commercially successful. Smith claimed he would break up the band immediately if they ever hit number one. That in no way, of course, prevented the Cure from releasing single after single, video after video, touring the biggest venues they could fit into, night after night, for years. Oh, how he loathed it all. But did he ever return, in disgust, any of the vast sums of money he had earned? No. (He does, however, contribute large amounts to charity.)

When "Lullaby" hit number five in the United Kingdom, a new high for the Cure, Smith insisted to *The Times* (U.K.) that he was unaware of the song's chart position and that he never wanted it as a single anyway given that it's his least favorite song on *Disintegration*. He said the same of "Lovesong" after it hit number two in the United States, despairing that such a lightweight throwaway, which had now replaced "Lullaby" as his least favorite on the album, was the song to become such a big hit. When "The Walk" broke through to become the Cure's first top-twenty hit in the United Kingdom, Smith lamented that surely a lot of very stupid people were buying it.

Smith performed an astonishing balancing act when "Let's Go to Bed" was released in 1982, an incredible left turn to commercial synth pop after the heavy rock gloom of the Cure's prior three albums. He reveled in trashing the single in the press at every opportunity, thus inoculating himself in case the experiment failed. Smith was, after all, far too cool to dig a perfect pop song (even if he had created it).

He managed to play both sides of the fence brilliantly, raking in dollars from a crass commercial sellout while maintaining his vaunted dignity by pretending the whole thing was some kind of weird lark. He said it was terrible, awful, horrendous. It's so bad, in fact, that the Cure has played it live in concert only 588 times since its release (making it number eleven on their list of all-time played songs). His deft management of this balancing act has been key to his success with the Cure, allowing him to preserve integrity while simultaneously scoring big hits under his own terms.

It's very difficult to find anyone with a past or current association with Robert Smith who is willing to say anything negative about him, publicly or privately, and the admiration and respect is genuine. He can be ruthless when he needs to be, such as with lineup changes, but he doesn't make such moves lightly. Part of the reticence to speak negatively about Smith is surely unease. As Chris Parry once said, "Robert can be very cold, you see, and one has to be wary of it." Nearly everyone involved in the Cure has discovered this at one time or another over the years.

There has been talk over the years that Smith runs the Cure with the iron fist of a tyrant, making personnel decisions capriciously and blocking creative input by his bandmates. The long trail of lineup changes cannot be denied, and it is also true that Smith often plays multiple parts on the Cure's studio albums, sometimes erasing and replacing instrumentation recorded by one of his bandmates. But he gets very defensive at the suggestion that he fires purely by whim, pointing out that he remains on good terms with almost all of the prior members and that each move was made for legitimate reasons. He is fiercely loyal to his friends and bandmates, and he individually thanked each member, past and present, at the Rock and Roll Hall of Fame induction ceremony.

Smith also defends his role as the band's chief executive and decider-in-chief in matters both creative and business. He told *Select* magazine in 1991, "I don't want to be in a group that does things I don't like, and if the others felt strongly that I was wrong, I hope they would have the courage to say, 'I'm leaving.'... But the buck has to stop somewhere. I learned a long time ago that you can't run a group by committee." It's hard to argue his point. Robert Smith has more invested in the Cure than anyone else by far, and he's the one blamed when things go wrong. It would be ludicrous for anyone else to have final say on anything related to the Cure.

Robert also learned over the decades the value of trusting his instincts, sometimes stubbornly. Robert reasons that the fans will have similar inclinations to his, generally. He told *Rolling Stone* in 2004, "I always place myself as the archetypal Cure fan. I'm the wrong age, but I still think that if like anything particularly, our fans will."

Robert was once asked what five words describe him, and the answer is illuminating: "Inquisitive. Thoughtful. Stupid. Wishful. Alien." These words taken together could mean a lot of different things, but they ring undeniably true. Nearly fifteen years ago, Smith told *SPIN* magazine, "I will most certainly not be wearing black and lipstick in 2011. That's a guarantee"—another promise broken, but this time it's one that fans can celebrate.

In June 2018, Robert Smith told the *Irish Times*, "I think you'd be hard-pressed to find many artists who don't like The Cure. I think people admire us, even if they don't particularly get the music. It sounds very conceited, but it's not about me, it's about the band. We've stayed true to ourselves . . . I think people admire our tenacity." He's right.

Somehow, despite no new studio material in over a decade and no hits in over two decades, the Cure have managed to keep climbing the ladder, esteem for them growing more profoundly every single year, until finally they made the Rock and Roll Hall of Fame. Smith stood triumphant on that Barclay Center stage on March 29, 2019, in New York, as the Cure was inducted into the Rock and Roll Hall of Fame. The brightest spotlight in the rock 'n' roll universe was on the Cure in those moments, and it had to feel satisfying for Smith and the rest of the band, given how many battles they had fought to be able to do exactly what they wanted to do.

Robert beamed, a bit anxious to stop talking and start playing music, but he gave a short and gracious speech. He was himself—a bit self-deprecating, humorous, and clearly proud of his collective colleagues, especially those currently in the band. Then he and his mates got behind their instruments and did what they do best, thundering through a five-song set that rendered doubters with no arguments left to make.

The future of the Cure is hard to predict. There's only one person who charts that course, and he surely doesn't know it yet either. One thing we do know: whenever the end finally arrives for the Cure, it will be Robert Smith who decides that it's over.

Robert Smith's Solo Recordings

"Pirate Ships" (1989)—Judy Collins cover, released on 2010 *Disintegration* deluxe reissue

"A Sign from God" (1998)—COGASM (Cooper, Gabrels, Smith), *Orgazmo Soundtrack*

"Very Good Advice" (2010), *Almost Alice* (music inspired by *Alice in Wonderland*)

"Small Hours" (2011), *Johnny Boy Would Love This… A Tribute to John Martyn*
"Witchcraft" (2012), *Frankenweenie* soundtrack
"C-Moon" (2014), *The Art of McCartney—Tribute to Paul McCartney* (Amazon .com exclusive bonus track)
"A Few Hours After This" (2015), rerecording of the Cure B-side, for the BBC TV series *Luther*

Robert Smith's Collaborations

(excluding Siouxsie and the Banshees and the Glove)
Tim Pope—"I Want to Be a Tree" (1984)
The Stranglers—*The Stranglers and Friends Live in Concert* (recorded 1980, released 1995)
(Robert plays guitar on "Get a Grip" and "Hanging Around")
"Yesterday's Gone" (1999), *Ulysses* —Reeves Gabrels
"Believe" (2003), *Zig Zag*—Earl Slick
"Perfect Blue Sky" (2003), *Radio JXL: A Broadcast from the Computer Hell Cabin*—Junkie XL
"All of This" (2003), *Blink-182*—Blink-182
"A Forest (a cover)" (2004), *Monument*—Blank & Jones
"Da Hype" (2004), *Trust It*—Junior Jack
"Truth Is" (2004), *2 a.m. Wakeup Call*—Tweaker
"To Love Somebody" (2005), *TheFutureEmbrace*—Billy Corgan
"Spiders, Crocodiles, & Kryptonite" (2006), *To All New Arrivals*—Faithless
"Please" (2007), *The Ideal Condition*—Paul Hartnoll
"J'aurai tout essayé" (2010), *Self-Titled*—Anik Jean
"Not in Love" (2010), *Crystal Castles II*—Crystal Castles
"Take Forever" (2011), *Controlling Your Allegiance*—the Japanese Popstars
"Come to Me" (2011), *We Were Exploding Anyway*—65daysofstatic
"Please" (2015), *8:58*—Paul Hartnoll
"There's a Girl in the Corner" (2015), "It Never Was the Same" single, the Twilight Sad
"In All Worlds" (2015), *Dead Planet*—Eat Static
"Strange Timez" (2020), *Song Machine, Season One: Strange Timez*—Gorillaz
"How Not to Drown" (2021), *Screen Violence*, CHVRCHES

2

So Close to Something Better Left Unknown: The Formative Years

In the wake of punk rock's cultural explosion, the dreary town of Crawley gives birth to an Easy Cure.

In the late 1970s, England struggled under austere economic conditions. High unemployment, alcoholism, violence, racism, and a malaise of hopelessness were endemic through vast swathes of the country. This was certainly true for Crawley, the squat unlovely mushroom of a town in West Sussex where the Cure formed. All three original members and three future members grew up in or near Crawley. The region boasted few enticing prospects for young men apart from endless toil stretching long into the future until their bodies grow old and tired.

Crawley's dullness is partly attributable to its drab architecture, a relic from the post–World War II population expansion. The band members have also cited the presence of several foreboding mental hospitals as contributing to Crawley's singular bleakness. There was no easy respite, either. It was possible to escape to London, but opportunities were limited by a difficult twenty-five-mile drive with no direct highway.

Against this backdrop, it's easy to understand why the talented young musicians who became the Cure were so insistent on getting away. Original drummer Laurence Tolhurst credited the "awfulness" of Crawley as key to their drive to succeed. As for Robert Smith, he said of Crawley in a 1987 interview with *Creem*, "It's like a pimple on the side of Croydon. It's not a very nice place." Over the years in subsequent interviews, when asked about Crawley, he said much the same. His opinion never changed.

Crawley was the incubator from which the fledgling Cure would emerge, and the process started when they were very young. Both Smith and Tolhurst were five years old when they first met in September 1964 while standing with their mothers waiting for the bus to St. Francis of Assisi Catholic School. Tolhurst had a difficult upbringing with an alcoholic father who was either distant or a raging drunk, although he had a strong bond with his mother Daphne.

The three young musicians who would eventually record *Three Imaginary Boys* first jammed together all the way back in 1972. They were all students at Notre Dame, a Catholic middle school that strived for a reputation of independence and free thought. Robert Smith already had an electric guitar that his brother Richard had given him as a Christmas gift after Robert had essentially appropriated it. He soon became friends with Michael Dempsey, another big music fan who was also a fledgling guitarist.

Once a week, Smith and Dempsey gathered with other students in the Notre Dame music room to practice whatever instruments they could get their hands on, often bashing out covers of current hits. Smith invited Lol Tolhurst to join them when he learned of their shared love for Jimi Hendrix. Tolhurst had no instrument, but he managed to excavate an old forgotten drum kit from a dusty jumble of musical debris in a corner of the music room. It turned out to be a fortunate find, as the cymbal rescued from that refuse pile is the same one used to make those distinct crashes on the Cure's first single, "Killing an Arab," several years later.

Robert Smith's first "band" was a family affair including siblings Richard and Janet and an ever-shifting casts of friends and acquaintances, including Tolhurst and Dempsey. They called themselves the Crawley Goat Band and then later simply the Group. It was obviously just for laughs, but they tried taking it a bit more seriously when they scheduled an end-of-school-year performance for April 1973. The earliest embryonic version of the Cure, barely a cluster of cells, was formed for a single year-end show at Notre Dame in April 1973 under the name the Obelisk. With his more accomplished classmate Marc Ceccagno on guitar, Robert Smith reverted to piano. Dempsey had yet to switch to bass and also played guitar, Lol Tolhurst played drums, and their classmate Alan White played bass. It was a disaster, but things improved rapidly.

By the time he was sixteen, Robert Smith was well on his way to becoming a serious rocker. He owned a thirty-watt Watkins Electric Music guitar amp and a Woolworths Top 20 guitar. Working to improve his guitar skills, Smith frequently jammed and practiced with Dempsey and Ceccagno. While at St. Wilfrid's Comprehensive School, Ceccagno built a group called Malice around himself on lead guitar, Robert on rhythm guitar, Michael Dempsey on bass, and eventually Lol Tolhurst on drums.

Malice rehearsed once a week at a local church hall, playing mostly covers. The band had yet to play a single gig when Ceccagno left in April 1976. A much more proficient musician than his bandmates, Ceccagno decided to pursue his love for jazz rather than the ragged proto-punk that Malice was playing.

After the departure of their leader, Malice added two additional members: vocalist Martin Creasy and Porl Thompson, already well known locally as an ace guitarist. Lol Tolhurst was already friends with Thompson, who had been dating Lol's sister Carol. Thompson worked at Cloake's Record Shop in Crawley, which meant, of course, that he was already friends with the voracious vinyl enthusiast Robert Smith.

Malice notched up the intensity in their attempt to become a tight unit during the summer of 1976. The highlight came when Robert Smith's parents decided to go on vacation, leaving their son in charge of the house and thus allowing the band unfettered access for nonstop immersion in their music. It became an extended house party/rehearsal session combo. It brought the band closer together and established the spare annex in Robert's house as a perfect rehearsal space.

Smith had upgraded his guitar to a Gibson Explorer replica, Porl Thompson was playing a black imitation Les Paul, and Michael Dempsey already owned the brown Guild bass that he'd play through the *Three Imaginary Boys* era. Lol would bash away to his heart's content on the Pearl Maxwin drum kit his mom bought for him. The four of them were in a zone of adolescent musical bliss, powering through song after song with manically charged energy, smoking cigarettes, and sometimes taking breaks to play records, mainly borrowed from Robert's older brother.

Meanwhile, the reality of maintaining real jobs to earn cash had intruded on Lol and Porl, who were heading back to their jobs, while Michael and Robert were getting ready for college. It was a period of reflection for Robert as he tried to determine what he should do with his life. Lol had watched his father slave away at a meaningless job he hated for his entire life until he died. His only purpose in life was to get up, go to work, come home, and repeat. Both Robert and Lol were absolutely determined to avoid that fate. All the answers kept coming back to music—it was the only way out.

This lineup—Smith, Dempsey, Tolhurst, and Thompson—rehearsed through the fall. Vocalist Martin Creasy never showed up for practices but did turn up for performances. Their first gig (sort of) for Malice was on December 16, 1976, at a church in Sussex called Worth Abbey (where, nearly twelve years later, Robert Smith and Mary Poole would be wed). The band couldn't use the name Malice, as it was too menacing. The fledgling musicians played an all-acoustic set with Tolhurst banging on bongos. It was a Christmas party for Upjohn, which was managed by Robert Smith's father. Alex Smith had arranged for the band to play, another example of how Robert's parents helped with the Cure's progress in any way they could.

The first real Malice gig was on December 20 for a special performance at St. Wilfred's annual Christmas concert. Previous performances in years past had included Handel's *Messiah* and Tchaikovsky's *The Nutcracker*. Smith told the headmaster he was arranging an orchestral pop concert. The headmaster liked to cultivate a reputation at the school for the talent of its students and to boast about their cultural accomplishments, so he readily agreed. Porl Thompson made posters for the show, describing the gig as "A Special Christmas Bumper Bundle Party," which would also include Marc Ceccagno's new group Amulet.

But instead of a choral group with brass or some sort of celestial orchestral pop, the audience at St. Wilfred's, expecting a festive musical delight, was instead treated to a brain-searing noise-fest by a very raw rock group called Malice. They tried a series of covers, but the sound was awful, and everything was drowned in earsplitting feedback. Presumed vocalist Martin Creasy showed up for the gig but was clueless since he hadn't been to any of the rehearsals. And it was loud—very loud. Most of the horrified crowd scurried for the exits.

That was the end of Malice—not an auspicious beginning for what would eventually morph into the Cure. Creasy was out by early 1977, leaving a lineup of Smith, Dempsey, Tolhurst, and Thompson. Malice was deemed an unsuitable name, so to come up with a replacement, the band wrote potential names on little pieces of paper so one could be picked randomly. The lucky draw was the Easy Cure, submitted by Lol Tolhurst after an early song he had written.

Around this same time, punk rock was reaching critical mass as culture tsunami that helped bring new urgency to the group's drive for success. Spending their formative years in Crawley had a discernible impact on the direction of the Cure's music. There wasn't much cause for cheer, which is reflected in the wry cynicism of their early material and in the aching melancholy and raging angst that would follow.

Punk was born from the same stew of woe and restless discontent, and while the Cure was never quite punk, they certainly fed off that same energy. They performed for many of the same crowds as the punk bands did and witnessed firsthand the fervor of the movement at its peak. Crawley was large enough to draw early visits from the Clash, the Jam, and the Stranglers, among others. Robert Smith and Lol Tolhurst went to as many of these gigs as possible, each one filling their heads with inspiration and determination.

Through early 1977, the band tried out a few potential new vocalists before settling on Peter O'Toole in April. Their first show with their new name and lineup was a belated birthday party for Robert Smith held on April 22 at St. Edward the Confessor's Church. On May 6, the Easy Cure made the first of many appearances at the Rocket, a seedy pub in Crawley that became their regular haunt.

The Easy Cure's infamous dalliance with Hansa/Ariola Records started in April 1977 when they spotted an ad the label placed in major British music magazines soliciting new talent for possible auditions. Feeling that this was an opportunity they couldn't pass up, they decided to submit a demo tape. The Easy Cure huddled at Robert's house with a tape recorder and laid down "Killing an Arab" and "10:15 Saturday Night" for their submission.

Much to his surprise, Smith received a telegram from Hansa almost immediately, and the Easy Cure auditioned for the label on May 13 at Morgan Studios in London. After hearing the band tear through a few originals, Hansa representatives were impressed enough to offer a five-year, £1,000 contract only five days later. The guys gleefully invested their rather hefty advance on new equipment, optimism soaring.

The band's live slate increased during the summer of 1977, particularly at the Rocket. They were drawing larger crowds partly because Porl Thompson was quickly earning a reputation as a blazing guitar talent. His popularity was also a big reason the Easy Cure kept getting regular gigs. Despite his ability to draw fans, Porl's status as local guitar hero quickly became a thorny problem.

His freewheeling guitar acrobatics, earsplittingly loud and often drenched in feedback, overshadowed the rest of the band. Robert Smith and the others felt that nobody in the audience was paying attention to the music anyway and that their primary purpose was to be background noise to accompany the patrons' inevitable descent into drunkenness. Smith seethed with frustration over the situation given the hard work they put into the music, but with demos for Hansa on the horizon, a lineup change was not in the cards.

One more domino fell on September 12 when Peter O'Toole left the band after returning from a kibbutz in Israel. Fed up at dealing with the uninspiring vocalists he'd worked with in Malice and the Easy Cure, Robert Smith decided to take on the role himself. He figured that since he was the songwriter, he'd understand what the song required more than anybody else could. They'd struck out so far with vocalists, and Smith had felt all along he could do better.

This was all well and good in theory, but Robert did not anticipate his incredible stage fright going into his first show as lead singer. It was an open-air concert held at the Crawley Bandstand on October 9, 1977, and dubbed the "Peace Party." Before the show, Robert drank himself into near insensibility to summon the courage to go onstage and sing, and when he finally did, he started in with a song different from what the rest of the band was playing.

Smith didn't have time to stew about his failures, as the very next day, the Easy Cure gathered at Sound and Vision Studios in London and cut five demos for Hansa. Only "Meathook" would survive to make their first album, while "Pillbox Tales," "I Just Need Myself," and "I Want to Be Old" were left off *Three Imaginary Boys*. The last song, "See the Children," has never been released, and Robert has said that it might be the worst song in the band's history.

The Hansa personnel on hand were not impressed. They weren't keen on the original material, preferring the Easy Cure record covers, like "I Fought the Law" and "The Great Airplane Disaster," which they refused to do. A month later, they returned to Sound and Vision Studios for another session. They tried two originals, "I'm Cold" and a slowed-down version of "Killing an Arab," along with three covers at Hansa's insistence: "I Saw Her Standing There," "Little Girl," and "Rebel Rebel." Neither side walked away from the session happy.

The situation between Hansa and the Easy Cure deteriorated rapidly. The label offered to allow them to record songs originally intended for the teen group Child, which Hansa had been trying unsuccessfully to break internationally. The band flatly refused, and a stalemate ensued. Hansa wanted to market the Easy Cure for their looks, while the band had no intention of being forced to do music they hated.

The two sides agreed to one more studio session to see if they could reach some sort of understanding. This time at London's PSL Studios in January 1978, Hansa brought in a higher-level producer, Trevor Vallis, with hopes that the band would benefit from his guidance and might churn out a few potential hits.

Once again, the session went nowhere. The Easy Cure managed to get through four songs, three originals ("I Just Need Myself," "Plastic Passion" and "Smashed Up"), and another go-around with Bowie's "Rebel Rebel." It was clear to all involved that the situation could not be salvaged. In the midst of his disgust over Hansa, Robert Smith realized that most of the originals they played for Hansa were crap anyway, and he was sick of them.

Although they had no clue at the time, the Easy Cure's next gig at the Rocket on February 19, 1978, held special significance. The support band was a ramshackle punk outfit called Lockjaw, which had already released a single, "Radio Call Sign." Lockjaw was soon forgotten, but their bassist at the time was Simon Gallup, who would eventually become an integral part of the Cure.

A few weeks later, it was officially over with Hansa. The label declined to release "Killing an Arab" as a single, and the contract was dissolved. Robert Smith was shrewd enough to ensure that the band kept their initial advance and retained the rights to the songs recorded during the demo sessions. The entire experience with Hansa was dispiriting, and they put their frustrations into a mocking new song, "Do the Hansa," which quickly became a live favorite and eventually ended up as a B-side.

Shortly thereafter, Robert Smith invested in new equipment that would serve him well in the months ahead. On April 17, 1978, he purchased his famous Woolworths Top 20 guitar, along with a Bontempi organ and a WEM amp. This is the setup that would get Smith through the band's early years until money started coming in. But just as he was upgrading, the band had reached a crossroad.

Smith was insistent that Porl Thompson no longer be part of the band, as his lead guitar style was simply at odds with the skeletal material Smith wanted to play. Tolhurst and Dempsey agreed given that Thompson drowned them out onstage with his blaring guitar. The situation was delicate in part because Thompson was dating Robert's younger sister Janet.

Eventually, they took the passive-aggressive way out of the dilemma. They paused rehearsals for a few weeks and then didn't bother telling Porl when they resumed. Thompson took his ouster in good stride and understood that it wasn't really a good match considering the direction the band was taking. Now a trio, the "Easy" was also dropped, and the Cure was finally born. Robert Smith always hated "the Easy Cure," claiming that it sounded like a group comprised of California hippies. He thought the Cure was more immediate and impactful, allowing for a more intense sound.

The final gig for the Easy Cure was on April 22, 1978, at Montefiore Institute Hall, and on May 18, 1978, the Cure debuted at their favorite haunt: the Rocket. The band held a special show at the Rocket on July 9, 1978, called "Mourning the Departed," in which they paid homage to Porl Thompson, who showed up in costume as a surprise guest. It would be this show that Robert Smith would erroneously call the band's first performance as the Cure forty years later when celebrating its anniversary in Hyde Park (it was actually their third).

May 27, 1978, turned out to be one of the most important dates in the Cure's history. The newly revamped trio booked time at Chestnut Studio in Sussex to record a new demo tape to send around to all the labels. The four songs on which they pinned their hopes were "10:15 Saturday Night," "Boys Don't Cry," "It's Not You," and "Fire in Cairo." They sent the tapes out, and very quickly the rejection letters started flowing in.

That might have been the end, with the Cure struggling along as a local band until they finally gave up and gave in to whatever alternate futures they might have lived. Fortunately for them and for music fans around the world, they got a lucky break. Chris Parry at Fiction Records, a division of Polydor, noticed the "drip drip drip" on "10:15 Saturday Night" while randomly listening to the dozens of tapes he received on a regular basis—and suddenly the Cure's future became very bright indeed, even if they didn't know it yet.

3

Radio-Friendly Unit Shifters: Chris Parry and Fiction Records

Chris Parry signs the Cure to Fiction Records and helps guide them to unimaginable heights.

To create, one must first imagine, which is simply a dream. Artists are dreamers. So many dreams die on the shelf, the flames of inspiration and ambition flickering less bright with each passing year.

For a band ripping through their songs at full volume in a garage or basement, pumped with aggression and tenacity, a demo tape is their best shot at making it. These tapes are capsules of hope, dream applications stitched together by sacrifice. They represent endless hours of rehearsal, writing, and performing; the money spent and the money lost from pathways not pursued; the time away from friends and family; and the drudgery of driving from gig to gig, lugging equipment, often to play for a few dozen people barely paying attention as they drink, chat idly with friends, and stare at their smartphones.

Once a demo tape is sent away, there is a palpable sense of anticipation and apprehension. Hopes rest on them, and they are mostly dashed—but not always.

The Cure's demo tape turned out to be a direct hit that slammed talent and determination into opportunity, resulting in the highest high a band could possibly dream. The demo session was financed by Ric Gallup, brother of eventual bassist Simon. Ric was a friend and supporter of the band who worked at a local record shop and had seen them perform numerous times. Ric felt they were good enough to put their ambition into motion, so he paid for a session at

Chestnut Studio in Sussex so that the Cure would have a high-quality recording of their best songs to send to record companies for consideration.

The songs chosen for inclusion were "Boys Don't Cry," "It's Not You," "Fire in Cairo," and "10:15 Saturday Night." They sent it to every major record label and hoped for the best. Although United Artists and Stiff professed potential interest, it was nothing but rejection letters until they heard from A&R man Chris Parry at Polydor Records.

Chris Parry was on a hot streak, having recently signed the Jam and Siouxsie and the Banshees to Polydor, where both had already scored hits. As part of his search for new talent, Parry routinely spent hours listening to some of the dozens of demo tapes sent in every week. He popped in the Cure's, not really paying that much attention until the "drip drip drip" of "10:15 Saturday Night" caught his ear. He stopped what he was doing, rewound the tape, and played it all the way through. Chris Parry liked what he heard.

Parry wrote to Robert asking for an audition. Smith suggested they meet first, which happened on August 10, 1977, at Parry's office in London. They got along well from the beginning. Parry thought that Robert was a bit odd and wasn't quite comfortable in his own skin but was obviously intelligent. He liked the band's looks and thought the Cure's music was unique and off-kilter enough to be compelling. Robert Smith liked Parry's obvious enjoyment of his job and that he didn't seem to take himself too seriously.

Parry told the trio that he was forming his own independent label, Fiction Records, to be distributed by Polydor and that he wanted the Cure to be Fiction's first signing and flagship artist. This threw the band for a loop initially, as they had assumed Parry would be signing them to Polydor, a major label. Parry countered that he would sign them directly to Polydor if they chose, but as he told the Cure more about how they fit into his plans for Fiction, their hesitation thawed, and they warmed to the notion of being on an independent label with the promise of more artistic freedom.

At Robert's suggestion, Chris Parry caught the Cure performing on August 27 at Lakers in Redhil, and the band managed to impress him with their sound and style. While watching them perform that night, Chris Parry had a premonition that the Cure would someday be very famous and would make him a lot of money. His instincts proved accurate. Two weeks later, the Cure signed a six-month deal with Fiction.

Chris Parry wasted no time in getting the band into the studio. Only a week after the contract was signed, the Cure found themselves in Morgan Studios, where they recorded their first five songs for Fiction: "Killing an Arab," "10:15 Saturday Night," "Fire in Cairo," "Plastic Passion," and "Three Imaginary Boys."

He immediately booked the Cure higher-profile gigs, including a few opening slots for Generation X, the band fronted by future star Billy Idol. They also landed two dates with Wire in early October. The Cure was dazzled by Wire's sonic power and the sheer force of their presence onstage. The shows made a lasting impression on the Cure, and they knew they needed to up their game.

On October 12, they were back in Morgan Studios. The band was essentially running through all of the songs in their repertoire live in the studio. To save money, the Cure recorded during the overnight hours, with Chris Parry producing and Mike Hedges engineering. Parry and Robert Smith bickered a lot about the sound of the album, but Smith didn't yet carry the leverage to win those battles, and Parry got his way. That would change when Smith seized creative control for the Cure's second album, *Seventeen Seconds*, but Parry remained the band's label boss, manager, and a trusted voice who understood Robert Smith and the way he worked.

Chris Parry and Robert Smith were similar in many respects. Neither of them wanted to play the usual record industry games, which allowed the Cure to operate much more independently than most artists. Smith respected Parry, which was key because when it came down to it, Parry was one of the few people the front man would listen to. The awkward suburban English teenagers and the laid-back New Zealander became unlikely partners. The talent was in Robert Smith and his bandmates, but it was Chris Parry who guided them out of Crawley. He is the man responsible for the Cure's ascension into the rock 'n' roll stratosphere.

Chris Parry, born near Wellington, New Zealand, was a music fan from childhood with a passion for drumming. By 1964, he had landed a gig drumming for the local band Sine Waves. They changed their name to the Insect and then to Fourmyula. Their sound was pop with a folk twist, and they became enormously successful in their native New Zealand.

By 1968, Fourmyula was scoring major hits in their native country. That year, they scored three top-ten singles in New Zealand: "Come with Me," "Alice Is There," and "I Know Why." They hit number one in New Zealand in 1969 with "Nature" and had eleven hit singles overall. Even though they toured the United Kingdom and other parts of Europe, Fourmyula was never able to break out of the New Zealand market. They broke up in 1971. In March 2010, a box set collected much of the group's catalog.

Parry first traveled to London while touring with Fourmyula and relocated there after the band's collapse. In 1973, he landed his first record label job in the International Department of Phonogram Records. The following year, he took a marketing position at Polydor but was soon working as a talent scout in their A&R department. In 1975, he made his first signing to Polydor: the Chanter Sisters.

Things changed in 1976 when punk exploded across the cultural landscape. After seeing the Sex Pistols at Barbarella's in Birmingham, Parry tried in vain to convince his bosses to sign them. He was also rebuffed by Polydor when he tried to sign the Clash, growing increasingly frustrated with the label's insistence that punk was a passing fad not worth pursuing.

Parry's big break came when he saw the Jam perform at the Marquee in January 1977. Parry signed them to Polydor, and by April, they had their first top-forty U.K. single with "In the City." The Jam went on to become massively successful and influential, with number one singles like "Town Called Malice," "Going Underground," and "Start!"

Parry rolled the dice with Siouxsie and the Banshees. They were a hot band around London by early 1978, but they insisted on complete artistic control, and thus far no record label was willing to make that offer. Chris Parry saw their long-term potential and wisely signed them in June 1978, giving them the control they sought. Only two months later, Siouxsie and the Banshees hit the top ten with their debut single: "Hong Kong Garden." By this time, Chris Parry had already spearheaded Fiction, with the Cure deemed its signature artist.

There were several clashes between Robert Smith and Chris Parry over the years, but one of the most momentous was over the 1982 single "Let's Go to Bed." Robert decided at the last minute that he didn't want the pop frivolity to come out under the Cure's name. Parry balked and refused to budge, overruling Smith's objection. Given that the song paved the way for the Cure's massive expansion of sound and their blockbuster hits, Robert Smith should be saying prayers of thanks to Chris Parry for that one.

Parry said in a 2010 interview that he and Robert Smith are still in touch, but their relationship became a bit strained when Parry sold Fiction to Universal. Although Smith will not speak publicly about it, there have been signs of tension. Smith yanked the Cure from Fiction after their last contract expired, and Lol Tolhurst said that in 2000, he was told by Smith that Parry had "gone crazy." But Robert Smith is well aware how vital Chris Parry is to the Cure's story. Of note, Parry was the only nonmember of the Cure whom Robert thanked by name during his acceptance speech at the Rock and Roll Hall of Fame.

Chris Parry managed the Cure until 1988, and Fiction released their music until 2000, when Parry sold the label to Universal Records. Fiction signed a few artists in the early days, most notably the Associates and the Passions, but the label soon became primarily a vehicle for the Cure. Parry again expanded the label's roster in the late 1980s and early 1990s, but by 1995, it again catered only to the Cure.

After the sale to Universal Records, the Cure left, and the label was eventually revived in 2004 as a brand for Universal to issue releases by mostly edgy guitar-rock bands. Fiction still exists as a label under parent company Universal Music Group and has issued albums by multiple influential artists of the last decade, including the Naked and Famous, the Yeah Yeah Yeahs, Crystal Castles, Snow Patrol, Death from Above 1979, and Tame Impala.

Chris Parry also became deeply involved in the radio business, cofounding XFM (later Radio X) in 1992. Robert Smith has also dabbled in the radio business, becoming deeply involved with XFM. Parry reunited with Fourmyula in 2010 and sat behind the drum kit for a couple reunion shows in New Zealand. Chris Parry is mostly retired now and still lives in New Zealand, spending much of his time boating.

Chris Parry will always be remembered for being the man who discovered and signed the Cure. He was able to guide the intractable Robert Smith through the early days of playing in raucous local bars to headlining stadiums. Parry remained a pivotal adviser who earned and kept Robert Smith's trust (not an easy task) but didn't hesitate to stand up to the mercurial and often stubborn rock star when needed. He was smart enough to allow Smith to follow his own musical path, providing suggestions and ideas along the way, but he didn't hesitate to stand up to the mercurial and often stubborn front man when he deemed it necessary. They were fortunate to have found each other, and it's a partnership whose importance perhaps gets overlooked. Without Chris Parry, the Cure may never have existed beyond the dive bars of Crawley and its surrounding villages.

4

Degenerate the Faithful: "Killing an Arab"

The Cure's debut single launched their career, but not without controversy.

At some point, existential angst seems almost inevitable. After all, look at the world around us, the unimaginable vastness of the universe. Can any of this ever be adequately explained? We humans have been trying to know the unknowable in outrageously inventive ways since the earliest of civilizations. How many Gods have been created and forgotten over the eons?

Mythology rules our world now as much as ever, for all our vaunted knowledge. Yet it's all an absurdity. No human can know the truth or even begin to envision the ultimate possibilities of the universe. There is no divine awareness, no purpose, no meaning. Therefore, life is meaningless, death is meaningless. It doesn't matter if we all die. To the universe, the death of a random stranger who is simply standing on a beach is much like a pebble tumbling from its perch on a cliff into the vast sea below.

Serious thoughts for anyone and certainly for a high school student suddenly questioning everything he or she has been told since birth. It's not unusual for students with even a hint of literary pretension (and Robert Smith had substantially more than a hint) to enter that phase of existential angst that requires an important rite of passage—the reading of the 1942 novel *The Stranger* by Albert Camus.

Camus was a French Algerian philosopher and writer tied, along with Jean-Paul Sartre, to the existentialist movement, although he always rebuffed such labels. *The Stranger* is the most widely known piece of literature explicitly drawn through this prism. It's about a meaningless killing. Murder and violence committed in a flash, one man's life extinguished and another's changed forever, for nothing.

Robert Smith got his hands on the book during high school, and it prompted what would eventually become a historic recording: the Cure's first single and the most controversial of their entire career, "Killing an Arab." Fittingly, many years later as the band's popularity soared and a huge new audience was exposed to "Killing an Arab" via the *Standing on a Beach* singles compilation, the song inspired a new generation in turn to discover Camus' novel.

"Killing an Arab" is one of Smith's earliest songs, written in 1975 when he was sixteen. It became a staple of the band's gigs from the early days as the Easy Cure, and the song stayed with them through every important step that led to a record deal with Fiction and finally to its release as the Cure's first single.

Like with the Beatles' "Love Me Do" and so many other debut singles, it's hard to imagine listening to "Killing an Arab" forty years ago and envisioning even a small iota of the success the Cure would experience. But experience it they did, and say what you will about its sophistication (or lack thereof) and

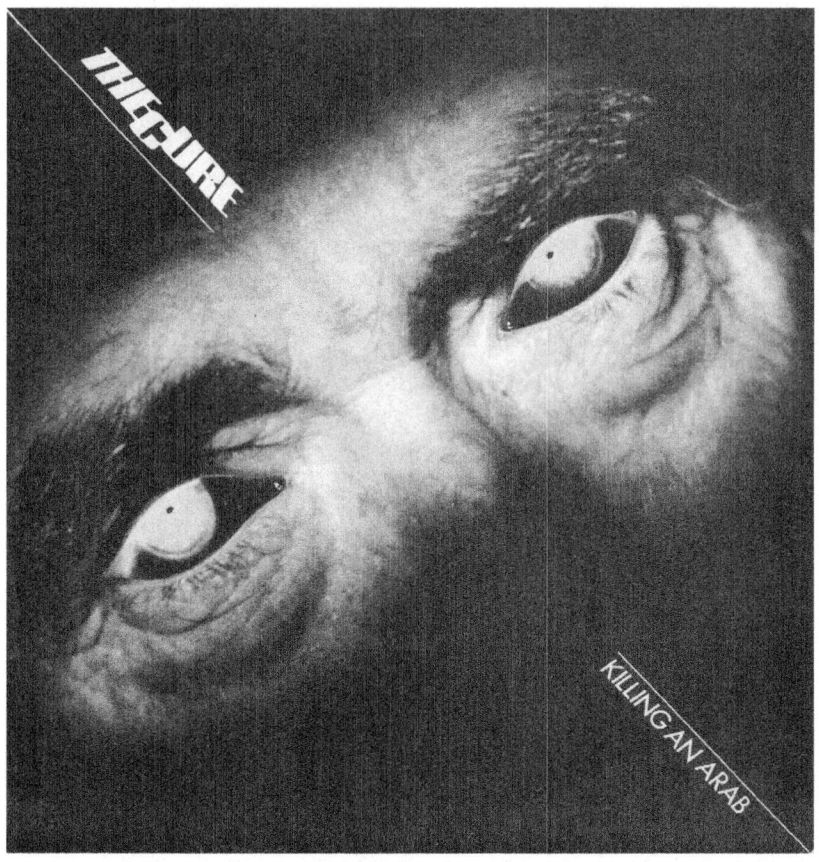

The Cure's controversial debut single is still capable of stoking debate over 40 years since its release even though it never made an appearance on the singles chart.   *Author's Collection*

depth, but "Killing an Arab" is the song that set the Cure on the pathway to greatness.

The Cure had tested a much slower version of the song when it was demoed at Sound and Vision Studios in London in November 1977 for Hansa Records. Their relationship with Hansa finally reached its inevitable conclusion when the two sides reached an impasse over what to record. Even as the Easy Cure in early 1978, the band insisted that "Killing an Arab" backed with "10:15 Saturday Night" be its first single. Hansa refused to even consider it, and by the end of March 1978, the band and the label officially severed ties.

Robert Smith, shrewd even at such a young age, insisted that the Cure would retain the rights to the original material they demoed, including "Killing an Arab." The bemused suits at Hansa didn't object in the slightest; it's interesting to consider how different the band's career may have been had the label refused to budge.

Chris Parry of Polydor signed the Cure to his new label Fiction, and his attitude about the song was much different. Parry had no problem with Robert Smith's vision of the jagged minimalist rockers "Killing an Arab" and "10:15 Saturday Night" as the Cure's first 45-rpm (although Smith wanted a double A-side, which Parry smartly refused). Smith thought the two songs were an absolute touchstone on what the Cure is about, edgy and tense with a detached laconic vocal and plenty of mystery.

"Boys Don't Cry" clearly had the most commercial potential out of any of the era's tracks, but Parry thought it would pigeonhole the Cure into the power-pop niche if it became a big hit out of the gate. He wanted to cultivate an edgier image for the Cure, and "Killing an Arab" would deliver that.

Nobody in and around the Cure felt that "Killing an Arab" would be a big hit, but Parry pinned his hopes on music critics appreciating the song as well as the more obsessive music lovers who follow their favorite artists religiously. He felt both groups would like "Killing an Arab" and generate buzz and momentum around the band that would lead to a big breakthrough with "Boys Don't Cry." Credibility first, then shoot for the top.

Both "Killing an Arab" and "10:15 Saturday Night" were recorded during sessions for the Cure's debut album, *Three Imaginary Boys*, which began on October 12, 1978, at Morgan Studios. The band essentially ran through their entire roster of songs in the studio, and not all of them turned out the way Smith had hoped.

Fortunately, they nailed "Killing an Arab." Robert Smith's deadpan vocal delivery of the tightly horizontal melody is so offhand as to almost seem spoken rather than sung, perhaps to emulate the detachment exhibited by the killer in Camus' novel. It's clear from their very first single that Robert Smith had confidence in his abilities and wasn't afraid to do something audacious. Musically, the song hints at Middle Eastern–influenced mysticism, with its oud-style guitar introduction and vaguely exotic guitar pattern throughout, punctuated by cymbal crashes and powered by a propulsive rhythm and bass.

December 1978 was a crucial month for the Cure. Their trajectory was trending upward thanks to Chris Parry nabbing them opening slots for bands like Generation X, Wire, and the U.K. Subs. The Cure played their first session for John Peel at BBC Radio on December 4, which was an important boost leading up to their debut single.

"Killing an Arab" was initially released on December 22, 1978, on the tiny Small Wonder label. Chris Parry farmed the song out to the smaller label for a limited initial pressing since Fiction's parent company, Polydor, was reluctant to put any weight or money behind the Cure or "Killing an Arab." Both the Cure and Chris Parry wanted the single out before Christmas, but a disinterested and unenthused Polydor was moving at a snail's pace, so Parry made the Small Wonder deal. After the 15,000 copies printed by Small Wonder sold out, it was reissued by Fiction and distributed by Polydor in January 1979.

The single helped catch the attention of the British music press almost immediately. *New Music Express* (*NME*) named "Killing an Arab" the Single of the Week and described Smith's guitar work as "full of eerie promises, slithering like the sprog of some belly dancer and a poisonous reptile." *NME* also praised the Cure's live show and soon had mentions of them regularly as the band expanded their tour dates. Other publications were just as positive. *Melody Maker* compared it to Siouxsie and the Banshees' recent top-ten breakthrough "Hong Kong Garden," and *Sounds* issued a glowing review.

The song was controversial even in the early days, as Crawley was infiltrated by a large contingent supportive of the racist National Front, a hate group whose slogan was "Keep England White." They, of course, completely misinterpreted the song, assuming it to be anti-Arab. At some of the Cure's shows in the area, on discovering the rest of the band's set was nothing like "Killing an Arab," some hard-core skinheads from the National Front loudly berated the band, shouting and even screaming verbal abuse.

The Cure said it didn't faze them, but it's hard to imagine not feeling at least somewhat roiled in that scenario. Extra security was added to the tour, and it kept hitting bigger and bigger places. The group knew there were people there who wanted to see them, so they went on with their complete shows. Once the "Killing an Arab" single was released, Smith was obliged to give several interviews patiently explaining how the song came about and why it is not racist.

The most serious flashpoint in the song's controversial history came in 1986 following the inclusion of "Killing an Arab" on the massively successful singles compilation *Standing on a Beach*. Even though it was the Cure's debut single and had been released eight years prior, this compilation was the first time most U.S. fans had been exposed to it. Unfortunately, "Killing an Arab" was again misinterpreted by some, and this time, the stakes were much higher.

The American-Arab Anti-Discrimination Committee (ADC) expressed concern about "Killing an Arab" directly to Elektra Records, the Cure's U.S. label, in the spring of 1986 immediately after a board member noticed the title in a review for *Standing on a Beach*. The pressure intensified when, according to the ADC, a student deejay at WPRB Princeton in New Jersey introduced the track with obvious approval of it, encouraging the "killing of A-Rabs" (although it should be noted that the deejay strongly denied the accusation, and others who heard the broadcast also disputed the ADC's characterization of the on-air comments).

The ADC also pointed to several other alleged incidents in which deejays played the song while making reference to the high-profile U.S. air strikes carried out in April 1986 against Libyan dictator Muammar Gaddafi in retaliation for a deadly bombing carried out in a West Berlin nightclub earlier that same month. They launched a telephone and letter campaign against Elektra and its parent company Warner Communications, demanding that "Killing an Arab" be deleted from future pressings of *Standing on a Beach*.

Elektra took the issue very seriously and asked Robert Smith and Chris Parry to drop the song from the album. Smith refused, citing the patently ridiculous nature of the misinterpretation and the song's pivotal role in the Cure's history. Smith offered to simply halt production of the entire album for the U.S. market. Elektra had no intention of cutting off an album that had already become the Cure's biggest-selling U.S. release by far, so Smith held the upper hand.

A resolution was reached when Smith agreed to pen a message to be included on a sticker prominently placed on the cover of all copies of *Standing on a Beach* that read, "The song "Killing an Arab" has absolutely no racist overtones whatsoever. It is a song which decries the existence of all prejudice and consequent violence. The Cure condemn its use in furthering anti-Arab feeling."

Smith also issued a statement to the American press via Chris Parry that said in part that he had been informed that "Killing an Arab" is being used by "certain reactionary factions of the media, most notably by some particularly brainless and irresponsible deejays, as part of a wave of anti-Arab feeling currently existing in some parts of America. I would therefore like it to be known that I and the rest of The Cure totally condemn this misrepresentation and consequent misinterpretation of the song."

In the years ahead, Smith would go even further in dampening any potential misinterpretation of the song. The Cure played the song less frequently than they once did, and often they used an alternative title, most frequently "Killing Another." They seemed to have disowned the song entirely when it was the only period track not included on the two-CD deluxe reissue of their debut album, *Three Imaginary Boys*, in 2004.

As time has passed, Smith's thinking on the issue seems to have evolved yet again. For the final three nights of the Cure's 2016 tour at Wembley in London,

"Killing an Arab" was reintroduced in their set, the only shows during the entire tour in which it was played. The original lyrics were used and sung with feverish intensity.

Most notably, at the Cure's highly publicized fortieth-anniversary show at Hyde Park in London on July 7, 2018, the Cure ended their special celebratory concert with "Killing an Arab," the lyrics unaltered. Many were surprised by the choice to end such an important show with the song, and it seemed like a bold statement given that Robert Smith clearly selected the set list very carefully to represent the band's forty-year career.

Of course, inevitably, more controversy ensued with discussion over the merits of the song and the wisdom of the Cure's decision to once again fully embrace it. Bloggers opined about it endlessly, articles in major publications discussed it, and Cure fans reacted with near universal approval. "Killing an Arab" served its purpose well as a debut single and is a classic post-punk nugget, but it's the controversy that will likely always define it. From 1978 to 2018, "Killing an Arab" has been and likely will always be a lightning rod for strong opinions and even stronger crashing cymbals.

5

You Would Cry Too: *Three Imaginary Boys*

The Cure's quirky post-punk debut hints at greater things to come.

Released: May 8, 1979
Fiction Records—FIX 1, 2442 163
Running time: 33:44

1. "10:15 Saturday Night" (3:42), 2. "Accuracy" (2:17), 3. "Grinding Halt" (2:49), 4. "Another Day" (3:44), 5. "Object" (3:03), 6. "Subway Song" (2:00), 7. "Foxy Lady" (2:29), 8. "Meathook" (2:17), 9. "So What?" (2:37), 10. "Fire in Cairo" (3:23), 11. "It's Not You" (2:49), 12. "Three Imaginary Boys" (3:17), 13. "The Weedy Burton" (1:04)

The prognosis for a band's long-term success is impossible to determine from their debut. Some deliver a knockout punch in the form of a classic first album, perhaps heralding the arrival of a major new talent. If the second album tanks, though, things can change quickly. The music industry is fickle and unpredictable. A big splash with a first album could launch a long and magnificent career, or, given our culture's tendency to tear down hard what has been lovingly propped up for years, it could just as easily be the mountaintop before an avalanche into oblivion.

The Cure's 1979 debut, *Three Imaginary Boys*, likely would have gone down as a mostly forgotten post-punk trifle if their popularity hadn't exploded. Their fame allowed an album that yielded no hits and barely grazed the U.K. album chart to eventually reach a larger audience. Robert Smith has dismissed *Three Imaginary Boys* as not representative of the Cure and has referred to its follow-up, 1980's *Seventeen Seconds*, as the band's first "real" album. That said, he has always maintained his fondness for certain songs of the era, several of which remain part of the Cure's live performances.

The punk-influenced power pop exhibited on *Three Imaginary Boys* is lean and sparse, with Smith sneering dourly through many of his earliest compositions. He chronicles the routine drudgery of everyday life with cynicism, sardonic wit, and earnest self-reflection. Drummer Laurence Tolhurst's technical limitations necessitated keeping the songs simple, which suited Smith perfectly because this limited the more lyrical bassist Michael Dempsey's ability to stretch beyond what the singer wanted while reducing the potential for conflict.

Robert Smith had intended to play the cheap Woolworths Top 20 guitar made by Teisco that he'd been using at shows, but Fiction label boss and producer Chris Parry was aghast at the notion and promptly bought the front man a new white Fender Jazzmaster. Smith decided to take the pickup from his Woolworths Top 20 and install it into the Jazzmaster, and it was this that he played throughout the *Three Imaginary Boys* sessions.

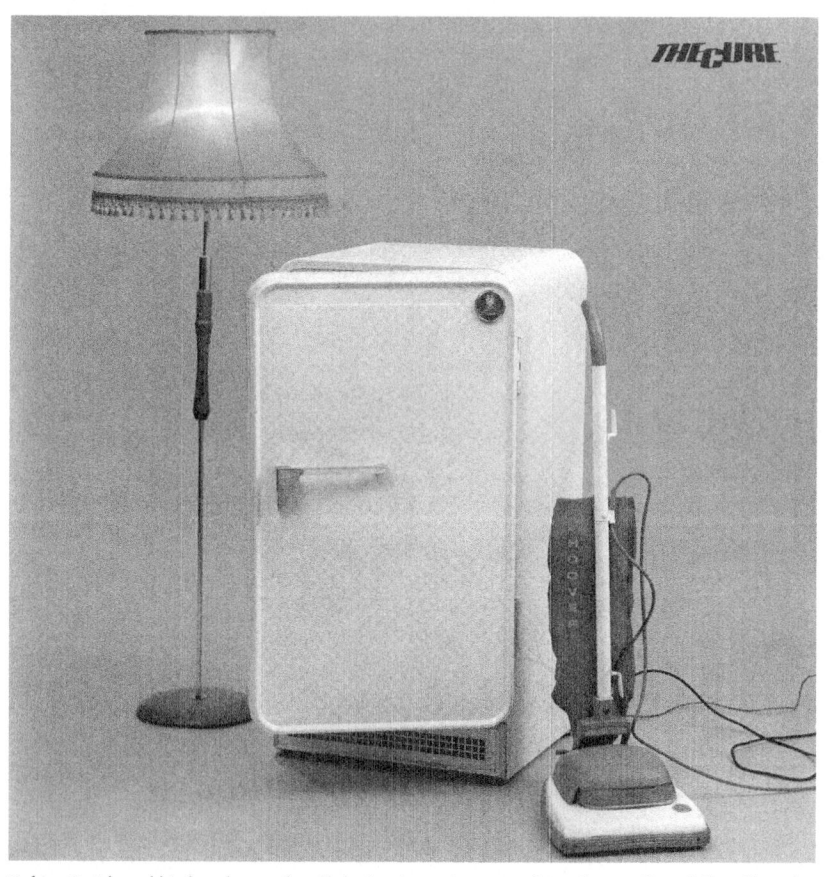

Robert Smith and his bandmates hated the "no image" concept foisted upon their debut album by Fiction boss Chris Parry in which the three band members were represented by mundane objects. It strangely suited the content of the album, *Three Imaginary Boys*, 1979.   *Author's Collection*

Smith's vocals at this stage are quite different than on later albums. He was just learning to be a singer, and his youthful voice is angular, sometimes angst-ridden or shiningly sincere, but more often indifferent. The youthful Smith had not yet developed the remarkably rich and nuanced instrument we hear on albums like *Disintegration* or *Wish*. Still, the traits and instincts that would come to define him as a songwriter and performer were already creeping through on standouts like "Another Day" and especially "Three Imaginary Boys," which points most directly to the band's future work.

At this point, Smith's songwriting may not approach his finest work, but it is nonetheless impressive for a writer of his young age. Many of the early tracks can best be described as sneering post-punk apathy, ranging from throwaways like "So What" and "Object" to a few much stronger nuggets in the same mold, like "Killing an Arab," "I'm Cold," "Plastic Passion," and "Grinding Halt." Smith balanced these spiky rockers with lower-key, more sparse and atmospheric material ("Accuracy," "Another Day," and "10:15 Saturday Night") with a few gleaming power-pop gems thrown in for good measure ("Boys Don't Cry," "Jumping Someone Else's Train," and "Fire in Cairo").

The Cure entered the sessions with a stockpile of original material developed over several years. Fiction Records boss Chris Parry produced the album with a miniscule budget, so they worked secretly in the middle of the night at Morgan Studios in London. *Three Imaginary Boys* was recorded in its entirety over five nights scattered from September 1978 through February 1979. The band quickly ran through their entire repertoire of about thirty songs, mostly just plugging in and playing the tracks live in the studio one after the other. Many of the recordings that made the album are first takes.

Parry produced *Three Imaginary Boys* to his own liking, aiming for cool detachment as an appropriate vehicle for the band's expressions of cynicism and boredom at the mundane. The demos and live recordings of the era show that the Cure possessed more innate power and ferocity than they exhibit on the album. Robert Smith realized during the sessions that Parry wasn't capturing the Cure's sound, leading to frequent arguments between them over the album's direction. In retrospect, it's clear that Smith had a valid complaint. All one needs to do is compare the band's propulsive take on "Grinding Halt" for *The John Peel Show* in May 1979 to the comparatively hollow album version to understand the discrepancy.

Even the demos show more bite. The early take of "Meathook" demoed at Sound and Vision Studios for Hansa Records in October 1977 is rough but has far more energy and force than the comparatively limp album version. Live performances of "Killing an Arab" have always been far more savage than the studio version. Yet it must be said that the atmospheric detachment of Parry's vision for the song creates a certain mystique that works to its advantage.

Ultimately, Chris Parry got his way because he held the leverage: Parry was experienced, while Smith was a studio novice. Parry also controlled the purse strings; he selected the track list and sequencing, and in collaboration with Polydor's art department, he helped create the cover art that the band unabashedly loathed.

Going for a "no image" concept that fit in with the detached nature of the music and the incorporation of the mundane in many of the songs, Parry had the three band members represented by a refrigerator, a lamp, and a vacuum cleaner, all on a bright pink background. Instead of song titles on the back cover, symbolic drawings were used to represent the songs. It was confusing to say the least.

The cover was ridiculed by some in the press, but it did get the Cure some attention. After the album was released, most reviews were positive (although *NME* writer Paul Morley savaged the album in a nasty review that irked Robert Smith even though he agreed with some of Morley's points). *Three Imaginary Boys* sold reasonably well, reaching #44 on the U.K. album chart, which was strong enough to bump up the Cure's profile and give Robert Smith the momentum he needed to seize control of the band's creative process.

Three Imaginary Boys

"10:15 Saturday Night"

The first recording of "10:15 Saturday Night," one of Robert Smith's earliest compositions, was conceived at his home on his sister Janet's organ. It was an important song in the Easy Cure's set from the very beginning, and the concept of a "Killing an Arab"/"10:15 Saturday Night" debut single was one that Smith held for a long time until it finally came to fruition. He nails a savage tremolo bar solo shredded by distortion. Chris Parry smartly included it as the leadoff track, thus giving it more exposure.

"10:15 Saturday Night" resonates with fans who understand the dispirited malaise being expressed. It was the hypnotic repetition of the "drip drip drip" that caught the attention of Fiction label head Chris Parry as he sorted through seemingly endless tapes of demos sent by hopeful artists. It seems appropriate that a song written about (and in a state of) boredom tinged with rejection and depression in a very real way launched the Cure's career. It was written by a fifteen-year-old Robert Smith in a setting exactly as described in the song.

Collectors salivate over a rare French promo single pressed in 1979 on Polydor with "Foxy Lady" as the B-side. A commercial release followed in 1980, again exclusive to the French market, this time paired with "Accuracy." The song remains a frequent part of the Cure's live shows, as they usually include it as part a set-ending encore of four or five early staples.

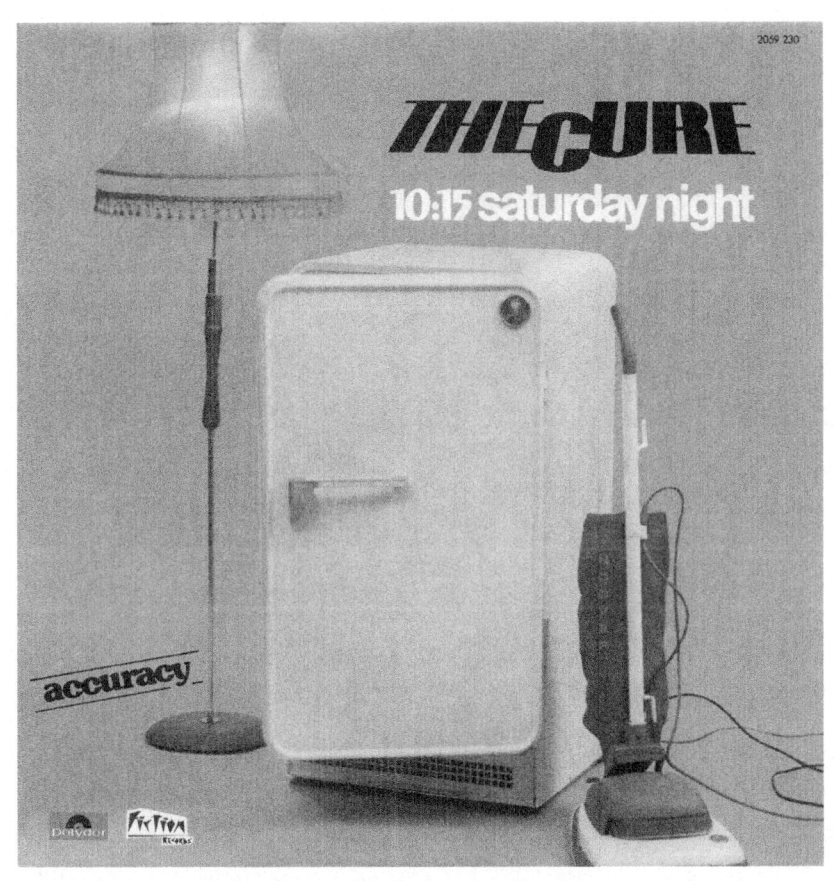

Robert Smith wanted this track to be a double A-side with "Killing an Arab" but Chris Parry smartly refused, although it did snag a spot as opening track for the debut album. Only in France was it released as a single.   *Author's Collection*

"Accuracy"

Robert Smith has named "Accuracy" one of his favorites on the album, as it points to the minimalism that the Cure would explore on *Seventeen Seconds*. The dead aim described by Smith in the song is the uncanny ability that humans have to say or do the precise thing that hurts a loved one the most.

"Accuracy" fit so well with the band's next two albums that it remained a regular part of their live sets all the way through the *Faith* era, one of the few tracks from the early days with that distinction.

"Grinding Halt"

Chris Parry pegged this spiky punk-pop nugget as the follow-up single to "Killing an Arab," resisting Smith's choice of "Boys Don't Cry," as he felt that such an obvious hit might trap the band into a stylistic box. He wanted a harder image for the Cure as they built their audience. The word snippets at the beginning of each line originate from lyrics written by Tolhurst but clipped by Smith to give it an edgier sound.

Parry had promo singles sent to local deejays, but a tepid response dashed plans for the single. *NME* critic Ian Penman wrote a short, negative, but ludicrously incomprehensible review, calling it a "hype." Copies of the promo single, backed with "Meathook," are now a highly sought-after collector's item.

Chris Parry wanted this spiky post-punk nugget to be The Cure's second single, and Fiction Records pressed a small number of 12" promo singles to send to DJs to guage interest.

Author's Collection

Chris Parry did manage to find a spot for "Grinding Halt" on the soundtrack to the 1980 film *Times Square*. An expression of the apathy that saturates much of the band's early material, "Grinding Halt" is a single that almost was and probably should have been. It still occasionally shows up in the band's live sets, usually during an encore of their early material. Of the five classic early era songs the band performed at their fortieth-anniversary show on July 7, 2018, in Hyde Park, in addition to the obvious choices of "Boys Don't Cry," "Killing an Arab," "10:15 Saturday Night," and "Jumping Someone Else's Train," the fifth selection was "Grinding Halt," emphasizing the song's importance among the Cure's early material.

"Another Day"

Given its sparseness, it's not surprising that Smith noted "Another Day" as another early song that he appreciates. It was added to the Cure's regular set about midway through their 1980 trek in support of *Seventeen Seconds*, but unlike its sonic cousin "Accuracy," "Another Day" was neglected for more than three decades before finally being performed again. As with other pieces on *Three Imaginary Boys*, "Another Day" is an expression of a dreary everyday existence trapped in monotony.

"Object"

Robert Smith has always expressed disdain for "Object," understandable given the sheer nastiness of the lyrics and delivery. In a 1988 interview, Smith named it his least favorite Cure song. It's a shame because the track is actually a potent rocker with plenty of attitude to spare and a decent melodic hook. Perhaps a rewrite of the lyrics could have salvaged it because there's just no way of getting through the last verse in particular without cringing.

"Subway Song"

Inspired by a railway underpass in Lol Tolhurst's hometown of Horley, "Subway Song" is suitably atmospheric and chilling with eerie harmonica and a whispered vocal by Smith. Its ending, a (spoiler alert) shocking scream that comes after a long fade-out, will make you jump if you're not ready. Barely grazing the two-minute mark, "Subway Song" is one of the shortest in the Cure's oeuvre.

"Foxy Lady"

All members of the Cure were Jimi Hendrix fanatics, and many years later, a very different lineup of the band would record an outstanding cover of "Purple Haze." This awkward run-through of "Foxy Lady," which they played in rehearsals and sound checks, has been cited by Smith as one of the reasons he regrets Chris Parry choosing the songs for *Three Imaginary Boys*.

It's hard to imagine what Parry was thinking, especially considering that he placed it prominently as the opening track of side 2. Bassist Michael Dempsey wanted to sing on a track, and rather than give him an original composition, Robert Smith chose this cover. Dempsey does his best, but nothing can salvage this throwaway, one of the Cure's least consequential recordings.

"Meathook"

This sinister ditty had been part of the Cure's live sets since early on. They demoed it for Hansa a year and a half prior to the album's release. Its off-kilter oddness is essential early Cure, even though Robert Smith has said it's one of their worst. It wasn't included on the compilation *Boys Don't Cry*, which sought to compile the strongest early material from the album and the various singles and B-sides for countries like the United States where *Three Imaginary Boys* hadn't been released.

"Meathook" is the kind of absurdity that would make the cutting room floor for almost anybody else, but in a way, it shows the fearless approach that has defined the Cure's career over four decades. If they have the balls to put a track like "Meathook" on their debut, then they can do anything.

"So What?"

Robert Smith hadn't bothered to write proper lyrics for this standard post-punk trifle, so when it came time to record, he just drunkenly sang from the back of a bag of sugar about a cake decorating set. It's bewildering that a song like this made it onto the album considering that there was much better material available, but its random nature fits nicely with the impersonal "no image" concept that Parry had concocted.

"Fire in Cairo"

"Fire in Cairo" was a key track in the band's live sets during the early years, and the studio version could easily have been a single. The melodic hook in the chorus consists of Smith spelling out the song's title repetitively, and despite its simplicity, it works rather well. "Fire in Cairo," with its almost reggae-influenced Police kind of vibe, is the kind of upbeat guitar pop from which Smith quickly wanted to distance himself, yet it remains one of the true gems of the era.

"Fire in Cairo" still appears occasionally in the band's live sets. Particularly noteworthy was the solo performance Robert Smith delivered during the final encore of a 50-song behemoth concert held in Mexico City on Robert's 54th birthday, April 21, 2013. At four hours and 16 minutes, it was the longest Cure show ever.

"It's Not You"

This snide rocker is one of four songs (along with early mainstays "Boys Don't Cry," "10:15 Saturday Night," and "Fire in Cairo") the band recorded at Chestnut Studios for the all-important demo that resulted in their signing to Fiction.

Smith later soured on "It's Not You," and it was left off when Chris Parry compiled the *Boys Don't Cry* compilation. It's so close to "Object" in tone and subject matter that it's overkill for both to be on the same album. "It's Not You" tries for a tough edge and attitude that it doesn't quite achieve, and the lyrics are aptly described by Smith himself as hateful.

"Three Imaginary Boys"

Stark and dramatic, "Three Imaginary Boys" points directly toward the band's shift in styles for their next two albums. Robert Smith's darkly poetic lyrics were inspired by a dream. They exhibit a depth of feeling that hadn't yet appeared in a Cure song, and Smith delivers them with palpable emotion. "Three Imaginary Boys" reaches its apex with a searing guitar solo that rises out of the somber accompaniment like a white-hot razor.

"Three Imaginary Boys" still features regularly in the band's set, and it ranks along with "Boys Don't Cry" as the very best of the Cure's early output.

"The Weedy Burton"

"The Weedy Burton" is a tossed-off instrumental bit of jazzy nonsense tacked on to the end of the album as an uncredited extra track. Michael Dempsey coined the name after reading *Play in a Day* by Bert Weedon, a 1950s-era British guitarist who was enormously influential to Robert Smith, among many others.

Non–Album Singles and B-Sides

"Boys Don't Cry"

The shining star of the Cure's early years, "Boys Don't Cry" is a 1960s guitar-pop pastiche with a killer melody and guitar riff. It was Robert Smith's attempt to write a perfect pop song in homage to the Beatles and other bands of the era, and he nailed it. His vocal delivery captures the sentiment in the lyrics to perfection: winsome, vulnerable, genuinely regretful, but still with a mischievous

The Cure's second single didn't chart at the time of its release, but over four decades later it's an undisputed classic. *Author's Collection*

spark. Smith's exaggerated accent gives the song a working-class, homespun vibe brimming with sincerity and the brashness of youth.

Robert Smith and Chris Parry knew that "Boys Don't Cry" had the potential to be a major hit, but Parry worried that it would typecast the Cure as too pop when he wanted to project an edgier image so that they'd be taken more seriously. Thus, it was passed over as the band's first single in favor of the spartan "Killing an Arab." Parry also left it off the Cure's first album to be saved as a single, which was finally released in June 1979. It did not become the massive hit that Parry and the band envisioned, a failure that Parry laid at the feet of Polydor for their failure to provide an enthusiastic promotional push.

Knowing it to be a great song, when the time came to record it, the Cure was up to the challenge and delivered a knockout performance in the studio. The double-tracked guitar runs are rather simple but tight and irresistibly catchy.

The middle eight conforms to guitar-pop convention and sets up the final verse deftly, allowing Smith to inject a deeper level of yearning into his vocal.

There are legitimate criticisms to be made about Chris Parry's handling of the Cure's early material in the studio, but "Boys Don't Cry" is a superb recording with a sharp sonic clarity and a timeless quality that transcends the decades.

Over the years, "Boys Don't Cry" has risen to become one of the Cure's signature songs, even though the original single was never a hit. Its inclusion on their popular 1986 singles compilation *Standing on a Beach* helped expose it to a wider audience. Robert Smith even took the opportunity to record a new vocal for a promotional remix single to amp enthusiasm for the compilation, which finally landed the song into the British top thirty.

It's amazing to think that a single released in 1979, selling very few copies and not even reaching the lower reaches of the pop chart, could become a beloved classic recognized the world over, yet that's exactly what happened with "Boys Don't Cry." Decades later, when the Cure performs "Boys Don't Cry," always near the end of the final encore, every audience member stands and gleefully sings along with every word. It's a chill-inducing display of musical magic, shared connection, and love for a song and a band in its purest form. "Boys Don't Cry" is a smash hit that never was, an all-time classic that broke all the rules.

"Plastic Passion"

"Plastic Passion" was pegged as the B-side to "Boys Don't Cry" and was left off *Three Imaginary Boys*, although its inclusion would have strengthened the album. A sharp and tightly wound slice of post-punk, "Plastic Passion" was one of the earliest songs recorded with Parry at Morgan Studios along with "Killing an Arab" and "10:15 Saturday Night." It was included on the *Boys Don't Cry* compilation of the band's best early material.

"Jumping Someone Else's Train"

The final single of the early era, "Jumping Someone Else's Train" is a bustling rocker with a hopping bass line that served as a swan song for Michael Dempsey, as it was his final recording with the Cure before being replaced by Simon Gallup. By this time, Robert Smith knew the band would be changing directions away from the jumpy punk pop represented here, but they needed a new single to keep their momentum humming along, and this bouncy rocker, about mindlessly following trends, had been part of the band's live set for some time. It was also a perfect showcase for Michael Dempsey.

Released in late November 1979, "Jumping Someone Else's Train" failed to chart. Only a few months later, the band would be ensconced in the studio working on music with a vastly different sound. This track closed the door on the Cure's early years, but at least it did so with an infectious manic energy that still comes through loud and clear.

"I'm Cold"

With a slick new A-side in the can, the band turned to a much older song, "I'm Cold," for the flip-side. Part of the band's live set dating back to the Easy Cure days, "I'm Cold" was demoed for possible inclusion on *Three Imaginary Boys* but didn't make the cut. The version recorded for the B-side is notable for the intricate vocal layering cleverly arranged so that a melody develops within its jittery snippets.

The lyrics are reminiscent of the nastiness inherent in "Object" and "It's Not You" but are much more effective and are delivered with a renegade snarl that's far more convincing. "I'm Cold" was played with an upbeat tempo live, and that's how the music was recorded, but Smith slowed it down to half speed to allow room for some savage psychedelic guitar licks. With its ominous, motoric groove, "I'm Cold" has a very different atmosphere than anything else the Cure had recorded to that point.

Siouxsie Sioux and Steve Severin stopped by the sessions to tell Robert Smith that he'd nabbed the fill-in spot on guitar for the Banshees' *Join Hands Tour*, replacing the departed guitarist John McKay. With the Cure already in place as openers, Smith agreed to fill the role as long as it didn't endanger the Cure's spot on the tour. Seizing on the rare opportunity that Siouxsie's presence provided, Smith prevailed on her to add some wordless wailing deep in the mix toward the end of "I'm Cold." Although the bands became intertwined in the years ahead, this was the only appearance Siouxsie ever made on a Cure record.

Extras

The Cure had a surplus of material to use for their debut album and accompanying singles, leaving several leftover tracks to stew on the cutting room floor. Many of these early songs remained unreleased until their inclusion on the two-CD deluxe reissue of *Three Imaginary Boys* in 2005.

Several of their early originals were demoed at Sound and Vision Studios in October 1977 for Hansa Records. Of those, only "Meathook" made the album. "I Want to Be Old" and "I Just Need Myself" are nothing special, and the band probably made the right decision setting them aside. Other outtakes included on the deluxe edition are "Winter," "Faded Smiles," "Play with Me," and an early live performance of "Heroin Face."

Also included on the reissue is the seedy, slow-grooving rocker "World War," a throwaway that Chris Parry for some reason found worthy of inclusion on the *Boys Don't Cry* compilation. Robert Smith has derided the track as one of the Cure's worst, yet they tore into an incendiary version of it during the special 2011 *Reflections* performance of the first three albums in Sydney, Australia. The studio version is a murky mess with unsteady vocals, but even worse is "See the Children," which is so putrid that it was even left off the reissue, although it circulates on bootlegs.

Much better is the hard-charging rocker "Pillbox Tales," another song from the October 1977 session that was eventually released (along with "Do the Hansa") as a B-side to the 1986 rerecorded version of "Boys Don't Cry." Smith rerecorded his vocals for both tracks, so although studio demos of these two early songs have frequently appeared on bootlegs, the original recordings remain officially unavailable.

Three Imaginary Boys and its associated singles exhibit the Cure before they really owned their sound. The album provided an important launching point from which the band grew in popularity and visibility as they simultaneously became more confident in their musical direction. While not on par with the Cure's finest work, *Three Imaginary Boys* holds up well as an awkwardly idiosyncratic record of late 1970s post-punk with a pop twist. It's *almost* there.

Robert Smith has called *Three Imaginary Boys* his least favorite Cure album, citing his lack of control over song selection, production, and artwork. After what was ultimately an unsatisfying experience, Smith was determined to never again allow someone else control over his work, and that's a promise he's mostly kept.

6

Ticking Away the Moments: *Seventeen Seconds*

Robert Smith is now firmly in creative control as the Cure records the first album that truly represents their sound.

Released: April 22, 1980
Fiction Records—FIX 004, Polydor—2383 574
Running time: 35:40

1. "A Reflection" (2:12), 2. "Play for Today" (3:40), 3. "Secrets" (3:20), 4. "In Your House" (4:07), 5. "Three" (2:36), 6. "The Final Sound" (0:52), 7. "A Forest" (5:55), 8. "M" (3:04), 9. "At Night" (5:54), 10. "Seventeen Seconds" (4:00)

The Cure's crucial second album, *Seventeen Seconds*, is the foundation on which all their future triumphs would be built. After the off-kilter power pop of their debut, an album on which Fiction label boss and producer Chris Parry was very much in control, Smith was determined to seize the reins and reproduce the sound ringing through his head. The album was preceded by a key lineup change, with Smith firing bassist Michael Dempsey and replacing him with bassist Simon Gallup and keyboardist Matthieu Hartley.

Smith had already explored some degree of minimalism with *Three Imaginary Boys*, particularly on "Accuracy," "Another Day," "10:15 Saturday Night," and "Three Imaginary Boys." With *Seventeen Seconds*, he would strive for and accomplish a more austere and skeletal atmosphere. It was a sharp turn toward the melancholy darkness that would come to define the band over the course of their following two albums and, to a certain degree, their subsequent career.

Perhaps it started with a gig opening for Wire at Kent University in London on October 5, 1978. Both Smith and Tolhurst were struck by the raw power that Wire exhibited with their jagged and hard-edged sound and their striking image onstage. Smith's brief stint touring with Siouxsie and the Banshees also inspired him to think about a starker, more potent sound.

Robert Smith had a cassette of four songs that he played obsessively with the intention of somehow merging their styles into what he wanted: Van Morrison's "Madame George," Nick Drake's "Fruit Tree," "Gayaneh Ballet Suite No. 1" from Stanley Kubrick's tense cinematic masterpiece *2001: A Space Odyssey*, and Jimi Hendrix scorching his way through a live performance of "All Along the Watchtower." Along with his oft-stated affinity for David Bowie's *Low*, these influences steered Smith's musical direction, and he was intently focused on achieving the exact sound he wanted.

Smith wrote most of the lyrics for *Seventeen Seconds* one turbulent night after a show with Siouxsie and the Banshees on October 3, 1979, in Newcastle. He got into a fight with three businessmen in the hotel elevator that then progressed into the hallway. Smith slammed one of them into a glass door, cutting them both, after which the guy's two buddies proceeded to kick the crap out of him. Smith's bandmates finally chased off his assailants, but by then, their front man was bruised and bloodied. That night in his hotel room, Smith stayed up for hours writing lyrics infused with the anger and loneliness that enveloped him, and the resulting album would come to reflect it.

After the band finished their tour opening for the Banshees, Smith began the task of painstakingly assembling the new material. Back at his parents' house in Crawley, Smith plugged his new Fender Jazzmaster guitar into his sister's Hammond organ, which was complete with a built-in drum machine, bass pedals, and a cassette recorder. With these primitive methods and using his lyrics from that bloody night in Newcastle, Smith sketched out the first batch of songs in about a week. The direction of *Seventeen Seconds* was already taking shape, and it would result in a fissure that would change the band forever.

By the time the band finished touring behind *Three Imaginary Boys*, Smith knew he wanted to make a change. The tour had become a joyless slog, with tension escalating between him and Dempsey. As the band opened for Siouxsie and the Banshees and Smith ended up taking on dual roles as guitarist for both bands, Dempsey started to resent the time Smith spent with his other group, which included his riding on their tour bus while Dempsey and Tolhurst were stuck driving Smith's tiny car. Dempsey had never shared the tight connection of friendship that Smith and Tolhurst enjoyed, and differences of opinion over the band's direction started coming to a head. Dempsey was a florid bassist who preferred upbeat and lively material, while Smith was running full throttle in the opposite direction.

Both Smith and Tolhurst had known bassist Simon Gallup for years. They'd been friends from the early days, as Smith lived in Crawley and Gallup lived in nearby Horley along with his older brother, who boasted a record collection that ended up being a huge influence on the young musicians. Smith knew that Gallup was unhappy with his current band, the Magspies, and felt he would fit in perfectly with the Cure.

He used a one-off side project as a test run. In July 1979, Smith and Tolhurst assembled Gallup and his Magspies bandmate, keyboardist Matthieu Hartley, along with guitarist Porl Thompson and Robert's sisters Margaret and Janet, Robin Banks and Nick Loot of Fiction label mates the Obtainers (so that it wouldn't appear as if he was simply replacing Dempsey), and a local Horley postman named Frank Bell who fancied himself a potential rock star.

With Bell singing and a general sense of frivolity in the studio, they recorded two tracks, "I'm a Cult Hero" and "I Dig You," which a bemused Chris Parry agreed to issue as a single on Fiction under the name Cult Hero. Fiction pressed 2,000 copies in the United Kingdom and gave the single a December release, but it went nowhere (except in Canada, where "I Dig You" became a surprise hit after an unofficial club mix created by a deejay became unexpectedly popular). It hardly mattered, as sales weren't really Robert Smith's main priority. The positive experience recording this just-for-fun novelty convinced Smith that Gallup was his man.

The final straw was Dempsey's reaction to the homemade demos Smith had created. Tolhurst was enthusiastic, but Dempsey seemed uninterested at best. An incensed Smith went straight to Gallup's house to play him the demos, and Gallup loved them. It was the right answer. Smith offered him a spot as bassist for the Cure right then and there, and Gallup happily agreed. Chris Parry landed the task of calling up Dempsey to inform him that Robert no longer wanted to work with him, and Dempsey took the news stoically. He soon became bassist for the Associates, another band on the Fiction label.

Feeling that things would go easier on Gallup if he wasn't the only new guy in the band, Smith also decided to bring in keyboardist Matthieu Hartley, Gallup's bandmate in the Magspies. Smith figured that the new songs could benefit from the added color of a keyboard. Hartley played the perfect instrument for Smith's minimalist vision, a Korg Duophonic synthesizer that would only allow two notes to be played at once. The new four-piece started rehearsals immediately.

Chris Parry was apprehensive at first when Smith broke the news of the lineup change. Parry had appreciated the Cure as a great power-pop trio and thought they had enormous potential in that direction. On meeting the new members, Parry bonded with Simon Gallup right away but not so much with Hartley. After hearing them play, his enthusiasm surged. While he was surprised by the markedly downbeat nature of the new material, he felt reassured by Smith's confidence and obvious artistic progression.

A few of the new songs—"Play for Today," "M," and "Seventeen Seconds"—had been part of the Cure's live set for a while, and others were worked up as the tour continued. The new four-man Cure convened at Smith's house in January 1980 to continue rehearsals and flesh out some of the lyrics. An early version of "In Your House" bore strikingly different lyrics, and "Secrets" was still instrumental, but most of the songs were ready for the studio.

Just days after finishing rehearsals in Crawley, the band gathered at Morgan Studios to record, with Mike Hedges coproducing with Smith. Chris Parry showed up on the first day, but Smith peremptorily shooed him out of the studio. To Parry's credit, he didn't take offense and was intrigued by Smith's drive and determination.

In only eight days beginning on January 13, 1980, the Cure recorded all ten album tracks plus a B-side, then returned on February 4 to mix the album, which took another week. A meager budget between £2,000 and £3,000 meant that the band worked exceedingly long hours to maximize studio time. On day one, Hedges and Smith set up the studio to their specifications and left it alone for the duration, saving time and giving the album an unusually cohesive sound since all the tracks were recorded similarly.

Developing the songs over weeks of live performing helped speed the process, although Smith was still rewriting some of the lyrics in the studio. The band slept at Morgan to save money so they could have extra studio time. Morgan was a converted church, and the spooky nighttime ambiance lent itself to the mood of the recordings.

Hedges, his assistant Mike Dutton, and Robert Smith experimented with several innovative techniques on *Seventeen Seconds*. Hedges's creative setup of the microphones on Tolhurst's kit produced the distinctly dry and precise drum sound for which the album is known. A Synare 3 drum pad, best known for the distinct "crack" sound in "Whip It" by Devo, "Bette Davis Eyes" by Kim Carnes, and "Cars" by Gary Numan, was used minimally but effectively. Flanging, tape delays, drum loops, and other sonic tricks helped forge a distinct vibe.

Despite the grim material, the mood was upbeat in the studio. It was the first time recording an album for Gallup and Hartley, and they were excited about the process and experience. Robert reveled in the creative freedom, while Lol appreciated the new musical direction and the sense of being part of something serious. The songs weren't old enough to be stale and in some cases were still being written in the studio, allowing a thread of creativity that didn't exist with their debut. Robert Smith and Mike Hedges tried to keep the sessions spontaneous, which is apparent in an album that pulses with energy even at its most melancholy.

While several earlier tracks are classics, it was *Seventeen Seconds* that first etched the Cure's true musical identity on an unsuspecting world. With a miniscule budget and a mere two weeks in which to work, they delivered a landmark album that started small but has ballooned in status infinitely. Robert Smith knew while it was being recorded that they were achieving the sound and vibe that he'd gone into the sessions hoping to capture. There is no overstating its importance. *Seventeen Seconds* is the foundation on which all the Cure's future work is built. Robert Smith's bold statement that it's the most important album the Cure ever recorded is fully justifiable.

Seventeen Seconds

"A Reflection"

This short and somber instrumental sets the tone for the album. Guitar and piano ring out slowly and carefully, almost as if afraid of disturbing something. A wisp of a ghostly wail rises briefly from the mist before retreating and then returning with more force.

"A Reflection" is cinematic, the haunting first moments in a film that eases you forward all in black until the camera moves slowly into focus on something that you're not sure you want to see. The moods vary somewhat from song to song, but "A Reflection" introduces the album's dominant sonic theme: isolation sheathed in an icy shell of detachment, almost quivering with barely restrained tension. It's beautiful, but it rings a warning note, a hint of foreboding.

"Play for Today"

Although technically never a single, if there could be said to be a follow-up to "A Forest," it would be "Play for Today." The Cure filmed a bare-bones performance clip for it for use as a video. It was included on the CD version of the 1986 hits compilation *Standing on a Beach*, and Smith looks suitably malicious sneering out the venomous lyrics. He plays a sociopath convincingly well, surpassing prior efforts like "Object" and "I'm Cold." "Play for Today" is propelled by Gallup's motoric bass and Tolhurst's driving beat, with Smith's rhythm guitar clean and precise.

A synthetic whip crack (created, like the other drum effects on the album, with a Star Synare 3 synthesizer pad) on every third beat amps the song's frantic edge, but it's Hartley's simple, sinuous keyboard riff that, despite being well down in the mix, provides the song's primary melodic hook. Crowds sang along with that wordless melody when the song was played live from the early days, a fan tradition that has endured through the years. Perhaps the best available example of this is wonderfully captured on the band's 1993 live album *Paris*.

The shadowy textures and soundscapes on The Cure's second album were a stark departure from the quirky power-pop of their debut. (*Seventeen Seconds*, 1980)   *Author's Collection*

"Secrets"

A brief instrumental opening leads to the whispered warning "keep quiet," which Smith heeds tremulously. His vocals are buried so far in the mix that they barely exist. Smith delivers two distinct parts: one a mournful phantom, the other more clipped and tethered to the furtive, shadowy reality of infidelity and regret hinted at in the barely sketched lyrics.

The long instrumental passage that closes "Secrets" is simple and beautifully constructed, with Smith contributing an acoustic solo followed by a softly shimmering piano, echoing the rich countermelody that Gallup plays in the instrumental breaks after each verse.

"In Your House"

Opening with a skeletal rhythm that fades in, a simple line of keyboard, and a repetitive finger-picked guitar pattern, "In Your House" is one of the band's earliest exercises in slowly building layers and layers of sound, a technique they would master in years to come. One of the final lyrics finished for the album, "In Your House" provides just brief impressions of brooding imagery over the pensive and stately accompaniment.

The impressionistic imagery in the lyrics suggest the struggle to keep going and stay level while living in a home of anguish and misery. Like much of *Seventeen Seconds*, "In Your House" is music for languidly gazing at the midnight sky or gently drifting in cool, dark water, "pretending to swim" while all sound slowly fades to black around you.

"Three"

Opening with discordant shards of sound that seem unlikely to form an actual song, "Three" finally coalesces into a stark rhythm carrying portentous shards of keyboard and guitar through a brief but disturbing aural nightmare. Smith's voice can barely be heard, trapped under ice or maybe locked in a dream that ends with a sudden and shocking blunt-force trauma.

An even eerier version, featuring more prominent keyboard and clearly inspired by David Bowie's *Low*, was included on the album's deluxe reissue in 2005.

"The Final Sound"

The melancholy fifty-two-second instrumental that opens side 2, "The Final Sound," was going to be a much longer piece, but the tape ran out while it was recording (which can be heard at the end of the track). The band's budget was too tight to use another reel, and Smith liked the audio vérité, so he left it.

"A Forest"

Although the Cure performed an early version of "A Forest" throughout late 1979, by December it was still known as "Into the Trees" and wasn't fully developed. The foundation was built: the keyboard introduction, with its ringing lines of guitar, and the protracted ending, with the instruments falling away one by one. The tempo, however, was much faster and more aggressive in its earlier stage, and the lyrics were incomplete.

By the time the band reconvened at Smith's house to resume rehearsals in early January 1980, the name had changed to "A Forest," the tempo slowed, and the lyrics were the familiar ones we know from the final version. "A Forest" was lavished with more time and attention than any other song on the album, as the band and producer knew early on that it would be the stand-out cut.

Opening with a haunting four-note beam of keyboard that repeats throughout the song, a stately and simple guitar pattern emerges, followed by Gallup's pulsing bass, which was inspired by the playing of the Stranglers' J. J. Burnel, and the sharp rhythm. Stark tension builds for nearly two minutes before Smith begins his remote, dream-shrouded vocal about a man haunted by the vision of an imaginary girl lost in a forest.

His heavily flanged Jazzmaster is bathed in reverb, creating a surreal effect that adds to the song's sense of mystery. "A Forest" becomes a behemoth in concert, often stretching well past its studio length, building to an immense climax with Smith restlessly calling out the song's final line "again and again and

The Cure's first entry into the U.K. Top 40, "A Forest" was the foundation upon which all the rest of their career was based. *Author's Collection*

again and again and again . . ." with manic intensity, leading the band into the protracted full-throttle ending that slowly collapses one instrument at a time. The keyboards stop first, then at some point the drums give out while squalls of guitar continue over the thumping bass. Finally, the guitar slithers away, and only the solitary bass survives for ten more seconds. "A Forest" is the Cure's first real masterpiece, a monolith of anxiety, isolation, and dark fantasy.

Once it was finally mixed to their satisfaction, they called Chris Parry over for a listen. Parry was pleased with the track but suggested a remix to make it more palatable for radio. Smith balked, flatly informing his label head, "This is how it sounds. It's the sound I've got in my head."

Parry shrewdly made the calculation that it was best to back away and allow the mercurial young talent to follow his vision, and he was right. "A Forest" was released on March 28, 1980, nearly a month prior to the album. Sales dwarfed the band's prior three singles, and it was their first charting single in the United Kingdom, peaking at #31.

"A Forest" is arguably the most vital track in the Cure's history. It was featured during their first live TV appearance on December 8, 1979, at Theatre de l'Empire in Paris. Over the years, the Cure has performed "A Forest" more than 1,060 times, far more than any other song ("Boys Don't Cry is number two, with just over 900 plays), including at the induction ceremony for the Rock and Roll Hall of Fame in March 2019.

"M"

"M" was the nickname Robert Smith used for his girlfriend Mary Poole; they met as young teenagers and have been together ever since. If she inspired this track, though, it must have been the result a bit of a rough patch in the relationship. A melodic, mid-tempo ballad, "M" is infused with longing and jealousy, with Smith dolefully predicting that she'll fall in love with somebody else. "M" is almost akin to a third single from *Seventeen Seconds* that was never actually released; it has been played more times by the band in concert than any other tracks from the album apart from "Play for Today" and "A Forest."

"At Night"

A lurching midnight leviathan, "At Night," with its monolithic wall of guitar followed by a corresponding wash of keyboard, is the closest thing on *Seventeen Seconds* that points to the direction of their third album: *Faith*. It's the bleakest track on the album—Smith's voice brims with desperation as he ends with a yearning plea that is clearly never going to be answered. It was inspired by the short story of the same name by Franz Kafka.

"Seventeen Seconds"

The album's finale and title track, which the band used as their show opener during the fall of 1979, is the most skeletal piece yet, opening and closing with Tolhurst's simple, unadorned drumbeat. Smith's vocal is dry, untreated, matter-of-fact, and beaten by reality.

There are no happy endings on *Seventeen Seconds*, only a bleak assessment of our all-too-brief passage through life as parceled out in arbitrary measurements created by mankind but with no real meaning other than what we bestow upon it.

B-Side: "Another Journey by Train"

Originally dubbed "Horse Racing" until the band realized it sounded more like a runaway train, this brisk instrumental B-side to "A Forest" had been part of the band's live set for some time. Musically, it's closely related to their third single, "Jumping Someone Else's Train," and eventually the band started appending it to the end of that song in live performances. Many years later, during the 2011 *Reflections* tour, fans were delighted when the band ended their first encore with a burst of energy by reviving this old favorite for the first time in thirty years.

Despite its decidedly noncommercial nature, *Seventeen Seconds* was a substantial success for the Cure, and Mike Hedges credits the album with boosting his demand as a producer, citing its popularity with musicians. *Seventeen Seconds* not only pointed the band's way forward stylistically but also proved popular enough that Smith was permitted by his record label to continue following his own vision.

Robert Smith credits the genuine emotion and passion behind the music for why it performed better than the ostensibly more commercial material on *Three Imaginary Boys*. Not only did "A Forest" become their first U.K. hit, but it expanded their horizons globally as well. They toured Europe and were a smash in New Zealand and Australia, where extra tour dates had to be added, as the album charted well in both countries. *Seventeen Seconds* hit number twenty on the U.K. album chart, a major improvement over their debut. The band was particularly popular in the Netherlands, where the album reached number fifteen.

They had also played their first American shows, although the album had not yet been released there. The Cure was becoming an international band, and they were doing it on their own terms. The momentum would only continue to grow in the years ahead.

7

Thunder in Our Hearts: Simon Gallup

The Cure's bassist for most of its existence, Gallup is Robert Smith's collaborator and an electrifying presence onstage.

Given Robert's Smith propensity to build everything else around a bass line, the role of bassist has always been of oversized importance in the Cure compared to most other bands. The bass part, bolstered by the rhythm of the drums, is the center of gravity for most Cure songs. All other sounds swirl around it like celestial bodies that flit in, out of, and around the reliably steadfast pulse of the bass.

Apart from Smith, Simon Gallup has been the most important influence on the Cure's songwriting, overall sound, and massive success. Gallup is second only to Robert Smith in number of years in the Cure. He is a supremely talented and intuitive bassist and has proven himself the perfect musical partner for Smith. Gallup's openness to follow in just about any direction has been a huge factor in the Cure's dizzying musical versatility. Just as important, he is not afraid to speak up and let his opinion be known when he thinks things are going off the rails.

Simon Jonathon Gallup was born on June 1, 1960, in a tiny village in Surrey. A year later, his family moved to Horley, about an hour and forty-five minutes from Crawley, where Simon would meet the young musicians who would become the Cure. Gallup's love of music centered around Kiss and whatever his brother Ric, who worked at a small record store in Horley, happened to be playing at the time. Simon knew Lol Tolhurst vaguely through friends, and Robert Smith knew his brother Ric through his many record-shopping excursions.

After learning the bass and becoming somewhat proficient, Simon joined the punk band Lockjaw, formerly known as the Guernsey Flowers and then the Amazing Doctor Octopuss. Lockjaw had already released one single in 1977:

"Radio Call Sign." Gallup has since admitted with wry amusement that Lockjaw was pretty awful, and his bandmates' names were as ghastly as their music: Bo Zo, Micky Morbid, and Oddly Ordish. Simon, tagged with the infectious alias of Andy Septic, was on board for Lockjaw's second single, "Journalist Jive," and B-sides "I'm a Virgin" and "A Doonga Doonga," released in November 1978.

Once Lockjaw began opening for the Easy Cure, Simon became tight with Robert Smith and Lol Tolhurst. Lockjaw quickly fell apart, and by 1979, Gallup was in the Magazine Spies (the Magspies for short). By this time, Robert Smith knew he wanted to replace Michael Dempsey on bass. Dempsey was talented, but his ornate style was at odds with the austere and stark direction Smith envisioned for the Cure's second album: *Seventeen Seconds*. He had also never managed to connect on a strong personal level with Smith and Tolhurst, whereas Simon got along with them immediately.

Smith was already convinced that Gallup was the guy, but he wanted to arrange an audition for him without tipping off Michael Dempsey. He asked Gallup to play on the one-off novelty single "I'm a Cult Hero"/"I Dig You," which was recorded in one drunken afternoon session at Morgan Studios by a rather bemused Chris Parry, who agreed to release the single on Fiction under the name Cult Hero.

A Horley postman named Frank Bell must have felt like a rock star singing vocals on the two songs backed with a lineup of Robert Smith and his sister Janet, Laurence Tolhurst, Simon Gallup, and Porl Thompson. They had a blast during the session, and Robert became convinced that Simon should be in the Cure.

Michael Dempsey participated in the recording of the "Jumping Someone Else's Train" / "I'm Cold" single in November, and shortly thereafter, the bassist was out. Along with Simon, Smith added keyboardist Matthieu Hartley, also a member of the Magspies, so that Gallup wouldn't be the only new guy and to provide additional color to the music. The new four-piece version of the Cure, featuring Gallup and Hartley, played its first gig on November 16, 1979, at Eric's in Liverpool.

Gallup continued as part of the Cure's lineup up through their fourth album: 1982's *Pornography*. During that span, he quickly grew into a major contributor to the Cure's sound. His bass line for "A Forest" is one of his most renowned, and on *Faith*, his bass was particularly high in the mix and often provided the song's melodic hook.

Tension within the Cure's lineup first started to build during the overly long sessions for *Faith* and the grueling tour in support of the album. The bad feelings continued to escalate, and the *Pornography* tour turned into a bitter and angry trek across Europe fueled by drugs and alcohol. Gallup was often at odds with his bandmates, and he had clashed with Robert Smith frequently in years past. This time, things were worse, and the relationship became toxic.

Simon Gallup performs with his band the Cure at the Glastonbury Festival, Somerset, England, June, 2019. *Grant Pollard/Invision/AP/Shutterstock*

After Gallup and Smith got into a fistfight at a bar after a show in Strasbourg, France, both of them angrily abandoned the tour despite several shows remaining on the schedule. They separately flew back to London, and it looked like the Cure might be finished. Several shows had to be canceled before the two could be cajoled back to finish the tour, the specter of major financial losses being enough to overcome the hard feelings and antipathy. The last show of the tour in Brussels marked the end of Gallup's first tenure with the Cure. The band effectively ceased to exist, and Simon Gallup and Robert Smith wouldn't speak again for a year and a half.

In June 1982, after his departure at the end of the *Pornography* tour in Brussels, Simon Gallup existed in a state of limbo. He heard nothing from Robert Smith, and his pride prevented him from picking up the phone and giving him a call. It turns out that Smith left him hanging and apparently had no intention of telling him he was out of the band.

His banishment from the Cure was a difficult period for Simon to endure. He returned to Crawley and attempted to launch his own musical vision, the Cry, with former Cure keyboardist Matthieu Hartley. It was a short-lived project, and Hartley soon left, so Simon brought in former Cure roadie Gary Biddles to sing for his new band: Fools Dance. Neither band made much of an impact, although Fools Dance eventually released two EPs: *Fools Dance* (1985) and *They'll Never Know* (1987).

During his banishment from the Cure, Simon spent much of his time hanging out with Biddles getting sloshed out of his mind at the local bar. A bitter divorce with his wife Carol sunk him further into despair. For a time, Simon was reduced to living at the office of Fiction. He received a call one day from a Cure fan asking to know where Robert Smith and Lol Tolhurst were recording. Until that moment, Simon didn't know for certain that he was out of the band. His first impulse was to try to talk things through, but he knew that Robert would never back down. Stubbornness and pride on both sides resulted in Simon Gallup being out of the band, although it would be temporary.

Simon has admitted to struggling to cope with the Cure's massive commercial success after his ouster. He watched with bitterness as they climbed the charts and played *Top of the Pops* with hits like "The Walk" and "The Lovecats." He later remembered thinking at that time that it should have been him on that stage playing on those songs and hamming it up in the videos.

In retrospect, it seems like a forgone conclusion that Robert Smith and Simon Gallup would not stay angry at each other forever. Gary Biddles harnessed some Christmas spirit and managed to get Smith and Gallup together at his place for drinks on December 25, 1984. The bond between them was strong enough that their friendship was renewed stronger than ever almost immediately.

Following the departure of Phil Thornalley, who played bass during the band's world tour in support of *The Top*, Robert asked Simon to rejoin the Cure in time for *The Head on the Door* sessions. Simon agreed, an easy decision that without question helped to cement the Cure's future. After its release in 1985, *The Head on the Door* was the band's biggest hit yet, and the resulting tour blew the doors off anything the Cure had done before. They would get only bigger from there, and this time Simon would be right in the center of it all rather than watching bitterly from home.

Robert has said many times over the years that Simon is his best friend and confidante and his most reliable and enthusiastic collaborator. This became even more evident in 1988, as Simon Gallup stood as Robert Smith's best man as the front man wed his longtime partner and high school sweetheart Mary Poole.

Simon Gallup is a natural talent, agile and aggressive, and bristling with raw power that generates propulsive and melodic pick-style bass lines that often form the heart of the song he's playing. He looks as badass as his instrument sounds—muscular, lean, and taut, sporting a quiff and often an Iron Maiden T-shirt and his body marked with tattoos. He's an enthusiastic video gamer, bicyclist, and footballer. Simon has been an avid mountain biker for many years and competes in races. For example, he rode for Team RideForMichael in the twenty-four-hour endurance event at Mountain Mayhem to raise money for a good friend who was paralyzed in an accident.

Although a pivotal part of the Cure's success and an able road warrior, playing one long marathon set after another onstage with his longtime musical partner, Simon Gallup has endured some serious health issues that has at times prompted Robert Smith to hire a fill-in. During the Cure's extensive European tour in support of 1992's *Wish*, Gallup was hospitalized after an October 31, 1992, show in Italy for what the band announced was a serious case of pleurisy. There was a bit more to it than that. Gallup's health had been declining for a while, thanks in large part to his bouts with depression and his massive alcohol intake.

Smith had been concerned for his friend's health for some time, and his deterioration alarmed him greatly. Gallup had a breakdown prior to the October 31 show but was able to go on with the performance. After the show's end, he was flown to a hospital. Simon's departure changed the mood of the tour, and the band struggled to get through the long trek. They were all exhausted.

Former Associates and Shelleyan Orphan bassist Roberto Soave filled in for Simon starting with a November 2, 1992 show in Marseille, France. Soave remained with the tour through the November 21 performance in Edinburgh, Scotland. Two nights later, Simon was back in the lineup for the first of two shows in Manchester.

Apart from that, he was away for what he has described as "holidays" in 1994 and again for a period leading up to the *Wild Mood Swings* sessions in which he was away from the band dealing with illness.

As with all members of the Cure, Simon Gallup has generally kept his personal life out of the press as much as possible. His brother Ric was an important part of the Cure family early on, as he helped bring Simon into the band in the first place. Ric also helped with the band's early artwork designs, and he created short films that were projected onstage prior to the tours supporting *Faith* and *Pornography*.

Simon's first marriage was to Carole Joy Thompson, a former secretary who had also contributed backing vocals for the Magspies and Porl Thompson's sister. Before divorcing, they had two children together: Eden and Lily. In December 1997, Simon married his second wife Sarah. They have two children together: Evangeline, born in 2000, and Ismay, born in 2007.

Eden Gallup has made a name for himself recently following in his father's footsteps—literally. Eden, who has Robert Smith for a godfather, is Simon's bass tech and an accomplished musician in his own right. He heads the band Violet Vendetta. On July 28, 2019, at the Fujiama Festival in Japan, Eden gamely stood in for his father when Simon was unable to travel to the gig because of what was later described as a "serious personal situation."

While the exact nature of Simon's absence isn't clear, Eden did a marvelous job under trying circumstances filling in for him. After Eden deftly negotiated his father's slippery bass line in "Lovesong," a clearly impressed Robert Smith announced to the crowd that there was a different Gallup onstage tonight. Robert said in an interview after the show that the band had to make a quick decision to proceed, and that Eden did so well that they couldn't even tell that Simon was missing from the lineup. The elder Gallup returned to the lineup for the next show.

Robert later said that there were some tense moments earlier before the show, as the band and management discussed whether to go forward with the show or cancel it. Canceling such a high-profile festival show would have disastrous financial consequences and would be a major burden on the venue, promotors, fans, and everyone else involved in the massive undertaking. Eden was well known to all in the band, having been Simon's bass tech on the road, and he knew all the songs. He was cool under pressure and convinced Robert that he could do it—and he did.

The same thing happened when the Cure returned to the United States for the October 12, 2019, show at *Austin City Limits*. Simon was unable to appear, and Eden stepped in with no problems. The Cure has never issued an official explanation for Simon's absences on these tour dates other than to say the issue is a "serious personal situation affecting our bassist Simon."

On March 29, 2019, Simon Gallup stood proudly onstage with his bandmates while Robert Smith offered a gracious speech to accept the Cure's induction into the Rock and Roll Hall of Fame. He then did what he does best: rolling thunder through the arena as the Cure ignited the place with a five-song set that was easily the high point of the night. Watching Simon perform that iconic bass line from "A Forest" in the most prestigious event of them all was an amazing moment in a career filled with them.

Simon Gallup's contributions to the Cure extend well beyond simply playing bass. He's blessed with a strong sense of melody and a knack for writing catchy pop tunes. Some of the Cure's catchiest pop hits started life as Simon Gallup demos, including "Lovesong" and "High." Simon's electrifying stage presence jolts energy into the Cure's live shows as he stalks aggressively across the stage in stark contrast to the mostly stoic Robert Smith. He made important creative contributions to the Cure's most celebrated albums—*Kiss Me, Kiss Me, Kiss Me* (1987), *Disintegration* (1989), and *Wish* (1992)—during their halcyon days.

Although his favorite is undoubtedly the Gibson Thunderbird, Simon switches his bass depending on the needs of the album and song. He's played a Rickenbacker prominently, and particularly on *Disintegration*, it was a custom Washburn semi-hollow. Simon recently followed Robert Smith in working with the California-based guitar manufacturer Schechter to create a custom guitar available to the public. The Simon Gallup Spitfire Ultra Bass, a striking yellow and black instrument, follows the Schechter 40th Anniversary Gallup Ultra Spitfire LTD Bass from 2018.

Although Simon doesn't consider himself to be an overly technical player, he is highly regarded among his peers. He's well-known for his low-slung bass position on stage. He describes his bass sound as "simple." Gallup described his tone to *Bass Player* magazine: "It goes heavy on the bottom. I take out the middle, and it's heavy on the top. On a graphic EQ the shape is like a chevron." He mostly used the same familiar pedals he's had for over a decade, including the BF-2 Flanger, CE-4 Chorus Ensemble, Boss MT-2 Distortion, DD-3 Digital Delay, and NS-2 Noise Suppressor. Like Robert Smith, he resists newer models that he doesn't know how to use for the old and familiar that he trusts.

Simon Gallup is, next to Robert Smith, the most important piece of the Cure puzzle, which is massive and complicated beyond belief with too many pieces to count. His melodious bass lines, rock steady and reliable, are a vital part of the Cure's sound, and he's a big part of why the Cure's live performances are so revered. And the swagger—Simon delivers it in spades. The Cure wouldn't be nearly as badass as they are without him.

8

The Ghosts of My Life: *Faith*

The Cure's spiritual third album was conceived out of desperation but emerged with beauty and with a glimmer of hope.

Released: April 14, 1981
Fiction Records—FIX 6, Fiction Records—2383 605
Running time: 36:54

1. "The Holy Hour" (4:25), 2. "Primary" (3:35), 3. "Other Voices" (4:28), 4. "All Cats Are Grey" (5:28), 5. "The Funeral Party" (4:14), 6. "Doubt" (3:11), 7. "The Drowning Man" (4:50), 8. "Faith" (6:43)

Bolton Priory, in the village of Bolton Abbey within the Yorkshire Dales, is barely an outline, hardly recognizable as a structure at all in the dense gray wash of fog on the cover art that Porl Thompson created for the Cure's third album: *Faith*. It is a holy place, though, and ancient. The site depicted so abstractly by Thompson has been a continuous location for worship since 1154. And even after all the people who bared their souls on this sacred ground have lived and died through countless centuries, nobody has ever known the truth. But only with faith does hope exist—without it, there is nothing left.

Robert Smith did not have much faith in anything on September 9, 1980, when the Cure gathered at his parents' house in Crawley to rehearse song ideas for their third album. Barely a week had passed since the end of a successful but arduous twenty-four-show trek through Australia and New Zealand in which they left a trail of trashed hotel rooms as evidence of increasingly hedonistic tendencies. Hordes of fans filled the sold-out venues night after night, and additional shows kept getting added, but the band was on the verge of collapse.

By the end of the tour, Matthieu Hartley could take no more of the Cure, and the feeling was mutual. He hated the band's grim musical direction and was dissatisfied with his keyboard parts, which he considered simplistic. Hartley could never bond with his bandmates on a personal level, and he kept to himself at every opportunity.

Hartley was ill suited for life on the road, and his constant complaining drove the others nuts. Eventually, Smith stopped speaking to him at all unless it was absolutely necessary. Once the band returned to London, he phoned Robert Smith to announce his departure from the Cure. Smith was relieved to have been spared the trouble of firing Hartley himself, although odds are that he would have delegated the responsibility or simply reconvened the Cure without bothering to tell him he was out.

The Cure's punishing 1980 touring schedule left them drained of energy and with no time to write new material for the next album. In addition to exhaustion, Robert Smith was suffering from severe depression. As he would explain years later, even though he was only twenty-one at the time, Smith felt incredibly old, and he held little hope for the future. Even so, the Cure's contract with Fiction required an album a year, and if they were going to record one quickly enough to get it into stores during the first half of 1981, there simply was no time to waste.

Chris Parry scheduled three days at Morgan Studios in London from September 27 to 29, 1980, for the Cure to record demos of the new songs they'd been rehearsing at the home of Robert Smith's parents. For three days, they tried coaxing life into "Primary," "The Holy Hour," "All Cats Are Grey," and an up-tempo number, called "Going Home Time," that didn't make the album, but everything sounded dull and dreary. Smith's temper frayed easily, and Chris Parry started avoiding them altogether.

Nothing usable came from the sessions, and only a couple days later, the dejected band members were back on the road for a series of European dates beginning in Sweden. Unfortunately, things would only get worse. The experience of recording *Faith* shattered any illusions the band may have had about confidently assuming that the process would be as easy as *Seventeen Seconds* had been.

The Cure reconvened during dreary February 1981 at Morgan Studios with Mike Hedges once again producing. Robert Smith has said that, initially, *Faith* was intended to be an upbeat album, but the natural mood of the band—faced with exhaustion, personal turmoil, and loss—seeped into the music. In one night, he wrote both "The Funeral Party" and "All Cats Are Grey," completely changing the tone of the album. The final product is a muted and bleak album that Smith has called "the sound of complete desolation" and reflects the genuine feelings of the band at the time.

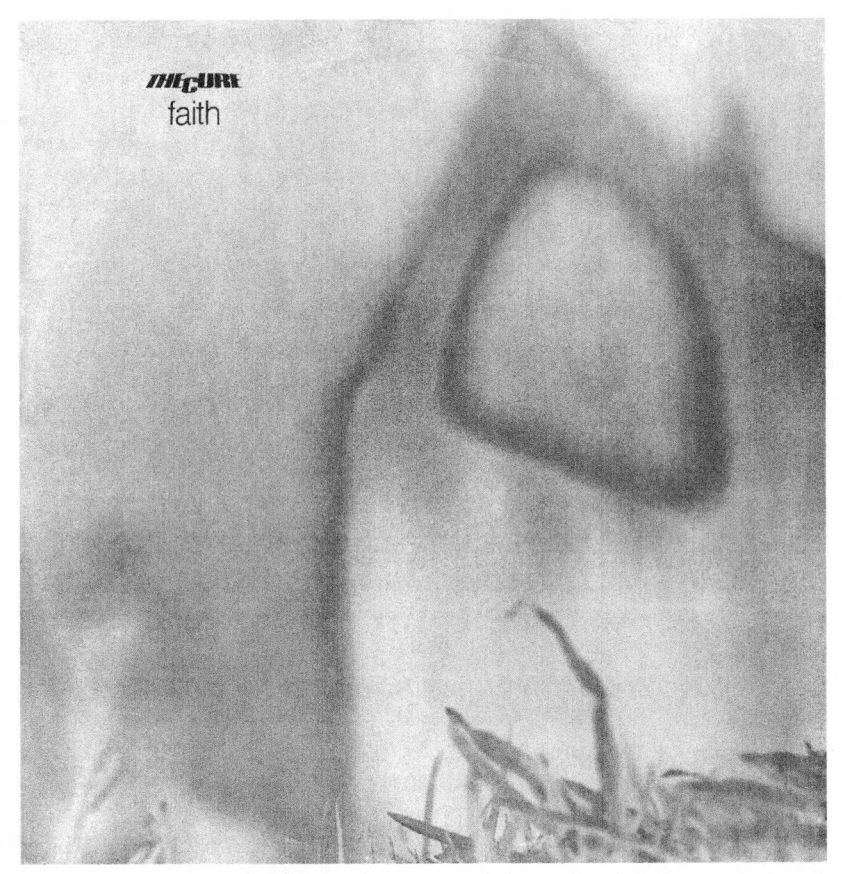

The Cure's third album ventures into the meaning of faith, and the human capacity to believe in the face of abject misery and sorrow (*Faith*, 1981). *Author's Collection*

Robert Smith's exploration of themes relating to faith—or the lack thereof—became a conceptual framework. Smith would sit in church pews watching the worshippers and attempting to understand the nature of their belief, what it meant to them, and why his own lack of faith scared him so much and left him feeling like an outsider.

Thoughts of mortality and loss hung over the band like a dark cloud. Robert Smith's grandmother had passed away, and the band learned early in the album's sessions that Daphne Tolhurst, Lol's mother, had been diagnosed with a terminal illness. Lol was very close to his mother, as were Robert and Simon. Daphne Tolhurst had been friends with Robert's mother Rita since he and Lol were young schoolchildren, and she supported the band enthusiastically. Her illness cast a pall over the sessions.

Tempers frayed as the recording sessions lasted well beyond the initial two weeks scheduled at Morgan Studios, as the drugs and alcohol flowed, seriously impacting the band's ability to function. The songs were written mostly in the studio, as Robert Smith spent endless hours trying to record his quiet and solemn vocals to his satisfaction. Mike Hedges struggled to keep the proceedings moving forward as the band mired down, recording multiple takes of the same song, trying to capture what Smith was hearing within the confines of his own skull.

The Cure abandoned Morgan after their allotted time expired with the album still unfinished. It required multiple sessions at four different studios—Trident, the Roadhouse, Red Bus, and Abbey Road—to finally complete the project. Chris Parry intervened to get Smith and Hedges working together again after their relationship deteriorated so badly that everything ground to a halt. Although they would collaborate again, Mike Hedges never again produced a Cure studio album following *Faith*.

Eventually, Chris Parry pulled the plug on the money flowing in from Polydor, and he advised Smith that the company would no longer cover the skyrocketing costs caused by delays. The Cure had no choice but to use their own funds to wrap up the sessions. Robert Smith said that when he completed his vocals at Abbey Road studios, all he felt was a vast emptiness instead of joy that it was finally over.

It's a credit to producer Mike Hedges that he somehow kept things together and to the band for completing an album that emerged with majestic power and a flowing beauty that belies its laborious gestation. For all its somber nature, *Faith* is very much alive with emotional intensity. In retrospect, Chris Parry, so concerned during the process, considers it outstanding. He admired Smith's tenacity and his songwriting, saying, "I think Robert plunders the inner self, that ground between what is going on in your life and what is going on in your head."

The arrangements are fuller and more complex than their prior work. The richly layered keyboard arrangements are far more elaborate than the simple lines used on *Seventeen Seconds*. Simon Gallup's bass is high in the mix, and Laurence Tolhurst's drum work is sparse and effectively simple. Smith's heavy reliance on the Fender Bass VI, an essential part of the Cure's overall sound, began with this album.

One of the most important factors on *Faith* is the growing confidence of Robert Smith as a singer. His vocals are a richer and more expressive tenor, stretching his previously tightly clipped punk-inspired phrasing to new limits. He also had become a far more nuanced singer, injecting "Primary" and "Doubt" with more post-punk aggression than any of the band's other recordings from that era and the solemn "All Cats Are Grey" with a serene gravitas.

Robert Smith wanted to make an album of emotional weight and power that would be taken as genuine. He was stung by the criticism that some leveled after the death of Joy Division's Ian Curtis following the release of *Seventeen Seconds* that the Cure was comparatively shallow and inauthentic. While recognizing the importance of *Faith* in retrospect, Robert Smith has expressed mixed feelings about it. Since it's a highly personal album, when Smith hears it, he is naturally drawn back to the emotional turmoil that inspired it. The Picture Tour in support the album was grueling, as the band relived night after night all of the dark moments that led to each song's creation. It wasn't a particularly cheery album or tour.

Faith

"The Holy Hour"

Simon's resonant bass introduction to "The Holy Hour" is an appropriate start to the lovelorn and spiritually bereft *Faith*, especially since his bass lines dominate the album's musical direction. Robert Smith's rhythm guitar is precise and restrained, boxed in by Lol's spartan rhythm. "The Holy Hour" rests solely on two chords that echo back and forth with perceptively tightening tension. A line of keyboard mimics the ghostly tolling of a church bell, a prayer for respite from the misery evident in the song's foreboding atmosphere.

"The Holy Hour" contemplates the rapt devotion beaming on the faces of worshippers attending mass. Robert wrote the lyrics while in church, observing rational adults so in thrall to supernatural fables that they pattern their own lives according to their dictates—or pretend to. For many, the adherence lasts until they are home, where they blithely settle back into their own unholy behaviors, their carefully sanctimonious expressions set aside until dusted off a week later when they are obliged to worship yet again.

"Primary"

"Primary" is human instinct at the most basic level, urgent and obsessive, and the loss of innocence that invariably comes from giving into it. By far the most commercially viable track on *Faith*, "Primary" was released as the album's only single and scaled to number forty-three. The Cure promoted it with an appearance on *Top of the Pops* along with a couple slots on Dutch TV.

On an otherwise somber album, "Primary" crashes like a boulder through wooden church pews, sending splinters in every direction. With Smith on his Fender VI, he and Gallup play concurrent bass riffs that endlessly spiral in and out of phase and send the track into motoric overdrive.

The "Primary" single cover art was the first of many to be designed for the Cure by former and future band member Porl Thompson and photographer Andy Vella, who collaborated under the name Parched Art. The duo would be responsible for most of the Cure's artwork going well into the future.

The only single taken from *Faith* is known for its driving rhythm and thundering bass parts.
Author's Collection

"Other Voices"

The core of the hypnotic "Other Voices" is, once again, Gallup's taut bass, around which Smith's guitar skitters as if held in orbit by the deeper instrument. The band and producer Mike Hedges create an ambience that's vaguely exotic but steeped with gloom. The lyrics, inspired by Truman Capote's haunting 1948 southern gothic novel *Other Voices, Other Rooms*, are intoned by Smith in a reverb-drenched voice.

"Primary" was the only single from *Faith*, but "Other Voices" was almost the second. A video was prepared, and the track was included on the CD version of the *Staring at the Sea* singles collection in 1986.

"All Cats Are Grey"

The night Robert Smith wrote the music for "All Cats Are Grey" was a turning point for *Faith*, as its sound spread to encapsulate much of the album. A repetitive triplicate drum pattern cascades and echoes dimly under a solemn swell of keyboard. Smith's faint vocal could very well originate from the same caves mentioned in the lyrics.

Lol Tolhurst has insisted that he wrote the lyrics to "All Cats Are Grey," and in a way to stake his claim, he recorded a cover of the song with his post-Cure band Levinhurst in 2007. Robert didn't seem to notice or care much, as he allowed Lol to play keyboards on the song when the Cure reunited with Tolhurst for the May 2011 *Reflections* shows in Sydney.

"The Funeral Party"

Sometimes detractors or writers who are simply lazy label the Cure "mope rock," a derisive tag that is wholly inaccurate, as anybody who knows the band's body of work can attest. If one song might fit that description, it's "The Funeral Party," music more suited to a crumbling mausoleum than a venue hosting a rock show. It's built largely around a heavy wave of synthesizer played on a Roland RS-09.

Although much humor and breezy jubilance can be found in the Cure's output, *Faith* is a singularly humorless album, with "The Funeral Party" representing the nadir of its despondency. Smith wrote the song about the death of his grandparents, which was his awakening to death as a real thing staring him in the face rather than an abstract thought far off in the distant future. Slow, sluggish, syrupy, and shrouded in woe, "The Funeral Party" captures a mood unlike any other song in the Cure's catalog.

"Doubt"

Coming out of the sea of melancholy into a crash of post-punk with "Doubt," Smith affects a heavily accented and exaggerated approximation of the thinner developing voice we heard on *Three Imaginary Boys*. He rails against the absurdity and pointlessness of human existence, harkening back to the existential angst of his youth. Savage and ragged, "Doubt" drives a stake through the heart of the album's gray-cloaked woe, a much-needed jolt of energy amongst the solemn hymns.

"The Drowning Man"

The second song after "All Cats Are Grey" on the album inspired by Ser Mervyn Peake's gloomy psychological fantasy series *Gormenghast*, "The Drowning Man" is the sound and the sight of Lady Fuchsia Groan, a young girl who rejects the grim realities of life by reading her cherished fantasy stories. Unable to cope with the perpetual horror of her surroundings, she affects an exaggerated, child-like enthusiasm that is wrenching to read.

Fuchsia's death, which Smith retells in "The Drowning Man" with some of the album's most poetic lyrics, comes after a lingering depression that she can't shake. She drowns when she accidentally strikes her head on a windmill, knocking her helplessly into swiftly flowing floodwaters that have been surrounding the castle.

Lady Fuchsia is a symbol, personifying the good and beautiful and hopeful things that we let slip away from our lives and/or from the world on a continual basis. "The Drowning Man" reflects this as a question of faith. It's a central tenet of doubt, of atheism or agnosticism. Quite simply, why would a benevolent God allow such innocence, goodness, and beauty slip to through his fingers completely?

Fuchsia dreamed of death so many times, yet it arrived at a time and place not of her choosing, and in the end, all she could do was claw feebly at nothing. The listener is in that moment, with Smith's spectral vocals and grimly poetic lyrics draped in a perfectly symbiotic musical arrangement. The relentless sway of the chord progression and rhythm evokes the captive feeling of drowning amongst the waves of cold dark water, the mist swirling just out of reach, fading from vision as the darkness becomes all.

"Faith"

The Cure has often closed albums with lengthy pieces of dark power, and "Faith" might be the finest of them all. Like its immediate predecessors "Three Imaginary Boys" and "Seventeen Seconds," "Faith" overflows with intensity, but it goes beyond the first two. At six minutes and fifty-nine seconds in length, its epic scope, spiritual yearning, and painful expressions of betrayal produce more deeply emotional live performances by Robert Smith than any other song. He's frequently said it is his favorite by the Cure. It's actually a forlorn and somewhat desperate surge of hope, amidst the turmoil and tragedy, that perhaps tomorrow will be better.

In concert, "Faith" is somewhat akin to a spiritual communal ceremony, with Smith baring his soul through powerful vocals and the band often extending the song far beyond its studio length, with the audience bathed in the simmering doubt and hope that has run like a chord through the whole album, manifesting itself most powerfully in its finale.

Smith doesn't add "Faith" to the band's set very often anymore, but sometimes when the mood is right, that bass line reverberates over the crowd, and those in attendance suddenly become an even deeper part of something larger than themselves.

B-Sides

"Descent"

The Cure brought one of their most obscure B-sides, originally the flip to "Primary," to a majestic level when they unearthed "Descent" for the *Reflections* shows in 2011. It's extraordinary to think that thirty years later, this brooding piece of atmospheric studio experimentation would be delivered to powerful effect at such a huge event. During live performances, Robert and Simon faced each other solemnly strumming their parts while, behind them, Jason Cooper rolled his mallets on the cymbals for dramatic effect. The Cure elevated it to a level far beyond what it had been by creating a more percussive and compelling version of a song forgotten by most.

"Charlotte Sometimes"

Needing a new single to fill the gap between albums, Smith once again mined his love of literature for ideas. Both "Charlotte Sometimes" and its B-side were inspired by the 1969 children's book of the same name by British writer Penelope Farmer, the final installment in the popular *Aviary Hall Trilogy*.

In "Charlotte Sometimes," the title character is a young girl who travels forty years back in time and begins an entirely different life as a girl named Clare. The story shifts back and forth through time, the point of view shifting from Charlotte to Clare as they attempt to communicate to each other by writing in a diary.

Charlotte's struggle to cling to her own identity is the central theme of the story and of the Cure's single. Charlotte is an outsider who is forced to come to terms with a society completely unfamiliar to her. She struggles to hold on to her true self while banished in an unfamiliar place where she is alone and doesn't belong.

Keyboard heavy and notable for a dramatic double vocal that mimics the personas dueling in Charlotte's head, "Charlotte Sometimes" has an oddly flat and muted sound unique in the Cure's catalog. The band was exhausted when they recorded it with Mike Hedges at his Playground Studios on July 16, 1981, while on a short break from their long and grueling Picture Tour, but they nailed the performance from the first take. It was released on October 5, 1981, reaching a U.K. peak of number forty-four. Despite the song's decidedly uncommercial gothic vibe, Smith had anticipated the single doing much better and was disappointed with the outcome, although the song is now an undeniable classic met with wild enthusiasm when played in concert. In 1986, "Charlotte Sometimes" was released as the third promo single from the *Standing on a Beach* compilation in much of Europe, where the Cure's popularity was skyrocketing.

Mysterious and haunting, "Charlotte Sometimes" filled the gap between albums but wasn't as successful as the Cure had hoped. *Author's Collection*

Penelope Farmer, the author who wrote the book that inspired "Charlotte Sometimes," wrote a truly fascinating piece about her experience with the song and Robert Smith himself. In 2007 for her blog *Rockpool in the Kitchen*, Farmer detailed the history of her encounters with the Cure's song from her perspective. Nobody contacted her or her agent prior to the single's release, she states, and she was never paid any royalties.

She initiated a copyright dispute, but she backed down when the chances of success seemed remote, and a win would have probably cost her money since the song had helped spike interest in her book. One interesting note: she mentions that Fiction was willing to go so far as to delete the song from availability to prevent a potentially costly lawsuit.

On May 31, 1996, as the Cure was starting the Swing Tour, Farmer decided she should go see the band and try to meet Robert Smith. After Farmer and her agent reached out to Cure management, it was all set that she would meet Robert prior to the show. She describes the brief and touching moment that they met and talked about her book. Robert told her that his brother read it to him when he was young, and that's how he learned it.

Farmer was clearly delighted by the meeting with Robert, his sincerity, and his warmth, and she was blown away by the show itself. Robert had promised that they'd play "Charlotte Sometimes" during the encores, and sure enough they did—and he pointed to her, as did the spotlight, leading a beaming Penelope Farmer to wave and smile to the massive crowd cheering in her direction. If the Cure never did anything else with that song, it was worth it for that one night when Penelope Farmer was for a brief moment a rock star herself.

"Splintered in Her Head"

The rhythm-heavy B-side "Splintered in Her Head" is like an echo of the A-side's concept being rattled around a cavern in purgatory, beset by odd sounds and visions. A deranged harmonica peals out of the darkness like the cries of a tortured night bird, and Robert Smith delivers a detached demonic vocal that seethes with unease. It sounds nothing like "Charlotte Sometimes" and instead clearly foreshadows the much denser intensity exhibited by the band's next album, *Pornography*, which completes the journey from perdition straight down to Hell.

Tolhurst laid down the drums first, based on a beat that had been bouncing around in Robert Smith's head, and they slowly worked through Gallup's bass parts and the guitar. It's a song built from the ground up, with no clear plan in place except to capture a forbidding atmosphere, which they clearly did.

"Carnage Visors"

At more than twenty-seven minutes, the stately instrumental "Carnage Visors" was recorded by the band to be played while an avant-garde film of the same name, created by Simon Gallup's brother Ric, was projected onto the stage prior to the start of their shows on the Picture Tour. Ric Gallup shot the minimalist film in his garage over a two-month span, but a mistake with the light exposures resulted in a frantic last-minute reshoot. The Cure had no choice but to record the piece without seeing the film. After two days of rehearsals, they recorded the long, bleak soundscape, nailing it in one take. Guitar and keyboard overdubs were quickly added, and the piece was complete.

Stark and repetitive, "Carnage Visors" is not going to inspire repeated listens, but there is a certain hypnotic quality to the droning drum machine, bass, and simple lines of guitar drenched in reverb. It's essentially a long showcase for Robert Smith's new obsession with his Bass VI guitar. Esoteric and lengthy as it is, "Carnage Visors" is something of a cult favorite among Cure fans who love its foreboding atmosphere of paranoia and unease.

The piece also inspired the creation of one of the biggest rock hits of the end of the millennium. John Frusciante, guitarist for the Red Hot Chili Peppers, cited "Carnage Visors" as being the primary musical inspiration for the smash 1999 single "Californication."

Critics were generally divided over the Cure's gray-skied third album, although many praised its solemn beauty and tense spiritual angst. Given its dark and deeply melancholy nature, *Faith* was instrumental in developing the Cure's reputation as a goth band despite their reflexive dismissals of such labels.

Faith became the Cure's most successful thus far, reaching number fourteen in the United Kingdom and launching their most lavish live outing yet: the Picture Tour. There is a level of emotional desolation on *Faith* that goes beyond anything the Cure had ever recorded. Even the darkest tracks on *Seventeen Seconds* maintain a raw edge of detachment.

On *Faith*, the heart in the music is much more exposed, its sorrow drawn from feelings so genuine that the songs are weighed down by clouds of sorrow. There is still a barrier there, a refusal to let go completely. Robert Smith still sings from a distance and never loses control, but the barrier is weakening. It would be gone completely by the next album.

Bereft in Deathly Bloom: The Cure in Goth

The Cure is one of the most influential goth bands in history, even if they don't admit it.

In 2018, four decades into the Cure's existence, it still happens all the time. When music writers aim their finely honed analysis in the Cure's direction, they face an almost irresistible compulsion to include certain well-worn clichés like "gloomy," "doom merchants," and "mope rock." It's sadly inevitable.

These throwaway words help bolster the marginalization of the Cure as a caricature not to be taken seriously. Many critics can't get beyond Robert Smith's hair and makeup and actually listen to the music with an open mind, and thus they rely on lazy, derisive crutches. There is one word, however, frequently used alongside the vapid space fillers to describe the band that is indeed meaningful to a large portion of the Cure's fan base: goth.

The goth subculture emerged in the late 1970s and early 1980s in England, a twisted, spooky branch spindling away from post-punk and taking a decidedly darker and more sinister turn. Goth is marked by an aesthetic inspired by sources such as 19th-century gothic literature and horror films, its fashion often incorporating mostly dark clothing and hair and very pale makeup often with jewelry and/or tattoos frequently inspired by the occult, but there are endless variations.

Although most Cure fans don't identify as goth, there are many who do. Feelings are divided. For some, a strong personal connection with the music of the Cure and other artists considered goth inspires them to adopt a different persona, individualized yet within certain recognizable parameters.

The Cure is often mentioned as one of the most influential goth bands in history, and Robert Smith is widely considered a major figure in gothdom. It's a topic that fascinates journalists, as they seem to delight in asking the Cure about it despite the band's obvious exasperation with the topic. The Cure has firmly and repeatedly disavowed any connection to the goth movement. Robert Smith doesn't typically bash or belittle goth culture, although he has poked a little fun in the past. He loves the fact that goth fans tend to be deeply knowledgeable about the music, and he admires the sense of community that exists at Cure shows in particular, but he has been steadfast in his insistence that the Cure is not goth.

One reason the Cure prefers not to be plastered with the goth label is to avoid limiting their appeal by placing themselves into a stylistic box. What they don't seem to understand is that it's not their place to decide. Robert Smith likes to be in control of all aspects of the Cure's music and everything else associated with the band, but by music's very nature, it's impossible for that to last indefinitely.

Once a new album is released and it's out there in the ether, it's up to the listeners to decipher it and determine where it fits. The Cure has no choice but to keep it unreleased or simply throw it into the wind and let it go. Fans, writers, musicians, and the public at large get to view it how they view it, and goth is a pretty reasonable conclusion to reach for a big chunk of the Cure's music. Whether or not the band intended it as such is irrelevant.

What is goth exactly? Writer and photographer Mick Mercer, who has chronicled goth music and culture more extensively than anyone, has said it's a state of mind. Given the propensity for music writers to expound on goth even if they know absolutely nothing about it (which is normally the case), I asked Andi Harriman, goth expert and writer of the acclaimed *Some Wear Leather, Some Wear Lace: The Worldwide Compendium of Postpunk and Goth in the 1980s*, to give her thoughts. She echoed Mercer and said, "It's about embracing darkness and appreciating the more macabre aspects of life, with elements of drama and romance. Most of all, Goth is about the music.... Without the music there would be no subculture."

Each person's perception of goth is different, much like the music that inspired it. The term first seems to have been applied to rock music in October 1967, when music writer John Stickney refers to the Doors as "Gothic rock." Stickney cites the "violence" in the Doors' music and their dark atmospherics in concert. He notes these gothic tendencies as a stark contrast to the fey hippy breeziness of the day. Black Sabbath and others of the late 1960s and early 1970s could also be considered goth in many respects.

The term became more widespread in the post-punk era of the late 1970s and into the 1980s, as bands with brooding theatricality and tense, dramatic power, like Echo and the Bunnymen, Magazine, Joy Division, and Siouxsie and the Banshees, have all been called goth. Others took their obsession with mortality and the occult to deeper levels, like Bauhaus, which might be considered the ultimate goth rock band. Critics also noted the Cure's balance of darkness, melancholy, and introspection, beginning with their second album, *Seventeen Seconds*, to be a perfect template for goth rock.

The notion that the Cure represents goth is so widespread as to be ubiquitous and unquestioned. The cliché is so ingrained in the media and mainstream fans' perceptions of the Cure and its music that it's hard to avoid. Smith has expressed frustration at the media's continued propensity to label them, complaining, "It's so pitiful when 'Goth' is still tagged onto the name the Cure. We're not categorizable. I suppose we were post-punk when we came out, but in total it's impossible. How can you describe a band that put out an album like *Pornography* and also *Greatest Hits* where every single song was top 10 around the world? I just play Cure music, whatever that is."

Other members of the Cure have also weighed in on the goth conversation. Simon Gallup said the Cure was never a goth band but only perceived as such because of "some of the more atmospheric tracks we've done. We've never sung about graveyards and bats and things like that." Of course, singing about such things has never been a prerequisite for goth. Lol Tolhurst has been rather congenial about goths, although he does go for a bit of a caricature in his memoir *Cured*: "Contrary to popular belief, we were not pale-faced Goths who sat in dark rooms with candles and cried all the time." On learning of the Cure's induction into the Rock and Roll Hall of Fame, Tolhurst told *Rolling Stone*, "I've got my Goth-tux ready!"

Robert Smith credits his stint as guitarist for Siouxsie and the Banshees for establishing himself and the Cure as firmly in the goth world. He told *Time Out London* in June 2018 that he was roped into adopting a goth look because he had to "play the part" as a member of Siouxsie and the Banshees. He said, "Goth was like pantomime to me. I never really took the whole culture thing seriously."

Smith also notes that the goth look was simply part of an overall presentation that he downplays as part of the necessary trappings of performing, saying, "It's just a theatrical thing. It's part of the ritual of going on stage." He also blames his looks for the need to wear stage makeup: "I have ill-defined features and naturally pale skin."

Despite his frequent rejection of the goth label, Smith has been quick to express his appreciation toward his fans who embrace the culture, the fans who love to come to the Cure's shows dressed in similar fashion as the band. In a recent interview with *Time Out* in which he was promoting the Meltdown Festival, Smith said, "Every Goth I've ever met has been very nice, you know? As a subculture, I think it's full of wonderful people. But I have never liked what's classified as Goth music."

Yet, apart from perhaps one specific example, it's not like the Cure has shied away from goth music or imagery, even after expressing annoyance about their association with it. Robert Smith's often ghoulish appearance is so perfectly goth that it may as well have been designed specifically to fit that designation. For what it's worth, Siouxsie Sioux, also considered a goth icon, has claimed that Smith merely adapted her look for himself.

Seventeen Seconds, with its sonic space and tortured lyrics, fits into the subgenre but perhaps would not have been enough by itself to place the Cure firmly in that camp. But there can be little doubt that its sequel, *Faith*, is goth to its core, more so than any other Cure album. *FACT* magazine, one of the most popular and influential music sites on the Web, placed *Faith* at number three on its 2010 list of the "20 Best Goth Records Ever Made," behind only Bauhaus's "Bela Lugosi's Dead," which is clearly the "Stairway to Heaven" of goth, and Joy Division's *Closer*.

It's on *Faith* in particular that the Cure's protestations against being goth ring the hollowest. The album's relentless downpour of weary sorrow, so genuine and soul-baring that it could have been created only from spiritual angst, clearly places it in that realm. The cover art of an ancient abbey certainly shuffles the band closer to that shadowy corner where goth exists. The melancholy and abject sorrow reflect the feelings of many who seek out the connections found in the goth world.

Look at the video for "Lullaby," the spiderweb-coated slice of creepy-crawliness from director Tim Pope. It's about as goth as it gets, and Robert Smith didn't seem to mind doing the video despite knowing that it would feed into a perception he's tried to deny. *Disintegration* and *Bloodflowers* are goth through and through, and so is "Burn" from the very goth film *The Crow*.

In *Post-Punk.com*'s "40 Years of Goth: Essential Albums from the Genre's Beginnings," published in October 2017, *Pornography* ranked number seven, and the writer went so far as to call it perhaps the first truly gothic album (a ridiculous assertion). The 1981 single "Charlotte Sometimes" and its accompanying video are goth in every conceivable way, from the mournful washes of keyboard to the ghostly echoes in the double-tracked vocals.

Even in recent years, the Cure has travailed this dark path. Much of *The Cure* and parts of their last album, *4:13 Dream*, certainly belong to the shadows, not the light. "Underneath the Stars," the opening track to *4:13 Dream*, is a midnight gothic slow dance. Robert Smith jumped at the chance to create a spookily clever remake of the Frank Sinatra hit "Witchcraft" for Tim Burton's *Frankenweenie*, with no apparent worries that his gothness would be once again on display.

Smith has moved away from the darkness intentionally a few times in his career. One was with the 1990 remix album *Mixed Up*, which Smith hoped would be something fun for the fans after the doom and gloom of *Disintegration*. More notably, after the band's crack-up at the end of the *Pornography* tour, Smith practically hurled himself into a bright musical orgy of colors that would last several years.

One of Robert Smith's motivations for moving away from the dark and turgid gloom rock of *Pornography* and toward the frothy synth pop of "Let's Go to Bed" was the increasingly disturbing makeup of the crowd that the Cure was generating. Smith was dismayed night after night looking out into the crowd

Bereft in Deathly Bloom: The Cure in Goth 87

The Cure at a promoshoot in Konstanz, Germany, 1995.

dpa picture alliance / Alamy Stock Photo

and seeing strange and outlandish caricatures of himself looking sickly pale in their makeup, looking up at the stage like zombies mouthing the words to his songs. It was disconcerting.

Smith and the band had taken to wearing heavy red lipstick around their eyes and mouths so that the sweat made it seem like they were bleeding. With the heavy material night after night and the worsening inner turmoil within the band, it was clear that the Cure and their fans were becoming increasingly insular, mirthless, and joyless.

After shifting to the peppy synth pop of "Let's Go to Bed" and subsequent hit "The Walk," when the Cure started touring with a new lineup, Smith was pleased at the change in the band's audience. Looking back twenty-two years later, Smith told *Rolling Stone* that after their pop success, the Cure's shows "went from intense, menacing, psychotic goths to people with perfect white teeth. It was a very weird transition, but I enjoyed it. I thought it was really funny."

The Cure was always drawn back into the darkness, though, which is their natural abode. The light frothy pop has been the exception, not the rule. Robert Smith said that he considered the Cure's 2002 *Trilogy* concerts, in which the band played three of their darkest albums in sequence (*Pornography*, *Disintegration*, and *Bloodflowers*), as the best representation of what the Cure is all about. And Robert Smith has said that their long-awaited next album will be as dark as anything they've ever done.

Given Robert Smith's instinctual disdain for the media, the likely root cause of any real antipathy toward the goth subculture is how incessantly it's overplayed by writers. Almost every article about the Cure mentions goth at least once, and frequently the tone is mocking and condescending. Some of the designations given to Smith relative to goth are mind-numbingly stupid. In a July 2004 piece for *SPIN*, Smith is anointed "the spokesman for a generation of lipstick smearing, hair-teasing, Goth-romantics."

When the Cure's fortieth-anniversary show at Hyde Park made headlines in July 2018, nearly every article used goth as a descriptor of the band and/or the audience. For example, *The Independent* referred to Smith as a leading figure in the goth subculture of the 1980s. *Rolling Stone* elevated him further in its July 8 concert review as a bold subheadline no less: "With sun beating down, Goth King Robert Smith still commanded a set that resonated with tens of thousands of concertgoers."

There are references that are wry and clever and those that clearly *try* to be clever but end up only wallowing in shallow, mean-spirited snark. For a cringeworthy recent example, one need look no further than Setlist.fm's October 2018 article about the Cure's first Scottish show in twenty-seven years. The writer opens with "Keep your black eyeliner handy" and directs the article to "all you Scot goths." As if the joke wasn't already tired, it's reinforced yet again in the second paragraph, which begins by referring not to the Cure but to "The Goths." If not for the dimwitted media portrayals and odious clichés, the band might not be bothered by the designation at all.

Robert Smith has made it clear that he considers the Cure's music universal and not aimed at a particular group. This is another reason why he doesn't plug the band into the confines of one genre, although it's worth noting that referring to the Cure as a goth band wouldn't exclude them from other designations. It hardly matters—it's not like Robert Smith is going to change his tune and no longer deny the undeniable like he's done for decades. The connection is real and inescapable. As of this writing, printed next to the Amazon.com listing for *Disintegration* is the proudly unfurled digital banner "#1 Best Seller in Goth!" Pretty good for a thirty-year-old album by a band that insists they aren't goth and never were.

Although it began in the late 1970s and proliferated during the 1980s, you can walk through most malls in America today and see that the goth subculture is still alive in 2021. The black wardrobe, eyeliner, and black or red lipstick are still embraced. Some things have changed, and now in the world of the Internet and Hot Topic, it's easier to be goth than ever—or at least to look goth. Actually being goth is a state of mind that can't be purchased at the mall.

10

Sex Is Violent: *Pornography*

The Cure's darkest musical extremity brings them crashing down to nothing.

Released: May 3, 1982
Fiction Records—FIXD 7, Fiction Records—2383 639
Running time: 43:29

1. "One Hundred Years" (6:42), 2. "A Short Term Effect" (4:25), 3. "The Hanging Garden" (4:32), 4. "Siamese Twins" (5:35), 5. "The Figurehead" (6:15), "A Strange Day" (5:06), 7. "Cold" (4:26), 8. "Pornography" (6:28)

This is it: the end of the Cure is at hand. The portentous thought was stubborn, and Robert Smith could not shake it as he began preparing material for the Cure's fourth album: *Pornography*. He was spent; the Cure was spent. The arduous sessions for *Faith* and its emotionally draining tour left him angry and depressed, yet the Cure was more popular than ever.

Smith has stated that his intent with *Pornography* was to make the ultimate "fuck-off" album. The Cure succeeded in creating an album uncompromising in its despondent outlook, a bleak assessment of the human condition that ends with a thread of desperate determination. It's harrowing and personal, the lyrics weaving an individual's struggles with a dim view of the world through the prism of abject hopelessness. Nothing matters anyway, but we might somehow fight this sickness. It doesn't matter if we all die, now, but perhaps at some point it will matter. Perhaps.

Pornography's colossal volcano blast of sound is a fiery wall so dense and impenetrable that Phil Spector would have given every frazzled hair on his head achieve it. The Cure amps up the intensity level past the red line with a bold and extreme approach that gives little thought to commercial considerations—massive drums and layers of turgid guitar and demon-warped vocals that veer from blistering rage to disgust to abject despair.

Robert Smith was determined to capture the relentless hammering against the insides of his skull that demanded release—a raucous maelstrom of whirlwinds and corrosive thunder with endless spikes of red flashing lightning. The cold and lonely beginnings of the project started in December 1981 as Smith huddled at Rhino Studios in Surrey, where he hammered out about a dozen demos that would form the core of a new album. Steve Severin popped in to play bass on a few tracks. Many of these demos can be heard on the two-CD deluxe reissue of *Pornography* released in 2005.

After working with Mike Hedges as engineer and producer on the first three albums, Smith decided that the Hellish aural brew percolating in his head required new blood. He and Hedges had endured a rocky road making *Faith*, and at one point, their relationship was very close to the breaking point. Hedges joined up with Siouxsie and the Banshees to produce their next album, *A Kiss in the Dreamhouse*, so the Cure would have needed a new producer regardless.

The Cure had never before been faced with the task of choosing a new producer for an upcoming studio album. There was some initial uncertainty about who might replace Hedges. Renowned German producer Conny Plank, known primarily for his work with "Krautrock" artists like Can, Kraftwerk and Neu!, was a serious contender. A collaboration between Robert Smith and the highly accomplished but notoriously strong-willed Plank would have been interesting indeed. Smith and Tolhurst even went so far as to have a meeting with him, but nothing ever came of it.

Smith's particular point of focus at the time was the massive drum sound he wanted, which is one of the main reasons he chose twenty-two-year-old Phil Thornalley to produce the new album. Smith loved the drum sound that Thornalley helped achieve as engineer for producer Steve Lillywhite on the Psychedelic Furs' 1981 album *Talk, Talk, Talk*. Lillywhite personally recommended him, which carried a lot of weight. Another plus was Thornalley's relative youth and inexperience, as he'd never produced an album and Robert didn't want the clash of wills he'd experienced with Mike Hedges.

Thornalley was engineer at RAK Studios in St. John's Wood, London, a converted Victorian schoolhouse with a rich ambiance that has hosted numerous top-tier artists. Robert had no desire to return to the familiar confines of Morgan Studios, and RAK was located conveniently close to their record label headquarters. The band slept at the Fiction offices during most of the sessions, becoming increasingly bedraggled as the album progressed.

The Cure convened in January 1982 to begin the sessions, working through the night, fueled by cocaine and acid. Robert worked to darken the mood and wring the most savage performances possible out of everyone involved, although Phil Thornalley remembers a far more genial studio experience.

Sex Is Violent: *Pornography* 93

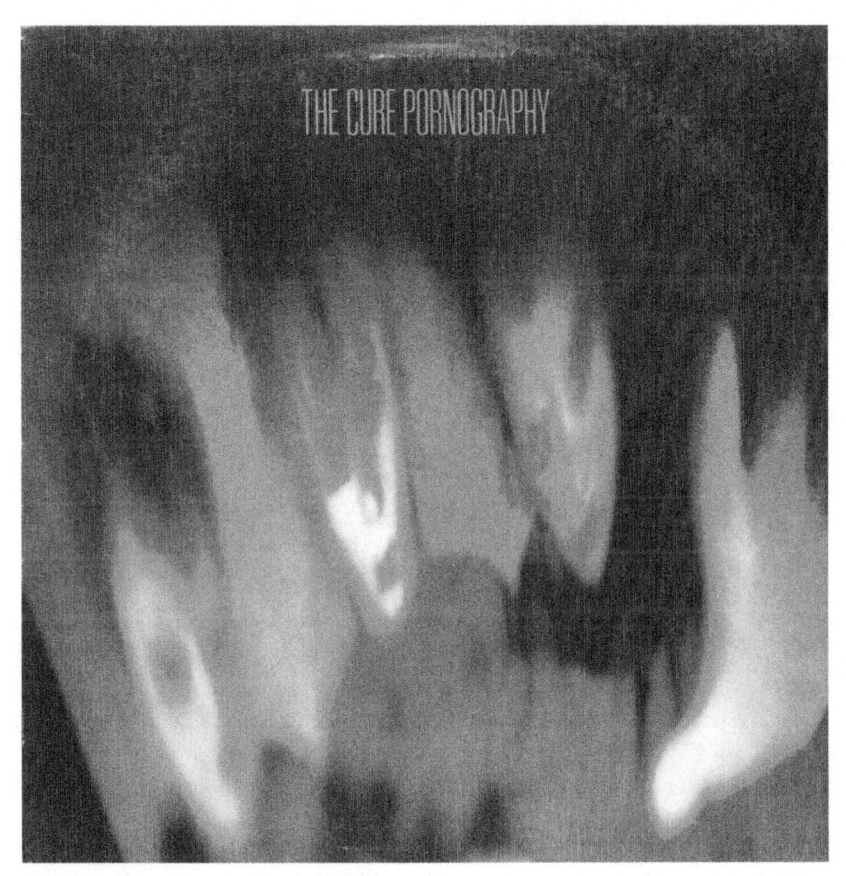

The Cure's darkest and most overtly goth album, *Pornography* (1982) is unrelenting in its anger and misery. *MPVCVRART / Alamy Stock Photo*

Robert Smith has described the sessions as vicious, horrifying, and anarchic, and certainly all three of those words can be used to describe the music, yet there is also some mythmaking in play here. Robert claims they watched disturbing film footage, pornographic and violent, and he remembers wondering afterwards if all that debasement was worth it.

Thornalley admits some of the tales about the album's creation are true, including the band sleeping at the studio. As he told *Songfacts* in September 2015, "All the nutty stories you've read . . . they're all true. It was just over the top. . . . There was this great legacy of this album that you put on and go, 'That's something different. . . .' The mythologizing, I guess maybe it has got something special about it. . . . So, long may the myths continue!"

Lol Tolhurst delivered some truly demonic percussion, helped in part by the RAK's large, cavernous studio with high ceilings. Robert Smith later claimed that he and Simon had to play Lol's drum parts alongside of him because the drummer was so weak from drugs and alcohol, but Tolhurst and Phil Thornalley dispute this. That said, Lol did admit in a 1991 interview to going on vacation for a while at the time *Pornography* was recorded.

Despite the heavy material, Thornalley got along well with the band and remembers no major problems. Robert has claimed the producer tried to temper the album to be more palatable to consumers and to more reflect the Cure's prior work. Robert Smith resisted this, wanting *Pornography* to be a different beast entirely. Thornalley remembers only one minor tiff but no major drama. He found Smith very receptive to ideas, such as his suggestion for some of the effects beamed onto the title track similar to the "found music" approach used by Brian Eno and David Byrne.

Chris Parry didn't hang around the sessions, as the peculiar madness Smith was delivering didn't appeal to him. He was, however, alarmed that once again, there did not appear to be a possible hit single, and he latched on to "The Hanging Garden" as the best possibility. He asked Smith and Thornalley to try to smooth out the song's edges so that it could be presented to radio as a single, so they obliged him and tried to give it more of a sheen. "A Strange Day" was identified as the other possibility, but realistically, there wasn't much that could be done to make any of these songs smash hits.

The name also caused headaches, as Polydor initially balked at the idea of putting it out under the name *Pornography*, which was meant to convey human debasement at its most vile. The label executives weren't thrilled, but little could be done given Smith's contractual guarantee of artistic control. Too much money had gone into the album for Polydor to hold it up, and the Cure was, after all, becoming more and more popular, so they needed new product.

Porl Thompson had been working on a gruesome painting of animals spiraling down from the sky to be the album's cover, but he couldn't get it wrapped up in time, and they settled for an angry red-tinged distorted photo of the band. Thompson's artwork was used instead as the backdrop for the band's stage set when they toured in support of the album.

Robert Smith was certainly pleased with the final product, and Polydor needn't have worried. Released on May 4, 1982, to mixed reviews, *Pornography* soared to number eight in the United Kingdom, their highest-charting album thus far. "The Hanging Garden" performed moderately well, scraping to a respectable number thirty-four even though it's not exactly the kind of song that mainstream radio is open to embracing.

In only three years, the Cure's sound and depth progressed with amazing rapidity, from their debut album in 1979 to that monolith of venomous rage and despair: *Pornography*. Although successful, the dark cloud of despondency and rancor that hovered around the Cure during the album's creation thickened after its release. The band was almost sunk by the same bad feelings on which *Pornography* fed for survival.

At the time, it seemed impossible for the Cure to continue, so Smith didn't hold back, wanting to make the album as confrontational and uncompromising as possible. Exhausted from the nonstop toll of touring, writing, recording, and tension with bandmates and depressed and wrung dry, the music was no longer about glamorous notions of rock stardom that the band may have harbored in the relatively prosaic days leading up to *Three Imaginary Boys*. The music was different now—it was real and all-consuming, a noxious vicious cycle ending with *Pornography*.

Pornography

"One Hundred Years"

"It doesn't matter if we all die" pretty much sums it up. "One Hundred Years," the nearly seven-minute opening grenade on this nonstop sonic assault, is a sharp expression of nihilism and hopelessness. The setting seems to be a lawless and violent dystopian near future along the lines of David Bowie's "Diamond Dogs," but the underworld that "One Hundred Years" inhabits is a far more deadly and decayed reality.

"One Hundred Years" is the powder keg that sets *Pornography* ablaze. Solos rise like whirls of fire from the swaying, heavily flanged rhythm guitar inferno. The jittery polyrhythms twitch like dead bodies jolted repeatedly by a relentless stream of electricity, thanks in part to the Cure's judicious use of a Boss DR-55 drum machine. Robert Smith seethes with desperation and anger, practically spitting the bleak and despondent lyrics. At its center, "One Hundred Years" is another of the Cure's "being and nothingness" songs, but they've gone way beyond Camus and *The Stranger*.

Provocative, fearless, and tense as razor wire, "One Hundred Years" is the hardest-rocking track the Cure had yet recorded. It's been a regular part of the band's live sets ever since and is always a harrowing leviathan in concert. Although never released as a single, there is a rare twelve-inch single promo that fetches premium dollars on auction sites.

"A Short Term Effect"

"A Short Term Effect" is restrained within the album's lines of hellish stateliness, a death march by legions on a shadowy road to battle in the underworld. As with the rest of *Pornography*, everything here is slathered with reverb, and Smith's vocals echo downward like the ripples of a stone getting smaller and smaller as it disappears into the murk. The lyrics are about a drug whose effects aren't quite as short term as expected.

Strangely, "A Short Term Effect" has been a rarity in the Cure's live sets. They've performed it far fewer times than any other track on *Pornography*. It's been dormant since the 2002 *Trilogy* shows during which the Cure played the entire album. Before that, twenty years had passed since it was performed on that fateful final night of the *Pornography* tour.

"The Hanging Garden"

With a thunderous tribal rhythm and wildly throbbing bass, "The Hanging Garden" is the fiercest Cure single yet and a most unlikely entry into the U.K. pop chart at number thirty-four. The track offers nightmare visions of primal animalistic lust, the inner beast taking control and cavorting with other creatures of the wild, all reveling in their dominance and power—not typical top-forty fare.

"The Hanging Garden" was the first single since "Killing an Arab" for which the Cure didn't include a non–album studio track as the B-side instead opting for a live version of "Killing an Arab." A "double-pack" version dubbed "A Single" also includes "One Hundred Years" and a live recording of "A Forest."

"Siamese Twins"

"Siamese Twins" is a slow, sinuous, poisonous screed of revulsion at giving in to the primitive lust of meaningless sexual debauchery. Wracked with self-loathing, Smith wails and moans his way over a rhythm that's every bit as plodding as a murderer in shackles being walked slowly to the electric chair. Musically, it has a faintly exotic air, its line of guitar rising and falling like a snake charmer trying to kiss a cobra. "Siamese Twins" is an anti–love song, sexually twisted and tormented.

"The Figurehead"

Side 2 begins with the anchor of the album, "The Figurehead," a death march as unstoppable as the tide. The base of the structure is the honest dialogue in the center room around which all of *Pornography* spins. It's as detached as Smith is able to get on the album, trying to view things with some space and distance. The imagery is arresting, a merger of purest loathing, animal need, and hopelessness—all themes that recur throughout the album.

"The Figurehead" is six almost unbearably tense minutes of compelling melodrama. It's always a welcome surprise when this old bedraggled warhorse is hauled out into the light and performed in concert.

Sex Is Violent: *Pornography* 97

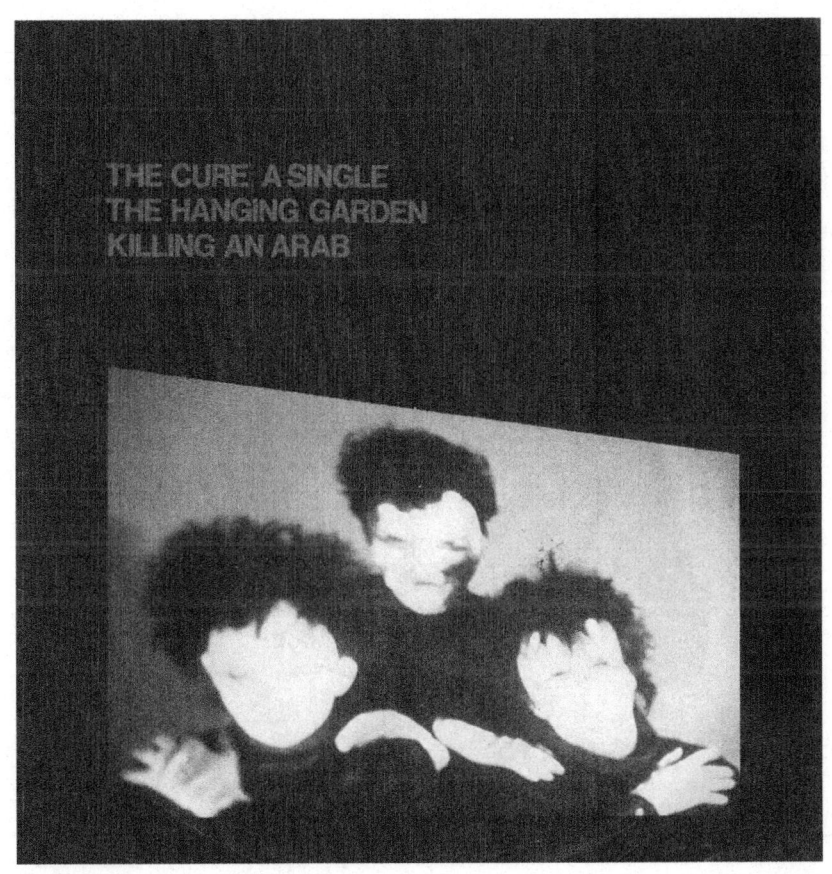

"The Hanging Garden" was the obvious choice for single, and managed to make the U.K. Top 40 even though the video was atrocious. *Author's Collection*

"A Strange Day"

In many ways, the Cure's music was still fairly raw at this point. Tolhurst's drum work was undoubtedly effective for the material they were creating, but it also prevented them from going in different directions. Although he was continuing to develop as a songwriter, Robert Smith had spent the last three albums chasing after a particular sound rather than focusing on creating the most engaging songs. This dynamic would change, but had it not existed, we wouldn't have a piece of sheer brilliance like "A Strange Day."

Had there been a second single from *Pornography*, there is little doubt "A Strange Day" would have been the choice. It's the most accessible track on the album, and the guitar work is phenomenal, especially during the brief instrumental section when the drums fall away and the layered guitar is prescient of the golden days of shoegaze and My Bloody Valentine.

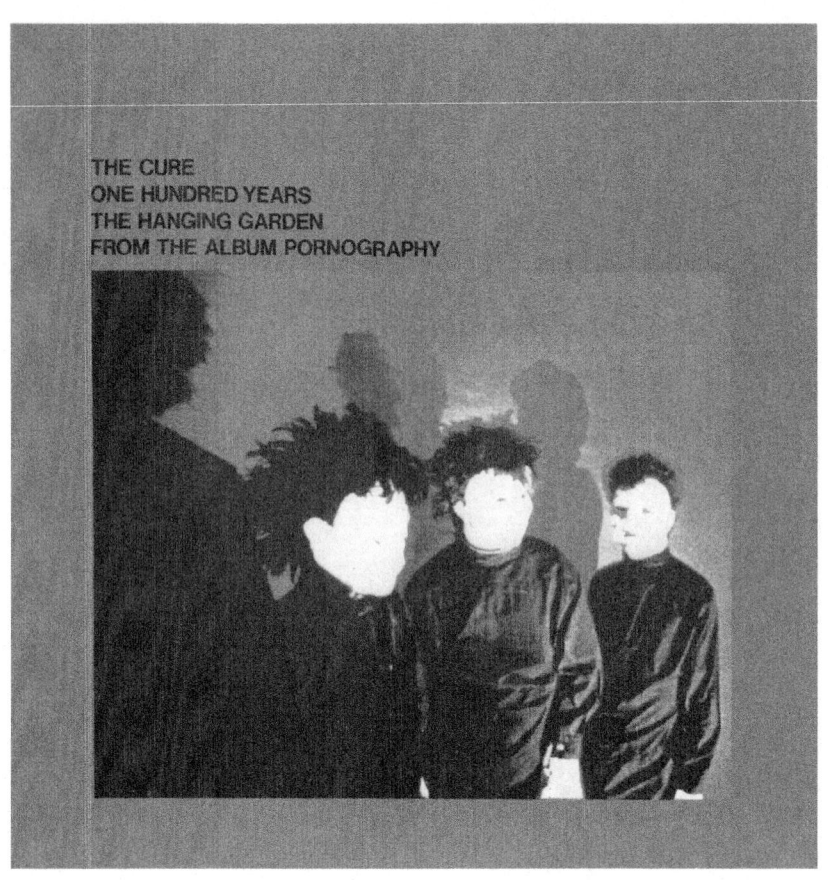

It was never a single, but the the 12" promo for "One Hundred Years" is now a rare collector's item. *Author's Collection*

"Cold"

It *sounds* cold and ominous, with icy synthesizers like skates keening across a frozen river at midnight. "Cold" is the most compact and disciplined recording on the album, carefully arranged and in perpetual motion like a half-frozen river winding through a desolate winter forest.

"Pornography"

The title track ends *Pornography* with a maddening whirlwind of sound, a hurricane psychosis that sends us careening through the air and pelted by debris. "Pornography" is disorienting, with sounds effects, screams, and strange voices fading in and out of the mix like a radio broadcast from beyond the veil.

Tolhurst's drum work is distant and low in the mix, like he's battened down in a basement somewhere, frantically pounding out an ancient rhythm meant to ward off evil. It doesn't seem to be working.

Somehow, drowning in despair and sickness, battered, broken, and cold, Robert Smith finds a glimmer, just a piece of sand really, of determination. He resolves that "we" must stand up, we must fight the sickness, we must find the cure. To what?

There is no one thing that *Pornography* points to as the cause of all our problems; rather, it's the human condition. We are all alone, and we battle through each day, clawing sometimes, failing, desperate to give in, against odds that are overwhelming. Fight this sickness, with what? By remembering that we as humans are all in this together—and, of course, through love. *Pornography*, as used in the context of this album as all that defiles, is the opposite of love. What else could possibly be its nemesis?

Bonus Tracks

"Airlock: The Soundtrack"

As he did for the Picture Tour, Simon Gallup's brother Ric created an abstract film to be projected onstage immediately prior to the Cure taking the stage for the 1982 *Pornography* tour. The Cure once again recorded the accompanying music, this time in the form of a thirteen-minute ambient instrumental called "Airlock: The Soundtrack."

The piece is suitably foreboding as is fitting for an introduction to the barrage of darkness to come. Built from weird noises, sound effects, and creepy bits of discordant piano, "Airlock" could almost be considered an extended coda following "Pornography," which employs similar effects. The first official release for "Airlock: The Soundtrack" was on the deluxe two-CD reissue of *Pornography* released in 2005; before that, it was largely unknown. For most fans, it probably still is—it's not the type of thing that inspires repeated listening.

"All Mine"

Like "Forever," "All Mine" is an always changing improvisation that was a constant part of the Cure's set during their 1982 tour but has never been released as a studio recording. The version on the deluxe *Pornography* reissue is the same one included on the 1982 *Anomalies* collection that the Cure appended to the cassette version of *Concert* on the B-side.

Recorded at the Hammersmith Odeon in May 1982, the sound quality is not the greatest, but its inclusion on the reissue was exciting for many fans, as

"All Mine" had developed a mythic quality over the years and had been widely bootlegged in various forms.

"Ariel"

Robert Smith recorded this much-bootlegged demo in July 1982 during the same session that resulted in "Temptation," the instrumental track that later became "Let's Go to Bed" and a demo that was never fully developed: "You Stayed."

"Ariel" was performed on October 24, 1982, for the *Kid Jensen Session* radio show on BBC along with "Let's Go to Bed," "One Hundred Years," and "Just One Kiss," and the version from that broadcast has been widely circulated among Cure collectors for years. The demo, which is a slow and ghostly piece with vocals reminiscent of the *Faith* era, was released for the first time on the 2006 deluxe reissue of *The Top*.

When asked about the song by *The Cure News* fanzine in December 1990, Robert Smith said it was part of his "mysterious solo project." More information dribbled out in an interview the following year in which Smith claimed that "Ariel" is part of an acoustic-based solo project inspired by Nick Drake.

It's a miracle that the Cure ever clawed out of the emotional wreckage wrought by the *Pornography* album and tour. They almost didn't. The tour was soaked in drugs and acrimony. The band members were emotionally battered anew each night by reliving yet again the malice and bad feelings that generated the new material in the first place.

Robert Smith has said that the album reminds him of things he'd rather not remember, that he was disturbed and out of sync at the time. The tour amplified cracks that already existed within the Cure while creating new ones and ultimately expanding them beyond the breaking point.

Pornography is a finality, a soundtrack for a fractured mind imprisoned by hallucinations and frayed nerve endings and wrenched by pain that seems to have no cure. No other Cure album reaches this same high-wire level of intensity, but that seems an impossibility anyway, as they couldn't possibly have survived it. No other album sounds like it in all of rock music, period. It's a singular accomplishment.

Robert Smith realized that the Cure no longer had a path to follow after *Pornography*. What came after was totally unexpected, and it had to be. The next door he opened would sweep him away to completely different shores, to a fantasy world that would get only bigger and stranger.

Once Upon a Time in a Land Called Fantasy: The Pop Singles

Tired of channeling misery, Robert Smith turns to whimsical pop to breath fresh life into the Cure.

June 11, 1982, Brussels. The *Pornography* tour thuds to a dismal ending, with bassist Simon Gallup storming away after months of tension, culminating in a fistfight with Robert Smith at a bar. The band's disintegration was all but complete. The Cure no longer existed as a functioning band.

Robert Smith abandoned his dingy apartment in London and retreated to the comforting familiarity of his parents' home in Crawley, where he spent weeks recuperating, getting sober, and dusting the accumulated cobwebs from inside his skull so he could think more clearly. He and his girlfriend Mary Poole took a short vacation driving and camping through the countryside of Wales. He stayed out of contact with Chris Parry of Fiction, who had no idea where his label's signature star had gone, or what the current status of the Cure might be.

The time spent at home with his family and on holiday with Mary seems to have rejuvenated Robert Smith. After his much-needed recuperation, he returned to London to record a one-off track for *Flexipop!* magazine and discuss the future of the Cure with Chris Parry. It turns out that they were thinking along the same lines. Parry wanted Smith to write an upbeat pop single that would shatter the creative box and mythology that surrounded the Cure after three straight dark albums considered by many as goth.

Chris Parry's idea fit perfectly where Smith's head was at the time. After the band's recent debacle, Smith was unsure whether the Cure could or should continue to exist. He was sick of what the band had become and of his own tormented-goth persona. Smith was not by nature the type of person who had been completely consumed by the melancholy and discord in which he'd been immersed for the last two albums and tours, and it became suffocating. He wanted to destroy the Cure and rebuild it by making a left turn no one would expect. Robert Smith, the pop star, was about to be born.

It's not like Smith hadn't expressed his pop sensibilities before—anyone familiar with "Boys Don't Cry" knows he can write a classic pop tune. Robert was eager to revisit that side of his musical brain again. It seemed logical, anyway. How could he possibly out-gloom *Faith* or out-anger *Pornography*? Smith's experience with *Pornography*, the album and tour, left him reeling. The sessions were tense and joyless, the music derived from anger, despair, and self-loathing. The tour was miserable. There was no going forward on that route, there was nowhere left to go.

Freed from the shackles of expectations, Robert Smith realized that he had the opportunity to reinvent the Cure in a radical way, and that's exactly what he did. It was time to have fun again. The trio of pop singles released over a year's span from November 1982 to October 1983 marked a tectonic shift in the band's direction.

It may have gone ever farther than it did, as there were hints in the media in late 1982 that the Cure would be rerecording twelve older songs for a new updated "hits" collection. It's a bit surreal to imagine what the 1982 synth-pop edition of the Cure may have done with songs like "Primary," "Boys Don't Cry," and "A Forest." This project never materialized, which may be for the best, but the period did result in about an album's worth of the Cure's own twisted vision of what pop music should be.

The Pop Singles

"Lament" (*Flexipop!*)

It was hard for anyone associated with the Cure to see how they could go forward after their tumultuous 1982 tour. Yet, as if by some magical spell woven just for the sake of defying everyone's expectations (which is a bit of a Cure specialty), only two short months after the last tour ended in chaos, in August 1982 a very strange and unlikely new Cure song popped up in the most unlikely of places: on magazine stands, attached to *Flexipop!*

From 1980 to 1983, *Flexipop!* was a popular British publication created by Barry Cain and Tim Lott, two journalists formerly of *The Record Mirror*. They came up with a brilliant idea—to tape a flexi-disc containing an original song by a major artist on the cover of each edition. They became enormously popular, with exclusive tracks by top-tier artists such as the Clash, the Police, Depeche

Mode, Boy George, the Stranglers, Siouxsie and the Banshees, the Psychedelic Furs, George Michael, Adam Ant, David Bowie, Duran Duran, Queen, Spandau Ballet, and many more.

When *Flexipop!* contacted Robert Smith to inquire about the possibility of the Cure's contributing a track to the popular magazine, it caused a bit of a dilemma. Would he admit that the Cure no longer existed, which would surely get blown up in media coverage, or perhaps he could record something quickly under the Cure's name for the magazine to use. He could also just punt, decline the offer with no explanation, and make a decision about the Cure's future later.

The fact that the Cure still owed several more albums to Fiction Records under the terms of their contract surely helped to make Robert Smith's decision, as he could have faced hefty financial consequences for breaking the deal. Of course, even if that had not been a factor, it seems unlikely that Smith, who spent much of the 1980s and 1990s compulsively writing, recording, and performing Cure songs, would have decided to let it end then and there.

Smith booked time at Garden Studio in London and called up close friend Steve Severin for help. They quickly cobbled together the woozy electronic experiment "Lament," a complete departure from anything released under the Cure's name up through that point. It was the first new song that Smith had written in quite some time, and he felt relief and satisfaction over it even if it was rather rough. The track strongly foreshadows the work that Smith and Severin would do together as the Glove.

Smith's wails are garbled and muted, as if recorded from a broken telephone over a great distance or perhaps beyond the grave. Swirling around him are whirls and woos of keyboard, the shrill keening of wooden flutes, and a slithery riff played on his old familiar Woolworths Top 20 guitar. Everything is weirdly off-key, with a primitive drum machine.

The result sounds more like an amateurish demo than a completed song, and in a way, it is given the superior version recorded not long after for *The Walk* EP. Compared to the finished track, the *Flexipop!* recording is merely a rough sketch—but an interesting one and critically important. After all, if not for that call from *Flexipop!* and the impromptu session that led to this half-finished curio, who knows if Robert Smith would have continued the Cure. Fortunately, the answer to that question is moot.

"Let's Go to Bed"/"Just One Kiss"

Rarely has a band made such an abrupt left turn and survived, but the Cure did it and thrived. At the end of the *Pornography* tour in June 1982, the Cure had collapsed. Simon Gallup was gone, and Laurence Tolhurst was increasingly inhibited both by his limited drum technique and by his rampant alcoholism.

Chris Parry challenged Robert Smith to come up with a hit pop song, and Smith produced the synth-pop classic "Let's Go to Bed."

The blueprint for the single was an instrumental demo Smith had recorded called "Temptation." The singer played every instrument apart from drums, for which he hired former Graham Parker and future Gang of Four drummer Steve Goulding. Years later, Lol Tolhurst denied that he was unable to handle the part himself, saying that he could have used the "Lol disco beat" for the song, whatever that might be.

Smith was dismayed with "Let's Go to Bed" from the very beginning and was unsure throughout the recording process if he wanted to release it under the Cure's name. It was a mad gamble, the type of sudden pivot that rarely works for an artist who isn't named David Bowie or Prince.

At the last minute, unable to accept the release of a song he couldn't bring himself to like, Robert Smith balked. He told Chris Parry that if Fiction wanted to release the single, it would have to be under a name other than the Cure. In a rare show of defiance, Chris Parry refused to change plans for the single and insisted that "Let's Go to Bed" be attributed to the Cure. Robert Smith almost always got his way, but this time, he should be eternally grateful that he didn't.

Chris Parry's decision to release "Let's Go to Bed" as the next Cure single is without question one of the most important turning points in the band's history. It opened the floodgates, forever changing the band's trajectory and infinitely expanding what the Cure could be. This paradigm shift would lead directly to the Cure's most successful period, both artistically and commercially. It was also the Cure's first single in the United States.

The significance of "Let's Go to Bed" in the Cure's overall career arc goes far beyond its relative strength as a composition and recording, which is certainly debatable. It's not a bad song, certainly—a witty synth-pop frivolity with catchy melodic hooks in both the vocal and the keyboard riff. The Cure has recorded many better songs during their career, but sometimes it's about the right song at the right time, and that's the case here.

Lyrically, "Let's Go to Bed" is a bit daft and meaningless, but when contrasted with the dense hallucinogenic diatribes on *Pornography*, it's evidence of Robert Smith's remarkable range. Smith delivers his wry and quirky vocal with easy confidence, slipping into a persona diametrically opposed to the punishing material he was recording only months earlier. The change from "One Hundred Years" to "Let's Go to Bed" seems so effortless. Smith does it with such panache that it's hard to believe this hadn't been his style all along.

There's more to this shift than just a shift to a synth-pop style of music. A new craftiness, a new level of deviousness, had suddenly appeared. The Cure no longer exclusively wore their hearts or pain on their sleeves. Sometimes they'd hide behind masks, invent characters, and adopt coy smiles, ambiguity, or mystery, all within the confines of a four-minute pop song.

"Let's Go to Bed" was released on November 15, 1982, just six months after the *Pornography* album and five months since the end of the tour. It didn't exactly burn up the charts in the United Kingdom, peaking at number forty-four. Robert Smith openly trashed the single during interviews at every opportunity, and Chris Parry has blamed this for the single's lack of chart success.

The Cure's image makeover was remarkable. Robert Smith transitioned from malignantly ghoulish and demented on their last tour to an enigmatic but cuddly oddball in the "Let's Go to Bed" video. The softened image also helped motor the Cure to the commercial success that had thus far been elusive. "Let's Go to Bed" set the stage for the next single, "The Walk," to be a huge breakthrough. More important was its impact on the Cure's overall sound. The Cure's sonic palette widened exponentially. If "Let's Go to Bed" could be the Cure, then they could do anything, go anywhere. And so they did.

In 1986, the Cure's North American record label Elektra chose "Let's Go to Bed" as the first promotional single for the *Standing on a Beach* singles compilation in the United States and Canada instead of "Boys Don't Cry," which was the pick for most of the world.

Although the B-side "Just One Kiss" lacks the obvious commercial appeal of its A-side, Robert Smith considers it to be far superior to "Let's Go to Bed," and it's hard to argue with this. "Just One Kiss" practically quivers with tension stoked by its frenetic percussion and wildly pulsating bass. Its sharply taut rhythm guitar and dramatic flourishes of keyboard add a sense of exotic mystery and increased potency.

Smith could have backed "Let's Go to Bed" with a synth-pop frivolity, but instead, he jumped right into his new ocean of possibility by creating something substantial. On "Just One Kiss," the Cure's dueling personalities balance in perfect harmony by marrying the brooding melancholy of *Seventeen Seconds*, *Faith*, and *Pornography* to a fresh emphasis on pop songcraft. "Just One Kiss" can be viewed as a template of sorts for the Cure's decades of enduring success. Pretty impressive for a B-side.

They didn't toss out throwaways—the Cure always put everything into what they recorded regardless of Smith's sometimes derisive commentary about their pop hits. These songs may not have the same emotional weight as the Cure's darker work, but they are cleverly conceived and beguiling. Actions speak louder than words. The Cure excels at creating timeless pop music. Although Robert Smith may have once repudiated these songs, in reality, he's embraced them by keeping them a staple in the Cure's set lists and by unloosening the screws and allowing the band's pop side to come out and play at least briefly on each album going forward.

"The Walk"/"The Upstairs Room"/ "The Dream"/"Lament"

During May 1983, Robert Smith recorded the Glove's *Blue Sunshine* album with Steve Severin (and featuring Andy Anderson helping on drums) while also working on *The Walk* EP for the Cure at Jam Studios in London. Smith chose producer Steve Nye for the project, who is otherwise best known for producing Japan's 1981 new wave classic *Tin Drum*. It was Robert Smith's admiration for that album that led him to seek out Nye, and the collaboration proved fruitful. The five-day sessions yielded four completed tracks, one of which became the Cure's biggest single yet.

Released in July 1983, "The Walk" appeared in slightly different formats depending on the country. In the United Kingdom, it was issued as a 45 backed with "The Upstairs Room" and a twelve-inch single, including "The Dream" and the rerecorded "Lament." In the United States, Sire Records chose to release the set as a six-song EP, including the four songs above while adding the extended version of "Just One Kiss" and the single mix of "Let's Go to Bed."

Bolstered by an irresistible synthesizer riff, "The Walk" is hyper–New Wave pop, an instant earworm that easily became the Cure's biggest hit thus far, going all the way to number twelve. The Cure finally had that big signature hit they'd thus far been lacking, and their visibility in the media rose substantially. As with "Let's Go to Bed," Robert went out of his way to slag "The Walk" in the press, but it became a hit anyway. The Cure appeared on *Top of the Pops* twice to perform the song.

New Order's Peter Hook accused the Cure of ripping off "Blue Monday" since the rhythm and bass on the two tracks are similar. "Blue Monday" was released on March 7, 1983, just as the Cure was beginning the sessions for "The Walk" and its B-sides. Robert Smith flatly denied the accusation, suggesting that if anything, "The Walk" was inspired by Japan.

"The Walk" sessions also exposed a rift between Robert Smith and Lol Tolhurst that would continue to gradually widen. Smith bought an expensive Oberheim OB-8 synthesizer and DSX sequencer for Tolhurst, who had ostensibly switched from drums to keyboard, and gave him three months learn how to operate it. Instead, Smith says, Lol spent the time taking drugs and learned nothing about the equipment.

Steve Nye was the key to unlocking the new machine and getting the sound out of it that Robert wanted. At one point, after watching Tolhurst twiddling ineffectually on the machine for hours, Nye snapped at him to "read the fuckin' manual!" It doesn't appear that the advice ever completely took hold. Years later, Tolhurst said rather feebly that he did try to learn it but that he would have needed a "degree in physics" to work things out.

"The Walk" became The Cure's first big pop hit in the U.K., a major breakthrough that helped usher in their most successful period. *Author's Collection*

"The Upstairs Room" was written by Robert Smith during the period when he was sleeping on the floor of Steve Severin's flat, as were many other songs from this period that ended up on multiple different projects. Upbeat and melodic with a driving bass line and jagged guitar riff, had these tracks been recorded for a full album, "The Upstairs Room" might have made a great single. "The Dream" is a synthesizer-driven pop nugget specifically inspired by Japan and was performed largely on the same Oberheim synthesizer that Smith used on "The Walk."

Robert Smith's favorite song on the EP is the reworked "Lament," the song he wrote with Steve Severin in June 1982 and recorded a primitive version for *Flexipop!* The final version follows the general blueprint of the earlier recording but has a much more elaborate arrangement and a newly written set of lyrics that are suitably haunting for the spectral music.

"The Lovecats"/"Speak My Language"/ "Mr. Pink Eye"/"A Hand inside My Mouth"

For the all-important follow-up to the Cure's first major hit, Smith conceived his most beguiling pop creation yet. Inspired by the Disney animated classic *The Aristocats*, "The Lovecats" is a colorful jazzed-up frolic that sidles up to that thin line between the sublime and the ridiculous and manages perfect balance. Smith's gifts as a vocalist are often overlooked. He's gifted at understanding and capturing the mood of a song and its lyrics in his vocals. Appropriately enough, given the setting of the film that inspired the song, the sessions for "The Lovecats"—its two B-sides and an unreleased track—took place in mid-August 1983 at Studio des Dames in Paris.

Phil Thornalley, producer for *Pornography*, fills a very different role here, as his swinging bass line is one of the signature elements of the song. He coproduced the sessions as well, and of all the work he did with the Cure, he points to these sessions as the best. Andy Anderson's nifty brushwork helped him to snag a spot in the band for the Cure's next album and tour.

"Speak My Language" is another jazz-pop pastiche, the garbled lyrics improvised by Smith on the spot. "Mr. Pink Eye" is a frenzied rush of self-loathing, written by Robert Smith after catching a glance at himself in the mirror after a long night of drinking. He expressed his disdain with a whirlwind cacophony of maddening harmonica and heavy drums that speed up like a boulder careening down a mountainside and flattening everything in its path. It wasn't rated as highly as the others by Smith at the time. Placed as an extra track on "The Lovecats" twelve-inch single, "Mr. Pink Eye" was the only track released during this period not included on the *Japanese Whispers* compilation.

Also recorded during the Studio de Dames sessions but abandoned (for the moment anyway) was "A Hand inside My Mouth." Robert Smith recycled the basic concept of the title for the B-side "A Man inside My Mouth" during *The Head on the Door* sessions, but it has little to do with this original version. The lyrics are entirely different, as is the music. "A Hand inside My Mouth" has a bit of a swing vibe, consistent with the other songs in the session, but seems a bit tentative. Smith evidently lost interest in the track, and it remained unreleased until it was included as part of the bonus material on the 2006 deluxe reissue of *The Top*.

"The Lovecats" was the Cure's biggest single yet, soaring to number seven in the United Kingdom. It was so popular that they performed it three times on *Top of the Pops*, turning Robert Smith into perhaps the most unlikely pop star ever to grace the cover of a teen magazine. For his part, Smith made sure to downplay it, calling it "amateurish" and "a joke." Of course, he'd made similar comments about "Let's Go to Bed" and "The Walk." Years later, though, he'd change his tune about the pop songs.

Robert Smith took a sharp left turn with "Let's Go to Bed" from turgid rock to bouncy synth-pop, and in the process opened up the Cure's potential sound canvas exponentially.
Author's Collection

Smith told *Spin* in July 2004 that when the Cure scored pop hits in the 1980s, he didn't think it would compromise everything the band had done to that point. He said, "I thought it was fucking great we were being played on the radio. Why would we have ever made those songs if I didn't think they were good songs?" He worried at times that doing pop songs would interfere with the perception of the Cure as artists, but eventually he realized what a ridiculous notion this was. The Cure's ability to embrace pop confection turned out to be vital to the band's overall career arc. It allowed them to have fun again after they had been treading down a very dark path and gave them the freedom that Smith always desired for the Cure—to do whatever they want for as long as they want.

12

Pictures Came and Broke Your Heart: The Cure in Video

The Cure's international profile continued to rise through the 1980s with eclectic and memorable videos mostly directed by Tim Pope.

The Cure's long string of visually striking music videos have been a key component to their success over the years. Although they filmed a few primitive clips for their early singles, it wasn't until "Let's Go to Bed" in 1982, their first collaboration with video director Tim Pope, that they really got into the format. Pope stayed on with the band for most of their biggest albums, directing some of the most memorable videos of the MTV era, including "Close to Me," "Why Can't I Be You?," "Just Like Heaven," and the ghoulish fantasy "Lullaby."

Videos

"10:15 Saturday Night" (1979), Director: Piers Bedford

The Cure's first video is a fascinating glimpse of the young musicians as middle-class suburban geeks. Robert Smith is all sullen adolescent petulance topped by a bowl cut. Lol Tolhurst is already in stone-faced mode, a long mop of curls hanging nearly to his shoulders. Michael Dempsey thrusts his hips like a 1970s glam-rock road warrior. He puts as much gusto into the ultrasimple bass part as possible, but it's clear from his mannerisms that he longs to really cut loose.

"A Forest" (1980), Director: David Hillier

There's something fitting about the low-budget, bare-bones clip that David Hillier directed for "A Forest," one of the Cure's most important songs. Hillier kept it simple, just splicing band performance footage with images of a random forest. Its rudimentary nature vibes nicely with the stripped-down recording, and the video holds together with distinct charm. "A Forest" was the first-ever music video for Hillier. He worked mostly in TV but did go on to shoot a number of other promo clips for multiple artists, with Murray Head's 1985 smash "One Night in Bangkok" his most widely known.

"Play for Today" (1980). Director: David Hillier

Although never a single, "Play for Today" should have been, especially since the band recorded what might be considered their first real video for the song. David Hillier shot the basic performance clip of the band with an all-white background, so the guys stand out starkly. It's simple but effective, and it's remarkable to see how much more self-assured they look barely over a year since the "10:15 Saturday Night" clip.

We get to see Robert Smith snarling out the viperous lyrics, Simon Gallup sporting a leather jacket and already looking totally badass, and Lol Tolhurst banging out the rhythm with gusto. Matthieu Hartley can be seen fingering that iconic keyboard riff that fans still sing along with decades later. It's difficult to understand why this was never issued as the follow-up to "A Forest," as in retrospect its commercial appeal seems strong.

"Primary" (1981), Director: Bob Rickerd

The obvious single from the *Faith* album, "Primary" came very close to following "A Forest" into the U.K. top forty, stalling just shy at number forty-three. The video is a simple performance clip of the band backed by darkness, with hazy images of mysterious young schoolgirls, presumably echoing the single's cover art, occasionally interspersed through the clip. The most notable aspect of the video is that we finally get to the hair-and-makeup phase of the band's career.

Robert Smith is now sporting lipstick (although it would get much more smudged in the years to come), and we get to see his famous hair in progress with an early prototype style that would rapidly progress into a much larger fixture perched precariously atop his head.

"Other Voices" (1981), Director: Bob Rickerd

As with "Play for Today" from the band's prior album, "Other Voices" was never released as a 45, although it clearly should have been. After all, they went through the trouble of filming a beautifully eerie video for the track, with the band blurred amongst the shadows inexorably assailing the ghostly light that surrounds them. Director Bob Rickerd helmed only two music videos in his career, but at least they are great ones—"Primary" and "Other Voices"—both of which were filmed on the same date.

"Charlotte Sometimes" (1981), Director: Mike Mansfield

Rightly deemed an embarrassment by the band, the video for "Charlotte Sometimes" is every bit as atrocious as the song itself is brilliant. The irredeemably tacky video was at the time the most elaborate concept piece the Cure had filmed by far, retreating to Holloway Sanatorium, where a young girl wanders through the halls in apparent reference to the Charlotte in the song, who is struggling to retain her sanity.

"The Hanging Garden" (1982), Director: Chris Gabrin

Speaking of miscalculations, here is another big one. "The Hanging Garden" is the sole single to have been issued from the Cure's landmark album *Pornography*, but its video is irrefutable evidence of the band's hapless inability to translate their musical power into effective visuals.

The issue may have been director Chris Gabrin. The band hired him because of his work with Madness, and they wanted to follow that whimsical direction—which seems singularly ill-suited for the turgid lust-fest "The Hanging Garden." Gabrin, to his credit, wanted more serious, but when gauging the unintentional hilarious end result, it's hard to say which side won out.

"Let's Go to Bed" (1982), Director: Tim Pope

Following a long string of mostly inept videos, the Cure finally enter the video age properly with director Tim Pope in the fold. Pope would end up collaborating with the band on all of the most celebrated clips through their most successful period. "Let's Go to Bed" wasn't a truly auspicious start, but it's certainly a step up.

As difficult as it may be to fathom, the ludicrous paroxysms plaguing Lol Tolhurst throughout the video are apparently intended as dancing. At one point, when his silhouette is seen dancing behind a curtain, he is in fact completely nude. The highlight from Robert Smith is his dramatic performance miming intently to the two shapely eggs he holds and then smashes together, perhaps in homage to some obscure rite of fertility that, along with this video, really never should have been permitted to escape from the 1980s.

Still, easy as it is to point and laugh at this and many other 1980s videos, it's important to note that this marks the emergence of Smith's singular style, which would soon grace magazine covers and appear in the upper reaches of the pop charts the world over.

"The Walk" (1983), Director: Tim Pope

"The Walk," the Cure's biggest hit up to that point, is much stronger than "Let's Go to Bed." The surreal video shows Robert Smith getting more comfortable in his skin as a pop star, a role he would never relinquish. Pope's video is abstract and hyper, as is fitting for the song, and the look devised for Smith couldn't be more appropriately silly yet has a hint of queasy sordidness. Things were starting to turn around for the band, and the progression evident in their video time line hints at the enormous push that would eventually lead them to bigger and better things.

"The Lovecats" (1983), Director: Tim Pope

Easily the best video the Cure had released to date, "The Lovecats" also gave the Cure their first top ten single in the United Kingdom. Smith and his bandmates romped with playfulness and good cheer through the clip, with Tolhurst good-naturedly pretending to play the jaunty piano and Andy Anderson making his first appearance with the band on drums. Only the crustiest curmudgeon could watch the sweet and endearing "Lovecats" without a smile.

"The Caterpillar" (1984), Director: Tim Pope

Robert Smith's hair had gotten even bigger. That's not the only notable thing about the video for "The Caterpillar," the only one created for *The Top* album. Both bassist Phil Thornalley and guitarist Porl Thompson are seen, although they aren't on the recording, and Tolhurst shows once again that he's better at pretending to play the piano than actually playing one. Smith is in full spaced-out mode, averting his eyes from the camera with a vague (probably high)

Inspired by *The Aristocats*, "The Lovecats" charmed its way to #7 in the U.K., their first Top 10 single. *Author's Collection*

expression on his face. Filmed at Syon Park Conservatory in London, "The Caterpillar" feels a little more forced than "The Lovecats," with some of the darkness inherent to *The Top* having seeped in.

"In Between Days" (1985), Director: Tim Pope

The Cure's arrival in full flowering bloom is captured beautifully by Tim Pope in this exuberant clip. In it, the camera moves in a circular pattern, while Smith spins around the room joyously. Colored socks spin over the live footage of the band. It all seems so carefree and innocent, in a way that the band had never really captured before or since.

"Close to Me" (1985), Director: Tim Pope

One of the Cure's signature videos, "Close to Me" portrays the band in a wardrobe that falls over the side of a cliff (filmed at Beachy Head, East Sussex) and sinks to the bottom of the sea, where the water starts seeping in. The wardrobe opens, and the band starts swimming amongst the clothes and the fish, and they all seem to be having a wonderful time. "Close to Me" is visually arresting and fun at heart. It is without question one of the Cure's finest video moments.

"A Night Like This" (1985), Director: Tim Pope

Although never technically a single, a haunting promotional clip was filmed for this dark and dramatic album track using a live performance of the song rather than the studio version. The nighttime setting, shadowy and mysterious, suits the vibe of the track well, and Robert Smith shows that, after a couple of upbeat videos, he still can deliver penetrating and serious just as compellingly.

"The Blood" (1986), Director Gerard de Thame

The Cure released a very limited number of promotional singles for this flamenco-flavored track from *The Head on the Door* only for the Spanish market. In the years since, the single's scarcity has made it one of the rarest items for Cure collectors to seek for their collections. Director Gerard de Thame created a stylish mishmash of images from various sources. "The Blood" single wasn't technically an official Cure release, and it's never been included in their hits or video collection. Yet it's a fascinating curio and worth checking out for fans who haven't seen it.

"Boys Don't Cry" (1986), Director: Tim Pope

For their 1986 singles compilation *Standing on a Beach*, the Cure rerecorded "Boys Don't Cry" to put out as a promotional single, and, for the video, they look back nostalgically at their past. While three young boys perform the song onstage, on the curtain behind them looms the shadows of Robert Smith, Tolhurst, and Michael Dempsey, whom Smith brought back for his only appearance with the band since 1979.

"Killing an Arab"/"Jumping Someone Else's Train" (1986), Directed by Tim Pope

In conjunction with their 1986 *Standing on a Beach* singles collection, the Cure also issued a VHS collection of nearly all their video clips: *Staring at the Sea—The Images*. For many fans, especially in the United States, it was the first time they'd been able to view early clips like "A Forest," "Primary," "Other Voices," and "Play for Today" that weren't exactly MTV staples. Robert Smith and Tim Pope collaborate on the video collection, adding bits of footage from through the years between cuts and creating clips for two major early singles that didn't previously have videos: "Killing an Arab" and "Jumping Someone Else's Train."

Neither of the clips featured the band, and both were very simple. Pope traveled to the small coastal town of Rye in East Sussex to visit the elderly gentleman on the cover of *Standing on a Beach*, retired fisherman John Button. Shot in grainy black and white, the video shows close-ups of Mr. Button on what looks to be a frigid winter day as he gazes out into the sea in apparent contemplation. There are shots of him lighting a cigarette or simply walking around his snow-covered fishing town. What it has to do with the song itself is not readily apparent.

"Jumping Someone Else's Train" is simply a take of train tracks disappearing ahead, and the camera, from the point of view of the train conductor, takes the viewer on a high-speed trip that stops right as the song ends. It's a cool little visual that doesn't really add much, but it doesn't need to. It serves its purpose to be a visual accompaniment for the song to help ensure that it wasn't forgotten.

"Why Can't I Be You?" (1987), Director: Tim Pope

This high-energy song demanded an over-the-top clip to match, and Tim Pope and the Cure delivered with a hysterical dance romp for "Why Can't I Be You?" Smith hams it up gleefully while dressed in a bear suit and the rest of the band dance and zip around madly. The clip received tons of MTV airplay and went a long way toward bringing the Cure to large-scale U.S. audiences for the first time.

"Catch" (1987), Director: Tim Pope

Filmed on location in Cannes, France, at the home of an elderly French lady and near where the band recorded *Kiss Me, Kiss Me, Kiss Me*, "Catch" is a beautifully languid clip that perfectly matches the genial vibe of the song with its lazy accordion and Smith's disarmingly relaxed vocal. Gorgeously filmed, it reflects the bittersweet nostalgia expressed in the lyrics with gracious beauty. Tolhurst adds violin to the long list of instruments he's pretended to know how to play, but he does this so ineptly that it ultimately detracts from the video's otherwise glowing beauty.

"Just Like Heaven" (1987), Director: Tim Pope

The Cure filmed their breakthrough U.S. hit "Just Like Heaven" largely at Pinewood Studios in Buckinghamshire, although it looks as if it really takes place on the side of a cliff overlooking the sea. Shots of the water were lifted from extra footage shot for the "Close to Me" video a couple years prior. The beautiful nighttime segment features Smith's wife Mary Poole, a glowing apparition in white gracefully dancing with her husband like a fallen angel.

"Hot Hot Hot!!!" (1988), Director: Tim Pope

The final single taken from *Kiss Me*, "Hot Hot Hot!!!" was filmed in black and white and intended to be sufficiently bonkers to fit the hyperkinetic track. Smith had cut his hair short and looks rather dapper, although Simon Gallup more than makes up for it. Lol Tolhurst mimes the trumpet this time, looking like he's in pain, and he probably was given his wretched state at the time.

"Lullaby" (1989), Director: Tim Pope

One of Tim Pope's deftest creations is for "Lullaby," a song with imagery that practically begs for a cinematic representation. Inspired in part by David Lynch's *Eraserhead*, the atmosphere and set design are suitably creepy, and the makeup is worthy of a haunted house maze where parents pay to have their children frightened during Halloween. The giant spider, though, as adorable as it is, hasn't really aged well, the poor thing. It looks like a Hostess Cupcake with the filling oozing out. Considered by many as their finest video, "Lullaby" won Best Video at the 1990 Brit Awards.

"Fascination Street" (1989), Director: Tim Pope

One of the Cure's greatest singles, "Fascination Street" helped bring them enormous American success thanks to heavy play on MTV and modern rock radio. The atmospheric video highlights the band performing intensely on a set designed to look like a forbidding street late at night. Pope keeps it fairly simple as he highlights the complex instrumental arrangements and the band's stellar musicianship. In retrospect years later, Robert Smith was cool to the video, stating they didn't quite capture what they sought with it.

"Lovesong" (1989), Director: Tim Pope

Tim Pope has said that the cave in the "Lovesong" video is intended to be the spot where Robert Smith and his bandmates end up after all being eaten by the giant spider in "Lullaby," although if this were truly the case, the giant spider is much larger than it seems to be initially and should really see somebody about all those mineral deposits coating his innards—it can't be healthy. The plan was to film at the Cave of Souls at Cheddar Gorge, Somerset, England, but they were unable to secure permission to do so and ended up in a sound studio.

Although Smith has made clear his disappointment in the final result, it is in fact a lovely video. The camera spends much of its time focused squarely on the lead singer as he sings his most direct and simple love song with a mournful quality (and he isn't exactly bursting with good cheer in the video). "Lovesong" rocketed up the U.S. singles chart and became the band's biggest hit, a feat aided no doubt by MTV playing the clip in heavy rotation.

"Pictures of You" (1990), Director: Tim Pope

The fourth and final single from *Disintegration* got shortchanged. As Robert Smith didn't want to repeat the time and effort that went into the clip for "Lovesong," the band decided to keep things simple. They decided to simply use grainy footage taken on a cheap Super-8 of the band performing and acting generally goofy in Ballachulish, Scotland.

While there is a somewhat beguiling innocence to the clip, it somehow seems comparatively shallow given the enormous feeling conveyed in the song itself. But perhaps that's the point, as it's so heavy and personal that the video is meant to puncture it a little and bring it all back down to earth and remind ourselves that laughing and smiling is nothing for which to apologize.

"Never Enough" (1990), Director: Tim Pope

One of the Cure's best videos arrived with "Never Enough," the only newly recorded single from the *Mixed Up* remix project. They filmed the clip at the end of Hastings Pier in Sussex. The band appears in an elaborately designed freak show as one of the spectacles with filters and camera angle trickery distorting their already wild appearance. The Porl Thompson–heavy song is a hard rocker that translates brilliantly to visual interpretation. Chris Parry has a cameo as the Freakmaster.

"Close to Me (Closer Mix)" (1990), Director: Tim Pope

Polydor Records wanted to follow up "Never Enough" with an edited version of the Paul Oakenfold/Steve Osborne mix of "Close to Me," but Robert Smith refused unless the label agreed to bankroll a new video for the single. The result is a more modern revamp of the original classic video, and although it's really just harmless fun, it feels a bit empty and is nowhere near as endearing as the original.

"High" (1992), Director: Tim Pope

Filmed in Mexico City during a searing heat wave, Robert Smith has bluntly described the making of "High" as a nightmare. Although the song is a bouncy delight, the video isn't one of their more memorable. Still, it gained a reasonable amount of MTV airplay, sending the song to number one on the modern rock chart.

"Friday I'm in Love" (1992), Director: Tim Pope

The band's biggest single of the 1990s features an appropriately silly video that was the last in a highly influential string of clips in which the Cure worked exclusively with Tim Pope going back to "Let's Go to Bed" ten years earlier (they'd work with Pope again in 1997 with "Wrong Number").

It's an appropriately zany performance clip with the band surrounded by people (including several members of their inner circle, such as producer Dave Allen and engineer Steve Whitfield) running on- and off-screen, bringing costumes and various theater props, in constant motion and constantly changing. The video took only a few hours to shoot, which is no doubt part of the reason why Smith has consistently named it one of the best the Cure ever did.

"A Letter to Elise" (1992), Director: Aubrey Powell

The third single from *Wish*, "A Letter to Elise" is a nice enough song, but it was a questionable choice as a single, and the video only makes it worse. It was shot during a sound check before a date on the Cure's marathon U.S. tour, making for a dreary and melancholy performance by a weary band that would clearly rather be doing anything else at that particular moment.

"The 13th" (1996), Director: Sophie Muller

It's too bad the Cure didn't collaborate more frequently with Sophie Muller, a legendary video director whose previous credits to that point included the Eurythmics, Sade, Bjork, Hole, and Jeff Buckley, among many others. Her work on "The 13th" is typically brilliant, and Robert Smith plays his part to perfection.

"The 13th" is a madcap delusion, surreal, amusing, a little scary, and an absolutely insane choice to be the lead single from a major new album. But that's the Cure, and they wouldn't be as great as they are if they were any other way. Smith plays guitarist/singer duetting with a beautiful Latina vocalist on a TV show. One of the show's panelists is a sexy blond bombshell (who also happens to be a serial killer) who sets Smith in her sights. She kidnaps him, and Smith ends up battered in her motel room as she dances maniacally to the broadcast of the show they filmed earlier.

Before she can make him her latest victim, though, the young Latina singer comes to save him. The ladies get into a knock-down, drag-out fight while Robert is grinning madly and singing into the mirror like the Joker after an all-night bender out in the seedier joints of Gotham. It's a cunningly created song, and Muller's superb video fits it perfectly. It is unfortunate that the single did so poorly and was just too weird for most, and most fans slag it not because of its artistic vision but because they blame it for the failure of *Wild Mood Swings*. The truth is that it may be the finest video of the Cure's career, and it richly deserves a re-evaluation.

"Mint Car" (1996), Director: Richard Heslop

For the video to the second single taken from *Wild Mood Swings*, the Cure goes full-in pop mode with "Mint Car," although even Robert has slagged it a bit as "Friday"-lite. Still, it's a tight little track, and the video looks like it was good fun. Directed by Richard Heslop at a studio in London, it's some unabashed silliness, with Robert hamming it up with various costumes. Robert wrote the list of set scenes to be used, Heslop set it up, and it was done with a minimum of fuss.

"Gone!" (1996), Director: Steve Hanft

Needing to promote their ongoing Swing Tour in support of *Wild Mood Swings*, the Cure opted to shoot the video for "Gone!" during an August 10 show at the Forum in Inglewood, California. Director Steve Hanft splices live material with candid and usually funny tidbits of the band behind stage, interacting with fans and goofing off.

The live version used in the clip is far superior to the vapid studio recording, but unfortunately it drags a bit and would have benefited from an uptick in tempo and energy.

"Wrong Number" (1997), Director: Tim Pope

After a five-year absence during which the band worked with multiple different directors, they reunited with Tim Pope for "Wrong Number," a new track recorded for the hits collection *Galore*. After an emotional chance meeting at a David Bowie concert, Smith felt that Pope, who directed clips for many of the hits featured on the upcoming compilation, should be given the chance to wrap things up with the final track.

Although it's not on par with most of his classics, the "Wrong Number" video is distinctly Tim Pope. It's frenetically paced and wildly colorful, with lots of slithery things sliding all over the place. It also marked the starting point of a second chapter of collaboration between the Cure and Tim Pope, leading all the way up to the present.

"Cut Here" (2001), Director: Richard Anthony

The somber video for "Cut Here," one of two new tracks released on the band's 2001 *Greatest Hits*, is fitting given the track's poignancy. The band performs it stoically, and Smith's anguish is obviously genuine as he sings about his late friend Billy Mackenzie. The flashy imagery that one would normally expect in a Cure video is appropriately absent, although this perhaps guaranteed that it wouldn't garner much play.

"Just Say Yes" (2001), Director: Richard Anthony

The Cure pairs the dour "Cut Here" with an expression of exuberant positivity with the other new track released on *Greatest Hits*. "Just Say Yes" is a duet with Saffron from Republica, and the video shows the pair fronting the band on a soundstage and obviously having a good time as they jump around the stage smiling and showing off for the camera.

"The End of the World" (2004), Director: Floria Sigismondi

For the lead single from their 2004 self-titled album, the Cure chose Italian director Floria Sigismondi, who had worked with a diverse range of artists, including Rihanna, Justin Timberlake, David Bowie, Marilyn Manson, and Bjork, and also directed *The Runaways* biopic. She gives "The End of the World" an innovative look, using stop-frame animation and other effects to show Smith wandering around a house that is rapidly tearing itself apart, an allusion to a disintegrating relationship.

"Taking Off" (2004), Director: The Saline Project

Another visually striking video from *The Cure*, this time Robert Smith descends on wings to join the rest of the band performing on what looks like an island oasis existing in a puddle of bacterial goo—or something you might expect to find under the microscope lens of an infectious disease researcher not afraid to look at the creepiest crawlies mucking about the bowels of the earth.

In reality, the acclaimed directing team the Saline Project (brothers Adam and Ben Toht and 3D artist/designer Jesse Roff) was inspired by the paintings of Darren Waterston, an American artist known for his fluid and abstract imagery.

"alt.end" (2004), Director: The Saline Project

The Saline Project once again lend their distinct style to "alt.end," a hard-rocking track that was the second U.S. single from *The Cure*. Robert Smith is wandering his way through a forest at night, illuminated by a giant moon and encountering various oddities and interesting characters along the way. At the start and again at the conclusion, we see Smith pecking away on an old typewriter, giving the impression that all the surreal weirdness he just experienced was a dream that caught him up during a brief bout of exhaustion between lines.

"The Only One"/"Freakshow"/"Sleep When I'm Dead"/"The Perfect Boy" (2008)

Although the Cure reportedly filmed four traditional videos for the singles that preceded the release of their *4:13 Dream* album, these remain stubbornly unreleased. Instead, eschewing their typically colorful weirdness, the band opted to simply use their performances of four songs at MTV Studio, filmed in black and white. It's a grittier and more personal look at the band, as they aren't hidden behind mountains of costumes, makeup, and elaborate sets. Three other singles taken from the album—"Freakshow," "Sleep When I'm Dead," and "The Perfect Boy"—were filmed at the same time in exactly the same style. Sorry, but boring! Too easy.

Video Collections

1984—*The Tea Party (Japan Only)*
1986—*Staring at The Sea: The Images*
1991—*Picture Show*
1997—*Galore: The Videos 1987–1997*
2001—*Greatest Hits*

13

Twisted Under Sideways Down: The Glove's *Blue Sunshine*

Robert Smith and Steve Severin take listeners on a freaky psychedelic joyride fueled by limitless hallucinogens and wickedly trashy B-movies.

Released: August 23, 1983
Wonderland label –SHELP 2
Running time: 43:10

1. "Like an Animal" (4:44), 2. "Looking Glass Girl" (4:56), 3. "Sex-Eye-Make-Up" (4:24), 4. "Mr. Alphabet Says" (3:50), 5. "A Blues in Drag" (3:12), 6. "Punish Me with Kisses" (3:40), 7. "This Green City" (4:34), 8. "Orgy" (3:19), 9. "Perfect Murder" (4:28), 10. "Relax" (6:03)

Prior to Robert Smith's last touring stint with Siouxsie and the Banshees, he and Banshees bassist Steve Severin, along with vocalist Jeanette Landray, indulged in a wildly creative psychedelic side project called *Blue Sunshine* under the name the Glove. Despite a decent amount of press attention, *Blue Sunshine* was mostly ignored by the public on its release, being lost in the shadows of more successful projects by the Cure and Siouxsie and the Banshees. *Blue Sunshine* has aged very well, sounding remarkably fresh and immediate thirty-five years after its release, and has become something of a cult classic.

Blue Sunshine was the culmination of drug-induced audio experiments that Smith and Severin recorded under the name the Glove, which was inspired by the slightly twisted 1969 animated Beatles film *Yellow Submarine*. The album

The side project between Robert Smith and Steve Severin didn't sell many copies but has become a cult favorite among fans of psychedelic pop. *Author's Collection*

owes more to the Beatles than just its name. *Blue Sunshine* plays like *Sgt. Peppers'* dark underbelly, the soundtrack to the hours spent by the Lonely Hearts Club Band after the show is over, lurking in their shadowy hideouts late at night, the air thick with the smoke from any number of the substances that the band members habitually ingest so that they may ride out their visions until darkness finally takes them for a few precious hours of sleep.

Robert Smith and Steve Severin first met in 1979, not long after the Cure had released *Three Imaginary Boys* and shortly before the Banshees were set to go on tour in support of their second album: *Join Hands*. The Cure opened for them on that tour, during which Smith becoming an emergency fill-in on guitar when two members of the Banshees abruptly quit. Smith and Severin remained friends and had discussed a side project as early as 1980. Their original vision for it was an "art experiment," which is pretty much what it turned out to be.

The Glove was initially slated to release just a one-off single or perhaps a series of singles. With that in mind, Smith and Severin demoed "Punish Me with Kisses" in October 1982. Coincidentally perhaps, Siouxsie Sioux and Budgie had jetted off to Hawaii on New Year's Eve 1981, and over the span of ten days in early January, they recorded the album *Feast* as the Creatures with the Cure's former producer Mike Hedges. It was the second release for the side project, following the 1981 EP *Wild Things*.

Shortly after the Creatures wrapped up work on *Feast*, Steve Severin and Robert Smith amped up momentum for the Glove considerably. Severin has insisted that the timing had nothing at all to do with the Creatures release. The project morphed into a full album after the duo churned out a wealth of strong material very quickly. They cowrote the music, while Severin wrote most of the lyrics, except for "Like an Animal," "Sex-Eye-Make-Up," and "A Perfect Murder," which Smith wrote, and "Punish Me with Kisses" which was a collaborative effort. They created demos for sixteen tracks by the end of January 1983.

In March 1983, the pair booked ten days of studio time at Britannia Row, during the same time frame that Smith was working at Jam Studios on new synthesizer-based material that would become "The Walk," "Lament," "The Upstairs Room," and "The Dream." It was a busy time for both, as only a month later, Smith and Severin would be working on the next Siouxsie and the Banshees album: *Hyæna*.

The sessions ran from early evening to around daybreak, when the duo would return to Severin's flat to watch horror films and cheesy B-movies for hours while tripping on various hallucinogens. These mind-bending adventures in shifting perceptions were a primary fuel for the swirly and twisted imagery and musical ideas spinning through the album, and even inspired its title. *Blue Sunshine*, a 1978 cult horror film written and directed by Jeff Lieberman, is about a strain of LSD that causes users to lose their hair and become homicidal maniacs years after their acid trip.

Smith described the album as a "real attack on the senses," and it is. The sessions were a drug-fueled circus, with partying with a constantly rotating cast of guests going on for hours, interrupted by relatively brief bouts of recording. At the end of the Britannia Row sessions, the album remained unfinished, so they had to fill in the remaining holes during multiple sessions at the Garden, Morgan, and Trident Studios.

The project hit a snag when Chris Parry of Fiction Records reminded Smith that his contract did not permit him to sing on any releases other than by the Cure. Parry was concerned about the Cure's precarious state of existence since the band was down to Smith and theoretical keyboardist Laurence Tolhurst, and their future was far from certain. Parry sought to rope Smith into maintaining his commitment to the Cure, as he feared that a project like the Glove was exactly the kind of thing that could bring the momentum of Fiction's most important asset to a screeching halt. Parry agreed to allow Smith to sing two songs on the condition that neither would become singles ("Mr. Alphabet Says" and "A Perfect Murder").

Jeanette Landray, former girlfriend of Siouxsie and the Banshees drummer Budgie and a good friend of Steve Severin's, was brought in to handle vocal duties on the rest of the album. Landray was a member of the dance troupe Zoo, which appeared weekly on the popular U.K. show *Top of the Pops*, and had never before been a professional singer, but her unpolished voice fits the material to perfection.

Musically innovative, the Glove was license for Steve Severin and Robert Smith to go beyond what they were able to do with their main bands in terms of open experimentation. The synthesizer parts are mesmerizing throughout, played mostly on a Roland Jupiter-8 over rhythms built mainly on a classic Roland CR-78 drum machine (supplemented by Andy Anderson on some tracks). The album was colored with exotic instruments, like a koto and a dulcimer.

Steve Severin ended up finalizing the project mostly on his own, as Robert Smith had Cure duties to attend to. Severin came up with the group and album name and the conceptual framework for the art and color scheme. *Blue Sunshine* was considered part of a Steve Severin's solo deal with Polydor, so it was released on the Swedish independent Wonderland label rather than Fiction.

The album was largely ignored on release, which shouldn't have been a surprise to anyone involved. There aren't any obvious pop hits on it, and the esoteric nature of the music should have inspired little confidence that it would catch fire with the public. For years, *Blue Sunshine* was mostly a colorful curio of interest only to diehards, but its reputation has grown over the years, and it was subject to a lavish reissue project in 2011 containing substantial bonus material and a limited edition pressed on swirling blue and white vinyl.

Blue Sunshine

"Like an Animal"

The closest thing to a typical pop song on *Blue Sunshine*, "Like an Animal" was released on August 12, 1983, as the album's lead single. Robert Smith wrote the lyrics based on a news story about a woman who went insane and started dropping various objects from the window of her apartment on people walking below.

An extended "club remix" was issued on the twelve-inch single, and the non–album track "Mouth to Mouth" landed as the B-side, but despite these bonuses, the single went nowhere.

"Looking Glass Girl"

This languid ballad easily could have been a single. The swaying string arrangement is gently beautiful, and Landray gives one of her loveliest performances on the album.

"Sex-Eye Make-Up"

Easily the strongest track on *Blue Sunshine*, "Sex-Eye Make-Up" is one of several songs Smith wrote that was at least partially inspired by the Nicolas Roeg film *Bad Timing*. Smith said he wanted to keep this track for *The Top*, and he clearly goofed by not doing so. Fortunately, Smith managed to hold on to two other songs from this period that were inspired by the same film: both "Give Me It" and "Piggy in the Mirror" became standout tracks on *The Top*. This sharing of material from the same well of inspiration, along with the unhinged and feverish nature of both projects, makes *Blue Sunshine* and *The Top* companion albums of sorts.

"Sex-Eye Make-Up" would certainly have been a perfect addition to *The Top*. A slithery rhythm and sinuous guitar line provide a decadent underground sex-club vibe. Jeanette Landray responds by delivering her finest vocal on the album, brazenly sensual and confident. Smith's provocative lyrics are straight from the dark sexual nightmares of some poor (or lucky?) soul chained to the wall of the seediest red-light district dungeon that's ever been dug.

"Mr. Alphabet Says"

The first of two *Blue Sunshine* tracks on which Robert Smith maintains his lead vocal, "Mr. Alphabet Says" is a nifty little vaudeville charmer with jaunty piano and cinematic strings. It's endearing and a little mysterious, with a strong melodic hook. Smith's earnest delivery is just the right tone for the impressionistic lyrics composed by Steve Severin. It's one of the few instances of Smith singing someone else's words except for cover versions or collaborative songs on someone else' project.

"A Blues in Drag"

A truly gorgeous instrumental, melancholy and filled with a regret expressed more beautifully by the flickering light of a piano than any words could have managed. Robert Smith originally planned to keep "A Blues in Drag" for the next Cure album, and it would have been a beautiful addition. It's one of Robert Smith's loveliest creations, sublimely woozy with a wonky groove and an elegant piano sent from the ballrooms of the bizarre.

"Punish Me with Kisses"

The earliest track that Smith and Severin recorded together with the Glove in mind, "Punish Me with Kisses" had been demoed on October 1982 at Playground Studios. Mike Hedges remixed the track for release as the album's second single, but it failed to chart. "Punish Me with Kisses" is the album's most goth track, and it was a favorite at the Batcave, the famous goth club in London.

The Glove mimed "Punish Me with Kisses" for the BBC arts program *Riverside* in 1983 with Andy Anderson appearing on drums. The clip is worth seeking out on YouTube, as it's a fascinating time capsule of the era. Steve Severin and Robert Smith look sharp in their matching white jackets while Jeanette Landray sashays away like nobody's business. Smith, smiling coyly, is clearly stoned out of his mind.

"This Green City"

One of the lesser tracks on *Blue Sunshine*, "This Green City" isn't as melodic as most of the others and seems a bit dull in comparison. In retrospect, *Blue Sunshine* would have been much stronger if "This Green City" would have been left off the album and instead replaced by eventual B-side "Mouth to Mouth," an electronic sliver of art-pop deliciousness.

"Orgy"

The most exotic and otherworldly of all the Glove songs is "Orgy," a heart-pounding belly dancer's freak-out. "Orgy" is built around two repetitive circular patterns, one of flute-like keyboards and the other a byzantine violin that buzzes like a billion insects in a mating frenzy at dusk.

Robert Smith has said that he wanted to stretch the limits of his vocal abilities on *The Top*, but it's clear from listening to the *Blue Sunshine* demos that this process was already well under way with the Glove. "Orgy," in particular," has Smith singing through a filtered effect that sounds nothing remotely like anything he had previously recorded. On the other hand, is it possible that Robert Smith recorded the vocal parts to these demos in preparation for the reissue? It doesn't really sound like the 1983 version of his voice.

"Perfect Murder"

The second Robert Smith–sung track, "Perfect Murder" is another song that, just like "Mr. Alphabet Says," surely would have been a substantial hit if released under the Cure's name. Severin's lyrics were inspired by Nabokov's *Lolita*. With swirling electronics and Robert Smith's chilled-out vocal, "Perfect Murder" is one of the more tantalizing gems to emerge from the Glove project.

"Relax"

Closing the album is this surreal instrumental, colored with unusual instrumentation and sound effects that are scattered throughout the song. It's a twisted dream of an ending, the perfect distillation of everything that came before it.

Blue Sunshine is often ignored by casual fans of both the Cure and Siouxsie and the Banshees, although it has become a cult classic of sorts among psychedelic music aficionados. It shouldn't be, especially given the existence of the superb 2006 deluxe reissue, which includes all of the original demos with vocals by Robert Smith intact (perhaps). It's trippy and whimsical at times, sinister and laced with menace at others, but always as inventive as the human mind can be on an acid trip. Seven years after the album's release, Robert Smith reflected to the fanzine *Curenews* that while Severin's lyrics are "patchy" and he wished all the vocals were his, he still viewed the project as "good deranged fun."

14

A Siren Singing You to Shipwreck: Robert Smith as a Banshee

Robert Smith's sojourn as a Banshee raised his profile and got him better drugs, but not without a price: he had to face Siouxsie's fearsome ire.

No, it wasn't at a secret clandestine meeting held in the lower reaches of the Batcave where Robert Smith first met Siouxsie Sioux and bassist Steve Severin of Siouxsie and the Banshees, although it should have been. The reality is much more prosaic—at the London YMCA. It was August 3, 1979, and the unlikely venue was hosting a thoroughly exciting double bill featuring Throbbing Gristle and Cabaret Voltaire.

At this point, the Banshees were ahead of the Cure in career development and popularity. The Banshees had already notched three top forty U.K. singles, including their hit debut, "Hong Kong Garden," which made a big splash and reached number seven. While the Cure's *Three Imaginary Boys* had just arrived in stores three months prior and would miss the top forty, Siouxsie and the Banshees' widely acclaimed debut, *The Scream*, had been out since November of the prior year and hit number twelve.

Their second album, *Join Hands*, was only a few weeks away from release. This dynamic would change in the second half of the 1980s as the Cure's popularity skyrocketed, but at this point, there was no question that Siouxsie and the Banshees stood higher on the food chain. Siouxsie and the Banshees were a featured act on Polydor and were a big coup for Chris Parry, who also signed the Jam and the Cure.

The Cure landed the opening slot for the Banshees' tour starting that fall to promote their hard-hitting second album, *Join Hands*, a brutal assault on the senses that represents the Banshees at their most extreme. They would temper their sound bit by bit as the years passed, getting more proficient at stringing together melodies and playing more complex arrangements. In their early years, though, they were rough, abrasive, and punishingly loud, as they were on this tour.

This would be the final string of dates for the Banshees' original lineup, the most electrifying they ever assembled: guitarist John McKay, drummer Kenny Morris, bassist Steve Severin, and, of course, fierce in every possible sense of the word, Siouxsie Sioux. She owned the stage, stalking restlessly while unleashing her discordant wail. Her voice cut through the jet-engine blasts of guitar not cleanly but serrated and barbed. There was nothing sweet and gentle about Siouxsie and the Banshees.

After only three gigs, the *Join Hands* tour came to a grinding halt on September 7, 1979, in Aberdeen, Scotland. Guitarist John McKay and drummer Kenny Morris had felt marginalized for some time, and tensions between them and the band's leaders, Siouxsie Sioux and Steve Severin, continued to simmer. Things came to a head at a record-signing event held at the local shop only hours before the show. McKay was already angry that nobody had bothered to tell him about the signing, causing him to arrive late. He then made a bit of a scene by pulling the band's latest album, *Join Hands*, off the store's turntable at the store, proclaiming loudly that he "fucking hates" the record before blasting a Slits album through the store's speakers. Siouxsie was incensed.

The mood was already sour because Polydor had failed to send enough copies of *Join Hands* for the band to sign, leading McKay and Morris to sign and give away promo copies which of course angered the store managers. Siouxsie started berating them for that, leading the pair to angrily stalk out of the shop and away from the Banshees forever. They went to the hotel, packed their things, and caught a train out of Aberdeen without a word of warning to anyone. By the time Sioux and Severin realized the two had departed for real, it was nearing showtime.

The Cure played their set at the Aberdeen show while the Banshees' team frantically tried to find the wayward duo, to no avail. The Banshees' tour manager, Dave Woods, begged the Cure to play longer, so the band improvised as long as they could, adding some new unfinished tracks that would appear on their next album. Eventually, Siouxsie and Severin joined their openers onstage to tell the crowd about the departures and to promise full refunds. They joined the Cure for a cathartic rendition of the Banshees' signature freak-out "The Lord's Prayer," and that ended the show.

That night backstage, Robert Smith had a long drinking session with Sioux and Severin, and the trio bonded and got to know each other on a deeper level than they had before. Smith offered then and there to step in on guitar, as he was keen for the tour to continue given that it was a prime slot for the Cure, but they were noncommittal. The Banshees had to cancel several dates while news about the departures swirled in the press and they tried out potential guitarists. Siouxsie was outspoken about the departures, calling McKay and Morris "spineless prima donnas" in *NME*.

Drummer Kenny Morris was replaced by former Slits drummer Budgie, who would stay with the band for the rest of its existence. On guitar, after trying out several potential replacements, Siouxsie and Severin opted to go with Robert Smith after all. The Cure was recording a new single, "Jumping Someone Else's Train," at Morgan Studios in London when the pair stopped by to give Smith the news (and Siouxsie provided some background wailing on the B-side, "I'm Cold"). Initially, the Banshees didn't want the Cure to continue being the support act, arguing that there was no way Smith could play both sets back to back, but Robert insisted he'd fill the vacant role only if the Cure stayed on the tour.

Finally Robert Smith got his way, and he made his first appearance as the Banshees' guitarist on September 18 in Leicester. Siouxsie said at the time that Smith would be a perfect permanent replacement for John McKay if only he didn't drink so much but that he would never leave the Cure anyway.

Robert Smith was a quick study in every respect. He was able to pick up the Banshees' catalog fairly quickly, although the darkly abrasive parts were quite different from what he played in the Cure. He also benefited from being onstage next to an audaciously gifted performer, Siouxsie Sioux, every night. Years later, Steve Severin attributed Smith's study of Siouxsie as the reason Smith gained a better understanding of how to perform for an audience and was able to come out of his shell as a front man.

After the tour, Smith parted ways, but they remained friends and close associates. The Banshees scored an excellent new guitarist, John McGeoch, and drifted in a more psychedelic direction with acclaimed albums *Kaleidoscope*, *Juju*, and *A Kiss in the Dreamhouse*. "Christine" was a crossover hit, reaching number twenty-four in the United Kingdom. "Spellbound" and "Arabian Knights" were also substantial hits. The Cure scored minor hits with "A Forest," "Primary," and "Charlotte Sometimes," and their 1981 album *Faith* became their biggest yet. Both bands were on an upward trajectory.

Robert Smith and Steve Severin in particular remained tight and spoke frequently about collaborating. Their friendship was predicated in part on their shared love of acid, and the hallucinogen would play a big part in their collaboration when it finally emerged. Severin took part in some of the demo sessions that Smith held for *Pornography*, and they had discussed doing a side project as far back as 1980.

Their relationship often created problems for Fiction head Chris Parry, who relied on the Cure as his label's signature act. Around the time of *Pornography* in 1981, Severin was actively trying to sabotage the Cure, pestering Robert to leave the band and join the Banshees full-time. That dynamic continued during the next couple years when Smith found himself leading dual musical lives.

Siouxsie and the Banshees' 1982 album *A Kiss in the Dreamhouse* was their biggest yet, but guitarist John McGeoch wasn't able to handle the pressure of the band's increasing visibility and success. During a performance in Madrid, Spain, the strain got to him, and he had a nervous breakdown. Once again, they turned to Robert Smith to be an emergency fill-in. The timing was fortuitous because the Cure had recently disassembled following a meltdown at the conclusion of the *Pornography* tour.

The Cure's future was uncertain at best. Simon Gallup was out of the band, leaving just Robert Smith and the musically challenged Lol Tolhurst as a duo. Chris Parry and Smith were feuding over the "Let's Go to Bed" single. In hindsight, the single proved a major turning point for the band, but at the time, it was a source of turmoil and a chance to either reinvent the Cure or destroy them for good. Uncertain that the Cure would even continue, when Severin called Smith about filling in for McGeough, he jumped at the chance to rejoin the Banshees full-time, and he stayed for the remainder of the tour in support of *A Kiss in the Dreamhouse*.

In January 1983, Smith and Severin finally began serious work on their long-discussed side project. They quickly wrote and recorded a large batch of demos that they recorded in March and released as the album *Blue Sunshine* under the name the Glove. The album was a departure, a drugged-out psychedelic whirlwind of strange effects and imagery. Smith and Severin consumed copious amounts of hallucinogens and other drugs during the album's creation. The album sold poorly but has since become a cult favorite.

Chris Parry had tried to put a halt to the Glove project, as he was again concerned about the future of the Cure. He pressed Smith to get to work on the next Cure album, but Smith felt it important that his time with the Banshees be documented in a studio album, so Parry would have to wait. The Banshees continued to press him in the other direction, urging him to dump the Cure and join full-time. They were increasingly annoyed that Smith had scored such major hits with what they considered throwaway joke singles—"Let's Go to Bed," "The Walk," and "The Lovecats"—to the point where the Cure's success now outstripped their own.

Wanting to get a single in the stores pronto, in September 1983, Siouxsie and the Banshees, with Robert Smith in tow, entered Angel Studios in Islington, Sweden, to record "Dear Prudence." The band wanted to do a Beatles cover from the *White Album*, and while Budgie and Siouxsie pressed for "Glass Onion," the only one Robert Smith was familiar with was "Dear Prudence," and Severin took his side. The single became a major smash, hitting number three in the United Kingdom, the Banshees' highest placement yet. Despite the success of the single, the recording of the full album frayed Robert Smith's relationship with Siouxsie until eventually it was impossible for them to continue collaborating.

Robert Smith and the Banshees struggled through the creation of *Hyæna*. Smith was perpetually exhausted, and his shambolic mumbling demeanor started grating on the always direct Sioux. She called him "Fat Bob" and mocked what she considered his tendency to copy her and Severin's clothing and makeup style. The songwriting and recording process was slow and laborious. The Banshees began to seriously doubt that Smith really cared much about the album. He didn't seem fully invested, caring more about the new Cure project that he was recording simultaneously: *The Top*.

When the album was finally complete, it garnered mixed reviews and didn't score any hits that approached the success of "Dear Prudence." In the United States, the Beatles cover was added to the track list and became a hit on college radio. The lead single, "Swimming Horses," is a dark pirouette and undoubtedly the most Cure-like track on the album. The psycho-glam "Dazzle" opens the album with tawdry gilded excitement, but much of the rest is rather desultory. The high point is "Bring Me the Head of the Preacher Man," which burns with feverish insurgent power. Robert Smith said after the album's release that four songs were good and that six were boring. For her part, Siouxsie said testily that "Fatboy Smith has nothing to do with the new album, except that he plays on it."

Finally bowing to pressure from Chris Parry and aware that his contract required a new Cure album every year, Robert Smith entered the studio in early 1984 to record *The Top* while simultaneously trying to finish the drawn-out *Hyæna* sessions. Smith's health suffered from the work schedule, coupled with overindulgence of drugs and alcohol, to the point that Chris Parry became so concerned for him that he urged Smith to see a doctor right away. When he did, the horrified physician warned him to stop doing whatever it was he was doing to put him in such a state. Smith was suffering from blood poisoning and was on the very brink of mental and physical collapse.

With a Banshees tour on the horizon to promote *Hyæna*, Robert Smith realized that he simply could not continue with them. He wanted to focus on the Cure and felt that his time with the Banshees was finished. Not long before the tour's start, Smith informed the band he could not do it, citing illness, extreme exhaustion, and the need to focus on *The Top*. He even provided them a doctor's note explaining why he couldn't do the tour.

They had already been losing patience with the Cure's front man, but now the Banshees were livid. Siouxsie Sioux went into an apoplectic rage on hearing the news, and her relationship with Robert Smith never recovered. Siouxsie, never one to hold back or mince words, said flat out, "I never trusted Robert." She felt that he was merely using the Banshees as a pedestal to raise his publicity and, by extension, that of the Cure. She pointed out that it was Robert who took "Dear Prudence" in a commercial direction and that, around the same time, the Cure enjoyed their biggest hit yet with "The Lovecats."

Smith's relationship with all of the Banshees was damaged by the move, including his close friend Steve Severin. But he could no longer cope with being in a band in which he could not assert any control or authority given Siouxsie's fierce determination to have her own way and Severin's equally dogged approach. The press lapped up the upheaval, while Smith simply focused on getting the next Cure album ready for release. Siouxsie made her displeasure at the situation very clear, and the anger never really abated.

More than two decades later, in a 2005 issue of *Uncut* magazine, Sioux said, "It wasn't like he was ill. He was one of those people who just didn't say 'no' to anything, so when it's self-induced it's hard to have sympathy. To actually say two days before a tour that's been planned in advance that he can't do it—fuck off! What a lightweight." Robert, on the same subject, said, "I think Severin understood and, by then, my mind was made up. After all, I'd given them two weeks' notice, which was longer than any guitarist had given them before!"

It's pretty obvious that Robert Smith was significantly influenced by his time with Siouxsie and the Banshees and, in particular, with Severin, with whom Smith had become particularly close, much to the annoyance of his Cure bandmates. Smith wanted to play with the Banshees at first because it was an exciting prospect and a challenge. Given that the Cure was still finding their way and the Banshees had quickly established themselves as a creative force, he knew that associating with them would benefit his band.

With the Banshees came more of the traditional trappings of rock 'n' roll, including drugs and big money. It was always a circus surrounding them, and while being part of their peculiar brand of madness, Robert Smith learned much about music and the record industry. He also had a great time going out onstage playing big power chords and cranking the volume beyond capacity. Ultimately, it was never going to last given his need for control, something he would never have with Siouxsie and the Banshees.

15

Feed Your Head: *The Top*

Essentially a Robert Smith solo album, *The Top* takes the Cure's manic weirdness to twisted new levels.

Released: April 30, 1984
Fiction Records—fixs9
Running time: 40:55

1. "Shake Dog Shake" (4:55), 2. "Bird Mad Girl" (4:05), 3. "Wailing Wall" (5:17), 4. "Give Me It" (3:42), 5. "Dressing Up" (2:51), 6. "The Caterpillar" (3:40), 7. "Piggy in the Mirror" (3:40), 8. "The Empty World" (2:36), 9. "Bananafishbones" (3:12), 10. "The Top" (6:50)

The Top is the sound of Robert Smith's head unraveling. Fortunately, he's such an intuitive and prodigious musical mind that the end result is as brilliant as it is absolutely mad. *The Top* is a glorious sprawling mess, hallucinations and fears that are twisted by chemicals and fun house mirrors, spun through a prism of obsession and paranoia, blowing clouds of every color twirling through hallways that shift and shake and wobble and quake.

The Cure had ceased to exist following the *Pornography* tour, with Simon Gallup out the door and Lol Tolhurst banished from the drums because Robert Smith was tired of dealing with the limitations that his drumming skill level put on the band's music. Tolhurst ostensibly switched to keyboard, but the reality is that he couldn't play. The band officially stayed a duo through "Let's Go to Bed," "The Walk," and "The Lovecats" while relying heavily on outside producers and session musicians. When the time came for the next Cure album, Robert decided to simply do it himself, and why not? Fewer people to argue with. He even told *No. 1* around the time of the album's release, "I *am* The Cure," which is a surprise considering he's always stressed the importance of his collaborators. Robert was simply speaking the truth.

Smith was on overload at the time, which no doubt contributed to the manic nature of *The Top*. He spent the prior year working with Steve Severin on the Glove project and scoring the biggest pop hits of the Cure's career. These singles exposed the Cure to a large new pop-oriented audience, and the opportunity to build on that success sent Smith into a frenzy of writing. The new material sprang from the same well of demented psychedelia that yielded the pop singles, their more experimental B-sides, and the eccentric loopiness of the Glove's *Blue Sunshine*.

Chris Parry at Fiction had been agitating for a Cure album; all the while, Robert was busying himself writing and recording with the Banshees. He was burning himself to a crisp living a dual life, recording two albums for two bands simultaneously. After a long day of laboring over *Hyæna* with the Banshees at Eel Pie Studios in Twickenham, Smith would taxi an hour to Genetic Studios in Streatley, where work on *The Top* would typically begin at 2 a.m.

The whacked-out schedule wrecked Robert Smith's health, and his mass consumption of drugs and alcohol didn't help. The onerous recording obligations forced Smith into a steady diet of junk food, which caused him to gain so much weight that Siouxsie Sioux started mocking him as "Fat Bob." Chris Parry was openly concerned about Robert's health to the point that he tried to intervene and convince his friend and the primary income source for Fiction to get to a doctor.

Somehow, he pulled through it, although engineer Dave Allen, who would go on to coproduce the four classic Cure albums on the horizon, called the sessions "terrifying" as Robert Smith spiraled farther down the rabbit hole to battle his own obsessions and Lol simply took up space and ingested whatever substances happened to fall into his hands. He said of the sessions that while he was physically in the studio every day, his "soul was elsewhere, looking down into that horrible abyss which nowadays I am thankfully free of."

By mainstream standards, *The Top* has never been considered one of the Cure's greatest albums, but it's an important one. For those who relish in the dynamic range of the Cure, it is essential. It is a stand-alone record that takes the listener on a wildly erratic journey of Robert Smith's making. He combines a newfound pop sensibility with the darker edges from the Cure's earlier albums, fueled by substance abuse. Smith also experiments more freely than ever before, adding exotic and more diverse instrumentation and focusing more on his vocals and singing style. The result is the Cure's most eclectic and diverse album by far to that point in their career.

With no band surrounding him, *The Top* essentially became a Robert Smith solo album in all but name. He holed up in a trio of studios (Garden, Trident, and Genetic) with engineer Dave Allen. Drummer Andy Anderson, who played so deftly on "The Lovecats" and contributed to the Glove's *Blue Sunshine*, was hired to provide the drumming for the sessions (he also provided a brew of mushroom tea that he and Robert swilled like water).

The Cure had almost ceased to exist after *Pornography*, and as a result *The Top* (1984) is mostly a Robert Smith solo project. *Author's Collection*

Robert's erstwhile partner in the Cure, Lol Tolhurst, is listed as cowriter on "Bird Mad Girl," "The Caterpillar," and "Piggy in the Mirror." Robert has said many times that he played all the instruments apart from Anderson's drums, and Tolhurst is credited rather sardonically with "other instruments" on the album. Apparently, imaginary ones.

With such scant assistance from collaborators, *The Top* was Smith's mad vision, a harrowing carnival ride buffeted by hallucinations that could be ethereal and gorgeous or horrifying and vicious but usually a combination of them all. Smith has been very open about his elevated drug use during this period, and this comes through in the music. There's no denying that *The Top* is drug soaked, both the music and the artwork drenched in acid. It's a wild musical trip, bold and fearless.

Although appreciation for *The Top* has grown over the years, it was tepidly received at the time of its release. It is now often viewed by fans and writers as the Cure's most underrated album. *The Top* is a transitional album connecting the Cure's first experiments with synth pop to the full flowering of their dramatically expanded palette on *The Head on the Door*. It also connects with their past, being the first Cure album to combine their newly discovered frivolity with the darker edginess searing through the veins of tracks like "Doubt," "Play for Today," "Primary," and the entire *Pornography* album.

Despite its defiant weirdness, *The Top* was another commercial success for the Cure. The lead single, a campfire sing-along fueled by copious amounts of psychotropics called "The Caterpillar," became a substantial hit everywhere but America. Although *The Top* fell two slots below the number eight showing for *Pornography*, it still made the top ten in the United Kingdom and performed well internationally. In the United States, it earned the Cure their first appearance on the *Billboard* album chart.

The Top

"Shake Dog Shake"

The album's opening salvo is a lethal sonic missile dominated by a ferocious guitar riff and incendiary drum work by Andy Anderson. It's clear right out of the gate that adding a talented and versatile drummer like Anderson opens up the Cure's musical possibilities considerably. The lyrics are savage, dripping in blood and animal lust, and Robert's searing vocal delivery is his most intense since *Pornography*. A raging torrent of the madness courses through even the poppiest moments on *The Top*, but with "Shake Dog Shake," it's on full unhinged display, its debasement unfurled for the world to examine.

For a while, "Shake Dog Shake" was considered the likely first single from *The Top*, and it was even mentioned in the British press well before the album's release. It was even issued as a promo seven-inch in France, copies of which are now prized by Cure collectors. In hindsight, "The Caterpillar" was obviously the correct choice, and "Shake Dog Shake" occupies the same exalted status among Cure songs as if it had been a single as well. They've performed it live more often than any other song from *The Top* by a wide margin. "Shake Dog Shake" has been a thunderous opener for many Cure shows over the years, including their landmark performance captured in *The Cure in Orange*. In tribute to Andy Anderson, "Shake Dog Shake" was the kickoff to the Cure's five-song set at the Rock and Roll Hall of Fame induction ceremony in March 2019.

Feed Your Head: *The Top* 143

"Shake Dog Shake" was only released as a promo single in France, although it has become a key song in the Cure's history. *Author's Collection*

"Bird Mad Girl"

If Robert Smith and Chris Parry wanted a pop sequel to "The Caterpillar," then "Bird Mad Girl" would have been the logical choice. They considered it and even tested the waters by pressing a twelve-inch promo single that is now a rare collector's item. In the end, it was not to be, and "The Caterpillar" ended up the lone single from *The Top*.

"Bird Mad Girl" was inspired by the Dylan Thomas poem "Love in the Asylum." Despite its charm, the Cure has dusted it off in concert only five times since the 1984 tour. Quirky but not as keenly demented as much of *The Top*, "Bird Mad Girl" has a melody beguiling enough to have sent it right into the top twenty just as "The Caterpillar" did had it been given the chance.

"Wailing Wall"

The Cure's first foray into the type of exotic sonic hypnosis they'd perfect with "The Snakepit" a few years later, "Wailing Wall" is a sound painting inspired by the sacred site in Jerusalem. Robert had traveled there with Siouxsie and the Banshees and found himself intrigued. It explores the intense devotion of those who hold religious devotion to their core, consuming their very being, permeating the pores of their skin and the tangled threads of their psyches.

Slow and languid, with exotic flourishes and a wild flute piercing the somber psychedelia below, Smith's vocals are heavily echoed and clearly inspired by the drugged-out experiments with Steve Severin on The Glove's *Blue Sunshine*.

"Give Me It"

"Give Me It" is a manic eruption, a frantic dive into a boiling sonic hell every bit as brain-searing as anything on *Pornography*. It's a cacophony of multilayered drums, shrill spears of guitar, and manic peals of saxophone. Robert Smith howls the lyrics with a manic animal intensity, like a distant soul in desperation being battered by debris in the midst of a hurricane.

The wild urgency of "Give Me It" is unique among Cure songs, with its closest relative probably "Shiver and Shake" on *Kiss Me, Kiss Me, Kiss Me*. "Give Me It" rides the edge of pure white-hot razor madness, sonic psychosis that disorients even as it thrills.

"Give Me It" is also notable as the song that helped bring longtime associate and early band member Porl Thompson back into the fold. He contributes the unhinged squeals of sax that rip through the song like steam blasting from an inferno.

"Dressing Up"

Smith had already expanded the range of his voice on singles like "Let's Go to Bed" and "The Lovecats," but he goes full throttle on *The Top*, sometimes descending into discordant wails that may follow a basic melody but that waver in and out of key like a drunken bard staggering through the maze of a freak show long after most of the cotton candy has been eaten, with popcorn now strewn about the ground.

Smith's elongated enunciation and lunatic howling on "Dressing Up" stand in sharp contrast to the song's music, neatly packaged with a circular keyboard pattern and embellished with peppy backing vocals. Had he gone a more conventional route, "Dressing Up" might have become one of Smith's most arresting pop creations. Instead, he chose to sabotage it with a slurred

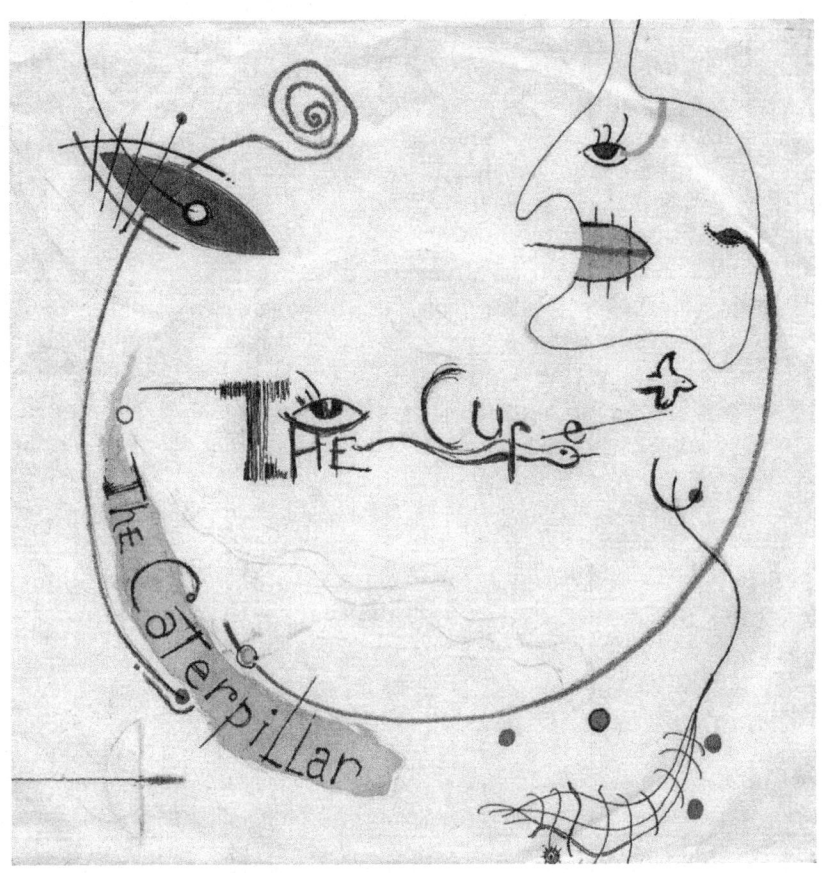

A delightful acid-trip singalong, "The Caterpillar" continued the Cure's string of hits with a strong showing. *Author's Collection*

and drunken nightmare vocal, ruining the song's potential beauty. "Dressing Up" is deliberately obtuse, like spraying a line of black paint across a trippy kaleidoscopic painting.

"The Caterpillar"

A buoyant acid folk trip, "The Caterpillar" is often unjustly overlooked as one of the band's major pop singles. It's one of the Cure's most joyous creations, with Smith's dreamy vocal quavering over the happily strumming acoustic guitars and spritely twinkling piano. The long introduction is unique among songs heard on pop radio, with an agitated fiddle mimicking a butterfly zipping about the loveliness. Sunshiny backing vocals complete the effect, a wildly happy and wonderfully weird confection that sounds like nothing else.

Idiosyncratic like only the Cure could manage, it's hard to imagine any other band pulling a track like this out of the rabbit hole and making it a hit single, yet "The Caterpillar" proved disarming enough to swirl and swing its way to number fourteen in the United Kingdom.

"Piggy in the Mirror"

Grim and sordid, "Piggy in the Mirror" is a sinister immersion in protracted self-disgust, reminiscent of *Pornography* but with more varied instrumentation, including keyboards that swoosh back and forth and against each other.

You can almost feel the revulsion oozing like fat rivulets of sweat streaming down Robert Smith's face. It's tempting to speculate that Siouxsie's recent needling of him as "Fat Bob" may have helped amplify and put into focus his unhappiness with himself when looking into the mirror.

Smith affects an oddly strident vocal accent, which seems to have been part of Smith's concept for the song early in the process, as he uses a similar voice in the demo and it certainly adds to the song's eccentricity. "Piggy in the Mirror," like "Give Me It" and the Glove's "Sex-Eye Make-Up," was partially inspired by Nicolas Roeg's *Bad Timing*.

"The Empty World"

One of the more disciplined and tightly wound creations on this generally freewheeling collection is "The Empty World," a sequel of sorts to "Charlotte Sometimes." Smith revisits the character with just a slice of a moment, not really telling a story or giving anything beyond a short snippet of her fractured psyche. "The Empty World" is a reflection of a mind inventing wars between facets of itself, as echoed by the martial beat and the sound of a fife played on keyboard.

"Bananafishbones"

Robert often mines literature for inspiration, but with J. D. Salinger's *A Perfect Day for Bananafish*, he only borrows the title. The inscrutable lyrics are another of Robert's frequent expressions of self-loathing. "Bananafishbones" has been excavated and unexpectedly added to the Cure's live sets in recent years, and it has been a welcome addition. The instrumentation is the album's tightest, and Smith delivers a kick-ass vocal. If the album's vibe could be distilled in one song, the wickedly evocative "Bananafishbones" would be the one.

With the 2004 reissue, Smith was finally able to correct an error in mastering that has led "Bananafishbones" to be slower than it should be all these years, allowing fans to hear this delightful oddity the way it's meant to sound only three decades after its release.

"The Top"

Then we get to the "The Top," the epic title song, the ending of a wild, haphazard journey, the tethering of the big circus tent post to the cold concrete slab of reality. All of the dreams, mad capers, sex, and drugs give way to catharsis because they must. It has taken its toll and eventually has to end.

Dark and dramatic, "The Top" is a stripped-down monument of melancholy. The instrumentation is a music-box motif that's like a twisted version of the Bangles' "Eternal Flame." Smith pleads in his vocals, but it's clear that his wish will not be fulfilled, and the end comes with a top spinning slower and slower until it falls over on its side with a clank.

B-Sides

"Throw Your Foot"

Released as the B-side to "The Caterpillar," the catchy and upbeat "Throw Your Foot" not only is strong enough to have been on the album but also, with a tighter vocal performance, might have made a great single. It's the danciest track from the period, a bit like a much more demented version of "Let's Go to Bed." The madcap layering of Smith's wildly overwrought vocals in his higher register hints at better things to come—he'd master his particular technique on "Why Can't I Be You?"

"Happy the Man"

Robert focused on expanding his vocal possibilities on *The Top*, as reflected most directly in "Piggy in the Mirror," "Dressing Up," and the B-side "Happy the Man." With its grossly elongated vocals, "Happy the Man" is perhaps too similar to "Dressing Up" for both to have made the album.

Robert made the right move by ditching "Happy the Man," which is arguably the most gruesomely awful song in the Cure's repertoire, and banishing it to curio status as an extra track for "The Caterpillar" twelve-inch. Smith later described his performance as "confusing and confused" and suggested it was likely the by-product of a super-strong batch of drummer Andy Anderson's magic mushroom tea.

The Top is Robert Smith as obsessive studio recluse, twisting in turmoil and bedecking the pain with shiny baubles of every imaginable color. Smith exhibits a musical range and proficiency beyond anything he'd ever done, managing to pull off an album that's wild and colorful but also haunted by playing nearly all the instruments himself.

Smith has reflected that *The Top* might have been better had he made it his primary focus instead of spreading himself thin. He wanted two of the Glove's strongest tracks—"Sex-Eye Make-Up" and "A Blues in Drag"—for *The Top*, but they ultimately got away from him. He wasn't overly happy with the album on its release, but he had no time to tweak it because of touring commitments with the Banshees (from which he ultimately backed away, citing exhaustion and illness).

In retrospect, *The Top* came out far better than it seemed at the time. Robert Smith has warmed to it over the years and has added several songs from it to the band's live set. The album's oddball and un-self-conscious nature is unique among The Cure's studio output. Never again would the Cure release an album so carefree and unrestrained from concerns over how it might be received. *The Top* is the sound of Robert Smith in his musical playground, his version of dancing like nobody's watching.

16

Lost in Motion, Locked Together: The Extended Cure

The Cure's lineup has evolved numerous times, with each member contributing yet another dose of imagination and creative power.

The Cure's Lineup

Perry Bamonte

Born in London on September 3, 1960, Perry Bamonte was a member of the Cure from 1990 to 2005, initially playing keyboard as a replacement for Roger O'Donnell before switching to guitar, his primary instrument, following the departure of Porl Thompson.

Perry and his brother Daryl Bamonte have been involved with music most of their lives. As a teenager in the late 1980s, Daryl was guitarist for the Spurts, which changed names to the School Bullies in 1980. Perry Bamonte entered Cure world in 1984 as a roadie and guitar tech. He was nicknamed "Teddy" because, according to Robert Smith, he hangs his head like a teddy bear.

Over the next six years, he became a prominent member of the Cure's road crew and a good friend of the band. He worked the back line for the Head Tour in 1985 and the Beach Party Tour in 1986, and he was elevated to assistant tour manager for the 1987 Kissing Tour. For the 1989 Prayer Tour, he was designated guitar tech.

During the 1986 sessions for *Kiss Me, Kiss Me, Kiss Me* at Château Miraval in France, Robert Smith's sister Janet, wife of Porl Thompson, taught Perry Bamonte the basics of playing piano. This would be turn out to be a major factor a few years later when the Cure needed a keyboardist to replace the recently ousted Roger O'Donnell. Putting a higher premium on chemistry than musical ability, Robert Smith tapped Perry for the role in 1990. Although Roger O'Donnell is a gifted musician who brought whole new dimensions of sound as a member of the Cure, O'Donnell had a prickly side that made him a sometimes difficult fit. Bamonte was a fixture in the Cure family who got along with everyone, and although his primary instrument is the guitar, he was proficient enough on the keyboard to make it work, and he knew all the songs.

Three years later, after the departure of Porl Thompson following the *Wish* tour, Bamonte stepped in to fill his shoes in the lead guitar spot. Bamonte has had the unenviable task of replacing two of the most technically gifted players in the Cure's history, and while he never had the musical chops of Roger O'Donnell or Porl Thompson, Bamonte still managed to carve his place in the Cure by working hard and playing with genuine heart and emotion.

His younger brother, Daryl, has also worked with the Cure as their tour manager and also for Depeche Mode in the same manner. In 2005, Perry and Daryl were abruptly fired from the Cure, and Perry was, ironically enough, replaced as guitarist by the man he replaced: Porl Thompson.

Michael Dempsey

The Cure's original bassist, Michael Dempsey was with the band from the very early days as a schoolmate of Robert Smith and Lol Tolhurst in Crawley. He was in the band's earlier versions, Malice and the Easy Cure, and then recorded as part of the trio for their debut album, *Three Imaginary Boys*, and the classic non-LP singles "Killing an Arab" and "Boys Don't Cry" and for his final appearance with the band: "Jumping Someone Else's Train." Dempsey is also the only band member other than Robert Smith ever to sing lead on a Cure track—he did the vocals for their throwaway cover of Jimi Hendrix's "Foxy Lady."

Dempsey's ouster from the Cure came about for a few reasons. Although he was friends with his bandmates, he never had the tight personal relationship that Robert Smith and Lol Tolhurst did. Musically, he was out of step with the disciplined, minimalist approach that Smith wanted to take. Dempsey is a florid, imaginative bassist whose style was much more ornate than Smith wanted for the stripped-down sound that he envisioned for the band. The two of them clashed frequently over the bass parts.

After Smith secretly arranged a recording session with Simon Gallup of the Magspies, he knew that he had found the perfect bassist for the Cure and that Dempsey had to go. Dempsey's final live performance as a member of the Cure was on October 15, 1979, at London's Hammersmith Odeon on the last night of the Cure's tour in support of Siouxsie and the Banshees.

In 1980, Dempsey joined Fiction label mates the Associates for a brief two-year stint that included the band's commercial and artistic pinnacle: *Sulk* (1981). The sessions for *Sulk* are legendary for the massive amounts of money the band spent on wild extravagances, including mountains of cocaine.

Dempsey tried to be a tempering factor in the band, but he left along with everyone else when the Associates fell apart in 1982. Lead singer Billy McKenzie carried on the band name for years with what was really a solo project, but he could never let it go. His 1997 suicide inspired Robert Smith to write the Cure single "Cut Here," about the last time Smith encountered McKenzie prior to his passing.

Since leaving the Associates, Michael Dempsey has kept busy over the years with a variety of bands and projects, including collaborating with former Cure mate Lol Tolhurst in Levinhurst. Dempsey has also composed film and television scores and music for animated features and the British television series *PB Bears & Friends*.

Michael Dempsey doesn't seem to harbor any hard feelings over his ouster from the Cure after only one album, or at least he successfully suppresses him. In October 1992, Dempsey said in an interview that the Cure was making some of the best pop music in the world and that they were doing it on their own terms and with complete integrity.

He called the Cure the perfect model for any artist, no matter what medium, in terms of being firm in the pursuit of a singular creative vision. Dempsey was recognized for his contributions as a founding member of the Cure in March 2019 when he was included in the band's induction into the Rock and Roll Hall of Fame. He was clearly happy to be with his mates, wearing a broad grin as he stood onstage all those years later, finally recognized for pivotal role during the early stages of the Cure's history.

Reeves Gabrels

The newest member of the Cure, Reeves Gabrels joined during the summer of 2012 and has toured with the Cure ever since. He has yet to appear on a Cure studio album. Born in New York City in 1957, Gabrels is the only American member in the Cure's history.

Gabrels is a veteran guitarist best known for his work with David Bowie as a member of Tin Machine and for his heavy involvement as cowriter and coproducer on Bowie's 1997 album *Earthling*. Other Bowie projects on which Gabrels contributed include *Black Tie, White Noise*, *Outside*, and *Hours*.

Robert Smith met Reeves in 1997 at David Bowie's star-studded fiftieth-birthday gala, and they quickly became friends. The same year, Reeves collaborated with the Cure on their new single "Wrong Number" from the *Galore* hits collection. They also collaborated on the track "A Sign from God," released under the name COGASM for the 1998 film *Orgazmo*. In 1999, Robert Smith cowrote and performed on Gabrels's solo track, the haunting "Yesterday's Gone," which could be considered a Cure song in all but name.

Although he's appeared on only one studio track with the Cure (until, presumably, the new album finally hits), Gabrels was inducted into the Rock and Roll Hall of Fame with the rest of the band on March 29, 2019. He wasn't initially part of the list but was later added, reportedly because Robert Smith was so vexed at his exclusion that he threatened to boycott the ceremony unless Reeves was included. That in and of itself speaks volumes about Robert's high regard for the guitarist.

Gabrels is arguably the most technically gifted member in the Cure's history. Robert Smith has always valued chemistry, cohesion, and feel over pure musical chops. With Reeves Gabrels, Robert had a guitar virtuoso on his hands and a steadying influence. He transforms songs with his sizzling guitar work—for example, "A Night Like This," where there used to be a sax solo, is now a guitar flameout that shows in just a handful of bars the new level of excitement Gabrels has brought to the band.

Matthieu Hartley

Matthieu Hartley, born on February 4, 1960, in Smallfield, England, was the first keyboardist for the Cure. Prior to the recording of the Cure's second album, *Seventeen Seconds*, in 1979, Robert Smith decided he wanted to replace bassist Michael Dempsey with Simon Gallup. At the time, Gallup and Hartley were both members of the Magspies. Smith decided to invite Hartley along with Gallup so that the bassist wasn't the only new guy and had someone with whom he had already played in the band. Smith also felt that the Cure's sound would expand and that the addition of keyboards would be welcome.

Hartley never quite grasped the musical direction that Robert Smith wanted to take the Cure. Robert wanted simple, stark lines of keyboard. Hartley played as Smith directed on *Seventeen Seconds*, but he was bored by the single-note simplicity of Smith's sonic design, and the dark tone of the music didn't interest him.

The issues with Hartley intensified during the long tour in 1980 supporting the album. Hartley was a complainer who seemed to have issues with everything, and he kept himself apart from the rest of the band whenever possible. Eventually, Robert Smith stopped talking to him altogether except when absolutely necessary. The rest of the band felt that Hartley wasn't suited to life on the road, and Hartley was disenchanted by the Cure's musical direction.

After a turbulent tour of Australia that ended on August 31, 1980, the Cure returned to London with everyone aware that a change would have to be made.

Shortly after arrival, Hartley called Smith to tell him he was leaving the band. Smith was relieved, as he was spared the task of firing the keyboardist. Interestingly enough, when Smith was asked in December 1990 by the fanzine *Cure News* to describe each former member with a word, "unreasonable" was his choice for Hartley.

Matthieu Hartley was around for only one album and tour, and although he considers himself the "least important" member of the Cure, he left an indelible mark on the band's sound. Hartley played two classic monophonic analog keyboards with the Cure: the Korg MiniKorg-700 and the Roland RS-09.

His synthesizer parts on "A Forest" and "Play for Today" are iconic, and his subtle play throughout *Seventeen Seconds* adds just the right touches where needed. After Hartley's departure, the Cure continued as a trio, but keyboards remained in the formula and have been a vital part of their sound over the years. More than a decade after his ouster, he wasn't impressed with his former band's music, calling it "confused" and insisting that there are much better bands than the Cure.

In 2019 at the Cure's Rock and Roll Hall of Fame induction, Robert Smith thanked Hartley during his speech as part of a rundown of prior Cure members. Hartley was one of three former members not to be inducted with the band.

Roger O'Donnell

By the time the Cure had finished their massive South American tour in April 1987, it was clear that they needed help at keyboard. Lol Tolhurst was officially the band's keyboardist since switching from drums at the end of the *Pornography* tour, but he could barely play and seemed to have little interest in learning. Porl Thompson had been helping on keyboard in addition to his guitar duties, but it was increasingly difficult for him to fill both roles, especially given the prominence of the keyboard parts in much of the new material.

With their popularity skyrocketing and a long slate of high-pressure North American and European dates on the horizon, Robert Smith decided to take advantage of a three-month break and bring in a new touring keyboardist.

Drummer Boris Williams suggested his friend Roger O'Donnell, whom he knew from his time with the Thompson Twins. Shortly after O'Donnell's arrival, it became clear that the technically gifted keyboardist was exactly what the Cure needed to replicate their ever-expanding sound live onstage. His first appearance was on April 24, 1987, as the Cure performed "Catch," "Why Can't I Be You?," and "Hot Hot Hot!!!" for last-ever episode of Channel 4's *The Tube*. His first show was on July 9 in Vancouver, the first date of the North American leg of the Kissing Tour.

Roger O'Donnell was a key component of the Cure's peak years as the only member during that period exclusive to keyboards and for his songwriting contributions. His creative apex is *Disintegration*, an album with lush synthesizers and complex keyboard arrangements far beyond anything the Cure had previously attempted. O'Donnell was deeply involved in the album's programming and sampling, collaborating with Robert Smith on such pivotal moments as the grandiose string patterns on "Plainsong," the breathtaking introductory piano on "Homesick," and the forlorn organ sample that drives "Lovesong."

As much as he shined in the studio where his creative and technical abilities were of great value, O'Donnell struggled on the road. He grappled with the stress generated by the Cure's enormous success and the expectations of the Prayer Tour. The complex keyboard arrangements were a nightly challenge, requiring a convoluted setup involving a combination of preprogrammed samples and live playing.

Given that O'Donnell's parts would be the most easily heard if a screwup were to take place, he had to be absolutely on point every night to a degree higher than that of any of the other band members. Maintaining that level of perfection over sets that had grown to be longer than two hours was an intense challenge. Even Robert Smith would often wander off the reservation with lyrics he improvised on the spot and by turning missed key changes and mistakes into improvisations, but that was impossible for O'Donnell.

O'Donnell also struggled with the personal dynamics within the band, a pressure point exacerbated by the Cure's new level of fame. O'Donnell had alienated Simon Gallup and Boris Williams so badly that by the time the band gathered in Sussex to prepare new studio material for the *Mixed Up* album, he had become such a focal point of bitter internal squabbling that Robert Smith ejected him from the Cure.

Whatever acrimony existed dissipated rather quickly, and in late 1994, Roger was brought back into the Cure for work on the *Wild Mood Swings* album. Porl Thompson was out, and drummer Boris Williams, who had left following the *Wish* tour, had been replaced by Jason Cooper. As Perry Bamonte slid from keyboard to guitar to replace Thompson, O'Donnell replaced the man who had replaced him when he was fired for the first time (how very Cure).

O'Donnell was once again key in the studio for *Wild Mood Swings*, and he was part of the touring lineup. He stayed in the fold through *Bloodflowers* (2000) and *The Cure* (2004), touring for both albums. When Smith decided to reconfigure the Cure as a hard-edged rock trio in 2005, O'Donnell was fired a second time, along with Perry Bamonte, as Porl Thompson returned to the lineup (replacing Bamonte, the man who replaced him).

O'Donnell found himself back in the Cure six years later in time for the enormously important May 2011 *Reflections* shows in Sydney, joining on keyboard to play through *Seventeen Seconds* and *Faith*. He's been part of the Cure ever since.

On March 29, 2019, he and his bandmates were be inducted into the Rock and Roll Hall of Fame.

In an interview on SiriusXM's *Feedback* morning show given the day of the announcement, O'Donnell called the induction the "cherry on top" and was clearly delighted by the honor. He also correctly predicted that no former members would be part of the group's live performance, stating that the Cure felt that the current lineup represented the best they've ever been.

Pearl (Formerly Porl) Thompson

Everyone who knows and loves the Cure is familiar with their incredibly talented longtime guitarist Porl Thompson. Thompson is regarded by many as the most technically gifted musician ever to play in the band, along with Reeves Gabrels perhaps. Put simply, he is a fiend on the guitar and has been since he was very young. Porl Thompson has been part of the Cure's universe almost from the beginning and stayed with them well into the new millennium.

Paul Stephen Thompson was born on November 8, 1957, in Surrey. He was part of the Cure going all the way back to the very early years. Porl (a name he adopted in 1976) worked at L & H Cloake's record store in Crawley, so it's no surprise that he met the rabid vinyl junkie Robert Smith, and the two became friends over their passion for music. A talented guitarist from a young age, Porl soon joined Robert, Lol Tolhurst, and Michael Dempsey for their regular rehearsals at Robert's house. It was during these rehearsals that he met Robert's younger sister Janet, and in short order, the two of them were dating.

Porl was a member of both pre-Cure groups: Malice and the Easy Cure. He became something of a local guitar hero around the Crawley area, as he was a far more advanced musician than his bandmates. To the annoyance of the others, Porl tended to showboat with flashy guitar acrobats and earsplitting feedback that overshadowed everybody else onstage. His status as a popular guitarist brought people to the Easy Cure's shows, but it soon became clear to all that Porl and the rest of the band were not on the same page musically.

Porl left the band on May 3, 1978, by mutual agreement. His flashy style was at odds with the minimalist approach that Robert Smith wanted for the Cure. This vision for the band left Thompson feeling restrained, and he agreed it wouldn't work for him. He took time to study fine art and painting. Even when not in the band itself, Porl remained part of the Cure world. He and Janet Smith eventually married and had four children.

One of Porl Thompson's more noticeable contributions to the Cure's catalog is the cover art he developed with artistic collaborator Andy Vella as part of Parched Art. The first piece of cover art for Parched Art was for the "Primary" single in 1981 and its accompanying album *Faith*, and the two have handled most of the band's album and single artwork ever since.

Porl's first musical contribution to a Cure record was his blasted demonic hellfire saxophone squealing on "Give Me It" in 1983. This led to his return to the band for *The Top* tour, for which he played keyboard in addition to guitar and other instruments.

His first studio appearance as guitarist for the Cure was in 1984 for *The Head on the Door* sessions. That album became the Cure's major breakthrough, and Porl was along for the wildest rides and biggest albums, including *Kiss Me, Kiss Me, Kiss Me*, *Disintegration*, and *Wish*.

In the studio with the Cure, the bulk of the guitar parts, even on albums like *Wish*, where they are particularly emphasized, are played by Robert Smith. Even the guitar solo on "From the Edge of the Deep Green Sea," one of Thompson's standout moments during a Cure show, is played by Smith on the album. Thompson avoided the studio to reduce the potential for conflict with Smith during the process of putting the final track list together and deciding what parts to use in a song. He preferred to simply play the parts and find out how things ended up when hearing the final product.

Thompson left the Cure in 1994 to play with Jimmy Page and Robert Plant during their 1995 tour. He went on to work with Plant extensively, joining his band for 2002's *Dreamland*. He rejoined the Cure for a third time in June 2005, touring with them multiple times and appearing on their 2008 album *4:13 Dream* before setting aside his music career entirely in 2012.

Porl Thompson was always an exciting presence in the Cure. In the early days, his guitar histrionics brought crowds to the shows, and when the band reached their pinnacle, Thompson had the presence to stand right alongside Simon Gallup and Robert Smith and not fade into the background like most would. Although revered for his playing, his flamboyant clothes and appearance helped make Porl a fan favorite. His body is covered with intricate tattoos of deep personal meaning, many of which also ended up as artwork on his guitars.

Visual art is as important if not more so to Porl than his music. In 2002, Porl's artwork was featured in an exhibition called "100% Sky," with the premier held at the Homer Watson Gallery and Museum in Ontario. He and accomplished art and photography editor Sarah Brittain cowrote a book in conjunction with the exhibition.

In 2015, Thompson reached a major turning point, leaving behind the name Porl to become Pearl Thompson. Friends had called him Pearl for years, and he felt the name represented a new beginning. He began wearing makeup, long hair, and sometimes women's clothing. However, he has not transitioned from male to female but rather is reflecting every aspect of himself to which he feels a strong enough connection to inform his perceptions in a significant way.

In March 2015, Pearl accomplished a feat quite different than blazing his wicked guitar solos in arenas packed with screaming fans. His artwork was showcased for the first time at a major exhibition, "Looking through the Eyes of

Birds," at the Mr. Musichead Gallery in Hollywood. The collection was twenty years in the making and reflects Pearl's love for the Malibu canyons and the surrounding desert landscape.

Thompson's impressive legacy with the Cure earned him a slot in the Rock and Roll Hall of Fame. He was inducted along with his bandmates on March 29, 2019, standing on stage with the rest as Robert Smith accepted the honor. It would have been amazing to see him perform with the band again, although Smith opted to just have current members play. That caused a bit of consternation, but at the end of the night it was about 40-plus years of the Cure, in all its versions, and that includes Thompson right up at the top. No Cure fan could ever forget his blazing solos on "From the Edge of the Deep Green Sea."

Phil Thornalley

Although he was with the Cure for only a brief time, Phil Thornalley made significant contributions that helped shape the band during their most successful period. A bassist and a talented technician in the studio, Thornalley began working as a recording engineer in 1978 at RAK Studios in London for producers Mickie Most, Steve Lillywhite, and Alex Sadkin.

As the Cure prepared to record their fourth studio album, *Pornography*, in early 1982, the first thing they had to do was find a producer. They eventually decided on Phil Thornalley, engineer for highly respected producer Steve Lillywhite. Lillywhite went so far as to put in a personal call to Robert Smith endorsing Thornalley, which meant a lot. Robert also liked the drum sound that Thornalley achieved on the Psychedelic Furs album *Talk, Talk, Talk*, for which he was engineer, and he was focusing on the drum sound in his head for the new album.

Pornography was Thornalley's first time producing a full album, and it ended up a classic. Dense walls of guitar and thunderous rhythms combined to create a cacophony over which Robert Smith wailed his angst-ridden and mournful lyrics of doom. Despite the album's content and the drug-addled condition of the band, Thornalley successfully navigated the personalities of the band to get through it with few problems. Helming the sessions for *Pornography* greatly impacted his career, as he received many of his future production gigs directly as a result of his work on it.

He went from producer to member of the band when the Cure needed a bassist to fill in for the departed Simon Gallup for some shows scheduled in 1983 in support of the recent pop singles the band had released. Thornalley had been a bassist since age fourteen, and the idea intrigued him, so he jumped on board. His tenure was brief. The debauchery on the road was not something he was used to, and he stuck around only through *The Top* tour in 1984.

During that tour, he helped make a pivotal membership decision for the Cure. Drummer Andy Anderson was ousted from the band after a fiasco in Tokyo in which he ended up in a fight with hotel security. The Cure had more shows only five days away and no drummer. It was Phil Thornalley's extensive industry connections that helped the Cure land a temporary fill-in with the Psychedelic Furs' Vince Ely.

Ely could stay for only a short time, but it gave them time to look for a permanent drummer. Once again, Thornalley was able to save the day by getting the band in contact with former Thompson Twins drummer Boris Williams, who stayed for ten years and was the rock-steady beat behind the Cure's best albums. If not for Phil Thornalley, the Cure's history would be very different.

Thornalley has been a successful performer, producer, and songwriter for many years. He joined British pop group Johnny Hates Jazz as lead singer in 1988. They reached number two in the United States and number five in the United Kingdom with "Shattered Dreams," which was sung by original vocalist Clark Datchler. Thornalley replaced Datchler, but the group was unable to sustain its chart momentum. Thornalley later scored three number one hits in the United Kingdom as co-writer for pop singer Pixie Lott: "Mama Do," "Boys and Girls," and "Cry Me Out." His greatest success came with the global number one "Torn" by Natalie Imbruglia, a song he cowrote with Scott Cutler and Anne Preven. Phil Thornalley maintains his work as a sought-after touring bassist and session musician, while continuing to pursue his own work. In 2018 he released a new solo project: *Astral Drive*.

17

Never Quite as It Seems: *The Head on the Door*

The Cure's disparate sonic elements all come together with their strongest batch of songs yet, sparking their Golden Era.

Released: August 26, 1985
Fiction Records—FIXH 11 (United Kingdom), Elektra—60435-4 (United States)
Running time: 37:46

1. "In Between Days," 2. "Kyoto Song" (4:16), 3. "The Blood" (3:43), 4. "Six Different Ways" (3:18), 5. "Push" (4:31), 6. "The Baby Screams" (3:44), 7. "Close to Me" (3:23), 8. "A Night Like This" (4:16), 9. "Screw" (5:54), 10. "Sinking" (4:00)

There are many paths an artist's recording career can take. Some ignite immediately with a killer debut, although such an auspicious blessing also comes with inherent peril. The long shadows these classics cast can be hard to escape or match. The "sophomore slump" is not just a tired cliché; it's an often unavoidable and sometimes fatal pressure point in the music industry.

Then there are those like the Cure who slowly build over years and multiple albums to reach their peak period of artistry and success. This room for growth is a luxury that many artists are never afforded given the music industry's laser focus on unit shifting. Things were a bit different in the post-punk era. The punk ethos didn't emphasize musical proficiency (certain members of some of the most famous bands of the era could barely play at all), and that anything-goes mentality spread as bands expanded the boundaries of the genre and moved into a more fully developed and song-focused direction, darkness and despondency often replacing sheer rage and vitriol.

There is a certain raw naïveté to *Seventeen Seconds*, *Faith*, and *Pornography*. All three are brilliant and distinct but still very much embryonic statements.

Then came a detour into fanciful pop, followed by the violent melding of Smith's dueling personalities in *The Top*. With *The Head on the Door*, Smith finds the sweet spot of balance, the darkness and light intertwined and working in harmony. His songwriting had never been sharper, and, vitally, the Cure became a real band again.

A daring but imminently accessible collection of pop nightmares both shadowy and fanciful, *The Head on the Door* marked a new artistic and commercial pinnacle for the Cure. The music is perfectly represented by the darkly fanciful cover, created by Porl Thompson and Andy Vella and based on a photograph that Porl took of his wife Janet, Robert Smith's younger sister.

In retrospect, it's easy to see the path that led to *The Head on the Door*, which was sparked by Smith's desire to elevate the stature of the band and bring their music to a wider audience. He took some time off following the arduous tour in support of *The Top* to listen to hundreds of hours of live tape to compile the acclaimed *Concert*, released in October 1984. Smith also officially cut his ties with Siouxsie and the Banshees, knowing that his obligations with the Cure would no longer permit the luxury of divided attention.

Swallowing the toxic feelings that led to Gallup's acrimonious departure following the *Pornography* tour, Smith reconciled with the bassist and brought his longtime colleague back into the fold. Smith also lured the talented drummer Boris Williams away from the Thompson Twins, with whom he was on tour. Smith also brought in old friend, Porl Thompson, on guitar. He was in the group early on and then departed prior to the recording of *Three Imaginary Boys* since his showy style didn't fit the minimalist vibe of the material at the time. The Cure's palette had expanded vastly since then, and suddenly, Thompson was the perfect fit. It's as if he was waiting for the band to catch up to him, and they finally did.

Robert Smith produced the album with Dave Allen, the engineer who had successfully navigated the singer's fractured neuroses and helped keep *The Top* sessions from derailing completely. *The Head on the Door* was recorded largely at Angel Studios in Islington, London, a former congregational chapel built in 1888 (Adele later used the studio for her 2011 global smash *21*).

The Cure's new lineup convened in February 1985 to start brainstorming with the set of demos Robert Smith had been toying with, and by March, the band was set at Angel Studios to finish writing and then record the new album. All the songs were written in under three weeks, with Smith focusing on more immediate and direct material. His goal was to harness the electricity of the new band and pump out the strongest batch of songs they could create, culminating in a classic pop album.

Smith reigned in his vocals from the wildly elastic swoops and wails that he often employed on *The Top*, delivering more disciplined and nuanced performances. The more self-indulgent impulses were held in abeyance (although Smith would let them out of the bottle to roam free on the Cure's next album).

Finally, it all came together for the Cure as *The Head on the Door* (1985) opened the band up to a vast new audience. *Author's Collection*

The final release exceeded all expectations and ended up being exactly the breakthrough Smith had been seeking. *The Head on the Door* exhibits a much higher level of ambition and professionalism than the Cure had ever presented before. It was mostly recorded live studio performances, which is reflected in the album's exuberant energy.

The Head on the Door was praised by critics, and fans couldn't get enough. As Robert Smith had hoped, it elevated the Cure's international profile, and his music was indeed being heard by more people. They booked larger venues than ever before, with tickets in high demand. Through parts of Europe (especially France, the Netherlands, and Belgium) and in a few other spots, the Cure had reached Madonna and Michael Jackson levels of adulation.

Although they weren't yet in the top forty, *The Head on the Door* significantly upped the Cure's visibility in America. MTV provided a boost by playing both of the album's quirky Tim Pope–directed videos—"In Between Days" and "Close to Me"—on a regular basis. Increasing spins on college radio helped lift the album to number fifty-nine on the *Billboard* "Top 200," by far their best showing to date.

The Cure were suddenly legitimate rock stars. Robert Smith's pale face, with his trademark spiderweb hair and smudged red lipstick, peered mischievously from the covers of just about every music magazine on the stands. He delighted in toying with gullible interviewers and took pleasure in making outlandish and contradictory statements and would often make these just for the fun of it. He cultivated a persona that dominated the band's image and helped distinguish them from the endless parade of U.K. bands that grew out of the late 1970s and early 1980s.

The Head on the Door marked the beginning of the Cure's "golden age," a span of eight years covering four remarkable studio albums and their subsequent tours. The Cure's legacy as one of the decade's most important bands was already cemented by the quality of their prior work, but *The Head on the Door* brought a much higher echelon of success, opening up the world to their deviant brand of musical weirdness.

The Head on the Door

"In Between Days"

Opening with a quick crashing drumroll, "In Between Days" is a fizzy whirlwind of acoustic guitars, keyboards, and Robert Smith's perpetually lovelorn vocal set to his purest pop melody since "Boys Don't Cry." It was recorded in a single take, exuding delectable charm despite its wistful, bittersweet sentiment.

"In Between Days" is the first taste of a new version of the Cure—more powerful, capable, and at ease. It was their most immediate and mature radio single by far. All those years of endless dreaming, rehearsing, writing, fighting, and working to realize a singular uncompromising vision that was Robert Smith's from the beginning was about to pay off big time.

The song arrived very quickly and almost fully formed, as if beamed from pop music heaven directly into Robert Smith's brain. He'd just bought a new six-string acoustic guitar, and as soon as he started playing it the first time, the chords to "In Between Days" came to him right away. That ease is translated into the final recording.

"In Between Days" was slated to be the lead single from the moment it was recorded, and it turned out to be the rocket launcher that lifted the Cure into the stratosphere. The lyrics are about as simple as you'll find, but sometimes, the right sentiment can be conveyed very simply. "In Between Days" pulls our kite strings for a few breathtaking swirls through the clouds, heartbreaking and joyous, much like life itself.

"Kyoto Song"

After opening with dizzy euphoria, Smith draws us right back into his feverish underworld with the stately death march "Kyoto Song," as if to make sure we don't get too comfortable with all that fresh air. Smith claims that the haunting imagery he conjured in this tense, exotic fantasy is a combination of two vivid nightmares (one by him and one related to him by his wife), but it's also surely inspired by an acid trip(s).

"Kyoto Song" first emerged during the drug-addled sessions with Steve Severin for *Blue Sunshine*. The keyboard riff offers a tinge of Far Eastern mysticism, and the gruesome lyrics are shrouded in cinematic violence and dread, a late-night subtitled horror movie that you wish to God you hadn't watched.

"The Blood"

Overindulgence on the Tears of Christ, a Portuguese wine, inspired Robert to pen this flamenco-flavored acoustic rocker. Swirling and percussive, the guitar work is particularly tight, and the arrangement is compact and punchy.

"The Blood" was released as a promo single with unique cover art in Spain only but in very limited quantities. These days, it's nearly impossible to find copies in excellent condition, making it a holy grail of sorts among Cure collectors.

"Six Different Ways"

Unlike prior albums, *The Head on the Door* was overflowing with potential singles, including the endearingly loopy "Six Different Ways." It's built on a circular keyboard riff adapted from a similar part Smith played on Siouxsie and the Banshees' much more sinister "Swimming Horses" single recorded six months earlier. It's as if Smith wasn't satisfied with the prior track and decided to remake it more to his own liking. He does so with a sweetly winsome vocal and a bubbly joyous feel despite the ambiguity of the lyrics.

"Six Different Ways" shows the immediate dividends that the addition of Boris Williams reaped for the band. His skittery rhythm is the key to the song, and the deft touch required to accomplish it is more than either of the band's two prior drummers could have accomplished. Its 6/8 time signature also lent itself to the song's title, which was first coined during moments of silliness as the band discussed the number of ways there are to skin a cat. Six, as it turns out.

The breezy acoustic-pop swirls of "In Between Days" proved irresistible to fans, who bought the single in droves and sent it well into the Top 20. *Author's Collection*

"Push"

"Push" is an emphatic exclamation point to end side 1, an arena-rock locomotive that roars to powerful life in concert as the band feeds off the amped-up crowd energy the song always generates. The long instrumental opening builds anticipation for fans to throw their hands in the air and sing along when Smith finally leaps into his spirited vocal.

Like many Cure songs, "Push" isn't structured in the traditional verse–chorus–verse pop-rock convention. The main melodic hook is the vocal introduction, which is followed by three verses before ending in a long rock-out of power chords and Boris Williams slamming into his kit with maximum velocity.

"The Baby Screams"

Even on this strange catalog of dreams, "The Baby Screams" must be the product of a particularly sweat-soaked night. One of the edgier tracks on the album, "The Baby Screams" opens side 2 with a wail and a skittery beat tripping with a madly hopping bass. Smith's elongated vocals foreshadow some of the intensity he'd pour into the band's next album: *Kiss Me, Kiss Me, Kiss Me*.

"Close to Me"

The Cure had never released two singles from the same album, but the success of "In Between Days" and the presence of a surefire hit made "Close to Me" a no-brainer. It's ingeniously constructed around a snappy hand-clap skip of a beat and a jumping bass with a nifty little keyboard hook in its mouth.

Tim Pope's video of the band in a wardrobe has become one of the Cure's most iconic visual clips.   *Author's Collection*

The single version is jolted with the manic energy of a New Orleans–style brass section played by Rent Party, leaving the album version feeling somewhat undressed. "Close to Me" wasn't considered a strong contender to make the album until near the end of the recording process when Smith delivered his superbly nuanced anxiety-sown vocal. The breathless panting between the beats injects the listener straight into his skull as he tries to claw himself awake in a frantic retreat from a nightmarish apparition that's bounding ever closer.

"Close to Me" is derived from childhood memories of horrifying scenes he'd imagine forming in beams of light coming into his room from the hallway and splaying ghoulish shapes on his wall.

"A Night Like This"

The seed of "A Night Like This" was born in the band's early days, in 1976, when Porl Thompson was in the Cure the first time around. It was performed in their second gig as Malice, although that early version morphed into "Plastic Passion," and this is an entirely different song.

One of the album's finest moments, "A Night Like This" is a melancholy rocker with Smith delivering a knockout vocal performance that matches the piercing intensity of lyrics filled with regret and a determination to make amends.

The fiery sax solo is played by Ron Howe, with whom Simon Gallup was familiar through Fools Dance, a side project that Gallup helped create during his brief banishment from the Cure. Howe delivers an element of drama that only amplifies what is already a potently emotional track.

Although never officially a single, "A Night Like This" was the focus of the four-track EP *Quadpus* along with three B-sides. The Cure also filmed a shadowy performance clip for the song, promo singles were sent to deejays in some markets, and it was included on the band's seminal 1986 singles collection *Standing on a Beach* (the CD and VHS versions only). It remains a staple of the band's live shows, and these days Reeves Gabrels inserts a jaw-dropping guitar solo where the sax used to be.

"Screw"

Built around a jagged bass line, Smith attributes "Screw" largely to its drug use. It's never been a regular part of the band's live shows, and following their 1985 tour in support of *The Head on the Door*, it disappeared from their set for more than three decades. They dusted it off for eight performances on their 2016 tour, surprising and delighting fans who are always eager to hear a lesser-known gem.

"Sinking"

The Cure saves the best for last. "Sinking" is the album's most genuine emotional expression, the despair of growing older and drifting farther away each year from the life you thought you would have or should have. With the realization of years speeding by while you are slowly sinking into the bubble world of your own creation—knowing it yet not having the ability or perhaps the drive to change it—you fill your time with baubles, possessions, sex, drugs, or whatever it takes to fill the emptiness—existential angst.

Simon Gallup's bass line throbs through the listener's skull, and an amazing vocal by Smith sears with angst and fear. With lofty synthesizers acting as a string arrangement above the hypnotically repetitive backdrop and heavily treated piano that rings in a jittery countermelody, "Sinking" is a superb finale that ties the band's newly expansive sound to the brooding melancholy of *Faith*.

B-Sides

"The Exploding Boy"

A song as catchy and immediate as "The Exploding Boy" would be a surefire single for most bands, but the Cure's wealth of strong material was such that this melodic guitar-pop gem was left off *The Head on the Door*. Perhaps in retrospect, it's a bit too similar to "In Between Days," the song for which it ended up as a B-side. Smith achieves that lush guitar sound by using a cap on his Bass VI and slathering it with a heavy chorus effect.

"The Exploding Boy" is about excess, drawing in too much, seeking too much, wanting too much—a theme that has recurred multiple times throughout the band's catalog. The Cure performed it only once, in 1985, while touring for the album, but they resurrected it thirty-one years later, delighting fans with five performances.

"A Few Hours after This . . ."

All lush orchestral swirls and echoey vocals, "A Few Hours after This . . ." is a beguiling delight that Smith claims never really came together. It's hard to imagine why.

Cinematic and bracing, pulsing with majestic grandeur, "A Few Hours after This . . ." is one of the many lesser-known Cure songs that more casual fans would no doubt adore if they ever had the chance to discover it. Diehards already love it. In 2015, a new Robert Smith solo recording of the song was produced for the BBC series *Luther*.

"New Day"

"New Day" is perhaps the least consequential of a very strong batch of B-sides. It's an improvisation that Smith devised while out of his mind on drugs, and it sounds like it. "New Day" was born from a demo that was originally recorded during the Glove period and that appeared on the bonus disc of the 2005 reissue of *The Top* as "Sadaic." Musically, the final version still has that raw demo-ish sound, and while the verses hold a certain intrigue, the song consists mostly of Smith wailing "NeeewwwwwwwwwwwEEEWEWAAAWWWEEEEeewwww Day!" like he's in some twisted version of primal scream therapy.

While it grates on the nerves very quickly and isn't likely to end up in heavy rotation for most fans, "New Day" is a demented curio, one of the Cure's most eccentric songs, and further evidence that Robert Smith was still utterly fearless in what he wanted to release.

"Stop Dead"

"Stop Dead" is a melodic synth-pop nugget with a propulsive bass line and catchy keyboard riff. Robert Smith delivers an unhinged vocal that points to his wild performance on "Why Can't I Be You?" Although it's easy to understand why "Stop Dead" didn't make the album, the potential is there for it to have been a serious contender for inclusion with a bit more refinement and a stronger, more focused vocal performance.

"A Man inside My Mouth"

One of Smith's most demented auditory hallucinations, "A Man inside My Mouth" is a neurotic sexual nightmare burning with fever. Smith's vocal is completely berserk, and the band churns out a manic groove that feels charged by an overdose of stimulants. It seems likely that Smith knew that this track wouldn't make the album, so he went all out on the weirdness and in the process created a strangely dangerous vibe that brings the listener right into the midst of a sweat-soaked night horror whether we wish it or not.

The title was borrowed from an entirely different song, "A Hand inside My Mouth," recorded in Paris in 1983 during the same session that yielded their smash hit "The Lovecats." This vaguely jazzy number with different lyrics and melody than the eventual B-side that borrowed its name was set aside and left unreleased until finally appearing as a bonus track on the deluxe reissue of *The Top* in 2005.

The band surprised fans when they performed "A Man inside My Mouth" live for the first time ever at three consecutive shows at the Eventim Apollo in

London on December 21–23, 2014, the only shows at which the song has ever been played.

Since it touches on most aspects of the Cure's musical lexicon, it is loaded with killer tunes, and none of the material is overly difficult, *The Head on the Door* is the studio album most often mentioned as the ideal starting point for would-be Cure fans. Nonthreatening and concise, its mixture of light and darkness is what the band is all about.

On its release, critics were generally favorable to *The Head on the Door*, although like all of the Cure's albums, it has garnered more respect retrospectively than it did at the time. There were better albums to come, but this was the beginning of the period that most fans associate with the Cure, including their biggest hits and most widely acclaimed releases—their golden years.

18

Hold on to These Moments as They Pass: The Cure Compiled

The Cure has been subject to numerous compilations over the years, some of which are vital components of the band's catalog.

As with most artists who've enjoyed some degree of longevity, the Cure has released multiple compilations over their career. Record labels tend to see a "Greatest Hits" package as a cheap way to sell product given that expenses are minimal and the hits easy to market. They can also be useful for an artist to stay on fans' radar during a gap between albums or if one more release is needed to wind down that pesky recording contract.

Sometimes these collections are thrown-together afterthoughts with little or no involvement by the artist at all, but obviously, that's not the case with the Cure. All of their compilations are worthwhile to varying degrees, with some aimed for casual fans and a few designed more for loyal diehards.

Compilations

Boys Don't Cry (February 5, 1980)

Many fans, especially in the United States, don't realize that *Boys Don't Cry* is a compilation rather than a proper studio album. It's often considered their debut album in the States, and in a way, it is. With *Three Imaginary Boys* out in the United Kingdom along with a trio of strong singles, Chris Parry decided to package the best album tracks along with the singles and key B-sides to create

Boys Don't Cry as a way to introduce the Cure to North American and European mainland markets.

One can argue that *Boys Don't Cry* is easily the better of the two releases, as it omits some of the more egregious throwaways from the official debut and includes the classics "Killing an Arab," "Boys Don't Cry," and "Jumping Someone Else's Train." The cover is borrowed from the imagery used for "Fire in Cairo" as part of the thematic artwork scheme on *Three Imaginary Boys*.

. . . Happily Ever After (September 8, 1981)

The Cure's American label, A&M Records, issued this two-LP set in September 1981, merging *Seventeen Seconds* and *Faith* into a single package with unique artwork.... *Happily Ever After* was released only on LP initially and then on cassette and CD in 1987 after A&M revamped the Cure's back catalog in the wake of their recent success. It made little impact and is now mostly just an interesting but pricey curio for completists.

Japanese Whispers: The Cure Singles Nov 82 : Nov 83 (December 12, 1983)

Another compilation that many wrongly assume to be a regular studio album is *Japanese Whispers*, which was released in late 1983 to capitalize on their recent trio of pop hits. "Let's Go to Bed," "The Walk," and "The Lovecats" are all classic singles, and with B-sides added, they work well as a coherent album. One B-side from the period, "Mr. Pink Eyes," is missing.

Japanese Whispers has become so ingrained in the consciousness of Cure fans that many consider it a proper studio album. It also has the distinction of notching the Cure's first appearance on the *Billboard* "Top 200" album chart in the United States, peaking at number 181. Just a taste of things to come.

Curiosity (Cure Anomalies 1977–1984) (October 16, 1984)

Fans who bought the cassette edition of the Cure's outstanding 1984 live album were gifted with an unexpected exclusive bonus on side 2. *Curiosity (Cure Anomalies 1977–1984)* is an eclectic ten-track mix tape of previously unreleased live recordings and rarities from the band's early years that until recently were officially available only on the *Concert* cassette.

It opens with the first official release of the early track "Heroin Face," recorded at the Rocket in Crawley. The audio has a very rough bootleg quality, but it allows us to experience the Cure in their formative years, brash and loud, if only for a

A collection of the "Fantasy Singles" and most of the B-sides, many fans consider *Japanese Whispers* an album in its own right. *Author's Collection*

few minutes. "Heroin Face" bristles with punk energy, far more abrasive than the stripped-down and detached tone they adopt for *Three Imaginary Boys*.

The sprightly demo of "Boys Don't Cry" was recorded at Chestnut Studios in May 1978 more than a year before the single's release. Recorded live in Amsterdam prior to the *Seventeen Seconds* sessions, "In Your House" is presented in early form with different lyrics. The chilling take on "The Drowning Man" recorded in Australia may be superior to the studio version on *Faith*. "Forever" is a haywire improvisation that often served as the band's finale and was never played the same way twice.

Curiosity is more than an offhand collection of throwaways, helping to fill in the blanks to the Cure's early years in ways that the albums can't accomplish. While this compilation has never been officially released in any other format, all of the tracks are included on their associated CDs as part of the deluxe reissue series of the band's first four albums in 2005, so fans can burn their own CD version or create a playlist. For those of us who have listened to the collection in sequence on headphones over and over again, this is a must.

Standing on a Beach (aka Staring at the Sea) (May 19, 1986)

Standing on a Beach holds a place of exalted importance in the Cure's catalog far beyond a normal hits collection. After *The Head on the Door* expanded the band's global audience and made inroads into college radio in America, the timing was perfect for a compilation to expose the Cure's extensive back catalog to a wider audience. Their earlier singles had mostly been mostly unheard in the

This pivotal hits collection was a huge factor in the Cure's risiing success globally, especially in the U.S. where it introduced many fans to their earlier material for the first time.

Author's Collection

United States, and thus *Standing on a Beach* helped songs like "A Forest," "Charlotte Sometimes," "Primary," "The Hanging Garden," and others become popular internationally despite never being major hits, even in the United Kingdom.

Although the album made sense for the band, it came about because of record label maneuvering. The Cure's deal with Polydor was about to expire, and there was a big deal on the table from Virgin. If they ended up taking the deal, the Cure would be stuck with Polydor being able to put out whatever compilation they wanted with no input from Robert Smith. This, of course, could not be allowed to happen, so Smith wanted to do the compilation to his liking if it was to be done anyway. Of course, they ended up resigning with Polydor, so it became a moot point, but it turned out to be a major boon for the Cure.

Sequenced chronologically, *Standing on a Beach* traces the band's development from the raw beginnings of "Killing an Arab" to the power pop of "Boys Don't Cry" and "Jumping Someone Else's Train" and through their darker episodes on *Seventeen Seconds*, *Faith*, and *Pornography*. Then comes the irresistible pop of "Let's Go to Bed," "The Walk," "The Lovecats," and "The Caterpillar" before it wraps up with their most complete work yet from *The Head on the Door*. A newly recorded version of "Boys Don't Cry" was issued as a single to promote the set and became a moderate hit in the United Kingdom and Europe, but it wasn't included on the collection itself. In America, Elektra had the bright idea to release "Let's Go to Bed" instead, and it went nowhere.

The project also included a home video anthology dubbed *Staring at the Sea* (this alternate name was also, perversely, given to the CD version, making it inexplicably different than the cassette and the LP). The VHS (still not available on DVD) includes all the Cure's videos so far plus additional footage.

For many fans, the best part is the cassette version's legendary side 2, which compiles the Cure's eccentric and endlessly creative B-sides minus those already widely available on *Boys Don't Cry* and *Japanese Whispers*. This was their first opportunity for most Cure fans to hear these strange gems. Presented chronologically like the A-sides, it's an alternate history of the Cure heard through the twisted prism of their most obsessive impulses. From the weird bass instrumental "Descent" to the percussive night terror "Splintered in Her Head" to the poppy, could-have-been-singles "The Exploding Boy" and "Throw Your Foot," the B-sides collection exposed the Cure's vast diversity and more experimental tendencies.

With its now iconic cover art dominated by the craggy visage of an elderly fisherman, *Standing on a Beach* became a vital part of the Cure's commercial development, unusual for a hits project. It reached new album chart highs for the band in both the United Kingdom (number four) and the United States (number forty-eight). The compilation easily outsold all of the Cure's prior studio albums in the United States and set the stage for the dizzying heights they'd hit in the years ahead.

A continuation of *Standing on a Beach*, this latest hits collection covered everything from *Kiss Me* through the end of the '90s. *Author's Collection*

Galore: The Singles 1987–1997 (November 3, 1997)

This late 1997 release takes up where *Standing on a Beach* leaves off, beginning with "Why Can't I Be You?" and continuing through the 1990s. It includes one newly recorded single: "Wrong Number." *Galore* is a good source for the seven-inch mixes from the period, especially Mark Saunders's excellent work on the *Disintegration* singles, which are sharper and more immediate than the album versions. The cover cleverly flips the motif of the old man on a beach, this time with an infant holding an ice cream cone.

Galore sold poorly despite containing material representing the Cure's commercial pinnacle. It reached only number thirty-seven in the United Kingdom and number thirty-two in the United States, a grim reflection of the band's diminished standing. The one bright spot was the single "Wrong Number," a track first attempted with Mark Saunders during the sessions for "Never Enough." Smith resurrected and drastically altered it with the help of guitarist Reeves Gabrels and producer Mark Plati, giving "Wrong Number" a vastly different sound than anything else the Cure has released. Its driving electro-rhythm and heavily processed guitar is very much in line with Gabrels's work on David Bowie's *Earthling* released earlier in the year.

"Wrong Number" didn't catch on in the United Kingdom, stalling at number sixty-two, but it was a hit on alternative radio in the United States, and it remains a regular part of the Cure's live shows.

Greatest Hits (November 12, 2001)

In a contractual obligation to close out the Cure's relationship with Fiction Records, the company with whom they'd been from the beginning, Robert Smith agreed to do another *Greatest Hits* collection on the condition that he select the tracks.

Greatest Hits merges songs from both *Standing on a Beach* and *Galore* in an attempt to boil down the biggest hits of the band's vast catalog to a single CD. It skips through the Cure's catalog like a stone on the surface of a lake. The North American and European versions are slightly different: in North America, it's an eighteen-track set including "The Walk," but in Europe, "The Walk" is dropped in favor of "The Caterpillar" and the single edit of "Pictures of You," creating a nineteen-track version.

By its very nature, a project like this is aimed primarily at casual fans, but Smith tried a couple of angles, hoping to convince the diehards to buy yet another singles collection. Two new songs were included: the deeply moving "Cut Here" and the less substantial "Just Say Yes" with guest vocalist Saffron from Republica.

For the two-CD deluxe edition, the band recorded all new acoustic versions and dubbed it *Acoustic Hits*. These unplugged takes are nice enough, but they are generally perfunctory run-throughs and don't offer much in the way of revelation or excitement.

Join the Dots: B-Sides & Rarities 1978–2001 (The Fiction Years) (January 26, 2004)

A history of the Cure from the other side of the mirror, *Join the Dots* is the treasure trove that fans had been hoping for years would come to fruition. When it finally did, the package exceeded even the loftiest expectations. *Join the Dots* collects all of the Cure's B-sides into a lavish four-CD box set with extensive liner notes by Robert Smith in which he provides candid and frequently amusing commentary on each track. It's a dazzling collection of some of the band's

This compilation, incorporating early singles plus the strongest album tracks, was the first Cure album for many Americans. *Author's Collection*

most relentlessly intriguing work, presented with care and attention to detail that underscores Smith's keen understanding of how important these tracks are to his fans.

Many of the Cure's B-sides are easily strong enough to have been album tracks or singles in their own right. The set also marks the first time that many of the classic B-sides that fans revere so deeply from side 2 of the *Standing on the Beach* cassette had ever appeared on CD. Also included are rarities and covers from various compilations albums, such as the band's take on David Bowie's "Young Americans" and the smooth electro-pop "More Than This" from *The X-Files: The Album*. One of the Cure's most popular tracks of the 1990s, "Burn" (from *The Crow*) finally finds a home on a Cure collection, where it belongs.

Smith also unearths previously unheard nuggets, like the abandoned Bob Clearmountain single remix of "How Beautiful You Are," a twelve-inch extended mix of "Doing the Unstuck" that never saw the light of day, and the previously unreleased "Possession," recorded early in the *Bloodflowers* sessions. Every track is remastered and presented with outstanding sound quality. Smith also took the time to make much-needed tweaks, including correcting the mixing error in "Fear of Ghosts" that resulted in a dropout and a sudden increase in sound on the original B-side version.

Join the Dots is clearly a labor of love for Smith, and the set was received euphorically by most fans, with little to complain about and very few things missing. *Join the Dots* presents a vast portion of the Cure's catalog that sits alongside and in tandem with their studio albums yet in a separate dimension.

Started Out Down a Dirty Road: The Cure in Concert, Part 1 (1976–1986)

The first decade of the Cure's long journey as one of the world's top concert draws.

The Cure's thirteen excellent studio albums do not represent a full picture of the band's music, even if you include the B-sides. Fans have long known that the Cure's music is best experienced in a live setting. Their shows are always thrilling and unpredictable, and since they often last three hours or longer, they are a hefty time commitment.

They've notched more than 1,500 shows in dozens of countries and in just about every venue imaginable, from the tiniest clubs to massive stadiums. They've trekked endless miles through Europe and North America, South America, Australia and New Zealand, Russia, Japan, Hong Kong, and Singapore. In March 2019, the Cure played on the African continent for the first time, with two colossal shows held in Cape Town and Johannesburg, South Africa.

Concert Tours

Three Imaginary Boys Tour/Join Hands Tour/Future Pastimes Tour (1979)

Before the Cure's official birth, Robert Smith and his mates were part of earlier bands dating to 1973, including the Obelisk, Malice, and the Easy Cure. Malice played a gig in 1976, their one and only performance. The three-piece lineup of the Cure, including Robert Smith, Michael Dempsey, and Lol Tolhurst, played

CURE - U.K. punk rock group lead singer Robert Smith about 1976.
Pictorial Press Ltd / Alamy Stock Photo

their first show under that name on May 18, 1978, at the Rocket in Crawley. If ever there were a Cavern Club equivalent for the Cure, the Rocket would surely be the place.

More shows followed through 1978 as the Cure signed to Fiction Records and began preparation for their first single and album. Fiction boss Chris Parry was able to get them higher-profile gigs right away. In early October, they opened for the live powerhouse Wire and were blown away by what they saw and heard.

On November 24, 1978, the Cure played the first of seven high-profile shows supporting punk rockers Generation X, led by future superstar Billy Idol. They were kicked off the tour after Lol Tolhurst accidentally peed on Idol's foot while the singer was leaning back against a urinal, purportedly getting head from a female fan.

The Cure wrapped up a very busy 1978 with a flurry of dates, their last on December 26 at the famous Marquee Club in London. Over the course of 1978, which culminated with the release of their debut single "Killing an Arab," the band showed significant progression.

The Cure's tour in support of their debut album, *Three Imaginary Boys*, launched on May 16 in Cheshire. Most nights, they opened and closed with "10:15 Saturday Night," in between which they rocked through most of the album plus associated singles and B-sides.

On July 29, the band played their first show outside the United Kingdom at the rain-soaked Stars in the Forest Festival in Groningen, the Netherlands. On September 12, the Cure raised their profiled by joining Siouxsie and the Banshees for twenty-seven dates in support of their album *Join Hands*. A whirlwind 1979 finished with the Future Pastimes Tour, a package deal headlined by the Cure with Fiction label mates the Associates and the Passions opening. Opening night was on November 16 at Eric's in Liverpool, which marked the debut of new bassist Simon Gallup and keyboardist Matthieu Hartley after Michael Dempsey was fired.

Seventeen Seconds Tour/Get a Dose of the Cure Tour/1980 Tour/Primary Tour (1980)

The Cure had already finished their second album, *Seventeen Seconds*, by the time they played their first show of the 1980s on March 6 at the Marquee Club in London. With the new album due in April and "A Forest" poised to become their first U.K. top-forty hit, the Cure was on the rise. Their three-night stand at the famed Marquee Club, where the Rolling Stones played their first gig, was generating significant buzz. The band's popularity in France was soaring, and on March 14, they headlined the second of three nights at the Europe Rock 80 festival in Nogent-sur-Marne.

The Cure played in the United States for the first time on April 10 at Emerald City in Cherry Hill, New Jersey. The venue had an illustrious history, originating in 1944 as a nightclub called the Latin Casino and hosting some of the greatest artists of the twentieth century, including Frank Sinatra, Liberace, Sonny & Cher, Lena Horne, Louis Armstrong, Harry Belafonte, Sammy Davis Jr., Nat King Cole, Pearl Bailey, and many others.

By the time a dour foursome from Crawley, England, stumbled onto its stage, the club had moved from Philadelphia to nearby Cherry Hill to escape onerous restrictions on the sale of alcohol. It went through a phase as a seedy disco club before ending its life as a rock club that hosted the likes of the Go-Go's, XTC, and the Talking Heads. Emerald City shuttered in 1982, and given its history and stature it was certainly an appropriate venue for the Cure's first American performance.

Before an enthusiastic crowd, Robert Smith ambled up to the microphone for a bashful "Hello," and Lol Tolhurst counted out the stately march that began "Seventeen Seconds," the opener for most of the tour. The performance can be found online from various sources (none of them official), and it's worth tracking down since the band has released precious little archival concert material from this era. A white-hot take on "Play for Today" stoked the crowd's already surging electricity. All those hours spent rehearsing and performing had paid off, and the Cure had developed into an airtight, cohesive sonic locomotive.

Knowing they'd just delivered a jaw-dropper, Robert Smith said with cool nonchalance, "We're the Cure, and this is our first time playing in America!" before blasting through a trio from the first album: "Three Imaginary Boys," "Grinding Halt," and "Fire in Cairo." The encore included a typically unhinged improvisation of "Three" (which would eventually morph into "Forever") and a merciless take on "Killing an Arab." It was a debut performance worthy of the career they'd have going forward.

The guys were excited to be in the United States, and, assuming they'd never have the opportunity again, they made sure to see as much of the cities, though it was a bit surreal. They treated the jaunt like a holiday and had fun seeing Washington, D.C., New York, Philadelphia, and Boston. The *Seventeen Seconds* tour officially began on April 25 in Cromar, England, and crisscrossed much of western Europe.

The Cure had almost no time before getting to New Zealand to start their first tour "down under," the Get a Dose of the Cure Tour, with a show on July 29 in Auckland. They were popular there thanks to radio support and import copies of their albums, and they endured a punishing schedule, often playing two shows a night. They wrapped up on August 31 in the final show for Matthieu Hartley.

Started Out Down a Dirty Road: The Cure in Concert, Part 1 (1976–1986) 185

THE CURE U.K. rock group with Robert Smith about 1980. *Jason Tilley / Alamy*

Dubbed the 1980 Tour, this twenty-seven-date roller coaster through Europe required the Cure to jam in all those shows from October 2 in Göteborg, Sweden, through November 2 in Rotterdam, the Netherlands. They introduced a few songs that would be on their next album, *Faith*, including "The Holy Hour" (which became the new opener), "Primary," and "All Cats Are Grey." The Cure played an astonishing 133 shows in 1980, a number they'd never reach again in a single year.

Picture Tour/Eight Appearances Tour (1981)

The Cure's third album, *Faith*, was released on April 14, 1981, and only four days later, they started the Picture Tour in Aylesbury, England. The main set was thick with the somber spiritual brooding of the new album, which they augmented with select older cuts that flowed right into that sea of woe, like "In Your House," "M," "Seventeen Seconds," "Accuracy," "At Night," and "Three Imaginary Boys."

Instead of mixing it up with older material with more energy, one plodding song followed another. Most nights, the first truly up-tempo rock track played would be "Primary," usually in the eleventh slot. The audience caught a respite during the encore, which typically included "Jumping Someone Else's Train," "Another Journey by Train," and "Killing an Arab." "Boys Don't Cry" was played on average in only one out of three shows.

The night started as somber as a séance as well. Projected onstage each night was an abstract film created by Simon Gallup's brother Ric called *Carnage Visors*, which was accompanied by a long instrumental track the band had recorded. The Picture Tour inescapably painted the Cure with the brush of goth.

The Cure was exhausted before the tour even started. The sessions for *Faith* were fraught with tension. The final album was intense and beautiful, but replicating that mood nightly was an emotional drain. Drug and alcohol use escalated, and the band's infighting was worse than it had ever been. Making matters worse, they were hit hard by family tragedy. Robert Smith's grandmother had recently died, and Lol's mother, Daphne Tolhurst, an enthusiastic supporter of her son and the Cure, died on June 24 while the band performed in the Netherlands. They flew back to London the next day for Mrs. Tolhurst's funeral and made it back in time for their next gig, which is exactly what she would have wanted.

The bleakness of the music soaked downward and impacted the band members, who were unable to rise above the thick sludge of gloom they had painted around themselves. The audiences were uneasy, and media reports noted that the mood seemed tense as the Cure slogged through one turgid dirge after another as if on a mission that they couldn't fathom but knew was very serious business. They took on an aura of self-important, self-righteous melancholy and built an entirely new persona around the band based on this. They even began to lose connections with old friends, and Robert Smith said they grew more "insular."

In the midst of this misery, the Cure planned a special gift for their Dutch fans, who had been incredibly supportive of the band. In the midst of the tour, they schedule a ten-date run in the Netherlands they dubbed the Circus Tour. Each night, the Cure performed the singularly humorless show in a circus tent with a capacity of about 2,000. The logistics were nightmarish, and the band encountered various technical challenges nightly. For their Dutch fans, though, it was certainly a chance for a surreal if not entirely pleasant music experience.

The European tour finally and blessedly ended on July 5 at the Werchter Festival in Belgium. The band had a couple weeks off before starting North American dates on July 23 for the first of two nights at the Ritz in New York, after which they jetted to the West Coast for four nights in Los Angeles and San Francisco. After stops in Australia and Canada, the Cure headed to France, where their popularity was soaring, for a grueling string of nineteen additional shows kicking off on September 30 in Caen.

The Cure's extensive 1981 touring obligations finally wound to a close with the aptly titled *Eight Appearances* tour, for which the band took their stunted melancholy into classic and no doubt haunted old venues all over England, starting on November 25 at the Lyceum in Sheffield and ending at the Hammersmith Palais in London on December 3. The tour was finally over, and the pressure on Europe's supply of antidepressants suddenly eased.

Fourteen Explicit Moments Tour/*Pornography* Tour (1982)

In support of their 1982 album *Pornography*, the Cure started where they left off the prior year by playing unique historic venues as a prelude to the main tour, ending on May 1 at the Hammersmith Odeon. After their warm-up shows, the *Pornography* tour ran for twenty-nine shows throughout the Netherlands, Belgium, Germany, Switzerland, and France.

The tour was notable for tense feelings that mirrored the album being promoted. Simon Gallup's mood darkened as the tour progressed, Robert Smith found the circumstances unbearable, and Lol Tolhurst drank himself into oblivion while trying to keep the peace. The tour's unruly road crew created additional problems. The tension finally erupted after the May 27 show in Strasbourg, France. Smith and Gallup got into a fistfight at a bar, after which both jetted home to Britain to nurse their wounded psyches.

The next two French dates, in Epinal and Annecy, had to be canceled, and the rest of the tour teetered in the balance. With multiple shows still on the calendar and the specter of serious financial losses looming, the sullen pair returned. Robert's father, Alex, was key in getting his truculent son back on the road, reminding him that fans had paid for tickets and would be disappointed if they bailed.

Smith and Gallup made it back in time to salvage the May 30 show in Montreux, Switzerland, and then came a brutal stretch of nine more shows in which they endured each other's hostility onstage and offstage while playing an aggressively hellish collection of songs each night to increasingly listless and uninterested crowds.

THE CURE - U.K. group about 1986 with Robert Smith at left.

Pictorial Press Ltd / Alamy Stock Photo

The final night was June 11 at the Ancienne Belgique in Brussels, and it was high melodrama from start to finish. The songs were partially improvised and drenched in feedback, and the band members switched up their instruments haphazardly. Their only encore was a dismal improvisation, "The Cure Are Dead," sung by the roadie Gary Biddles. And indeed, for at least a while, they were.

1983 Tour (1983)

The Cure didn't really exist as a band anymore by 1983, but somehow, they were more popular than ever thanks to their smash pop single "The Walk." Asked to play the Elephant Fayre in Cornwall, Robert Smith—who had been moonlighting as guitarist for Siouxsie and the Banshees—decided it was time to get back to playing live dates with the Cure, so he cobbled together a new lineup. He was joined by *Pornography* producer Phil Thornalley on bass (replacing the departed Simon Gallup), Lol Tolhurst on keyboards, and new addition Andy Anderson on drums.

The first gig for this new-look Cure was on July 27 at the Midnight Express Club in Bournemouth. Another warm-up gig in Bath followed, and then came the Elephant Fayre, at which they focused on the darkest parts of their catalog rather than the newer pop songs. Smith said that given the band's new direction, which he expected to continue in the future, it might be the last time they could play such a dark set. The Cure then turned to the United States in New York City at the Ritz on August 4 and 5 before wrapping up with four dates in California.

Top Tour (1984)

With Smith's obligations to the Banshees complete, it was time to promote the next Cure album with a proper world tour. Porl Thompson's brief cameo on *The Top* led to his return to the band as touring guitarist, his first time back in the lineup since the Easy Cure days. Beginning on April 25 in Newcastle, the Cure played to capacity crowds in theaters and concert halls all over Britain, concluding at the Hammersmith Odeon in early May.

The Cure spent the rest of May touring mainland Europe, then took a break for most of the summer before hitting Australia and New Zealand for the first time in three years. Next came three shows in Japan, ending in Tokyo on October 17.

This was the final gig for Andy Anderson, who was fired in Tokyo because of erratic behavior. With North American shows looming in just five days, the Cure needed an emergency fill-in. Phil Thornalley knew Psychedelic Furs drummer Vince Ely from his work as engineer on their *Talk, Talk, Talk* album, and Ely jumped at the chance to play a fill-in role. After only two days of rehearsals, Ely took the stage on October 22 in Vancouver.

He was only a temporary fix, and his last show was on November 4 in Houston. Former Thompson Twins drummer Boris Williams joined in time for the November 7 show at First Avenue in Minneapolis and stayed on for the ten most successful years in the Cure's history.

1985 Tour/Head Tour (1985)

The ten European shows the Cure played prior to the August 26 release of their breakthrough album *The Head on the Door* were the first with their new lineup, which saw Robert Smith joined again by longtime bassist and collaborator Simon Gallup, who had departed after the *Pornography* tour. Porl Thompson did double duty on guitar and keyboards, and new addition Boris Williams rocked the drums. Laurence Tolhurst rounded out the lineup, playing as much keyboard as he was able.

The Cure began supporting the new album in earnest with the first date of the England leg of the Head Tour on September 8. With sales of *The Head on the Door* soaring, the sets featured new material more prominently. The opener was "The Baby Screams," with most nights going over twenty songs and three encores. They shifted to North America beginning on October 2 in Vancouver. The venues were smaller than in Europe, but it was their most extensive North American exposure yet. They wrapped up with a high-profile gig on November 1 at Radio City Music Hall.

1986 Tour/Beach Party Tour (1986)

With *The Head on the Door* already the Cure's biggest-selling album so far and a new lineup delivering the most dynamic shows of the band's career, the triumphant Cure took a break during early 1986 as Robert Smith readied what would prove to be a major breakthrough in the United States: the *Standing on a Beach* singles collection. The career-spanning set exposed some of the Cure's older classics to newer fans for the first time.

The first five gigs of the year started at the Royal Albert Hall on April 25, followed by several festival shows, including their historic first headlining slot at Glastonbury on June 21. They headed next to North American, where they sought to capitalize on the strong U.S. sales for their singles collection with the Beach Party Tour. They played seventeen shows from July 6 to July 27. An incident just prior to the final show on July 27 at the Los Angeles Forum put a dark cloud over the finale. A thirty-eight-year-old man who had been recently released from a mental hospital stabbed himself repeatedly with a hunting knife, evidently in an attempt to impress a female Cure fan. The man was taken by paramedics and released without life-threatening injuries.

The Cure resumed play on August 2 in San Sebastián, Spain, where they played "Why Can't I Be You?" for the first time. They played five high-profile shows, ending with their historic August 9 performance at Theatre Antique D'Orange, which was immortalized in the concert film *The Cure in Orange*, directed by Tim Pope.

20

There's Fever in the Funk House, Now: *Kiss Me, Kiss Me, Kiss Me*

The Cure's sprawling double album elevated them to dizzying new heights of success around the world.

Released: May 25, 1987
Fiction Records—FIXH 13 (U.K.), Elektra—9 60737-1 (US)
Running time: 74:35

1. "The Kiss" (6:17), 2. "Catch" (2:42), 3. "Torture" (4:13), 4. "If Only Tonight We Could Sleep" (4:50), 5. "Why Can't I Be You?" (3:11), 6. "How Beautiful You Are ..." (5:10), 7. "The Snakepit" (6:56), 8. "Hey You!!!" (2:22), 9. "Just Like Heaven" (3:30), 10. "All I Want" (5:18), 11. "Hot Hot Hot!!!" (3:32), 12. "One More Time" (4:29), 13. "Like Cockatoos" (3:38), 14. "Icing Sugar" (3:48), 15. "The Perfect Girl" (2:34), 16. "A Thousand Hours" (3:21), 17. "Shiver and Shake" (3:26), 18. "Fight" (4:27)

Anybody with a cursory knowledge of rock history will understand that double albums are tricky to pull off with any degree of success. Too often, they reek of self-indulgence or tedium or are so ambitious that there is simply too much information for the listener to reasonably absorb. Putting together enough strong material to span a single LP is challenging enough, and doubling that task makes it all the more onerous.

That said, if an artist rolls the dice and is able to pull it off, a double album can become an important career cornerstone. The best examples tend to be wildly diverse quiltworks of style that allow an artist to stretch and explore in ways that a standard single LP does not allow. Perhaps the greatest example of all is the Beatles' *White Album*, their undisciplined 1968 grab bag of styles that meandered in every direction imaginable. Every double album has detractors who claim it would be better as a more concise single release—after all, do we really need "Why Can't We Do It in the Road," "Wild Honey Pie," and Ringo's shambolic "Don't Pass Me By"?

Of course, we do. The idiosyncratic, offhand nature of some of the material is part of what makes the *White Album* so disarming and appealing in the first place. In many ways, it set the template for how a successful double album can work. Fleetwood Mac's *Tusk* works as a mashup between the graceful pop artistry of Christine McVie and Stevie Nicks with Lindsey Buckingham's crabbed and defiantly neurotic outbursts. The Clash lets loose on *London Calling*, an epic and harrowing barrage that would be impossible to achieve on a single disc.

Two of the greatest double albums in rock history emerged in 1987 within a couple months of each other. Prince unleashed perhaps the finest work of his career in March with *Sign o' the Times*, an album often cited as an example of Prince's musical genius. He had planned an even more ambitious three-album set, but even whittled down to two, it shows Prince's peerless capacity to shine at any genre or style that he chooses.

Two months later, on May 5, the Cure released *Kiss Me, Kiss Me, Kiss Me*, easily their grandest musical statement yet. It exhibits the band's dizzying versatility, adventurous songwriting, and innovative musical impulses. Robert Smith and his bandmates hit new highs in audacious self-confidence, showing no hesitation in exploring any sonic fancy that arose from their imaginations.

It's no accident that the album is all over the place musically. That's exactly the direction Robert Smith wanted to go, and unlike *The Head on the Door*, for which he was almost exclusively responsible for the songwriting, Robert actively sought his bandmates' input.

The Cure convened in March 1986 to play each other their latest demos and discuss ideas. In short order, they amassed a sizable batch of new material and retreated to the south of France to begin sessions for what was initially to be called *One Million Virgins*.

The freewheeling sessions were the band's first outside of a traditional studio, and they enjoyed it so much that this unconventional setup became their norm. They set up at Miraval in Correns, France, a residential studio where another famous double album was recorded: Pink Floyd's *The Wall*. On prior albums, the Cure kept people away from the studio as much as possible, but this time, it was a party vibe with people always around, including girlfriends, wives, and families. The relaxed and amiable but chaotic atmosphere recalls the Rolling Stones' infamous sessions for their similarly wide-ranging double album *Exile on Main Street*, also recorded in the south of France.

If the Cure could ever be said to have a perfect song, there's no doubt it would be "Why Can't I Be You?"
Author's Collection

An endless stream of musical ideas flowed along with the copious amounts of alcohol. For the first time, Robert Smith opened the door for his bandmates to comment and make suggestions about the songs he had written. Smith took parts he liked from song ideas by Simon Gallup, Boris Williams, and Porl Thompson, worked them up further, and played them back to the band for feedback. Never before had the Cure worked in such a collaborative fashion. The only member not meaningfully participating was Lol Tolhurst, whose uneven behavior and ever-increasing alcohol intake made it impossible for him to function. He became the frequent target for jokes and ridicule. Porl Thompson and others tried to get Lol into rehab, but he wasn't having it.

As the sessions progressed and the songs kept piling up, discussions about what should be on the album led to the realization that a single disc simply wouldn't do. No combination of songs seemed to make the right mix, and they

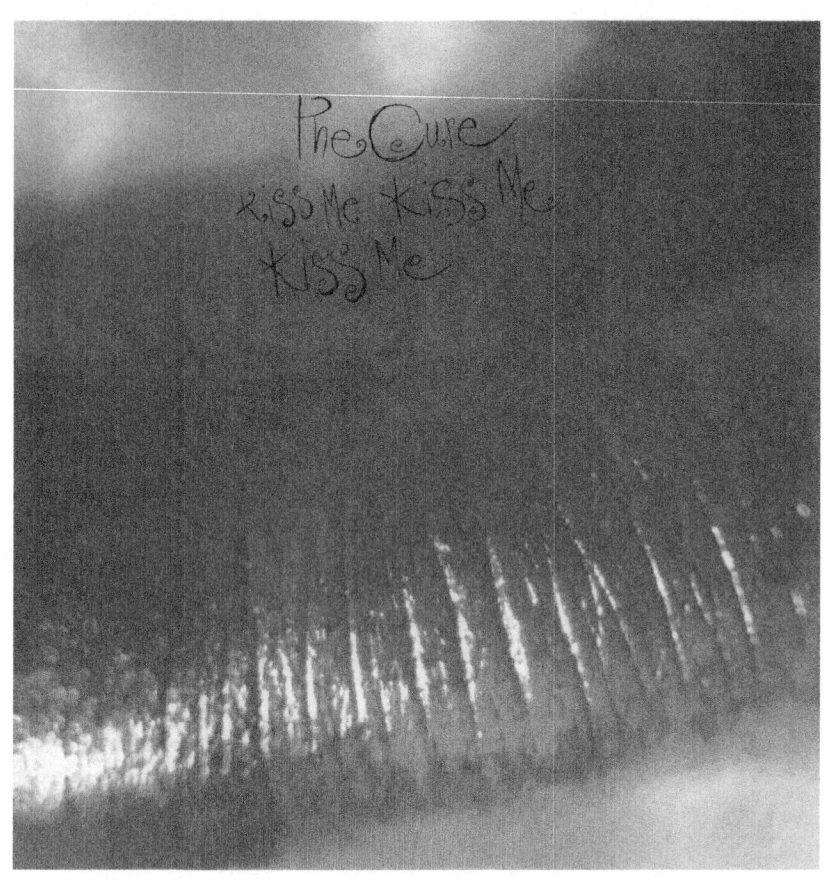

The Cure's landmark double album brought new levels of global success on the strength of truly classic singles (*Kiss Me, Kiss Me, Kiss Me*, 1987). *Author's Collection*

decided that, given the strength and diversity of the material, it would work well as a double album. They had generated so many strong demos that only half of them made it to completion and final release.

Robert was unable to finish the lyrics and vocals by the time the lease at Miraval had ended. After the band and their guests dispersed, he set off for Compass Point Studios in Nassau, Bahamas, with Chris Parry and Dave Allen to finish his vocals and mix the album. Robert immediately hated the outdated equipment there, so they headed to ICP Studios in Brussels to finish the album.

The final product, one of the great double albums in rock history, is worth all the effort that went into its creation. Bold and musically accomplished, it covers an amazing amount of stylistic territory while making it seem effortless. The Cure's U.S. record label, Elektra, and Chris Parry of Fiction were convinced they had a smash on their hands, so boatloads of money were poured into its promotion.

It worked. *Kiss Me* was a massive global success, yielding four major singles and fueling skyrocketing demand for tickets to the Cure's Kissing Tour. The Cure's popularity in the United States soared, as the album's crown jewel "Just Like Heaven" became the band's first top-forty hit. Critics praised the wide-ranging diversity, the strong musicianship, and the songwriting.

Kiss Me, Kiss Me, Kiss Me is the point at which the band's multiple personalities and differing impulses mesh into something timeless. The Cure instilled their deepest and most compelling songs yet with the fearlessness that has always been their driving force. Everything rings true—all the sonic colors take the songs where they are meant to go. More great albums would follow, but the Cure would never again burn with such white-hot fever as they did on *Kiss Me, Kiss Me, Kiss Me*.

Kiss Me, Kiss Me, Kiss Me

"The Kiss"

It doesn't sound like an opener for a huge hit album—"The Kiss" is the Cure's most imposing and monolith of angst since "One Hundred Years" on *Pornography*. String synthesizers from the Solina glide above snarled tangles of raging guitar like a cool layer of water over a cauldron of bubbling lava. Robert Smith's voice boils over with hate and fury, fully exposing those vile impulses that often writhe within the human psyche but are usually kept hidden.

"Catch"

This loopy but gentle acid-washed memory is a swift turn away from the roiling psychedelia of "The Kiss." "Catch" is a romantic dream, hazy and cloaked in bittersweet nostalgia. The lyrics were inspired by a recurring daytime hallucination that Robert Smith experienced at age ten when he suffered a concussion after falling off his bike. The image of a girl came to him sporadically, but the visions halted two years later after a plane ride through turbulence resulted in nausea, vomiting, and a terrible migraine. This seemed to "undo" whatever neurological happening caused the original visions. The song idea came when Robert met a girl in a New York airport who looked strikingly like the girl in his old visions.

An easygoing shuffle laced with accordion that gives it a distinctly European vibe, "Catch" was the album's second single everywhere but the United States, as Elektra Records deemed it too weird for American audiences and passed on it.

"Torture"

After a brief whimsical detour, the Cure dive back into frayed-edge anguish and hard rock intensity on "Torture," a potent counterpoint to the album's euphoric pop and solemn meditations.

"If Only Tonight We Could Sleep"

Based on a Porl Thompson demo, "If Only Tonight We Could Sleep" is an aural narcotic. The long instrumental introduction is exotic and beautiful, with a chiming sitar over a hypnotic rhythm. When Smith's voice finally emerges, it is plaintive and intense. The atmosphere is eerie, shrouded in shadows with sliding lines of guitar that feel like glowing beams of light shimmering through a dark red fog.

"Why Can't I Be You?"

The hyperkinetic first single "Why Can't I Be You?" packs a nuclear punch thanks to an ultra-tight groove, blistering rhythm guitar, and a horn riff so exuberant that it will ring through the listener's head for days. Robert Smith's deliciously bonkers lyrics and madcap vocal are so disarming that it's easy to lose sight of how artfully conceived and clever they are.

A pop rocket with more punch than any of the Cure's prior singles, "Why Can't I Be You?" earned significant airplay on U.S. radio, where it reached number fifty-four in spite of its wonderful weirdness. MTV embraced the playful zaniness of the video, setting the stage for even greater success to come.

Some of Robert Smith's finest vocals among the more popular tracks are on "Why Can't I Be You?," an absolute freak-out on which his manic voice zips up and down the gamut of his vocal range, with squeals and weird left turns and spins, and somehow it all works. It seems so haphazard and wild that it's easy to miss how carefully layered it is, superbly arranged with the multiple vocal parts combining for a mass effect of wild weirdness that no other singer could possibly get away with.

"How Beautiful You Are . . ."

Planned as the possible single, "How Beautiful You Are . . ." got as far as having a radio mix created by Bob Clearmountain before it was canceled. It's easy to understand why "How Beautiful You Are . . ." almost got the nod, as it's a strongly melodic up-tempo track that occupies the same bittersweet melancholy of "Just Like Heaven."

Inspired by a poem written by Charles Baudelaire in 1869 called "The Eyes of the Poor," the lyrics are a bleak and pointed parable about how even those we think we know the best often have facets of their personalities that can be shocking when revealed.

"The Snakepit"

"The Snakepit" revisits the rhythmic motif from "Wailing Wall" but with swollen scope and ambition. Smith's deadpan vocals are layered with an effect he'd revisit for "Plainsong" on *Disintegration*. "The Snakepit" is seven minutes of sustained unease and haunting atmospherics, with razor shards of guitar and keyboard coiling through a drum pattern dusted with sedatives, suggestive of snakes sliding through dark corridors. Like the equally hypnotic "Like Cockatoos," "The Snakepit" originated with a demo by Boris Williams and Porl Thompson.

"Hey You!!!"

The simmering tension of "The Snakepit" erupts into a boiling mass of raw energy that ends the album's first half. "Hey You!!!" is like aural smelling salts to pull the listener out of the dark reverie induced by its lengthy predecessor. Driven by a locomotive rhythm section and a frantic guitar riff, "Hey You!!!" is two minutes and twenty-three seconds of the Cure at their most manic, a tightly wound ball of restless energy.

"Just Like Heaven"

If ever the Cure created a slice of perfection, then it's "Just Like Heaven." Robert Smith has named it the finest pop song the Cure ever recorded, and he's right. The hard kick of an opening drum fill revs up a motoric rhythm and bass that provide the song's foundation. Every sound is perfectly placed. The soaring synthesizers, the ascending/descending guitar pattern, and the deft little piano countermelody are all intertwined in perfect symbiotic harmony.

Robert Smith delivers what might be the best vocal of his career. His wistful lyrics are romantic but laced with pathos. "Just Like Heaven" is exquisite, a prime example of how pop music can touch our souls and move us just as strongly as anything else in life.

"Just Like Heaven" became the first of three top-forty pop hits for the Cure in the United States. After spending two weeks at number forty-one, it got just enough of a nudge to hit number forty before falling back out of the mainstream, which is where the Cure happily resides.

"All I Want"

After the elegant beauty of "Just Like Heaven," Robert Smith descends to debasement with a hard rock expression of raw animal lust so overwhelming that it obliterates all thought. Built around torrid guitar riffs, "All I Want" pummels listeners with the sheer ferocity of its emotional and sexual urgency.

"Hot Hot Hot!!!"

A fiery, tight-as-nails groove propels "Hot Hot Hot!!!" into the funk-rock stratosphere, once again illustrating The Cure's peerless versatility. As with many Cure songs, the bass dominates, with a hard-edged and jittery guitar line punching through like barbed wire. Smith unleashes one of the most manic and daft vocals of his career, restlessly sliding and twisting up and down the scale.

There are many drug references in Smith's lyrics, although these allusions can sometimes by shadowy and veiled. Not so with "Hot Hot Hot!!!," a feverish and sweat-soaked vamp that vividly describes how it feels to slam a certain speedy substance into the veins. Robert Smith has, in a strange way, performed a valuable harm reduction service here. No need for curious dabblers to take a risk so insane as actually trying it. Crank "Hot Hot Hot!!!" to eleven and you'll understand very well what that lightning feels like.

"One More Time"

This gentle ballad opens with a long instrumental passage before Smith's gentle vocal rises over above the sweet interplay of keyboard and guitar. His intensity builds to an emotional apex, before fading back at the end into sublime calm and beauty.

"Like Cockatoos"

Here we get to the dark heart of *Kiss Me, Kiss Me, Kiss Me*, the darkly evocative "Like Cockatoos." An expression of heartrending separation and the desolate feeling of loss, "Like Cockatoos" exposes that painful moment of dissolution and the shattering of illusions like a sheared nerve dangling in the wind.

The lyrics, inspired by the short story "The Cockatoos" by Australian writer Patrick White, are some of the most poetic that Smith ever penned. His hazy vocal rises from the murk of a repetitive acoustic guitar pattern, speckled with ominous cries and sounds of night birds preying in the darkness. "Like Cockatoos" originated from a demo collaboration between Boris Williams and Porl Thompson.

"Icing Sugar"

Smith lets saxophonist Andrew Brennen go wild with a wickedly demented solo that adds gasoline to an already raging inferno. Simon Gallup wrote the basic demo for "Icing Sugar," and his bass is the throbbing heart at the center of the song. Boris Williams is a maniac on the drum kit, slamming with full force and restless abandon.

"Icing Sugar" is a needle pulsing out of the vein as the blood pumps through, a vision of defilement so gripping and urgent that there is no time for regret or reflection, only need. It courses through the body so strong and hot that you can feel it behind your eyes, you can taste it.

"The Perfect Girl"

This bouncy pop-rock nugget would have surely been a single for most bands, but *Kiss Me, Kiss Me, Kiss Me* has so many strongly commercial tracks that this one remains a deep cut. Based on a demo by Simon Gallup, "The Perfect Girl" is supremely catchy and endearing although perhaps a bit lightweight next to the album's five-star pop classics. Robert Smith allows his voice to warble and wander all over his register, adding some much-needed flavor and weirdness to what otherwise might have been a fairly pedestrian tune.

"A Thousand Hours"

Hidden away near the end of this long sonic trek is "A Thousand Hours," a relatively minor piece that's overshadowed by the bolder material surrounding it. A slow and solemn march, it's notable for the lovely interplay between a piano and a silvery line of string synthesizers. Robert Smith's full-throated vocal is rich with palpable longing, a howl in the darkness rooted in pure loneliness.

"Shiver and Shake"

Every once in a while, like on "Give Me It" from *The Top* and "The Scream" from *4:13 Dream*, the Cure exhibits manic paroxysms of loathing and disgust set to raging guitars, lunatic beats, and Robert Smith howling like a madman. "Shiver and Shake" is that moment on *Kiss Me* when everything goes haywire, a runaway train careening down a mountainside, awaiting the cataclysmic crash that surely awaits it when the wheels go off entirely.

If it sounds particularly convincing, there's a good reason: the song is a hate note to Lol Tolhurst, who by this time was making no musical contributions whatsoever. During Smith's legal battle with Tolhurst in 1994, the singer explained in a written statement to the court that he had written "Shiver and

Shake" about his former childhood friend and made him stand in front of him when he recorded the vocals so that he could sing it with more feeling.

"Fight"

The Cure is often accused of being merchants of gloom, and anyone with a cursory knowledge of their catalog will know this for truth. Of course, there is often hope hidden away in the despondency if you dig deep enough to find it. The Cure is just as capable of writing uplifting pop songs or songs meant to inspire, like the jagged rocker "Fight," the album's finale. It's based on an early demo by Porl Thompson and Boris Williams.

"Fight" is pure instinct, an expression by Robert Smith of never giving in, of grasping life until the very last flicker of flame winks out. There's a particular urgency to "Fight" that almost feels like desperation. Smith gives it his all, pulling from deep within to deliver a hair-raising vocal.

"Fight" ends the album on a note of defiance and confrontation but also of self-empowerment. Stand up to yourself and don't let the sickness world around us defeat you. Fight dirty if you have to, but most important, just fight.

B-Sides

"A Japanese Dream"

Probably the most prominent of the strong crop of B-sides to emerge from the *Kiss Me, Kiss Me, Kiss Me* singles is "A Japanese Dream," which debuted on the flip side of the "Why Can't I Be You?" single. "A Japanese Dream" is a jagged rocker with swirls of electric guitar and a vaguely Eastern-sounding keyboard riff that follow the rise and fall of Simon Gallup's bass. Boris Williams shows once again why he was such an important addition to the Cure given this song's complex and frenetic rhythm.

Robert Smith has said that it was strongly considered for inclusion, and unlike most Cure B-sides, "A Japanese Dream" was performed live as part of the band's regular set in support of the album from which it was left off.

"Snow in Summer"

It's hard to envision "Snow in Summer" as a serious contender for inclusion on the album, although it's not without appeal. With a stuttery rhythm that seems to fall in on itself and a genuinely sweet vocal by Smith, there is a lovely warmth to the track, but ultimately it comes and goes without making much of an impact. Robert Smith dismissed the track as "slightly awkward" in the liner note for the *Join the Dots* B-sides collection.

"Sugar Girl"

Perhaps the slightest track released during the *Kiss Me* era, "Sugar Girl" is charming all the same, built around a jaunty line of keyboard and touched with a bit of the same hazy dreaminess that makes "Catch" such a delight.

"Breathe"

"Breathe" shines with beauty, built on a wash of sweeping, layered keyboards, each following its own melody. Smith's subtle vocal, awash in echo, is deep in the mix and sparse, floating amongst the keyboard like a yearning plea to someone no longer there to listen.

"A Chain of Flowers"

This "Just Like Heaven" B-side is majestic and haunting, a throwback to the era of *Faith* but fully within the realm of the *Kiss Me* sound. Smith's furtive vocal is especially poignant, and the interplay between guitar and piano is beautifully conceived. The lyrics are reminiscent of a distant memory or perhaps a dream that takes place in the gray ghostly netherworld surrounding the church on the cover of *Faith*.

"To the Sky"

Recorded early on in the *Kiss Me* sessions, "To the Sky" is a graceful and stately guitar piece that Robert Smith never quite liked, insisting that the band could never get it to feel the way it was intended. It wasn't even deemed good enough for release as a B-side, and thus "To the Sky" remained unheard until Smith allowed Chris Parry to include it on the *Stranger Than Fiction* sampler in 1989.

Stranger Than Fiction is a six-song compilation of old nuggets from the early days of Fiction to newer material. It includes Cult Hero's "I Dig You," which was mostly the Cure, recording with Simon Gallup for the first time with vocals by postman Frankie Bell. Another Cure-associated track is "I Want to Be a Tree" by the band's longtime video director Tim Pope, recorded with the band during the 1984 sessions for *The Top*. The Associates track is an old demo from 1979, and songs by Eat and Die Warzau were intended to showcase Fiction's two newest signings. The sampler quickly became a collector's item.

Kiss Me, Kiss Me, Kiss Me may have some moments of sadness, but the album as a whole is too raw, with too many nerve endings frayed, to give in to solitary depression and suicidal oblivion. There is fire being wrought here, built from numerous sources: the despondency that permeates *Faith*, the stark hopelessness of *Seventeen Seconds*, the grisly rage of *Pornography*, the innate pop sensibilities of "The Walk" and "The Lovecats," the feverish experimentation of *The Top*, and the full complement of the band finally coming together on *The Head in the Door*.

Kiss Me, Kiss Me, Kiss Me is the culmination of everything that came before, the ultimate expression of the Cure in full bloom, exhilarating and exhausting and frustrating and brilliant and spine-tinglingly beautiful and ugly all at once. The album skips from loopy pop to thunderous intensity, a reflection of life itself, the real world around us that we struggle to traverse day by day. The fact that the album ends on an exhortation to fight as hard as possible reminds us that though life is never easy, moments of beauty remembered are just flame enough to spark that fight instead of a surrender.

21

What You Had and What You Lost: *Disintegration*

The Cure's greatest studio achievement explores the jumbled emotions of staggering personal loss.

Released: May 2, 1989
Running time: 71:47

1. "Plainsong" (5:12), 2. "Pictures of You" (7:24), 3. "Closedown" (4:16), 4. "Lovesong" (3:29), 5. "Last Dance" (4:42), 6. "Lullaby" (4:08), 7. "Fascination Street" (5:16), 8. "Prayers for Rain" (6:05), 9. "The Same Deep Water as You" (9:19), 10. "Disintegration" (8:18), 11. "Homesick" (7:06), 12. "Untitled" (6:30)

The Cure has released thirteen studio albums of varying quality over the span of their forty-year career. All of them are worth picking up, most of them are outstanding, and several—*Faith*, *Seventeen Seconds*, *Pornography*, *The Head on the Door*, and *Kiss Me, Kiss Me, Kiss Me*—are alternative rock classics.

As good as these are, one album towers above them all: the darkly majestic *Disintegration*. It's often called the Cure's masterpiece, and while that word gets thrown around a lot in rock music, in this case, it's not hyperbole. *Disintegration* is epic in scope yet intimate enough to be deeply meaningful at a personal level.

Music means different things to each listener, and there is no right answer. For some, music is just another form of entertainment, like a sitcom or the latest Xbox game. It's a beat to dance to at the club or a chorus to sing along with in the car on a road trip. For others, rock music has the power to grab them by the soul with a personal connection that can be intense and very real. When an album has that kind of impact on significant numbers of people, it can become a cultural landmark.

This unique Spanish 7" promo with "Disintegration" backed with "Plansong" is one of the rarer items in the Cure's catalog. *Jose Ramon Garcia Alvarez*

Disintegration is one of those albums. Released on May 2, 1989, its lush sonic textures and emotionally compelling songcraft swept into listeners' minds like a flood and swirled around for months as enthralled fans listened to the album over and over again. *Disintegration* is music for darkness. It should be played late at night in solitude, lying back, relaxing, and listening start to finish.

Unlike with *Kiss Me*, commercial expectations for *Disintegration* were fairly low in America. One executive with the band's U.S. label, Elektra Records, went so far as to call the album "commercial suicide." They couldn't have been more wrong. Shattering expectations, it punched through to number twelve in the United States and number three in the United Kingdom and rocketed into the top ten around most of the world. Even though *Wish* charted higher on release in 1992, *Disintegration* remains the Cure's highest-selling album globally. It yielded four major singles, including the Cure's career-best pop chart placements in both the United States and the United Kingdom with "Lovesong" and "Lullaby," respectively.

Disintegration touched countless listeners as profoundly as is possible for rock music. The lush sonic textures are deep enough to lose yourself. Everyone hears it differently. For some, it's nothing but sullen mope rock with a couple good singles; others regard it with sacred reverence. Esteem for it has grown in recent years, in tandem with respect for Robert Smith and The Cure generally. A compendium of "best rock album" surveys compiled from various publications by *Newsweek* in September, 2020 ranked *Disintegration* at #34, ever. That's heady stuff.

The Cure's prior album, 1987's *Kiss Me, Kiss Me, Kiss Me*, showcased the band's versatility thanks in part to Robert Smith's insistence that his bandmates bring ideas to the sessions. Smith still considered the rest of the band's contributions for *Disintegration*, but he focused on those that best fit the cohesive sound he hoped to present.

Smith had been preoccupied with the fact that his next birthday would be his thirtieth. He viewed the day, still months into the future, with simmering dread. Thoughts of mortality gnawed at him, but he also felt the quickly spinning hands of his artistic time clock moving faster and faster. Smith pondered all the artists who'd recorded their best work in their twenties and wondered if he'd allowed his prime creative years to slip through his fingers without producing anything truly meaningful.

Despite its breakthrough success or perhaps because of it, Robert Smith dismissed *Kiss Me, Kiss Me, Kiss Me* as a "party album" and rebelled against expectations that the Cure would once again serve up tasty pop confections like "Why Can't I Be You?" and "Just Like Heaven." Smith had become leery of impending fame, and if he wasn't already there, he was certainly on the cusp. The Cure was on the edge of mass success that most bands would give anything to accomplish but that Robert Smith had come to dread.

Smith wanted a return to the discipline of creating a thematically cohesive sound akin to what the band did during their dark trilogy of *Seventeen Seconds*, *Faith*, and *Pornography*. He also wanted listeners to perceive how much care and effort went into the album's creation. Robert Smith was well aware how much the Cure's music meant to countless individuals, and he wanted these people to know that he took it seriously even if he didn't always take himself too seriously. He was also keen to test the seriousness and musical acumen of those fans the Cure had picked up in recent years with their pop hits. Could they follow the Cure back into darker territory?

Smith prepared his demos in isolation at his home in London. Many of the instrumental pieces he developed were long and dramatic, in part reflecting his increasing interest in film music. As the Cure's popularity soared, filmmakers contacted Smith requesting that he create music for their projects, and although

Smith had no choice but to decline because of the time commitments involved, he was intrigued by the idea of pursuing more expansive and cinematic pieces.

After the completion of the demos, as Smith prepared to present them to his bandmates, he thought the tracks might be unsuitable for a Cure album and might instead become his first solo release. That mind-set changed when the Cure assembled for two weeks at the home of drummer Boris Williams in June 1988 to record demos. Smith played his recordings for the band, and they were so enthusiastic that the idea of using them for a solo album melted away.

The band's stay at Williams's home was a great move. The Cure enjoyed the sun-soaked country weather in the wilds of Devon, and the good vibe seemed to lend itself to productivity. They rehearsed and recorded with a basic setup, playing live in an unused room into two microphones connected to a simple four-track recorder. The Cure cranked out more than thirty demos to work with for the upcoming album, including the songs Smith brought with him, new material Smith penned since arriving, and more than a dozen other tracks.

The Cure took a break from working on new music for a rather special day. After a fifteen-year romance that began at St. Wilfrid's Comprehensive School in Crawley, Mary Poole and Robert Smith married on August 13, 1988, at Worth Abbey in West Sussex. Simon Gallup stood as best man. At the very same church nearly twelve years earlier, on December 16, 1976, a young group of musicians called Malice, with Robert Smith on guitar, performed at a holiday party held by his father's company. The party lasted all night, with Smith playing deejay, in control of the music as he always likes to be.

In September, the Cure reassembled at Boris Williams's home to nail down the best of the demos and work up the strongest material in preparation for studio sessions. With the songs now taking shape, Robert Smith took a couple weeks to work on lyrics before the band gathered in October 1988 at Outside Studios in Hook End Manor to record. The large rural manor house located in Oxfordshire was owned for many years by David Gilmour of Pink Floyd.

Robert Smith has said that the *Disintegration* sessions were far more intense than the laid-back and amiable demo sessions held over the summer. He recalls being deeply depressed and had been drinking a lot and using hallucinogenic drugs. One night, a fire broke out in Robert's room at the manor house, and he barely managed to save a satchel containing all of the album's lyrics. As a result, he had to move to a room in a different part of the manor, further isolating him from the rest of the band. The sessions stretched through the winter, and eventually, Smith wrapped up the overdubs and mixing with help from Dave Allen at RAK Studios in London.

By this time, the Lol Tolhurst show had reached peak inanity. He was constantly drunk, unable to contribute anything, and was the subject of nonstop ridicule and cruelty at the hands of his bandmates. He spent most of his time during the sessions drinking and watching MTV. Robert Smith insists that while

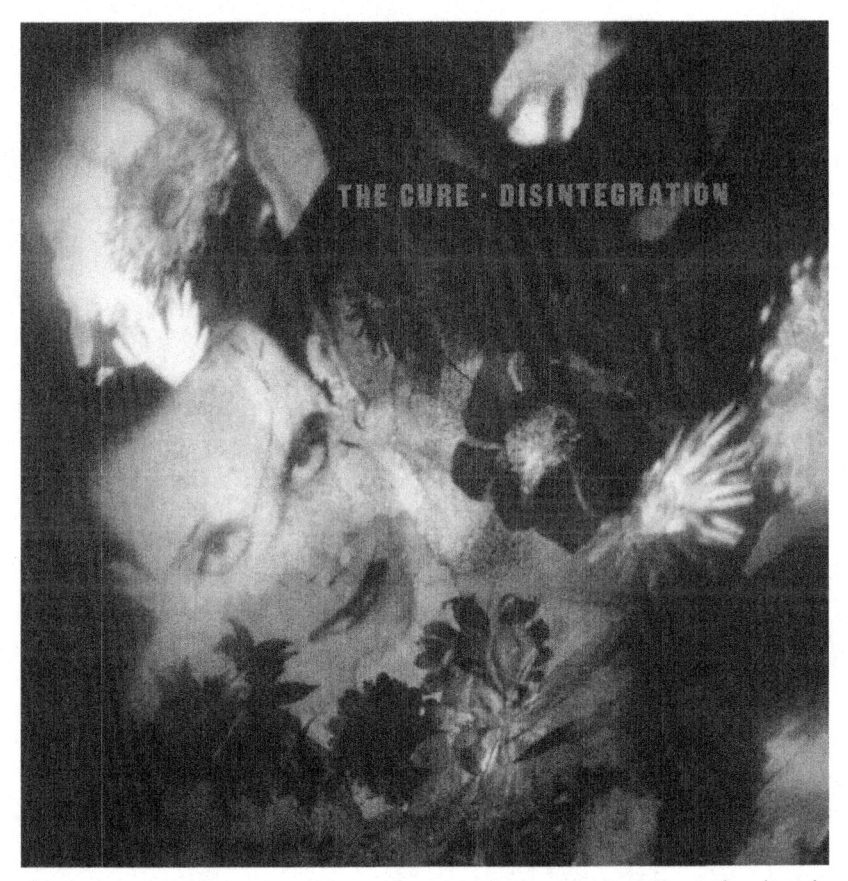

The Cure's greatest album, a towering masterpiece, *Disintegration* (1989) is a cultural touchstone with very few peers. *Author's Collection*

was physically in the building, he never actually stepped foot in the recording studio at all during the album's sessions. Both Porl Thompson and Simon Gallup urged Robert to fire Tolhurst once and for all, both threatening that they would boycott the Cure's tour in support of the new album if Lol were invited along.

During the final week of December 1988, when the Cure gathered at RAK to hear the final mix of the album, Tolhurst finally crossed the point of no return. While the band sat listening quietly to an album that Robert Smith had poured everything he had into, Tolhurst made a loud and drunken spectacle of himself, roaring that the album was crap. A few weeks later, he received a handwritten letter from Robert Smith, his friend since both were five years of age, that he was no longer in the band that the former drummer had cofounded.

As painful as the Tolhurst situation undoubtedly was, *Disintegration* was everything Robert Smith had hoped it would be. The last three albums had been all over the place stylistically, especially the madly diverse *Kiss Me, Kiss Me, Kiss Me*, but *Disintegration* was a cohesive piece of melancholy at its grandest scale. Emotional and poignant, it has remarkable depth, but there are still plenty of great hooks. *Disintegration* received excellent reviews on release and has since been widely recognized as one of the essential alternative rock albums of the 1980s.

"Plainsong"

Disintegration begins with the quintessential Cure concert opener: "Plainsong." Twenty seconds of sparkling chimes, as faint as distant stars, are swallowed by an ocean of synthesizers. The sound is enormous and moving, a sweeping drift of melody that's stately and riven with sadness. A line of guitar emerges after ninety seconds, gliding with the waves along the surface, descending for only a minute or so for Robert Smith's heartrending vocal, a recitation of a remembered conversation, a painful memory of someone slipping through the grasp of his fingers, and there's nothing he can do to stop her from sliding away.

A plainsong is a Catholic liturgy, such as a Gregorian chant. Robert Smith was raised in a Catholic household, although he long ago professed his atheism. His version of a plainsong is not about a connection between an individual and an eternal deity but rather about the eternal human capacity for love that survives even sorrow and loss.

"Pictures of You"

No other song gets to the heart of what the Cure is all about as completely as "Pictures of You." Rarely has bittersweet melancholy been expressed with such transcendent beauty. "Picture of You" is human emotion in musical form. Robert Smith's vocal is rich with genuine yearning and regret. Tangible loss seeps through every note, vulnerable and dignified.

Interestingly, Robert Smith once compared "Pictures of You" to "How Beautiful You Are...," which contemplates how we cling desperately to an image or perception of a person that would be painful to finally let go. It's an aspect of "Pictures of You" not often discussed, but it's fascinating to think that the woman in the photos is not a real representation of who she was but rather his own idealized version of her. The truth is often difficult to face, especially if it means the change of something that will never be regained. Once a mental picture of a person changes, it's never going to be the same.

Smith showcases his Bass VI as part of the interplay between multiple melodic guitar parts. Leisurely paced at seven and a half minutes, "Pictures of

the cure pictures of you

The album's fourth single, "Pictures of You" was edited down from nearly 8 minutes to a more manageable length, but the song was still largely ignored by mainstream radio in the United States. *Author's Collection*

You" is given time to fully develop into an epic hymn of regret. It builds tension like tightly strung guitar strings wrapped around a heart multiple times, tighter and tighter, biting into the flesh deeper with each pass.

The exalted place in the Cure's catalog held by "Pictures of You" was emphasized yet again on March 29, 2019, as the Cure was inducted into the Rock and Roll Hall of Fame. It was the song played after Trent Reznor finished his stirring speech and members of the Cure past and present shambled up the steps from the audience and onto the stage.

On April 1, 2019, Robert Smith announced that he and keyboardist Roger O'Donnell had collaborated with the string ensemble Quartet Voluté to record a stark and haunting new version of "Pictures of You" for the documentary *Dead Good* about a group of women in the United Kingdom working to change how people reflect the lives of loved ones during the ritual funeral process.

"Closedown"

A long introduction with a tribal rhythm somewhat reminiscent of "The Hanging Garden," "Closedown" is built on waves of string synthesizers, a simple guitar pattern, and a deep bass pulsing along with the rhythm. It's instrumental for the first two minutes, and when the vocals finally begin, they are a desperate plea for the capacity to feel love.

There's a heartbreaking majesty to "Closedown," a beauty that ends unexpectedly on a discordant swell of synthesizers, sparking dread and the emotional shutdown the song portrays.

"Lovesong"

It seems strange to imagine the Cure in the top ten on the U.S. pop singles chart, let alone threatening to hit number one, but that's exactly that happened with the second single from *Disintegration*: "Lovesong." Starting at number fifty-eight, it hit number two in its eleventh week on the *Billboard* Hot 100 after a rapid ascent: 58, 46, 36, 31, 27, 22, 16, 10, 7, 4, 2.

Although it couldn't break the four-week reign at the top by Janet Jackson's "Miss You Much," it's still a remarkable achievement for a band whose only prior top-forty hit in the United States, "Just Like Heaven," barely made the cut and stalled after a peak at forty. In March 2019, "Lovesong" was one of the five selections the Cure chose to perform at their Rock and Roll Hall of Fame induction ceremony.

"Lovesong" originated as an instrumental demo by bassist Simon Gallup. Robert Smith wrote the lyrics as a gift to his wife Mary when they wedded in August 1988. The words are romantic, yet Smith sounds dejected and melancholy. His wistful allusions to feeling "fun again" and "young again" hint of memories from happier times.

Opening with a bright slash of guitar, "Lovesong" is driven by Boris Williams's simple but insistent rhythm. Countermelodies on keyboard, bass, and guitar groove alongside and around each other, like pieces of a musical jigsaw puzzle. The line of keyboard that is the track's sonic signature is an organ sample fed through an E-mu Emulator II Vox, which was then played through a studio amp to add subtle distortion. It sounds like it's on the cusp of overload, giving it a vaguely 1960s rock vibe. Simon Gallup's florid but disciplined bass follows the melody of the keyboard with added flourishes.

"Lovesong" falls somewhere in between the Cure's mad lurches from fizzy pop to melodramatic rock. The lyrics and the tone are at odds, leaving what many see as one of their more straightforward songs open to interpretation. Part of the Cure's appeal is their mystery. Just when you think you have them pinned down, they slither away.

The Cure's biggest commercial hit in the United States, "Lovesong" reached #2 and was kept out of the top by Janet Jackson's "Miss You Much." *Author's Collection*

"Last Dance"

Savage guitars roil over a jagged rhythm on "Last Dance," easily the most venom-soaked track on the album. Robert Smith's vocal is thick with obvious loathing, although whether it's directed internally or to the person pointed at in the lyrics is unclear. Smith has said that "Last Dance" is about seeing someone after a very long time and realizing that the strong feelings once held have disappeared somewhere along the way.

"Lullaby"

Robert Smith wrote the music to "Lullaby," the first single from *Disintegration* in the United Kingdom and most of the world, during the band's summer rehearsals. It's a deliciously creepy fable inspired by Robert's memories of somewhat disturbing and traumatic bedtime stories told to him as a child by an uncle.

Several different melodic hooks on guitar and keyboard play off each other like slick magnetized coils that repel each other in a constant swirl that becomes a dance. Smith lays the ghoulishness on thick with a whispery vocal so extravagantly macabre that it should be ridiculous, but he has the dramatic presence to pull it off perfectly. Singing is a form of acting, in some songs more than others, and on "Lullaby," Robert Smith displays his preternatural ability to paint his words with just the right shading and nuance to make something that should sound hokey and contrived into a beautifully genuine rendering of a story-time nightmare.

"Lullaby" was a huge success in the United Kingdom, hitting number five, a career-high chart peak for the Cure that they've never surpassed. The spooky video by director Tim Pope won the Brit Award for Video of the Year. In the United States, as the album's third single, "Lullaby" wasn't able to cross over to the mainstream and couldn't build on the momentum created by "Lovesong," as it limped to a peak of number seventy-one.

"Fascination Street"

An ingenious arrangement, "Fascination Street" rests on Simon Gallup's elastic bass and Boris Williams's deft syncopated rhythm. Differing parts of guitar and keyboard come into the song one at a time, complementing and building on each other. Smith's desperate vocal and cunning wordplay add a sense of unease and mystery.

The simmering tension builds as the song progresses, and finally, all the overlapping parts combine into a breathtaking cacophony. "Fascination Street" is the Cure at their best, and Elektra Records chose it over "Lullaby" as the album's lead single. It proved a shrewd choice. MTV jumped on the video, and alternative radio loved it. "Fascination Street" spent seven weeks at number one on the modern rock chart, and despite its absolutely noncommercial nature, it almost hit the top forty on the pop chart, stopping shy at number forty-six.

"Prayers for Rain"

With dense guitars and a cascading rhythm, "Prayers for Rain" is high drama. There are two main instrumental hooks that follow in succession, one a pulsing bank of string synthesizers, the other a simple guitar pattern. Robert delves into his deepest levels of agony and spits out the pain-infused lyrics with primal force. Never once does Robert Smith sound phony on *Disintegration*. Never once does he seem to be going through the motions. He lives every moment of this album.

"The Same Deep Water as You"

The first of two titans that form the climax of *Disintegration*, "The Same Deep Water as You" is a slow-developing, mesmerizing piece with a stunning vocal by Smith. The sound of the rain and wind fall relentlessly in the background, and the musical arrangement is calm, simply precise and elegant. The power builds as the song slowly unfolds, Smith's vocal becoming more urgent with each verse. "The Same Deep Water as You" burns with a quiet but breathtaking intensity, a potent counterpoint to the raucous release of emotion that follows it.

"Disintegration"

For an album this compelling and vast in scope, the title track must be a knockout. "Disintegration" is a smoldering rocker, like a boulder rolling downhill, crashing everything in its path into shards of nothing, getting faster and hitting with more force as it goes.

At eight minutes and twenty seconds, Robert Smith has plenty of time to detail in searing verse the complete unraveling of a relationship. He spits the lyrics with toxicity, sparing no word of tenderness and making excuses in a wordy diatribe that he clearly poured his soul into to be able to articulate the genuine passion in the song. A powerhouse of even higher stature when played live, "Disintegration" is often the final track of the Cure's main set, prior to the encores. Despite its length, "Disintegration" was issued as a single in Spain only, backed with "Plainsong."

"Homesick"

With a long introduction of piano and guitar delicately playing off each other, "Homesick" is a languid meditation on conflicted loyalties and uncertainty sung by Robert Smith in his lower register. It came about when Simon Gallup and Roger O'Donnell came back to the studio after a long dinner and lots of wine. They improvised the beginning section on piano and bass, and the song was born.

"Untitled"

Like "Fight" on *Kiss Me*, the Cure ends *Disintegration* on a hopeful note with "Untitled." It's like the first hint of dawn after a long, tortuous night. Set to a background of accordion and bright guitar patterns, "Untitled" is a leisurely shuffle that tries to inject hope into a constant barrage of bleakness.

B-Sides

"Babble"

The Cure issued four previously unreleased studio recordings as B-sides to the *Disintegration* singles, and while all of them are top-notch, it's clear why none made the album. They simply don't fit the vibe. "Babble" is a surreal, sound effect–laden rocker soaring with keyboards that provide the main melodic hook. Thematically, it seems well suited to have been on *Kiss Me*, although it has hints of the madness of *Pornography* as well.

After a long instrumental opening, Robert Smith delivers a blistering vocal before it descends once again into madness.

"2 Late"

The Cure's B-sides should never be considered "lesser" material just because they didn't fit onto the album for which it was recorded. The jaunty guitar pop of "2 Late" would have been an outlier on *Disintegration*, but had it been a single, there is no question that it would have been a hit.

Robert Smith has expressed his fondness for "2 Late," calling it one of his favorite B-sides. Smith also thought that "2 Late" was certain to be a single but that it never really fit in with the album. The Cure never played the song in concert until that epic forty-five-song show at the Royal Albert Hall on March 28, 2014, for the Teenage Cancer Trust benefit show.

"Fear of Ghosts"

This long, psychedelic drone originated with a demo from keyboardist Roger O'Donnell. At nearly seven minutes, "Fear of Ghosts" is far more substantial then the B-sides offered by most bands. Robert Smith's whispery vocals, miked closely and then pushed high in the mix, bring an air of dread and suspense. "Fear of Ghosts" would have been a perfect addition to the sound track of some creepy supernatural thriller.

"Out of Mind"

One of the Cure's more straightforward rockers is "Out of Mind," which was based on a demo by Roger O'Donnell and then radically reworked. "Out of Mind" is more immediate and urgent than much of the album material and doesn't fit stylistically, but it might have made a great single as an extra track on a hits collection or as a soundtrack single.

The first single in the U.K. and the rest of the world was passed over in the United States, where the edgy psyschedelic rocker "Fascination Street" got the nod instead. *Author's Collection*

"Delirious Night"

When the three-CD deluxe reissue of *Disintegration* hit stores in 2010, it was obviously loaded with a lot of extras. Demos for every album track and B-side are fascinating to hear for die-hard fans interested in how these epics songs developed; however, more casual fans are likely to skip over them. More interesting are the demos for songs never before released, especially the swirling psychedelic "Delirious Night," which is polished enough to be a final version.

Based on a demo by Porl Thompson, "Delirious Night" is a trippy and exotic drone with rhythmic acoustic guitar colored by swirls of layered synthesizers and bleary, unintelligible vocals by Robert Smith that blur in and out of the mix. The end result is like an aural acid trip shimmering through the darkness. It's a shame that a track this fascinating and well conceived was wasted for so many years sitting on a shelf. Fortunately, it's now available, but only the most devoted of fans willing to wade through the deluxe edition bonus material are ever likely to hear it.

Disintegration is one of those essential albums that music fans, even if they aren't particularly into the Cure, are likely to seek out simply because it's so widely revered and famous. It's a landmark album, like Radiohead's *OK Computer*, U2's *The Joshua Tree*, or the Talking Heads' *Remain in Light*.

As *Disintegration* reached the thirty-year milestone in 2019, it was a year of celebration and rediscovery of the classic album. The Cure performed *Disintegration* in its entirety during four exclusive performances in May for the Vivid Live festival in Sydney. They headlined the same festival in 2011 for *Reflections*, in which they played their first three albums in sequence.

After the runaway success of the stylistically diverse *Kiss Me*, Robert Smith wanted to see if the Cure could make an album of substance, expressing genuine human emotion with depth and seriousness. No doubt, the Cure accomplished what they set out to do. *Disintegration* works because the emotion is real and comes through despite a painstaking recording process marked by careful attention to every detail. The songs are engaging and disarmingly creative, memorably but not overtly commercial. Each track is distinct, yet all fit within a sonic atmosphere that is entirely cohesive.

In the liner notes, in all caps, listeners are notified, "This music has been mixed to be played loud so turn it up." Excellent advice.

22

Playing That Organ Must Count for Something: Laurence Tolhurst

The Cure's cofounder spiraled out of control and out of the band, but the passage of time and *Reflections* brought two imaginary boys back together on stage.

Laurence "Lol" Tolhurst cofounded the Cure with Robert Smith and Michael Dempsey, and he was the band's original drummer. Both his admirers and his detractors would agree (albeit for different reasons) that he filled the drummer's role in a way nobody else could have done. Lol was a stoic rhythm machine behind the kit, and his simple but precise beats are an integral part of the distinct sound of the Cure's first four albums. Of course, Lol was also at the center of the worst period of turmoil and public acrimony in the Cure's long history.

It's ludicrous to imagine the sparse rhythms of *Seventeen Seconds* originating from Boris Williams or Jason Cooper. The simple repetitive beats lulling listeners into a trance on *Faith* require an intuitive feel for the music, not technical wizardry. The album would have lost much of its stately grace with someone other than Lol Tolhurst overcomplicating it.

Pornography wouldn't have the same frightening martial aspect, its stark rhythms like soldiers of Hell marching in formation to battle amidst the flames. Tolhurst's thunderous cacophony, disciplined and powerful, is the sound of the harrowed surface as it's clawed and ripped by all the other sonic elements battling each other in the album's pernicious maelstrom of sound.

Many drummers and music fans would raise an eyebrow or two, if not laugh outright, at the assertion that Lol Tolhurst was a great drummer. If they do, they are missing the second part of the equation: he was great for the Cure, at the time. The parts of the band were what they needed to be, assembled as required, at that particular time and place, for the Cure to emerge from Crawley and achieve international success. Nobody will ever mistake Lol Tolhurst for Neil Peart or Stewart Copeland. Yet Lol Tolhurst could deliver *Seventeen Seconds*, *Faith*, and *Pornography*, while Peart or Copeland could not have done so. Sure they could have played his parts, but they would not have generated them. These classics would not have been possible and would sound inescapably different.

Without Lol Tolhurst, Robert Smith might now be a retired schoolteacher or perhaps a local business owner in Crawley instead of a rock icon. Those rhythms built into Lol Tolhurst and no one else were completely essential to the Cure's sound.

Over the course of multiple lineup shifts, members of the Cure have ranged in level from amateur to elite musicianship. Robert Smith, Porl Thompson, Reeves Gabrels, Roger O'Donnell, and perhaps Boris Williams are in that top tier. Tolhurst, Mathieu Hartley, and Perry Bamonte, when he was on keyboard, are in the bottom group. The others are all somewhere in between on a continuously changing spectrum. The Cure has never been about how many notes a guitarist could play in a minute. No matter how technically gifted, if someone doesn't fit easily into the Cure's vibe and understand the feel and meaning of the music, they won't be around long.

Yes, Lol had limitations, and the Cure was able to expand their sonic possibilities immensely once Robert Smith yanked him from behind the drum kit. But without Lol Tolhurst, there would be no Cure. And although he tried to put on a good show of competence when playing keyboard, Lol does generally admit to his shortcomings, if not to their full scope. In his 2016 memoir *Cured: The Tale of Two Imaginary Boys*, Tolhurst makes perhaps the understatement of the decade: "Although I have always felt like a creative musician, I will be the first to tell you that I am not a virtuoso drummer or keyboardist."

Lol first started exploring music in a quasi-serious way by the summer of 1970 when he began borrowing as many LPs from the local library as was permitted. He soon began snagging bargain-bin vinyl at a shop his hometown of Horley, citing *It Crawled into My Hand, Honest* by the Fugs as his first purchase. The angst-ridden music appealed to the young Tolhurst, and this led him to grab whatever American rock import he could get his hands on.

At Notre Dame Middle School in Crawley, Tolhurst spent much of his free time with fellow music junkies Robert Smith and Michael Dempsey. They would hang out in the library talking music, or they would listen to records in the band room. They were soon immersed in their earliest attempts to make music together.

As a thirteen-year-old in 1972, Lol spent hours playing records in his bedroom, which he'd transformed with colorful paint and a red lightbulb. He'd gaze at the covers and imagine them as little windows into an unknowable world of wonder far away from the dreary confines of West Sussex, England. Robert Smith's older brother Richard (dubbed "The Guru") helped both Robert and Lol build their knowledge and love for rock through his music collection. Lol liked hanging out at Robert's house for this music but also partially as a refuge away from his father.

Lol earned money for new music by delivering newspapers on his bike. By the summer of 1972, his record collection had outgrown his brother Roger's, who asked him to deejay a party being thrown for their brother John. It was at this party that Lol had his first experience with alcohol, the malignant spirit that would torment him for many years.

He started drinking wine, loving the feeling it caused, the warm glow of friendship and of feeling fine. Of course, those good feelings evaporated rather quickly when he was bent over the toilet puking his guts out. It was the first time but wouldn't be the last. He blacked out, again the first of many such occurrences. Lol was just getting acquainted with his demons. He would come to know them much more intimately as the years went by.

As they grew into their teens, Lol, Michael, and Robert continued practicing and learning their instruments. They were persistent, rehearsing whenever they could. Smith was the true musical mastermind, but Tolhurst certainly contributed. He cultivated an image in the early days as a leather-clad tough guy, a heavy drinker who was always quick to defend himself and his friends in the rough-edged world the boys inhabited. The specter of constant fighting and violence was never far in those days, and all three of them were capable of standing their ground. Those years brought an edge that has never left.

By 1978, the Cure was officially born, with Lol, Robert, and Michael the founding members. They were a tight unit, playing gigs around Crawley and the surrounding area. Tolhurst never had the musical gifts of Robert Smith, but fortunately, his limited technique was perfect for the minimalist vibe of the songs Smith was writing. Lol managed nicely on the band's first album, *Three Imaginary Boys*, his unyielding rhythmic box keeping the more elaborate flourishes favored by bassist Michael Dempsey to a minimum, much to Robert's delight.

Lol was often Robert's right-hand man in those early years, and he frequently tried to act as conciliator between Robert and Dempsey's replacement, Simon Gallup, as the two strong-willed and sometimes volatile musicians weren't always on the same page. Lol was always something of a mascot or court jester in some measure, certainly by the time of the later years of his tenure, and that all stems from his desire to generate smiles and keep the peace.

As the band transitioned from the *Three Imaginary Boys* period to the more pivotal *Seventeen Seconds*, Tolhurst's distinctly simplistic technique become the foundation on which the band's sound was built. His drums were high in the mix, implacable and relentless. He and producer Mike Hedges added the distinctive crack of the Synare 3 drum pad to his sound.

Tolhurst's unique style helped set the Cure apart from the countless other bands emerging from the post-punk scene in Britain at the time. His presence was also important to the band's image in that era, with the stone-faced visage he affected lending a sense of both toughness and detachment. He's always considered himself a punk-rocker in his approach and attitude, if not always musically.

For *Seventeen Seconds*, his sparse rhythms played well into the haunting austerity echoing in Smith's head. *Faith* wasn't much of a departure, and Tolhurst's delicate play on tracks like "All Cats Are Grey" contributes mightily to their beauty and mesmeric appeal. For *Pornography*, he was able to channel his aggression into a ferocious sonic assault.

When the Cure pivoted to synth pop in 1982 on "Let's Go to Bed," they also became a duo. Smith and Gallup's fistfight near the end of the *Pornography* tour led to the bassist's exit from the band. It wasn't the only change—after four albums behind the drum kit, Lol Tolhurst was told by Robert Smith that he could no longer be drummer for the Cure.

It was obvious for years that the Cure had no ability to make significant advances in musical development with Tolhurst as drummer. His limitations were just too profound, and they finally caught up with him. Robert Smith told *Select* magazine in 1991, "When we did 'Let's Go to Bed,' he tried to do the drumbeat for about three days, and it cost us a fortune in studio time. In the end we got a session drummer. He was going to pretend he'd played it until I pointed out to him that if he had to play it somewhere and he couldn't, he'd be humiliated."

Lol could stay in the band by learning keyboard, but he was also encouraged to dabble in new technologies and innovative avenues of creativity. Lol agreed but struggled immediately in his new role. He gamely delivered positive spin to the media, but he couldn't play keyboard, and it was obvious that he wasn't inclined to put in the work necessary to learn.

Although Tolhurst tried to contribute ideas, the Cure was essentially a solo project for Robert Smith until *The Head on the Door* three years later. Lol had not advanced beyond beginner's level on keyboard in a three-year span since he switched. He could usually manage simple melodies that didn't require more than one finger. Robert implemented a system of colored stickers that he placed on the keys so that Lol knew what notes to play, but his mistakes were still frequent. These problems were amplified by Tolhurst's erratic behavior as he became increasingly incapacitated by drug and alcohol use.

Lol was given every chance to get his act together and remain part of the Cure, but he was simply incapable of doing so. As the band's popularity grew with smash hits from *Kiss Me, Kiss Me, Kiss Me*, Tolhurst's gutter dive headfirst into endless a perpetual flow of alcohol only worsened. His behavior became dangerously unstable, and he suffered frequent blackouts. As he relates in his memoir, even as the band was riding new heights of success, Lol felt empty and alone, aware that his substance abuse was like a boulder careening downhill, completely out of control, but he seemed unable to do anything to help his situation.

Exasperated by his behavior, his bandmates would sometimes subject Lol to ridicule and mean-spirited pranks. He made no meaningful creative contributions. He was in the band only because Robert Smith respected his standing as a cofounder of the Cure and still held out hope that Lol would get his act together. Smith made his feelings clear to Lol often, such as the session for the hate-fest "Shiver and Shake," in which the singer asked Lol to stand in front of him so that he could sing the venomous lyrics with more fervor.

The final straw came at the end of the sessions for *Disintegration*. Robert and his bandmates had poured everything they had into a profoundly personal epic. Tolhurst had contributed nothing whatsoever to the creation of the album and was a drunken mess most of the time he was at the rural manor that housed the studio. Robert Smith claims that Tolhurst never once stepped foot in the actual recording studio at all during the sessions. The days when Lol was the amiable fool, the drunken toady who could play court jester and still get laughs, were gone. Any remaining sympathy for him had evaporated almost completely.

Smith spoke with the others to get their views on what should be done about Lol, and they were unanimous in their desire to see him gone. Both Porl Thompson and Simon Gallup, who had known Lol since they were teenagers in Crawley, were so hardened against him that they warned Smith that they would not go on tour to support the album if Tolhurst wasn't fired. Simon, who was Robert Smith's best friend and best man at his wedding, was particularly adamant.

Tolhurst received a call from Fiction Records in late December to come to RAK Studios in London to join the rest of the group to hear the final mix of the album. The band and some of their associates in the production and management team gathered in the studio's control room, where Robert Smith hit "Play" and the album unfolded before them. As he listened, Lol grew increasingly depressed because he knew that *Disintegration* was great, and he felt completely removed from it. Shame and the regret of missed opportunities echoed through his mind, and the music almost seemed to mock him with its majestic grandeur.

Lol had been drinking heavily as the playback progressed, so he was good and drunk by the time Robert paused the music for a brief break. The moment of silence was broken by Lol blurting out loudly that the album was shit and that half of it didn't even sound like the Cure at all—this from someone getting money and credit for playing and writing for the album even though he did no such thing, surrounded by all those whose hard work and sacrifice had indeed combined to create a classic.

Moments of stunned silence followed his proclamation, after which Robert silently pressed "Play" again so they could hear the rest of the album. As Lol relates in his memoir, at that moment, he knew he had finally gone too far. Everyone in the band and the crew avoided him after the playback until Lol ran out of the studio alone in tears. Robert Smith and the rest of the band were incensed over the situation, and although there was no big scene or discussion with Lol at the time of the incident, there seemed no doubt that his long tenure in the band was over.

Friends and bandmates many times urged Lol to get help, and though he tried a few times, he continued to worsen. Likewise, everyone had been pleading with Robert to get rid of Lol for years, but Smith resisted. He found himself unable to do so any longer.

Lol knew what was coming as the winter of 1988 stretched into the new year. He dreaded it daily. It finally arrived in the form of a handwritten letter by Robert Smith telling the cofounder of the Cure and his lifelong friend that he was out of the band. Tolhurst's exit was much discussed in the press, and the truth of his limited musical contributions and his chronic alcoholism became more widely known.

Many fans were not happy that such a pivotal member of the band was summarily dismissed. As James Murphy of LCD Soundsystem told *The Guardian*, "I was someone who grew up obsessed with bands, how they were and how they treated one another, and how they treated fans. You know, it mattered to me when Lol Tolhurst left the Cure. I was heartbroken." He wasn't the only one.

As the months passed, Tolhurst watched in sullen sadness as the Cure reached a level of success unimaginable when he helped to start the band as a schoolboy all those years ago. He benefited from it since Robert Smith had given him songwriting credits on *Disintegration* even though he did nothing at all, but that didn't matter.

Tolhurst had been stewing about perceived injustices at the hands of his old friend, and that bitterness only escalated as he watched the Cure soar to previously unheard-of heights with the success of the album that led to his ouster: *Disintegration*. The back-and-forth between he and his former bandmates became increasingly bitter. Robert Smith didn't hold back, calling him "useless" in a 1989 fanzine interview and saying that he only pretended to be part of the group.

Meanwhile, Lol's only real brush with the possibility of musical success outside of the Cure came in 1991 with his band Presence, with former Cure roadie

Gary Biddles on vocals, keyboardist Chris Youdell, and drummer Alan Burgess. They released a single, "In Wonder," a goth rocker with a dance kick to it that received a decent amount of press. Unfortunately for Lol, the single was forcibly removed from stores shortly after its release thanks to an injunction by a London band that claimed they had rights to the name. The injunction was overturned, but the damage had been done.

Tolhurst, egged on by his wife, her family, and their attorneys, became convinced that he wasn't receiving a fair share of the band's publishing and that he should be owed a lot more money. In 1994, Laurence Tolhurst sued the Cure and Fiction Records over royalties and joint ownership of the Cure's name. The case weighed mightily on Robert because, as unlikely as a Tolhurst victory was, if it happened, it could seriously impact the Cure and cost enormous amounts of money.

Eventually, the case came down to a lurid, widely covered courtroom trial in which Tolhurst sat stone-faced as Smith regaled the court with tales of Tolhurst's utter inability to participate in any meaningful way in the creation of the band's music. The height of irony is that Smith ensured that Tolhurst was given credit along with the other band members for work on *Kiss Me, Kiss Me, Kiss Me* and *Disintegration* that Tolhurst did not (and could not) actually produce. Smith was also open about Tolhurst's lack of musical ability in the press, escalating a bitterly divisive feud and exposing one of the key fractures that the Cure's existence has always straddled: Tolhurst's paltry musical ability.

Tolhurst whined in the press that Smith was critical of others' mistakes but not so much his own, adding that the singer frequently forgot lyrics and that when he played wrong notes on the guitar, he would repeat them in an attempt to make his mistakes seem like an intentional improvisation. He should have known that he was opening a line of discussion and inquiry that would not go well for him.

Robert Smith rebuked Tolhurst harshly in a statement to the court, which must have been painful for his former friend to read. Smith states that he allowed Tolhurst to remain in the band even though he wasn't contributing only out of sympathy and a hope that he would somehow conquer his self-destructive drinking and become a functioning member of the group again.

Obviously, this didn't happen. Smith concludes his damning indictment by reflecting that while Tolhurst "started out as a keen, if limited drummer, full of enthusiasm and drive, he ended up as a tired and shambling shadow of his former self." Ouch. Smith doesn't hold back in that statement, but then this was serious business, and the Cure could have lost millions of dollars and part ownership of the band name had they lost. Smith was giving the unvarnished truth.

It was obvious from the proceedings that Tolhurst's case was weak and that he was poorly counseled. In the end, the court found Tolhurst's claims unfounded, and Robert Smith was vindicated. It was a huge moment of relief for Smith and the band, and the cloud that the lawsuit had created and that hovered over the band for years had finally lifted.

For Tolhurst, that was it, the last bite at the apple smacked away, the final bridges irrevocably burned. Rather than realizing his hope for a financial boost from the lawsuit, Tolhurst was destroyed financially, losing vast amounts of money to attorneys' fees and having his paychecks garnished 75 percent by the court in order for him to pay the assessed penalties.

Further salting the wound, Justice Chadwick wrote in his decision that he was satisfied that Tolhurst had ample opportunity to continue with the Cure largely through Robert Smith's generosity and that "his musical services were not required for their own sake." Ouch, again.

Lol Tolhurst lost everything. Shortly after the court ruling and after enduring the wrenching pain of the loss of a daughter during childbirth, Tolhurst's wife divorced him. Robert Smith, who had been so enraged at his former friend for filing the lawsuit and who had said such bitterly nasty things about him, ended up feeling sorry for Lol. Ironically enough, his main source of income was the royalties he was raking in from being included, solely through Robert Smith's generosity, as cowriter and performer for songs on the Cure's biggest-selling albums of the 1980s, for which he contributed next to nothing.

Tolhurst was cast adrift and found himself wandering in the California desert of all places, where he was finally able to enter treatment and successfully achieve sobriety. As they tend to do, years and hindsight can change everything. Tolhurst worked hard to stay sober and eventually came to the inescapable conclusion that the lawsuit had been a fiasco entirely of his own making, and he came to regret it bitterly.

Eventually, Lol worked himself up to do what he had wanted to do for years, and in the winter of 2000, he penned a long, emotional and cathartic letter to Robert Smith in which he apologized for his actions, including the lawsuit, and attempted to explain the situation through his point of view as candidly and as openly as possible. Lol told Robert in the letter that he would like to meet and make amends with him in person rather than just via correspondence.

Robert Smith replied, asking Lol to come and meet him when the Cure played at the Palace in Los Angeles on February 19, 2000, on their tour in support of *Bloodflowers*. Tolhurst reached the venue, was let backstage and then led straight to Smith's dressing room.

In the dressing room, Robert Smith and Lol Tolhurst saw each other for the first time since the last day of trial six years earlier. They stood quietly for a moment, then hugged, and Robert asked everyone else in the room if they could leave them alone for a bit. Then it was just the two of them, passengers together on a journey far more incredible than anything they possibly could have imagined in the late 1970s as two young dreamers back in Crawley. They were dreamers, still.

Lol said that he wanted to make amends and that he was sorry for all of the hurt he had caused. Robert just smiled, and after a long estrangement, the friends since age five were reconciled. Tolhurst and his wife watched the Cure's shows, happy beyond words. Robert dedicated "The Figurehead" to him, and those stern martial opening beats took him back to another lifetime to which he once again felt connected. Then again, the infamous "Shiver and Shake," essentially a hate letter to Lol, was also included in the set, a rarity on this tour. Perhaps it was a joke, or perhaps things would always remain a bit complicated.

The next step would be bigger yet. When Lol noticed that the thirtieth anniversary of *Faith* was rapidly approaching, he wrote to Robert Smith suggesting that the original lineup for that album reunite and perform it from start to finish.

It was a shot in the dark, and Lol had no reason to think that Robert would be agreeable, even with their recent reconciliation. He didn't hear from Robert Smith for a while, but when he did, the news was far beyond what he expected. Smith suggested that instead of just playing *Faith*, the Cure's third album, they should play the first two albums as well. It would be *Three Imaginary Boys*, *Seventeen Seconds*, and *Faith* in sequence by (almost) the original lineup. Tolhurst was overwhelmed by the news, and arrangements were quickly made for the Cure to do these shows over two nights, May 31 and June 1, 2011, at one of the world's most iconic venues: the Sydney Opera House.

In a business where happy endings can sometimes be only a fond dream, this reconciliation was genuine. The relationship was repaired to the point that Tolhurst was able to join his former bandmates onstage for the *Reflections* shows in 2011, during which the band played their first three albums in their entirety. The band rehearsed for months in preparation for the show, but it wasn't quite like old times. There was some drinking but nothing like in the old days, and the atmosphere was much more distant and workmanlike.

Much had changed in the decades since Tolhurst was last in the band. Tolhurst appeared onstage to play some keyboard parts for the *Faith* segment, and his extraordinary joy at returning all these years later onstage in front of fans who still loved him despite the drama was the stuff of rock 'n' roll dreams.

Tolhurst has maintained generally good relations with Smith, although some of the other band members have not been so keen. In 2016, he released his memoir, *Cured: The Tale of Two Imaginary Boys*, which details his history with Smith and the Cure, focusing mainly on their friendship, the debauchery that led to his downfall, his agonizing regret over the lawsuit, and his ultimate reconciliation.

There is not a whisper of negativity toward Smith to the point where its exclusion is almost obsequious, yet Tolhurst has come to recognize the sheer musical genius and the towering presence of his grade school friend in the music industry and respects it. He is also justifiably proud of his contributions to the music when he made them, particularly when he was drummer for the first four albums.

Memoirs, particularly by rock musicians, tend to have a streak of score settling to them, as the writer rehashes a long inventory of grievance and slights and relitigates them from his or her point of view with the benefit of hindsight. Tolhurst intentionally avoids this. He had read numerous rock biographies in preparation for his own memoir, and he was determined not to sully the band's reputation in any way—and he doesn't. *Cured* is basically a long public penance. Robert Smith hasn't commented publicly on the book, and Lol said during one interview that he hadn't heard from Smith since its publication, but he noted wryly that if Smith didn't like it, he'd certainly let Lol know.

While Lol demurs and is intentionally vague about any substance abuse issues faced by Smith and the rest of the band (even though Smith has been generally candid about his drug use), he is open and honest about his own struggles with addiction, then recovery, and ultimately sobriety, a keenly human story to which many can relate and which brings an element of humanity to what can sometimes be a persona that's hard to penetrate.

He endured banishment and redemption, and these days, Lol Tolhurst can be seen at book signings or sometimes at Cure shows, often interacting with fans, who love him for his part in the band's history, his unique style and personality, his down-to-earth approachability, and his happy ending. He goes to arts festivals and does question-and-answer sessions at which he is always quite affable and has created music for films. He is also outspoken on contemporary social justice issues.

Lol was ecstatic when the Cure was inducted into the Rock and Roll Hall of Fame, and he grabbed some media attention with an interview with *Rolling Stone* the morning of the announcement. Tolhurst said he was looking forward to seeing the band at the ceremony, and he joked to *Rolling Stone* that he'd have his "goth tux" ready for the show.

Some members of The Cure evidently weren't so pleased with Lol's induction and his eager media presence around the Hall of Fame. Tolhurst eased his way onto multiple media platforms giving interview after interview opining about all things Cure, especially the Rock and Roll Hall of Fame induction, his book and his relationship with Robert Smith. His earnest and sincere persona, which seemed fake and self-serving to many Cure insiders, earned him a sharp rebuke from Robert O'Donnell, who openly questioned in the press why Tolhurst should be inducted.

Despite any hard feelings that may have existed or backhanded comments or whispers or laughs, the Hall of Fame induction must have been an enormous event for Tolhurst. Perhaps it offered him some closure and finality to be celebrated for his contributions to the band as a founding member, musician, collaborator, and, for a long time, tragicomic foil who thankfully was able to pull himself together in a way that few who are down as far as he was could realistically hope to do.

Lol said in an interview that after his memoir was published, Simon Gallup sent him a letter saying, "If I do have any regrets, I wish that we were kinder to each other when we were younger." Lol Tolhurst said of the Cure recently that they are not like his family—they *are* his family.

23

Feel Like Swirling and Dancin': *Mixed Up, Torn Down*, and the Remixes

The Cure is not known primarily as a dance band, but they've allowed different spins to be put on their music with remixes.

While the roots of the modern remix can be traced to Jamaican dance hall culture of the late 1960s and early 1970s, it was the sleek disco grooves pounding at full volume at the decadent nightclubs of the 1970s that caused an explosion of the remix into popular musical consciousness. Deejays in the 1970s would twist and spin and swirl radio-size disco singles into eight- to eleven-minute dance floor behemoths. Producers and deejays became musical icons in their own right, like Larry Levan and Giorgio Moroder, whose trance-inducing masterpiece with Donna Summer, "I Feel Love," became one of the most important recordings of the decade.

It was too good a concept not to spread, and soon remixes were routinely created for pop and even rock songs by the late 1970s and into the 1980s. Every pop star riding the airwaves in the 1980s seemed hell-bent on working with brand-name producers who'd turn their latest single into a massive club anthem.

The twelve-inch single format, allowing longer lengths for extended dance remixes, became increasingly popular thanks to the likes of Shep Pettibone, Jellybean, François Kevorkian, and others, all of whom scored multiple smash hits. Artists like Madonna, Prince, Janet Jackson, and many others used the format to their advantage, extending the shelf life of their singles and bringing their music to new listeners around the world who might not listen to the radio much but surely loved to dance all night at the club on a Saturday night.

The popularity of the twelve-inch extended mix wasn't exclusive to pop stars. Edgier, "alternative" artists frequently used them to amplify the visibility and sales of their latest single and to provide some artistic license to provide fans with extra B-sides and the opportunity for the A-side to be shown in a different light. Siouxsie and the Banshees jumped on the twelve-inch single bandwagon quite early with a string of excellent mixes, including "Cities in Dust" and "Dazzle." The Shep Pettibone mix of New Order's "True Faith" is arguably the quintessential version of the song.

The 1990s pop/dance scene was dominated by of high-profile deejays and their reswizzled versions of the electronic dance music (EDM) standards of the day. Sometimes, a track would be released on a CD single, sometimes in several parts (especially in Europe), and might feature as many as six or more different mixes. Generally, they are difficult to sit through as a listening experience and exist more for the sweat-soaked exploits of 3 a.m. in the club.

As technology advanced, the process of creating these extended mixes changed. Through the late 1980s, artists would often record additional parts to extend their singles in new and exciting ways. By the 1990s, just about everything was fed into a computer, and the floodgates of possibility opened for different mixes that could often radically change the vibe of a song. Sometimes, these consisted of endlessly repeated loops and generic dance beats with snatches of vocal or melodic hooks that were even more focused at the dance floor rather than listeners at home. The number of mixes exploded, but the days when an extended version would get played on the radio or would become a particular fan favorite were largely gone.

The Cure was never exactly known for their dance material, yet they took advantage of the twelve-inch single format, and over the course of their career, many of their singles were turned into extended mixes. Some were aimed at the dance floor, and some were just extensions of the singles. Their first twelve-inch single was "A Forest" in 1980, but it simply contained the album version with the same B-side as the 45: "Another Journey by Train." The Cure's first extended mix was "Primary," the lead single from *Faith*, released in 1981. As remixes go, the twelve-inch version of "Primary" is about as basic as it gets. Extra bars of the hard-driving instrumentation bloat the compact three-minute and thirty-nine-second single version to five minutes and fifty-six seconds, but with no additional sonic elements, it feels unnecessary.

As the Cure's music shifted away from the turgid rock of *Pornography* to more radio-friendly fare, generating strong twelve-inch mixes became more important, but it took a while before it became a major point of emphasis. "Let's Go to Bed," released in 1982, has a rather pedestrian extended mix, but its B-side, "Just One Kiss," was the first time the Cure really used the format to provide something enticingly different, as the mix is a dramatic departure from the shorter version, with different elements.

Next came "The Walk" (1983), their big commercial breakthrough in Britain. Reaching number twelve, it was extended to seven minutes and forty-four seconds but again contained no new sounds. It was comprised simply of longer keyboard riffs and sections of instrumentation. They got more creative with "The Lovecats," as the extended version includes a unique instrumental section to the beginning, although it gained only a minute in length.

Two years passed until the next Cure single was remixed, and again, it was with a light touch, as "In Between Days" earned an extra minute with a longer instrumental section at the beginning. The nifty rhythm and bass on "Close to Me" is emphasized on its twelve-inch mix, which stretches the song beyond the six-minute mark, but, of course, the most notable addition is the woozy New Orleans–inspired brass provided by the U.K. jazz combo Rent Party.

To promote their pivotal 1986 hits collection *Standing on a Beach*, the Cure hired Mark Saunders to rework their seminal classic "Boys Don't Cry," for which Robert Smith provided a new vocal. The 1979 original single, despite its enduring global popularity, never made the pop chart so Saunders's "New Voice Club Mix" gave the song its first chart run when it peaked at a modest #22. The mix wasn't included on the singles compilation, though, and has since faded a bit from consciousness.

All things considered, the Cure were latecomers to the remix game, but when they embraced it, they did so full throttle. It finally happened in 1987 with their brilliant double album *Kiss Me, Kiss Me, Kiss Me*. Robert Smith finally seemed to grasp the artistic possibilities that the twelve-inch single format and remixes in general could provide. For the band's first truly high-profile remix, they turned to François Kevorkian and Roy St. Germain, who turned in an exhilarating eight-minute take on "Why Can't I Be You?" Kevorkian followed that up with a kinetic revamp of "Hot Hot Hot!!!" that remains one of the finest twelve-inch mixes the band ever released. An extended mix of album track "Hey You!" appears on the B-side.

Mark Saunders's work on the *Disintegration* singles is superb. Saunders is an innately creative producer with a great musical mind and is particularly known for bringing the strongest melodic hooks to the forefront while adding elements that fit into the canvas of the music comfortably without ruining the vibe of the song. His radio mixes for "Lullaby," "Lovesong," and "Fascination Street" are arguably better than the album versions, a rarity indeed for singles.

The spacey keyboard riff in "Fascination Street" had been part of the song's arrangement in demo form and has often been added to the mix when played live. It had been dropped from the album version, but Saunders injects it into the twelve-inch mix. He added bits of bubbly synthesizer in "Lullaby," which are like a witch's cauldron boiling over, and turned in an extended take on "Lovesong" that was popular enough to be frequently played on U.S. radio stations as an alternative to the single version.

Robert Smith's interest in remixes peaked in the 1990s. He was faced with the enormous pressure of following up the phenomenally successful *Disintegration*, and, like many artists and fans in the early 1990s, he was enthralled by the rave culture and club scene that had become a global cultural wave. He decided that the best way to uncork the pressure of following up a masterpiece was to make a dramatic left turn, much as he did with "Let's Go to Bed" following *Pornography*, and explore the potential of classic Cure songs being turned into electro-pop anthems.

Mixed Up

By 1990, as dance music dominated top-forty radio, the popularity of remix albums exploded after a series of trailblazing 1980s classics like New Order's *Substance*, Pet Shop Boys' *Disco*, and Madonna's popular *You Can Dance*. Remix albums were suddenly in vogue. Many of them were disposable, cheaply made products intended as a quick cash grab with little in the way of artistic merit. But the Cure has never gone down that path, and *Mixed Up* was no exception.

Mixed Up is a combination of previously released twelve-inch versions like "Hot Hot Hot!!!" and "Fascination Street" with newly remixed tracks that Smith produced with Mark Saunders. It was clearly not intended solely as a high-energy dancefloor soundtrack, given the set opens with the meditative trance-like Mark Saunders mix of "Lullaby." Several songs, including "The Walk" and "A Forest," were completely rerecorded, as the original masters were not readily available for use. "The Caterpillar" received the remix treatment for the first time with the "Flicker Mix." Ironically, for the one newly recorded track to make the album, the Cure veered away from electronica in favor of the rolling guitar epic "Never Enough." It was included in extended form as the "Big Mix" and the single version became a big hit on alternative radio in America.

The Paul Oakenfold / Steve Osborne mix of "Close to Me" dubbed "Closest Mix" was released as the second single from *Mixed Up*, and while it was largely ignored in America, it hit an impressive #13 in Britain. Robert was sufficiently enamored by the easy-going trip-hop take on the track that he included the remix on the band's hit collection *Galore*. The third single chosen was Mark Saunders's superb "Tree Mix" of "A Forest," arguably the finest of the new mixes on the album. The sparse and creepy electro take on the classic fit the original's vibe perfectly, but alas it may have been a bit too esoteric to take off on pop radio.

Going forward, the band continued using the remix to their advantage, generating excellent takes on "High," "Friday I'm in Love," and "A Letter to Elise" from the 1992 *Wish* album. The slick "Fix Mix" of "Open" is reason enough to track

Feel Like Swirling and Dancin': *Mixed Up, Torn Down*, and the Remixes   235

The Cure's decision to follow-up *Disintegration* with a remix album proved to be a smart move.
Author's Collection

down the "High" CD single. "Doing the Unstuck" even received a reworking, although it was shelved after the track was skipped over as a single, and finally unearthed years later on *Join the Dots*.

By 1996 and the *Wild Mood Swings* album, remixes were more popular than ever, and all of the singles from *Wild Mood Swings*—"The 13th," "Mint Car," "Gone!," and "Strange Attraction"—had multiple remixes, most of them forgettable. The best mix from the period is "This Is a Lie (Ambient Mix)" by Tim Palmer, which Robert Smith praised in the liner notes to *Join the Dots* and said it should have been a single. There were also multiple mixes for the sizzling electro-rock "Wrong Number," released as a single for their 1997 hits collection *Galore*.

The next two Cure albums (*Bloodflowers* in 2000 and *The Cure* in 2004) didn't particularly lend themselves to the remix concept, although both "Maybe

Someday" and "Out of This World" were tweaked for promo single versions and several other mixes. Most notably, Paul Oakenfold was commissioned to mix "Out of This World," and the band's early era producer Mike Hedges created a unique mix of "Maybe Someday," but these weren't given a commercial release until included on the *Join the Dots* box set. Additionally, renowned British producer Underdog reworked "Watching Me Fall" for use on the soundtrack to *American Psycho*, getting it down to a much more manageable length in the process.

A hidden gem in the Cure's library of remixes is the 2001 "Cut Here (Missing Remix)," which was mixed by Robert Smith himself. The other new single from the band's 2001 *Greatest Hits* was "Just Say Yes," and the industrial-flavored 1990s alternative rockers Curve transformed it into a hard-edged rocker, but it wasn't released until its inclusion on the *Join the Dots* box set.

It wasn't until 2008 and the *4:13 Dream* album that the band delivered to fans their first significant remix project since *Mixed Up*. This arrived on September 13 in the form of a five-track remix EP called *Hypnagogic States*. It contains mixes of the album's four singles by current artists: "The Only One" by Thirty Seconds to Mars, "Freakshow" by Wolves at the Gate, "Sleep When I'm Dead" by Gerard Way and Julien-K, and "The Perfect Boy" by Patrick Stump and Pete Wentz.

All profits generated by the EP went to the International Red Cross. Initially, there was a bit of a kerfuffle over the £7.99 price tag in the United Kingdom. Smith went so far as to suggest to fans that they not buy the album until the price was lowered, which it was rather quickly after Smith went public with his frustration.

In 2009, Danny Lohner stripped down "Underneath the Stars" from *4:13 Dream* and cleaned the vocals from the layered effects, making it a much more effective song. It was used on the soundtrack to the film *Underworld: Rise of the Lycans*. In 2012, Lohner gave the same treatment to the *Wish* ballad "Apart" for the film *Underworld: Awakening*, and once again, his stripped-down approach works. His version of "Apart" is slower and haunting and is a guide for how the Cure could proceed sonically in a way that sounds modern but retains the classic Cure sound.

Torn Down

In 2018, the Cure's best remix projects took a big turn in the spotlight as Robert Smith presented the band's first major archival release since the deluxe *Disintegration* reissue in 2010. First appearing on picture-disc vinyl for Record Store Day in April, the newly refurbished *Mixed Up* incorporated mixes that were omitted from the original version, including the original extended versions of "Let's Go to Bed" and its B-side, "Just One Kiss," from 1982 and mixes of "Primary," "Let's Go to Bed," and "Just Like Heaven" that were done by Saunders for the original projected but ended up as B-sides. Smith even dusted off the extended twelve-inch version of the excellent *Kiss Me*–era B-side "A Japanese Dream," one of the relatively few B-sides that Smith ever bothered turning into an extended mix.

The real thrill of the expanded set is a third CD that was sold separately as a two-LP vinyl set titled *Torn Down*. Treated by most as a curiosity at best or a side project accompaniment to *Mixed Up* (in part because it's saddled with the subtitle *Mixed Up Extras*), *Torn Down* is actually one of the more interesting releases by the Cure in ages.

Torn Down plays like an alternate greatest-hits collection, as Smith selected one song from each album to rework and then sequenced them chronologically. The set opens with him wailing "Can you help me?" on a stark electronic reworking of "Three Imaginary Boys," and it only gets better. Rarely does an artist have the luxury of looking back over such a vast career and selecting choice nuggets to revisit and reimagine, and Smith clearly relishes that opportunity here.

The new versions are largely thoughtful in their treatment of the original and provide an interesting spin, but some work better than others. The jaunty rhythm on "A Night Like This" doesn't quite connect, but the stunning deconstructed take on "A Strange Day" more than makes up for it. The songs chosen are among those Robert Smith has praised over the years as personal favorites, making *Torn Down* unusually penetrating for a compilation.

The "New Blood" mix of "Shake Dog Shake" maintains elements from the original, with an emphasis on Andy Anderson's opening drum barrage, but its updated vibe, with cool effects and eerie keyboards weaving ominously between the crunch of the guitars, is even more menacing. The tracks that Smith includes from the band's most recent two studio albums are perhaps a bit surprising: "Lost" and "It's Over," both of which are far superior to the original versions. The production on *4:13 Dream* is particularly bad, and the version of "It's Over" presented here shows it could have been a much better album had the material been given a chance to shine.

The Cure has never really been a "dance" band, although it's true that some of their songs are capable of getting even the stodgiest wallflower onto the floor. They aren't nearly as reliant on remixes as some bands are, but when they've chosen to do it, for the most part they've been highly successful. Given the size of their catalog, remixes will never play as large a role for the Cure as they do for many other artists, but it would a mistake to overlook them. They rarely if ever surpass the original versions, but the top tier—like "Hot Hot Hot!!!," "Lullaby," "Cut Here," and "Lovesong"—are essential in their own right.

24

I Will Rise... and You'll See Me Return: *Wish*

The Cure faced enormous expectations for their studio follow-up to *Disintegration*, and they delivered the biggest album of their career.

Released: April 21, 1992
Fiction Records—FIXH 20, Polydor—513 261-1
Running time: 65:42

1. "Open" (6:51), 2. "High" (3:37), 3. "Apart" (6:40), 4. "From the Edge of the Deep Green Sea" (7:44), 5. "Wendy Time" (5:13), 6. "Doing the Unstuck" (4:24), 7. "Friday I'm in Love" (3:39), 8. "Trust" (5:33), 9. "A Letter to Elise" (5:14), 10. "Cut" (5:55), 11. "To Wish Impossible Things" (4:43), 12. "End" (6:46)

Robert Smith's vision for the Cure never included international stardom. Filling arenas worldwide, selling millions of albums, and hitting the top of the charts have never been his goal. His ambition for the band had always been simple: to be able to continue playing the music he wanted for as long as he wanted. Smith has said he'd prefer a small audience that cared deeply about the music than a much larger one that didn't. In interviews, he's often expressed horror over the idea of the Cure becoming too big.

Yet, by the dawn of the 1990s, the success he spent all those years dreading had become the Cure's new reality. They never chased this level of fame, and commercial considerations were not the main driving factor behind their music. Nobody could have predicted the juggernaut *Disintegration* had become. The Cure did everything on exactly their own terms, maintaining their integrity, and still became huge. Robert Smith didn't back away from it, but he didn't completely embrace it. The Cure played bigger venues and did higher-profile events, yet they didn't take all the steps they could have to maximize commercial potential. They threaded the needle very carefully.

Even though he hadn't sold out, Robert Smith still found himself uncomfortable with the scope of the band's enormous popularity and he found it difficult to cope with the various pressures this brought. How to continue the Cure—or even if it should be continued—weighed heavily on his mind.

Disintegration, an album that the Cure's U.S. record label considered commercial suicide, instead became a cultural touchstone that was almost impossible to follow up. He decided to punt the next studio album and instead put his efforts into a remix collection: *Mixed Up*. This allowed him to present the fans with something fun after the deep melancholy of *Disintegration*, and it also took pressure off himself and the band because expectations for a remix collection would be far different than a new studio album. Smith was also increasingly interested in the electronic music inspired by rave culture that had taken the United Kingdom and the rest of the world by storm, so *Mixed Up* served multiple purposes.

Perhaps most important, *Mixed Up* helped fill the three-year gap between *Disintegration* and *Wish*, the longest stretch between studio albums of the Cure's career thus far. They collaborated with producer Mark Saunders on new single, "Never Enough," a blast of Porl Thompson's guitar that seemed to wipe away the cobwebs of the past couple years. It was a major hit at alternative radio in the United States and helped keep the Cure's visibility high.

The band's lineup had shifted since the *Disintegration* sessions. Keyboardist Roger O'Donnell was ousted from the group following the Prayer Tour, and Smith handed the slot to longtime guitar tech Perry Bamonte. He wasn't the most proficient keyboardist, but he knew all the songs and, most important, got along with everyone in the band. That had been an issue at times with O'Donnell, whose personal entanglements with Simon Gallup and Boris Williams in particular made it difficult for Robert to keep him in the group at the time (though he would of course be back).

Lol Tolhurst was ejected prior to the start of that tour, but his specter still loomed large when news broke in August 1991, just as the Cure was entering the studio, that Laurence Tolhurst was threatening legal action against the band and Fiction Records. The former Cure drummer and alleged keyboardist asserted that the 1986 contract between the Cure and Fiction/Polydor handed an oversized share of the band's profits to Robert Smith and Chris Parry. Tolhurst also claimed part ownership of the Cure's name and that he was owed massive sums in back royalties.

Robert Smith dismissed Tolhurst's claims as frivolous and ridiculous. Most around the Cure and Fiction were shocked, especially since Smith had gone well beyond normal generosity by keeping Tolhurst in the Cure and handing him songwriting credits even though Lol contributed nothing creatively to the band for years because of his alcohol abuse and musical limitations. The band members were consumed with rage over what they viewed as a cheap attempt at payback. Even though they were confident and were publicly dismissive of the claims, the news weighed heavily on the band as sessions for their vitally important follow-up to *Disintegration* approached.

The Cure gathered at Shipton Manor in Oxfordshire in September 1991 to begin recording *Wish*, with Dave Allen once again producing. The rural mansion-turned-studio was owned by Virgin head Richard Branson, and the band had stayed there while preparing for their high-profile gig at Glastonbury earlier in the summer.

Going into the sessions, the band members collectively contributed nearly forty instrumental sketches for consideration. The band gathered to listen and offer commentary on each of the song ideas, a process that could be heated and intense. Robert took these opinions into consideration as he narrowed the material down to twenty-six tracks that he chose for additional studio workup to contend for a spot on the album(s).

With such a wealth of material, the Cure planned for two separate studio releases: the all-instrumental *Music for Dreams*, and an upbeat collection of potential singles with the working title *Higher*. The instrumental album was eventually shelved, although a four-track EP of instrumental demos called *Lost Wishes* was issued as a limited-edition promo on cassette only. Twelve songs survived the arduous process to make the final cut for the retitled *Wish*, with six additional tracks landing as B-sides.

The mood at Shipton Manor was generally upbeat. The Cure tried to recapture the party vibe of the *Kiss Me* sessions with friends and family present rather than the insular process of *Disintegration*. It wasn't quite Miraval, but there was still plenty of alcohol flowing through the proceedings.

The recording sessions, however, were grueling as the band struggled with so much new material and the pressure of following up a classic. The lineup change impacted the sound, as Roger O'Donnell was gone and his replacement, Perry Bamonte, was more a natural guitarist than keyboardist. The music shifted to more guitar-heavy material with starker arrangements. The sweeping waves of synthesizer that fans had grown used to on *Disintegration* were mostly absent, resulting in a leaner and tougher sound on *Wish*.

As the shifting conceptual framework suggested, the Cure struggled with an overall direction for the project and with deciding which songs would make the final product. Everything was in flux. Early in the process, the lofty and dramatic "The Big Hand" was slated to be the lead single, and the beautifully lush album artwork even included a specific visual reference to the song. It ended up jettisoned from the album completely after Robert Smith decided the band hadn't really captured the song as he intended.

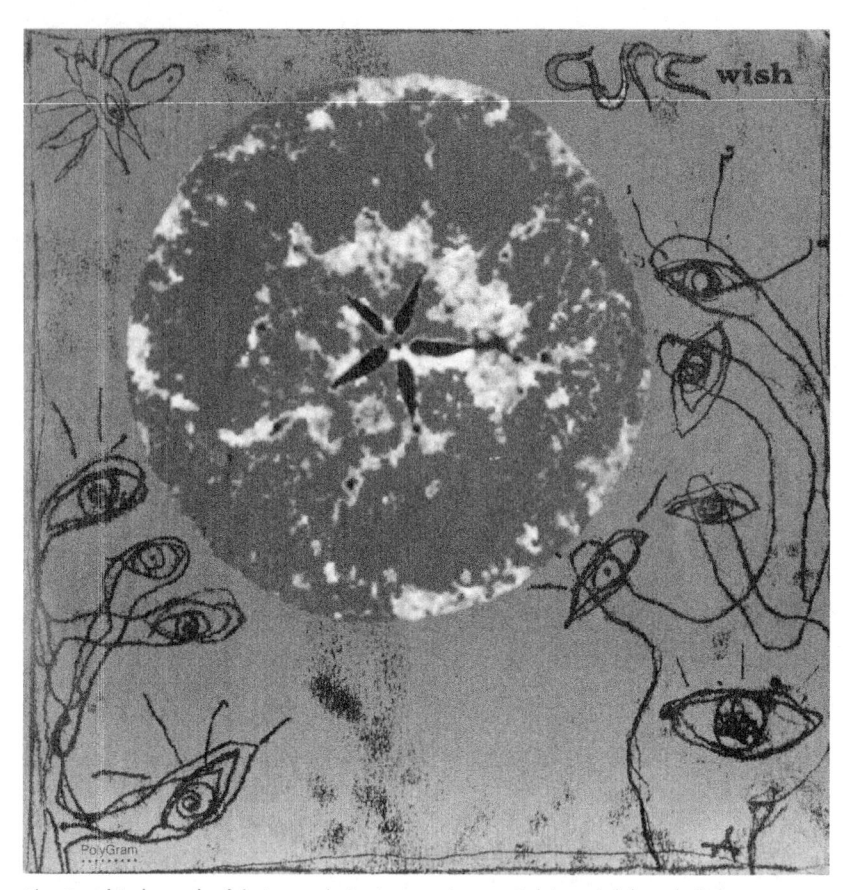

The Cure hit the peak of their popularity in America as *Wish* (1992) debuted all the way at #2, and launched a massively successful tour.
Author's Collection

Smith grew increasingly frustrated with what he considered his bandmates' lackadaisical approach to the entire album process. He later griped that for much of *Wish*, the band wasn't sufficiently invested in the project, and it often felt like he was the only one who cared whether the album was ever completed. It all seemed somehow rote in comparison with the deeply meaningful *Disintegration*.

Although the mix is murky, somehow *Wish* came together and was finally released on April 21, 1992. It became the Cure's highest-charting release the world over. It debuted at number one in the United Kingdom, their first chart topper there, and at an astounding number two in the United States, unable to knock Def Leppard's *Adrenalize* off the top spot. The *Wish* tour that followed was the most ambitious of their career, and it yielded two live albums and a concert video.

Given the expectations for the Cure's first post-*Disintegration* album, it's not surprising that *Wish* left some fans feeling empty. It's stylistically diverse like *Kiss Me* but more mature and lacking the feverish energy. The piercing introspection that marks *Disintegration* and *Faith* is missing. Robert Smith's songwriting turns outward on *Wish*, and for some listeners, that will never hold the same emotional impact as songs that are more personal.

It may not scale the same heights as its immediate predecessor, but that's an impossible challenge to meet. *Wish* holds up well. The songwriting is stellar, and there are some audaciously inventive arrangements. A remix to scrape the sludge off the top would be welcome, and hopefully that will happen with a deluxe reissue in the near future.

Wish

"Open"

It's serious business out of the gate with "Open," the Cure's heaviest guitar number since "Shiver and Shake," "Torture," and "All I Want" from *Kiss Me, Kiss Me, Kiss Me*. An epic rocker of swaying disorientation and woozy guitars, "Open" is about going to a party, getting whacked out on drugs, and hallucinating.

Robert Smith has always been fond of using literary devices in his lyrics, going all the way back to the Cure's debut single. In "Open," the repeating line "and the way the rain comes down hard, that's the way I feel inside" is an allusion to Sylvia Plath, who wrote in *Letters Home: Correspondence 1950–1963*, "I am glad the rain is coming down hard. It's the way I feel inside."

"High"

Released several weeks prior to the album, "High" was the high-stakes choice as first single for such an important album. Robert Smith obviously had confidence in the song, as it was once the de facto title track when the album was planned to be released with the name *Higher*. It was a smart choice, as "High" delivered the boost the Cure needed at a critical juncture. Like many of the band's best pop songs, it's based on a Simon Gallup demo.

Opening with chiming guitar arpeggios, "High" is built around two different patterns from Smith's Bass VI. For such a bouncy and engaging pop gem, its arrangement is deceptively complex. The colorful lyrics show Robert Smith once again getting away with lines that would sound utterly ridiculous coming from anybody else. The song's whimsical nature comes in part from its inspiration, a young girl Robert knew, a daughter of a friend of his, who was truly convinced

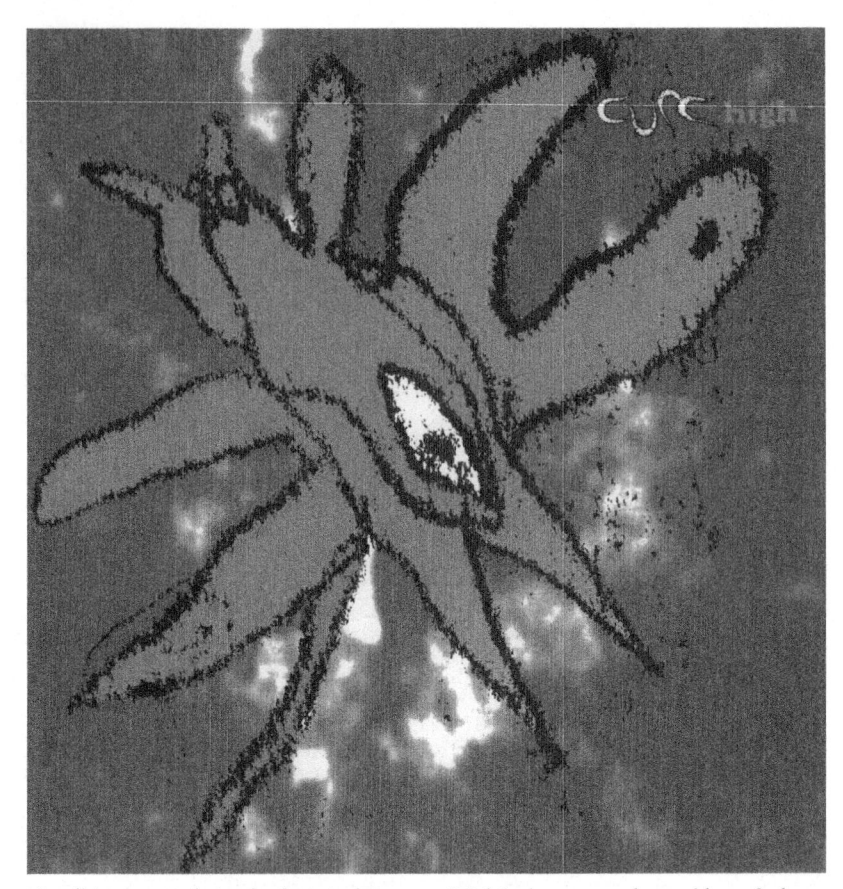

The all-important choice for first single went to "High," a buoyant and superbly-crafted pop gem that remains a constant in the Cure's live sets. *Author's Collection*

she could fly. Her uniquely droll way with words inspired some of Robert's lyrics in "High."

A buoyant introduction to the new album, "High" fell just shy of the *Billboard* top-forty pop chart in the United States, peaking at number forty-two, but it was enthusiastically embraced by alternative radio and spent four weeks at number one on the modern rock chart. In the United Kingdom, "High" reached number eight, becoming the Cure's third top-ten hit following "The Lovecats" (number seven) and "Lullaby" (number five).

"Apart"

Being in a relationship that is slowly but inexorably falling apart is a heartrending experience. It's like watching bricks fall one by one from a foundation, feeling the structure quaver, knowing it's only a matter of time before a stiff wind knocks it to the ground. "Apart" is an expression of wrenching disbelief that a relationship that had once seemed indestructible could somehow be unwinding.

The couple in "Apart" no longer listens to each other, they don't understand each other, and they don't really try to. All it would take is one step across the breach by either side, but pride too often gets in the way. They also mourn for what could have been, the years wasted, a future imagined in the fond days of optimism that seems like nothing but a dim memory.

"Apart" was remixed in 2012 by Danny Lohner for the sound track to the popular action/horror film *Underworld Awakening*. His stark, stripped-down approach gets to the core of the song, revealing the naked human emotion laid bare, that emotion to be heard intimately.

"From the Edge of the Deep Green Sea"

A swirling wildfire of blazing guitar and kinetic drum work, "From the Edge of the Deep Green Sea" is the emotional heart of *Wish*. It's nearly eight minutes of tension and drama as Robert Smith delivers his most impassioned vocal on the album.

Although the studio version is a powerhouse with numerous vocal and instrumental tracks woven together into a hazy inferno of sound, it really comes alive in concert, with the audience always obliging Robert Smith when he pleads with them to put their hands in the sky.

The freakout guitar solo was Porl Thompson's chance to go wild when the track was played during the *Wish* tour, but on the studio version, all of the guitar parts are performed by Smith. After playing around with the sound to get it exactly how he wanted, he nailed the solo on his first try, and Porl Thompson felt he had nothing to add.

"Wendy Time"

Lifting off with a howl and a blast of drums, "Wendy Time" is a white-hot groove, tight as nails, with Simon's popping bass adding a twisted funk vibe not normally associated with the Cure. With a remix edit to tighten it up (the album version runs past five minutes) and the word "fuck" edited, the infectiously catchy "Wendy Time" might have made a killer single.

"Wendy Time" was one of the first songs on *Wish* to be performed live, as an early version of it was included in the Cure's secret show on January 17, 1991, at London's Town & Country Club. Strangely, even though it's a stand-out cut on the album, "Wendy Time" had been performed seven times total prior to the band's 2019 stadium tour of Europe. Prior to that, it was last played on May 17, 1992, at the Spectrum in Philadelphia, only the fourth show into the North American *Wish Tour*, after which it was dropped from the set and has been completely ignored by the band ever since.

Until June 8, 2019, at Malahide Castle & Gardens Malahide in Ireland. "Wendy Time" made a surprise appearance between "Never Enough" and "The Walk," which seems like a logical spot. But it didn't last long in the set. Maybe Robert got bored with it or didn't think it translates well live, but like in 1992 it was cut short—only six appearances, and then it was dropped from the tour.

"Doing the Unstuck"

Sheer bliss, "Doing the Unstuck" is Robert Smith at his most fanciful and joyous. It's a response to negativity, an attempt to lift oneself and others out of their bustling world of stress and heavy blue depressions into a delirium of glee. There is a bit of a manic edge to it, almost desperation, as if one moment longer without some release would be too much to take.

Smith intended "Doing the Unstuck" to be a single, and a twelve-inch mix was created (and ultimately released on the *Join the Dots* set), but the record label preferred the comparatively sedate "A Letter to Elise" instead. Robert has always spoken of "Doing the Unstuck" as if it was a definite hit that should have been, and perhaps he is right, but it is difficult to conceive American radio, at least, embracing a song so manic and frantic, albeit jubilant.

"Friday I'm in Love"

This one had "pop hit" stamped in bright bold letters on its forehead from the moment of its conception on a carefree Friday afternoon. Although it may seem a bit twee, the eminently catchy "Friday I'm in Love" should not be dismissed as throwaway pop. Like "Boys Don't Cry," Smith intended this to be a perfect pop song in the vein of the Beatles, and while it may not quite be fab-four level, it absolutely gleams on the radio. Smith plays one of his favorite guitars on the track, a Gretsch Chet Atkins Country Gentleman.

"Friday I'm in Love" benefits from a common pop music studio tactic to maximize commercial potential. Smith sped up the tape so that it's a quarter-tone sharp, which gives the song a brisker, more vibrant sound.

Released as the second single from *Wish*, "Friday I'm in Love" reached number eighteen in the United States, their second-highest charting hit behind "Lovesong," and became their second straight chart topper on the modern rock chart. It reached number six in the United Kingdom, giving them two top-ten U.K. singles from one album for the first and only time in their history.

The Cure hit mainstream pop success again as "Friday I'm in Love" became their final (so far) Top 40 pop hit in America. *Author's Collection*

"Trust"

This lush, sorrowful ballad with soaring synths and elegant piano could have fit nicely on *Disintegration*. "Trust" is a plea for someone to stay despite having lost trust, and the argument being made—basically, I love you, so why can't you just believe me, and, by the way, nobody else trusts me either—isn't exactly persuasive.

Once trust is broken, it's extremely difficult if not impossible to truly recapture. Trust defines the bond in a relationship, delineating the limitations and borders. In a partnership that is supposed to be a lifetime commitment, the loss of trust is often the fatal blow dooming it to failure.

"A Letter to Elise"

A heartfelt mid-tempo guitar number, "A Letter to Elise" captures some of the same nostalgia in mood and tone as "Pictures of You." It was inspired in part by *Les Enfant Terribles*, a novel by Jean Cocteau, but it also feels very personal.

Issued as the third single from *Wish*, "A Letter to Elise" was a commercial misfire. It reached number twenty-eight in the United Kingdom but was unable to crossover to the U.S. pop chart, missing the Hot 100 entirely. It did manage to reach number two on the U.S. modern rock chart and might have been the Cure's third straight to reach the top if not blocked by the six-week run at number one by Morrissey's "Tomorrow."

Robert Smith has complained that "A Letter to Elise" was a poor single choice that was foisted on him by the record label when he wanted "Doing the Unstuck." While there's no doubt that the Cure's inability to sustain the momentum generated by the strong performance of "Friday I'm in Love" was a blow, it's hard to see how Smith could blame the label. He's bragged about his vaunted artistic control for decades, but when something goes awry, the blame tends to be placed elsewhere. It's hard to see how label executives could have been so gung ho over "A Letter to Elise" that they'd go to battle with Robert Smith to ensure its release as a single. And it's far from certain that the frantic hyperkinetic "Doing the Unstuck" would have been a hit. It's certainly difficult to imagine it getting much pop airplay in America.

"A Letter to Elise" was always a major song in the project. It was earmarked as a projected title song for a planned EP as far back as the summer of 1991. The EP would have been "A Letter to Elise," "The Big Hand," a still-unreleased song called "A Wave," and "Wendy Time." Smith ultimately decided that an EP at that point would be a poor strategic decision that could negatively impact the new album's reception, but it was clear a year before the album's release that he considered "A Letter to Elise" to be single-worthy.

And the reason it was always a major song in the project is that it's one of the strongest on the album. Wistful like a sibling of "Pictures of You," "A Letter to Elise" is a masterful composition, musically dazzling with layers of exquisitely arranged guitar work and heartrending lyrics. Robert Smith nails one of the finest vocal performances of his career on what might rightfully be considered one of the most underrated Cure songs of their entire output.

"Cut"

This jagged-edged rocker is an amp of adrenalin, a jolt of pure vitriolic energy that brings the band closer to the sound of *Pornography* than anything else on *Wish*. Porl Thompson goes wild with the feedback, especially in concert, when he delivered a torrent of liquid guitar fire each night on tour.

Along with "Wendy Time" and "The Big Hand," "Cut" (then known as "Away") was one of three as yet unreleased songs that the Cure premiered at a secret show at London's Town and Country Club 2 on January 17, 1991. It had the staying power to remain on the album through all its twists and turns until its release more than a year after it was first played.

"To Wish Impossible Things"

The last and best of the album's three superb ballads, "To Wish Impossible Things" is a stately and emotional beauty, one of the most gorgeous pieces the band ever recorded. It has a faintly exotic air thanks to a lovely string section and judiciously used finger cymbals.

Robert Smith's vocals are consistently strong throughout the album, but he really shines here. The dramatic moment at two minutes and thirty-five seconds when the double-tracked vocals kick in is spine-tingling. The sublime viola is performed by Katie Wilkinson. "To Wish Impossible Things" is the putative title track of sorts, a jaded and morose rejoinder to *Faith*. Encapsulated here is the essence of what "Faith" is truly about: wishful thinking.

"End"

The album's closer is a lumbering powerhouse of angry guitars and swirling vocals. Smith lashes out with all his resentment at having his motives misunderstood, for being caricaturized and idolized. It's just a rant, as if he hated the music business so much, why continue? But it's an effective rant, psychedelic and hard-edged, making a great closing number for both the album and the main set of the *Wish* tour.

B-Sides

"This Twilight Garden"

Lush and romantic, "This Twilight Garden" is a song of late summer evenings into dusk, smelling the lush flowers and trees and luxurious vines. Secret shadowy corners where lovers may hide in the evening, reveling in their solitude, the beauty around them, and, most of all, each other's presence. "This Twilight Garden" is love at its most elegant, the lyrics soft and exquisite, without guile or irony or a hint of underlying sorrow.

Robert Smith has expressed his admiration for "This Twilight Garden," reflecting that it should have been a single and that it's a true shame it was left off the album. He's certainly correct on the second point, although that can be said about all but one of the album's magnificent set of B-sides. It's hard to envision "This Twilight Garden" gaining much airplay as a single, being so soft and awash in keyboards, the melody so subtle and languid. It's not an immediately catchy pop song, but then again, who knows? Sometimes a song is so good that those normal considerations don't matter.

The Cure rarely plays B-sides in concert, but fans were delighted when the band performed it for the first time ever in New Orleans on May 11, 2016 (and a more perfect city to debut this particular song could not have been chosen). They played it ten more times over the course of the 2016 tour, plucking one of many B-sides from obscurity and shining the spotlight on it. It's taken only fourteen years, but some good things are worth waiting for.

"Play"

Hopefully, the wait for "Play" will be over soon since as of this writing, it has never been performed live by the band—a sad missed opportunity because it's a powerfully emotional song, a devastating heartsick contemplation of a relationship that is ending in bitter and acrimonious fashion. "Play" was a chance for Robert Smith to be the villain again like he's done in past numbers, such as "I'm Cold" and "Object," only this time he's much older—therefore, much more devious and calculating, and far less snide.

"Scared as You"

This hard-rocking track was incredibly personal to Robert Smith. He's said that he was actually weeping in the studio while recording his vocal part. "Scared as You" is an edgy, emotional track with an arresting melody and a restless vibe. Like most of the B-sides from this period, it's just as good as most of the tracks that made the album.

"Halo"

A gentle pop song with guest vocals by Caroline Crawley of the band Shelleyan Orphan, "Halo" is pleasant in a folksy, sunshiny kind of way. It has a wide-open sound and melody and a winsome appeal that would have potentially worked well on radio. In retrospect, "Halo" may have been the best choice for third single had it been included on the album. It's easy to imagine it doing better than "A Letter to Elise" or "Doing the Unstuck," which Robert Smith claims to have favored.

"The Big Hand"

One of the first tracks written for *Wish* and the first recorded, "The Big Hand" was considered a likely candidate for first single. The album's artwork even reflects the song's conceptual theme. Although it was a favorite of the band members and had already been performed in concert, in the end, it was left off the album because Robert Smith felt it hadn't really come together the way he envisioned. It's a shame because "The Big Hand," another of Robert's musings on addiction, offers a powerful message and is musically gorgeous.

"A Foolish Arrangement"

The only B-side not completed during the *Wish* sessions, "A Foolish Arrangement" was only an instrumental demo until the Cure needed a track for the "A Letter to Elise" single. While on tour in Australia, Robert Smith wrote the lyrics and finished the track with Simon Gallup's assistance in a Sydney recording studio.

Inspired by the Samuel Taylor Coleridge poem "Christabel," "A Foolish Arrangement" is the least impressive of the stellar *Wish*-era B-sides. Musically, it still feels like an unrefined demo, and the melody isn't compelling enough to really capture the listener's attention. This one needed a bit more time under the fire.

Lost Wishes

In November 1993, the Cure released *Lost Wishes*, a four-track EP of dreamy instrumentals recorded during the *Wish* sessions. It was available to members of their fan club via mail order only and only on cassette. All proceeds from the sales were donated to Portsmouth Down Syndrome Trust. Given that *Lost Wishes* was a limited edition and not available through normal retailers, it quickly became a highly sought-after collector's item for fans.

"Uyea Sound," "Cloudberry," "Off to Sleep," and "The Three Sisters" all sound more like demos than completed songs, but they are lovely nonetheless. Robert Smith promised during a radio interview in April 2018 that an expanded reissue of *Wish* was ready for release that would presumably include the *Lost Wishes* tracks.

As of this writing, Cure fans are still waiting. With a new studio album on the horizon, and COVID pushing the world back essentially an entire year, this wait may increase. Or not. Robert Smith does things according to his own off-kilter calendar, so it's hard to predict. Here's one prediction (or call it a fervent wish): perhaps a Record Store Day limited edition vinyl EP of *Lost Wishes*?

All things considered, *Wish* is exactly the album that the Cure needed at that particular moment in time. *Disintegration* part two was out of the question. The sound shifted with a newly guitar-heavy lineup, and the material was shaped with that direction in mind.

Although the album certainly sold well and burned up the charts, the seeds of the Cure's future sales swoon were already planted. An argument can be made that *Wish* tailed off very quickly, with only two substantially successful singles. The Cure was not able to capitalize on the success of "Friday I'm in Love," a failure that marked the end of their commercial golden era in America.

Part of this is can be blamed on the record label's decision to issue "A Letter to Elise," a rather noncommercial track, as the third single. An edited remix of "Wendy Time" or "Doing the Unstuck" likely would have performed better, but the most obvious single after "High" and "Friday I'm in Love" was demoted to B-side status: "Halo."

The deeper issue from a commercial standpoint is that *Wish* is not the "up collection of singles" that Robert Smith promised in August 1991 when the album's working title was *Higher*. Perhaps this is the result of a merger with other tracks not initially earmarked for the project or simply that the Cure does not determine what makes an album based on the prospects for pop radio airplay. Perhaps it was even intentional—after all, Robert Smith was struggling with the idea of the Cure as massive stadium rock band.

Regardless, while some fans are cool to *Wish*, many fans consider it to be the Cure's last truly great album. There is certainly a parade of great songs on the album, with moments of pure genius. Yet the highest highs on the album ("Open," "A Letter to Elise," "High," and "To Wish Impossible Things"), don't quite reach the band's career best, and it's hard to shake the notion that some of the better options were left to waste away as B-sides. Solid, strong, even excellent *Wish* might be, but it feels like a loping triple that with a little bit more oomph could have cleared the wall.

25

Reach Out and Touch the Flame: The Cure's Live Albums and DVDs

The Cure has chronicled their history as one of the world's premier concert draws with multiple outstanding live albums and videos spanning most of their career.

From the very beginning in 1976, when the original members of the Cure were still playing in Malice, through the band's final festival date of 2019 at Austin City Limits, the Cure has played 1,541 shows in thirty-nine countries. Given the marathon nature of Cure sets, that's an astonishing amount of music. Many of these shows were played during tours in support of their studio albums, but the Cure often tours during years in which they have no new product to support, and it's still a major event.

Some of these tours have been chronicled in the extensive series of live albums and videos the band has released spanning much of their career. Each one tells a different story, as every show is a different set list and there are variables between the tours, including how the band approaches the show, the particular lineup at the time, and the various ways the music is presented, whether via audio alone or visually. There are several "must-haves" for fans to get a taste of the Cure as a live band, although the best way to do that, of course, is to get to some actual shows.

Live EPs and Albums

The Peel Sessions EP (1988)

On December 11, 1978, the Cure got a big early boost when the trio played legendary BBC One broadcaster John Peel's radio show. In 1988, four tracks ("Killing an Arab," "10:15 Saturday Night," "Fire in Cairo," and "Boys Don't Cry") from the performance were released as an EP on John Peel's Strange Fruit Records. These recordings illustrate how much more aggressive the Cure sounded in live performance than on their debut album.

The Cure played for the Peel show multiple times, and although there has never been an official release compiling all of these appearances, they do exist on many bootlegs.

Concert: The Cure Live (1984)

Raw and unrefined, the Cure's first live album, *Concert*, was recorded very simply on a mobile unit during three stops on the band's tour in support of *The Top*: May 5, 1984, at the Apollo in Oxford and May 9–10 at the Hammersmith Odeon in London. The plain black cover with white text and grainy images reflects the album's audio vérité; there are no glossy studio overdubs or technological trickery here.

Concert presents the essence of a hard-edged band ripping through ten career-spanning songs with a ferocity that might surprise fans who jumped on the Cure bandwagon only because of the pop hits. *Concert* shows a side of the Cure that had never been captured in the studio. It's a low-budget production, as Robert Smith and Dave Allen spent only a few days mixing it. Robert described it as intentionally "trashy" to the *Record Mirror*.

The lineup of Robert Smith, Porl Thompson, Andy Anderson, Phil Thornalley, and Lol Tolhurst wreck their way through a selection that emphasizes the Cure's harder-rocking tendencies. It opens with an incendiary take on "Shake Dog Shake" before ripping through "Primary," "Charlotte Sometimes," and "The Hanging Garden." Singles like "Let's Go to Bed," "The Lovecats," and "Boys Don't Cry" are passed by in favor of edgier material, like the psychotic freak-out "Give Me It," which closes the first side.

The second half opens with a rocked-out take on "The Walk," followed by the punishing "On Hundred Years" and the album's high point, "A Forest," taut as a high wire blazing with electricity. This recording of "A Forest" was issued as the A-side of a twelve-inch promotional single release called *An Excerpt—The Cure Live*, with "Primary" chosen for the B-side slot. They close the album with two older numbers, and both rock hard: "10:15 Saturday Night" and a tough-as-nails rampage through "Killing an Arab" that is much more potent and harder-edged than the comparatively limp studio version.

It's unfortunate that *Concert* has largely been ignored by the Cure since its release. It wasn't included in their 2006 reissue series and has never been remastered or expanded—a shame, as Robert Smith spent endless hours going through live tapes to select the songs that make up the album, and the result more than justifies that effort. The cassette version was a particular delight to fans, as side 2 included an exclusive ten-song compilation of rarities, demos, and live tracks dubbed *Curiosity (Killing the Cat): Cure Anomalies 1977–1984*.

The Cure Live in Japan (1985)

The Cure's first concert video is also the hardest to find. Filmed in Tokyo at the Nakano Sun Plaza Hall on October 17, 1984, *The Cure Live in Japan* captures the last of three stops the band made in that country in support of *The Top*. It was issued exclusively for the Japanese market on VHS and Beta only and has never been upgraded to DVD.

High-quality original copies can fetch hundreds of dollars, but the average fan can probably make do with finding it streaming online.

It's a solid show and showcases Andy Anderson on drums. The set is heavy on tracks from *The Top*, like "Bird Mad Girl," "Wailing Wall," and "Piggy in the Mirror," that fans rarely have the chance to see live. Also included is the B-side "Happy the Man," which the band played only during their 1984 tour and haven't dusted off since.

The Cure in Orange (1987)

Théâtre antique d'Orange, a first-century AD Roman theater in the French countryside, proved a majestic setting for those mopey British malcontents the Cure to film one of the best concert films of the decade: *The Cure in Orange*.

Directed by Tim Pope, the man behind the Cure's most celebrated string of music videos stretching from 1982 to 1992, the performance was filmed on August 9, 1986, on the last date of the band's massively successful Beach Party Tour, with close-ups and extra footage added at a mock-up shoot the following day.

The performance was a high-pressure moment for the band, as there would be no second chances if things went awry, and a lot of money was already on the line. With only one night to film, they had to nail it, and that's exactly that the Cure did. Unintimidated by the massive crowd, the magnificent historical venue, or the high expectations for the live shoot, the Cure seems relaxed and completely at ease, leaving no doubt from the beginning that they belong on

This Tim Pope-directed concert film is widely regarded as one of the best of the '80s (*Live in Orange*, 1987). *Author's Collection*

that hallowed stage. Robert Smith sent Cureworld into a minor tizzy when he casually threw the giant spidery wig on the top of his head into the crowd during the opener and thereby revealed that he—gasp—cut his hair! Some fans have never fully recovered from the shock.

The film represents one of the band's signature triumphs. *The Cure in Orange* runs nearly ninety-five minutes and features twenty-three songs played by the classic lineup of Robert Smith, Simon Gallup, Porl Thompson, Boris Williams, and Lol Tolhurst. The set covers the length of the band's career, from early gems like "Three Imaginary Boys" and "10:15 Saturday Night" to their newest material from *The Head on the Door*.

The show begins with an absolutely brilliant opening sequence including "Shake Dog Shake," "Piggy in the Mirror," "Play for Today, "A Strange Day," and "Primary." Other high points include powerhouse versions of "Sinking" and

"Faith" and crowd-pleasing pop hits like "In Between Days," "The Walk," and "Let's Go to Bed."

Despite its stature as the best loved of the Cure's concert films, *The Cure in Orange* has still never been issued on DVD or Blu-ray. Fans hoping to watch it must find a dusty VHS tape, a LaserDisc, or an online stream. In October 2009, Robert Smith indicated that *The Cure in Orange* would finally be available on DVD in 2010, but it never materialized.

Entreat (1991)

Recorded at Wembley Arena in July 1989 during the Cure's Prayer Tour, *Entreat* was originally intended simply as a promo disc for the French market. It featured eight songs from *Disintegration*, several of which had already been used as single B-sides. Those hungry for anything Cure related in the wake of their big breakthrough snatched up import copies, and the disc improbably became popular among fans. Many became angry at facing extortionate import prices, leading Robert Smith to eventually agree to release the set outright.

In 2010, when *Disintegration* was remixed and remastered for vinyl release, an expanded twelve-track version of *Entreat*, now encompassing a live performance of *Disintegration* in its entirety, was also presented for the first time.

Show (1993)

An elaborately produced live album and video from the Cure's grueling trek in support of *Wish*, *Show* was recorded over two nights from July 18 to 19, 1992, at the Palace of Auburn Hills in Auburn Hills, Michigan. It hit stores more than a year later on September 13, 1993, as a two-disc set in most countries, and the concert film was available on VHS and LaserDisc.

Show was trimmed to a single disc in the United States at the insistence of Elektra Records, and the missing tracks ("Fascination Street," "Let's Go to Bed," and "The Walk") were instead sold separately as the EP *Sideshow*.

Most of *Wish* is included, and the live versions often outshine the originals. "From the Edge of the Deep Green Sea" is a behemoth that pulses with energy, becoming more substantial as a centerpiece of the Cure's live performances than as an album track. The heaviest tracks from *Wish*—"Open," "Cut," and "End"—are dispatched with hurricane ferocity. The pop numbers "High," "Friday I'm in Love," and "Doing the Unstuck" all bounce with verve and feeling. Scattered throughout are hits from the Cure's golden era, including "Just Like Heaven," "Pictures of You," "In Between Days," and "Never Enough."

Unfortunately, the set is missing the encores for the Auburn Hills shows, including "To Wish Impossible Things," "Primary," "Boys Don't Cry," "Why Can't I Be You?," and "A Forest." The live concert film was a huge undertaking, as

Robert Smith had to laboriously rework the footage after he loathed the original director's cut. Sadly, *Show* has never been refurbished or upgraded. In late 2009, Smith posted to thecure.com that *Show* would be newly reissued on DVD/Blu-ray the following year, but, like the similarly promised *The Cure in Orange*, this has yet to occur.

Paris (1993)

A companion album to *Show* to further document the Cure's massive *Wish* tour, *Paris* was recorded at Le Zénith de Paris over three nights from October 19 to 21, 1992. It's more raw and less refined than *Show*, giving it the vibe of an excellent-quality bootleg. *Paris* highlights some of the darker and more obscure tracks played during the *Wish* tour, including "The Figurehead," "At Night," "In Your House," and "Dressing Up."

Two songs stand out in particular: a thrilling take on the classic "Charlotte Sometimes" and a high-energy performance of "Play for Today" that features perhaps the best example on record of the audience singing with joyous abandon along with the keyboard riff.

Although *Paris* may be the least well known major release from the Cure among more casual fans, vinyl record collectors should be familiar with it. Given it was such a small vinyl pressing when released, copies can be exceedingly difficult to track down and prohibitively expensive—several hundred dollars easy, depending on the condition.

Five Swing Live (1997)

Following the Swing Tour, the Cure released a little thank-you to fans that has since become an expensive collector's item. Fiction issued the *Five Swing Live* EP exclusively through thecure.com, limiting it to 5,000 numbered copies. The tracks selected ("Want," "Club America," "Mint Car," "Trap," and "Treasure") are among the strongest cuts from *Wild Mood Swings*, and the performances, recorded in December 1996 as the tour wound through Birmingham, Sheffield, and Manchester on its final three stops, are outstanding.

Trilogy (2002)

David Bowie was one of Robert Smith's most important musical influences, so perhaps it's not surprising that a Bowie concert would inspire Smith to undertake one of the most ambitious live projects in the Cure's history. While on tour for his brilliant 2002 album *Heathen*, Bowie's set consisted of the new album in its entirety and then most of his 1977 masterpiece *Low* during one long segment. When Smith attended Bowie's July 29, 2002, performance at the Royal

Festival Hall in London, he was blown away by both the performance and the conceptual aspect of the show, and he immediately resolved to stage something similar with the Cure.

Plans developed quickly for the *Trilogy* concerts, held in Brussels on November 7, 2002, and then for two nights in Berlin on November 11–12. The Cure planned to perform their "dark trilogy"—*Pornography*, *Disintegration*, and *Bloodflowers*—all the way through, in sequence. The lineup of Smith, Simon Gallup, Perry Bamonte, Jason Cooper, and Roger O'Donnell was at its very best.

The intensity and emotional depth of the performances came shining through on the beautifully filmed DVD set released on June 3, 2003, called *The Cure: Trilogy (Live in the Tempodrom Berlin November 2002)*. The nearly four-hour presentation includes the three featured albums played in their entirety plus an encore of two songs that fit the sequence perfectly: "If Only Tonight We Could Sleep" and "The Kiss" from *Kiss Me, Kiss Me, Kiss Me*.

Robert Smith considers *Trilogy* to be a celebration of the albums that best represent the Cure's first twenty-five years of recording. *Trilogy* has never been released as an official audio CD (a lavish multidisc LP box set would be a vinyl lover's dream), making the DVD or Blu-ray release an essential purchase for Cure fans.

The Cure Festival 2005 (2006)

Released on DVD in late 2006, *The Cure Festival 2005* documents the band's summer European festival shows as seen through the camera lens of fans and crew. The rough look of the visuals matches the hard edge of the music. The Cure was a four-piece at the time, with Porl Thompson's guitar taking oversize prominence as they toured in support of their hard-rocking 2004 album *The Cure*. Missing is a lot of the subtlety we are used to hearing from the Cure, and the absence of keyboards leaves a gaping hole in their signature sound.

Despite an outstanding set list including lesser-played cuts like "The Blood," "Shake Dog Shake," "The Kiss," "A Strange Day," and "A Drowning Man," *The Cure Festival 2005* is one of the more difficult Cure offerings to sit through. With sound quality that's on par with a decent bootleg rather than an official release, *The Cure Festival 2005* is likely to be of interest only to completists.

Bestival Live 2011 (2011)

One of the lesser-known Cure live releases appeared on December 6, 2011, barely more than two months after the show was recorded. *Bestival Live 2011* documents the band's performance at that year's festival on the Isle of Wight, a frequent stop on the Cure's concert schedule.

Bestival Live 2011 offers a look at the touring lineup of Smith, Gallup, Cooper, and the return of Roger O'Donnell. The keyboards are much welcome, and the set is outstanding, with a few songs from the most recent studio album, *4:13 Dream*, interspersed with the expected hits and deep cuts. Unfortunately, the sound is lackluster and there's not much to generate excitement. As with *Festival 2005*, *Bestival* can safely be skipped unless one is attempting to soak up the Cure's entire vast catalog. Not a bad idea, to be sure, but there are far better examples of the Cure in a live setting.

40 Live Curaetion 25 + Anniversary Deluxe (2019)

When the Cure announced the forthcoming release of this lavish box set covering two of the most consequential shows in the band's history, it became pretty clear that despite Robert Smith's promises, there wouldn't be a new studio release in 2019. While that was a disappointment to fans, *40 Live Curaetion 25* is about as good a consolation prize as the band possibly could have delivered.

Forty years into its history the Cure is in prime form, unleashing two knockout performances in high profile, high pressure settings. This collection documents two singular triumphs and helped usher in a period for which appreciation of the Cure has skyrocketed. The moment it was released, *40 Live Cureation 25* overpowered the competition to comfortably assume its position as the finest live document the Cure has yet released.

The deluxe edition which includes four audio CDs and two DVDs, and a book, all presented beautifully, is well worth the investment.

Cureation-25: From There to Here—From Here to There was held on the last night of the 25th Meltdown Festival on June 24, 2018 at the Royal Festival Hall in London. The ten-day event was curated by Robert Smith, who unsurprisingly was able to pull a stellar lineup of artists to perform, including Nine Inch Nails, My Bloody Valentine, Deftones, Placebo, Manic Street Preachers, the Psychedelic Furs, the Church, Suzanne Vega, and the Twilight Sad, among many others.

For the Cure's final-night headlining performance, Robert and the band planned something special and unique: *From There to Here—From Here to There*. The Cure covered its entire history by playing just one song from each studio album from start to finish chronologically, and then do a second set of songs in reverse order. It worked to perfection. The intimate crowd was perfect for such an unusual show, and Robert smartly mixed some well-known songs with a lot of deep cuts. The band absolutely nailed the performances, sounding every bit as good as they ever have—perhaps better.

The Cure opened with "Three Imaginary Boys" representing their debut album, and off they went with "At Night," "Other Voices," "A Strange Day," "Bananafishbones," "A Night Like This," "Like Cockatoos," "Pictures of You,"

This excellent live document of the *Disintegration* era was issued on vinyl for the first time in 2010 (Entreat Live Concert, 1990). *Author's Collection*

"High," "Jupiter Crash," "39," "Us or Them," and finally "It's Over" representing their most recent studio album, *4:13 Dream*. The Cure ended set one with "It Can Never Be the Same," an unreleased track they first played in concert during their 2016 tour.

For the return trip second set, they again started with a previously unreleased song, "Step into the Light," which was also first performed live in 2016. The Cure then rollicked back through their career in the opposition direction, ending like a boulder thundering downhill with a series of hard rockers. Starting with the most recent this time, the second representative from *4:13 Dream* is the album's best song, "The Hungry Ghost," then back step by step with "alt.end," "Last Day of Summer," "Want," "From the Edge of the Deep Green Sea," "Disintegration," "If Only Tonight We Could Sleep," "Sinking," "Shake Dog Shake," "One Hundred Years," "Primary" (a last-minute replacement as "Faith" was on the printed set list), "A Forest," and then back to the start again with "Boys Don't Cry."

The box set gives fans the opportunity to watch the show via DVD or Blu-ray, and the audio is presented over two discs. The film is beautifully directed by Nick Wickham, who'd already killed it with *Trilogy*, the Cure's former high-water mark for a concert film. The vibe is chill and relatively sedate, to be expected given the small indoor venue and a song selection that skews to the downbeat and includes multiple relative obscurities. It was a much larger crowd a few weeks later for another historic London show by the Cure, their fortieth-anniversary performance on July 7, 2018, at Hyde Park. More than 60,000 jammed together on one of the hottest days of the summer to help the Cure celebrate four incredible decades of music. Again, the band was on point with a performance that met the lofty expectations. The carefully selected set is similar to the band's recent festival outings, focusing mostly on well-known material. The crowd responded with enthusiasm by singing along, dancing, swaying, cheering, screaming—and some were tearful at times.

The Cure's longtime video director Tim Pope took the reins again this time, and he does a masterful job bringing the moment to us as we watch. We see the Cure up front and personal, blemishes and wrinkles and all, and are able to occupy a prime viewing location to observe the band's tight and sometimes intense connection with the music and their fans. The mixing and editing are great, and the audio is crisp, clear, and dynamic—miles away from the murky *Show*.

The shows were so good, it was only a matter of time before an audio-visual documentation of them was presented for fans to enjoy, and the band prepared for it all along. Fortunately, the box set *40 Live Cureation 25* is every bit as good a presentation as is the music inside.

26

The Rhythm Has Control: The Drummers

Multiple drummers have contributed to the band's music, each with a distinct style and approach.

Andy Anderson

Andy Anderson entered the Cure's universe when they were set for an April 1983 appearance on BBC's *The Oxford Road Show*. It was too high profile a television spot for the Cure to miss, but they were not exactly ready for prime time. At this point, it was questionable whether the Cure truly existed anymore, as they were down to just Robert Smith and former drummer and presumed keyboardist Lol Tolhurst. They needed a new drummer ASAP.

Chris Parry knew Anderson through his work with Steve Hillage, Brilliant, and Sham 69's, a band that Parry signed to Polydor. After nailing an audition in front of Parry and Robert Smith, Anderson joined the Cure that very day. He made the TV appearance, which was supposed to highlight the new single "Let's Go to Bed" and "Just One Kiss." At Robert's insistence, they instead hammered through the dark and menacing "One Hundred Years" and "The Figurehead."

During his time with the Cure, Andy Anderson played on "The Lovecats" single and its B-sides "Speak My Language" and "Mr. Pink Eyes," performed on the Glove's *Blue Sunshine*, and was drummer for *The Top* album. He was part of the lineup for the handful of 1983 shows the band performed and again for their more extensive 1984 tour. His superb drum work can be heard on the *Concert* live album.

The Cure's 1984 tour in support of *The Top* was Anderson's final stand with the group. His behavior had grown increasingly erratic as the trek progressed, stemming at least in part from heavy substance abuse. Robert Smith later commented that Anderson simply kept "flipping out." The drummer was arrested in Nice, France, after an altercation with a security guard.

The situation finally grew untenable while the Cure was in Tokyo on the Japanese leg of their tour. Anderson got into a violent confrontation with hotel security and with members of the Cure's own entourage, and his hotel room was utterly trashed. Robert Smith had no choice but to fire him. Lol Tolhurst later complained that while the band was encouraged to hire Anderson, those recommending him neglected to mention that Anderson "went crazy" while on the road.

Anderson later attributed his behavior to hypoglycemia, and he said in a 1992 interview with the French magazine *BEST* that he left the Cure voluntarily because he had different opinions than the rest of the band and management.

Whatever the circumstances of his departure, Andy Anderson made valuable contributions during his time with the Cure, including the loopy percussion on "The Caterpillar" and his rapid-fire blasts on "Shake Dog Shake." Anderson was ferocious onstage, bringing a fire to songs like "Give Me It" and "One Hundred Years" that was unmatched by any other Cure drummer. After leaving the Cure, Anderson continued his long association with British guitarist Steve Hillage and worked with Iggy Pop, Peter Gabriel, and Lol Tolhurst's post-Cure band Levinhurst.

Time dulled whatever hard feelings, if any, may have existed between Anderson and Robert Smith. After the Royal Albert Hall show in 2014, Anderson reported that Robert dedicated "Shake Dog Shake" to him and that they met for a brief conversation after the show and it felt like no time had passed at all. Even though he was not selected for induction, Andy offered warm congratulations to his bandmates and expressed gratitude to Cure fans everywhere when the Rock and Roll Hall of Fame announced the band's inclusion in December 2018. Sadly, he was in declining health at the time. Robert Smith was aware of Anderson's health woes and lobbied unsuccessfully to get him inducted into the Hall of Fame with his bandmates, knowing it would be a huge deal to the terminally ill drummer. Unfortunately, the Hall of Fame wouldn't budge.

On February 17, 2019, Anderson announced on his Facebook page that he was suffering from terminal stage 4 cancer. He posted, "There is no way of returning back ... it's totally covering the inside of my body, and I'm totally fine and aware of my situation. I've gone for a no-resuscitation." Despite the grim prognosis, Anderson urged fans to remain positive: "Please, no boo-hooing here, just be positive. For me it's just another life experience and hurdle that one has to make.... Be cool, I most definitely am, and positive about the situation." Anderson died nine days later on February 26 at age sixty-eight.

The Cure posted in tribute, "In memoriam Andy Anderson, a great drummer and a great man." Lol Tolhurst, who had stayed in touch with Anderson throughout his illness, commented on Twitter that he was a "true gentleman and a great musician with a wicked sense of humour, which he kept until the end." Iggy Pop said of Anderson, "Andy was a great guy. He was one of the nicest people I've ever met or worked with. I'm really sorry he's gone." During the Rock and Roll Hall of Fame induction ceremony, Robert thanked the late drummer during his acceptance speech, and the Cure performed his signature number, "Shake Dog Shake," as their opening song of the Hall of Fame set in his honor.

The drummer's funeral took place in his hometown of Chelmsford, where he was known simply as Cliff (his birth name was Clifford Leon Anderson). His funeral was as memorable as his fiery onstage performances—the coffin was made to look like a drum case with a custard cream lid, and the names of the bands he had played for were emblazoned on both sides.

Anderson played for the Cure for only a brief time, but nobody can doubt the impact he made musically. Anderson was regarded by his bandmates with warmth and respect, and esteem for him and his work will continue to grow as the years go by and new generations of fans discover the Cure's catalog and in particular, a peculiar album midway through called *The Top*.

Boris Williams

After Andy Anderson was fired in Tokyo on the Cure's 1984 tour in support of *The Top*, they needed a drummer immediately, as North American dates were only five days away. Bassist Phil Thornalley, well-connected in the industry, was able to help get Vince Ely from the Psychedelic Furs on a temporary basis. Ely was a short-time fill-in because of other commitments, but Thornalley once again saved the day by helping to lure the talented Boris Williams away from the Thompson Twins.

It was a whirlwind preparation for Boris Williams. He was in California on vacation when he received Thornalley's call. He jumped at the opportunity to join the tour even though he'd be taking a substantial pay cut. He rushed out to buy the Cure's entire back catalog, and they sent him a tape of all the songs being played on tour. Williams flew out to Minneapolis to meet the band, they had two sound checks, and he was deemed ready to perform that night at the famous First Avenue on November 7, 1984.

Boris Williams felt like a part of the band almost immediately, whereas with the Thompson Twins, he was treated like an employee. With the Thompson Twins, the live performances were largely mechanized and reliant on tapes, so his creative input was limited. He was unrestrained onstage with the Cure, who played completely live every night and were not caught up with making sure the songs sounded exactly the same from show to show. The Cure and their crew were also far more fun to be around, especially since Boris liked to drink, a vice that the Thompson Twins strictly forbade while on tour.

Robert Smith was so impressed that after the tour, he invited Williams to officially join the band, which was the start of a ten-year tenure that encompassed the Cure's "golden years." He's widely regarded by fans as the best of all the Cure's drummers.

Williams's versatility and skill opened a world of possibilities for the Cure. They had been constrained on the early albums because of Lol Tolhurst's limitations, but there were no such problems with Williams. Although he didn't consider himself a technically gifted drummer, Williams had an intuitive feel for a song and what it required. His parts are often quite simple, with superb timing and discipline, with flashes of technical wizardry when needed. He's adept at creating hypnotic cyclical patterns that provide the foundation for many Cure songs. He helped the Cure build a wider sonic canvas for their greatest albums: *The Head on the Door*, *Kiss Me, Kiss Me, Kiss Me*, *Disintegration*, and *Wish*.

Boris Williams (nicknamed "The Count" by the band) also submitted demos for Robert Smith and the rest of the band to consider during the initial songwriting process for a new album, often in collaboration with guitarist Porl Thompson. His drum technique, loose and fluid with creative rolls, was instrumental in the creation of such key songs as "Fascination Street" and the ferocious "Icing Sugar." It was Boris Williams who delivered the deftly motoric rhythm and those perfect fills that made "Just Like Heaven" possible.

After a decade with the Cure, Boris decided it was time to move on. He left in 1994, not long after the end of the arduous *Wish* tour, so that he could work with his girlfriend Caroline Crawley in the group Babacar. His final studio recording with the Cure was on "Burn" from the 1994 soundtrack to *The Crow*.

Williams made a brief return behind the drum kit for the Cure for the 2001 acoustic recording of their biggest singles for the bonus disc to their *Greatest Hits* album. He also attended a few sessions for the band's 2004 self-titled album produced by Ross Robinson. Boris Williams stood proudly with his bandmates in March 2019 as the Cure was inducted into the Rock and Roll Hall of Fame.

Jason Cooper

After the departure of Boris Williams in 1994, the Cure planned to use session drummers for their next album: *Wild Mood Swings*. Several drummers appeared on the album, but with an ambitious tour schedule looming, a permanent solution was needed.

They decided to place a blind ad in *Melody Maker* that read, "Very famous band requires drummer, no metal-heads." An avalanche of audition tapes had to be sorted out to determine who would get an in-person tryout. The final stage would be an actual jam session with the band. The Cure had no shortage of options, as multiple heavy-hitting drummers with serious professional experience auditioned.

But in true Cure fashion, it was an inexperienced newcomer that got the gig over the wizened pros. Jason Cooper, only twenty-seven years old, had been in the Brit pop group My Life Story before rolling the dice for a famous unnamed band. While he lacked the experience and technical skills of the other candidates, Cooper had one major factor in his favor—he was a ginormous Cure fan.

Cooper's father had worked for Virgin Records, building their megastores in various markets, and he was a huge music fan. Jason got *Seventeen Seconds* from him at age twelve, and he couldn't stop playing it. He also grew to love *Faith* and *Pornography* and saw the Cure perform at Glastonbury. Robert Smith and *Wild Mood Swings* producer Steve Lyon thought Cooper would be a good fit with the band's peculiar mix of personalities, always a huge factor with the Cure. His youth and enthusiasm certainly helped as well.

Jason Cooper got the job, and he's been the Cure's drummer ever since. Robert Smith's initial instructions to him were to play in the spirit of the music. Replacing the gifted Boris Williams would be daunting for anyone, but the spirited Cooper took the challenge in stride. He doesn't have Williams's deft touch and intuitive feel for the music, and he occasionally sounds clunky and disconnected. Some fans complain that he often goes overboard with too many cymbals, and his fills are sometimes poorly placed in the context of the music. However, he can also be downright phenomenal, and he's put in the work and effort to continue to improve.

A vocal segment of Cure fandom still insists that Cooper has never really fit in, but it's hard to argue with the results: the "new guy" has been part of the band longer than any drummer in their history (twenty-three years). When the Cure was nominated for the Rock and Roll Hall of Fame in 2012, Jason Cooper's name was left off the ballot. Robert Smith was irate and publicly scolded the Hall of Fame selection committee.

They got it right the second time around. Jason Cooper, Boris Williams, and Laurence Tolhurst, three of the Cure's drummers, were all enshrined into the Rock and Roll Hall of Fame with their bandmates.

Believe Me, I'm Going to Be Big: The Cure in Popular Culture

With Robert Smith's larger-than-life persona and well-loved songs that transcend generations, the Cure are deeply ingrained in modern popular culture.

David Bowie sang about "Sound and Vision," and he was a master at both, combining the elements to stunning effect. He was the ultimate shapeshifter, his persona and music changing regularly as he scored one landmark album after another. Robert Smith latched onto him as a young adolescent when, like so many others in the United Kingdom, he was jolted by Bowie's game-changing television performance of "Starman." There's no question that his careful study of Bowie's career was an enormous influence on his own.

It was a major awakening for Robert Smith as he realized the opportunities presented by merging music and visuals into one complete package. While nobody can hope to equal Bowie, Robert's deft mix of whimsy and woe has built the Cure into pop-culture titans with a career spanning forty years and counting to their credit. His shrewd understanding of how music and visuals can work together has been a major factor in the Cure's cultural ascendance.

One of the keys to entering the public's consciousness in a lasting way is creating a memorable identity, which Robert Smith has certainly done for himself and the Cure. That briar patch of twisty black hair, his ghoulishly pale face with eyeliner and smeared red lipstick, and the formless black clothing that just seems to hang on him in layers help create a persona that is an effective vehicle from which the Cure's music can flow. It all fits like a rumpled glove, the light and darkness both visually and musically.

Legendary rock band, the Cure, inducted into Hollywood's Rockwalk, 2004.
Credit Tsuni / USA / Alamy

Robert Smith's appearance as himself on the American animated series *South Park* is perhaps the most famous instance of the Cure's ability to transcend upward and outward to infiltrate the work of others. Creators Matt Stone and Trey Parker, massive fans of the band, worked Robert Smith into an episode called "Mecha-Streisand" in which he battles a monster born from the image of Barbra Streisand. After turning himself into a giant moth, he defeats Mecha-Streisand and is hailed as a hero by the town's citizens. As Smith walks away, one of the show's main characters, Kyle Broflovski, calls out to him the now famous line: "*Disintegration* is the best album ever!"

Airing on February 18, 1998, as the twelfth episode of season 1, "Mecha-Streisand" set a new high for viewership for the show. A bemused Robert Smith had delivered his lines over the phone and didn't really understand what the episode was about, in part because his script was intentionally left incomplete. Although it's been more than twenty years since the episode aired, Smith still fondly notes it as one of his favorite projects, mostly because being on *South Park* rendered him far cooler in the eyes of his nieces and nephews than simply being the lead singer for the Cure.

Smith had a chance to contribute to another 1998 Stone and Parker project, offering the track "A Sign from God" for use in their film *Orgazmo*. Robert Smith recorded it with Cure drummer Jason Cooper and future Cure guitarist Reeves Gabrels at the same session that yielded the single "Wrong Number," which became a substantial hit for the Cure. "A Sign from God" was issued under the name COGASM, which combines the first two letters of each member's name, although it had every bit as much right to the Cure name as "Wrong Number." It seems a shame that the upbeat electro-rock track was relegated to obscurity—it might have made a great follow-up single to "Wrong Number."

The Cure was almost an even bigger focus in a feature film. Famed 1980s filmmaker John Hughes very nearly put a Cure song front and center in one of his films. Shortly after Hughes's shocking 2009 death of a heart attack, actress Molly Ringwald, one of Hughes's greatest collaborators, told *Vanity Fair*, "When *The Breakfast Club* ended, [Hughes] started writing a script called *Lovecats*, because I played him that song by the Cure... I was obsessed by the Cure—still am. I think Robert Smith is an underrated songwriter. Anyway, I played this song for John, and he started writing a script, and he gave me a mix tape of what the soundtrack was gonna be. Which was pretty much Dave Brubeck, with the last song by Bob Dylan."

The Cure's biggest movie hit came in 1994 with "Burn," the searing opener for *The Crow* soundtrack. James O'Barr, a big fan of the band, included the lyrics to "The Hanging Garden" in his original comic on which the film is based. When Robert Smith was asked for permission to use the song in the film, he instead offered to write and record a new track specifically for the project. The movie was a box office smash, prompting a high-profile sequel, and *The Crow* soundtrack hit number one on the *Billboard* Album Chart.

Not quite as successful is "Dredd Song," the band's grandiose theme for *Judge Dredd*, a 1995 action sci-fi behemoth starring Sylvester Stallone. The Cure gamely tried to go the Hollywood route, and along with producer Steve Lyon, they put their all into creating a cinematic rock epic. Unfortunately, like the film itself, the song didn't quite come together. *Judge Dredd* was a noteworthy failure, and "Dredd Song" is not likely to be featured in the band's live set anytime soon.

The vast majority of Cure songs featured in films or on TV were not written specifically for the project. The slithery keyboard carousel of "Six Different Ways" is used to creepy effect in the smash Stephen King adaptation, *It*, a box office behemoth. It's also highlighted in the 2002 adaptation of Bret Easton Ellis's *The Rules of Attraction*. Two years earlier, an Underdog remix of "Watching Me Fall" was included in another Ellis film adaptation: *American Psycho*. Two excellent Danny Lohner remixes of Cure songs were featured on the soundtracks to two *Underworld* films: in 2009, "Underneath the Stars" was used for *Underworld: Rise of the Lycans*, and in 2012, *Underworld: Awakening* included "Apart."

"All Cats Are Grey" and "Plainsong" are in *Marie Antoinette*, "Grinding Halt" in *Times Square*, and "Fascination Street" on *Lost Angels*. "Plainsong" appears briefly in the superhero film *Antman*. "In Between Days" is on the soundtrack for the 2016 film *Sing Street* and made a memorable appearance in *Gross Pointe Blank*. Several major films have been titled after Cure songs, including 1999's

Boys Don't Cry and 2005's *Just Like Heaven*. "Boys Don't Cry" has had a few memorable appearances, like in *The Wedding Singer*, *The Beach Bum*, and *Moi et toi*.

On a couple occasions, Robert has recorded new versions of classic Cure songs for a visual project. He and Roger O'Donnell reworked "Pictures of You" for the 2019 documentary *Dead Good*, and in 2015, he recorded a new version of the B-side "A Few Hours After This" for Idris Elba's BBC crime drama, *Luther*. The show's creator, Neil Cross, considers himself an "obsessive Cure fan since age 13," and he was over the moon excited when Robert Smith agreed to re-record the old obscurity.

Television has been home to Cure music as well. The popular and much-discussed HBO show *Westwood* included a chilling instrumental piano version of "A Forest" in the season 1 episode "Dissonance Theory" in 2016. *Cold Case* was perhaps the most effective use of the Cure's music in a television show overall (or at least the most extensive). From 2003 through 2009, seven Cure songs were scattered over six episodes: "Other Voices," "Secrets," "A Forest," "Lullaby," "Just Like Heaven," "Pictures of You," and "Lovesong." *One Tree Hill* also featured multiple Cure songs; between 2004 and 2009, the show included "Pictures of You," "Fascination Street," "Prayers for Rain," "To Wish Impossible Things," and "Apart" in five different episodes. "Lovesong" was included in an episode of *Vampire Diaries*.

In 2015, *American Horror Story* memorably used two of the Cure's creepiest tunes: "Lullaby" and "Siamese Twins." "Pictures of You" has been used in a multiple television shows, including *Gilmore Girls*, *The Politician*, and *The Vow*. "Friday I'm in Love" was used in *Melrose Place*, *S.P.U.N.G.*, *The Worst Week of My Life*, *Chuck*, *My Mad Fat Diary*, *Ghosts*, and others. "Just Like Heaven" has been in *the Goldbergs*, *New Tricks*, and others.

These mere handful of examples is just a tiny sampling; the Cure's music has proved compelling enough that at last count, according to the experts at IMDb (the International Movie Database), a song by the Cure has appeared in a major film or television series a whopping 179 times, but it seems surely more than that. The first Cure song to appear on a television series was 1979, when "A Forest" aired during the show *Something Else*. Their first song to nab a slot in a major motion picture was "Grinding Halt" in 1980 in *Times Square*.

The band has also performed on numerous daily shows and variety shows over the years, exposing many of their songs to large TV audiences. Their songs have been featured in reality shows like *Dancing with the Stars*, *The Masked Singer*, *The Voice*, *So You Think You Can Dance*, and others.

Directors will sometimes use Cure-related props, such as a big "Boys Don't Cry" poster hanging on a dorm room wall or a Cure t-shirt that's constantly worn, to help suggest certain characteristics. Martha Plimpton's character wore an "In Between Days" t-shirt in the 1987 film *Shy People*, for instance. Cure

The Cure performing on stage at the "MTV Icon of 2004" tribute to the band, held at the Old Billingsgate Market, London. *PA Images / Alamy Stock Photo*

posters and other memorabilia are sometimes seen in bedrooms, or a Cure song might be played in the background—or any other association with the Cure or Robert Smith, really, that can bring an immediate additional level of understanding to a character's personality.

What they are essentially doing is feeding on stereotypes, and many longtime Cure fans can speak with endless frustration about being subject to these personally. The stereotypical Cure fans might be smart, acutely emotional, and is likely viewed internally and by others as a misfit or an outsider, with artistic talent but often self-destructive tendencies. There might be some tendencies toward goth subculture. Might be the smartest kid in the class, but is more likely than not to be shy, may grapple with depression and anxiety, but has a good heart and good intentions, exhibiting loyalty and a fierce sense of humor that flashes when least expected. None or some or all of these may apply, of course, but they all are perceptions of Cure fans that a director might use to paint a character.

Robert Smith had promised never to allow the Cure's music to be used in commercials, although he backed away from that vow a couple times. "In Between Days" was used for Punto and Fiat automobile ads, and more controversial was "Pictures of You" for a Hewlett-Packard ad. Smith later said to *Spin*, "I agonized about the Hewlett-Packard ad that used 'Pictures of You.' I was backed into a corner with that and I still feel really bad about it.... 'Pictures of You' is a huge song in the Cure canon. It means a lot."

Robert Smith revealed to *NME* that it was necessary for the Cure to earn the money for those ads so that they could keep control of their catalog as their deal with Polydor was nearing its end. He said, "I'm so against music in adverts, it fucking killed me even agreeing to that, but it was the only way. The money generated from those adverts went into buying me control on our back catalogue, otherwise it would have been like mortgaging the band." Thanks to their inherent gloom and overexaggerated melancholy and, of course, Robert Smith's outlandishly ghoulish appearance, the Cure has often been on the receiving end of parody. Although he's often noted as morose—and indeed much of his music is—Smith's sharp sense of humor is often missed in caricatures of him.

For instance, during an episode of *The Mighty Boosh*, a British show featuring skits performed by the popular comedy troupe of the same name, an advertisement appears for "Goth Juice, the most powerful hairspray known to man... Made from the tears of Robert Smith." *The Mary Whitehouse Experience*, another British comedy show, often pointed witty barbs the Cure's way, usually with actors portraying members of the band. Robert Smith took the ribbing with good humor, even going as far as appearing on the show for the season 2 finale.

Robert Smith's stage appearance has been a huge source of inspiration for countless fans and artists. Tim Burton based his title character to *Edward Scissorhands* primarily on Smith, and even asked him to do the score for the film. He sent Smith a script, but the Cure was too busy working on *Disintegration* for Robert to take the job. They would eventually have the opportunity to work together, as Smith recorded a couple of soundtrack tunes for him. It's easy to see the Robert Smith influence in Tim Burton's aesthetic, though, from *The Nightmare before Christmas* to *Frankenweenie*.

The Cure's music has been immeasurably influential for a huge range of artists, and many of them have acknowledged this. Blink-182's Tom Delonge, for example, cited the Cure as a band that changed his life, and his bandmate Mark Hoppus has said that Robert Smith's appearance on the 2003 Blink-182 track "All of This" is one of the highlights of his career.

More recently, Robert recorded a vocal part for the currently popular Scottish synth-pop group the CHVRCHES for their 2021 single "How Not to Drown" from their new album *Screen Violence*.

The band's manager attempted to contact Smith about the CHVRCHES possibly opening for the Cure for some dates on their next tour, but the discussions instead led to a superb guest vocal by Smith on an exciting electroclash single that will hopefully elevate the CHVRCHES' visibility.

CHVRCHES' vocalist Lauren Mayberry said of Robert Smith, "We are all huge Cure fans.... He has chosen to take the path to be just a really cool, nice guy who's still interested in music and still creating." Multi-instrumentalist Martin Dohery said, "He's a genius.... I'm stating the obvious, but even now... every intricacy in the record, he stayed involved. Loads of thoughts and loads of really great insight. We're obsessed with the Cure. *Disintegration is* my favorite album; I wouldn't be in this band if it wasn't for his music."

Billy Corgan of Smashing Pumpkins has long considered the Cure one of his most pivotal influences. The Pumpkins recorded a cover of "A Night Like This" as a B-side, and Corgan had Robert Smith guest on his solo LP *The Future Embrace*. Interpol vocalist Paul Banks said every member of his band was heavily influenced by the Cure. Jonathan Davis of Korn said to *Kerrang* of the Cure's music, "That's my teenage years right there," and he said one of his proudest moments was when the Cure performed with the band during Korn's taping of *MTV Unplugged*. Billy Howerdel of A Perfect Circle cited Robert Smith as an influential guitarist whose technique he could never quite master. Philip Anselmo, former front man of groove-metal powerhouse Pantera, told *LouderSound*, "I have an incredible amount of respect for [the Cure]." He named *Seventeen Seconds* his favorite Cure album and said that their music "definitely touches a spot in my heart." Soundgarden named them a major influence. Brand New borrows a line of lyric from "Close to Me" for their 2001 track "Logan to Government Center." The superb "shoegaze" band Slowdive are fans and have been open about the Cure's influence on their musical development.

When Robert Smith turned sixty on April 21, 2019, ace Rage Against the Machine guitarist and Rock and Roll Hall of Fame committee member Tom Morello took to Instagram to express his admiration. He wrote, "Happy 60th birthday.... *Disintegration* is one of my favorite albums of all time. Dark, beautiful, romantic, and deep as a troubled sea. I lobbied hard for their well-deserved admittance to the Rock Hall."

Pop artists have also been swept up by the Cure's music and not always during times of glee. One of the biggest stars on the planet, Lady Gaga, told *The Guardian* that "Never Enough" could be the theme for her "lost weekend." She said, "My cocaine soundtrack was always the Cure. I love all their music, but I listened to this one song on repeat while I did bags and bags of cocaine. 'Whatever I do, it's never enough.' Isn't that funny?"

As is inevitable for a band of the Cure's stature, there have been countless cover versions recorded of their songs by artists of every conceivable genre. Rock, pop, metal, EDM, easy listening, reggae, classical, jazz, swing, country, rhythm-and-blues, and rap artists have all tried their hand at interpreting a Cure song. There's even a complete album of Cure songs recorded as children's lullabies.

Even if an artist doesn't get around to recording a Cure cover in the studio, many have performed one or more of the band's songs in concert. In 1999, No Doubt sometimes included a bouncy rendition of the early pop-punk gem "Jumping Someone Else's Train" during their encore. Smashing Pumpkins frequently did "Friday I'm in Love" with James Iha on vocals in 2019. David Gray,

Counting Crows, Natalie Imbruglia, and Crowded House have also performed the 1990s pop nugget in shows.

"Lovesong" is, of course, a favorite, with Adele and Tori Amos both delivering dazzling renditions in concert. It's also been performed by artists as diverse as Death Cab for Cutie, Snake River Conspiracy, Tracy Chapman, Good Charlotte, 5 Seconds of Summer, and Imagine Dragons. The edgy 1990s alt-rock group 311 had a moderate hit with their 2004 cover of "Lovesong," recorded for the Adam Sandler comedy *50 First Dates*.

There have been numerous attempts to rework the band's classic 1980 single "A Forest," with varying degrees of success. Synth-goth gloomsters Clan of Xymox give it a try on their 2012 covers album *Kindred Spirits* to mediocre results, and even worse is the plodding and graceless 2017 cover by the British doom metal band Alunah. One of the finest is the icy-cool take by Frankie Rose from her 2017 rerecording of the entire *Seventeen Seconds* album.

Indie rockers Luna tackle a less obvious choice, frequently incorporating the early gem "Fire in Cairo" into their shows. Goth rockers The Mission has done "A Night Like This," and the popular industrial/alternative group of the 1990s, Stabbing Westward, dug deeper in the catalog for a couple performances of "Give Me It." Brit-pop pioneers the Charlatans gave "The Caterpillar" a whirl with excellent results.

When guitarist Porl Thompson toured with Robert Plant and Jimmy Page in the 1990s, in the mix right alongside the blues covers and Led Zeppelin standards was the Cure's "Lullaby." Editors, Bat for Lashes, Elbow, and numerous others have also played the spooky hit in concert. Piano whiz Ben Folds often performs a peppy version of "In Between Days," which has also been regularly performed by Manic Street Preachers, Amanda Palmer, Pete Yorn, the Cranberries, and Natalie Merchant. Paramore played the song in 2013 for a gig at Sirius XM Radio.

When Temple of the Dog, the Seattle-based grunge supergroup, performed shows in 2016 for their twenty-fifth anniversary, a searing take on "Fascination Street" was part of the extended encore. Arena rockers Matchbox 20 also performed the song at a 1998 show in Orlando, Florida.

Dinosaur Jr. has the honor of recording the Cure cover that Robert Smith has often named as his favorite. Their raw and blistering grunge cover of "Just Like Heaven" was released just on cassette single back in the same year as the original, 1987. Fast-forward three decades, and Dinosaur Jr. not only still plays the song live, but often closes their sets with it. A long list of artists have covered "Just Like Heaven," not surprising given its status as a perfect pop song, including Dashboard Confessional, Katie Melua, 10,000 Maniacs, Goldfinger, Linkin Park, Better than Ezra, Cat Power, Edwin McCain, the Ocean Blue, and Christian-rock band Jars of Clay, among many others.

The emo band the Get Up Kids contributed their straightforward rock take on "Close to Me" for the 1999 Vagrant Record compilation *Before You Were Punk 2: Another Punk Rock Tribute to 80's New Wave,* and later included it on their 2001 collection of covers, B-sides and rarities, *Eudora.* It has remained a staple of the band's live shows, usually in the encore. Other artists who've incorporated the track into their shows include KT Tunstall and Of Monsters and Men.

Another emo band, AFI, frequently played both "Just Like Heaven" and "The Hanging Garden." In October 2020, pop diva deluxe Miley Cyrus, who was born the same year *Wish* was released, performed "Boys Don't Cry," a sure sign of the Cure's escalating popularity among a younger generation of fans.

Cutting-edge modern pop vocalist Morgxn recorded an emotional cover of "Boys Don't Cry" for his 2018 album *vital* with Robert Smith's approval. In May 2018, Morgxn penned an essay for *Billboard* relating the song to the death of his father. He wrote in part, "Boys don't cry ... boys actually weep. It is ok to show how much it hurts.... And for my father, that I'm sorry for not understanding him before he was gone. I'm sorry that I didn't say I love you enough when I had the chance." Morgxn also reveals that "Robert Smith did hear my version, and the note from his publisher was 'Robert Smith approves, which is rare.'"

Green Day also performed "Boys Don't Cry" once, in their early days, at a 1990 show in Minneapolis. The classic 1979 single which wasn't even a hit at the time has also been performed in concert by the likes of Guster, Idlewild, the Libertines, Sheryl Crow, Grant-Lee Phillips, Chris Martin of Coldplay, and many others.

New wave revivalists the Killers, one of the most popular bands in the world today, perform an electrifying version of "Push" in concert, much to their fans' delight. Placebo occasionally plays "Let's Go to Bed." Duncan Sheik has done "Kyoto Song," the Gaslight Anthem performed "A Letter to Elise" at a 2008 show in Baltimore. British rockers Hard-Fi did "Killing an Arab" in 2011, and Interpol dusted off the *Head on the Door* album cut "Screw" for their support slot at the Cure's 2018 40th anniversary show at Hyde Park.

Some other lesser-known standouts: Santigold patterned her ferocious performance of "Killing an Arab" during her 2009 tour after the Cure's powerful live renditions rather than the more staid studio version. *Give Me the Cure,* a compilation of Cure covers by Washington, D.C.–area artists to benefit AIDS research, is highlighted by Shudder to Think's scalding take on "Shake Dog Shake." Editors' tense and feverish recording of "Lullaby" is worthy of such a classic tune.

According to the invaluable concert stats website Setlist.fm, there are seven Cure songs that have been played by other artists in concert by a wide majority over the rest of the band's catalog: "Just Like Heaven" is by far the most-played, followed by "Lovesong" and number two, then "Boys Don't Cry," "Friday I'm in Love," "In Between Days," "A Forest," and "Close to Me" in descending order. Then comes a substantial drop-off before the top ten most played Cure songs

The iconic British group the Cure, led by singer and guitarist Robert Smith, signs autographs and take pictures with their fans outside the Fasano Hotel in Sao Paulo, 2013.

GADE/AKM-GSI / Alamy

by other artists in concert winds down with "The Walk," "Lullaby," and perhaps surprisingly their early classic "10:15 Saturday Night" at number ten.

The best Cure cover? There are so many, it's hard to even come up with a short list, but a strong contender is the smoldering version of "Seventeen Seconds" by Cowboy Junkies from their 2004 album *One Soul Now*. They already scored arguably the greatest Lou Reed cover with "Sweet Jane," so why not the Cure as well?

There are artists whom Robert Smith is very vocal about liking and some he could definitely do without. He's never really been shy about calling out artists for whatever reason, and when he was younger he would sometimes come off with slightly caustic comments about certain artists. He doesn't really do that anymore, but he did get plenty of media attention when he called out Radiohead in 2010 for their Internet "pay what you want" price scheme for their instant classic album *In Rainbows*. Robert was incensed at the devaluation of the music and what it meant for artists less fortunate than Radiohead.

Of course, not everybody is on the same page when it comes to music, and contrarians abound, such as Morrissey. It's almost impossible to envision a scenario in which Morrissey could have ever appreciated Robert Smith and the Cure. They beam with sincerity and emotion leaking from every note, while Morrissey is sheathed by acerbic cynicism and mordant negativity.

The Cure delights in sometimes creating music made simply for the sake of enjoyment; Morrissey disdains everything. He would sniff in revulsion at a frivolity like "Let's Go to Bed" or "The Caterpillar," while Smith could never quite capture the barren self-pity that permeates all of Morrissey's music. Both express woe and sorrow, but that's where the similarities end. It's only natural that Morrissey would be a vocal antagonist against the Cure and everything the band stands for.

It would be overstating it to call it a feud, although that may be true between some members of the two fan bases. Perhaps it's Robert Smith's perception that the Smiths are favored by critics and the rock music intelligentsia, and maybe Morrissey is edgy over the Cure's staggering commercial success versus his own. Whatever the source of the ill feelings, the two alternative-rock icons have exchanged barbed one-liners and withering rejoinders in the press over the years.

In 2019, though, it seems that Morrissey has finally come to terms with Robert Smith, and it's not all bad. In an interview on his website, Morrissey professed to be sorry for saying nasty things about Robert back in the 1980s. Robert, for his part, seemed bemused by the whole thing. Responding to queries about Morrissey's apparent apology, he said with a laugh that he wasn't really thinking all that much about it, and he wasn't sure what the hard feelings were supposed to have been about anyway. Yeah, a whole lot of silliness but part of the fabric of the strange histories of two seminal bands.

28

We've All Gone Crazy Lately: *Wild Mood Swings*

A shifting alternative-rock landscape and other factors helped the Cure's tenth album become the first of their career to sell fewer copies than its predecessor.

Released: May 7, 1996
Fiction Records (United Kingdom) FIXLP 28, 5317931/Elektra (United States) 61744-1
Running time: 61:36

1. "Want" (5:07), 2. "Club America" (5:01), 3. "This Is a Lie" (4:31), 4. "The 13th" (4:06), 5. "Strange Attraction" (4:19), 6. "Mint Car" (3:32), 7. "Jupiter Crash" (4:15), 8. "Round & Round & Round" (2:38), 9. "Gone!" (4:31), 10. "Numb" (4:49), 11. "Return" (3:28), 12. "Trap" (3:37), 13. "Treasure" (3:45), 14. "Bare" (7:57)

Longevity in the music industry inevitably means peaks and valleys. Sales figures from one album to the next don't increase forever, and eventually, the sustained whirlwind of an artist's peak years will subside. That reality hit the Cure when their tenth studio album, *Wild Mood Swings*, became the first in the band's history to sell fewer copies than its predecessor. The fact that an album could hit number nine in the United Kingdom and number twelve in the United States, sell more than 1 million copies worldwide, and still be considered a commercial disappointment is a testament to how big the Cure had become.

Wild Mood Swings doesn't deserve the scorn that's been heaped on it if the entire output of the period is considered. The biggest problem is sequencing and song selection since several of the strongest tracks were left off the album. The best songs of the period—"Want," "Jupiter Crash," "A Pink Dream," and

"Adonais"—are strong enough to sit alongside the band's finest work. With a different configuration and a better lineup of singles, *Wild Mood Swings* could have been a worthy follow-up to the commercial juggernaut *Wish*.

Robert Smith decided to hold the sessions at St. Catherine's Court, a brooding sixteenth-century manor house in the countryside outside of Bath and owned by actress Jane Seymour (the following year, Radiohead used the same space to record *OK Computer*). His most immediate problem was finding a band. By 1995, after a major lineup shift following the marathon *Wish* tour, the Cure had melted away to just Smith and Perry Bamonte.

Drummer Boris Williams rebuffed Smith's request that he stay, leaving the Cure so that he could record with his wife, Caroline Crawley, former vocalist for Shellyanne Orphan. Porl Thompson was asked to join the Robert Plant and Jimmy Page tour, an impressive acknowledgment of the guitarist's talent and a chance he simply couldn't pass up. Simon Gallup, struggling through serious health issues related to years of heavy drinking, was unable to join Smith and Bamonte as they spent months (and massive amounts of money) at St. Catherine's Court writing songs and preparing the space for the sessions.

Slowly, the new-look Cure started taking shape. The task of replacing guitarist Porl Thompson was a daunting challenge, and Smith decided to simply bump Perry Bamonte from keyboard to guitar, which is his primary instrument anyway. Simon Gallup was eventually able to return on bass, and keyboardist Roger O'Donnell, an essential component of the band's sound for *Disintegration*, returned to the lineup.

Choosing a new drummer was a more arduous process. Initially, Robert Smith intended to record the album with multiple session drummers. Realizing they would need a permanent member for the upcoming tour, he decided to find a more permanent solution. The Cure took out an ad in *Melody Maker* that read, "Very famous band requires drummer, no metal heads," and waded through hours of audition tapes from hopefuls.

They narrowed the choice to seven candidates, and several songs on *Wild Mood Swings* feature drummers who were in the running. Mark Price is on "Mint Car," "Trap," and "Treasure"; Louis Pavlou rocks out on "Club America"; and Ronald Austin provides the stately rhythm on "This Is a Lie." Ultimately, the relatively inexperienced Jason Cooper was chosen. Despite his lack of professional chops, Cooper's enthusiasm and love for the Cure's music helped nab him the spot. Robert and producer Steve Lyon were confident he would fit into the band's complicated dynamic, and they were right. He's been the Cure's drummer ever since.

Robert intended the new album to replicate the dizzying versatility of *Kiss Me* and allowed the sessions to progress with no real direction. Steve Lyon described it as simply working on a batch of songs. For a while, it seemed that a more austere collection might emerge, as the band considered an

Wild Mood Swings (1996) struggled with a difficult first single and botched sequencing as the Cure faced a much less favorable musical landscape than four years prior with *Wish*.
Author's Collection

acoustic-based album of downbeat tracks to be called *Bare*. The possibility of a double album—half acoustic based and half more pop and eclectic material—was also considered.

They almost released a four-track EP highlighted by "Mint Car" during the summer of 1995 as a teaser, but that idea was abandoned. In the end, the band ended up with a boatload of material, and it just came down to picking and choosing what made the cut and what was cast adrift.

The title was borrowed from a proposed Robert Smith solo album that had been percolating in 1983 but never materialized. The recording of *Wild Mood Swings* stretched late into 1995, as Smith tinkered endlessly with the production and arrangements. For the first time, the Cure relied heavily on computers in the studio, and the change in atmosphere from prior albums is striking. There's a coldness and emotional detachment on *Wild Mood Swings* that makes it harder for fans to develop a deep connection to it.

Smith's vocals are cleaner, the simple and direct arrangements a stark contrast from the group's prior work. The carefully layered harmony vocals that had been such a huge part of the band's sound are almost completely absent. The mixing was farmed out to multiple producers because the band simply ran out of time. They were frantically scurrying to finish the album after setting a release date, with promotion and touring obligations set in stone and rapidly approaching. As leisurely as the pace was to prepare and record it, in the end, *Wild Mood Swings* was rushed.

The project veered off the rails almost immediately thanks to Robert Smith's insistence on releasing "The 13th" as first single. Audacious, brilliantly demented, and defiantly uncommercial, Smith had an image for the video that he was so keen to make that he ignored the advice of everyone around him.

The weird salsa-flavored oddity was paired with an equally superb and madcap video, but the wildly unconventional song was the wrong choice to lead off a new album project. There was zero chance that a track this weird would end up a hit, and indeed, after the initial curiosity wore off, it was only the diehards who paid it much attention. The album never recovered from that fatal stagger out of the gate.

Everything can't be blamed on the choice for lead single, though. A combination of factors conspired to result in *Wild Mood Swings*' failure. The Cure no longer fit into the concept of the "now" musically; they were already being viewed through a nostalgic prism, a 1980s band still hanging around. They were no longer cutting edge or exciting to a younger audience. Artists labeled "Brit pop" or "grunge" had changed the mood of alternative rock considerably, and although Robert Smith later professed that the Cure was relieved, as they were more comfortable outside the mainstream, he was still bitterly disappointed in the album's poor performance.

Casual fans jumped off the bandwagon after *Wish*, and *Wild Mood Swings* failed to connect with many dedicated fans who lambasted it as trite, overproduced, too clean, and computer driven at the expense of genuine feeling. It didn't help that songs like "Strange Attraction" and "Gone!" sounded like calculated artifice. Even "Friday I'm in Love," obviously conceived specifically to be a radio single, has a genuine buoyancy that is palpable.

Wild Mood Swings was the first major failure in the band's career and the first Cure album to sell fewer albums than its predecessor. They never recovered their commercial cachet from a sales or critical standpoint with their studio work. Their albums don't sell nearly at the level of their peak years, although their live shows remain hugely popular.

Considering that most of their contemporaries borne of the late 1970s and into the 1980s were either no longer together or treading water, with many already on the "oldies" circuit, the Cure was still doing extremely well. But after the heights of *Wish*, disappointment over the swoon was probably inevitable.

Smith was stung by the failure of *Wild Mood Swings*, having invested more than a year's worth of effort into the album's creation. It hardened him against paying much attention to what others thought about the Cure's music or what it should be. Smith blamed the record label for not knowing how to properly market the album or figure out where the Cure fit in. Given how the album was presented, though, it's hard to imagine what the record company could have done differently. The reality is that "The 13th" was never going to be a hit, period, and it was a difficult commercial landscape for the band to begin with.

The amount of time and money spent on it is staggering, especially compared with previous albums, most of which were recorded very expeditiously. Smith sought the same diversity as *Kiss Me, Kiss Me, Kiss Me*, but the album ended up simply disjointed. He tried to inject humor and whimsy as a major component in their sound, but it didn't always seem genuine. Smith did the most promotion of his entire career to support the album, giving interview after interview, as the band went out full throttle to make the album a success. In the end, though, it wasn't enough.

Wild Mood Swings

"Want"

Wild Mood Swings opens with the blistering "Want," an exercise in slow-burning tension that builds with each added layer of sound until a devastating climax in which Smith delivers a gripping vocal performance in the final verse. Thematically, "Want" returns to a concept Smith has written about a number of times, including on "Never Enough" and "The Hungry Ghost": need, whether it's money or sex or possessions or the overwhelming compulsion to consume more drugs. It's an endless cycle central to the human experience: want/need, achieve/respite, want/need more.

"Want" is by far the strongest track on *Wild Mood Swings* and unlike the rest of the album remains a regular highlight of the band's live shows. Given the hard-edged vibe of the song, Smith and Steve Lyon assigned the mix to Alan Moulder, who has worked with Nine Inch Nails, Smashing Pumpkins, and Ride, among many others. The end result is a ferocious molten blast on par with other classic Cure openers like "The Kiss," "Open," "Shake Dog Shake," and "One Hundred Years."

"Club America"

Once considered a front-runner to be first single, "Club America" is a swirling, guitar-heavy rocker somewhat similar to "Never Enough" but with a rawer, hazier edge. Smith snarls in his lower register, heaping scorn and derision on the facile elite of wealthy narcissists living in a bubble of easy luxury and entitlement.

It was the only track on the album mixed by Paul Kolderie and Sean Slade, a duo known mostly for their work with alternative rock bands like Belly and the Circle Jerks. Powered by Louis Pavlou on drums, "Club America" has a grittiness that is lacking from much of the rest of the album.

The potent one-two punch of "Want" and "Club America" starts *Wild Mood Swings* with an adrenaline rush that the Cure is unable to sustain as the album lurches untethered from one style to the next.

"This Is a Lie"

Built around a simple but elegant string arrangement, "This Is a Lie" is Robert Smith's attempt to convincingly sing lyrics that convey a sentiment he doesn't believe. The song explores whether the concept of monogamy provides any hope for a lifetime of love and happiness, however that is defined. He's been with the same person for forty-five years and believes that it is possible, as Smith explained when discussing the song. However, the narrator takes a different view, bitterly denouncing the concept as untenable and a brazen falsehood that ends up causing only unnecessary turmoil. Or perhaps things haven't been as prosaic as fans have assumed and the song is more personal than it seems at first glimpse.

Either way, "This Is a Lie" doesn't quite carry the emotional heft to convincingly pull off the necessary emotion. Robert needed the same soul-baring intensity he delivers in epics like "Sinking" and "Prayers for Rain," and his vocal just never gets there. He never lets go completely. It's too measured and sedate, always staying within the same sterile lines and never striking any measure of intensity.

"The 13th"

Named "The Two Chord Cool" until very late in the process, "The 13th" is a lunatic mariachi nightmare unlike anything else the Cure has ever conceived. The listener gets to hear the psychosexual inner dialogue taking place in Robert Smith's warped mind as he fantasizes an encounter with the object of his lust as she performs with the band he's watching.

Smith's admiration for the evocative and madly creative "The 13th" is understandable, especially given the wickedly clever lyrics. The video is as genius as the song, but it was still a terrible choice to be the album's first single. His insistence on "The 13th" was hotly debated by the band, production team, and record label executives and continues to be a discussion point among fans. Steve Lyon and others pushed for "Mint Car," the most radio-friendly song on the album by a mile, and "Club America" was also seriously considered. Smith was adamant, though, and the results speak for themselves.

"Strange Attraction"

The Cure tentatively tiptoe back into the realm of synth pop with the oddly hollow "Strange Attraction." While it offers an interesting story line based on real correspondence, it's so labored that any potential charm it may have possessed is obliterated.

"Strange Attraction" has the air of being an obvious attempt to create a hit, which is not the Cure's usual method of operation. The attempt failed: "Strange Attraction" didn't make so much as a ripple when released as the album's third U.S. single, sinking without a trace.

"Mint Car"

One of the earliest tracks recorded, the relentlessly upbeat and deftly arranged "Mint Car" was the choice of label executives and producer Steve Lyon for first single, but Robert Smith feared it would be viewed as a "Friday I'm in Love" retread and quashed it in favor of "The 13th." By the time it appeared as the second single, momentum for the album had chilled so greatly that "Mint Car" substantially underperformed commercial expectations.

"Mint Car" exudes a feverish joy pushed to almost manic delirium over the need to experience it to the fullest before it's snatched away. The title was derived from Simon Gallup's weakness for expensive cars, which he'd often describe as "mint"—thus, the word became an in-joke of sorts referring to happiness, and "Mint Car" is nothing if not happy.

The video, directed by Richard Heslop, features Robert frolicking through various campy scenarios in different costumes, singing with exaggerated glee and theatricality. He's either genuinely having a blast or gifted at faking it. An earlier version that was intended to be the commercial video was filmed by Smith while the band was on tour. He edited fifteen hours of footage taken in locations such as Coney Island, Brazil, and London down to about three minutes. When it was finished, Robert deemed it too unprofessional for MTV and instead released it as an Internet exclusive, one of the first such endeavors for a music video.

Although a brilliant madcap song, "The 13th" was a controversial choice for first single and never had a chance to be a hit. *Author's Collection*

"Jupiter Crash"

This solemn acoustic piece is one of the most significant tracks from the sessions and one of the album's strongest moments. "Jupiter Crash" harbors more genuine feeling than most of the other songs and has strong echoes of some of the band's earlier morose triumphs.

Wry and resigned, sad and forlorn, "Jupiter Crash" is an expression of disappointment that is expected yet sorrowful all the same. The song's dreamy beauty is especially powerful when Smith begins double tracking his vocal, which is so striking that it makes the absence of harmonies on other tracks all the more glaring. Along with "Want," "Jupiter Crash" was selected by Robert Smith to represent *Wild Mood Swings* during the band's pivotal, career-spanning set on June 24, 2018, at the Meltdown Festival in London.

"Round & Round & Round"

Many fans dismiss this trifle, but "Round & Round & Round" is actually a disarming little song albeit inconsequential. The arrangement doesn't quite work, as it ends suddenly at the conclusion of the bridge when sonically it needs another pass-through of the chorus to wrap it up. Probably not strong enough to have been on the album, it likely would have been admired for its quirkiness had it been a B-side.

"Gone!"

Robert Smith has gone on record stating that one of the problems with *Wild Mood Swings* is its length, and he's singled out the slight jazz-pop frivolity "Gone!" as one that should have been axed. He's right. Released as the third single in most countries (the United States got "Strange Attraction" instead), "Gone!" crawled to number sixty on the U.K. singles chart, the lowest placement for the band since prior to "A Forest." It bears a striking resemblance musically and thematically to Siouxsie and the Banshees' "Got to Get Up" from their 1991 Stephen Hague–produced *Superstition*.

The album version is overly slick and sterile, perhaps a sign of having been tinkered with too long in the studio. When performed in concert, "Gone!" has a grittiness and punch to it that is completely lacking on the single. The Cure seems to have decided it's a song best left forgotten. They played it only sporadically on the Swing Tour, and it hasn't been dusted off since.

"Numb"

It's sometimes hard to know, given the continuous turmoil and heartache expressed through so much of the Cure's music, exactly how much of it is fiction and the work of imagination and how much of it is "real." There are other moments, however, that are more obvious, and "Numb" is one of those.

Lofty and dramatic, with tempestuous strings and a hint of exotic instrumentation, "Numb" is easily one of the more powerful tracks on the album.

"Return"

This exuberantly zany pop gem is much stronger than either of the two singles "Gone!" and "Strange Attraction" and has become one of the Cure's most overlooked pop songs. A new single remix might have been a great idea for *Galore* to go along with "Wrong Number"—preferably including the removal of the breathlessly zippy horn section that jolts the song into a level of hyper a couple notches over the "over-the-top" line.

Still, it's a fun song if not particularly meaningful, and "Return" would have made for a better single choice than either "Gone!" or "Strange Attraction." Instead, this potential pop hit was hidden away near the end of the album and has generally been ignored by both fans and the band over the years.

"Trap"

"Trap" occupies the same place on *Wild Mood Swings* that "Cut" does on *Wish*—a searing rocker that helps anchor the album's second half. "Trap" is crisper and tighter than the wild Porl Thompson guitar-fest that is "Cut," and part of that is new guitarist Perry Bamonte staying between tighter lines than Thompson ever did. He never really gets to break out on it, and his riffs are accented and partially muted by a horn section. The ending practically begs for a descent into a blazing guitar solo and then one more go at the chorus, but it doesn't happen. "Trap" is one of the more worthwhile tracks on the album and brings a much-needed rock 'n' roll kick.

"Treasure"

Sad and beautifully poignant, "Treasure" is built around a music box motif of a simple rhythm bracketed by repetitive strings and delicate lines of piano and guitar. Smith's gentle vocal, sung in his lower register, is sublime as he offers words of comfort from the point of view of someone who has died but is offering solace to those left behind. Inspired by the Christina Rossetti poem "Remember," "Treasure" is up there with "Want" and "Jupiter Crash" as among the finest moments on *Wild Mood Swings*.

"Bare"

The Cure would, of course, choose an epic finale, and "Bare" fits that slot nicely. It stretches to nearly eight minutes of somber meditation on the end of a relationship. Perhaps it's the same couple from "Mint Car," where everything is glorious and wonderful but a few years go by, and suddenly the romance has fractured, Smith's narrator coming to grips with that finality.

It's clear that this isn't a spur-of-the-moment breakup. The nerves are frayed at the end of a relationship in which the partners have literally laid themselves bare, both in the traditional sense and emotionally. "Bare" is a requiem for a love affair, much like "Disintegration," but absent the fiery passion and feeling. It's more sedate, solemn, and sadly resigned—the rage exhibited in "Disintegration" has already subsided here.

"Bare" is not the most immediate or engaging song and does not rank alongside closers like "Faith," "The Top," "Untitled," or "Sinking." Even so, "Bare" contains its own muted power and works well as a finale. Robert Smith's vocal is infused with genuine heartache as he contemplates the failure of something in which he invested so much.

B-Sides

"A Pink Dream"

Easily the album's finest pop song and clearly the best choice as first single, the magical sun-kissed "A Pink Dream" somehow didn't even make it onto *Wild Mood Swings*. A jangly guitar-pop number in the mold of "In Between Days," "A Pink Dream" is far more substantial than "Mint Car" or any of the other pop-oriented tracks on the album.

"A Pink Dream" is warm and nostalgic, with a winning melody and lyrics filled with the joy of memories past and of better days. It shares some of the same sense of bittersweet romanticism as "Catch." Robert Smith's vocal has real spirit, and there is a deep poignancy that is missing from inanities like "Strange Attraction" and "Gone!" Instead of being hidden away as a B-side, "A Pink Dream" should be sitting alongside the Cure's other great pop tunes on their *Greatest Hits* collection.

"Adonais"

Another of the strongest pieces from the *Wild Mood Swings* era, the taut and dramatic "Adonais" could have been one of the centerpiece tracks had it been included on the album. Its propulsive rhythm and cinematic strings bring a sense of urgency, and Smith's engaging vocal is one of his most effective of the era.

Inspired by the poem "Adonais: An Elegy on the Death of John Keats," written by Percy Bysshe Shelley in 1821, perhaps Smith thought it too idiosyncratic to be on the album and that it might not fit with the rest of the material. Its urgent propulsive rhythm, strings, and the effects-layered vocals create a dark and tense vibe that is among the Cure's finest recordings of the era.

"Ocean"

A delicate piece wreathed with strings, "Ocean" boasts one of Robert Smith's most effective and heartfelt vocals of the era, and the subtle double tracking lends a sense of mystery and tension. Moody, evocative, and darkly melodic, "Ocean" uses a toy box percussion motif similar to what the band employed on "Treasure."

"Home"

An acoustic ditty with lines of cello and accordion reminiscent of "Untitled," "Home" is brimming with sincerity and a level of comfort that is deeply appealing. While it's not a major song, "Home" has a sharp enough melody and enough heart that it, too, should have made the album over several of the tracks that did.

"It Used to Be Me"

Although "It Used to Be Me" would have added some grit and much-needed raw intensity to *Wild Mood Swings*, the album is better off without it (although it was appended onto the end of the CD for the Japanese market). Smith's strident vocal, becoming more feverish as the song progresses, foreshadows his approach on future albums, particularly *The Cure*.

Unfortunately, like on the band's 2004 self-titled album, Smith's vocal is way too high in the mix and becomes grating, overwhelming the excellent vibe of the stripped-down psychedelic-rock accompaniment. "It Used to Be Me" doesn't quite have the emotional power that it might with a tighter and more focused arrangement, but its searing intensity tops almost anything on the album itself with the notable exception of "Want."

"Waiting"

All six B-sides released on the singles of *Wild Mood Swings* are stronger than songs on the album, and "Waiting" is no exception. Another acoustic-based piece, up-tempo and engaging, "Waiting" is a sonic locomotive that surges with tension and anxiety.

Wild Mood Swings is an important album in the Cure's career arc because of what it represents in terms of the band's place in the world of popular music but also because it has some great songs. With the ever-changing industry landscape, it's hard to envision a scenario in which anything the Cure released, no matter how brilliant, would have made the commercial impact of *Wish*.

Smith has defended the album in subsequent years, at one point saying it's his favorite, but the band has mostly shied away from playing songs from it on recent tours. Only "Want" remains a regular part of the band's live set, with "Jupiter Crash" and "Mint Car" appearing less frequently. Fans will have another chance to discover this album on Record Store Day, July 17, 2021, as the Cure will release a twenty-fifth-anniversary vinyl edition of the album on picture disc. The new pressing was supervised by Robert Smith.

There has not yet been an announcement about a potential deluxe CD reissue as well, but there is reason for optimism. When *Mixed Up* was issued on picture disc for Record Store Day, the deluxe expanded CD came as well, and producer Steve Lyon has mentioned that Robert Smith contacted him requesting photos of the era for a deluxe reissue. Perhaps all these years later, *Wild Mood Swings* will finally get its due.

The Good Old Days May Not Return: The Cure in Concert, Part 2 (1987–1999)

The Cure is at the peak of their popularity, playing top venues around the globe in support of a string of classic albums.

Concert Tours

1987 Tour/The Kissing Tour (1987)

The Cure faced sky-high expectations in 1987. Over the prior two years, they reached new heights as a live band as they expanded their fan base exponentially with *The Head on the Door* and *Standing on a Beach—The Singles*. With the brilliant new double album *Kiss Me, Kiss Me, Kiss Me* set to be launched with a major promotional campaign, the Cure lined up their most extensive slate of shows yet.

By 1987, the Cure had become massively popular in South America. In the prior year, they sold nearly half a million albums there, and their decade-old "Boys Don't Cry" was the top-selling single in Brazil. They launched the Kissing Tour with an ambitious ten-date run through massive stadiums in South America, their first visit to the continent, beginning on March 17–18 at Estadio Ferrocarril Oeste in Buenos Aires.

The Cure, New York City, August 1989. *Frankie Ziths/AP/Shutterstock*

The shows were big news in Argentina, as the Cure was the biggest rock band to play Buenos Aires since the fall of the country's totalitarian government. Bedlam greeted the Cure in Buenos Aires, a surreal spectacle typically associated with megastars like the Beatles or Michael Jackson. A raucous crowd awaited them at the airport, and they were followed to their hotel, where legions of fans were waiting to greet them.

The Cure and everyone in their entourage were rattled by violent clashes at both shows in Buenos Aires. For the first night, organizers sold 19,000 tickets to a venue holding 17,000, and counterfeiters sold thousands of bogus tickets, leading to hordes of irate fans climbing fences to get in, only to be met by the Argentinian security force charged with preventing chaos. A melee broke out with dozens suffering injuries, and three policemen were killed.

The situation continued to deteriorate after the Cure took the stage. Robert Smith said that it looked like the stadium was on fire as he walked out front and center. Fans pressed inexorably forward and eventually rushed the stage. Dozens were trampled in the surge, with at least thirty people hurt, some of them seriously. Finally, things calmed down enough for the Cure to continue, and they riveted the audience with a set heavy on old material.

The second show was even uglier, as temperatures soared and security personnel continued to aggressively combat fans trying to climb fences to get into the show. In an attempt to prevent the violence of the first show, authorities erected a barrier to keep fans back from the stage, but it blocked the view of those near the front. Outraged fans disassembled the barriers, and fights broke out once again between fans and with security. The mood worsened as the night progressed until eventually some turned their anger on the Cure, and projectiles hurled from the crowd started landing onstage right in the band's midst. Porl Thompson was the first one hit, and he left the stage immediately.

The Cure at a Promoshoot in Konstanz, Germany, 1995.

dpa picture alliance / Alamy Stock Photo

A bottle of Coke thrown from the crowd hit Robert Smith square in the head during "10:15 Saturday Night," at which point he stopped playing and launched into a vituperative-filled tongue-lashing at the hooligans causing the violence. After the show, the madness continued outside the venue as the Cure was whisked away to their hotel. The two Buenos Aires shows were frightening reminders to the band of how vulnerable and exposed they were onstage, and as the tour continued, the safety of their fans remained a deep concern.

The Cure was happy to get out of Argentina and into Porto Alegre, Brazil, where another throng of screaming fans greeted their arrival. Technical problems during their March 20 show resulted in everyone onstage getting buzzed repeatedly by surges of electricity. Nobody was seriously injured, and the show went forward with a crowd so wildly enthusiastic that the band was overwhelmed. The following night in Porto Alegre was even more wild than the first, with fans excited to the point of hysteria. The unexpected level of frenzy that met the Cure was exhilarating but also amplified their feelings of unease.

The madness continued as they traveled through Brazil in devastating heat that refused to abate. The Cure performed to hordes of hyperexcited fans, with problems continuing to arise along with moments of unforgettable magic. The South American tour made a lasting impact on Robert Smith and his bandmates, who were shocked and a bit alarmed by the reception they received.

The Cure's biggest North American tour yet kicked off on July 9, 1987, at the Expo Center in Vancouver. Unlike the South American shows, which featured very little new material, the show was almost exclusively from *Kiss Me, Kiss Me, Kiss Me*. Of the sixteen songs played in the main set, all but three were new, with the oldies being "A Forest," "In Between Days," and "The Walk." The album was quickly becoming the major breakthrough their labels had predicted, ticket sales were through the roof, and the band was getting the superstar treatment everywhere they went.

The ruby-red cherry lipstick on top of the Kissing Tour cake was the sold-out tour finale on August 10 at Madison Square Garden in New York City. The twenty-five-song triumph was a bold statement on how remarkably high the Cure had ascended in America. A month later, Robert Smith described the show as "big and full and hot and loud and we played well and happily." They followed the next night with an incendiary performance before a packed house at the legendary Ritz.

The Cure had two months to recover before opening the European leg of the Kissing Tour on October 22 in Norway. They played in venues jammed to capacity all across the continent before wrapping up with a triumphant three-night stand at London's Wembley Arena in early December. Smashing all expectations, the Cure's popularity was now at a level far beyond anything they had ever imagined. Exhausted and overwhelmed, they needed time to decompress, reflect, and decide what (if anything) to do next.

The Prayer Tour (1989)

After the madness of 1987 and the Kissing Tour, it seemed impossible to imagine that the Cure would somehow get even bigger. They did. Their 1989 album *Disintegration* was the most celebrated of their career. Robert Smith claimed to the press that the tour supporting the album would be the Cure's last. It wasn't, but had it been, the Cure would have gone out on a remarkable high.

The main set for the Prayer Tour included much of the new album, with a handful of select older nuggets thrown in, opening with the crystalline chimes of "Plainsong" and concluding with the thunderous "Disintegration." After the heavy emotional lifting of the main set, the crowd was ready to dance, and the Cure obliged with a string of their color pop singles. Next came a searing rip through early material before they returned to melancholy grandeur with "Homesick," "Untitled," and "Faith" to close the show.

The Cure played to record crowds over fifty-two shows in Europe, concluding on July 24, 1989, at Wembley Arena in London with a legendary thirty-five-song, four-encore show. Ticket sales soared in America as the Cure's popularity reached a new high. In a surreal spectacle emblematic of their newly exalted status in the rock stratosphere, the Cure opened the twenty-four-show North American leg of the Prayer Tour on August 20 at Giants Stadium before nearly 45,000 fans. They also nabbed an impressive three-band lineup to launch the festivities: Shellyann Orphan, the Pixies, and Love and Rockets.

The Prayer Tour wrapped up on September 23 at the Great Woods Performing Arts Center in Mansfield, Massachusetts. Robert Smith promised another six or seven songs at the start of the third encore and told fans that if the venue switches on the lights while the band is still playing, "Don't take any notice cause we look just as ugly as you!" They knocked out a tense version of "The Figurehead" followed by a powerful string from their first four albums. The Cure's historic Prayer Tour ended with a cathartic rampage of the old improvisational freak-out "Forever," after which Robert Smith said, "Thank you very much and good night. And I'll never see you again. Thank you."

The Pleasure Trips Tour (1990)

Although Robert Smith promised that the Prayer Tour would be the Cure's last, he changed his mind rather quickly when the prospect of a dozen lucrative European festival shows arose. With no new studio album to promote, the band called the trek the Pleasure Trips Tour. The first date, June 21, 1990, at Fête de la Musique in Paris, was the first show for new keyboardist Perry Bamonte, who had replaced the departed Roger O'Donnell.

The Cure's headlining slot at the June 23 Glastonbury Festival drew 72,000 fans, a new high for the event, but was marred by chaos. Poor organization, lax security, and flimsy guard barriers led to fans surging tighter and tighter to the front, leading to dozens of injuries from trampling and asphyxiation.

The band stopped playing during "Fascination Street" so that a police helicopter could swoop in to rescue a woman near the stage who had nearly died. A horrified Robert Smith pleaded with the crowd multiple times to pull back. At one point, he promised nothing but slow songs if they continued pushing forward, and the band followed through with a solemn ten-minute take on "The Same Deep Water as You."

The show was such a fiasco that *The Telegraph* referred to it as "love and peace in a muddy war zone" that "began to resemble the Mekong Delta in the nightmare trench scene of *Apocalypse Now*." Robert Smith was furious after the show, calling out the organizers in the press and vowing to never play Glastonbury again (although he did relent eventually.)

The Cure spent most of 1991 working on their next album and played only three shows, all in January. The first was a secret gig at London's Town and Country Club on January 17 that they dubbed "Five Imaginary Boys." The set included three new unreleased songs: "The Big Hand," "Away" (an early version of "Cut"), and "Wendy Time." Two nights later, they headlined "The Great British Music Weekend" at London's Wembley Arena.

Their final performance of 1991 was an all-acoustic set for *MTV Unplugged*. Filmed before a small crowd at MTV Studios in London, the Cure mixed hits with lesser-known tracks and debuted one new song: "A Letter to Elise." The synthesizer riffs on "The Walk" were replaced by kazoos that were handed out to several members of the audience to play along with the band.

The *Wish* Tour (1992)

By the spring of 1992, the Cure was ready to take center stage with the most ambitious tour of their career in support of their first studio album since *Disintegration*. The lineup was the same five-piece in place since 1990: Robert Smith, Simon Gallup, Boris Williams, Porl Thompson, and Perry Bamonte.

The *Wish* tour commenced with eleven warm-up gigs at small, historic venues throughout the United Kingdom, and then it was on to North America for forty-four shows, opening on May 14 in Rhode Island at the Providence Civic Center and ending on July 3 on Long Island, New York, at the Nassau Coliseum. The Cure played to capacity crowds late into the night as the tour stretched across the continent. They prepared dozens of songs in rehearsal, allowing for diverse set lists blending new material, singles, and deep cuts for the hard-core fans.

After a ten-date tour of Australia and New Zealand, the Cure took a month off before hitting Oslo, Norway, on September 21 to start the tour's European leg. Ticket sales remained in high demand throughout the tour, and cash flowed

Arguably the Cure's greatest live document, *Show* (1993) captured them during their peak of the *Wish* era. *Author's Collection*

into the band's coffers. Strong album sales fueled high ticket demand, but none of it was easy given the grueling nature of their global *Wish* odyssey.

Health troubles started entering the public's awareness when the band announced to the press that all five members had contracted viral infections while in Australia, leading them to cancel a high-profile appearance at the MTV Video Music Awards. It was reported that while the rest of the group recovered, Simon Gallup became so ill, in part because he was "run down and exhausted," that he had to be admitted to a hospital.

Gallup played on October 31 at the Forum in Assago, Italy, which ended up a much shorter show than normal, as Simon could barely function. Bassist Roberto Soave of the Associates and Shelleyan Orphan, two bands very well known to the Cure, filled in for Gallup starting with a November 2 show in Marseille. Soave stayed in the lineup through the November 21 show in Edinburgh

Gallup returned on November 23 for the first of two shows at the G-Mex Centre in Manchester. They wrapped up on December 3 with a final show at the Point in Ireland.

After the arduous tour in support of *Wish*, the Cure was a scarce commodity in the coming years. They played only one show in 1993, "Great X-pectations," in London's Finsbury Park on July 13, with a unique lineup of Smith, Gallup, Boris Williams, and Perry Bamonte. They started the gig with the hate-letter to Lol Tolhurst, "Shiver and Shake," no doubt in response to his recent legal action against his old band. The Cure was dormant in 1994, with no live performances for the first year since 1988.

The Swing Tour (1996)

While working on *Wild Mood Swings* during the summer of 1995, the Cure once again hit the European festival circuit for eleven big shows starting on June 6 in Greece for the Rock in Athens Festival. They debuted three songs from the upcoming album: the opening number, "Want," along with "Jupiter Crash" and "Mint Car." This was new drummer Jason Cooper's first show with the band, filling out a lineup of Smith, Simon Gallup, Perry Bamonte, and keyboardist Roger O'Donnell, who was back in the Cure after a six-year banishment.

The Cure's place in the music industry had changed by the time they launched their 1996 tour in support of *Wild Mood Swings*. The new album didn't enjoy nearly the same level of success as *Wish* and *Disintegration*, and many fans who jumped on the bandwagon at the height of the Cure's popularity missed the new album entirely. With drummer Jason Cooper replacing the popular and ridiculously talented Boris Williams and former guitar tech Perry Bamonte in the lead guitar slot previously occupied by Porl Thompson, the lineup was an undeniable downgrade in terms of experience and raw talent. With a chip on their shoulders and something to prove, they brought everything they had to the stage and gave one great performance after another.

The Cure opened the first European leg of the tour in London with album opener "Want" opening their sets. The North American leg began on July 2 at the Centrum in Worcester, Massachusetts, and lasted forty-eight shows through the September 17 show at Radio City Music Hall in New York City. Then it was back to Europe, where the band played forty shows from October 12 in Rotterdam to December 16 at the National Exhibition Centre in Birmingham.

With no new material to promote, the Cure played mostly festivals in 1997 and 1998. Their final show of 1998 was a secret gig organized by the Miller beer company and performed for contest winners, journalists, and other lucky fans at the Forum in London. A year would go by before the Cure played their one and only show of 1999, at Sony Music Studios in New York on October 19 for VH1's

With a quirkier song selection, *Paris* (1993) is a companion piece to *Show* more aimed at die-hard fans. *Author's Collection*

"Hard Rock Live." It included three debuts from the Cure's next album: "Out of This World," "The Last Day of Summer," and the title song, "Bloodflowers."

30

Hello Darkness, My Old Friend: *Bloodflowers*

Robert Smith dwells again in the shadows for the final installment of a trilogy that includes *Pornography* and *Disintegration*.

Released: February 15, 2000
Fiction Records—FIX 31, Polydor—543 123-1
Running time: 64:29

1. "Out of This World" (6:44), 2. "Watching Me Fall" (11:13), 3. "Where the Birds Always Sing" (5:44), 4. "Maybe Someday" (5:04), *5. "Coming Up" (6:27), 6. "The Last Day of Summer" (5:36), 7. "There Is No If..." (3:44), 8. "The Loudest Sound" (5:09), 9. "39" (7:20), 10. "Bloodflowers" (7:31)
*Bonus track available on certain international pressings.

Released on February 15, 2000, *Bloodflowers* marked the beginning of a new millennium but also the end of an era. The album was the Cure's final new studio release for the record label which had been their home since "Killing an Arab" Fiction/Polydor. The wrangling with label executives had become increasingly difficult for the Cure in recent years, and the arduous process to get *Bloodflowers* into stores contributed greatly to their decision to leave. Although the album was completely finished and turned in for release in May 1999, it was pushed back almost a full year because the Polydor wanted to capture "post-millennial fever," according to Smith.

Whether it ever captured said fever is up for debate. While it's true that *Bloodflowers* was one of the first new albums of the 2000s by a major artist, that didn't translate to any significant commercial momentum. *Bloodflowers* debuted at number sixteen in the United States, down from the number twelve premier by its predecessor *Wild Mood Swings*. In the United Kingdom, its debut at number fourteen was the lowest for a new Cure studio album since *Faith* hit the same number back in 1981.

For most of the world, including the United Kingdom, "Out of This World" was the first promotional single, whereas the U.S. label opted for the harder-edged "Maybe Someday." The two were then reversed as the second offering, and that was basically the end of the promotional efforts for the album, as there weren't any obvious pop hits to be found.

Of course, *Bloodflowers* isn't an album geared for the mainstream, but then neither was *Disintegration*, which ended up being the band's biggest seller. Robert Smith tried to advance the noncommercial nature of *Bloodflowers* as a selling point. He boldly placed the album on the same plane as *Pornography* and *Disintegration*, billing *Bloodflowers* as the last of a "dark trilogy." That he placed the new album alongside two undisputed classics shows that Robert had no shortage of confidence in the new material, but the comparison to such pivotal albums created a standard that was nearly impossible to meet. *Bloodflowers* is solid on its own terms—dramatic, cohesive and with exquisite attention to detail, with a sonic clarity that is fresh and alive.

After the stylistic grab bag *Wild Mood Swings* suffered the indignity of mostly negative reviews and commercial disappointment, Robert Smith wanted the Cure's next album to be a more serious and cohesive work, something with substance. He decided to return the band to St. Catherine's Court in Avon, where the recording of *Wild Mood Swings* had been such a positive experience.

Initially, the Cure tried to incorporate more electronic elements into their sound so that they would remain relevant and modern while retaining their classic identity. Sessions began at St. Catherine's in September 1998 with Paul Corkett, who had mixed some of the tracks for *Wild Mood Swings,* lined up as engineer (he would eventually be handed coproducer credit for his assistance on the project).

This first round of sessions went nowhere. They were using loops, synthesizer bass, and other electronic equipment, but the songs just weren't there, and the vibe was meandering and unfocused. Robert Smith later said that too many drugs clouded the band's judgment, and although he may have been mythmaking with that assertion, it's certainly true that the Cure was straying off path.

Smith came to this realization when he wrote the solemn meditation on mortality "Out of This World," the song that changed the direction of the entire project. Suddenly, the focus they needed was in place. The band made the difficult decision to scrap half an album's worth of material to start fresh. The track "Possession," previously unreleased until Smith unearthed it for the *Join the Dots* box set, is an example of the protracted false start that was finally put to rest by "Out of This World." The only song from those early session to make the album is the electro-rocker "Coming Up," which is included only as a bonus track on some versions of the CD, and in the United States, it was omitted entirely. After

Robert Smith promised that *Bloodflowers* (2000) was on the same level as *Pornography* and *Disintegration*, but fans disagreed on whether this was achieved. *Author's Collection*

the dismal opening round, Smith and the band took six weeks off before coming back to try again.

Now determined to make a darkly emotional collection in line with *Disintegration*, Robert Smith took tighter control over the sessions than was his usual practice. Before they started, to give the band a sense of what he wanted, Smith played for them *Pornography* and *Disintegration* all the way through. He wanted to make the ultimate Cure album, an archetype of the melancholy side of the band that he views as their truest identity. The studio was available for only three months, a much stricter time limit than with *Wild Mood Swings*, which helped instill discipline into the proceedings and kept the material and keep it within the boundaries Smith had set. The sessions were intense, but Smith later said of them that *Bloodflowers* was his best experience in the studio since *Kiss Me, Kiss Me, Kiss Me*.

All of *Bloodflowers* was recorded at St. Catherine's except for the vocals, which Robert decided to do in the familiar confines of RAK Studios in London. The proceedings went quickly, with only a couple weeks being added to the albums' recording time. Feeling the need to get out of London, Smith mixed the album at the Farm, a recording studio created by the band Genesis and located in the Surrey countryside. Whatever the reasoning, the combination of locations and studios worked, as *Bloodflowers* is arguably the best-sounding album of the band's career.

Increasingly peeved by what he perceived as the record labels' laser focus on commercial success, Smith ensured there were no obvious singles on the albums. Robert later acknowledged that some of the songs meander too long. *Bloodflowers* is heavier than its immediate predecessors, with no light and frothy pop songs to offer respite from the albums relentlessly downbeat nature.

On its release, the reviews were mostly solid, and despite its gloomy nature, *Bloodflowers* sold well and was generally regarded by fans and critics as a return to form after the disappointment of *Wild Mood Swings*. The subsequent Dream Tour was one of the best of the Cure's career, and die-hard fans loved it as the band deemphasized the hits and played much of the *Bloodflowers* album and songs from the past that fit in with the new album's atmosphere. Given the uneven nature of the two studio releases that have followed it thus far (*The Cure* and *4:13 Dream*), and the long-delayed status of new studio material, *Bloodflowers* stands alone as the Cure's late-era high-water mark.

Bloodflowers

"Out of This World"

When Robert Smith penned the sublime "Out of This World," he knew that it was the crucial turning point he'd been seeking to breathe new life into an album that had thus far been a struggle. With a new centerpiece in place pointing the way forward, the Cure ceased their ineffectual dabbling at electronic rock and shifted to a more natural moody guitar-based vibe. As befitting a song that rescued the project, Robert decided to showcase "Out of This World" in the album's high profile opening slot. It holds up nicely against other classic openers like "The Kiss," "Want," "One Hundred Years" and "Shake Dog Shake."

"Out of This World" is a pensive expression of the human tendency to morbidly count down in our heads the ever-dwindling days remaining until we die. It's a reflection of grace and somber elegance tinged with a tangible regret that life is slipping through our fingers and that we'll soon be out of this world and, perhaps, someplace else.

Hello Darkness, My Old Friend: *Bloodflowers*

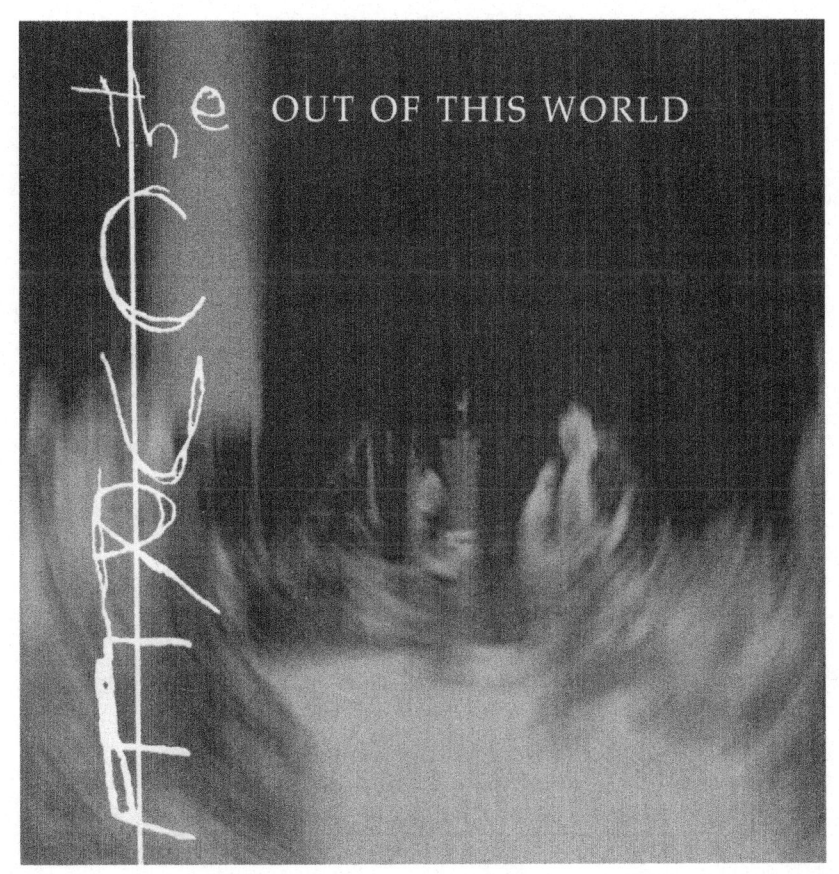

"Out of This World," the opening track for the new album, became another in a long line of great concert openers for the Cure like "Plainsong" and "Open." *Author's Collection*

Beginning with a few brushstrokes by Jason Cooper and then carried by the acoustic layered with slow, subtle lines of keyboard and guitar, "Out of This World" follows the classic Cure formula with precision. Yet it doesn't sound derivative or stale, as if all Cure albums must start in the same way. Smith's gentle, closely miked vocal is one of his loveliest and nuanced, and the gently swaying rhythm and musical swirls are warm and somehow comforting while undeniably sad.

"Watching Me Fall"

Robert Smith insisted that this lumbering eleven-minute death wish could not be edited down to a more digestible length, yet Underdog got it down to 7:42 in his remix for the *American Psycho* soundtrack. In the process, he created a much less punishing listening experience than the album version. The length wouldn't be such a problem if so much time wasn't devoted to Robert Smith's manic and unhinged wailing, which is unfortunately way too high in the mix. "Watching Me Fall" is the most egregious blot on the otherwise mostly-superb *Bloodflowers*. It's just too much.

"Where the Birds Always Sing"

Former Cure Guitarist Parry Bamonte, who delivers starkly powerful acoustic work on "Where the Birds Always Sing," has singled the track out as a striking reminder of Robert Smith's songwriting genius. He's right. The entire band shines on the track, and Robert's vocal is stellar as well. Smith sings in his lower register, imbuing his performance with nuance and genuine feeling.

"Where the Birds Always Sing" is an atheist's anthem, a song about the uncaring neutrality of the universe. There is nobody up there to answer all those endless hours of continual prayer, from the sidelines of a football game to the foot of a hospital bed. It's a cold dose of reality, the simple stark truth, powerfully told.

"Maybe Someday"

The most immediate and directly impactful song on *Bloodflowers* is undoubtedly "Maybe Someday," a torrid hard rocker that the Cure's label in the United States chose for first single. Robert Smith nails an absolutely spot-on vocal, spry and rich with nuance, especially in the run through the last verse. His voice, mixed with the heavy guitar riffs and jittery keyboards, stokes a fierce urgency to the red line, tight with pressure and ready to blow.

"Maybe Someday" is intense psychological drama, powerful and compact. It's a should-have-been classic Cure single that would sound great alongside their other singles on an ultimate greatest-hits collection. It did perform well on alternative radio in the United States, reaching number ten on the modern rock chart.

"Coming Up"

The earliest recorded song on *Bloodflowers*, "Coming Up" was part of the initial sessions during which the band had been exploring more electronic-based rock than most of what ended up on the album. Most of this material was abandoned with Smith came up with "Out of This World," but "Coming Up" was too good to let go (although it is omitted from the album in some countries, including the United States).

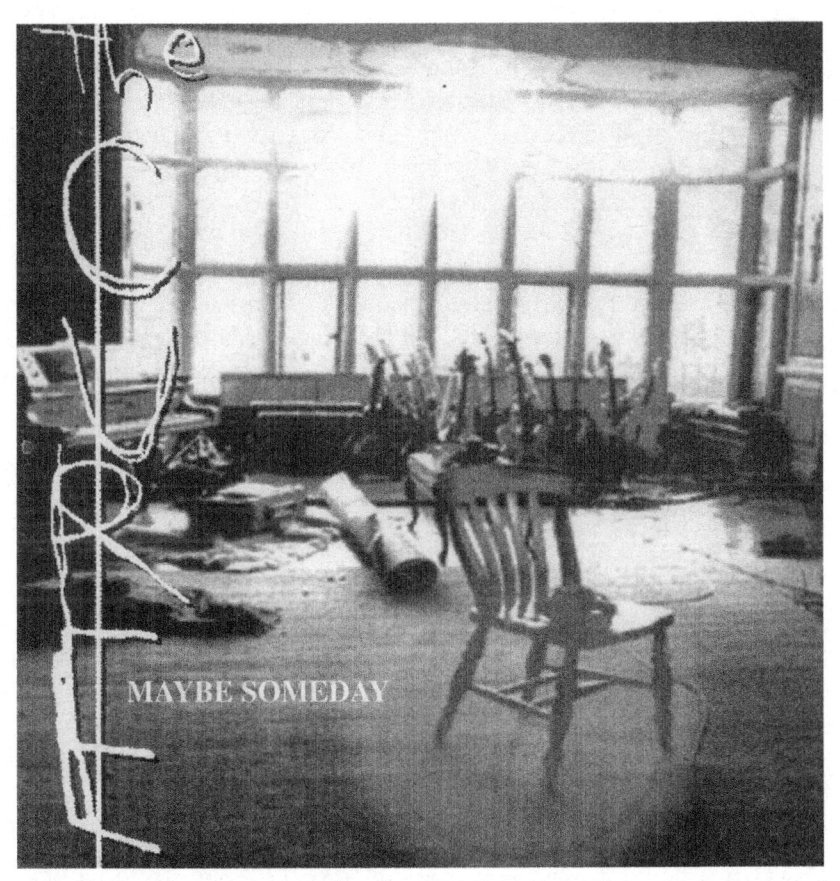

Although *Bloodflowers* wasn't a singles album, "Maybe Someday" is good enough to stand proudly alongside many of the Cure's classics. *Author's Collection*

"The Last Day of Summer"

The Cure's reputation falls heavily on the word *sorrow*, as in that is one of the most commonly used descriptors of the band's work in general, yet when you think of their catalog, how many songs actually express a feeling of sorrow specifically? By putting into short lines of poetry, stark and simple, building a deeper meaning through the said and unsaid, Robert Smith manages the writing trick of showing and not telling.

Here we have the last day of summer never feeling so old or cold. This is about the end of something, whether a relationship, a friendship, or something else. All the lines are terse, expressing a thought or emotion without overdoing it, impressionistic and emotionally cold, like a stone skidding across the top of an iced-over pond.

"The Last Day of Summer" had a long gestation and started in a different medium entirely. Robert Smith mentioned in a 1991 interview with *Select* magazine that he wrote a story with the same title sometime in between 1987's *Kiss Me, Kiss Me, Kiss Me* and 1989's *Disintegration* as part of an intended short-fiction collection.

Written out longhand, Smith says that the story was about "me as I would have liked to be as a little boy—an imaginary last summer, just as you're beginning to be aware you're growing up. It was all the missed opportunities, all the things I wished I'd done, written as though I'd done them." The concept is the same, with the lines filled in and the gaps closed. Had a third single been released from *Bloodflowers*, it may have been "The Last Day of Summer," as promo singles were issued in several countries.

"There Is No If . . ."

This delicate acoustic-based track is the calmest moment on *Bloodflowers*. The sonic clarity of the album is superb throughout but especially here. Robert Smith's vocals are bracingly high in the mix, which works better here than elsewhere on the album, and the instrumental background, notable for the lovely countermelody played on the Bass VI, is so sparse that he sounds vulnerable and practically naked with emotion. "There Is No If . . ." is a gorgeous song, one of the Cure's greatest hidden gems.

"The Loudest Sound"

There is a wounded dignity in the silent suffering of a disintegrating relationship, with each partner clinging to pride with every bit of strength they can muster. There is enough sonic space in "The Loudest Sound" that the listener can easily imagine within its languid echoes the two individuals who were once crazy about each other, excited to see one another, smiling, giggling, breathless. Then years bring familiarity, and things happen, fires erupt and they learn things about each other that slowly change their perception. By the time it reaches the point of such long frozen silences as described in the song, the tension has been so strong in their muscles and bones for so long that they don't even realize it's there anymore; it just feels natural.

Arguments and squabbles become increasingly bitter. They have heated clashes, shouting matches, and hurt words and feelings. Sullen silence becomes the norm. They have forgotten themselves and each other, forgotten what they meant and mean to each other, forgotten how to communicate, to forgive, to see things through the other's eyes.

If only once they could swallow their pride, let down their guard. Think. Remember. They are still the same two people who swept each other away at a time when nothing was more important than each other. They are both thinking it. "I wish things could be like they were before." "Why can't it be like it was before?" One of them could crack the facade, say the words. The other's heart melts after so much silent longing for these words to be said.

But no. Side by side in silence, the only words trapped in their own heads, held firmly by tongues in jaws set in expressions of determination, anger, hurt, depression, and sorrow.

"39"

This is such a Robert Smith way to approach a song or an event. On his thirty-ninth birthday, instead of celebrating with friends and family, Smith claims to have locked himself in a seclusion from which he emerged with this song.

"39" is about the inner fire that powers your ambition sputtering out more and more as you age, the motivation and drive to accomplish things that once seemed so exciting now fading into cynicism and indifference. The track is overly long, the keyboards are too far down in the mix, and Robert Smith spends too much of the song shouting, but the concept of the years whittling away your inspiration is one worthy of exploration.

"Bloodflowers"

Robert Smith tried to make this title song an ultimate Cure epic, but "Bloodflowers" doesn't quite get there, falling somewhat flat as the album's big finale. It seems overwrought and labored, like Smith was trying so hard that he ended up sapping much of the track's spirit. Compared with most of the rest of the album, "Bloodflowers" seems rote, Cure-by-numbers. It's not particularly compelling as a concept or a recording, and the lyrics are fairly pedestrian. It's also overly long—not the strong ending Robert Smith was seeking.

Bonus Tracks

"Spilt Milk"

The Cure revisits a track recorded in 1990 with producer Mark Saunders, "Ching Chang Chong," and keeps the same basic musical arrangement and melody but with completely different lyrics. Smith's vocal is higher in the mix, and the instrumentation is denser and more clunky. There is an airiness to "Ching Chang Chong" and a kick in the right spots that "Spilt Milk" completely paves over. The Cure would have been better off keeping "Ching Chang Chong" and issuing it as a B-side.

Despite its flaws, "Spilt Milk" would have been one of the more immediate tracks on *Bloodflowers*, but it doesn't quite gel stylistically with the rest of the album. It was issued as an Internet-only bonus track at the time of the album's release, but for reasons unexplained, it was left off the Cure's B-side compilation *Join the Dots*.

"Possession"

Recorded during the first round of sessions for *Bloodflowers*, "Possession" was released for the first time in 2004 on the *Join the Dots* box set. Robert Smith cites it as an example of the more electronic-influenced material the Cure was attempting to create early in the sessions. It's also an example of why those sessions didn't work. "Possession" has some good musical ideas (a couple of which were recycled on "The Loudest Sound" and "39") but lacks presence. This is a tame and diffident version of the Cure, unsure what to do and tentatively tiptoeing forward on slippered feet rather than their usual brash steel-toed march of confidence. It's easy to hear why Robert Smith jettisoned the aimless bubbling of "Possession" and other such tracks so that he could redirect the Cure back to its musical heart.

Robert Smith had grand ambitions for *Bloodflowers*, but despite a tremendous effort, it falls just barely short. Smith clearly developed the songs with a specific framework in mind and perhaps because of that songwriting sometimes feels a bit forced rather than the product of genuine inspiration. He's so jaded by age thirty-nine, and is so determined to use that milestone as a creative devise of angst, that the fierce primal intensity he seeks is lacking.

Smith tries, though, burrowing around for bits of wounded psyche to poke endlessly with a stick and squeeze out moments of inspiration. Unlike its predecessors in the trilogy, the songwriting on *Bloodflowers* is not compelling enough to overcome the strict stylistic box it occupies. A sameness creeps in, one that is amplified by several tracks being too long. Getting all the way through in one sitting is a weighty slog.

All that said, there is a lot to like about *Bloodflowers*. "Out of This World" has real heart and warmth. "Maybe Someday," "There Is No If...," "The Last Day of Summer," "Where the Birds Always Sing," and "The Loudest Sound" are all top-notch. The more overwrought tracks—"39," "Watching Me Fall," and the title song—get buried by their own excess. The vibe is hostile and unwelcoming, not the Robert Smith that ends *Disintegration* on a note of thoughtful optimism. *Bloodflowers* exhibits all the gloom and doom that many writers and the public associate with the Cure, and there is no respite at the end.

As good as this album is, it will never be seen as having lived up to expectations because Robert Smith himself set the bar unreachably high with his discussion of a trilogy and of *Bloodflowers* being the heir to *Pornography* and *Disintegration*. It's doubtful that he could have produced any album to meet that standard.

31

This and That, These and Those: The Cure's Hidden Gems

Outcast songs that don't fit anywhere else but shouldn't be forgotten.

Most artists who've been around for a while have at least a few of them—those scattered and often forgotten nuggets from soundtracks, compilations, and other sources that may not have been associated with a particular studio album but that deserve to be heard nonetheless. The Cure has quite a few, oddities and covers and spare parts, some vital and others of little consequence. These are the outcasts of outcasts, diverse and assorted, like multicolored caterpillars and cockatoos gone a little crazy from living too long on the island of misfit toys.

Hidden Gems

4play (2006)

As the remastered deluxe two-CD reissues of the Cure's first four albums—*Three Imaginary Boys*, *Seventeen Seconds*, *Faith*, and *Pornography*—the label issued a special promo CD *4play* to help generate interest. It included ten tracks from the three albums, including previously unreleased material that would appear on the accompanying bonus discs and a four-part interview recorded in 2005 in which Robert Smith discusses the albums.

Most exciting for fans, however, was the inclusion of newly recorded versions of all four title songs to the albums being reissued. Adding to the intrigue, these are the only recordings released by the unique summer of 2005 version of the Cure as a trio: Robert Smith, Simon Gallup, and Jason Cooper. They recorded the tracks with Mike Hedges, original engineer and producer for three of the first four albums. These rerecordings remain exclusive to this set, which was made available for fans to download on iTunes in the United Kingdom. Although they are fairly rudimentary run-throughs of these classic tracks and they don't improve on the originals, they are nonetheless an intriguing listen. Mostly of interest to die-hards.

"Burn"

The production for the 1994 film version *The Crow*, based on the 1989 comic book, made headlines when its young star, Brandon Lee, was accidentally wounded on set after being hit with a defective blank. He was rushed to a hospital but died during surgery. Lee had already filmed most of his scenes, and the film was finished and became a box office hit. The soundtrack is heavy on 1990s alternative rock, but it's the Cure in the prime leadoff spot.

James O'Barr, creator of *The Crow*, is a huge Cure fan and included the lyrics to "The Hanging Garden" in the original comic, which Robert Smith loved. Director Alex Proyas asked to use "The Hanging Garden" in the film, but Smith instead offered him a new song specifically composed for the film: "Burn." Over a two-day session, Robert played all the instruments except for Boris Williams's drum part, which was his last studio recording with the Cure.

The Crow was a massive box office success that ultimately generated a franchise including three film sequels and a television version. The soundtrack was also a huge success, reaching number one on the *Billboard* Album Chart in the United States and becoming one of the signature soundtracks of the 1990s. "Burn" is the only song by the Cure to appear on an album that has been to the top of the album chart in America so far.

"Burn" is an epic, nearly seven-minute seething rocker with a tribal rhythm in a nod to "The Hanging Garden" and discordant flutes during its eerie beginning. Despite its popularity, the Cure didn't perform "Burn" in concert until November 3, 2013, nearly twenty years after its release, at the Voodoo Music Experience in New Orleans. Since then, the song's profile has continued to ascend. It became a regular part of their 2016 set and was one of twenty-nine songs selected by Robert Smith to represent the band's forty-year history of performing during their July 7, 2018, anniversary concert at Hyde Park.

"Ching Chang Chong"

This "Spilt Milk" precursor was recorded in 1990 around the same time as "Never Enough" and "Harold and Joe" to be considered as a potential single for the *Mixed Up* project. The song was shelved, eventually morphing into "Spilt

Milk," an Internet-only bonus track from the *Bloodflowers* era. "Ching Chang Chong" is much better, with far more energy and personality. It's got a nice kick to it, and Smith puts his all into a charismatic multitracked vocal.

The track seems to have been forgotten by Robert when he compiled the *Join the Dots* box set, or perhaps he doesn't consider it a finished song, but with new expanded reissues presumably on the horizon, perhaps this gem will finally get its moment in the sun. Until then, it can be heard on Mark Saunders's website at https://www.marksaunders.com.

"Cut Here"

The Cure recorded three new songs for their 2001 *Greatest Hits* compilation, two of which ended up on the album—"Cut Here" and "Just Say Yes"—while "Signal to Noise" was relegated to B-side status.

The first single was "Cut Here," which Robert wrote about his last encounter with Billy Mackenzie only a few weeks before his suicide in 1997 at the age of thirty-nine. Mackenzie was vocalist for the Associates, a Scottish New Wave band that were Fiction label mates with the Cure in the early 1980s. They toured together, and Robert and Billy became close friends.

"Cut Here" is an unusually poignant and substantial recording for an add-on to a greatest-hits collection. Mark Plati's production work is clean and impactful, and Smith's vocal is thick with anguish and regret. During the deftly written rapid-fire chorus, Smith practically spits the lyrics with anger and self-recrimination over being caught up in the demands of an always busy life and not taking the chance to visit with an old friend. As it turns out, that chance was his last.

"Cut Here" is a gorgeous and heartrending piece of work that was sadly overlooked when it was released and deserves much wider appreciation as perhaps the Cure's finest single of the 2000s.

"The Dragon Hunter Song"

One of the Cure's greatest attributes has always been their willingness to do whatever they wanted to do, and that has led to some wonderful oddities, like the April 6, 2004, release "The Dragon Hunter Song." The band recorded it to be the theme song for the fifty-two-episode French cartoon series *Dragon Hunters* created by Arthur Qwak and produced by Futurikon. The song was later reworked with completely different lyrics as "Taking Off" from the Cure's self-titled album released in June of the same year.

"Dredd Song"

The first song to emerge from the Steve Lyon–produced sessions at St. Catherine's Court that culminated in *Wild Mood Swings* is this soaring orchestral-rock number recorded for the futuristic science-fiction thriller *Judge Dredd* directed by Danny Cannon. Robert Smith had always been a fan of the British comic book series on which the film was based.

The Cure and producer Steve Lyon tried hard to produce an epic track for the film, but "Dredd Song," despite an ambitious string arrangement and a spirited vocal by Smith, never quite gets there. Neither did the film, which was mostly panned by critics and landed with a dud at the box office.

"Forever" (Version)

"Forever" originated as an improvisation that grew out of a performance of the track "Three" from the *Seventeen Seconds* album. It took on a life of its own and became a regular part of the Cure's live sets for many years, almost always during the final encore and often as the final song. It changed from night to night, the lyrics never the same twice and the lengths varying each time it was played.

"Forever" is an abstract, totally unhinged freak-out, basically an excuse for the band to go wild and end their show with a bang. A nine-minute live version was included on the *Faith* deluxe reissue, but perhaps the most famous is the performance from May 1984 at Le Zenith in Paris that was released as "Forever (Version)" on the *Anomalies* compilation of rarities included on side 2 of the cassette release of *Concert: The Cure Live*.

"Harold and Joe"

Released in 1990 as the B-side to "Never Enough," "Harold and Joe" is based on a Simon Gallup demo inspired by characters in *Neighbors*, one of his favorite TV shows. It was initially earmarked as the likely new single that would be included on the *Mixed Up* remix collection.

"Harold and Joe" was the "electronic" track that Robert and producer Mark Saunders were tinkering with in the studio while the rest of the band, bored, galloped through a hard-rocking jam session centered around an edgy Porl Thompson guitar riff. The jam session eventually led to "Never Enough," which became the A-side, while "Harold and Joe" was demoted to B-side status.

A rumination on apathy, "Harold and Joe" is easily good enough to have been a single in its own right. Robert Smith delivers a beguiling lower-register vocal, over a typically peppy chord sequence devised by the band's pop-master, Simon Gallup.

"Hello I Love You"/"Hello I Love You (Slight Return)"

This outstanding cover of the Doors' 1968 chart topper gets the distinction of being the first new Cure release in the wake of the band's meteoric success with *Disintegration*. It was recorded for the collection *Rubáiyát: Elektra's 40th Anniversary*, for which artists on the Elektra roster cover some of the classic songs released over the label's distinguished history.

The Cure bashes out a daredevil garage-rock rendition of "Hello, I Love You," with gleeful abandon. While it's an undeniably electrifying take, it seems a shame that the band selected one of the Doors' most lightweight singles to cover. It's tantalizing to imagine what they might have done with something more substantial. Still, it's one of the band's best covers and there was such hunger for new Cure material that alt-rock radio programmers jumped all over the track, sending it to #6 in the U.S. at alternative radio.

The album ends with the "Slight Return" coda, which is ten seconds of the band thrashing through the song's chorus punk-rock style.

"Hello Goodbye"

The Cure's 2005 cover of John Lennon's "Love" wasn't all that inspiring, but they make up for it with this ebullient cover of the Beatles 1967 chart-topper penned by Paul McCartney, "Hello Goodbye." The band collaborated with Paul's son James McCartney, who plays keyboard and contributes backing vocals. It was recorded for the tribute album *The Art of McCartney*, in 2014, making it the first Cure studio release after the eight-year gap since *4:13 Dream*. With no new music yet as of this writing in 2021, "Hello Goodbye" remains the most recent Cure studio offering in existence and the only studio release from the band in the staggering gap between 2008 and (hopefully) 2021

The Cure's upbeat version has a jubilant quality that suggests that the band is genuinely having a great time. They don't stray too far from the original, but they don't need to. The video is a delight, with Robert swooning and swirling a great vocal at the mic and Simon Gallup gamely offering up Paul McCartney's famous bass runs in front of the superstar's son James, who looks a bit like a curious owl who has somehow fallen in with a pack of crows.

Robert Smith recorded a similarly good-natured solo version of "C Moon," an oddball McCartney B-side that bluffed its way into the U.K. 5 in 1972. Smith's shambolic take was included as an Amazon.com exclusive bonus track for *The Art of McCartney*.

"Just Say Yes"

The second newly recorded track featured on the Cure's 2001 *Greatest Hits* album along with the much-superior "Cut Here," "Just Say Yes" is a high-energy romp that doesn't quite work as intended. Robert Smith duets with Saffron, vocalist for the popular 1990s electro-rock group Republica, but their voices don't really work well together. It feels awkward and forced, one of the very few songs the Cure has released that seems inauthentic. After the chilly response to "Cut Here," the label decided to jettison the idea of a commercial single for "Just Say Yes" so it was released as a promo only, and promptly ignored.

"Love"

The Cure's cover of this John Lennon classic from his 1970 *Plastic Ono Band* album was recorded in June 2005 at Westside Studios in London with their collaborator from the early years Mike Hedges coproducing. It's the band's contribution to the Amnesty International Make Some Noise campaign and was released on December 10, 2005.

The Make Some Noise campaign was a benefit created in collaboration with Yoko Ono, who donated the recording rights to John Lennon songs exclusively for use by Amnesty International for various artists to record covers. Artists such as U2, Green Day, R.E.M., Maroon 5, Christina Aguilera, and others contributed John Lennon covers for the benefit. They all appeared on the album *Instant Karma: The Amnesty International Campaign to Save Darfur*, although the Cure's cover of "Love" was not on the U.S. configuration of the release.

Unfortunately, the Cure's take on the classic by Lennon is not one of their better efforts. They strip away the delicate beauty of the original and reimagine it as a sludgy rock track that plods along without much feeling. Kudos to Smith for trying to bring a fresh approach to the classic, but sadly it just falls flat.

"Love Will Tear Us Apart"

The Cure recorded Joy Division's titanic classic backstage at the Brisbane, Australia, Livid Festival on October 21, 2000, for Triple J Radio. It's never been released officially by the band but is widely available to stream online. Their cover is unfortunately rather pedestrian. Although Robert Smith's vocal is excellent, the cover is ruined by awful lead-footed drum work.

"More Than This"

Recorded in 1998, "More Than This" is a complete solo recording that Robert Smith did with *Bloodflowers* producer Paul Corkett. It was written specifically for inclusion on *The X-Files: The Album*, a sound track to the popular supernatural-themed television series. Smith was a fan of the show, although "More Than This" doesn't have any obvious thematic connection to it except for a vaguely foreboding feel to it. "More Than This" is a slowly shuffling electronic-based track that seems to fit right in with the type of material the Cure would pursue early on in the sessions for *Bloodflowers* (also with Corkett) before they switched course.

"Never Enough"

The band collaborated with producer Mark Saunders for "Never Enough," the one new song for their 1990 remix album *Mixed Up*. The six-minute album version is dubbed the "Big Mix," while the single edit was a major hit for the band, hitting number thirteen in the United Kingdom and spending three weeks at the top of the modern rock singles chart in the United States.

"Never Enough" was generated out of frustration. Saunders and Robert Smith were holed up in the studio working on "Harold and Joe," which at that point was planned as the one new song for the remix album. The rest of the band, bored from cooling its heels, started jamming on a riff that Porl Thompson had been blasting around the practice area. Saunders happened to walk in and hear what they were doing, and he grabbed Robert Smith to give it a listen. They abandoned the laborious "Harold and Joe," and "Never Enough" came together quickly.

The Cure's first single post-*Disintegration*, "Never Enough," is a hard rock rush built around Porl Thompson's blazing guitar heroics. Robert Smith's stuttery lyrics are a self-reflection on never being satisfied, a theme he has revisited multiple times over his career.

"Purple Haze"

Robert Smith has always maintained a love for Jimi Hendrix, so it's not surprising that they would appear on a tribute to the guitar master, the excellent "Stone Free" released in 1993. They contribute one of Hendrix's signature songs, and they do it justice with a trippy, electronic treatment that's radically different from the original. The band also recorded a more routine and traditional straightforward rock cover that remained unreleased until its inclusion in 2004 on *Join the Dots*. Smith commented in 2004 that he felt "Purple Haze" was the best cover the Cure ever recorded, and he may very well be right (although a decade later, they may have surpassed it with "Hello Goodbye").

"Signal to Noise"

The Cure recorded three new tracks to fill two spots as new singles on their 2001 *Greatest Hits* compilation: "Just Say Yes," "Cut Here," and "Signal to Noise." It was always a definite that "Just Say Yes," a duet with Saffron from Republica, would be included, but the decision between "Cut Here" and "Signal to Noise" went down to the wire.

Ultimately, it was "Cut Here" that made the cut, and "Signal to Noise" was relegated to B-side status. Robert Smith muses in the liner notes to the *Join the Dots* box set that perhaps the melodic rocker "Signal to Noise' would have been a stronger choice, and in a way, he's right—but it's the comparatively mediocre "Just Say Yes" that should have made room for it, not the superb "Cut Here." "Signal to Noise" was so close to getting on the hits collection that they even recorded an acoustic version for the bonus disc in case it was chosen.

"World in My Eyes"

Robert Smith recorded this electro cover of the Depeche Mode classic for the 1998 compilation *For the Masses*. The collection is a tribute to Martin Gore, one of the band's principal songwriters, and all of the songs selected were written by him. Smith's version is nice enough and follows the original closely. It may have been interesting to hear a more radical take, but it's undeniably solid. This was Smith recording all on his own, with none of the rest of the band involved.

"Wrong Number"

Originally attempted and quickly aborted during sessions with Mark Saunders for *Mixed Up*, "Wrong Number" was radically reworked by Smith with heavy input by Reeves Gabrels and Mark Plati. The only other member of the band to appear on the final version is drummer Jason Cooper.

"Wrong Number" was the featured new single for the 1997 *Galore* hits collection, and although it sounds more like Gabrels's work with David Bowie on *Earthling* than a Cure song, it performed well for the band on alternative radio in the United States. "Wrong Number" managed an impressive peak of number eight on the modern rock chart at a time when that genre was at an apex.

It was the Cure's first brush with any true commercial success in the United States since "Friday I'm in Love," and Smith commissioned several remixes for the CD-single release. The high-energy track remains a frequent part of the band's live shows, particularly in the United States.

"Young Americans"

It's a bit counterintuitive for the Cure to record cover versions given how much of their appeal is based on the personal and emotional nature of Robert Smith's lyrics. They have never really proven themselves gifted at interpreting the works of others, and their take on "Young Americans" is another example.

It's a very basic run-through of the David Bowie classic, recorded in 1995 for the *104.9 XFM* compilation, a benefit album to provide funding for a London radio station for which Smith and Chris Parry were on the board of directors. Produced by Steve Lyons in the lead-up to the *Wild Mood Swings* sessions, "Young Americans" was only available on the compilation until 2004 when it was included on the *Join the Dots* box set.

32

Just When You Think You've Got It Down: *The Cure*

Robert Smith hands the producer's hat to Ross Robinson for the band's hard-edged twelfth album.

Released: June 29, 2004
Geffen Records—B0002870-01, I Am—060249868461
Running time: 71:13

1. "Lost" (4:07), 2. "Labyrinth" (5:14), 3. "Before Three" (4:40), *4. "Truth, Goodness and Beauty" (4:20), 5. "The End of the World" (3:44), 6. "Anniversary" (4:22), 7. "Us or Them" (4:09), *8. "Fake" (4:43), 9. "alt.end" (4:30), 10. "(I Don't Know What's Going) On" (2:57), 11. "Taking Off" (3:19), 12. "Never" (4:04), 13. "The Promise" (10:21), *14. "Going Nowhere" (3:28), *15. "This Morning" (7:15)
* Not included on all pressings.

Given their diverse sonic canvas, it's sometimes easy to forget that the Cure is still just a rock band at heart. That's how they were conceived in the halcyon days of post-punk, and while they've expanded their sound exponentially over the years, the Cure has always been able to go full-throttle hard rock when the mood strikes.

Even the mournful *Faith* has the hard-edged "Doubt" and "Primary." For all its dark moods and gloomy ponderings, *Bloodflowers* has a rock 'n' roll power to it. A strong Cure compilation showcasing their harder-edged material would be a great listen: "Shake Dog Shake," "Give Me It," "Push," "All I Want," "Shiver and Shake," "Cut," "Scared as You," "One Hundred Years," "Grinding Halt," "Last

Dance," "Club America," "Maybe Someday," and "Never Enough" would be a good starting point. Then add a few tracks from their 2004 self-titled album, shake, and serve.

The Cure, the band's first self-titled album, was released on June 29, 2004. It's by far the heaviest rock album of their career. Smith wanted something completely different, and he wanted someone who would amp up every notch beyond maximum. In pursuit of this idea, for the first time Robert Smith allowed another producer to basically take over the project. He ran into Ross Robinson at the end of the Coachella festival in the California desert. The two started chatting music and quickly became friends. Smith has said that he knew he wanted to give Robinson the opportunity to produce the new Cure album after just one day.

It was an interesting combination, and it's likely that the Cure had no real clue what they were in for with the popular young American producer of hard rock bands that sold lots of records but didn't exactly thrill the critics. Of course, given Robert Smith's dim view of critics, that may have been another point in Robinson's favor.

Robinson respected the Cure, but he went into the sessions knowing he was not going to be stepped on by anybody, even a rock legend. Robinson is best known as a pioneer in the so-called Nu metal genre that reached mass popularity at the end of the 1990s and early 2000s with bands like Korn and Limp Bizkit. Robinson also produced heavy-hitting metal bands like Sepultura, Deftones, Slipknot, Fear Factory, and others (including an ignominious turn producing Vanilla Ice on his failed 1998 "comeback," *Hard to Swallow*, which indeed proved true to its name).

Recording in Los Angeles at their producer's insistence, the Cure tried to avoid the distractions of such alien territory by isolating themselves completely. They proved to be in a prolific mood, finishing nearly forty possible contenders for the album in demo form.

Robinson's goal was to distill the twenty-five years of the Cure's history to then culminate with this album. The sessions were structured to focus on one song per day, with Robert Smith standing to explain the song's lyrics and meaning to the other bandmates and the studio personnel. This typically led to a discussion, with emotionally charged comments and debates not uncommon.

The Cure's deeply ingrained English reserve was tested to the boiling point by Robinson's brash demeanor. Keyboardist Roger O'Donnell, for instance, loathed Robinson so much that he refused to participate in the band's impromptu group therapy sessions. On one occasion O'Donnell's started became so enraged he started screaming at Robinson, who only responded by cackling madly like a deranged evil scientist.

Bassist Simon Gallup, Smith's longtime right-hand man, was put off by Robinson's aimless experimenting to try to get a Cure bass sound that Gallup knew very well how to get. But not wanting to rock the boat, Gallup later said, "I didn't want to interfere too much." Robinson's technique and his freewheeling, often abrasive personality was a bizarre changeup for the veteran musicians. They weren't enjoying it, and they didn't think Robinson understood the Cure, but as long as Smith was on board, that was all that mattered. And he gave the producer the benefit of the doubt, hoping that a classic Cure album would arise out of the tension and chaos.

Most of the flaws on *The Cure*, which has some strong material from a songwriting perspective, can be laid at Robinson's feet. It's a shame that Robert Smith's principles had evidently changed since September 1992 when he said to Joe Gore of *Guitar Player* magazine, "We'd never have a producer who actually tells us what to do. I suppose I had the courage of my convictions very early on. I'm glad I didn't give in to people who thought they knew better than I did when I was young."

There were any number of producers who would have been a better fit, including some of their prior collaborators. Smith, however, seemed to delight in handing the power to the brash young producer and seemed willing to put up with almost anything to get an album that sounded current and relevant. It must have crossed Robert Smith's mind quite a few times that the Cure's last couple studio albums had sold rather poorly overall, and he undoubtedly wanted to reverse that trend.

The Cure was released on Robinson's I Am label, an imprint of Geffen, as the first of what was intended to be a three-album deal. The resulting album is hit and miss and remains divisive among fans. Robert Smith was enthusiastic about *The Cure* when it was first released, telling *The Guardian* that "anyone who doesn't like this just doesn't like The Cure." He also claimed that more passion went into the making of *The Cure* than any of their other albums. Given the intense sessions for *Faith*, *Pornography*, and *Disintegration*, that's a very strong claim to make.

The album's creepy child-drawn artwork was created by Robert Smith's nephews and nieces and then mashed together as "good dream" and "bad dream." Much of this album resides firmly in the "bad dream" territory, but there are many positives to be found as well.

Reviews for *The Cure* were chilly, and most fans had the same reaction. The album performed better on the charts, at least initially, than the Cure's prior two studio efforts. *The Cure* reached number seven in the United States and number eight in the United Kingdom, higher than both *Bloodflowers* and *Wild Mood Swings* in both countries. None of the singles—"The End of the World," "Taking Off," and "alt.end"—were significant hits, and only "The End of the World" has been a consistent part of the Cure's live sets in years since its release.

Almost all who disliked it pointed to Robinson's production as the main culprit. Robinson's guitar-heavy approach is light on the keyboards, thus minimizing Roger O'Donnell and removing a key component of the Cure's signature sound.

Also problematic is that Robert Smith seems to have forgotten to write any melodies for this album. He spends most of *The Cure* wailing at the top of his lungs, with his vocals front and center and way up too high in the mix. His voice is plastered all over what seems to be every second available on this seventy-plus-minute marathon with barely a moment's respite. Smith's caustic yell in "Lost," the political rage gone haywire in "Us or Them," the earsplittingly awful "Never," and the ten-minute ride through hell's bumpier back roads "The Promise" are all among the least listenable of the Cure's catalog. Just because you sing louder and yell into the microphone doesn't mean you're putting more passion into it.

Yet, despite the considerable legitimate criticism, there are some true gems hidden among the dross. "Labyrinth" and "Before Three" are strong, as are the three pop songs "The End of the World," "Taking Off," and "(I Don't Know What's Going) On." To Robinson's credit, the Cure does sound freshly energized on a few of the rockers, most notably "Fake" and "alt.end." The finest moments are two down-beat tracks that fit more naturally into the Cure's lush and funereal comfort zone: "Anniversary" and "Going Nowhere."

Thank whatever deities intervened to allow the stronger tracks to seep in because otherwise the end result is an album's worth of being screamed at incoherently. It's aesthetic can best be described as decidedly unpleasant. One might point to *Pornography*, almost universally acknowledged as a classic, as another album that isn't exactly loaded with memorable hooks. Yet *Pornography* captures a certain mood, a feverish place that only it occupies, and the stilted, doomsday vocals that Smith delivers there fit perfectly. Here, the only mood generated is anxious irritability, punctuated by frequent lurches by the listener to lower the volume when confronted by one of Robert's more garish earsplitting screams.

It's not believable in the way *Pornography* (or any of Smith's best work) is. *The Cure* sounds like the Cure trying hard to sound like the Cure at their most intense but then overshooting their target by a mile. They are simply over the top.

The Cure

"Lost"

The Cure opens with a bold declaration of the band's new sound, which they considered hard-hitting but just turned out to be loud flailing for the sake of it. It's as if Smith tried to compensate for the obvious lack of sincerity and true feeling in the music by wailing louder and louder until the listener's brain is vibrating with the sheer desperation of it all.

"Lost" is a punishing howl-fest that could have been so much better with a little restraint and some judicious lowering of Robert Smith's voice in the mix.

"Labyrinth"

One of the better tracks on the album, "Labyrinth" hangs on the repetition of a trippy exotic melody that, along with the locomotive rhythm, builds tension and mystery over the course of its five minutes. Vocally, Smith is gauzed in a digital shroud for the early part of the song, but then, unfortunately, he breaks into the open air and resumes the yelling that made up the majority of track 1. As usual, all the guitars are strangely tuned, with Simon Gallup's bass particularly off-kilter. "Labyrinth" is almost there in terms of listenability, but once again, pain mistaken for passion slams it off course.

"Before Three"

Finally, we get to the Cure of the album title. "Before Three" is smart and poignant, a man reaching near the desperation point to keep a flame alive that probably flickered out beyond hope ages ago, but he either doesn't realize it or won't acknowledge it. But maybe not. Things can turn around and get better—in a good dream.

"Before Three" is brimming with genuine emotion, just enough of a rock edge, and a good enough hook to have been a single had the Cure opted to go beyond the three they issued.

"Truth, Goodness and Beauty"

One of the annoying peculiarities of *The Cure* is that multiple configurations exist, depending on format and country, which makes it next to impossible to even determine the album's official track listing. In the United States, for example, "Truth, Goodness and Beauty" is available only on the vinyl edition. It's worth tracking down. This languid, almost bluesy number has plenty of sonic space and has the band grooving in slow motion under a thick cannabis cloud.

Smith's vocals are still a bit too present, but he instills the right feeling into a song about finding someone whom you think the world of and who would like nothing better than to leave the world permanently. There's always some disconnect between self-perception and reality, and the cliché but so often true phrase "I wish you could see yourself like I see you" comes to mind immediately.

"The End of the World"

The album's first single doesn't sound like much at first, but it's a grower. Repeated listens bring out its verve and zany charm. Despite a visually stunning video, "The End of the World" didn't have enough commercial punch to lift the album into public awareness, but, as we know, popular doesn't always equal good.

"The End of the World" is the only song from *The Cure* to be a regular part of the band's live set in the years after the album's release, and it was even played at their fortieth-anniversary show in July 2018 at Hyde Park, which says plenty about what Robert Smith thinks of the song. It also shows that Ross Robinson has a lighter touch than he usually exhibits and can rein it in once in a great while.

The first single from *The Cure* didn't gain much traction among fans, but it's stayed in the Cure's live shows and was included in their career-overview set at the 40th anniversary Hyde Park show in 2018. *Author's Collection*

"Anniversary"

A strong argument can be made that "Anniversary" is the pinnacle of *The Cure*, and back to back with "The End of the World," it certainly shows what a different album this might have been if Smith and Robinson hadn't been so determined to force the Cure's square peg into a trapezoidal hole with no lube—it was never gonna work.

"Anniversary," with its ominous vibe, eerily sinuous lines of keyboard, and a particularly haunting vocal by Smith, is the track on *The Cure* most reminiscent of their classic sound of the late 1980s in part because of the prominent keyboards. The lyrics are enigmatic enough to be open for interpretation, but the mournful tone suggests that things didn't end well.

"Us or Them"

What could have been an effective hard rocker is marred by the same flaw that infects most of *The Cure*: Robert Smith's vocals are way too high in the mix. There is some real grit and feeling here, though, and for a change, it doesn't feel like self-parody. It's almost enough to echo fondly back to the days of *Pornography*, but in that regard, the most likely result is for the listener to want to go back to that classic album and listen to it again.

It's the closest thing the Cure has done to a protest song, as Smith rails against the idiocy of religion, the policing of thought and ideas, and the narrow-minded mentality of a black-and-white world that's split into good and evil, or us and them.

"Fake"

One of the best songs on *The Cure* can't even be found on the U.S. pressing, but it's easy enough to track down. "Fake" is a mid-tempo rocker with an old-school guitar pattern, one of those single-note Robert Smith classics, with a New Wave synthesizer riff quavering in the back of the mix. The stripped-down approach on "Fake" works much better than the thick and surly wall of noise that makes up much of the album's sound.

"alt.end"

The second single in the United States is this outstanding rocker, the best hard-edged song on the album by a mile. "alt.end" sounds like the Cure, with Smith's vocals suitable to the rock setting but not out of control and irksome. Another stunning video accompanied the single, but rock radio sadly didn't pay much attention.

"(I Don't Know What's Going) On"

At under three minutes, the brevity and tight focus of this melodic pop gem should have made it a natural candidate to be a single, and it may have been had the earlier ones performed better. While not as light and frothy as "Taking Off," it has a quirky charm similar to "The End of the World" that is hard to accomplish while still sounding so natural. The most dangerous ear worm on the album, it will get stuck in your head for days.

"Taking Off"

The bright and upbeat "Taking Off" was released around most of the world as the album's second single (the United States got the hard-rocking "alt.end" instead). It's a worthy addition to the long list of great Cure melodies, and it's a shame that it wasn't a more substantial hit. One thing often neglected in discussion of *The Cure* is the string of terrific videos, and the goofy video for "Taking Off" certainly qualifies.

"Taking Off" had appeared a couple months prior to the album's release with entirely different lyrics as "The Dragon Hunters Song," the theme for the French cartoon series *Dragon Hunters*.

"Never"

"Never" is the first of a one-two punch that Smith obviously intended to be the album's emotional apex but instead is a punishing test of sheer will and endurance. Listening to "Never" and "The Promise" back to back and all the way through is like putting your head up to a fire truck siren and taking the full brunt of the piercing alarm directly into the brain, shattering both ears and your sanity in the process.

"The Promise"

The good thing about "The Promise" (and much of the rest of *The Cure* for that matter) is that the sound clarity is outstanding. The wrenching guitars come through like hot serrated wire slicing out of the speaker casing. We may have to hear Smith braying his venom and vitriol for ten long minutes, but at least the sound quality is good. The centerpiece of the album, "The Promise" is a mess, simply unlistenable. There's no power to it, just loud and angry sounds.

"Going Nowhere"

With a twinkling introduction lifted directly from "Pictures of You," the slow and solemn "Going Nowhere" is sublime enough to make you forget the worst of the sins you endured to arrive here (almost). The long instrumental introduction sways with a slow dance between a simple guitar pattern and warmly glowing piano, easing into a tune of romantic sorrow and hurt that is Robert Smith's specialty.

"This Morning"

Although available via vinyl only if you want a physical copy, you can catch this track streaming and via digital download. The bigger question is, why would you want to? "This Morning" is more than seven minutes of Robert Smith moaning more drearily that ever before, about, well, nothing really. And what does it matter? It's long and formless with no melody and nothing to hold the listener's attention.

B-Sides

"Why Can't I Be Me"

Turgid and dire, "Why Can't I Be Me" is a terrific example of the overexaggerated clichéd gloominess that Cure detractors think is the band's usual vibe. The song's dreadfulness is amplified by its ill-advised callback to the manic dance classic from which it derives its name. It's partially redeemed by some interesting guitar and rhythm parts, but Smith's tuneless vocal, with no discernible melody to be found, destroys any real value the song may have had.

"Your God Is Fear"

By far the better of the two B-sides, "Your God Is Fear" has all the searing intensity that several songs on *The Cure* grasp for and miss entirely. Even Robert Smith's rage-fueled vocal fits perfectly within the lines this time. He's already directed one song to the perils of closed-minded religion, "Us and Them," but this one is arguably better. Slow burning with a savage guitar solo buried deep in the mix, "Your God Is Fear" is a missed opportunity.

It's not really easy to claim that the Cure has never released a bad album because surely that's just a fanboy talking. Surely, every artist with ten or more records has had at least one bad one and probably more. With the Cure, it's dicier because there are only two candidates—*The Cure* and *4:13 Dream*—and while both of them are certainly problematic in various ways, the bottom line is that *The Cure* has nine songs that are on the good side of the ledger and *4:13 Dream* at least eight. While fans may love to hate Ross Robinson's production on *The Cure*, it's easy to lose sight of that fact that it has more good songs than bad and is worth getting.

The strong perception of *The Cure* being a really terrible record is likely caused by the low points being so damn low. Some of the worst things the Cure have ever done are on this record. Furthering that point, the high points are nowhere close to the best the Cure has to offer. While neither album may be "bad" per se, it's hard to argue that the quality of the Cure's studio albums has slipped. Of course, with only three exhibits to choose from since 2000, it's hard to know what the Cure might be doing if they weren't so allergic to the studio.

There is zero doubt that *The Cure* suffers from multiple issues, the most obvious being Robert Smith's voice being too high in the mix and too plastered all over the place and the absence of the vocal harmonies that have made so many Cure songs more memorable. More keyboards would have helped, too, and a few songs need to be reeled in dramatically.

It's easy to blame everything on Ross Robinson. There's no doubt his behavior was boorish and arrogant (at one point, he was flinging lit candles at the band members), but at the end of the day, Robert Smith is in charge. He could have stepped in at any time and kept this project from going completely off the rails, but strangely enough, that appears to be what he wanted.

Robert Smith said he wanted to do something different, a complete break with the Cure's past. In the end, he decided to call it *The Cure* because he thought it was the best thing they'd ever done and that it was the most Cure thing they'd ever done. If that's the case, it seems strange that after the tour in support of the album, almost every song disappeared from the band's live set completely, with only "The End of the World" being played on a regular basis.

Ross Robinson didn't understand the first thing about the Cure and was too arrogant to figure it out. Smith's bandmates hated Robinson, but that simply appeared to be evidence to Smith that the producer was shaking up the status quo.

Smith stood behind a guy who became famous for producing really terrible albums by really terrible bands and who treated his bandmates like crap instead of those very band members who have been with him for years and almost universally loathed Robinson. And for what? The disconnect between Robert Smith's perception of this album and its reality is a gaping maw of cognitive dissonance.

33

Seemed So Very Real: **4:13 Dream**

The Cure's most recent studio album (so far) is only a partial vision completed and is sadly not the sweetest of dreams.

Released: October 27, 2008
Suretone—B0010913-01, Geffen Records—B0010913-01
Running time: 52:28

1. "Underneath the Stars" (6:17), 2. "The Only One" (3:57), 3. "The Reasons Why" (4:35), 4. "Freakshow" (2:30), 5. "Sirensong" (2:22), 6. "The Real Snow White" (4:43), 7. "The Hungry Ghost" (4:29): 8. "Switch" (3:44), 9. "The Perfect Boy" (3:21), 10. "This. Here and Now. With You" (4:06), 11. "Sleep When I'm Dead" (3:51), 12. "The Scream" (4:37), 15. "It's Over" (4:16).

From 1979 to 1989, the Cure released eight classic albums: *Three Imaginary Boys, Seventeen Seconds, Faith, Pornography, The Top, The Head on the Door, Kiss Me, Kiss Me, Kiss Me,* and *Disintegration,* plus scattered singles and EPs, two live albums, two concert films, a best-selling singles compilation, a dizzying gaggle of B-sides, and an influential series of music videos—all while touring almost nonstop.

Looking at an identical stretch of time from 2008 through 2018, the Cure released only one studio album, and few would consider it a classic. After numerous delays, *4:13 Dream* finally appeared with a whimper on October 27, 2008. *4:13 Dream* exists within a malaise, lacking the spark needed to cut through the overly compressed production that Smith cooked up with engineer and coproducer Keith Uddin.

The first sessions at Parkgate Studios in April 2006 yielded the album's basic foundation, although work continued off and on for a grueling two and half years. More than twenty-five songs were recorded and ultimately abandoned. The protracted studio residency and never-ending tinkering were sure signs of trouble since the Cure usually records quickly. When the smoke finally cleared, thirty-three new songs emerged for what was planned as a double album.

More delays ensued. The band gridlocked on how to best present the voluminous and widely varied material to the world. Robert Smith was indecisive, as he was bombarded with conflicting advice and constant bickering. Some felt the Cure should focus on the darker material to appeal to their core base, while others argued for the most immediate and accessible material to reestablish their presence in the top forty. The original idea of a double album showcasing the band's diversity seemed to lack label support.

Smith's frustration boiled over, and eventually, he acquiesced to the label executives, who wanted a single disc. Beset by disagreements over what songs should make the final cut, Smith cobbled together the thirteen diverse tracks that became the final product. He promised that the remaining material, mostly dark and melancholy, would be issued as a separate album called *4:14 Scream*. Over a decade later, it still hasn't seen the light of day.

Unfortunately, few of the songs seem truly inspired, resulting in an album that is emotionally flat. The bigger issue, though, is the production and mixing. *4:13 Dream* is so dense and compressed that it's practically unlistenable. There is zero dynamic range. The return of guitarist Porl Thompson is welcome, but everything is such a mush of sound that it hardly matters.

Completed demos for three unreleased songs have leaked online—"Strum," "A Boy I Never Knew," and the absolute stunner "Please Come Home—" the last of which would have been the strongest cut on the album had it been included. These three tracks sound amazing in demo form and weren't compressed into thin aluminum wafers by whatever sonic filter of doom Robert Smith and Keith Uddin used to ruin the finished album.

"A Boy I Never Knew" was performed twenty-five times during the band's tour in support of the album. Smith mentioned two additional tracks that were slated for the album but eventually set aside—"Lusting Here in Your Mind" and "Christmas without You"—more than a year before *4:13 Dream* finally appeared.

It doesn't help that everything seems so contrived. *4:13 Dream* sounds like Robert Smith followed a checklist detailing all of the things a Cure album should contain. Epic, swirly, dreamy opener? Check. Manic guitar freak-out with Smith screaming like a tortured madman? Yup, the final two tracks. Goofy pop song? Got it. Breezy acoustic-flavored melodic pop rocker? Present and accounted for. It's Cure-by-numbers, going through the motions.

The band poured tons of energy and promotional muscle into make the album a success in the United States, but it was strangely timed. Several weeks after the album's release, they made the rounds of late-night TV, hitting Jay Leno, Jimmy Kimmel, and Carson Daly in a one-week span wrapped around their December 14 headlining slot at KROQ's Almost Acoustic Christmas. As with most Cure albums, reviews had been all over the place, although the band's website was quick to note *People* magazine bizarrely calling it a "damn near classic Cure album." They even performed the album in its entirety for an episode of *MTV Live*.

In the end, all of this activity failed to move the dial in the album's favor. Despite a wealth of material and the staggering amount of time and effort poured into the project by Smith and company, *4:13 Dream* was a major commercial disappointment. The album reached number sixteen in the United States, a nine-position dip from *The Cure* and tied for their lowest peak since *Disintegration*. The Cure's native United Kingdom offered a stern rebuke, as *4:13 Dream* crawled to a stunningly low number thirty-three, down from a number eight showing for its predecessor. Only their debut, *Three Imaginary Boys*, peaked lower, reaching number forty-four nearly three decades earlier.

The dismal response to *4:13 Dream* must have been painful for Robert since he expressed such pride and optimism during interviews surrounding its release. He told *Rolling Stone* that his standards were much higher than ever before, and he said flat out that any fan of the Cure would like *4:13 Dream*. He miscalculated somewhere along the way.

4:13 Dream

"Underneath the Stars"

The opening slot on a Cure album, at least since "One Hundred Years," is usually reserved for songs with truly epic scope and power. This is certainly true of "Shake Dog Shake," "The Kiss," "Plainsong," "Open," Want," and "Out of This World." For *4:13 Dream*, they turn once again to the dreamy epic template for "Underneath the Stars." The necessary ingredients are all there: shimmery keyboard chimes, echoey vocals low in the mix, understated lead guitar, and lyrics that hit just the right level of wistful romanticism.

"Underneath the Stars" has a lot going for it, and the potential is there for a classic Cure opener, but it falls just short. Robert Smith nails a terrific vocal, but the reverb is turned up to about twenty-seven. It plods a little and is lacking in grace. "Underneath the Stars" is earthbound when it could have soared, not quite transcendent but still good enough to qualify as the best track on the album.

Speaking of transcendent, "Underneath the Stars" was remixed by Danny Lohner for the 2009 soundtrack to the supernatural thriller *Underworld: Rise of the Lycans*. Lohner is a multi-instrumentalist and former close collaborator with Trent Reznor on various Nine Inch Nails projects. He supervised the film soundtrack, remixing multiple artists under the moniker Renholdër.

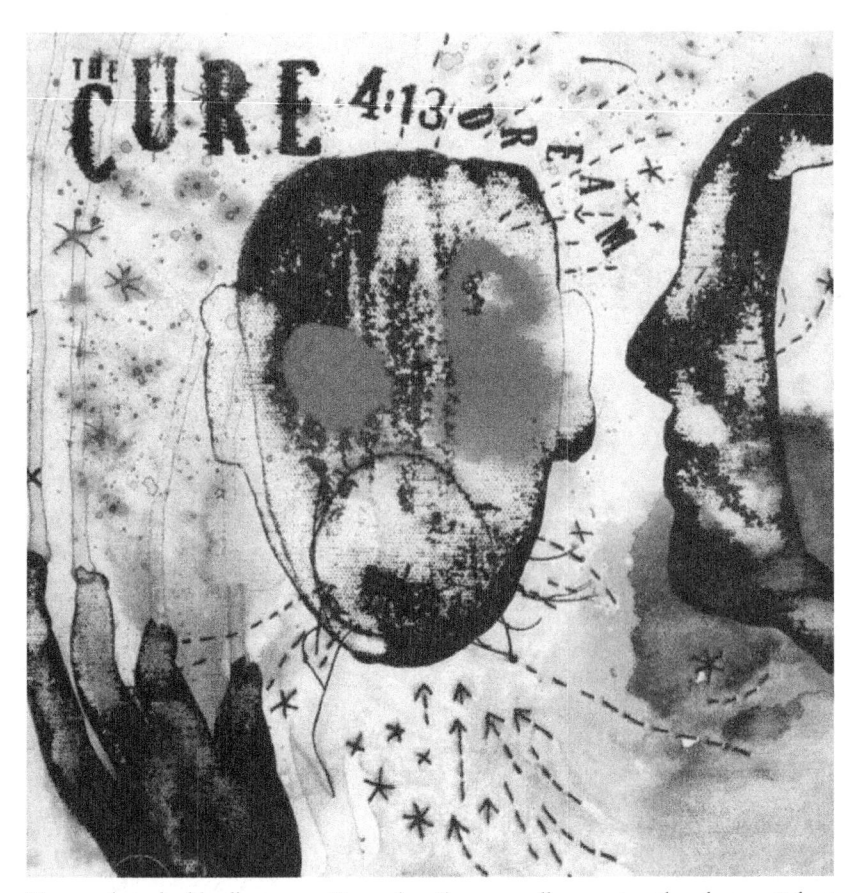

Meant to be a double album, *4:13 Dream* (2008) never really came together the way Robert Smith had hoped. *Author's Collection*

"Underneath the Stars (Renholdër Remix)" strips away the excess baggage of the original and gets to the heart of the track, exposing the song's innate theatrical power by allowing it to build as it progresses to a truly moving conclusion. Lohner adds a sublime vocal part by Milla Jovović, and her voice, alongside a bare-bones Robert Smith removed of all the effects and sonic tricks, is stunning. If nothing else, "Underneath the Stars (Renholdër Remix)" shows that Robert Smith is still capable of writing strong material but hasn't been as successful lately in translating his ideas in the recording studio as he has in the past.

"The Only One"

The album's lead single, "The Only One" is a brisk acoustic rocker, Robert Smith gliding above loopily in his higher register. It's pleasant and catchy but somewhat slight. It reflects rather dimly a series of earlier, superior pop songs, like "High," "A Pink Dream," "Friday I'm in Love," and "In Between Days."

Smith effectively presents his ebullient side, that head-over-heels, smiling-all-the-time romantic bliss that envelops a happy couple before the glow surrounding them starts the inevitable fade into recrimination, misunderstanding, and that all-too-familiar fusion of hurt and anger that consumes the soul. Smith has penned songs about that side of the relationship as well.

When "The Only One" was issued on May 13, 2008, it seemed puzzling that the Cure would choose such an ordinary song as the first single. When the album was finally released six months later, it made perfect sense given the lack of truly viable options available. Fans weren't impressed, and the single limped to number forty-eight in the United Kingdom, the lowest-ever chart placement of any lead single from a Cure album.

The single was barely acknowledged in the United States by radio and other media outlets, but the Cure's shrewd decision to issue physical CD-5 singles paid dividends. Although ubiquitous in the 1990s, by 2008 the CD-5 was an almost extinct format. With so few being released, it didn't take much in the way of sales to reach number one on the Billboard Singles Sales chart. And indeed, all four singles from *4:13 Dream* accomplished this, thanks to the exclusive B-sides each one boasted and thanks to the undying loyalty of Cure fans.

"The Reasons Why"

There are undoubtedly powerful moments on *4:13 Dream*, and one of them is "The Reasons Why." Robert Smith wrote it about a suicide letter he received in 1987 from a person he knew. The letter writer was the same age as Robert, who obviously was stricken by the situation given the searing intensity of the vocals. Life is so difficult that suicide sometimes looks like a viable option of escape. Avoiding reality altogether, a head-in-the-sand approach to life, is another method, although this can also be a precursor to suicide if the head simply can't remain in the comforting confines of the sand. "The Reasons Why" contemplates exactly this: how we can't stand to face certain things in our lives, how they get sluiced under the skin to fester, how others avoid mentioning things so we don't get upset, and how some traumatic events are never acknowledged at all.

"Freakshow"

Twisty with a rock 'n' roll punch, "Freakshow" is a delight even if it's obviously a conscious attempt to introduce the zany pop of "The Lovecats" or "Close to Me" into the album's mix. Songs are not required to have pure intentions free of all calculation to be good, and despite its derivative nature, "Freakshow" has

"The Only One" was a strong first single, but it mined the same territory the Cure had covered before more successfully. *Author's Collection*

a charm all its own. It feels looser and less self-conscious than anything else on the album and really comes alive in concert.

"Sirensong"

This sweet, swaying acoustic waltz is a definite highlight and a forgotten song that Smith would be wise to resurrect for the band's live sets. "Sirensong" is swooning midnight music, with glistening guitars and a jaunty keyboard riff that is classic Cure. The chorus gets a little cluttered, like an aural traffic jam, but that's a minor quibble. "Sirensong" is a lovely little ditty that's been hidden away and should be dusted off and brought out into the sunlight.

"The Real Snow White"

This gnarly rocker is another that just screams "what could have been." Jason Cooper's drum part is too busy, and Robert Smith occupies nearly every moment with his vocal, refusing to let the song breathe. As the emperor says in *Amadeus*, "Too many notes. Just cut a few, and it'll be perfect."

"The Hungry Ghost"

With a better sonic production, "The Hungry Ghost" might be a certifiable Cure classic. It's the strongest track on the album and is one of the few that sits comfortably alongside the Cure's best work. Even though it was never a single, "The Hungry Ghost" has remained a regular part of the Cure's live set, while the rest of the album is mostly ignored. Robert Smith has been effusive in his admiration for the song, but in concert, he wisely doesn't try to re-create the elevated vocal part he delivers on the album version. He'd likely hurt something if he did.

"The Hungry Ghost" revisits a concept that has recurred multiple times in Cure songs: the endless cycle of someone never getting enough of whatever it is they want, need, or are obsessed with. This cycle of greed is often generated as an attempt to fill a vast hole that somehow never stops being empty. In this case, it could be stuff, endless items that we don't really need or want, or wastes of money that do nothing but put you further in debt. Or it could be sexual addiction for someone who feels alone and unwanted. The two sides of the equation may not even be related, as one can try several methods to fill the same emptiness. Sometimes we have to deal with the reality that the emptiness is endless; it will never be filled but will rather remain a part of life forever.

"Switch"

The harder-edged tracks on *4:13 Dream* are generally a difficult listen, but "Switch" is a welcome exception. "Switch" bristles with electrifying haywire guitar work by Porl Thompson. Robert Smith puts real energy and force into his vocal without lapsing into that gruesome moan he splatters unbearably high in the mix all over *The Cure*. There's not much of a melodic hook, but "Switch" does possess an undeniable groove that's cleaner and punchier than just about anything else on the album.

"The Perfect Boy"

The fourth and final single from *4:13 Dream*, "The Perfect Boy" doesn't seem all that special at first, but it's a grower. Reading the lyrics bumps it up several notches, as it's a particularly crafty composition. The word "perfect" shows up frequently in Robert Smith song lyrics, but this time it's the focus of an exploration of how a word can mean something entirely different depending on one's perception. Perfection is an ideal that we seem to subconsciously seek as the benchmark, an impossible standard to meet.

It's not a new story, but Smith tells it with poignancy and grace. A woman falls deeply, madly, excitedly in love with a man whose attitude is more cavalier. It'll end in heartbreak, but, then, these things often do one way or another.

"This. Here and Now. With You"

Smith's weirdly compressed vocal is part of a problem that plagues the entire album, but on this track, it's particularly distracting and makes for a difficult listen. It's too bad since there is potential here for "This. Here and Now. With You," despite the cumbersome title, to have been more than just a novelty. As it is, hidden away in the last third of an album that's hard to get through anyway, it's one of those songs that seems destined to exist in obscurity, known only to die-hard Cure fans.

"Sleep When I'm Dead"

The third single issued prior to the release of *4:13 Dream*, "Sleep When I'm Dead" originated as an instrumental demo from the *Head on the Door* sessions. It was abandoned and forgotten until Smith discovered it two decades later while preparing bonus material for that classic album's deluxe reissue. It's easy to hear the musical similarities with the funkier tracks of that era, like "Screw," "The Baby Screams," "Stop Dead," and "A Man inside My Mouth."

Unfortunately, the final version is a murky mess that in hindsight should have remained abandoned and forgotten.

"The Scream"

With this one, it really depends on what you're going for. If you *want* a tense, nervous headache, then by all means find the "Repeat" button. Robert Smith's voice can be exquisitely beautiful, and sometimes when he's shouting above a rock epic or wailing over a dirge of deepest despondency, it can hold tremendous emotional power and nuance.

At other times, it's like an ice pick scraping along your skull from the inside, in circular patterns, over and over again. It's too bad that Smith goes down this road because the menacing first section of "The Scream" is great, with an atmosphere so threating that it practically sparks with dread. But as the wind builds and starts swirling faster, it erupts into a firestorm of unlistenable melodrama, over the top in all the worst ways.

"It's Over"

Finally. The Cure being who they are and possessing the talent they do, *4:13 Dream* is by no means a complete wash. A few songs are really quite strong, and most of the rest of the album is at least passable. But these last two songs—"The Scream" and "It's Over"—sound like castoffs from *The Cure* swept up from the cutting room floor and accidentally appended to their latest album.

"It's Over" was at one time called "Baby Rag Dog Book," or at least that's how it was referred to when performed during shows prior to the album's release. There's not much to say about it other than it's a noisy train wreck with a horrible vocal—unlistenable. When it finally ends, the feeling is of relief: whew, it's over.

B-Sides

"NY Trip"

A particularly Cure-ish phenomenon continues: the B-sides are better than the album tracks. In this case, it's true for three of the four. "NY Trip," the support song for "The Only One," is a dark and moody hard groover with the kick of a strong melodic hook in the chorus.

"All Kinds of Stuff"

Regret is once again the focus of a Cure song, but this time its angry, not wistful or nostalgic like on "Pictures of You." It's a bit of a mess, a riotous assault to the ears in the form of a hard-edged rocker that feels a bit chaotic. Like most of the songs from this period, it has an air of pointlessness, as if it's a song created just for the sake of having a song, which is a very un-Cure-like approach to doing music. This throwaway is the B-side to "Freakshow" and is the only one of the four whose addition would not improve *4:13 Dream*.

"Down Under"

Paired with the "Sleep When I'm Dead" single, "Down Under" is a surprising delight. It would have been a contender for strongest track on the album had it been included. The upbeat instrumentation is dense but seems to breathe more than the other tightly compressed songs of this era. The lyrics contain some of the loveliest imagery Robert Smith has devised since the start of the new millennium, and his breezy vocal is the most natural and nuanced of all the *4:13 Dream* material.

"Without You"

The relaxed acoustic rock of "Without You" most definitely should have been included on the album, which is mostly cramped and uptight. There's some nifty keyboard work here and a well-conceived arrangement. Robert Smith's dexterous vocal shows him in fine form and more at ease than most songs of this period. This is another hidden gem left to whither on the vine as a B-side, while far inferior songs nabbed album slots on *4:13 Dream*—wasted opportunities.

4:13 Dream is such an abuse to the ears because of its all-loud, tightly compressed sound that it's difficult to sit through one disc let alone a second, as was the plan. Yet the material here is mostly good to strong. The songs are better live, but it seems that Robert Smith and the band were sick of the material before it even had the chance to shine. It's been largely ignored in concert even when the band was ostensibly supporting it.

Out of fifty-six shows in 2008, only four songs from *4:13 Dream* were played twenty-five times or more—the three mentioned above plus "Sleep When I'm Dead." This problem was created by the incessant delays that plagued the album's genesis. The tour designed to promote *4:13 Dream* was almost complete by the time the album belatedly hit stores.

As for what was to be *4:14 Scream*, it's doubtful it will appear anytime soon, at least as an independent album under that name. Robert Smith seems to have lost interest in it as the years have passed, and the unreleased material grows ever more stale. He's also noted that the band that created that album no longer exists given the lineup changes. The new studio album that Smith had promised for 2019 initially, and is now presumably due for 2021, will contain all new and unrelated material.

Eventually, all of this will surely come out as an archival release, which, if done correctly, could have the potential to redefine and salvage this era in the Cure's recorded history. Even Robert Smith knows that *4:13 Dream* is a shambles, and he's made it very clear he wishes the bountiful material from the era had been handled differently. He still has the chance to execute some revisionist history and present all of the material in a manner more to his liking, but given the tepid response to the original album and with the passing of time, will anyone care? The short answer is yes. Their legions of fans who adore them will care very much, and that's all that matters to the Cure.

I Guess I'll Know When I Get There: The Cure in Concert, Part 3 (2000–2019)

The Cure has released only three studio albums in the 2000s, but that hasn't stopped them from taking the stage nearly every year.

Concert and Tours

Dream Tour (2000)

After warming up with ten shows that hit small venues in major markets in both Europe and the United States, the Cure kicked off the Dream Tour in support of their new album *Bloodflowers* on March 27 in Madrid with a lineup of Smith, Gallup, Cooper, Bamonte, and O'Donnell. The band walked onstage accompanied by Samuel Barber's "Adagio for Strings" and then opened with the instant classic "Out of This World," a sublime rumination on mortality that set a melancholy tone each night.

    The tour was a massive success, as the Cure performed for more than 1 million fans over a span of nine months. The band played most of the new album each night, with the live versions frequently blowing the doors off the studio recordings. The searing intensity of "Where the Birds Always Sing" sprayed from the concert stage like a molten blast of fire, and the gentle beauty of "There Is

No If…" held the audience in a spell of rapt silence. "The Loudest Sound" keeps a wounded distance on the album, but in concert, the band was able to draw from the shadows the aching poignancy and silent grief of a dying relationship that could be saved but is still inexorably slipping away.

Hard-core fans were delighted as the band dropped some of the pop hits in favor of darker album cuts, like "The Snakepit," "Jupiter Crash," and "Like Cockatoos," which fit better with the somber *Bloodflowers* material. The tour was well received and is still widely considered one of the Cure's finest. Fans gushed over the fiery darkness unleashed as the Dream Tour wound through Europe and North America. For the tour's final stand, the Cure staged seven spectacular shows for their fiercely loyal Australian fans, pulling out all the stops with marathon sets that delivered one gem after another. They wrapped up in style, headlining Livid 2000 on October 21 in Brisbane. The Cure topped a bill that also included Green Day, Lou Reed, and No Doubt.

Euro Festivals Summer of '04 Tour/Curiosa (2004)

The Cure spent early 2004 holed up with producer Ross Robinson bashing out their hard-rocking self-titled studio album, which they released at the end of June. They did take time on March 3 for "Passport: Back to the Bars," a benefit show in support of War Child and Shelter held at the London Barfly. The Cure went all out for this event, putting together their most fascinating and unexpected set list in ages.

They didn't bother with anything from the new album, and several rarities saw the light of day, including "Hey You!" The biggest surprise was the appearance by Frank Bell, the Crawley postman who sang lead on the novelty single "I'm a Cult Hero"/"I Dig You" and who took the stage during the encore to take another stab at the songs thirty-five years later. It was an incredible moment of Cure nostalgia and history.

In May 2004, the Cure headlined two high-profile U.S. events aimed at appealing to a younger audience and bringing new fans into the fold: the Coachella Valley Music and Arts Festival in the California desert and the HFStival at RFK Stadium in Washington, D.C. Next they were back in Europe to headline 14 major outdoor festivals from June 19 in Imola, Italy, to July 17 at the Vilar de Mouros in Portugal.

Only a week later in West Palm Beach, Florida, the Cure embarked on the highly publicized Curiosa Festival tour through the United States and Mexico. In an attempt to draw in new and younger fans, the Cure brought several support bands each night on two stages. All of the guests were influenced by the Cure in a major way, including some of the hottest bands of the moment, like Interpol, the Rapture, and Mogwai.

The Cure perform on stage at the "Ministry of Rock" Open Air Festival in Frauenfeld, Switzerland, July 2002. *Mario Gaccioli/EPA/Shutterstock*

The Cure continued without the support artists beginning with a spectacular five-encore show at the Everett Events Center in Everett, Washington, after which they headed to Mexico for four amazing performances with some of the longest sets they'd ever played, wrapping up on September 6 in Mexico City. They closed out a busy 2004 with a string of special radio and television performances in Europe running from September 17 through November 19.

As is usual for a non–album year, 2005 saw the Cure hitting the festival circuit. More lineup changes shifted the band, as Perry Bamonte was out but replaced on guitar by a familiar face, Porl Thompson, and Roger O'Donnell was once again ousted from the band. The newly refurbished four-piece Cure played their first show at the massive July 2 benefit concert Live 8 in Versailles, during which they performed five songs: "Open," "One Hundred Years," "End," "Just Like Heaven," and "Boys Don't Cry." The new lineup did not include a keyboardist, although Porl Thompson could jump from guitar to keyboard as needed, but the harder-edged songs were emphasized.

The first festival show was on August 5 for the Festival Internacional de Benicassim in Spain. The set lists was an unusual mashup of eras, focusing on edgier material, including surprises like "Signal to Noise," "The Baby Screams," and "At Night." More festivals followed, including one of only four shows the Cure has ever done in Hungary. They wrapped up 2005 with an astonishing five-encore marathon on September 3 at the Rock'n Coke Festival in Istanbul, their first and only performance in Turkey.

The Cure pose for photographers before a press conference during the Motorokrfest in Mexico City, 2007. *Mario Guzman/EPA/Shutterstock*

4tour (2007–2008)

The Cure performed only once in 2006, but they made it count. On January 4 at the Royal Albert Hall in London, the Cure performed for the Teenage Cancer Trust, delighting fans for a mesmerizing three hours that included several rarely played nuggets.

The Cure launched their next major excursion—the 4tour World Tour 2007–2008—on July 27 in Naeba, Japan, where they dusted off "Kyoto Song" for the first time in nearly twenty years. The lineup remained the same stripped-down, keyboardless four-piece—Robert Smith, Simon Gallup, Jason Cooper, and Porl Thompson—that had been in place since 2005, with the sets veering toward harder rock material. They next went to Hong Kong for the first and only time, playing on July 30 at the AsiaWorld-Expo, then two nights later, the Cure performed at Singapore Indoor Stadium. These historic dates were followed by shows in Australia and New Zealand, after which they dashed off for a long string of dates in North America scheduled to begin on September 13 in Tampa, Florida.

Much to the fans' consternation, the Cure canceled all but one of those U.S. dates, which were slated to last until October 17. The apologetic statement announcing the cancellations cited a tight schedule that allowed only a few weeks to finally finish what was then still being called a double album before the tour resumed (and, of course, when their next album finally emerged more than a year later, it was a single disc). The band also cited a desire to incorporate material from the new album into the sets.

That incorporation never materialized. When the tour resumed on October 20 in Mexico City, the only new song played was "The Only One." Otherwise, "Freakshow" was the only other track from the upcoming album to appear live in 2007. The entire European leg of the tour passed without another new song being added. It wasn't until May 9, 2008, the Cure's first U.S. show of the year, that a third track from *4:13 Dream* crept into the set as they debuted "The Perfect Boy" at the Patriot Center in Fairfax, Virginia. Another new track, "A Boy I Never Knew," became a regular part of the set, but it didn't make the album's final cut and has yet to be released.

They didn't try to make up for lost time the following year, as they only played three shows in 2009. One notable show was at the O2 Arena in London on February 26 for the Shockwaves *NME* Awards Big Gig. A night earlier at the O2 Academy Brixton, Robert Smith accepted the Godlike Genius Award from *NME* and performed a set of ten songs for the awards show. The Cure stayed off the stage entirely in 2010, but 2011 held something so special that it was worth the very long wait.

Reflections (2011)

"Light, Music, and Ideas" was the stated goal of the third annual Vivid Festival, slated to take over the iconic Sydney Opera House from May 27 through June 12, 2011. Stephen Pavlovic, head of the Modular record label, was to curate the ten-day Vivid Live portion of the festival, featuring live performances from a variety of artists. When Pavlovic first signed on, he could not have imagined the music history that would be made during his portion of the festival.

Rumors started swirling in April that the Cure was planning something big, possibly in Sydney and possibly very soon. The truth was probably more than even the most optimistic fans could have expected. On May 6, the *Sydney Morning Herald* broke the news that the Cure would perform two nights—May 31 and June 1—as part of the third Vivid Live Festival at the Sydney Opera House. Each night, the Cure would perform their first three albums—*Three Imaginary Boys*, *Seventeen Seconds*, and *Faith*—all the way through in sequence.

In addition, they'd be joined by Roger O'Donnell after a six-year absence, and, yeah, Lol Tolhurst would be back for his first show with the Cure in more than twenty-three years, dating to the last night of the Kissing Tour on December 9, 1987, at Wembley Arena in London. The last time Tolhurst played to a Cure audience from behind a drum kit was even farther back in the hazy recesses of the band's long history: June 11, 1982, in Brussels at the Ancienne Belgique, the final show of the *Pornography* tour.

Tolhurst was returning after years of drunken debauchery ruined his standing with the band, resulting in his ouster just as the Cure's greatest studio achievement, *Disintegration*, was finished. Tolhurst was being welcomed back onstage after having engaged the band in a bitter lawsuit that ate up massive amounts of time and money for the band and caused Robert Smith an immeasurable amount of anxiety—until Tolhurst soundly lost.

This was the reconciliation, the healing of the rift, that many fans had always hoped might occur. It's difficult to imagine that even at the darkest moments, deep down, Robert Smith and Laurence Tolhurst, two boyhood friends who'd traveled together on a most remarkable journey, didn't also secretly hope it would happen.

Once the news broke, the anticipation among fans was breathless. Smith took to thecure.com and, in his usual all caps, stated, "As of now ... *'Reflections'* is a special—a one time only (two times only?!!) event—filmed both nights with a view to creating a DVD.... As things stand we have no plans to play this show anywhere else." "As things stand" is a monumental qualification, and fans around the world hoped the Cure would plan additional nights in different cities. But news of that would have to wait.

Tickets were snapped up almost the instant they went on sale just two weeks before what was undoubtedly the most anticipated show in the Cure's history. Finally, the show arrived on May 31. The stage was stark black with just enough white light to see Robert Smith, Simon Gallup, and Jason Cooper walk calmly onto the stage. Robert and Simon picked up their instruments nearly simultaneously, straps over their shoulders, like they have done so many countless times before. In typically understated fashion, Robert Smith walked up to the microphone and greeted the crowd with a quick "Hello!"

The tapping drums of "10:15 Saturday Night" sent the crowd into a frenzy, and then they were off. The trio zipped through *Three Imaginary Boys* with alacrity and energy. The jagged post-punk of "Grinding Halt," the snarling nastiness of "Object," and the dark beauty of the title song all came to life.

Many of these songs hadn't been performed in years. The Cure hadn't played "Subway Song" since 1996, "It's Not You" since 1993, and the Hendrix cover "Foxy Lady" since 1992. The ambling jazz-pop gem "Accuracy" was last played in 1989, the year of *Disintegration*. Three of the songs—"Object" (which Robert Smith has always hated), the pensive "Another Day," and the slightly twisted oddity "Meathook"—were played for the first time since 1980, the year following their release. "So What" was played by the Cure in concert for the first time ever.

Even with all those early gigs and all the shows in the intervening decades, one song had never been played before until this night. Some thirty-two years since it was recorded in the dead of night with Robert Smith drunkenly making up lyrics on the spot by reading the back of a bag of sugar, "So What" was played by the Cure in concert for the first time ever. After the first album fades away,

The Cure perform live on stage at Mediolanum Forum, Milan, Italy, 2016.
Rodolfo Sassano/Alamy Live News

Robert Smith told the crowd cheerfully, "In the olden days that was it! But... see you in a few minutes!" And he was true to his word.

Keyboardist Roger O'Donnell joined them in place of Matthieu Hartley, as the Cure ripped through a tight-as-nails performance of their second album: *Seventeen Seconds*. The sound in the venue was immaculate, and Robert Smith's voice filled the room, intense and nuanced, as good as he's ever sounded. The audience sang along gleefully to the keyboard line on "Play for Today." Robert Smith delivered a full-throated vocal on "Secrets," a song normally reserved for whispers. The experimental "Three" was performed by the band for the first time in thirty-one years.

The massively powerful four-song stretch to close the album—"A Forest," "M," "At Night," and "Seventeen Seconds"—had the crowd stoked for the last part of the trilogy and a moment of Cure history nobody would forget.

In his 2016 memoir *Cured: The Tale of Two Imaginary Boys*, Laurence Tolhurst describes the moment he walked out on that stage in Sydney as "overflowing with pure joy." It had been a long road back, but there he was. He took position behind his percussion set, no sign of nerves, and waited for the sonorous tones of Simon Gallup's bass that open "The Holy Hour," the first track on *Faith*.

The Cure played the album straight through, driving hard with urgency on "Primary" and channeling ethereal beauty on "All Cats Are Grey" and post-punk angst on "Doubt," a song they had never before played live. The gothic majesty of "The Drowning Man" and the searing intensity of the title song back-to-back were breathtaking. It was a magnificent retelling of the album. Tolhurst doesn't just bang on the percussion, either; he's able to reprise his role as sometime keyboardist, playing those ghostly final notes on "All Cats Are Grey."

Then came the encore, which *Spin* aptly described as "an amazing fan fever-dream." The Cure roared through the era's non–album singles, including standards like "Boys Don't Cry," "Jumping Someone Else's Train," and their debut: "Killing an Arab." To the delight of die-hard fans, they also tackled the B-sides, delivering a red-hot take of the deliciously nasty "I'm Cold," the aural nightmare "Splintered in Her Head," and two songs that were played live by the band for the first time ever: the early cast-out "World War" and the mesmerizing bass-heavy B-side to "Primary": "Descent." They even rampaged through the rollicking instrumental "Another Journey by Train."

The Cure wasn't ready to call it a night just yet. Hours into the show, it was time for drummers Jason Cooper and Lol Tolhurst to wrench back into their reserves for the energy to play together on "The Hanging Garden," sounding epic and thunderous. Robert then cheekily that "something weird" happened after "The Hanging Garden," after coming back for the third time: "It was this," and the bouncy, playful idiocy of "Let's Go To Bed" must surely have been weird to fans who'd just made it out of the *Pornography* phase. They finally wrapped up with the cheesy yet fitting finale of "The Lovecats." After nearly four hours and forty-four songs, the Cure was finally done for the night. But they'd be back the following night and do it all again.

Although the two Sydney shows were originally intended to be a one-time occurrence, it was just too good to leave it at that, and more shows were added. Reflections was performed on November 15, 2011, at the Royal Albert Hall in London, then for three nights (November 21 to 23) at the Pantages Theatre in Hollywood before one final stand (November 25 to 27) at the Beacon Theatre in New York. That last show stretched to an amazing forty-eight songs and 150 minutes.

Then it was over, a concert series unlike any the Cure had ever performed, and in the process, they tied ends that had been loose for far too long.

Summer Cure Tour (2012)

The Cure returned to the road in 2012 for a run of summer festival dates throughout Europe, starting on May 26 at Pinkpop in the Netherlands. In the months since the Reflections shows, guitarist Reeves Gabrels, best known for his work with David Bowie as part of Tin Machine and on his 1997 album *Earthling*, was now the band's guitarist. The set was a fairly standard run-through of their hits and key album tracks with a few surprises. They'd play

The Cure headlining British Summer Time celebrating their 40th anniversary, featuring Robert Smith, Simon Gallup, Roger O'Donnell, Hyde Park, London, July, 2018.
Jason Richardson / Alamy Stock Photo

nineteen shows, including their first and only concert in Russia, before ending on September 1 in Stradbally Hall, Ireland.

LatAm2013 Tour/Great Circle Tour (2013)

Still no hint of new studio material, but that didn't stop the Cure from hitting the road in 2013. They opened their LatAm2013 Tour on April 4 in Rio, playing eight massive shows in Latin America, wrapping up on April 21 in Mexico City. Then it was on to the Far East and the Great Circle Tour, starting on July 26 in Ansan, South Korea, and then traveling to Japan, Honolulu, and the North American mainland, where they played seven more shows. They wrapped up 2013 with an infamous show at the Voodoo Music + Arts Experience in New Orleans, where they delivered one of their best sets ever, highlighted by the live debut of their epic 1994 classic "Burn" from the soundtrack to *The Crow*.

The band played only nine shows in 2014, but they ended it with a forty-one-song marathon lasting more than three hours on December 23 at the Hammersmith Apollo in London. The last of a three-night stand at the venue, the Cure pulled out all the stops with a set loaded with surprises like "Wailing Wall," "A Man inside My Mouth," and "Piggy in the Mirror" before closing with the first performance of the frenzied little gem "Hey You!" in more than a decade.

The Cure Tour 2016 (2016)

After a year away from the stage, the Cure returned for a massive new tour in 2016. Their seventy-six-show calendar was their most ambitious in two decades. Even with no new music to promote, the Cure filled arenas and amphitheaters wherever they went.

They opened on May 10 at the Lakefront Arena in New Orleans, winding their way through the United States and Canada before wrapping up on July 17 in Honolulu. Four nights later, they were in New Zealand for a six-show trek down under, after which they took a couple months off and landed in the United Kingdom to start the European leg of the tour on September 10 at Bestival on the Isle of Wight. They crisscrossed Europe, including dates in eastern European countries that they'd rarely had the chance to visit, before finally ending the trek with three triumphant nights at the SSE Arena Wembley in London. The Cure Tour 2016 was widely considered by fans as the Cure's best tour in many years, and they sounded energized and gave no indications of slowing down anytime soon.

The Cure in 2018

Robert Smith was asked to curate the twenty-fifth edition of the prestigious Meltdown Festival. He ended up with an impressive roster of artists who were only too happy to play a show at his personal request. They performed an acclaimed show the final night consisting of a run through their entire catalog, one song from each album, all the way up and all the way back. The Cure's second and final show of 2018 was a certifiable career capper. Before a spectacular audience of at least 60,000 on one of the hottest London nights of the summer, the Cure tore through a two-hour-plus set highlighting every stage of the band's career. Given the high-profile and historic importance of the show, the set list was selected carefully by Robert Smith to be truly representative of the band's forty-year career. Tim Pope turned this performance into a feature film that was shown in theaters all over the globe in July 2019. A deluxe DVD/CD box set documenting both shows was released in October 2019.

The Cure in 2019

With their induction into the Rock and Roll Hall of Fame already under their belt and a new studio album on the agenda, 2019 was to be one of the biggest years in Cure history. They scheduled an exhilarating lineup of live performances, and more are on the way.

The Cure's 2019 touring slate opened with two historic performances as part of the Rock and the Lawns Festival: March 16 on the Festival Lawns at Carnival

City in Johannesburg and March 18 at Kenilworth Racecourse in Cape Town. The shows marked the first time the Cure had ever performed in Africa, and the media coverage was enormous. The announcement was met with a frenzy of anticipation by fans, and the press in South Africa heralded the news as a huge get for the country, going to great lengths to emphasize the Cure's global popularity and status.

The shows were a spectacular success and generated ecstatic reviews. On the South African music news site Texx and the City, writer Graeme Raubenheimer captured the overall mood of the media coverage with an unusually heartfelt piece praising every aspect of the performance. He called Smith's presence "quirky and warm" and wrote, "For a 59-year-old man, Robert Smith's voice is a powerhouse. Not a single crack. Nothing." He called Simon "beast-like" on the bass and noted that the rhythm section was "exceptionally tight."

That was followed by another extraordinary event in Sydney, Australia. Following the Reflections shows held there in 2011, the Cure again headlined the Vivid Live Festival at the Sydney Opera House for five nights starting on May 24 to celebrate the thirtieth anniversary of their finest work: *Disintegration*. They performed the epic album all the way through in its entirety plus period B-sides for the first time ever ("Fear of Ghosts," "Out of Mind," and "Babble" were all extraordinary), and, astonishingly enough, demos released on the deluxe *Disintegration* reissue—"Esten" and "Noheart"—made their unexpected debuts as part of the Cure's concert lexicon.

Following those historic shows, the band has embarked on what can only be considered a victory lap, headlining major festivals in Europe. The extensive trek started on June 8 in Dublin at Malahide Castle & Gardens. They stuck with a set similar to the Hyde Park show but shook it up with a few new arrivals, including their stellar B-side "Just One Kiss," which they performed for the first time in seven years and which would become a staple the rest of the tour. "Last Dance" survived from the *Disintegration* anniversary shows, and they also added "39," "One Hundred Years," and "Doing the Unstuck." By far, the most unexpected was the rarely performed "Wendy Time," which the band hadn't played onstage since 1992.

A definite highlight was their triumphant appearance at Glastonbury, which was greeted by rapturous press reviews. The Cure played three countries for the first time ever: Romania, Serbia, and Croatia. They also returned to Russia for the second time, headlining at Kolomenskoe Park in Moscow on August 3, 2019. The Cure almost had to cancel a date when Simon Gallup was unable to travel to Japan for the Fuji Rock Festival because of "serious personal issues," leaving the band in a major lurch. Simon's son Eden, his bass tech while on tour and a talented musician in his own right, saved the day by stepping in on his dad's behalf without missing a beat. He was familiar with the material, and all the band members know him well (he is Robert Smith's godson.) The Cure wrapped up at the Rock en Seine in Paris on August 23 before heading west to California to headline the August 31, 2019, Pasadena Daydream Festival. The set list was the standard one played through most of Europe, with "Just One Kiss" being played for the first time ever on America soil.

After a brief break, the Cure returned to North America for three high-profile shows in October to wrap up their year. Bookended by dates at *Austin City Limits* on October 5 and October 12, the Cure headed down to Mexico City on October 8 for one of their trademark marathon shows at Foro Sol. This time the Cure played for nearly three hours, covering thirty-six songs. Simon Gallup was again unable to make the October 12 show in Austin, prompting another rescue appearance by son Eden.

35

They Shine for You, They Burn for All to See: The Cure's Legacy

The Cure's elite status in music history is cemented by their induction into the Rock and Roll Hall of Fame.

May 30, 2019. It had already been a glorious year for the Cure when they took the stage at the Sydney Opera House for their fifth and final performance at the Vivid Live! Festival to celebrate the thirtieth anniversary of their landmark album *Disintegration*, and it would only get better.

Two months prior, the Cure took the stage at the Barclays Center in Brooklyn to be inducted into the Rock and Roll Hall of Fame, an enormously prestigious honor that elevates them into the same rarified air as the Beatles, the Rolling Stones, and Elvis Presley. They delivered two historic performances in South Africa, their first time on that continent, and over the summer, they headlined a long string of summer festivals in Europe, dazzling fans in a victory lap from one city to the next with a career-defining set list loaded with classics.

They played three special U.S. shows and a monster show in Mexico City. It was a capstone year for the Cure, an extravagant series of successes that have raised the band's profile to new international highs. The Cure have never been more popular and vital than they are right now, and Robert Smith promises they aren't close to being finished.

"The thing about The Cure is that we exist in isolation. We're not in competition with anyone. One day I *suppose* we'll stop. But we'll never be replaced," Robert Smith told *The Quietus* in 1989, and, of course, he was correct. The truth of this statement, made barely a decade into the Cure's journey, grows move obvious with every passing year. Improbably, even with no new material to promote, 2019 became the biggest year in the Cure's colorful history. This singularity is key to the Cure's success and longevity. From the beginning, Robert Smith has done his best to ensure that the Cure operates with complete creative freedom, and that's what they have done. They reside firmly outside the mainstream of popular music, ignoring the music industry lines that restrict most artists.

The Cure have released dozens of singles stretching back decades, and yet they've hit the top forty on the U.S. pop chart only three times, the most recent nearly three decades: "Just Like Heaven," "Lovesong," and "Friday I'm in Love." That's it. Yet they are guaranteed to sell out large venues in most markets, and they still hit the top twenty with every new studio album. Their appeal stretches far beyond the confines of the top forty.

The Cure has been better able than most artists to withstand the inevitable peel-away of casual fans that comes with career longevity in the music industry. They've been able to cultivate a large and loyal global base of fan support over the years. These diehards will stick with the Cure no matter what until the very end. They have earned that kind of trust, and the band recognizes and returns it.

Despite this, it is undeniably true that the Cure no longer sells the number of records they once did. Obviously, the music industry has taken an enormous hit in terms of total sales figures over the past two decades, which is a big part of the decline. But even setting sales figures aside, the last several Cure studio albums have just not been able to notch anything close to the same cultural significance as their landmark predecessors. New studio albums sell robustly but are not greeted with the same enthusiasm, nor do they make the same cultural impact as the classics of their golden era.

Of course, this calculus may change with their first album in a decade, hopefully due in 2021, especially given all the attention they've received recently. No matter what happens with the new album, the Cure has nothing left to prove to anyone but themselves.

It's easy to understand why the Cure is suddenly being appreciated on new levels by the rock 'n' roll tastemakers that shunned them in the past. When the Hall of Fame news was released, journalists in papers large and small and in blogs waxed ecstatic and nostalgic about the Cure, their music, and what it meant to them and their peers. It was a victory, finally, for the outcast, the misunderstood, who have always connected so strongly to the Cure's music.

Because of their tight connection with the music and ardent dedication, Cure fans are sometimes caricatured in much the same way as the band. The Cure does not aim for a particular type of audience, and they are quick to note that there are Cure fans of every conceivable type. Yet the typecast emotional adolescent dressed in black while alone in the bedroom writing poetry still seems to be the image that many people will envision when asked to identify a Cure fan. That stereotype has stuck, as have others surrounding the band.

They Shine for You, They Burn for All to See: The Cure's Legacy

2019 Rock & Roll Hall of Fame Induction Ceremony: Robert Smith (C) and members of the Cure, March 29, 2019, Barclays Center, New York City.
Photo by Kevin Mazur/Getty Images For The Rock and Roll Hall of Fame

Not that any of this particularly troubles the fans or the band itself. They've been misperceived since day one, but that's partly attributable to their own desire to retain a sense of mystique, operating under a haze of mystery from behind a question mark.

The Cure has never been a darling of the critics. Although many of their albums are recognized now as classics, music writers have never been overly warm to them, and their disdain is largely a symptom of their own myopic tendencies. Part of this can be traced to Robert Smith's strangely ghoulish image, the wildly unkempt hair, the phantom-pale face, the smudged lipstick. It was hard for some of the old school to take him seriously, and some still don't.

Joe Gore of *Guitar Player* magazine stated it perfectly in a 1992 article: "To their gargantuan worldwide following, The Cure combine sublime pop and heartfelt expressivity; to a large segment of the music press, they're self-obsessed gloom merchants, purveyors of pessimism to suburban America's petulant teens. But many of the band's detractors have probably let Smith's personal flamboyance divert their attention from the band's phenomenal pop craftsmanship and stylistic range."

Their astonishing diversity is perhaps unparalleled by any other group with their stature in the rock era. *Kiss Me* alone is overflowing with a kaleidoscope of musical ideas. There is no sonic element known or unknown to human ears that could not somehow fit onto the Cure's canvas. They have produced a body of work so vast and diverse that, when amplified by the limitless variables flitting through our capricious minds, the result is an infinite musical explosion that will continue to expand in time with the universe.

The Cure's music resonates so strongly that they are often featured by event promotors and deejays for club nights, such as being paired with other bands perceived as similar. "The Smiths versus the Cure" is still a popular theme event, as are nights featuring the Cure and bands such as Sister of Mercy, Joy Division/New Order, Echo and the Bunnymen, and Siouxsie and the Banshees. The Cure is always a staple at 1980s nights and in darkwave- or goth-themed clubs and events. There are several different Cure cover bands with sizable followings. You can sing one of any number of Cure songs at your local karaoke bar. They have songs on popular gaming systems, like Rock Band and Guitar Hero. The Cure has permeated every aspect of entertainment culture.

In an interview about his curation of the 2018 Meltdown Festival with the Cure's fortieth-anniversary concert looming ahead, Robert Smith insisted that he views the Cure as being just as vital and relevant as the younger artists he's selected to perform. Although "10:15 Saturday Night" might be forty years old, it's every bit as immediate as a new song played by Editors or any of the other current bands performing at the festival.

"This band has got a couple hundred years of onstage experience between us now, I mean, we're all getting on," Smith said at the time, "but one of the weird things about music, when you play music particularly, even when you listen to it, it kind of acts like a time machine, and I start singing a song I wrote thirty-odd years ago, and I'm there!"

Smith is bemused at the level of esteem and admiration that has been lavished in his direction recently, especially after being sneered at for so long by the traditional types lapping at the boots of Bruce Springsteen and Bob Dylan. He says, "It's kind of odd that I'm being portrayed as this curator, legend kind of person that I'm not at all, it doesn't feel right. I live a kind of normal life." Smith seemed genuinely bewildered when he said it, and it's clear that he truly does not comprehend how the Cure reached this level of fame.

The numbers speak for themselves—the millions of albums sold, the longevity, the chart positions, the countless fans to whom they've played all over the world. Undoubtedly impressive, yet the Cure has never been about a set of statistics. The Cure has always been about the music. That is what is important to fans, and that is what will last when all of us are long gone. There is a reason it touches people so deeply and holds them through decades of fandom. The music is the Cure's legacy.

Now that legacy will be forever part of the shrine built to recognize that rock 'n' roll music has intrinsic value and must not be forgotten. The Rock and Roll Hall of Fame is an extravagant time capsule that archives for future generations the most vital artists to partake in that long, strange trip crossing many roads and rivers, multihued and shaped by infinite sonic possibilities.

The Beatles are there, with the Rolling Stones, Jimi Hendrix, Bob Dylan, Aretha Franklin, David Bowie, Michael Jackson, Prince, Madonna, Elton John, Metallica, James Brown, Bruce Springsteen, the Sex Pistols, Janis Joplin, Marvin Gaye, Nirvana, Neil Young, Patti Smith, the Clash, Black Sabbath, Talking Heads, and Joni Mitchell. And now the Cure.

When the Cure was nominated the first time, in 2012, Robert Smith went online to castigate the Hall of Fame for excluding drummer Jason Cooper. This time around, the lineup was initially Robert Smith, Simon Gallup, Porl Thompson, Boris Williams, Roger O'Donnell, Perry Bamonte, Michael Dempsey, Lol Tolhurst, and Jason Cooper. Weeks later, on February 7, 2019, current Cure guitarist Reeves Gabrels was added to the list because Robert Smith told the Hall that the Cure would not be appearing at the Brooklyn ceremony unless Reeves were included.

Missing were Andy Anderson, Matthieu Hartley, and Phil Thornalley. Robert Smith lobbied to have all thirteen inducted, especially Andy Anderson, who was battling terminal cancer and very much wanted to be part of the Hall with his bandmates. The Hall wouldn't budge, and Robert finally gave his okay, later expressing disappointment that Anderson wasn't included because it would have meant a lot to the drummer. Even with only ten inductees, the Cure now ranks third all-time for number of musicians included behind only the Grateful Dead (twelve) and Parliament/Funkadelic (sixteen).

The recognition is well deserved. While several American bands of the post-punk/New Wave era are already in (Blondie, Talking Heads, the Pretenders, and the Cars), the Cure's induction will be only the second for a British band of the period, following the Police, and of course two greats of the slightly earlier punk era, the Sex Pistols and the Clash. Cure fans are surely delighted that they get the nod ahead of other deserving British bands like the Smiths, Joy Division/New Order, Depeche Mode, and Eurythmics. All of these artists will likely be inducted sooner rather than later, but nobody deserves the honor more than the Cure.

Other artists inducted in 2019 were pop/rhythm-and-blues superstar Janet Jackson, British hard rock titans Def Leppard, that enchanting purveyor of dark magic Stevie Nicks for her solo career (she's already in as a member of Fleetwood Mac), art-rock pioneers Roxy Music, 1960s psychedelic rockers the Zombies, and trailblazing modern-rock visionaries Radiohead.

Although there was some speculation that the Cure might perform with a combination of current and former members, that was squashed rather quickly. The day of the announcement, Roger O'Donnell told SiriusXM's *Feedback*, "I think we're all decided that this is the best lineup that the Cure's ever been. So I think that would be extremely likely that we would involve any ex-members. Bands evolve, don't they?"

After a frenzy of anticipation, March 29, 2019, the date of the ceremony, was suitably surreal for the Cure's official entry into the rock 'n' roll stratosphere. During the obligatory preshow red-carpet appearance, the Cure shambled through the ever-present gaggle of media inanity with endearing awkwardness.

Robert Smith, looking slightly harried and with an "Oh fuck, I knew this was coming" expression on his face, was ushered right into the gaping maw of the sunshiney effervescence. Robert even managed to generate a minor media kerfuffle that was still generating news articles more than a week after the ceremony itself by gently swatting an overenthusiastic television interviewer with a sardonic one-liner.

Television personality Carrie Keagan chirped ecstatically, "Hi! Congratulations, the Cure! Rock and Roll Hall of Fame inductees, 2019!! Are you as excited as I am??"

Robert Smith deadpans, "From the sounds of it, no." Twitter goes berserk with delight.

Although the Hall of Fame has been vociferously criticized for multiple legitimate reasons, it is still widely regarded as a career-capping honor. It's taken seriously in the United States and generates significant attention and discussion. The Cure's induction was covered heavily in the U.S. media, bringing added visibility to the band at a critical time in their history. New Cure fans are born every day, and old fans who may have fallen off the wagon are climbing back on. Robert Smith, sometimes treated as a joke in the American music press, is now routinely described as a "living legend" or by a similar phrase. Multiple pieces have appeared in major publications from writers waxing nostalgic over the Cure's profound importance and influence in their lives and in the lives of fans all over the world.

The Cure's induction and performance generated significant buzz and approval. Their fans were beside themselves with delight, affecting none of the blasé indifference that many Radiohead fans, for example, exhibited. The Cure has always been viewed as the musical territory of weirdos and misfits, and these outcasts were now bursting with pride as their band crashed the party of the rock 'n' roll elite and were finally getting their due. It was almost overwhelming to imagine the hearts of Cure fans thumping in tandem with the thunderous rhythm as Jason Cooper did his best Andy Anderson as they opened their Hall of Fame set, unleashing all of their pent-up frustrating on behalf of themselves and their fans with an absolutely incendiary and totally uncompromising performance of "Shake Dog Shake."

After weeks of heavy promotion, cable giant HBO exclusively broadcast the highlights of the Hall of Fame induction ceremony during a three-hour special on April 27 in prime time, and they also streamed the show. HBO spent millions advertising the event, ensuring that the Cure and their fellow inductees would be seen by a massive global audience.

In the wake of their acceptance, the Cure's visibility has never been higher. Suddenly, band members are getting prime interview slots on satellite radio, and think pieces are showing up all over the Web as longtime fans who are now writers relish the opportunity to wax ecstatic about the heroes of their adolescence.

Robert Smith told *NME* on March 16, 2012, "I can't see our career arc any more. I've got absolutely no idea. We haven't signed to anyone since the last album came out and the contract was up. I'm not even signed as a writer. To be really honest, if we're gonna do something it has to be really good." Roger O'Donnell summed up the Cure very well when he said on SiriusXM, "Whenever anyone said, 'You've got to do this with your career,' we would always do the exact opposite." And the results speak for themselves.

The Very Last Thing Before I Go

Rock legend Robert Plant has called the Cure the last great English rock band. They are iconic, immediately recognizable by music fans the world over, even by those who have never delved into their music. The list of artists influenced by the Cure is unending, uncountable. It's possible to hear their fingerprints on a vast swath of modern rock and pop, it's obvious, and it's everywhere. Without the Cure, rock 'n' roll would not be the same. They have changed it immutably.

What if the Cure had never formed? What if that demo tape and its Saturday night drip, drip, dripping never made it to Chris Parry's desk? There would be a massive pop-culture void resulting in music and other creative mediums that are altogether more gray and less theatrical, resonant, and emotional than we hear currently, although we wouldn't know it. Endless positive things have been generated by the Cure and their music—among them a strong sense of community. Friends have been made, marriages celebrated, and children born, all because of a shared love for the Cure's music that threads through people of all backgrounds and fused connections that otherwise never would have happened.

The question remains—does it even matter if the Cure is still around? Shouldn't they just hang it up? After all, most fans didn't pay much attention to the last couple albums. They've played pretty much everywhere and played just about every song. Their recorded legacy is so strong that they have very few peers among rock bands to have emerged since the punk revolution. It's all been done before, so why spend endless hours writing, rehearsing, playing, traveling, promoting, and doing it all over again?

A few reasons. They are still having fun, and, as Robert Smith said in an interview following the announcement of a new album for 2019, they are still doing it for the right reasons. He described the rush of getting onstage each night as intense. And, most important, people still give a shit. If you really think that after forty years the Cure is just a nostalgia act and that they don't really matter anymore, all you have to do is read what South African music writer Graeme Raubenheimer wrote about the band's recent history-making performances in Johannesburg and Cape Town: "The Cure did not disappoint ... When they finished with 'Boys Don't Cry,' Smith stood to the side of the stage and waved to the fans ... As The Cure left the stage after a very long and satisfying encore, a ringing stayed with us. We left Kenilworth Race Course on a high. But as we headed home, the hangover started kicking in. The suburbs shrouded in darkness. The load shedding. And the realization that we may never see this band in South Africa ever again. It hit us hard. We can really only hope to see such rock brilliance again. Because that was just like a dream. Never think that The Cure no longer matters to people."

Anyone can hear it. Every music fan has the capacity to understand. It's very simple, and all you need is a good sound system or headphones. Choose an album, preferably *Three Imaginary Boys* since you really should start at the beginning of the story. Sit down and listen—all the way through. Get your face out of your phone, don't let anyone disturb you, and listen. Work your way through their body of music.

Listen to the deft musical interplay on "Lovesong" or "Lullaby." Hear the smoldering tension building second by second on "Want," "Open," or "One Hundred Years." Listen to the sonic space, the mystery, the precision of "A Forest"; the note-perfect arrangements of "Just Like Heaven" or "Fascination Street"; the natural gift for melody exemplified by "Boys Don't Cry," "Let's Go to Bed," "In Between Days," and "A Pink Dream."

Slowly submerge into the ghostly, soul-baring depths of "All Cats Are Grey," "The Same Deep Water as You," "Jupiter Crash," "To Wish Impossible Things," or "Sinking." Ride the sparkling, unfeigned, genuine joy flowing free on "High," "The Lovecats," "Mint Car," and "Friday I'm in Love" or the utter derangement unleashed in "Give Me It," "The Figurehead," "Bananafishbones," and "A Man inside My Mouth."

Hear the stunning beauty of "Treasure," "Out of This World," "Trust," and "Homesick"; the frothing rage of "The Kiss," "Prayers for Rain," "Shiver and Shake," "Pornography," and "Shake Dog Shake"; the razor-sharp musicianship of "Why Can't I Be You?," "From the Edge of the Deep Green Sea," and "Never Enough"; the lyrical dexterity of "Disintegration," "High," and "Like Cockatoos."

Experience the poignant emotion like blood coursing through every note of "Before Three," "Pictures of You," "The Loudest Sound," "Apart," "A Chain of Flowers," "Last Dance," "Scared as You," and "Faith."

Nearly thirteen years have passed since the last Cure album, and it seems that a large part of the reason is Smith's waning belief in his own ability to create. He told *The Guardian* in 2018, "I think there's only so many times you can sing certain emotions. I have tried to write songs about something other than how I felt but they're dry, they're intellectual, and that's not me."

If there is a new Cure album, and it seems very likely there will be, it will be only because Robert Smith believes in it. He will never allow the Cure to become self-parody. He told *The Guardian*, "I fucking hate the idea of the Cure that's going to embarrass me. I defend it passionately, because I've invested my adult life in the band." They will never simply churn out new albums to generate product and sales. Cure music means far more than that to Robert Smith, to the rest of the band, and to the fans.

Their fan base is enormous and always growing as younger generations discover music that speaks to the human soul like few others do. Cure fans exist in every demographic and in every country. Our lives would not be the same without the Cure—they speak to the outsider in us. They opened our eyes and imaginations to possibility. Each album represents memories more powerful than a book of photographs could ever be. The Cure's canvas is vast, their still-expanding journey endlessly fascinating.

The connection between the Cure's music and those who listen can be deeply felt and intense. It burns to the soul. Music is something that can be appreciated on multiple levels. There are casual fans who love the pop hits, and there are diehards who know the word to every B-side. When it comes down to it, music either means something or doesn't. Sometimes you feel it so strongly that it gets into your blood and moves you. The Cure's music, written largely by Robert Smith, has done that for countless individuals, humans who are often struggling to get through each day.

The music is real, and that is the Cure's true legacy. Everything else is a sideshow.

Selected Bibliography

"14 Things You Didn't Know about *The Crow* Soundtrack." *Revolver*, March 29, 2018.

Adams, Owen. "Admit It: The Cure Are Important." *The Guardian*, January 29, 2018.

Aniftos, Rania. "The Cure's Robert Smith Says a New Album Is Coming in Time for Rock Hall Induction." *Billboard*, December 14, 2018.

Anselmo, Philip. "Philip Anselmo: 'Why I Love The Cure.'" *Louder*, January 25, 2019.

Apter, Jeff. 2009. *Never Enough: The Story of The Cure*. New York: Omnibus Press.

Azerrad, Michael. "Searching for the Cure." *Rolling Stone*, June 25, 2018.

Barbarian, Steve Sutherland, and Robert Smith. 1990. *The Cure: Ten Imaginary Years*. New York: Omnibus Press and Schirmer Trade.

Bellia, Richard. "The Cure 1992." *BEST* (France), 1992.

Bradshaw, Calum. "'Killing an Arab': The Cure Try to Reclaim Their Most Controversial Single." *The New Statesman*, July 20, 2018.

Brewster, Will. "Gear Rundown: Robert Smith of The Cure." *Mixdown*, August 14, 2018.

Buskin, Richard. "Classic Tracks: The Cure 'A Forest.'" *Sound on Sound*, December 2004.

Cagnucci, Tonino. "The Crack Up." The Cure: Dressed in Red and Yellow (blog), October 11, 2014. https://thecuretc.wordpress.com/2014/10/11/the-crack-up-2

Christgau, Robert. "Creative Censorship." *Village Voice*, February 3, 1987.

Chun, Kimberly. "Now There's a Cure: Conversing with the Agile Robert Smith . . ." *San Francisco Bay Guardian*, October 3, 2007.

Crandall, Bill. "The Cure's Discography: Robert Smith Looks Back." *Rolling Stone*, January 2000, updated 2004 and 2014.

Cromelin, Richard. "Rock Group Withdraws 'Arab' Song." *Los Angeles Times*, January 21, 1987.

"The Cure's Robert Smith Explains Radiohead Bashing." *The Quietus*, March 2, 2009.

Davroy, Gabrielle. "Let's Talk about Sex: Porl Thompson The Cure." *RTBF Info*, April 10, 2016. https://www.rtbf.be/classic21/article/detail_let-s-talk-about-sex-porl-thompson-the-cure?id=9263832

Delingpole, James. "Love and Peace in a Muddy War Zone." *The Telegraph*, June 26, 1990.

Deserto, Frank. "40 Years of Goth: Essential Albums from the Genre's Beginnings." *Post-Punk.com*, October 31, 2017.

Dimery, Robert. *1001 Albums You Must Hear before You Die*. London: Cassell Illustrated, 2011.

Fonseca, Nicholas. "The Cure Play First Three Albums Live." *SPIN*, June 1, 2011.

Frost, Deborah. "Talking the Cure with Robert Smith." *Creem*, October 1987.

Gittins, Ian. *The Cure: A Perfect Dream*. New York: Sterling, 2018.

Gore, Joe. "Confessions of a Pop Mastermind." *Guitar Player*, September 1992.

"Goth—A Lifestyle Choice." *H2g2 The Hitchhiker's Guide to the Galaxy: Earth Edition*, December 19, 2000.

Di Perna, Alan. "The Gothfather." *Guitar World*, June 1996.

Greene, Andy. "The Cure's Lol Tolhurst on the Rock & Roll Hall of Fame: 'I've Got My Goth Tux Ready.'" *Rolling Stone*, December 14, 2018.

Grow, Kory. "The Cure Celebrate 40th Anniversary with Hit-Filled Hyde Park Show." *Rolling Stone*, July 9, 2018.

Hemmeter, Marcella. "The 10 Best Albums by The Cure to Own on Vinyl." *Vinyl Me, Please Magazine*, November 7, 2017.

"I'm a Cult Hero." *SPIN*, July 6, 2004.

Iqbal, Nosheen, and Tshepo Mokoena. "When Someone Great Is Gone: Is the LCD Soundsystem Comeback A Good Idea?" *The Guardian*, January 5, 2016.

Johnson, Derek, ed. "Banshees Bust-up: Walk-outs Hit Siouxsie Tour." *New Music Express*, September 15, 1979.

Kamal, Nathan. "13 Best Goth Albums of All Time." *Spectrum Culture*, March 21, 2013.

Keaveny, Shawn. "Exclusive Robert Smith Interview, 'I'm Probably Going to Do Something on My Own on Stage . . . but I Always Feel Lonely.'" *BBC*, April 10, 2018.

La Hart, Pug. "The Cure's Wild Mood Swings." *Circus*, May 15, 1996.

Lynskey, Dorian. "The Cure's Robert Smith: 'I Was Very Optimistic When I Was Young—Now I'm the Opposite.'" *The Guardian*, June 7, 2018.

Miller, Kirk. "Q&A: The Cure's Robert Smith on His Musical Influences." *Rolling Stone*, July 8, 2004.

Morton, Roger. "Cure Genius." *New Musical Express*, February 9, 1991.

O'Gorman, Martin. "The Cure's Lol Tolhurst: 'Boys Don't Cry' Was Like a Diary." *Radio X*, September 24, 2016.

Ohanesian, Liz. "How Three Moody British Bands Became the Holy Trinity for L.A. Misfits." *L.A. Weekly*, November 29, 2017.

Pattison, Louis. "The Cure's Robert Smith: 'I'm Uncomfortable with Politicised Musicians.'" *The Guardian*, September 9, 2011.

Paytress, Mark. *Siouxsie & the Banshees: The Authorised Biography*. London: Sanctuary, 2003.

"Pearl Thompson, from The Cure, 'Through the Eyes of Birds' Opening Art Reception." *LA Guestlist*, 2015.

Petridis, Alexis. "LCD Soundsystem's James Murphy: 'I Was a Joke. My Wife Said I Was Going to Die.'" *The Guardian*, August 31, 2017.

Pickard, Joshua. "Record Bin: How The Cure Reshaped Goth Rock on *Disintegration*." *NOOGAtoday*, November 14, 2015.

Radio X News. "Robert Smith: 'I Don't Want to Beat People over the Head with New Cure Material." *Radio X News*, March 30, 2014.

Reid, Alastair, and Press Association. "The Cure Wow Fans in Hyde Park Almost 40 Years since First Ever Show." *Independent.ie*, July 8, 2018.

Riefe, Jordan. "The Cure Guitarist Pearl Thompson's Art Goes on Display." *The Hollywood Reporter*, March 6, 2015.

Richin, Leslie. "Revisit 15 Classic Tracks by The Cure." *Billboard*, April 21, 2017.

Rocky II. Directed by Sylvester Stallone. United Artists, 1979. Transcript.

Roberts, Jo. "Sticky Carpet—Cure the Icing on Vivid Cake." *Sydney Morning Herald*, May 27, 2011.

"The Cure Reschedules 2007 Tour Dates." *BrooklynVegan*, August 24, 2007.

Sande, Kiran. "20 Best: Goth Records Ever Made." *Fact Magazine*, November 25, 2016.

Shah, Asal. "The Cure to Play First Scottish Gig in 27 Years." *Setlist.fm*, October 23, 2018.

Strickland, Britt. "Simon Gallup a Cure for the Bass." *Bass Player*, October 2004.

Thrills, Adrian. "Ain't No Blues for the Summertime Cure." *New Music Express*, December 16, 1978.

Trethan, Phaedra. "Recalling the Latin Casino: Showplace of the Stars." *Courier Post*, January 19, 2018.

Tolhurst, Laurence. *Cured: The Tale of Two Imaginary Boys*. London: Quercus, 2016.

Wenn. "The Cure Star Porl Thompson Still Can't Believe He Shared a Stage with Plant & Page." *Contactmusic.com*, March 10, 2015.

Wright, Alice. "40 Years of The Cure: One Our Most Underrated British Bands." *Metro*, September 9, 2017.

Zuel, Bernard. "Gloom to Be the Perfect Cure at Vivid Festival." *Sydney Morning Herald*, May 6, 2011.

Zaleski, Annie. "'Our Gang Was The Cure': Lol Tolhurst Opens Up about Growing Up with Robert Smith, Addiction and Redemption." *Salon*, October 11, 2016.

Websites

www.afoolisharrangement.com/Cure/cure.asp
www.apinkdream.org
www.curefandocumentary.com
www.picturesofyou.us
www.setlist.fm
www.thecure.com
www.thecure.cz
www.thecurerecords.com

Selected Index

2 a.m. Wakeup Call, 18
4tour (2007/2008), 350
65daysofstatic, 18
1983 Tour, 189
1985 Tour, 190
1986 Tour, 190
2018 Meltdown Festival, 362

Adele, 160
Adrenalize, 242
Aerosmith, x
A Kiss in the Dreamhouse, 92, 135, 136
Allen, Dave, ix, x, 120, 140, 160, 196, 208, 241, 254
Almost Alice, 17
Anderson, Andy, xvii, 106, 108, 114, 128, 130, 140, 147, 189, 254, 255, 263, 264, 265
Angel Studios, 136, 160
Anomalies, 99, 172, 255, 320
Ant, Adam, 103
Antman, 271
A Perfect Circle, 275
A Perfect Day for Bananafish, 146
Aristocats, The, 108
Art of McCartney, The, 18, 321
Associates, The, 30, 55, 183, 203, 301

Bad Timing, 129, 146
Bamonte, Daryl, 149, 150

Bamonte, Perry, xii, 149, 150, 154, 220, 240, 241, 259, 282, 290, 299, 300, 302, 347, 349, 363
Bangles, The, 147
Batcave, 130
Bauhaus, 84, 86
BD-2 Blues Driver, 14
Beach Party, The, 149, 190
Beach Party Tour, The, 190
Beachy Head, East Sussex, 116
Beatles, The, 34, 47, 126, 246, 296, 363
Bedford, Piers, 111
Bell, Frank, 55, 64
"Bette Davis Eyes," 56
Biddles, Gary, 65, 66, 189
Black Tie, White Noise, 151
Blank & Jones, 18
Blink-182, 18, 274
Bolan, Marc, 11
Boleyn, Anne, 1, 2, 3, 4
Bowie, David, 9, 11, 24, 54, 59, 95, 103, 104, 121, 122, 151, 177, 178, 258, 269, 324, 325, 354, 363
"Bring Me the Head of the Preacher Man," 137
Budgie, 127, 128, 135, 136
Button, John, 117

Cabaret Voltaire, 133
Cain, Barry, 102
Camus, Albert, 33

Cape Town, 181
Ceccagno, Marc, 20
Chameleons, The, x
Chateau Miraval, 150, 194, 196, 241
Chestnut Studio, 25, 28, 47, 173
Clash, The, 11, 22, 102, 194, 363
Closer, 86, 119
Coachella, 328, 348
Cooper, Jason, xvii, 79, 154, 219, 259, 260, 266, 267, 282, 302, 309, 318, 324, 343, 347, 350, 352, 363
Corgan, Billy, 18, 275
Corkett, Paul, 306, 322
Crawley, xvii, 5, 11, 12, 19, 20, 21, 22, 23, 29, 36, 54, 55, 56, 63, 65, 71, 101, 150, 155, 172, 183, 184, 208, 220, 221, 223, 226, 250, 266, 282
Creasy, Martin, 21, 22
Creatures, The, 127
Creem, 19, 370
Crow, The, 86, 178, 266, 271, 318, 355, 369
Croydon, 19
Crystal Castles, 18, 30
Cult Hero, 55, 64, 203, 370
Cured: The Tale of Two Imaginary Boys, 85, 220, 227, 228, 353, 371
Cure News, 100, 153
Cure Tour, The (2016), 356

Da Hype, 18
Dead Planet, 18
Death From Above 1979, 30
Def Leppard, 242, 363
Deftones, 328
Delonge, Tom, 274
Dempsey, Michael, xvii, 20, 21, 22, 25, 40, 46, 47, 49, 53, 54, 55, 64, 111, 116, 150, 151, 152, 155, 181, 183, 219, 220, 221, 363
Depeche Mode, 103, 150, 324, 363
Die Warzau, 203
Doors, The, 84, 321
Dragon Hunters, 319, 334
Drake, Nick, 11, 54, 100
Duran Duran, 103
Dutton, Mike, 56
Dylan, Bob, 362, 363

Earthling, 151, 177, 324, 354
East Sussex, 117
Easy Cure, The, 19, 22, 23, 24, 25, 34, 35, 42, 50, 64, 150, 155, 181, 189
Eat, 18, 203
Edward Scissorhands, 274
Eight Appearances Tour, The, 186
Elektra Records, 37, 159, 175, 193, 197, 206, 214, 257, 281
Ely, Vince, 158, 189, 265
Eurythmics, 120, 363
Eventim Apollo, 168

Farmer, Penelope, 79
Fear Factory, 328
Feast, 127
Fender Bass VI, 14, 74, 81, 167, 210, 243
Fender Jazzmaster, 40, 54, 60
Fiction Records, ix, x, 25, 27, 28, 30, 34, 35, 36, 39, 40, 41, 42, 47, 53, 55, 64, 71, 72, 91, 92, 93, 101, 103, 104, 127, 128, 135, 139, 151, 159, 177, 183, 193, 196, 203, 223, 225, 239, 240, 258, 281, 305, 319
Fleetwood Mac, 3, 194, 363
Flexipop!, 101, 102, 103, 107
Fools Dance, 65, 166

For the Masses, 324
Fourmyula, 29, 31
Fourteen Explicit Moments Tour, The, 187
Frankenweenie Soundtrack, 18, 86
Frusciante, John, 82
Future Pastimes Tour, 181, 183
Futurikon, 319

Gabrels, Reeves, xvii, 18, 151, 152, 177, 324, 354
Gabrin, Chris, 113
Gallup, Ric, 27, 63, 67, 81, 99, 186
Gallup, Simon, 4, 12, 13, 24, 49, 53, 55, 63, 64, 65, 66, 67, 68, 69, 74, 81, 85, 99, 101, 103, 112, 118, 136, 139, 150, 152, 154, 156, 157, 166, 167, 183, 186, 187, 189, 190, 195, 201, 202, 203, 208, 209, 212, 215, 221, 223, 229, 243, 251, 256, 259, 282, 287, 300, 301, 302, 318, 320, 347, 350, 352, 353, 363
Galore: The Singles 1987-1997, 121, 123, 152, 176, 177, 235, 289, 324
Geffen Records, x, 327, 337
Generation X, 28, 36, 183
Gibson Explorer, 21
Gibson Thunderbird, 68
Glove, The, vii, 103, 106, 125, 127, 128, 130, 136, 140, 144, 146, 148, 263
Gore, Joe, 329, 361
Gore, Martin, 324
Gormenghast, 77
Goth, vii, ix, xiii, 12, 82, 83, 84, 85, 86, 88, 89, 101, 102, 130, 274, 370, 371
Goulding, Steve, 104
Guild (bass guitar), 21

Hammersmith Odeon, 99, 151, 187, 189, 254
Hansa/Ariola Records, 23, 24, 35, 41, 46, 50, 51
Harriman, Andi, xvi, 84
Hartley, Matthieu, 53, 55, 57, 64, 65, 72, 112, 152, 153, 183, 184, 220, 353
Hartnoll, Paul, 18
Head Tour, The, 149, 190
Hedges, Mike, 29, 56, 62, 72, 74, 79, 92, 127, 130, 222, 318, 322
Hendrix, Jimi, 11, 12, 20, 45, 54, 150, 323, 352, 363
Henry VIII, 1, 2, 3
Heslop, Richard, 287
Hollywood, 157, 354, 371
Hook, Peter, 106
Horley, 55, 63, 64, 220
Howe, Ron, 166
Hyaena, 127
Hyde Park, xiii, 3, 4, 25, 38, 45, 88, 318, 332, 370, 371

Ideal Condition, The, 18
Indovina, Johnny, xvi
Interpol, xiii, 4, 275, 348

Jackson, Janet, 212, 231, 363
Jackson, Michael, 161, 296, 363
Jam Studios, 106, 127
Jam, The, x, 22, 28, 30, 133
Japanese Popstars, The, 18
Japanese Whispers: The Cure Singles Nov 82–Nov 83, xiii, 108, 172, 175
Johannesburg, 181
Johnny Boy Would Love This... A Tribute to John Martyn, 18

Selected Index

John Peel Show, The, 41
Join Hands, 126, 133, 134, 181
Join Hands Tour, 181
Joy Division, 84, 86, 322, 363
Judge Dredd, 271, 320
Juju, 135
Junior Jack, 18
Junkie XL, 18

Kaleidoscope, 135
Kid Jensen Session, 100
Kissing Tour, 149, 153, 197, 295, 298, 299, 351
Korg Duophonic (synth), 55
Korg MiniKorg-700 (synth), 153
Korn, 275, 328
Kraftwerk, 92
Kubrick, Stanley, 54

Landray, Jeanette, 125, 128, 129, 130
Lennon, John, 321, 322
Les Paul, 21
Levinhurst, 77, 264
Lieberman, Jeff, 127
Lillywhite, Steve, 92, 157
Limp Bizkit, 328
Lockjaw, 24, 63, 64
Lost Angels, 271
Lynch, David, 118

Mackenzie, Billy, 122, 319
Madonna, 161, 231, 234, 363
Manson, Marilyn, 122
Marie Antoinette, 271
Maroon 5, 322
Marquee Club, 183
Mary Whitehouse Experience, The, 274
McCartney, Paul, 18

McGeoch, John, 135, 136
McKay, John, 50, 134, 135
Mecha Streisand, 270
Melody Maker, 36, 266, 282
Meltdown Festival, The, 85
Michael, George, 103
Mighty Boosh, The, 274
Morgan Studios, 28, 35, 41, 49, 56, 64, 72, 73, 92, 135
Morgxn, 277
Morley, Paul, 42
Morris, Kenny, 134, 135
Morrison, Van, 54
Most, Mickie, 157
Mourning the Departed, 25
MTV, 111, 117, 118, 119, 120, 123, 161, 198, 208, 214, 275, 300, 301
MTV Unplugged, 275, 300
Muller, Sophie, 120, 121

Neighbors, 320
Neneh Cherry, x, xiv
Newcastle, 54, 189
New Musical Express, 42
New Order, 106, 232, 234, 363
New York City, 151, 189, 302
New Zealand, 29, 31, 62, 71, 184, 189, 300, 356
Nicks, Stevie, 194, 363
Nirvana, 363
Notre Dame Middle School, 20, 220
Numan, Gary, 56
Nutcracker, The, 22
Nye, Steve, 106

Oberheim OB-8 synth, 106
One Million Virgins, 194
Ono, Yoko, 322

Orgazmo Soundtrack, 17
Outside, 151, 208

Page, Jimmy, 156, 282
Parched Art, 75, 155
Parkgate Studios, 337
Parry, Chris, ix, x, xi, xii, xvii, 16, 25, 27, 28, 29, 30, 31, 35, 36, 37, 40, 41, 42, 44, 45, 46, 47, 48, 49, 53, 55, 56, 61, 64, 72, 74, 94, 101, 104, 105, 119, 127, 133, 135, 136, 137, 143, 171, 183, 196, 203, 240, 263, 310, 325
Passions, The, 30, 183
Peel, John, 36, 41, 254
Penman, Ian, 44
Phonogram Records, 29
Picture Tour, The, 75, 81, 82, 99, 186
Pinewood Studios, 118
Plank, Conny, 92
Plant, Robert, 156, 282, 365
Plastic Ono Band, 322
Plati, Mark, 177, 319, 324
Playground Studios, 79
Pleasure Trips Tour, The, 299
Police, The, 102
Polydor Records, x, 25, 28, 35, 36, 42, 48, 53, 74, 94, 119, 128, 133, 134, 239, 240, 263, 305
Poole, Mary, 21, 61, 101, 118, 208
Pope, Tim, 18, 86, 111, 113, 114, 115, 116, 117, 118, 119, 120, 121, 122, 162, 191, 203, 214, 255
Post-Punk.com, 86, 370
Prayer Tour, The, 149, 154, 240, 257, 299
Prince, 104, 194, 231, 363
Proyas, Alex, 318
PSL Studios, 24

Psychedelic Furs, 92, 103, 157, 158, 189, 265

Radiohead, 218, 282, 363, 369
Radio JXL: A Broadcast from the Computer Hell Cabin, 18
RAK Studios, 92, 93, 157, 208, 209, 223, 308
Raw Like Sushi, x
Record Mirror, The, 102
Red Hot Chili Peppers, 82
Reflections, 62, 79, 154, 219, 227, 351, 352, 354
R.E.M., 322
Rent Party, 166, 233
Republica, 122, 177, 322, 324
Rhino Studios, 92
Rickerd, Bob, 112, 113
Ride, 4, 285, 366
Rihanna, 122
Riverside, 130
Robinson, Ross, 266, 327, 328, 332, 335, 336, 348
Rocket, The, 5, 24, 25, 172, 183
Roff, Jesse, 123
Roland synth, 128
Rolling Stone Magazine, 3, 85, 88, 183, 339, 363, 369, 370
Rolling Stones, The, 3, 183, 363
Roxy Music, 11, 363
Royal Albert Hall, 190, 216, 350, 354
Runaways, The, 122

Sade, 120
Sadkin, Alex, 157
Saffron, 122, 177, 322, 324
Saline Project, The, 122, 123
Salinger, J. D., 146
Sartre, Jean-Paul, 33

SAV Studio, 35
Schecter, 14
Scream, The, 133, 201, 337, 344, 345
Sensational Alex Harvey Band, The, 11
Septic, Andy, 64
Sepultura, 328
Severin, Steve, 92, 103, 106, 107, 125, 126, 127, 128, 129, 130, 133, 134, 135, 136, 137, 138, 140, 144, 163
Sex Pistols, 11
Shelleyan Orphan, 67, 250, 301
Sigismondi, Floria, 122
Sinatra, Frank, 86, 184
Sine Waves, 29
Siouxsie & the Banshees, x, 28, 30, 36, 54, 84, 85, 92, 103, 125, 126, 127, 128, 131, 133, 134, 135, 136, 137, 138, 148, 151, 160, 163, 183, 189, 232, 370, 371
Sioux, Siouxsie, 85, 127, 133, 134, 137, 140
Slade, 11, 286
Slick, Earl, 18
Slipknot, 328
Slits, 134, 135
Small Hours, 18
Small Wonder, 36
Smashing Pumpkins, 275, 285
Smith, Janet, 155
Smith, Margaret, 10
Smith, Patti, 363
Smith, Rita, 10, 73
Snow Patrol, 30
Soave, Roberto, 67, 301
Solina String Ensemble, 197
Some Wear Leather, Some Wear Lace: The Worldwide Compendium of Postpunk and Goth in the 1980s, 84
Sound and Vision Studios, 41, 50
South Park, 270
Spandau Ballet, 103
Spector, Phil, 91
Spin Magazine, 17, 88, 109, 273, 354, 370
Springsteen, Bruce, 362, 363
Stallone, Sylvester, 371
Star Synare 3 (synth pad), 56, 57, 222
St. Francis of Assisi Catholic School, 20
St. Francis Primary School, 10
Stranger Than Fiction, 203
Stranger, The, 33, 95
Stranglers And Friends Live In Concert, The (1980 concert, released in 1995), 18
Stranglers, The, 18, 22, 103
Strasbourg, 65, 187
Studio des Dames, 108
Summer Cure Tour, The (2012), 354
Swing Tour, The, 258, 289, 302

Talking Heads, 184, 218
Talk, Talk, Talk, 92, 157, 189
Tame Impala, 30
Teisco, 40
The 1980 Tour, 185
TheFutureEmbrace, 18
Thin White Duke, 9
Thompson, Pearl (formerly Porl), xii, xiii, xvii, 21, 22, 23, 25, 55, 64, 67, 71, 94, 114, 119, 144, 149, 150, 153, 154, 155, 156, 158, 160, 166, 189, 190, 195, 198, 199, 200, 202, 209, 217, 220, 223, 240, 245, 248, 254,

256, 259, 265, 266, 282, 290, 296, 300, 302, 323, 338, 349, 350, 363, 370, 371, 372
Thompson Twins, 153, 158, 160, 190, 265
Thornalley, Perry, xvii, 66, 92, 94, 108, 114, 157, 158, 189, 254, 265
Thornalley, Phil, 92, 93, 94, 157, 158, 265
Throbbing Gristle, 133
Throw Your Foot, 147, 175
Time Out, 85
Times Square, 45, 271
Tin Drum, 106
Tin Machine, 151, 354
Tokyo, 189, 255, 264, 265
Tolhurst, Daphne, 73, 186
Tolhurst, Laurence, xvii, 10, 19, 40, 64, 74, 103, 127, 190, 219, 225, 240, 352, 353
To Love Somebody, 18
Top of the Pops, 11, 66, 106, 128
Top Tour, The, 189
Tower of London, 1, 2, 3
Triple J Radio, 322
Trust It, 18
Truth Is, 18
Tweaker, 18
Twilight Sad, The, 4, 18

U2, x, 218, 322
Ulysses (Della Notte), 18
Uncut magazine, 138
United States of America, The, 159, 172, 175, 193, 281
Universal Music Group, 30
Universal Records, 30

Vallis, Trevor, 24
Vancouver, 153, 190, 298
Vanilla Ice, 328
Vella, Andy, 155
Very Good Advice, 17
Vow, The, 272

Wales, 101
Warner Communications, 37
Watkins Electric Music (guitar amp), 20
Wellington, 29
Wembley, 37, 257, 298, 299, 300, 351, 356
West Berlin, 37
Westside Studios, 322
West Side Studios, x
West Sussex, 12, 19, 208, 221
Westwood, 272
We Were Exploding Anyway, 18
White, Alan, 20
Wild Things, 127
Williams, Boris, 153, 154, 158, 160, 163, 164, 190, 195, 199, 200, 201, 202, 208, 212, 214, 219, 220, 256, 265, 266, 282, 300, 302, 318, 363
Wire, 28, 36, 54, 183
Wish Tour, The, 242, 300
Witchcraft, 18, 86
Wonderland, 17, 125
Woods, Dave, 134
Woolworths Top 20 guitar, 20
Worth Abbey, 12, 21, 208
WPRB Princeton, 37

X-Files: The Album, The, 178, 323
XFM, 31, 325

Yeah Yeah Yeahs, 30
Yellow Submarine, 125
Yorkshire Dales, 71
YouTube, 130

Ziggy Stardust, 9
Zig Zag, 18
Zoo, 128

Printed in Great Britain
by Amazon

ELDER
ON MUSIC

ELDER
ON MUSIC

Sir Mark Elder in Conversation
with Raymond Holden

RAYMOND HOLDEN

ROYAL
ACADEMY
OF MUSIC
PRESS

First published in 2019 by
Royal Academy of Music Press

Royal Academy of Music
Marylebone Road
London NW1 5HT

Copyright © The Royal Academy of Music, 2019

www.ram.ac.uk

The author asserts his moral right to be identified as the author of this work. All rights reserved. No part of this publication may be reproduced, stored in a retrieval system or transmitted in any form or by any means, electronic, mechanical, photocopying, recording or otherwise, without prior written permission of the author.

While every effort has been made to trace the owners of copyright material reproduced herein, the authors and publishers would like to apologise for any omissions and will be pleased to incorporate missing acknowledgements in any future editions.

HB 978-1-912892-70-9
eBook 978-1-912892-74-7

Project management by whitefox
Designed and typeset by Tom Cabot/ketchup
Cover design by Alice Moore
Printed and bound in Great Britain by Clays Ltd, Elcograf S.p.A

CONTENTS

Foreword................vii

Introduction................xi

PART ONE: Becoming and being a conductor............1

PART TWO: The art and craft of conducting............31

PART THREE: German music............75

PART FOUR: Italian music............119

PART FIVE: British music............133

PART SIX: French, Scandinavian, Czech and Russian music..153

Coda............165

Index............167

FOREWORD

TRYING TO GAUGE WHAT MOTIVATES EMINENT MUSICIANS in their various pursuits is famously hard. Bruno Walter and Dietrich Fischer-Dieskau each wrote illuminating self-portraits but the majority of insights from such artists have mainly been derived from one-to-one interviews which, combined with parallel research, leads to fully fledged biography – Sir Nicholas Kenyon's work on Sir Simon Rattle or Richard Osborne's on Herbert von Karajan.

What most excites me about this book is that it's about Sir Mark Elder on music. Whilst a biography of Sir Mark would always be enlightening and profoundly entertaining, these pages are all about the art, the circumstances, the anomalies, the fantasy, the polemics, the mysteries, the delights and the key protagonists in all the theatres of musical accomplishment that he has visited over 60-odd years. Such is the kaleidoscopic range of Sir Mark's influence on international musical life – and his never-ending quest to reveal more and more about the music to which he is drawn – that a monograph of even mildly comprehensive coverage could appear prohibitively herculean. Raymond Holden's deft strategy to collect material from a number of public interviews seemed to present a promising template. The interviews themselves were memorable for the unpredictable turns in the discussions, the friendliness and fun of the exchanges and the passionately expressed and authoritative visions of musical life – past, present and future – which Sir Mark imparts with such compelling and mesmerising freshness.

As you will see in these discussions, here is a figure who proudly draws inspiration from tradition but then unashamedly defines it for his own times. This is the hallmark of his major positions held in the UK, most notably as Music Director of the English National Opera and the Hallé, where the legacies are rooted in an artistic zeal defined by deep regard and recognition for musicians and colleagues who allow him to 'make hay' with uncompromising results. The resonances from this collective approach make him one of the most popular musicians of recent times: a role model for young people alongside his genuinely impassioned support for musical communities, and their centrality to the health of society, education and identity. As our Barbirolli Chair of Conducting at the Royal Academy of Music and a regular visitor here, Sir Mark leaves no student in any doubt as to the importance he attaches to the potential role in the world of every person in the room.

Within these pages, we are offered a riveting view of a legendary explorer of unknown great music, the staunch and joyful enabler of new music, ambassador for British music, opera in spades, his tireless work with period ensembles and symphony orchestras of all shapes and sizes, and always with conviction, not only on the podium but famously in his pre-performance talks. His hypnotic way with audiences, both live and in all forms of media, remains memorable for millions.

ELDER ON MUSIC

This book could never be comprehensive but it provides wonderful insights into Mark Elder's brilliant and enquiring mind, his desire to communicate a deep knowledge drawn from broad experience peppered with childlike wonder. My thanks go to Sir Mark for his generosity and to Professor Holden for his tireless expertise at all stages of the process.

Professor Jonathan Freeman-Attwood CBE Principal
Royal Academy of Music London, 2019

INTRODUCTION

I F OSCAR WILDE WERE STILL ALIVE TODAY, he might observe of Sir Mark Elder: 'To save one great British cultural institution may be regarded as remarkable; to save two looks phenomenal.' Born in Hexham in the north-east of England in 1947, Sir Mark made his professional conducting debut in Melbourne in 1973. He went on to dazzle and enthral Australian audiences with performances that were both breathtaking and stylish at the newly opened Sydney Opera House. Such an outstanding talent was never going to remain Down Under for long, however. Britain beckoned and he quickly found his musical home at the London Coliseum. But the English National Opera lacked direction when he was appointed its Music Director in 1979 and was in need of an artist of vision and charisma to turn around its musical fortunes. Never one to shy away from a challenge, he set about reforming the company and soon left audiences, critics and musicians in no doubt that something wonderful was happening in St Martin's Lane. By the time that Sir Mark moved on, both he and the ENO had a reputation for artistic excellence and social relevance.

With his American orchestra, the Rochester Philharmonic (1989–1994), he continued to challenge audiences and artistic norms. But it was with his appointment as Music Director of the Hallé in 2000 that he once again strode into the musical fray. Facing bankruptcy, the orchestra needed a great figure to rejuvenate it musically and financially. Sir Mark did both. The orchestra was saved and audiences returned. A musical miracle had occurred in Manchester.

It is clear, then, that Sir Mark's career has been nothing short of extraordinary. For more than four decades, he has been at the forefront of British musical life and has been a welcome guest at all the world's great opera houses and orchestras. He has also worked indefatigably with young musicians throughout his career and has been a role model for two generations of aspiring conductors. I was keen, therefore, to chart at least part of his wonderful life. The principal forum for this exploration was the Barbirolli Lectures, the Royal Academy of Music's premiere interview series. Between 2013 and 2017, Sir Mark was my guest at six of these events during which we discussed a wide range of topics, including his life and career, the technical aspects of conducting and his thoughts on individual composers and schools of composition. Inevitably, the 12 hours of discussion that emerged from these interviews needed some rearranging and editing before they could be published. In transforming these discussions into a readable narrative, every care was taken to retain Sir Mark's tone, insights, passion and wit. It is no exaggeration to say that audiences hang on his every word and never fail to be entertained and educated by his unique blend of scholarship and linguistic elan.

Throughout the preparation of this book, I have received enthusiastic support from Sir Mark and Lady Elder. I would like to thank particularly my research assistant, Abigail Sin, for all her hard work in transcribing the interviews. I would also like to thank Professor

ELDER ON MUSIC

Jonathan Freeman-Attwood, Professor Timothy Jones, Mark Racz, Edward Gardner, Nicola Mutton, Janet Snowman, Philip White, Dr Stephen Mould, Marcus Dods, Andrew Hawkins, Rachael O'Brien, David Gleeson, Henry Kennedy, Jonathon Heyward, Paul Brooks, Francesco Bastanzetti and Peter Quantrill for their unstinting help, advice and kindness. I would like to acknowledge especially the photographers, Benjamin Ealovega (front cover) and Chris Christodoulou (back cover and inside front cover), for kindly allowing the Academy to use their superb images of Sir Mark Elder. But my greatest debt of gratitude is to my wife, Mary, for her unfailing optimism and encouragement. She sustained me throughout this project and without her support, this book would not have been written.

Raymond Holden
Professor of Public Engagement
Royal Academy of Music
London, 2019

PART ONE

BECOMING AND BEING A CONDUCTOR

RH: Sir Mark, you are numbered among the pre-eminent opera conductors of our time. Would it be reasonable to assume that the voice and vocal music have been important to you throughout your life?

ME: As a child I spent every morning bouncing up and down on my bed singing and inventing anthems. At an early age I was taken by my mother for a voice trial at a choir school. I found it natural to sing and it was something I did without realising I was doing it. It's such a natural part of music-making and the only form of music-making for which you don't need to buy an instrument. Everybody should try to sing and nobody should have a problem with it. I hope it never disappears from our lives and that schools will once again encourage young people to sing. As we all live and thrive in a multicultural and multi-faith society, I refuse to believe that singing in schools will disappear completely just in case somebody is offended by it.

RH: You made your recording debut as a chorister at Canterbury Cathedral singing Benjamin Britten's *A Ceremony of Carols*.

ME: We recorded it in the Chapter House, a spectacularly beautiful building. I still have an old copy of the disc. It was inspiring to make that recording as a boy. I sang the second of the two little solos for 'In Freezing Winter Night', which is in five beats to the bar. This was at the end of the 1950s and they couldn't get the microphones quite right. I had to stand on a collapsible wooden chair in the middle of the Chapter House. It was freezing cold and somebody kept spoiling take after take by getting the 5/4 rhythms wrong. I recall standing up there for hours waiting for this little top G. The harpist was Maria Korchinska, a very short, very round Russian lady. She was a wonderful musician, a brilliant artist and sounded like a thunderstorm when she played her harp. Every time we started to record, it was clear that she was much too loud and I was much too soft. Consequently, I would move closer and closer to the microphone and she would move further and further away. To do the solo again and again until they were satisfied with the recording was an incredible experience and one that taught me a great deal about balance. It was a beautiful work to sing and it was a fascinating challenge to try and master such difficult music when we were all so young.

Being a chorister is great training for a life in music. But many wonderful choristers decide not to become musicians in later years. One of my great friends at Canterbury was Oz Clarke. For a long time, he sang in *Evita* in the West End but is now a famous wine expert. What you gain by being trained as a chorister at the age of 8 or 9 is discipline, dedication and concentration. Those traits are a great help for whatever you do in life. To get up, sing a service at eight o'clock on a cold morning and produce the same level of performance day after

PART ONE: BECOMING AND BEING A CONDUCTOR

day: this is valuable training for a young child. And because of that training, I realised early on that my future would be in music.

RH: Have those early vocal experiences had an impact on your work as a conductor?

ME: All conductors should sing and, if you work in the theatre, you have to be prepared to sing any part at the drop of a hat. If somebody is ill – and singers are always ill – you have to be ready to fill in and sing whichever part isn't there. And you have to do it in such a way that makes it clear you understand what it's all about and you have a feeling for the music. It's an essential part of being an operatic musician.

RH: From Canterbury you went to Cambridge by way of Bryanston School in Dorset. How did those moves prepare you for the music profession?

ME: The decision of whether to go to a conservatoire or to a university after leaving secondary school is always hard. Down at Bryanston School in Dorset it was difficult to understand where I should go next, whether to one of the music colleges or to university. In the 1960s, it was felt that students were delaying the inevitable by going to university; the moment when they had to opt for a particular specialism. While that might not be the case today, I feel I was right to delay my decision as to which particular avenue of music I would eventually enter.

Nevertheless, it was during my years at Bryanston that I lifted a baton for the first time. As I am left-handed, the school's brass teacher, a West Country horn player, said, 'Dear boy, if you think they're going to follow your beat, you'd better use the other hand.' And I've been struggling with conducting ever since! I felt that going to university would expand my appreciation of music and that proved to be the case. Cambridge offered me the opportunity to hear music I didn't know existed, and it prepared me for the profession.

RH: During your time at Cambridge, one of your friends was David Pountney, now one of the world's most distinguished opera and theatre directors.

ME: David and I played in the same youth orchestra when we were 12 years old. After we went up to Cambridge together, he suggested that we should stage an opera. As we had no experience, I was somewhat surprised by the suggestion. But that didn't deter him and, as they say, the rest is history. We performed Alessandro Scarlatti's only comic opera, a beautiful piece called *Il trionfo dell'onore*, and approached it in an experimental way. It was the first time that David and I ever worked together.

RH: Was there a particular 'eureka' moment at either school or university when you realised that you were destined for a life on the podium?

ME: The short answer is 'no'. I played the bassoon, the piano, the harpsichord and the organ while I was an undergraduate at Cambridge, but I also acted a great deal. Even though I had acted at school before going up to university, it was at Cambridge that I was first exposed to the elemental and overwhelming power of opera. I came to realise that there was something fundamentally different between German and Italian opera, symbolised by the Alps which separate northern

PART ONE: BECOMING AND BEING A CONDUCTOR

and southern Europe. The 'Latinness' of the French, Spanish, Italian and Greek temperaments informs their languages which, in turn, informs their music. As I've always been interested in language, I found that incredibly exciting.

Although I didn't study German at school, I did learn French and Latin. Latin is so valuable for musicians; it is the root of so much that we use. During my first year at Cambridge, I felt that conducting could bring all these things together. I had an enormous amount of fun playing the bassoon and by learning music through the middle of the orchestra, but I knew that I didn't want to scrape reeds as a wind player for the rest of my life. Watching the Hallé musicians cope with this, and seeing the detritus around the bottom of their feet, I know that I made the right decision.

The first concert that I gave included Mahler's *Lieder eines fahrenden Gesellen* and Beethoven's Fourth Symphony. When you are young, and you know nothing, you don't know whether something is easy or difficult. And it's incredible the things we do before realising how tricky they are! I have rehearsed Beethoven's Fourth many times with different orchestras since that first Cambridge performance, but I still remember how strange it was to stand up and to do it for the first time. Nevertheless, I felt at home on the podium, even at that early stage. That feeling is an important part of being a conductor. Even though you might lack knowledge and experience as a young conductor, you need courage and strength of purpose. You just hope that you've learned the score well enough and that you have the ability to transmit the knowledge gained to the players.

But how should one study a score? What do you do? What does it mean to 'know' a piece of music? These are difficult questions that demand entirely personal answers. During those formative years, I remember feeling how motivated I was to learn my craft and to develop my skills. As to what would happen after that, I had no idea. It took another four years before I really had the confidence to give it a go. When I started being paid regularly for conducting, I remember thinking, 'Well, other people must think that I'm worth paying and worth entrusting me with the responsibility.' By saying that, I don't mean to be venal. In fact, the money wasn't great. For the first full opera I worked on at Glyndebourne, I was paid only £22 a week. But the *honour* of working for Glyndebourne!

RH: The music director at Glyndebourne was Sir John Pritchard, who, I know, was fond of you and admired your talent. He was also proud of the opportunities Glyndebourne offered young artists. Do you think that is still the case?

ME: I was still at Cambridge when I was given a walk-on part at Glyndebourne. The facilities there, the space, the sense of being away from the noise of city life, and the ability to make music in such incredible surroundings, all these things made a great impression on me. The company still has a great sense of tradition and continues to concentrate on young singers and musicians. Many artists started their professional careers at Glyndebourne. Janet Baker, for example, was in the Glyndebourne Chorus. It's a wonderful way to start your career, to meet your contemporaries and to form friendships that remain with you for the rest of your life.

I shall never forget the two summers I spent at Glyndebourne. It was a marvellous experience to watch opera being performed and to observe the process from a distance, without having any responsibility, apart from remembering to take my specs off when I walked on stage as a super. For one production, I had to wear a Renaissance costume, which, apparently, cost over £250, an enormous sum in 1968.

PART ONE: BECOMING AND BEING A CONDUCTOR

I felt embarrassed to be wearing such an expensive article of clothing and, one night, I suddenly realised that I could see the conductor and the audience. I still had my specs on!

More important, it was at Glyndebourne that I smelled a theatre for the first time. Every theatre has its own smell. That was particularly true of the old Glyndebourne house before it was completely rebuilt in the 1990s. Often the charm and the appeal of these smells can come from prosaic things such as what they clean the carpets with. But I adored the smell of Glyndebourne. Perhaps my attachment to the place stems from my years as a chorister at Canterbury. We were taken to see a dress rehearsal there and I shall never forget the impact of being in a theatre and watching an opera for the first time. As a young boy, I went to Glyndebourne on three occasions. I saw *Le nozze di Figaro* with Oliver Messel's designs from the 1950s, *La cenerentola* conducted by Vittorio Gui and, later, *Don Giovanni*. I remember going backstage and seeing the props, the fabric and the craft of the theatre. After that, I yearned on some level to get back there.

When I entered the profession, my work at Glyndebourne was crucial. It opened my eyes and ears as to what an opera house should be about. It was there that I met Sir John Pritchard. He was Music Director of Glyndebourne at the time and was a great support to me. He felt that he should help me, push me forward and give me opportunities. But there were many singers, too, whom I met there. Janet Baker came to work on Cavalli's *La calisto* with Raymond Leppard. We'd already been rehearsing and she arrived late one day to work on a particular aria. The three of us worked together in the sunset; an unforgettable experience. I had admired her so much from a distance and never imagined for one moment that I would meet her. I remember singing with her and Ray, who was such a brilliant conductor and support. She stopped at one point and said, 'I just want to say how wonderful it is to be here at Glyndebourne. I've had six weeks of opera elsewhere and the atmosphere was so tense. Nobody knew where they stood. The music-making was wonderful but it was difficult. Even though I loved being there, it's so nice to be here amongst the sheep.'

As a young conductor, it is inspiring to watch other musicians work, to think about how their approach affects you, to consider what they're doing and to question whether or not they are making the music better or worse: these things teach one how to listen. And one of the hardest things about being a young conductor is being able to listen as well on the podium as off it. We can all be at somebody else's rehearsal and say why he or she doesn't hear, can't hear or simply doesn't notice. But the moment you stand on that little box and everybody's focus and energy is physically centred on you, your perspective changes. Being entirely yourself, and hearing as much as possible, takes an enormous amount of practice, faith, hard work and aural training. Very few people have flawless ears from an early age; the rest of us have to work at it. We have to learn how to listen to an orchestra, how to improve its sound, how to balance its various instrumental voices and how to affect the type of sound it makes. Watching other conductors rehearse is a valuable way to learn, but we all need to get up and do it ourselves, however rare those opportunities are.

RH: Tradition at Glyndebourne was very important. Its connection with Richard Strauss through the activities of Fritz Busch, and his pursuit of Strauss's ideas on Mozart, was a defining feature of the old Glyndebourne house. Do you carry any of those traditions with you now?

ME: While I don't think I do, it's interesting that you should ask about the company's sense of history and tradition. There was an

PART ONE: BECOMING AND BEING A CONDUCTOR

extraordinary Austro-Hungarian personality who ran Glyndebourne's music staff during my time there, Jani Strasser. He was an incredibly gifted man, cantankerous and difficult to work with. But, for all that, he was a dear. I was one of the music staff always trying to get permission to miss rehearsals and get away to do other things. I used to queue up to ask for these things and he wouldn't take any notice of me. Then one day he said, 'Mark, my dear' – he had a rather strange voice – 'if you want to ask me a question, the answer is "no".'

Nevertheless, I learned an enormous amount about Mozart style from Jani. I learned the need for detail, the need to work with singers and the need to go on working with them. Having a quick rehearsal is of no value because of the muscles, body, psychology and psyche of the performers with whom you are working. Singers need time. They need to be taught how to interpret their roles and to be given the chance to absorb them. They need to understand how much they can colour their voice, how they can change their voice depending on the type of character they are portraying and how they can use their voice to express a particular scene. This isn't something that can be done quickly. It requires a great deal of care and consideration.

If the imagination guides the voice, the sound will change. You have to stimulate the imagination and that was what Jani did. It was amazing to watch him work and to see how he achieved his artistic goals through the music. I found that inspirational and it's something I think about regularly.

At that time, there was also a remarkable Italian man at Glyndebourne, the company's Italian coach, Ubaldo Gardini. I learned more about conducting from him than from anyone else. He was a difficult man who perspired all day long. But he was passionate about his work and brilliantly gifted. Many singers performing today learned their craft, art and Italian repertoire from him. For me, he was an inspiration, a magical musician.

RH: As a student in Sydney during the 1970s, I remember watching Jani Strasser work. I was fascinated by the effect that he had on members of the opera company there.

ME: He wore a toupee by then.

RH: Yes, it seemed to go before him most of the time. But not one singer there doubted his ability. Occasionally, he came to the conservatorium to work with us – which leads us to your Australian period.

ME: As a young répétiteur at the Royal Opera House, I met Sir Edward Downes. He was at my audition and asked me a tricky question that I didn't know the answer to. I completely fumbled it but he forgave me immediately. Not long after I had joined the music staff, Ted asked if I would like to live and work in Australia, as he had just been appointed Music Director of the Australian Opera. I hadn't met anybody quite like him at that time and what he gave me was something nobody else could possibly have given me: an opportunity that was invaluable and one I think about often.

His death – with his wife, Joan, a double suicide – made an enormous impact on us all. He and Joan were a wonderful team. It came at a time when the idea of assisted suicide was very much in our hearts and minds, because of Ted and also other people. It was a source of enormous discussion and disagreement. But their decision to end their lives was entirely characteristic of them. Ted was almost totally blind and on his way to becoming deaf. He was well into his 80s and Joan was dying of cancer. They made a joint decision and, in my opin-

PART ONE: BECOMING AND BEING A CONDUCTOR

ion, they were perfectly entitled to do so: it showed such strength of character and strength of personality. I found what they did very moving, no matter what anyone else might think or say.

RH: Sir Edward's impact on Australian musical life was profound. And it was thanks to him that you made your professional conducting debut. I was at your first performance in Melbourne and then at your second performance at the Sydney Opera House. I remember Prokofiev's *War and Peace* and a series of Verdi operas. But wasn't there also some Mozart?

ME: In Sydney, I conducted *Die Zauberflöte* for the first and only time; a special production for the opening of the Sydney Opera House. When Tamino charmed the animals with his flute in Act 1, all the creatures that came on stage were indigenous to Australia. It was a lovely touch which was greeted with hysteria by the public night after night.

The tenor singing Tamino was not so pleased, as he would sing a few notes and then a duck-billed platypus or kangaroo would appear. One 7-year-old boy was given a crocodile costume. All he had to do was come out of the wings, crawl to the centre of the stage, wait for two minutes, then turn and crawl back. One night this lovely boy crawled out beautifully but then lost his nerve on the journey home and began heading for the pit. That was a terrible moment: a young crocodile apparently making a suicide leap! Just as he got to the front of the stage and would have gone straight into the pit, around the proscenium arch came the bare arm of the director, who yanked him away to safety. I am sure the poor boy never got over it and I often wonder what he's doing now.

RH: And what a logistical challenge those early performances must have been for you. The opera theatre in the Sydney Opera House is small by international standards.

ME: When I did *Die Meistersinger* there, the opera theatre was so small that I had to *insist* that the management give me a fourth double bass. I said, 'You *cannot* do this piece with three double basses.' There is a wonderful book called *The Other Taj Mahal*, written by the journalist John Yeomans. The stories behind the design and the building of the house, and the painful and difficult things that were lived through before it could be opened, are in this book. I believe this book to be truthful and honest. What I heard at the time, and what I was told when I was in Sydney, was not.

It was important for the New South Wales government to make sure that the architect Jørn Utzon was the scapegoat. He was forced to resign and never saw the building completed. If you're on the harbour and taking photographs of Sydney, it's a beautiful sight, but it's an appalling, second-rate building inside. The opera theatre is a tiny part of the smaller shell. The bigger, main shell houses a concert hall and that is where the symphony orchestra plays.

When I first arrived in Australia, the Sydney Opera House was a building site and had been one for a long time. The time it took to build was such that when taxi drivers drove by it they used to ask me why I was there. I explained that I hoped to be working in the Opera House one day. With stunned amazement they would then say, 'There? They'll never finish that. That will never happen.' I would explain that I wanted to learn how to be a conductor and to conduct operas. Still unconvinced, they would continue with, 'Jeez, that's a great thing to aim for but it won't happen there.' That was in 1972.

PART ONE: BECOMING AND BEING A CONDUCTOR

When it eventually opened in 1973, it was an extraordinary moment. It struck me that the building replaced corks on hats as an image of Australia across the world: it was a milestone for the country. There was an enormous amount of expectation in the air, and a sense that the building would change the cultural life of the city – which in many ways it did. The problems were with the design, who was going to use it and what it was going to be used for. It became a source of incredible political confusion. Nevertheless, I was fascinated to learn about music-making, the world in general and Australia in particular. Ted Downes gave me the chance of a lifetime. I lived in Australia for two and a quarter years and conducted 160 performances. If I had stayed at the Royal Opera House, I might have been lucky to have conducted three.

RH: After Australia, you came back to England and to the English National Opera at a difficult time for the company.

ME: My immediate predecessor as Music Director of the English National Opera was Sir Charles Groves. He was a wonderful musician who did an enormous amount for the musical life of the UK. But he wasn't happy as Music Director of the ENO. He didn't feel fulfilled and he didn't feel at home there. He then had a moment of crisis and resigned. Lord Harewood asked me to take charge of the company overnight and I felt it was my responsibility to say 'yes'. That was at the end of the 1970s. I loved the company then and still do. Perhaps more importantly, I care for what the company stands for in the cultural life of London. The idea that there should be a theatre with performances in the language of its people is vital to me. Opera in the vernacular is incredibly hard to do well, but when it does succeed it can be life-changing.

At the beginning of the 1980s, the ENO lacked a sense of aesthetic purpose. It took little account of the exciting things that were happening in Germany, Austria and, sometimes, Paris. Opera in the UK was, with some exceptions, still rather homespun, narrow, inward-looking and not at all theatrically innovative. I made it plain that I thought this was something we could change and that it would be exciting to do things in a different way.

Of course, there were nights when we didn't get it right. I shall never forget the first time an audience booed at the London Coliseum. I can tell you exactly the place in Tchaikovsky's *Mazeppa* when it happened: after the ballet during which the orchestra played the famous 'Hopak'. The audience erupted and the orchestra was totally shocked and traumatised. They assumed that the audience were booing at the way they played the music. I tried to put them at their ease and said, 'No, no, no, it's all right. It's fine. You're great. It's obviously them.' As more people started to boo, others started to cheer – and at that point in the 1980s, boos of that energy had not happened in London. They were heard occasionally at Covent Garden but the whole idea of an audience booing is something that's now a refreshing and vigorous part of our lives.

In Italy, these things are a way of life. Some years ago, I was making a documentary about Verdi with the BBC and we went to a performance in Bologna in order to experience the flavour of an Italian audience. In the second act of *Simon Boccanegra*, one of the Italian singers gave a worthy interpretation of his difficult aria. It wasn't great, but his voice was virile and he sang it strongly. He got a smattering of applause but, just as the audience was settling down, an over-dressed young lady sitting by herself in the box next to me thought she'd try to keep the applause going. She leaned forward and screamed, 'Bravo, bravo, bravo'. At which point, two elderly Bolognese

PART ONE: BECOMING AND BEING A CONDUCTOR

matrons in the next box along looked with horror at this vulgar display of enthusiasm and immediately shouted, 'Boo, boo, boo'. Had my neighbour not clapped, they wouldn't have booed. They did this as a way of making public conversation.

It is entirely natural to behave like this if you have that sort of temperament. I think it's lovely. The worst thing in an Italian opera house is an audience's total silence. If you do something, and you think you've done it creditably, but silence reigns, then you should creep away into the night feeling fully shamed. Many years ago, one of my distinguished – or perhaps not so distinguished – Italian colleagues conducted the Prelude to Act 1 of *La traviata*. There is a tradition in Italy that it gets a round of applause. That night, total silence. He thought, 'Well, I'd better get on with the first act.' Just as he started the act, somebody in the gallery said, '*Ma*'. Just that. Nothing else. It fell like a stone. He meant: 'Couldn't you do better than that?'

RH: Let's chat about East Berlin and your encounters with Joachim Herz.

ME: Joachim Herz was an East German who, together with Götz Friedrich, made an enormous impact on the production styles of that country and, later, those of West Germany. In 1977, Herz came to London and directed *Salome* at the Coliseum. He was a huge physical presence and a bully. But he was a musician of the first order who knew every note of the score and whose command of what he wanted was fantastic. I'd never worked with anyone who was so autocratic, difficult and nervous about his own talent. Consequently, he was also nervous about the people with whom he worked.

Nevertheless, it was very exciting to do *Salome* with Herz, and after that production, he asked me to go and work with him in East Berlin on a staging of *Madama Butterfly* at the Komische Oper. I lived there for nearly two months: there were two months of rehearsals. All the singers I know feel that three weeks is quite enough and are confused as to why some directors need six. Even after such an extended rehearsal period, he was still dissatisfied with our work and put off the premiere. Although it was supposed to open before Christmas, he said, 'Right, we'll all go home for Christmas, come back in the new year, rehearse a bit more and then give the first night in January.'

If you run your own theatre, and you're in East Germany, you can do that. The singers were sort of captive. He simply told them what they would do and that they were not going to do the premiere. He felt it wasn't ready and wasn't good enough. Nevertheless, the experience of working with him twice – in fact three times, as he returned to London for a production of *Fidelio* at the Coliseum – was amazing. I'd never worked in German before and I had to learn the language as I went along.

Even though Herz was a difficult man, not at all easy or sympathetic, he was a great musician and a great director. I don't regret for one moment the difficult times that I spent with him, as it showed me another branch of my craft.

In East Berlin, I also came face to face with the difficulties of singing Puccini in German. Having been asked to conduct *Butterfly*, I attempted to coach the local singers in the vernacular. I was keen for them to sing with a sense of line and beauty so that every word would be audible. While that was something of a challenge for a young Englishman, I felt that it was important for the public to hear clearly the nuances of Puccini's score. Thankfully, the acoustics of the Komische Oper in East Berlin are fabulous. If only the ENO had that theatre, our whole awareness of what the ENO could be, and could achieve, would change overnight. As the Komische Oper is a large building, big-scale operas can be performed there with ease. And, as

PART ONE: BECOMING AND BEING A CONDUCTOR

the acoustic is so clear, all the work the company does on making every line of every opera understandable pays off.

The problem with the Coliseum is that it was never designed for sung speech. It was a variety hall designed with vaudeville in mind. It's very hard to be understood in there, and I spent years trying to make the text clear. In the Komische Oper, everyone understands everything. In the second act of *Madama Butterfly*, for example, when Pinkerton returns and Butterfly commits suicide, every single word on every single night was audible, understandable and *felt* by the public. That is so important in the theatre.

A member of the East Berlin orchestra asked me, 'Why have we got so few rehearsals?' I've never known an orchestral musician to ask such a question. It would be unheard of in the UK. I tried to justify our schedule by saying, 'I think we've got enough.' And he replied, 'Well, we are used to many more rehearsals here. Every word must be clear. The orchestra must never be too loud.' That's absolutely true. For an orchestra to be aware of that, to believe it and to want it, reflected the ethos of a company that understood the importance of communicating with its public.

Going to another country to learn one's craft, and absorbing things one cannot find in one's own country, is an important part of the developmental process. There are many young musicians who have travelled to England from other countries to try and make sense of our strange society. For me, going to Germany, and experiencing for myself the effect that the Wall had on Berlin, was important. For those who didn't see the Wall, and who didn't experience it first-hand, it can be difficult to understand fully the impact that it had on Berlin and Berliners. As you flew in, you'd see a bit here and a bit there of that grey worm that wriggled its way through the streets of the city. Then you'd lose it, then you'd see it again.

East Berlin broadened my horizons, just as Sydney had done all those years earlier. I was fortunate to get to know personally many of the members of the Komische Oper, and to learn that people actually *did* make a happy life there. They knew they had problems, and they were aware that things were difficult, but they still had joy in their lives and contrived to work within the system. It wasn't a fair system but perhaps it wasn't as bad as we now tend to think. Nevertheless, the sensation of leaving East Berlin, with its absence of light, and re-entering West Berlin, with all its flamboyant, neon-lit capitalism, was remarkable.

RH: You once remarked that 'an opera house must be a place of discussion and disagreement. It should be dangerous.'

ME: In countries where there has been a revolution, often the crucial moment happens in the opera house. An opera house is often in the city centre; it's a natural place for people to meet and to exchange ideas. It should be remembered that communication and intelligibility were fundamental to the design of a Baroque opera house. It was and still is a forum for public debate. I believe that the theatre should be at the centre of our lives, not a slightly risqué alternative for a cold night when you have nothing better to do. The task of theatre is to get us thinking about ourselves, to laugh at ourselves, to cry about our lives, to learn how to deal with the broader picture, to be moved and stimulated and to make us curious. It is fundamental to society.

RH: The Coliseum was once described as an artistic 'powerhouse', led by you as Music Director, David Pountney as Director of Productions and Peter Jonas as General Director.

PART ONE: BECOMING AND BEING A CONDUCTOR

ME: That word was a yoke around our necks. Everybody thinks we called ourselves that. We didn't, and we never did.

RH: But the whole point of being a cultural powerhouse is to drive society forward. Is it such a bad thing for the Coliseum to have occupied such a role?

ME: There was a time in the 1980s when the way we staged operas seemed to be more inspired by music. In a broader sense, the Coliseum seemed a bit more post-modern, avant-garde, dangerous and interesting than the National Theatre. For a time there was an idea that opera could lead the way theatrically. Such a time could return but one has to have the ability to fail.

RH: In the 1980s, Britain was undergoing a transformation, both politically and economically. The arts were badly affected by this transformation and suffered because of it.

ME: As the decade went on, things got tough financially, reaching a point of crisis around 1986. Every year, we cancelled things, went back on agreements, disappointed colleagues and let people down. It was horrid, and it was not the way to run a company that was striving for a future. How can you have a vision, which we're all encouraged to do now, if you can't see that vision through to completion? The 1980s were difficult years and I think we went as close to the edge as we dared. I know that when all three of us left, we left a substantial financial deficit. But it's impossible to run an opera company in the UK without that.

RH: My observation at the time was that standards were never sacrificed, even against the hugest odds. This was particularly true when it came to the orchestra. You worked it into a fantastic ensemble.

ME: When the ENO first went to the London Coliseum it was a combination of two opera companies. It was originally called the Sadler's Wells Opera Company. Sadler's Wells is a theatre in North London, but the Sadler's Wells Opera was also a regular touring company. If you could find someone who played the horn, for example, and who was prepared to take on all the touring dates, they would get the job. 'Can you play the horn? Can you play loud, soft, high, low? Right, you're in Hartlepool tomorrow night.'

That was in the 1950s and the 1960s. When Sadler's Wells Opera moved permanently to the Coliseum at the end of the 1960s, it was originally called 'Sadler's Wells Opera at the London Coliseum'. It was a combination of both the touring company and the company based in North London. So you had two first oboes, for example, and inevitably a discussion arose as to who was going to play first oboe at the London Coliseum. The Musicians' Union was adamant that there were to be no redundancies. But there were too many people and somehow it had to be sorted out. Who would be the leader, for example? There was an uneasy truce when this happened. Gradually, they settled down and, gradually, everybody realised that the Coliseum would be their new home. But when I took over as Music Director at the beginning of the 1980s, I found that the orchestra was rather uneven and had no true identity.

It is probably a shocking thing to say, but the players were not expected to treat the London Coliseum as their main job. If they wanted to play a concert somewhere else, or if they had a chamber music engagement, they were given permission to be absent. Worse

PART ONE: BECOMING AND BEING A CONDUCTOR

still, the musicians were allowed to appoint *and pay* their own deputies! Even though deputy rates are stipulated by the union, deals were made and there were jobs for the boys. It was not uncommon to hear, 'Come and do *Traviata* for me tomorrow night and I'll give you £55.' The deputy probably should have been given £70. But work is work, even if it wasn't quite as much as the deputy was hoping for. I thought this was very unhealthy and I didn't believe that the orchestra could develop unless such practices changed. Inevitably, things were rather tricky between us to begin with.

For the really difficult operas, I made it clear that the orchestra must be the same for every rehearsal and for every performance. If you conduct in Germany, it's not always a given that the musicians at the rehearsals are the same as those at the performances. When I conducted a Verdi opera in Munich many years ago, I was allocated some rehearsals, as they hadn't played the work for a few years; I think I had three. At one of these, a young German trombone player came up to me and said, 'You know, I've really enjoyed these rehearsals. I'm so disappointed that I'm not doing any of the performances.' Somewhat stunned, I replied, 'What do you mean you're not doing the performances?' Unfazed, he continued, 'No, no, I'm just here as a super, as a substitute for my colleague who's not available. But he'll be good, he'll be very good. He's doing the performance.'

This is normal in Germany. While 'I'm sorry I'm not free for the performance' is a cliché, it happens all the time. I was determined that we shouldn't do this at the Coliseum. I made it clear that for five operas a year we should have a fixed orchestra. Pandemonium! There were meetings, frowns and much shaking of heads. There were cries of 'impossible' and 'you don't pay us enough to tie us down'. We had arguments and discussions but we did try to do what we could about the money. Some players were on Schedule D for taxation and some were on Schedule E. That's really difficult for an orchestra. If there are two violinists sharing a desk, and one of them is on Schedule D, which means that they take home much more money than the other at the end of the week, it becomes a contentious issue. If you're on Schedule E, and you know that the Schedule D people have wonderful expenses that they can claim back from tax, then it also becomes divisive. Peter Jonas changed the atmosphere in the orchestra by ensuring everyone was on Schedule D.

RH: In the 1980s and the 1990s, you also worked closely with the BBC Symphony Orchestra, the City of Birmingham Symphony Orchestra, the London Mozart Players and the Rochester Philharmonic Orchestra in the United States. As Music Director in Rochester, you were active educationally, and you remarked at the time, 'As a relative newcomer to Rochester, I've already been struck by the seriousness with which the educational programmes are considered by the RPO. Where are the audiences of the 21st century in the Rochester area if they are not at the moment in various stages of their schooling? Our job at the RPO is to continue to make concert-going as entertaining and as much fun as possible. With this is mind, surely we should plan new ways of exciting our audience! No one should ever feel that the complexities of serious music need be a barrier to its being richly enjoyed.'

ME: There's one word in that quote I don't remember at all. It sticks out so clearly: the word is 'entertaining'. To what extent is art that strives to open the human soul and to deal with issues of the human condition entitled, or allowed, to be entertaining?

I believe that to be entertained is a broad term. Those of us of a certain generation might think of MGM, and being entertained by

PART ONE: BECOMING AND BEING A CONDUCTOR

Bob Hope. But I think that entertainment is to lose yourself in something, to find a different part of yourself through the experience of sharing something. We can be entertained by a performance of *Hamlet*, for example. We can be lost in it, moved by it and have our lives changed by it. I think *that* can be referred to as being entertained. I don't think it has to be jokes and superficiality. That's what I meant when I used the word.

So where does music fit in? In the UK, and in English-speaking countries generally, the relationship between creativity and the audience's desire to enjoy art – not only music but also poetry and drama – isn't the same as in other countries. We didn't write *Die Zauberflöte* and we didn't write 104 wonderful symphonies. We have to work for it. If you're a young child in Cologne, it's natural that your parents, grandparents and godparents will take you to see and hear the great German repertoire. It's there for the taking and it's part of your education. But it is now – more than ever before – part of our lives in the UK, too.

With my orchestra in Manchester, the Hallé, the director of educational work is a member of the senior management team, Steve Pickett. He's a composer, a communicator and a wonderfully inventive and heroic personality. The work that he does in north-west England is sensationally good and he's following a tradition of educational work that the Hallé has done for decades. Orchestras shouldn't simply bus thousands of children into their concert halls so that they can say proudly in their annual report the number of children who came. It's a matter of actually engaging the children's creativity. You do this, in my experience, much more successfully by going to them and by using their space.

In Manchester, we do this in a variety of ways. We devise projects based on our programmes. We take a single work and, months before, go into several schools and get them involved in creative work where the children are told about the piece, what it means and what it's trying to express. They listen to it with open ears. The success of this naturally depends on the quality and the talent of the teachers, but that applies to any subject. They then come to our concert having done their own version of the work or having created something themselves. They also share it with other schools. This is one tiny example of how one can reach out and show that being in a symphony orchestra in the 21st century is being part of a community. It is not good enough to live in a temple removed from life and hope that people will come and be interested in what you're doing.

Not unrelated to this is the way in which an orchestra continues to dress: they still wear what audiences wore in the 19th century. When will someone invent clothes for performing musicians that will be smart, elegant and of our time? I haven't worn tails for years. It is all a question of the relationship between the players and their public. An orchestra lives and works in a particular community. It exists to give that community something it would otherwise be much poorer without. That's why Charles Hallé went to Manchester. Hallé was a fine pianist and a renowned teacher. But in the 1850s he found himself with no pupils because of the revolutions that had taken place all over Europe. He decided, therefore, to come to England. The squalor and poverty of mid-19th-century Manchester was well known, but he thought that he could effect social change by forming an orchestra. At that time, there were no orchestras in England except for one-off concerts. By establishing his ensemble in Manchester, Hallé formed the first professional, working symphony orchestra in Britain. It's wonderful that he is still remembered in its name and it is one of the few orchestras in the world named after its founder.

PART ONE: BECOMING AND BEING A CONDUCTOR

RH: During the first half of the 20th century it was common to hear statements such as 'I learned my music from Sir Henry Wood', and later on 'I learned my music from Sir John Barbirolli'. Do you hope that one day Mancunians will say, 'I learned my music from Sir Mark Elder'?

ME: Part of me wants to say, 'I should be really upset if they don't', while the other part of me wants to say, 'I would be thrilled if they do'. Education is a crucial element of being a successful conductor. That said, I don't set out to educate. If people feel that they've been educated by the experience of listening to a concert of mine, of listening to me talk a little bit about the music, of coming to rehearsals or by working with me, then that's great. If it stretches their curiosity, and if it enlarges their perception, knowledge and taste, that's fantastic.

However, while it's possible for a conductor to have a strong educational role, I think it's dangerous to set out to teach audiences what they don't know. It's important to inspire people. The word inspiration comes from the Latin *spirare*, 'to breathe': inspiration is a vital part of success. Some conductors are not good technicians, but they are great inspirers. In the long term, they are much more valuable. The opportunities for conductors to reach out and to change people's lives – not only to entertain them but to make a difference to them in a profound way – are incredible. While those opportunities for change depend on many things apart from the conductor, the energy for it must come from him or her.

RH: You became Music Director of the Hallé in 2000, when its future seemed doubtful. It was struggling both financially and musically. You remarked at the time that 'the string playing and the wind playing lack personality'. It's clearly full of personality now. How did you go about making that transformation?

ME: I said to the orchestra, 'What you're doing is lovely. It's fine. But it doesn't interest me. It doesn't engage me. You don't seem to be playing with heart.' As the orchestra's financial situation worsened, and as its relationship with my predecessor deteriorated, the Hallé lost its way. That was towards the end of the 1990s. The musicians were frightened that they wouldn't have a job and they were fearful that the city wouldn't come to their rescue.

The fact is that bankruptcy would have happened two weeks later. But the city of Manchester *did* step in and *did* ensure that the Hallé didn't disappear. It was important for the players, and for me, to believe in the city's support. If you are number 12 of 16 violinists, and it is rumoured that there will be redundancies, you are sure to be unsettled. In Manchester, every player believed that the orchestra was nearly bankrupt and that it was close to being disbanded. But the Hallé has such a remarkable relationship with music-lovers around the world that disbandment was unthinkable. When I go to different countries, I meet people who say, 'If it wasn't for the Hallé, I wouldn't like music. My grandmother used to send me Christmas presents. They were always LPs of Barbirolli conducting the Hallé and that was the first music I ever heard.'

Such feelings remain vivid and real today. Even at its lowest point, there was a feeling that the Hallé's demise mustn't happen. The orchestra touched the lives of people far beyond the city of Manchester and the north-west of England. That's a reflection of the enormous work that Sir John Barbirolli did during and after the Second World War. He brought music back into people's lives. I wanted to do that again. I said to the orchestra, 'If you want the public to believe in us, and to keep coming to hear us, even on wet Manchester nights, you've got to give them an experience that they're going to take away and will keep them going until the next time.' That wasn't happening, though

PART ONE: BECOMING AND BEING A CONDUCTOR

the Hallé has always had a core audience that has supported it through thick and thin. It is no exaggeration to say the Hallé audience is wonderful. They are knowledgeable, passionate and full of heart. They're a great, great crowd.

RH: I know from personal experience the affection that the Manchester public has for you. For them, it seems that the Hallé has only had two conductors: you and Sir John Barbirolli. Somehow they've collapsed the whole of Mancunian conducting history to J.B. and you. Do you think that has to do with dissemination? In 2003 the Hallé established its own record label, which I think has been fundamental to its recent success.

ME: For an orchestra to be able to record and listen to itself, and to be judged on a world stage of great ensembles, is an important part of its development. The label was not founded so that the orchestra could get huge cheques every month after selling thousands of copies. It wasn't about that, or about money-making at all. We needed to do this to stretch ourselves and to have a vision for our artistic future that would take us far beyond where we were then and now. And the way to do this was to have our own label. But since it involved the orchestra, and it would have an effect on every aspect of the players' lives together, I wanted the musicians to be involved in the decision-making process.

RH: The label has built on the orchestra's history and traditions. Other conductors would have shied away from recording Elgar with the Hallé, as he was a composer closely associated with Barbirolli. But you looked at this music afresh and built on his legacy.

ME: Barbirolli was a fantastic character and what he did for Manchester was amazing. But conducting is not just charisma; it's also hard work. He was a great supporter of the city and its musical life.

Not long after I started in Manchester, I was particularly encouraged when Evelyn Barbirolli said to me how pleased John would have been with what I was doing. That's all I wanted to hear. But it's important to not be backward-looking. It's important to think of a way that the public in Manchester, or wherever we happen to be playing, will be interested in the Hallé now. I would love to think that if Barbirolli came and did a concert with my orchestra he would change the sound just by how he stood on the podium. He would probably have the violins make a slightly silkier sound. His sound would reflect who he was simply by the way he conducted. Nevertheless, I am sure that he would want me to continue to renew the repertoire, to be my own man and not to copy. Emulation is one thing. Imitation, never.

PART TWO

THE ART AND CRAFT OF CONDUCTING

RH: Let's talk about the nuts and bolts of being a conductor. What, for you, are the defining characteristics of a successful conductor and, probably, by extension, a great conductor?

ME: The key word here is 'probably'. A successful conductor isn't necessarily the same as a great conductor. There are many conductors I would call great but who wouldn't necessarily have been perceived as successful. Conversely, there are a number of successful conductors who could hardly be considered 'great' in any definition of the word. What defines success and greatness would fill a book.

The most important thing for a conductor is that whatever the situation – whether you are studying by yourself, in discussion with colleagues or actually trying to get an orchestra or a choir to make music – the music is the most important thing in the room. Not you, not your ideas, not your ability to make gorgeous gestures that impress everybody. A friend of mine once said, 'Oh, I must do *La bohème* again sometime, I can make some really good gestures in that.' The only thing that matters is the music. You must learn it and inhabit it, so that it comes out through you. It should not sound like anybody else. It must sound like you and only you.

Even though the essence of conducting is hard to talk about, I wish it was discussed more. Not all conductors want to talk about it. Klaus Tennstedt was principal conductor of the London Philharmonic Orchestra in the 1980s. He was an East German who had suffered greatly before becoming famous. He didn't like talking about music at all and never wanted to engage in conversation about it. He was also a great conductor. Conversely, I think that it's really helpful – particularly when young conductors are starting out – to try and talk about our art. Discuss what you believe in and talk about how the music strikes you. Revel in the fact that you might all completely disagree with each other as to how a piece of music should go. But *listen*. Conductors have to be the best listeners on the planet. We have to be able to listen to what is being said to us either with words or with music, but primarily with music. While we must always put the music first, conductors require other qualities. One of them is courage. In order to succeed as a conductor you have to stand alone. The quality of how you study a score privately is directly related to your ability to stand alone in front of an orchestra. When you address the orchestra, you have to emanate, or *'ausstrahlen'*, as the Germans say. Funnily enough, we don't have a word for that in English. You have to have such strength in your *'Ausstrahlung'* that you convince the orchestra that you have a clear picture of what you want the music to sound like. Only then can you begin to discover whether or not you can improve, grow and take charge of performances that honour the music.

'Successful' is the other half of the question. To be offered opportunities at the highest levels, to be given posts of responsibility, to be seen to be making recordings and to be praised and condemned in

PART TWO: THE ART AND CRAFT OF CONDUCTING

equal measure: these are generally considered barometers of success. The greatest conductor of our lifetime was Carlos Kleiber. We all adored him and couldn't believe that it was possible to be a greater conductor. Yet he performed Beethoven's Seventh Symphony with the London Symphony Orchestra at the Royal Festival Hall in 1981, and the reviews were full of poisonous vitriol. We all found ourselves thinking, 'What, even Carlos Kleiber gets a bad review? This is not possible.' People will say both wonderful and discouraging things about you. You have to keep them in perspective. If you get a good review, enjoy it and don't be falsely modest about it. If someone has something of importance to say to you, take it to heart and think about it. If you find that you don't manage your rehearsals well, and you always seem to run out of time, think about it, meditate on it if you like, but don't try and fix it like a plumber.

If conductors are to grow professionally, they have to be in touch with their inner selves and, in particular, their solar plexus region. This is where grief, experiences and difficulties are held. That's why the basic position for conducting must have some relationship with this area. If a conductor speaks to themselves and thinks deeply, then they may find a path to discovery. If they are constantly thinking, 'I could make a great effect with this piece, it's got such a wonderfully loud ending and the orchestra and the audience always like it', they may achieve some success but will never be a great artist. And, surely, the aim of every conductor should be to become an artist. But that requires long thought and much discussion.

I often find that people are good practitioners. They may play the clarinet beautifully, for example, but they don't touch me or interest me by the way they play. An artist has to engage an audience. Being a true artist means being able to recreate a composition in a way that is true to the spirit of the original. Playing the notes, even with a beautiful tone, without expressing the inner meaning of the text, is hopeless. There will always be people whom you can't admire and can't understand why they have such success. But, when you find someone whom you do admire, do so for the right reasons. It's a wonderful thing to be able to admire people and to discover what it is about them that appeals to you.

Then there is the 'I' word: 'integrity'. Everyone talks about the importance of integrity, but what does it mean? For me, it means wholeness. If a conductor doesn't have integrity, in his attitude towards both his work and the composer, the orchestra will suffer. Integrity implies a sense of the whole, understanding a work in its completeness. If you've been asked to rehearse a symphony next week, for example, it's important to sense its totality. I believe that all music has a narrative and that it is imperative not only to discover how the movements relate to each other but, also, to explore the music's story.

Some works have stronger dramatic narratives than others. When I am about to perform Sibelius's First and Second Symphonies, I feel that I am about to go on a great journey. When I was young, the second concert my mother took me to included Sibelius's Second Symphony. That was at the Royal Festival Hall with a dreadful conductor. Even at the time, I remember looking at him and agreeing with my mother that he wasn't very good. But, as it was one of the first pieces I heard, it is part of my musical heritage.

Coming back to your terms: to be successful and to be great are not necessarily wedded together unless you make them so.

RH: You touched on a conductor's ethical and moral imperatives. How should these manifest themselves? In 1990, during the Gulf War, you expressed your reservations about conducting Elgar's 'Pomp and Circumstance' at the Last Night of the Proms, for example, and that

PART TWO: THE ART AND CRAFT OF CONDUCTING

caused a stir. But you were in good company. That great Bismarckian Hans von Bülow didn't stop to think that he shouldn't speak to audiences about critical, ethical, moral and political issues. Do you think this is part of a conductor's job?

ME: I don't think it is part of a conductor's job and, I must say, I'm not very fond of the word 'job'. When you leave the pit after conducting *Götterdämmerung* in the US, it is common to hear, 'Great job, Maestro'. It's thrown at me all the time.

Being a musician brings with it certain responsibilities. To want to be an artist in a community, country or city means that you have to be a voice for contemporary thought and of that community's *Zeitgeist*. This can manifest itself in many ways. Being a conductor means having the potential to influence the life and soul of an orchestra, not simply the content of its concerts. A conductor may make an impact on the cultural life of a city just as a theatre director or a film director may do so. A good example is the film *I, Daniel Blake*, directed by Ken Loach. While it's very moving, it also sharpens our responses to those who are disadvantaged and the impact of the state on their lives. In music conservatoires up and down the country, professors, whose time would be better spent teaching, now fill out endless forms, as Blake does in the film. It's both terrible and tragic.

An artist working for a community has a responsibility to be a voice for that community. That doesn't mean to say you have to go on marches or make speeches at Speakers' Corner. It doesn't necessarily mean you have to speak at all. It can be done through your work. One relevant example is Dmitri Shostakovich and how he coped with the circumstances in which he found himself. I admire him enormously as a man, quite apart from his qualities as a composer.

RH: Let's discuss programming. How do you go about unlocking the mysteries of new music for a concert-goer, while ensuring that established masterpieces retain their power?

ME: Speaking more generally, there's no doubt that some composers inhabited their own ivory towers after the Second World War. That drove them away from the wider musical public and the complexity of late 20th-century music made it hard for many music-lovers to find a way in. But that was also true for music from the 1920s and the 1930s. While audiences from those decades probably also flinched when confronted with new works, I am convinced that they made more of an effort to come to terms with what they considered new. But the tide is turning. There are many talented and gifted composers who write music that speaks directly to us. Not long ago, I conducted the world premiere of a symphony by Huw Watkins. Although it's a really attractive piece, I was sure that the audience in Manchester would be wary of it, so I programmed it side by side with the *Rob Roy* Overture of Berlioz. In the end, the symphony was both a critical and a popular success. I was delighted by that, because Watkins is a powerful composer whose music is approachable, even on first hearing. But if you want to do something fresh and new, and if you want to keep the audience's curiosity engaged, you need to do it compellingly. I've never found any difficulty in getting audiences to enjoy going back to the Baroque and Classical periods by performing those works differently. Quite the opposite. Audiences are passionately interested in, and receptive to, innovation, as it makes the music come alive.

Because of music's place as a *lingua franca* in the 17th and 18th centuries, and the way musicians responded to each other, very few instructions were annotated. Composers didn't need to indicate crescendos and diminuendos; they were obvious to the players. Unlike music from the 1930s and the 1940s, for example, composers weren't so prescriptive and it was probably as a result of that need for clarity of instruction that so many performances of Classical and Baroque music from that period were unbelievably dull. Everybody spoke of the 'divine Mozart' but there was really nothing there. The musicians simply played the notes, as little else was written down to guide them. It is possible to change that mentality but some of the hardest people to change are the players.

RH: When Arthur Nikisch took charge of both the Leipzig Gewandhaus Orchestra and the Berlin Philharmonic in 1895, his approach to programming reflected the cultural and political imperatives of each city. Leipzig was an important provincial centre, while Berlin was the capital of an empire. Parallels can be drawn here with Manchester and London. If the Hallé was a London-based orchestra, would your approach to programming be different?

ME: There are some works that I could programme in London that I couldn't programme in Manchester. If I did, the audience figures would suffer. If I do a strong Romantic/early 20th-century programme, and insert a piece by a living composer, we lose between 300 and 500 people along with the concomitant money. That's fine. You can do it and you should do it. But you need to know how you're going to make up the money that you've lost on that concert in one of the other programmes. That way, over the whole year, you are in control of the budget and are budgeting appropriately.

Even though the Manchester audience is traditionally conservative, we seem to be making headway with young people. The problem is that we can never quite tell when students from the Royal Northern College of Music and the university are going to come in force. But, when they do, it's an extra 400 people. I remember a performance of Mahler's Fifth Symphony that was like a rock concert at the end of the evening. When I had the principal trumpet stand, the audience went wild. It was not only important for me but also for the older generation of concert-goers, as they were able to feel a new sense of excitement at their concerts. And it was clear that the excitement was not a transitory thing.

It is obvious to me that Mancunian audiences want this great art form to go on and to be heard in perpetuity. They want to feel that younger people actually enjoy what we do. Young people come for *Le sacre du printemps* and, when I conducted Wagner's *Das Rheingold*, the Bridgewater Hall was full. That rarely happens. In my experience, most modern halls are between 300 and 400 hundred seats too large. The deSingel hall in Antwerp seats 2,000. The Bridgewater Hall is well over that and is about the same size as the Royal Opera House or the Coliseum; somewhere between 2,200 and 2,300 seats. We would have a much better time of it if they had designed it for 1,800 and got people fighting for tickets.

RH: I attended that *Rheingold* and was impressed not only by the contingent of young people in the audience but also by the number of young players in the orchestra. The ability to programme *Rheingold* in that way, the response of the players and the reaction of the audience made it a remarkable evening. It is evident that the Manchester public is deeply proud of its pantheon of great conductors. Hans Richter, Sir Hamilton Harty, Sir John Barbirolli and now you have left deep impressions on the city's civic and cultural identities. So much so that when the Free Trade Hall was converted into a five-star hotel, its major public rooms were named after you all. Would the nature of your relationship with Manchester, its people and its orchestra be possible in London or New York?

PART TWO: THE ART AND CRAFT OF CONDUCTING

ME: A London equivalent is possible but it has to do with how much a conductor wants to work at it and how much money the orchestra's management is willing to spend on developing it. Concerts cost money! The only reason why we can complete the *Ring* in Manchester is because one benefactor has given us so much towards our artistic enterprise that we can afford to do it. If somebody was prepared to underwrite it, the same would be possible in London. Even though the business of developing relationships can be challenging, we achieved it at the Coliseum.

RH: When I first came to London from Australia, I was young and you gave me a great deal of time. Even though you were about to take over from Sir Charles Groves, which can't have been an easy period, you always made time for younger musicians. Looking back over your years in St Martin's Lane, I am struck by the company's *esprit de corps* and the ways in which the ENO was shaped in your artistic image. There was a similar *esprit de corps* evident in the London Philharmonic Orchestra around the same time, and it was fostered by Klaus Tennstedt, whom you mentioned earlier. With a much smaller repertoire than you, he still engendered great intensity.

ME: It was due to the quality of what Tennstedt produced with the orchestra and the way in which the players responded to his high standards. They adored him. While it is possible to do that now in London, you need to be able to talk openly about such relationships and to make the public aware of them. The present Music Director of the LPO is Vladimir Jurowski, whom I know well. I admire enormously some of the astonishing risks he has taken with his programming through his themed concert series. Sometimes they work, sometimes they don't. But at least he's trying. As the sheer number of musical events available to the public in London on any one evening is the biggest problem that that city's orchestras face, it's difficult for all of them to retain high profiles. Fundamentally, it depends on the personality of the conductor and how that personality manifests itself to the audience at its concerts. London orchestras also require a world-class concert hall, which they do not have at present. But does it have to cost £278 million?

RH: There has always been a kind of mindset in the UK that struggles with the idea of investing both financially and emotionally in the physical infrastructure of music-making. During the Second World War, the Queen's Hall was bombed and razed to the ground one night in May 1941. It had been a cultural landmark for almost half a century, and the first home of the modern Promenade Concerts. Even though audiences and performers were devastated by the hall's loss, no attempt was made to rebuild it at the end of the war. Whereas, when the Staatsoper in Vienna was reopened in 1955, the city shared in a collective sense of pride.

ME: This is a peculiarly British problem. Unlike in Germany, Austria and Italy, nobody has come to the realisation that live performance in the creative arts is something for everybody. If a German opera house wanted to stage a modern opera in the 1960s and the 1970s, but knew that it would be lucky to get a 40 per cent house, the government would subsidise it, say, with a 20 per cent grant. Governments there understood that it was part of their job to foster new work. Consequently, German opera houses felt that they were allowed to programme new operas with the assurance that they would not be penalised financially. While I am not sure precisely how much governments there gave, I know that they provided enormous amounts of money to foster new work. That's something that we simply don't do. That said, the Royal Opera is now reducing its prices for unusual and new works to encourage people to attend. The results are phenomenal and their approach is important. Musical patronage in the UK has been done in other ways and has never come from the top.

RH: One of the thorniest questions facing a conductor is whether or not to conduct from memory. Felix Weingartner was hauled over the coals at the Leipzig Conservatoire when he conducted without a score at his final examination. His professors considered it too 'Bülow-ish', as Hans von Bülow, who conducted a great deal from memory, was thought to be too radical a model and not one to be imitated by those aspiring to be a true German Kapellmeister. Bruno Walter was another conductor associated with Leipzig, and he argued that conducting from memory gave him a greater sense of freedom. Do you feel strongly about the practice?

ME: The short answer is 'no'. While it doesn't often happen because of the amount of repertoire that I have to study, I still do it a bit. There are certain pieces that I've always done from memory, such as Debussy's *La mer*, Elgar's 'Enigma' Variations, Sibelius's First Symphony, Dvořák's last five symphonies and some Verdi operas. It's to do with the way I prepare them. A few conductors have a natural ability to memorise the page. Then there are others who simply think it looks good to perform without the score.

Young conductors should feel under no obligation to perform from memory or to feel that they are less successful if they don't. If they *can* do it from memory, the advantage is that they have limitless and constant communication with the players. But if you don't know how to use that contact, there's no point in not having the score there.

I am reminded of that wonderful Klemperer story. 'Dr Klemperer, there's this marvellous new German conductor,' he was told by someone in the Philharmonia. 'He's just come out of college and we're inviting him to perform with the orchestra. He comes from Berlin and we understand that he conducts everything from memory.' To which Klemperer replied, 'I can *read* music.' You know, he *really* valued reading music and I value it all the time. But I also approve of Hans von Bülow's comment to the young Richard Strauss: 'You must have the score in your head, not your head in the score.' That doesn't mean to say you shouldn't have a score; I often use one to remind myself of one or two bars over the course of a page, it's part of the mechanics of conducting. If I realise that I've conducted a run-through and I don't need it, or I won't need it, that's fine. I can then focus completely on the players.

It is true, however, that if a conductor rehearses with the score, and then performs without it, it heightens the tension for the players. They will think, 'He's going to do it from memory. We've really got to concentrate, watch and make sure we're all together.' Whether or not that's a good tension depends on the orchestra and the conductor. Conductors should get to know a score really well and then decide. In many pieces, I stick lots of pages together with paper clips. If I need the first four pages, but then don't need the score for the whole of the development, for example, I might do 28 pages with one page turn.

Carlos Kleiber knew about this. When he conducted *Der Rosenkavalier* for the Royal Opera, he performed it all from memory until Act 3, where there's a passage that is extremely fast and easy for the orchestra and the singers to go wrong. It's *very* fast indeed! Instead of worrying about it, he just turned pages furiously. That was his way of saying, 'I don't know where I am, please get it right without me.' He was extremely 'psychological' in that way.

PART TWO: THE ART AND CRAFT OF CONDUCTING

RH: How does a conductor develop the skill of carrying a large work such as *Der Rosenkavalier* in the memory?

ME: It comes down to experience. If you coach the singers from the piano, assist the main conductor, conduct the off-stage bands and attend all the rehearsals and performances, you will learn the opera along with everybody else. The first opera that I conducted professionally was *Rigoletto*. I did 32 performances in 6 months and, by the time I'd done 10, not only did I know it, but I was also pleased that I knew something that well. As a result, I could then do it from memory. Perhaps I could have done it from memory the first time I did it, but there were so many things to think and worry about. So, it is possible but it takes time. Lorin Maazel conducted everything from memory. He had a photographic memory but that didn't mean his performances were better or worse because of it. He simply had a talent for memory.

One important early experience for me was to be a prompter. When I joined the music staff of the Royal Opera in 1970, every line of every opera was prompted. Hardly anyone wanted to prompt, but I found the idea of getting to know an opera by prompting enormously exciting. As it happens I prompted *Der Rosenkavalier*, an opera that I didn't know at the time. I was so terrified of misleading the singers that I really got to know it. As a prompter, you are in a position of trust with the singers on stage. It is easy to send the wrong cue at the wrong time, and they will respond accordingly. And prompting in German is different from prompting in Italian. A lot of Italian singers were not, and are not, terribly good musicians. If you cue them early, they will come in early. I remember one stupid tenor who sang an entire *cabaletta* in a Rossini opera a whole beat early, as he had misunderstood me. It was *so* embarrassing. Even though prompting has largely stopped today because directors don't want a prompt box to inhibit the performance space on the main stage, it is another way of learning a score from memory.

RH: *Der Rosenkavalier* is a notoriously difficult opera to pace. Sir Georg Solti went to see Strauss at his villa in Garmisch in 1949 and asked the composer, 'What are the tempi of *Der Rosenkavalier*?' Strauss replied, 'Just speak it exactly as Hofmannsthal wrote it and that will work.' There is a film of Strauss conducting the end of Act 2 at the Prinzregententheater a few weeks before his death in 1949, and he does just that.

ME: While Strauss's suggestion is largely true, it is not necessarily applicable to all operas. But it is certainly true of German operas where you have to conduct the text. For those, I just listen to the words. As I have to learn what the singers do, and not what I *hope* they will do, I listen to how they deliver the words. If you're teaching someone a part from scratch, you can make them do it as you want it. But you can't completely re-coach singers. When they come for two or three days of rehearsal in Manchester, I take what they give me. The way they pronounce the words is the way they're going to do it, as it is part of their muscle memory. Understanding that is a vital aspect of learning how to conduct singers.

RH: Let's discuss conducting technique. Have you developed and refined it over the years or did you establish it at the beginning of your career?

ME: My technique is constantly developing and changing. It is not something that I can talk about easily, as I don't quite know what I do.

PART TWO: THE ART AND CRAFT OF CONDUCTING

Nevertheless, technique *is* important. Effectively, it is the ability to make the best gesture to achieve the sound that you have envisaged. That is a completely different matter from what the trumpet section of an orchestra might think of as good conducting technique.

The further you are away from the beat, the more reassurance you want from the conductor. Players want to look up and see that you are giving them a beat in three or four. They want to feel comfortable and to be left in no doubt as to where they are in the bar. In my experience, orchestral musicians fail to appreciate the art of conducting, as so few of them are able to see beyond their own requirements. In contrast to the craft of conducting, the *art* of conducting is more intuitive, suggestive, malleable and inspirational. I can be clear when I decide that the musicians need clarity. And, by clear, I mean demonstrably and painstakingly clear, such as when I conducted *Das Rheingold* in Manchester. The first scene is completely in 6/8. After seven and a half minutes, there's a bar of 9/8 before going back to 6/8. I knew that the players wanted some reassurance at that point: I could see it in their eyes. I noticed during the first rehearsal that many of them were looking up to see whether or not I would conduct the 9/8 bar clearly. I knew that by doing so, I would give them the absolute confidence of knowing exactly where they were. If you have 53 bars rest in 6/8 and then, suddenly, there's a bar of three, that's a sort of milestone. I just did one, two, three and we all knew where we were. But, in the heat of the performance, there's no point doing it with dramatic gestures. That's more autistic than artistic.

RH: Tell me about the baton. It's a tool that everyone associates with the conductor. Yet, when Wolfgang Sawallisch and Herbert von Karajan conducted some choral works, they abandoned it in favour of bare hands. What are your thoughts on the use and non-use of a baton?

ME: It's not to do with the genre. I would never conduct Verdi's Requiem without a baton. It's to do with the type of sound that is required and the physical experience needed in achieving that sound. Determining the style and sound-world required for a particular piece is one of the greatest challenges – and pleasures – of being a conductor. It is not simply highfalutin' 'inspiration'. Many different factors come into play, and I often make decisions as I rehearse. At the Royal Albert Hall for the Proms, I did *Parsifal* without a baton but, at the Bridgewater Hall, *Rheingold* needed a stick.

RH: You often use the media as an educational tool and are adept at talking to camera. Is this a skill that young conductors should be honing in a multimedia world?

ME: Absolutely. Capital letters 'YES'. Every conductor should learn how to talk to their audience. But a little goes an enormously long way. Before you've communicated anything musically, the fact that you have turned and addressed the audience, and are happy to have made a connection with them, is already profound. It is appreciated and, if there are people who scoff at it, that's their problem.

In my early years of working with the Hallé, some of the music critics were against me talking to the audience. They felt that I was trying to teach them something that I thought they didn't know. The defensiveness was remarkable. I just kept going and gradually they stopped mentioning it. Eventually, the positive feedback was overwhelming. In talking to the audience, we can teach them how to listen and how to come to terms with unfamiliar pieces of music. The time I spent with the Rochester Philharmonic in the US was a valuable experience for me in this regard. After one concert – probably at the obligatory post-concert reception – a woman said to me, 'Maestro, it was really nice that you told us when that tune enters in the last movement. That it comes first of all on the flute and then it is played later by the oboe. That was so helpful. I was so grateful that you said that, as it all sounds the same to us.' The difference between a flute and an oboe is second nature to musicians. We don't even think it's remarkable that we know the difference. But the general public is often quite deaf and doesn't necessarily hear with expert ears.

RH: You're known for exploring different sound-worlds according to different composers. How do you focus on a particular sound-world and what are your criteria for that decision?

ME: When exploring the sound-world of a particular piece, there are specific questions one should ask. When was the work written? What were orchestras doing at the time? What do we know about the musical life of the period? How many players did the composer expect to hear playing his piece? Was that what he wanted or simply what he got? I am passionate about exploring original circumstances. With such an exploration comes a feeling that there is a sound that is both appropriate and contemporary. It won't be the same as what they had in 1740 or 1840, but that doesn't matter. And I'm not saying that it *is* the same. I am trying to reach back through whatever means I can to make a sound that I think makes the music seem most beautiful.

The starting point should be the recognition that there's more than one form of beauty. Herbert von Karajan thought the opposite. When he invited a friend of mine to conduct *Figaro* at Salzburg, my friend said, 'I'm interested in developing my knowledge and experience of Classical style.' Karajan replied, 'What do you mean by "Classical style"? This is Salzburg and we only have two styles: Mozart and Brahms. That's it. Good day.' Karajan put the phone down on him. But we should all be interested in this. The ability to turn your hand to different styles is now a requirement for every conductor.

The original-instrument movement, for want of a better title, has not only changed us all but has also changed what we expect of an orchestra. When I gave my first concerts with the Hallé some 17 years ago, we performed a Haydn symphony followed by a Mozart violin concerto. After the interval, we then gave Rachmaninov's Third Symphony. I remember thinking at the time: 'Will we be able to do this? Can I get them to play the Classical music differently from the Rachmaninov?' The same would be true if we were to perform works by Stravinsky and Rachmaninov. Stravinsky has quite a specific style and so does Rachmaninov. Stravinsky is as different from Rachmaninov as Haydn is from Rachmaninov. Haydn needs not so much a dry sound as a crackling attack, a sound with humour and liveliness. Haydn is wonderful for a symphony orchestra to tackle. The problem is that only half the orchestra gets to play it.

It would be so great to perform a Haydn symphony at the beginning with one half of the orchestra – and then the other half comes on to play another Haydn symphony straight after the interval. That would be really marvellous. We ought to do that, as the orchestra loves it when we reduce. They have a member of each string section who's responsible for organising whose turn it is to go home early. There's always a bit of discussion that I have nothing to do with. It would be wonderful to say, 'We're all going to do either of these pieces.' But the point is that I've gotten my orchestra to associate a certain attitude with a certain sound when performing Classical music. We don't talk about it now. If someone is new to the orchestra, has just joined as an extra, or simply doesn't realise what I'm after, he might start playing Haydn like Rachmaninov. If no one is playing with vibrato, and this chap is suddenly vibrating furiously, it looks like he is waving to his

PART TWO: THE ART AND CRAFT OF CONDUCTING

wife in the audience! I remember saying recently, 'You're still vibrating. Try it without. It's good!' Sometimes, people can't stop vibrating. They have practised vibrating all their life and then they are suddenly expected not to. Nowadays, it's possible to study two different styles in a conservatoire. There are now Baroque lessons but this was almost unheard of 20 years ago.

RH: When you're working with period-instrument ensembles such as the Orchestra of the Age of Enlightenment, how often does the sound-world that you are trying to cultivate come into conflict with the players' instincts?

ME: Given the kind of repertoire that I've performed with the OAE over the last 25 years, the short answer to your question is 'all the time'. While it started life as a Baroque ensemble before becoming a Classical orchestra, the OAE has gone on to perform late 19th-century music with me. It's inspiring to hear how they bring their Classical and Baroque playing into Mendelssohn, Berlioz, Donizetti and Verdi. Nevertheless, I have felt in the past that many of the players were resistant to my approach. Even though some of them are my friends and contemporaries, they would ask: 'Are you *really* sure you like conducting us with our sound?' As I am much more of a conductor than many of the musicians with whom they work, I would say, 'Absolutely! But I'm trying to see how your sound can be placed into this particular piece.' Sir Simon Rattle has also done a lot of work with them, but many of the people they perform with are not really conductors. As the group is often led from the keyboard or the violin, the sort of physicality that I demanded of them often seemed overwhelming. I wanted the music to be physically alive and precise. At first, they didn't notice I was there and just tried to play with each other, as that's what they tend to do. I would have to say, 'Could we just do it once more with *me* now?' Consequently, there was a lot of tension and I think that it's probably still there in certain cases. It's sort of endemic.

RH: When you conducted Verdi's *Falstaff* with the OAE at Glyndebourne in 2013, it was quite clear that you were moving them forward towards the turn of the 19th and 20th centuries. I assume that French bassoons and piston-valve, French-made F horns wouldn't be their natural hunting grounds. I assume equally that these instruments presented a challenge at times.

ME: Even though such instruments were a challenge, I would often say: 'This needs to sound a bit fatter. Not so lifted. It needs to sit a bit more.' They would try it again and I would then say, 'Much more like that. That's great.' But it wasn't the fatness that the London Philharmonic Orchestra would have given me. When you're performing an opera with the LPO, the players are always conscious of the words. The characters on stage demand the music to be played in a particular way and the only reason to perform opera is to find out how music can express psychology and character. How an orchestra breathes with the music is also essential, as a singer can't do a second phrase until they've taken a breath at the end of the first. Working with the OAE in that context was a very interesting experience.

RH: We touched earlier on your work in Rochester. Could you tell me more about your experience with US orchestras?

ME: As the American system is so inflexible, there is an overwhelming expectancy of competence. When I had an American orchestra,

PART TWO: THE ART AND CRAFT OF CONDUCTING

the union representative – he was one of the horn players – said to me: 'Mark, if we can't do it in four rehearsals, we shouldn't be doing it.' That's absolute nonsense. To get a good result from an orchestra, you need to plan the concert's rehearsal schedule according to the repertoire. For many programmes he's right, and four rehearsals might well be adequate for an adequate performance. But if you want to do something special, you have to be able to do different things with the time available. You can't do that in the US and God knows I've tried. Neither with opera houses nor with symphony orchestras. As they have a way of doing things, you're expected to play along. And it is necessary to conform to this approach because they are a machine producing a product for a public, a product that is regularly given with enjoyment and, often, with great quality. But conductors should not expect an American orchestra to sound like one from Europe. What a conductor should do is to indicate to the players how to change what they're doing in order to make a different effect. This can be done in little ways. For example: 'Horns, could you make the staccatos not so dry? Make it longer.' But sing the effect you want to the players so that it is clear. Any good American orchestra will oblige. Say to the strings, 'The sound should have a more concentrated vibrato; not so fast but narrower.' The sound should change instantly. But why would a conductor want to make them sound like a European orchestra? Why on earth would I want to make my Manchester orchestra sound like the New York Philharmonic when I'm conducting Charles Ives? I don't. I want the music to sing with these players in the way that *they* sing. As I said earlier, it's possible to have different forms of beauty. One of the interesting things about being a conductor, and conducting different orchestras, is how to make the soul of the music ring out with that particular ensemble. Let them be who they are.

RH: A tangible realisation of your argument was the way in which Wolfgang Sawallisch seated the Philadelphia Orchestra during his tenure as Music Director. He chose to go along with the classic American-English disposition with the cellos on his right and all the violins on his left. As a German conductor, this would not have been his usual seating pattern. Would you modify your approach in this manner?

ME: I change the seating of an orchestra if they let me. In Manchester, I have the seconds on the right; the way Mahler, Elgar and Sibelius knew it. When balancing a symphony orchestra, divided violins are absolutely basic to my concept of sound and it does so many things so much more easily. I love having the cellos inside playing out into the audience. I hate them on the side; I really don't like it. If I have to have all the violins on the left, such as in Washington, where they won't let me change it, I'll have the cellos inside and the violas on the outside. While I can get used to that, I really don't like hearing all the violins playing together. Stokowski was keen on having the violins grouped together, but I believe that was an act of necessity.

RH: In fact, necessity was the basis of the Stokowski sound per se. Much is made of the 'Philadelphia Sound', a sound that developed and adapted with each new music director. Stokowski's preference for free bowing and free wind phrasing is actually a product of his youth. He seems to have replicated Henry Wood's approach and seated the orchestra, at least initially, as Wood did. That pattern changed much later when he placed all the winds, brass and timpani to his right and the strings to his left and front; a seating pattern common in Dresden before 1846. Wood also put the harps on the apron of the stage, as Elgar did, and conducted piano concertos from the audience side of the piano.

PART TWO: THE ART AND CRAFT OF CONDUCTING

ME: And Barbirolli?

RH: Sir John Barbirolli, Sir Malcolm Sargent, Constant Lambert, Basil Cameron and even Richard Strauss, when he performed his *Burleske* at the Royal Albert Hall in 1947 with Alfred Blumen, all conducted over the top of the piano.

ME: Why would anyone want to do that?

RH: It seems that nearly all British conductors did it apart from Sir Adrian Boult, who appears to have been the only one to object to this method.

ME: But surely the conductor just hears the piano.

RH: There's a film from 1943 called *Battle for Music* which the LPO made after Sir Thomas Beecham dumped them when war broke out. In the movie, Eileen Joyce and Benno Moiseiwitsch perform excerpts from Grieg's Piano Concerto and Rachmaninov's Second Piano Concerto with Basil Cameron and Constant Lambert, both of whom conduct over the top of the piano.

ME: But when you say over the top, how can the orchestra see the conductor?

RH: They had exceedingly high platforms. Barbirolli did this even at the end of his life with Arthur Rubinstein in Houston and Julius Katchen in Manchester. This, along with Stokowski's free bowing and free wind phrasing, was in line with what Sir Henry Wood did. For Wood, however, these techniques were a necessity brought about by a lack of rehearsal time. When the French conductor Charles Lamoureux brought his orchestra to the Queen's Hall in the 1890s, Wood was impressed by their regimented bowing, fingering and phrasing, but he was unable to implement the approach of Lamoureux because of a paucity of preparation time.

It seems to me that musicians' childhood memories and experiences contribute significantly to the sound-worlds they establish. I am convinced that what Stokowski did was a direct result of what he had heard with Sir Henry Wood. Wood, like Stokowski, was something of a musical iconoclast and used French-made F horns and French bassoons in his Queen's Hall Orchestra as a direct result of his adoption of Continental pitch in 1895. When Beecham founded the LPO, he, too, changed the sound of the orchestra in Britain by using German bassoons and German horns. When that orchestra was launched in 1932, Beecham was filmed conducting a passage from Tchaikovsky's Third Symphony in the Queen's Hall using one French F horn and three German horns, and one French bassoon and one German bassoon. Eventually, those sections were unified by adopting German instruments throughout. It's fascinating how these sound-worlds changed and it is interesting how few conductors talked about emerging sonic environments. Even Strauss, who worked as a conductor throughout Europe and North America, doesn't talk about the sound of the orchestra. It doesn't seem to have occurred to him.

ME: You mean it doesn't occur to them that it might change?

RH: Conductors of that era seem to have adapted to whatever sounds the orchestra was making. They accepted that if they went to Russia, the horns vibrated in a characteristic manner and that French orchestras used the more nasal-sounding, small-bore French bassoon and the somewhat saxophonic, piston-valve F horn.

ME: If I were to conduct in Russia, I would want to hear the vibrato in the brass.

RH: Sadly, that sound has largely disappeared. With the fall of communism, everyone looked west and orchestras wanted to sound like the Chicago Symphony Orchestra. This meant that lucrative film scores could now be made with cheaper orchestras such as those in Prague. Even Sir Charles Mackerras said to me, 'I'm pleased it's gone'. By which he meant the characteristic sound of the Czech Philharmonic. I must admit that I was a bit shocked. The sounds that Tchaikovsky and Shostakovich would have heard are now gone. Isn't that a little sad?

ME: Whereas the general English orchestral style is not so interesting. It doesn't have so much personality. I often say to the Hallé – they know I do it just to goad them – 'It sounds so English!' when we're rehearsing Shostakovich or Tchaikovsky. Then they know that they've really got to put their feelings on the line. Shostakovich and Tchaikovsky are pointless unless everyone has the same attitude towards the sound. But when everybody does sustain the loud angry melodies, and plays with incredible rhythmic passion, the sound of the orchestra changes.

RH: Do you think there is such a thing as rehearsal technique? And when discussing instrumental technique with the players, how far do you go when instructing them as to what he or she should, or shouldn't, do? You have mentioned string vibrato but what is your approach, say, to oboe vibrato?

ME: It all depends on how vivid is the desired sound in my inner ear. If someone is playing really beautifully, but in a slightly different way from what I had hoped to hear, then I have a choice: to allow the player to sing it the way they're singing it, or to say that I want a different, specific tonal character. In the case of the oboe, I might want it bleak, cool and objective rather than warm and passionate. If it's a piece that the players don't know, they need you to guide them and to orientate them on the musical map. Let me give you an example. While Mahler often asks all three oboes to play *grell* ('harshly') in the Third Symphony, they never do. It's possible to achieve this effect but, unless the oboists are already aware of it, and are proud of the fact that they know what to do, it can be hard to address the problem in front of the orchestra. The player needs to put the reed further into his or her mouth to get the *grell* sound. By so doing, they have much less control and produce a more elemental sonority. It sounds like a medieval shawm and is not in the least bit elegant. But that's what Mahler meant: he wanted distortion and conductors must address that. But I would go much further. When the bassoonist has a problem – sometimes they haven't realised that I was a bassoonist – I always say with a smile, 'I'm on your side. Try this'.

A good understanding of string technique is vital, as there are important choices to be made when dealing with the strings. Everyone respects the fact that a good conductor makes these choices and will come having prepared them. If a string section plays something, and everyone is doing different things, they're waiting for you to make a choice. If you don't make the choice, you have failed. That is something a conductor must do immediately.

PART TWO: THE ART AND CRAFT OF CONDUCTING

Getting involved in the way musicians play is part of the fun of being a conductor. I always assumed it was what all conductors did. Then I found that there are two sorts of conductor: those who enjoy conducting and those who engage with an orchestra. I have always wanted to engage. But there are conductors who come to the Hallé and say, 'You sound absolutely marvellous! Just do that tempo change for me. I'll see you tomorrow.' The Hallé doesn't like that and they'll say, 'Now, wait a minute, why are you conducting this? You haven't told us. Why have you chosen this music? We don't know why it's so important for you. Show us. Then we'll do it especially for you. We don't want to do it like we played it for the bloody Music Director last year. We want to do it for you!'

It's important not to underestimate this. It's the way to an orchestra's heart if you appreciate the fact that they play something because they know you want it to be a particular way and that you love them for it. Understanding this can be the beginning of something special.

RH: How do you tackle the issue of intonation?

ME: Intonation problems must be addressed, but *not* the first time the orchestra plays something. If, for example, you repeat a passage because the horns and the woodwinds aren't agreeing, and it's still not right on the second attempt, you can show in your face that it's not quite correct. If the musicians can fix it themselves, they will. But, when you're facing an orchestra for the first time, it's always good to make sure that you can show them the quality of your ear at once.

Perhaps even more essential is the conductor's ability to communicate with both eyes and ears. An orchestra will sense immediately whether or not you can hear. You might need to say, 'The second horn is flat at the bottom of that chord. Can we just check its tuning?' Even after 17 years, I still need to do that with the Hallé. It helps them to apply themselves, knowing that I can hear. More importantly, it helps them to improve the performance because it makes them listen.

RH: Do you think your practical experience as a bassoonist helped to sharpen your sense of intonation compared with someone whose principal instrument involved a keyboard? There seems to be a clear difference between aspiring conductors whose early training is on an orchestral instrument rather than a keyboard when responding to intonation and rhythm.

ME: It's harder for a keyboard player to become an effective conductor easily and the way he or she conducts will quickly reveal their understanding of different instruments. If they have a knowledge of stringed instruments, it will affect their gestures. String players require particular gestures depending on the type of attack and sound that the music needs. Showing them when to play 'lumpily', and not with a lovely long line, is crucial. If you want a chord that has no strong front to it, and you want it to come in late, you make a gesture that *shows* that you want it late. But, if you want it absolutely precise, you must make that clear through a different gesture. I'll never forget watching Sir Georg Solti start Bartók's Concerto for Orchestra with the Chicago Symphony Orchestra at the Proms in 1981. Solti was something of a maniac as a conductor. One of the reasons why he was so maniacal – and as a young man I worked with him and had the opportunity of watching him at close quarters – was that he was terrified that his own rhythm was not good enough to keep the orchestra together. So, he used to conduct in an overtly hyper-rhythmic way which, of course, destroyed the rhythm.

PART TWO: THE ART AND CRAFT OF CONDUCTING

Orchestras don't need too much conducting. They need to be allowed to play with each other and he was always getting in the way. Nevertheless, the Chicago Symphony Orchestra was a wonderful ensemble that he had made into a particular instrument. It was hard-edged because he was always so tense himself. He conducted the first note of Bartók's Concerto for Orchestra as if he was going to conduct the first 'Pomp and Circumstance' March. It was an enormous upbeat. I felt so embarrassed. But, I suppose, they must have been so used to it by the time they came to London for that performance at the Proms.

RH: When one looks back over Solti's relationships with both the Chicago Symphony and the London Philharmonic Orchestras, there seems to be something of a schism. In the autobiography that Solti collaborated on with Harvey Sachs, he noticeably minimises his period with the London Philharmonic Orchestra. The LPO found it difficult to work with him; they felt that he wanted them to sound like an American orchestra. In complete contrast, all the singers with whom he worked absolutely adored him.

I remember seeing Solti conduct the Concerto for Orchestra with the LPO. It was at the Royal Festival Hall in the late 1970s in a programme that also included *Bluebeard's Castle*. At the beginning of the Concerto, he twitched at the wrists on the second beat and the double basses inadvertently twitched back. It was peculiar. In 1985 he conducted Beethoven's Fifth Symphony with the BBC Symphony Orchestra at the Royal Albert Hall for a charity concert, and one of the trumpet players told me that his colleagues only played after they heard Solti's cufflinks click.

Speaking of pacing, how do *you* pace a rehearsal? I once took a group of postgraduate conducting students from the Royal Academy of Music to the Royal Festival Hall to observe you rehearsing Berlioz with the Orchestra of the Age of Enlightenment. You literally took the rehearsal to the last minute. The students kept asking, 'Will he finish in time?' You paced it marvellously and you got to the end with ten seconds to spare. How did you learn that skill?

ME: 'Experience' is the answer. When working in the opera house, conductors are regularly faced with acts of operas that are more than an hour long. Rehearsing huge structures in the allocated time of three hours is taxing and this is particularly true of German operas. Conductors need to take the long view. Whether it's a symphony or an opera, you must know how long you've got to the end, where you are up to ten minutes before the end, and be aware of how long the remaining material will take in rehearsal.

With those priorities in mind, timings are invaluable. Even so, it is a difficult subject to talk about. These days, I plan my rehearsals meticulously, as that's the only way to get the best results. But it wasn't always like that. Twenty or thirty years ago, I often ran out of time. I felt terrible about it. Not that I hadn't done good work but the players need to have the certainty of the last rehearsal at the concert. You need to get to the end. If you don't, players must understand that you don't need the remaining time.

With the Hallé, there are certain pieces that I've done many times, both at the Bridgewater Hall and elsewhere. For these, I just rehearse the bits that I know we need. If there are one or two players who've never performed the work in question, and they're looking a bit green and shaky, I don't worry. While they'll look at it and be nervous, they'll get through it. I'll certainly help them if I know where they are seated. But it's important to think about the highs and lows of a rehearsal and to consider it from a player's point of view.

PART TWO: THE ART AND CRAFT OF CONDUCTING

I am conscious of the psychology of working with an orchestra: the first rehearsal is quite different from the last. It is always good to tell a joke when everyone is dying for a cup of tea and looking at their watches. It is important to change the energy by being humorous, being humane or by admitting that you've made a mistake; anything to break the regularity of the rehearsal.

Try not to use more words than you need. This is hard for us all and particularly hard for young conductors. They will often use ten words when six will suffice. Actively limit the number of words that you use and try not to use whole sentences with an orchestra. It's good if you just say 'Still out of tune. Again,' or 'Horns, the C sharp. Longer.' Don't be too explicit. It should be as if you are saying it in Morse code. In other words, it should act as a form of verbal semaphore that the players can decipher easily. If it's not too specific, they'll have to think and you'll force them to ask: 'Which C sharp? We've got so many. I think he means this one? Let's have a look.' They will then play some C sharps and look at me to see that I'm satisfied.

I remember Sir Charles Mackerras saying to the orchestra of the English National Orchestra, 'First violins! You know that bit after Letter B, you know it sort of ... you know it sort of goes up, you know it ... it doesn't ... it could be. Oh, play it again!' And it was much better. Everybody was thinking, 'What the hell does he mean?'

I always encourage young conductors to watch me, to see if I manage the rehearsal well and to see whether or not I've misjudged something. That way, we can learn so much from each other. They should question why I don't spend more time on a passage if it still doesn't sound good. Then, if the passage is better at the concert, perhaps they will question me as to why it improved of its own accord. That said, and to be perfectly honest, sometimes I guess and intuition kicks in. There's a voice inside me that says, 'Do it again. Do it three times.' When someone makes a mistake in a different passage, and I don't appear to be paying attention, what I'm actually thinking is, 'In the performance, I will have to be aware of this passage and to make sure that I will give the orchestra the energy to play.'

The business of how to steer an orchestra through a piece they don't know well, or even one they do know, is always tricky. When an orchestra *thinks* that they know a work, the question is: how well *do* they know it? All of this is part of the craft of conducting and conductors should be open about it. Bruno Walter makes it clear in his book, *Theme and Variations*, that he was ruthlessly self-critical when he was a young conductor. He constantly assumed that the result would have been better if he had done something differently in rehearsals. In performance, he assumed the opposite. He assumed that he was in charge and that nothing could go wrong. No matter whatever happened, he was going to be supremely confident and that the result would reflect him at his best.

This approach is invaluable. It's another way of saying that we can do something differently and, consequently, better. That can only be done in rehearsal and not in performance. During the performance, we need to take the long view and to give the orchestra a sense of momentum and enjoyment. You must communicate the fact that you love to hear them play and that your sense of enjoyment will be transmitted to the audience. More important, that's also how we can teach *ourselves*.

RH: You once said to me that it's very lonely being a conductor. Tell me about your relationships with players and how you balance those relationships, both as a music director and as a guest conductor.

PART TWO: THE ART AND CRAFT OF CONDUCTING

ME: You have to be able to be lonely. Actually, 'lonely' is not quite right: 'solitary' is a better word. At the end of a rehearsal, or at the lunch break, you should stand aside and not throw yourself into the middle of the orchestra having lunch. You should be alone. That way, you can make objective decisions about how to proceed, how to treat the players and how to improve the rehearsal process. That's not to say that you can't be approachable and can't enter into some enjoyable, funny, helpful and valuable conversations. But you need to be able to know when to withdraw and to take a step back from them all.

Young conductors who are just starting off should use every minute to learn and to think. They will wonder if the players are giving them enough and whether or not they are giving the players sufficient to achieve their own vision of the music. They may even wonder, 'Do the players like me, am I doing all right and why has that woman been glowering at me all morning?' But, when young conductors start to experience these emotions, I point out that the woman in question is probably glowering at you because you're in her direct line of fire. She's probably thinking that she forgot something in her online supermarket order, and her husband is going to be cross about it. Even if that is not the case, tell yourself that's what it is and that it's nothing personal. It *may* be something personal but, unless someone expresses it to you, you can't know. So, don't let it get to you.

The players' energies are all focussed on you, as they need to be sitting in such a way that they can see you. And, don't forget, you can see *them*. Orchestras might say that it only takes them five minutes to decide if a conductor's any good or not but, I say, it takes me only three minutes to decide whether an orchestra is any good. So, stand on your own two feet. Be happy to be the one who's going to make the decisions and to show the way the music's going to go. If you try it, but can't do that, don't be a conductor.

RH: When I work with students at the Royal Academy of Music, I look for their potential and it takes about two seconds to see from their eyes whether or not they are alive artistically and ready to work. While I am not making judgements about them as people, I am deciding how I can take them further, both educationally and musically. Presumably, as a conductor, you are looking for potential all the time.

ME: Absolutely. I look for potential in the players' eyes, as well as the potential deep within them.

RH: Looking back over the performance histories of some of your great predecessors – not only Sir John Barbirolli in Manchester – it was common for them to take charge of the vast majority of the concerts given by their orchestras. Even though the Cleveland Orchestra was a part-time ensemble until the late 1960s, George Szell was virtually ubiquitous and dominated their season. Similarly, Barbirolli was synonymous with the Hallé for nearly three decades and gave some 3,200 performances with it. Is that kind of omnipresent conducting still possible today?

ME: I didn't realise that Barbirolli did such an enormous number of concerts. What percentage of the orchestra's yearly output was that?

RH: During his first 14 years with the orchestra, it was more than 90 per cent of concerts. And, if one looks at particular years during the 1940s and 1950s, he conducted the Hallé five or six nights a week, often in different towns and cities. This was also true of his work with the British National Opera Company, with which it was not unknown for him to conduct two operas on the same day. Quite remarkable.

PART TWO: THE ART AND CRAFT OF CONDUCTING

The fact that he didn't have perfect pitch, that he couldn't play the piano and that he learned everything by solfège makes it even more remarkable. But to go back to my original question: is that kind of omnipresent conducting still possible today?

ME: A music director should commit to doing a certain percentage of the year. I do 15 weeks, sometimes 16, with the Hallé. While that doesn't seem a great deal, many music directors only do 12 weeks a year. That is a month less and too little. An orchestra should feel that it is developing with a music director. If a music director is away too much, then everyone becomes less sure. Not every conductor wants that responsibility. Many conductors just want to conduct an orchestra, make sure that it's tidy and enjoy the concerts. But they don't make good music directors. Carlo Maria Giulini was an Italian conductor whom I admired enormously. When the Los Angeles Philharmonic invited him to be Music Director, he said that he didn't want to have anything to do with the hiring and the firing of the players or anything else outside his concerts; he just wanted to conduct his performances. As he was a great artist and a wonderful conductor that was fine for him, but he wasn't a music director. A music director's role is much more important than that; it's profound. Conductors should not accept a music directorship for three or four years and then go off to accept another one. And they shouldn't have two symphony orchestras. Some conductors collect orchestras like other people shoot elephants. You can't do anything properly unless you're totally committed to it.

RH: Do you think that's why a visit to Bridgewater Hall feels like a familial experience, an experience that seems to be missing in London these days?

ME: One of the reasons why it doesn't happen in London is that it's essentially a huge pool of freelance players. Some of the players are given first call on the work of a particular orchestra so that they have a commitment to it. But every time I conduct the London Symphony Orchestra there are players whom I didn't see the previous time. It feels much freer, much more like swinging in the wind, and that is true of all the orchestra's sections. It is not uncommon to think: 'Who's the first oboe today?' It makes a conductor's life much harder when an orchestra is organised like that.

RH: A conductor's relationship with the players and singers is also linked to the choice of repertoire. For young conductors, this is a particularly tricky issue. How should they go about making repertoire choices and when should they accept or reject a particular work or works?

ME: This is a huge question. With very few exceptions, an aspiring conductor should always say 'yes' and accept the engagement provided the repertoire is right. But repertoire is everything and that is still the case for me now. If I'm asked to go to an orchestra that is new to me, the pieces that I do matter enormously. Let us say a young conductor of 25 or 30 is asked to do a concert because someone has fallen ill. The management says the advertised programme includes Dvořák's Eighth Symphony and an overture, and the young conductor is familiar with neither of them. It is perfectly acceptable for them to say, 'I've done the "New World" and the Seventh Symphony but I've never done the Eighth. I would rather not do it for the first time under these circumstances. Is there any way you could put on the Seventh or the "New World"?' They will not be laughed at and the management won't put

PART TWO: THE ART AND CRAFT OF CONDUCTING

the phone down. They will say, 'We particularly wanted the Eighth, as we haven't played it in such a long time.'

Then the conductor has to make a decision. He or she might say, 'I would be so grateful if you could talk to your colleagues and come back to me as to whether or not we could do either the Seventh or the "New World".' If the management come back the next day and say, 'the Seventh would be good', then the young conductor has to be sure that he or she really meant it and wasn't fibbing. The conductor must then say, 'Thank you. That would make a terrific difference to me. I've never done the overture but I've always wanted to do it.' That way, the young conductor will know the symphony and will only have to learn the overture.

The management may still come back and say, 'No, we are sorry but we really must programme the Eighth Symphony. Are you still able to do the concert?' My advice would be to reply, 'Give me twenty-four hours and I will see whether or not I am able to do it.' That all depends on how quickly a young conductor can study, how many days there are before the first rehearsal and how well they know the piece by sound, even though they have never conducted it before. If the management asks them to come back with an answer by 5.30 in the afternoon, and all those criteria are met, then take a deep breath and say 'Yes'. Cancel everything else. Get the score, look at it and then decide whether or not you would like to go ahead. Don't be ashamed or feel like you're letting yourself down if you decide that you can't learn it in time. But at least you tried to get a piece you do know. Sometimes it works and sometimes it doesn't. I once accepted an engagement that I shouldn't have done and spent many years regretting it. I said 'yes' to something that I should have said 'no' to and it stayed with me for a long time. In a way, that was simply bad luck and just a wrong choice.

RH: Presumably, choices also have to be made in the opera house. What are some of the challenges that you face when working with a stage director? How do you respond to a staging that doesn't coincide with your vision of the work?

ME: There's a great difference between a new production and a revival. If you're lucky, the original director might be there for a revival, but that's only 5 per cent of the time. For the rest of the time, an assistant will be in charge. If that is the case, it is essential to establish their ability, imagination and commitment to the original production. If it's a new piece of work, and directed by someone who's not much of a musician, my heart sinks. I recently did a production like this in New York. I realised after an initial telephone conversation that it was going to be difficult and I would have to challenge the director's use of sightlines and balance. A director may have wonderfully poetic ideas while lacking practical experience with a big orchestra and singers. Then you have to weigh in. I weigh in anyway; it's my nature. As I started my career in the theatre, I think about the opera psychologically and physically. While I am studying the piece in advance of rehearsals, I consider how it's going to work and how the music is best served. But the best directors will want a partnership and, if you encounter one who doesn't, all I can say is, do your best and never work with them again.

RH: Do you think that the route to the podium is different for a young conductor today? Many aspiring conductors now start their musical lives by attending conducting courses at university music departments and conservatoires. Does this not fly in the face of Sir John Barbirolli's dictum that 'conductors are born and not made'? Granted, he also felt they could be 'refined'.

PART TWO: THE ART AND CRAFT OF CONDUCTING

ME: What Barbirolli said is true. Genuinely talented conductors have a quality or, if you like, a force within them as musicians. That's a given and it's there at birth.

What does it mean, to teach conducting? The New York-based conducting pedagogue, Otto-Werner Mueller, insisted that everyone should wear the same clothes regardless of gender, do exactly the same things, bow to the audience in the same way and prepare for the downbeat in the same manner. He was extremely prescriptive. I knew one of his pupils and I asked her, 'How can you do this? It's so imposed. You were the second conductor on stage, but you did the same as the first conductor.' I think Mueller believed that his responsibility was to give everyone something to grab hold of. Presumably, he thought that when they flew the nest, and got on with their own lives, they would begin to alchemise what he had given them, change it and develop it. But it was extraordinary. I saw four conductors do a little concert and they all dressed the same, came on stage in the same manner and did the same things. They looked like clones to me. That's one way of doing it but it's not one that I am in the least bit interested in.

I never studied conducting. I learned by doing. It's important to distinguish between craft and art: craft is the skill and art is the vision. While conductors might be in pursuit of a particular vision – and surely this must be their ultimate goal – they must also be able to distinguish moment by moment between craft and art. Am I sorting out how this chord is made up? Can I hear it exactly? That is craft. The art, or vision, concerns how a conductor makes a performance whole.

Teaching operates at different levels and, while it is important to study conducting, there are different forums in which to do so. When I started off at university, I had to get the players out of bed and insist that they turn up to the rehearsals. It was my own strength of purpose that enabled me to do that. Conversely, when Mark

Wigglesworth was a student at the Royal Academy of Music, he got some of his mates together and formed a group called the Premiere Ensemble. It was a clever thing for him to do, particularly the name. He put his money where his mouth was, as it were, and ensured that every programme included a world premiere. He was then able to entice people to come and to listen to the new work. Consequently, the critics came and his talent was recognised.

While young conductors learn most by actually conducting, they can also learn a great deal by listening. Time and again, I come back to the importance of listening. I find that many young conductors with whom I work in Manchester don't know how to listen. They don't hear well enough, as they are often quite nervous. There's so much stress and so much worry. Imagine how many things are going through their brains as they stand up and conduct even a little piece by Stravinsky or something small-scale like a Mozart symphony.

Learning comes from doing. But it can also come from watching other people. Going to experienced conductors' concerts and rehearsals, and listening to whether or not they make any difference, is vital. A conductor may insist on something and you don't hear any difference at all. While, on the other hand, another conductor may say almost nothing but the orchestra seems to improve by itself. The experience of watching Pierre Boulez at work was particularly instructive. I was a young man when he first came to London and was thrilled by him. In fact, my whole generation was bowled over by him. While every conductor has to have a strong personality, his was never temperamental. His importance stemmed from his remarkable ability to hear so spectacularly well on the podium. There have always been great musicians with phenomenal ears – Hans Richter, a former music director of the Hallé, was one of them – but Boulez came at a time when nobody could touch him in that respect. He was an inspiration.

PART TWO: THE ART AND CRAFT OF CONDUCTING

He always managed to put his finger on what was wrong. And that's something that we all have to train ourselves to do.

RH: Sir John Barbirolli, Sir John Pritchard and Sir Charles Mackerras all left school in their middle teens to become jobbing musicians. Having cut their artistic teeth by working at the artistic coalface, they went on to make successful careers on the podium. Is that route still available today?

ME: Being an instrumentalist is a wonderful preparation for being a conductor. It's a question of the route and how long you pursue it for. The former principal clarinet of the Berlin Philharmonic, Karl-Heinz Steffens, was keen to become a conductor. At one point, he was near to giving up but felt so strongly about conducting that he eventually triumphed. He has since come to Manchester a few times and has conducted the Hallé. His natural passion for the music helped him through.

The problem faced by many orchestral musicians who aspire to be conductors is that they fail to realise that you have to have a technique. Conducting is as different from playing the cello as playing the cello is from ballet dancing. But everyone has their own way of doing it. While I think it's possible for a jobbing musician to become a conductor, the problem is that they are often stuck in a world which isn't quite the world they want to work in.

RH: Mark Wigglesworth and I were involved in a public interview, during which we discussed the German opera-house system and the career opportunities that it has traditionally offered young conductors. He felt that route was no longer as viable as it once was. Do you agree?

ME: While there are more opportunities now for young conductors in the UK than there used to be, many still find their musical feet by working in the German system. As one season ends, the treadmill slows down to allow people to hop off before allowing them to hop back on again in a different place. If a conductor becomes part of that world, it's sometimes hard for them to leave it. This is particularly true if a life is established there. But it is an experience and, after all, that is something we all need. We need people to trust us, to have confidence in us and to give us a go. To find the right circumstances in any one period of one's life, and to find the right opportunities, is phenomenally hard. Luck plays a big part. When young conductors give concerts, they should invite people to them. They should be bold, bloody and resolute. They must invite people without expecting anyone to reply or to turn up. If one person does, they should think, 'One person's coming. That's better than none.' One never knows what might happen.

I remember conducting a double-bill of two contrasted operas at Cambridge. To my surprise, there was an agent sitting in the audience who later introduced himself to me. We got to know each other and he wanted to help me. There are some agents who actually want to do that. Any agent of quality will be interested in the next generation, as they want to ensure their own ongoing success by developing young talent. Managers want to be able to say, 'Of course, I saw him before anyone else and I realised there was some talent there.' Young conductors today are lucky, as there is an emphasis on youth in the performing arts. Two or three decades ago that was not the case. People want the next young talent to be seen, encouraged and applauded.

RH: A route that wasn't so widely available to young conductors during the 19th and early 20th centuries is competitions. Competitions are now very popular. What are the pitfalls and advantages of competitions? Are you a supporter of them in general?

ME: I'm not, and I wouldn't go out of my way to establish a competition or to be on the jury of one. That said, there are two good things about them. Firstly, competitions make young conductors work. They make them concentrate and they give them something to work towards. If an aspiring conductor decides to apply for a competition, and is later invited to attend, it focuses his or her mind. It's really challenging. As there aren't so many experiences to be had elsewhere, it might be the first time he or she works with a professional orchestra. That has to be a good thing. Secondly, it brings a young conductor's name before the public, even if only for a short period of time. People read the names of those involved.

The person who gets first prize isn't necessarily the most successful person in the competition; this is also true of instrumental competitions. The fact that you get a prize is enough. Conversely, winning first prize won't automatically mean that your career takes off. These things are ephemeral and not easy to define. People tend to expect too much from a competition. People who aren't conductors don't know how to evaluate them. They are not sure whether or not they're looking at a hopeless case or at somebody who might later turn into something. This is more of a problem in conducting than in any other musical discipline.

PART THREE

GERMAN MUSIC

RH: When central European conductors write about the Austro-German canon, the word 'content' recurs time and again. It seems to refer not simply to the notes on the page but to some quality that underpins the music culturally, politically, socially, religiously and ethically. What is your take on this?

ME: For me, the crucial factor is that German music comes more from the mind rather than the heart. That's not to say that the heart is absent but Germans have been guided more by intellect than spontaneity. If Handel hadn't studied in Italy, his music would have been fundamentally different. Bach didn't study there and his music has an intellectual rigour that is part of its stature.

RH: Do you think your understanding of 'content' might be different to that of a musician born in a German-speaking country?

ME: I wouldn't have thought so. In studying German music, you take it, look at it and find what's in it. There's so much to glean in German music and it doesn't come easily. It needs time and preparation.

RH: Beethoven occupied a central place in the repertoire of Austro-German conductors from the late 19th and early 20th centuries. In their attempts to unlock its content, many of those conductors retouched and altered the orchestration of works such as the Ninth Symphony.

ME: But wasn't that just their desire to make it 'work better' with an early 20th-century symphony orchestra?

RH: Perhaps you are right. Perhaps it was simply for practical reasons. Even Sir Henry Wood stressed the need for retouching Beethoven. In Wood's opinion, the instruments of the early 19th century were incapable of expressing what the composer had in mind. He felt that the music would have spoken with greater tonal and cultural impact if only Beethoven had had the resources of the modern symphony orchestra. Nevertheless, I still have a feeling that it was more than that for German musicians. It was a way of getting to the essence of their artistic psyche and their cultural solar plexus.

ME: But the solar plexus of their culture is perfectly evident in the score of the Ninth Symphony. I see no reason to change a note of it. For me, unlocking the content of a German score comes from spending time with it, absorbing it and thinking about it. I want to explore what it expresses, the depths to which the music plunges and the ways in which an orchestra can come to terms with it.

PART THREE: GERMAN MUSIC

RH: In his book, *Of Music and Music-making*, Bruno Walter wrote this about the symphonies of Schumann: 'There are scores which, as it were, resist live realisation by an orchestra since they are written by an unskilled hand, or have not sprung from the spirit of the orchestra. This is the case with Schumann's symphonic work. His aural imagination was predominantly under the sway of the pianoforte. He was not at home with the orchestra. Here instrumental retouching becomes an unavoidable duty, for Schumann's original orchestration is unable to do justice either to the spiritual content of the work or to its thematic clarity, either to the spirit or to the letter.' I expect you would disagree with that argument!

ME: Completely!

RH: How, then, would you approach these works?

ME: It all depends on the instruments that you're dealing with. Bruno Walter wrote those remarks based on the orchestra that he knew and the ways in which it performed as an ensemble. I mentioned Karajan's response to the idea of 'Classical' style: for Karajan's and Walter's generations, the idea that anything would change between ways of playing Mozart and Brahms was unthinkable. And there are still many listeners of all ages who find it hard to go along with the entire wave of interest in what we now like to call 'Informed Performance Practice'.

Orchestras of Walter's era played Beethoven and Schumann in the same way and would sink themselves into Brahms and Wagner without hesitating. They wouldn't ask whether or not they should change. Walter's remarks were based on a sound that he was brought up with. In that respect, he did not belong to a generation that would consider change.

I encountered this approach as a young musician when I conducted Schumann's Second Symphony for the first time. A colleague offered me the chance to study George Szell's scores. He had been an assistant of Szell and told me how marvellous they were. He also told me that I couldn't possibly perform the work without Szell's amendments. As I thought this was going to be the secret to unlocking Schumann, I was initially very grateful. But I was astonished by the amount of instruments that were crossed out and how brutally the dynamics were changed. Perhaps it was a sort of abuse that I've never recovered from. I've never really had a chance to reassess these symphonies since that early encounter but I know what I'd do now: I would perform them as they are written. In the end, it comes down to style: Schumann style.

The work done by my colleagues in the original-instrument movement has shown us that it is possible to change. There are different forms of beauty. This is vital to me. I found music of the Classical era much easier to relate to, and to be excited about, once I began my relationship with the Orchestra of the Age of Enlightenment 25 years ago. Just by being with them, talking to them, learning about their sound-world, and what they expected me to like about it, affected me deeply. When we first worked together, they were wary of me. They were concerned that I wouldn't like what they brought to the table. They wanted reassurance that I didn't want to make them sound like the London Symphony Orchestra. It was their different sound that I found thrilling, interesting and ear-opening.

When performing works by composers such as Schumann, the questions that a conductor should always ask are: What is the sound-world inhabited by the orchestra you are about to conduct? How can you make it change? These questions lie behind my disagreement with Walter. To claim that Schumann's symphonies 'resist live realisation by an orchestra since they are written by an unskilled hand' is quite curious. His approach may well have been unskilled when compared to that of Mendelssohn or Berlioz. The truth is that Schumann needed to write for an orchestra in the way that his music needed to sound.

The orchestra that Bruno Walter led in 1955 was unlike any that Schumann would have heard in 1840. But, as Walter was not alone in taking this stance, this is a really interesting quote historically. Considering Walter's argument in the context of Schumann's overture to *Genoveva*, it is even further from the truth. Both the overture and the whole opera are beautiful, just as they are. When I conducted the overture, it never occurred to me to make changes or to send any of the instruments home: I just balanced it with my ears and with my heart. What *was* hard was getting the orchestra to understand the expressive nature of the music and how far they could go when playing it. That was a real battle.

Schumann's overture to *Manfred* is also a difficult piece to rehearse, conduct and play. You have to come at *Manfred* from the music which preceded it. We appreciate this now thanks to the work of the OAE and other period orchestras. To come at each decade of the 19th century through the music of the previous half-century is essential. What was Schumann listening to? How did it affect what he wrote? It is important to ask those questions rather than to say, 'Well, we play Brahms in a particular way, so we're going to perform Schumann with the same sound but with some small alterations.' Instruments, and the way sound is produced, have changed. The opening of *Genoveva* is a sublime moment of Romanticism. The pain in the music is really extraordinary. The sense of desolation and yearning that Genoveva experiences during the course of the opera is wonderfully portrayed and the work has an intensity and boldness that one usually associates with Wagner. Making an orchestra sound good in that music is no less demanding than making Stravinsky's *Le sacre du printemps* sound good with an orchestra that's never played it before. Both need a special sound and a special attitude. All music needs its own 'Orchestra of the Age of Enlightenment'. We need to be enlightened about all music.

RH: Do you think, though, that in some ways it's also down to the shift in how conductors now operate? Bruno Walter, Wilhelm Furtwängler and Otto Klemperer all aspired to be composer-conductors. Does that aspiration lie behind the urge to change the printed text? When it declined, in the generation of Herbert von Karajan and Wolfgang Sawallisch, so did the urge to reorchestrate. Karajan and Sawallisch were great Schumann conductors, but they were primarily conductors. Do you think that the shift from composer conductor to virtuoso conductor is important in this discussion?

ME: As I never talked to Karajan and Sawallisch about it, I've no idea. But I presume it must have been, as they would have approached a particular work with a different attitude. That attitude would have been based on whether or not they were performing it as if it were their own music. After the Second World War, things started to change seriously and everybody started to find new ways of making sound. As the old world had been discarded and destroyed, everybody wanted to strike out on new paths. As Britain is always a little bit behind the rest of Europe, it only gradually came to this country but we are now one of the leaders in the field of making new sounds and new beauty. Furtwängler was of his time and, understandably, wanted to change the music. I am from a later generation and would not change a note. It's just a matter of how you make music, the way you respect it and your belief in the printed score. That said, I might make little changes in the brass parts with modern instruments. I might add a note or two to the second horn, as we know it can play more notes than Beethoven's horns could. But I wouldn't do what one of my recently deceased colleagues did and put a whole chromatic timpani part in the slow movement of the 'Eroica'. It's something that would never occur to me.

I want to find out what Beethoven's orchestra sounded like. I don't want to presume that he was inept. I also don't want to presume that Schumann could have done better had he had a bit more training in how to write for the orchestra. If his music comes from the piano – and he wrote brilliantly for the piano – it may be that we have to change the way we play his music as an orchestra. But your original question was 'how does this relate to finding the content of the music?' My feeling is that, in the latter part of the 20th century, and certainly at the beginning of the 21st, our imaginative response to so much music has changed from our upbringing. I'm interested in the younger generation and in what they're finding in the music. They don't want to change Schumann's writing for the orchestra. They want to assume that it's good enough to go on with and to find the right way to bring it to life. I don't see the orchestra as this enormous, monumental, architectural weight that added certainty to serious artistic purpose.

RH: It is absolutely clear from what you have just said that you are passionate about the conductor as detective and about the importance of discovering composers' intended sound-worlds. When performing music from the 20th century, there are many sound recordings and films of composers performing their own works, notably Stravinsky. Do such documents render the conductor as detective redundant? How closely should artists observe these documents as performance models?

ME: Stravinsky was a great composer who had an unusual and unhealthy appetite for money. Although he was a fascinating and interesting personality who loved being paid to perform, he was not a terribly good conductor. As he composed so many iconic pieces around the beginning of the 20th century, it was inevitable that he should be asked to perform them. Even though his music is often regarded as the acme of precision, that precision was not reflected in his own performances. I find watching him conduct his own works unhelpful; it doesn't enhance what I can learn from the score.

That said, by not following his own metronome marks in performance, it allows other conductors to make tempo decisions for themselves according to the needs of the music. In other words, if you're not really convinced by the printed mark, you don't feel as if you're committing an artistic crime by not observing it. By performing his own music, Stravinsky broadened its audience base, especially in America. That was crucial, as Americans were fascinated by his personality. But the truth is that he wasn't in control of himself as a conductor and he couldn't control the orchestra.

RH: Many German musicians of the past saw their tradition as a natural consequence of cultural evolution and were adamant that Johann Sebastian Bach was fundamental to that evolutionary process. When I look at modern programmes, this seems to be changing. Do you think that Bach is still fundamental?

ME: He's fundamental to an appreciation of what music exists for. You need to start with Bach and to make him the inspiration for what came after him. He was an artistic giant and I miss his music. Even though I only conduct it occasionally, I love it.

PART THREE: GERMAN MUSIC

RH: I once asked a young Russian conductor, 'Do you conduct Bach?' He said, 'No, I leave that to the experts.' I was bewildered as to who those experts were. Do you think this is a typical modern response?

ME: Many modern symphony orchestras and their managements have come to regard both the Baroque and the early Classical periods as off limits. As their response is a backlash from the impact of the historical performance movement, it was perhaps inevitable. Even the Chicago Symphony Orchestra is now inviting specialists to come and to encourage the orchestra to play Bach in an informed way. But there are still people who've never given up performing Bach, and the other great masters of the Baroque, on modern instruments. How they perform those works is their choice and that, too, is really healthy.

Many years ago, I was asked to conduct a Mozart symphony with an orchestra not far from Cardiff and to introduce them to the idea of playing in an original, Classical style. I told the management that the only way we could do this was by having enough time and by introducing the new sound-world to the orchestra a little each day. The concert was on a Friday and I started work on the Monday by saying, 'We're going to try and do this in a different way. As we've got small timpani, I would just like to hear a couple of notes.' The percussionist obliged and produced a sound completely different from that which they were used to. Then I said, 'We've also got natural trumpets and they, too, are going to make a completely different sound. We've all got to change our sound and to try and play without vibrato today. I know that's going to be really hard, as we've trained ourselves to vibrate all the time. Although we've practised vibrating consistently, try not to do it at all.'

This was difficult for the musicians and they found it alarming. I said to the winds, 'When you play expressively don't add vibrato. Just keep the sound pure.' Somebody then said, 'So, you mean you want it to sound really ugly.' Undeterred, I said, 'As we're taking a new path, perhaps it *will* sound ugly today and perhaps it *will* feel uncomfortable.' In exploring these sounds, I have generally found – not so much now but 20 years ago – that orchestras thought that if they responded in an aggressive and negative way, I would just sigh and give up. They hoped that I would allow them to do what they wanted, which was great, as the battle lines were then drawn.

The last thing I was going to do was capitulate. Even though they tried, it sounded horrid, uncomfortable, nervous and out of tune. We tried a bit more and then went on to something else. Eventually I said, 'We'll leave it and come back to it tomorrow.' The next day, they all reconvened looking haggard and totally negative. I said, 'Okay. Let's go on to the second movement. Now, I know you probably think I'm completely crazy …' to which the first viola said, not quite quietly enough, 'God, he's psychic, too.' For me, it was a remarkable journey. As every day went by, they saw that I wasn't going to give up and that they had to try and play with a different type of beauty.

This journey is now completely habitual all over the world. When you do come across an orchestra that's never tried it, it now feels like the exception. Whether it's for Bach, Schumann or Rachmaninov, some of the world's greatest orchestras are now entirely adept at changing their sound. As I have pointed out, you cannot play Rachmaninov in the way that you play Brahms and you cannot play Brahms like you play Haydn. They each have a sound-world. It is part of the orchestra's responsibility, inspired and encouraged by its conductor, to find what makes each particular composer's music speak most tellingly.

RH: How would you approach the music of Handel in contrast to that of Bach?

PART THREE: GERMAN MUSIC

ME: Handel benefitted greatly from his time in Italy. His music is full of sunshine and sensuality, traits not always found in the works of Bach. Handel's music is completely irresistible. It has a lilt and lift to it that stems from its rhythmic mobility and vitality. One feels that Handel is the 'Vispring Earl' of Baroque composers. If I were to conduct Handel again, I would ask the orchestra to play cleanly and in a lively manner. I would have the strings lift their bows off the string and to get them to hold their bows further up, so that they can play as lightly as possible. I would choose tempi that were fleet, brilliant and mercurial, in the spirit of the Italy that inspired him so much when he was a young man.

RH: Have you considered performing Handel's *Messiah* orchestrated, say, by Sir Eugene Goossens, as recorded by Sir Thomas Beecham in 1959?

ME: As it shows how another generation viewed this great music, I would love to hear every different version of *Messiah* and to conduct one sometime. I have no doubt that the music would stand up to the treatment. It would still be there at the end and would still be loved and admired. It's wonderfully healthy that the musical perspective of each successive generation changes and adapts. It should never be considered a crime against good taste. Our own period of music history has done so much research into how music might have sounded at the time of its composition, and this has inspired us all to think about what we do. But I emphasise how it *might* have sounded in 1700 or 1750. What *is* impressive about Beecham's recording of *Messiah* is that everybody is totally committed to his interpretation. The *accelerando* at the end of the 'Hallelujah!' Chorus – unforgivable of course – is brilliantly conducted. I've never heard anything like it and it's absolutely marvellous. I would never turn my nose up at it: it's just of its time.

If you have a huge choir, and an orchestra that matches it in terms of instrumental detail, a reading like that of Beecham is inevitable. When I conducted *The Dream of Gerontius* with the Hallé Choir in Manchester, we used 190 singers. Not all the choir's members were regulars but what a terrific sound it made. It was perfect for that music. It had a scale of utterance that was in the composer's ear when he wrote it. Not only am I convinced Elgar would have wanted it performed in this way but it also matched the size of the hall in which it was performed.

That said, problems of size and familiarity might arise if I were to plan to do Bach's St John Passion next year. What would I say to the choir? Would I say, 'I don't want all of you, as I only want those who can come to the 16 extra rehearsals'? As an amateur choir thrives on sound, you don't necessarily get the same beauty of achievement if you halve it. There are so many beautiful performances done with minimal forces now that everyone's ear is being guided towards a different form of beauty. But large-scale performances are still valid and still have a place in our musical life. If one were to perform Mozart's orchestration of *Messiah* with a small choir, it might be prudent to announce it by saying, 'We're going to do something different this year. We are going to celebrate the work but we will be making it more late 18th century than Baroque.' Whichever approach you choose to adopt, the most important thing is to do it well.

RH: Perspectives on Mozart have changed radically during the last century. When Artur Schnabel began to champion the piano concertos in the 1920s, his efforts were met with disbelief. As he pointed out in his memoirs, those works were considered 'children's music'. Similarly,

PART THREE: GERMAN MUSIC

when Richard Strauss made his debut with the New York Philharmonic in 1904, he conducted the 'Jupiter' Symphony. The critics left the hall scratching their heads in bewilderment and were baffled as to why he chose to conduct a Mozart symphony at all. The response of *The New York Telegraph*'s critic, Gustav Kobbé, was not uncommon. He wrote 'the sound [that Strauss] evoked [in the 'Jupiter' Symphony] made one think of a man who, after finishing a set of exercises with Indian clubs, goes through them with toothpicks.' Strauss's works were the Indian clubs while Mozart's symphony was the toothpick.

ME: That was also true of opera. *Così fan tutte* is now performed regularly; it is an opera with which many young singers have had some of their earliest stage experiences. During the 19th century, however, this great and difficult piece was hardly performed at all. Its genius only became obvious through Fritz Busch's and Sir John Pritchard's performances at Glyndebourne during the middle of the last century.

Once again, we return to the issue of taste. How different societies view their art and culture, and the ways in which they celebrate it, is central to this discussion. A piece I enjoy conducting enormously is Bach's Fantasia and Fugue in C minor orchestrated by Elgar. Richard Strauss admired Elgar greatly. This support was significant for Elgar, as he was a deeply sensitive and neurotic man who needed tremendous encouragement. After the German premiere of *The Dream of Gerontius* in Düsseldorf in 1902, Strauss welcomed him and they got on terribly well together. In 1920 they agreed to share a project: one of them should orchestrate the Fantasia and the other should orchestrate the Fugue. They would orchestrate it in their own styles and in a manner appropriate for their own orchestras.

Even though it was a brilliant idea, Strauss went home to Garmisch, carried on with existing projects and never got around to it. Fed up waiting for Strauss, Elgar orchestrated the Fugue and then the Fantasia. Strauss's eventual non-involvement in the project was something of a guardian-angel moment for Elgar, as the result is a Fantasia orchestrated by him which we wouldn't have otherwise had. The orchestration is the work of a master.

In some ways, it has parallels with the Albert Memorial. For my generation, the monument opposite the Royal Albert Hall was a thing of horror. We couldn't understand why on earth it was there and why it was supposed to be so fabulous. Eventually, they covered it up, took much of it away and spent £11 million on restoring it. The result is a glorious celebration of Victorian values. The restoration revealed the panache, daring and sheer monumentality of the original conception in all its glory. And that's what Elgar did for the Fantasia and Fugue. It's a wonderful piece and great fun for the orchestra to play. They are delighted and astounded when the harps come in with the glissandos and when the tambourines get going. When I conducted it in Holland some years ago, the audience adored it. They thought it was thrilling. So, what is beauty? This is what it's all about.

RH: You are absolutely right about *Così fan tutte*. Even Karajan refused to perform it in the theatre and handed it over to Karl Böhm and then Riccardo Muti at the Salzburg Festival. But what about Haydn? How do you approach his music? And how does Haydn differ from Mozart?

ME: For me, Mozart, even in his more earthy compositions, seems to be in contact with something more distantly spiritual. With Haydn's music you feel that his feet were firmly on the ground. The fact that he was writing for musicians whom he knew personally is central to his symphonies. Haydn's humanity – not just his sense of humour – is one of his greatest qualities. He makes us smile not only by his daring but also by his ability to communicate that daring through his style. His works are like a constant conversation between the people involved in playing it. This is also true of Mozart in his operas and piano concertos. In the latter, there is always a sense that they have emerged from the theatre and that Mozart is giving himself a vehicle for his own virtuosity and Romantic personality. And here I use the word 'Romantic' in its broadest sense. He treats the orchestra as a cast of characters. Sometimes it's funny and sometimes it's rather touching.

But with Haydn you feel that you're living with a man who wanted to make music for his society. One feels that he was reaching out to players and listeners alike and that there was something collegial and communal about his music-making. I adore his music and one never knows what's coming around the corner. Every time I conduct one of his symphonies, I am tempted to claim it as my favourite, even though there are so many to choose from. Towards the end of his life, his great oratorios and masses took his achievements to an even higher level, perhaps even greater than Mozart's Requiem, a piece that has never appealed to me. I've never conducted the Requiem and I don't mind if I don't. I prefer *Die Schöpfung* and *Die Jahreszeiten* – which is a work of genius, full of contrast, colour, wit and pathos, all done with a rugged sense of communication. I adore it.

RH: While Mozart and Haydn influenced Beethoven, it was his symphonies that were heard most frequently during the late 19th and early 20th centuries. Do they still speak with the same intensity of a century ago?

ME: If they are done well, yes. I was in New York recently and I heard a 90-year-old conductor of great reputation and achievement conduct Beethoven's Seventh and Eighth symphonies. Even though he is now rather frail, he is a wonderful musician. By avoiding Furtwängler's expansive speeds, and by adopting modern tempi, the performances were very lively. But the orchestra played without any awareness at all of what I would call performance practice. They played with a sound that I said goodbye to many years ago, and I found it hard to hear the music performed in that way. That said, the audience's response to the performance was perfectly enthusiastic and everyone was thrilled.

Performance style in Beethoven has come a long way over the last 30 years. If you want to remain in the past, it's still possible to give great pleasure: Beethoven's Seventh Symphony is a great work whichever way you choose to do it. It is well known that Beethoven only had two double basses at the premiere and very few cellos. While it would be fascinating to hear it in the original performance space, Beethoven's genius, his indomitable will to conquer through his structures and his desire to say something truly original, mean that the work will survive regardless of the number of double basses used.

RH: I am interested to hear your thoughts on Beethoven's great contemporary, Carl Maria von Weber. How do you differentiate between the sound-worlds of both composers?

ME: I start by asking the orchestra to play Weber like Beethoven. As Weber's music was composed contemporaneously with that of Beethoven, the players need to make it sound as if it belongs to the same musical trajectory. The difference between conducting *Der Freischütz* and *Fidelio*, for example, is not so great. As both operas have a taut dialogue between good and evil, the issues that the orchestra must express through the way they play are quite similar.

The evil must then be presented in a powerful and real way but with Weber's art and imagination in mind.

Coming to know *Der Freischütz*, *Euryanthe* and *Oberon* has been exciting for me. *Der Freischütz* is a challenging work to perform. And it is so important for the history of German music, as it was the first time that a composer represented everyday country folk in opera. Nobody in Germany had previously dared to put simple country folk with all their legends and superstitions on the stage. Even though the opera house was traditionally a place for elevated subjects, the work had an enormous success thanks to the power and originality of Weber's music. While his operas are as fresh today as they were when they were first performed, their intrinsic faults lie in Weber's poor choice of librettists.

I love Weber's operas because of their freshness and because they reflect his abilities as a born theatre composer. Of the three operas, *Oberon* has the worst libretto but has some of the most gloriously original music. The topic is worth thinking about, as music for the theatre cannot be the same as music for the concert hall. Because it has to serve the drama, the process by which operatic music is conceived and written comes from a different part of the creative heart. This is necessary if it is to assist the flow, contrasts and issues of the drama. Late in life, Verdi said that opera composers should have the courage *not* to write too much great music and that poets should have the courage *not* to write too much great poetry. What *should* concern them is the drama. They should also think about the poor audience, who, by 9.45 pm, has sat through two long acts. The composer must control the direction of the narrative so that the audience remains involved until the end of the third act. If *Euryanthe* hadn't been written, Wagner's *Lohengrin* would scarcely be the same. While *Lohengrin* deserves to be heard more frequently, Weber's work acted as its model.

What Weber and Wagner had in common was an innate knowledge of how to write for the stage. They understood how to work within the context of the theatre and the role that music plays within the theatrical whole. In opera, music is not the be-all and end-all. If you want to write something where music is the only thing that matters, then write a symphony. While Weber and Wagner attempted to write symphonic music, their lasting contribution to art is in the theatre.

Weber died young of tuberculosis in London in 1826. At the time, he was working at Covent Garden, where he had just conducted the premiere of *Oberon*. After his death, he was buried first in a cemetery near London's Barbican. As one of Weber's most devoted admirers, Wagner was upset by this and was determined that his hero's body should be returned to Germany. With Weber's son Max – named after the character in *Der Freischütz* – Wagner started a fund in Dresden, Weber's adopted hometown, to raise enough money to disinter Carl Maria from the London cemetery and to have his body reinterred in Dresden.

The ceremony took place on a cold and wet day, and an orchestra of wind instruments met the cortège at the city gates. It processed through Dresden playing a symphony written by Wagner and based on themes from *Euryanthe*. I have a copy of the score and it is a series of great tunes from a wonderful opera in honour of a great man. For Wagner, Weber was an inspiration and a mentor. His works encouraged Wagner to reassess German opera and to shape its direction for the rest of the 19th century. While Wagner succeeded amazingly, and we still enjoy and discuss his great works today, Weber's part in all of this should never be forgotten: his operas are milestones in the development of German music.

RH: Have you conducted any stage works by Schubert?

PART THREE: GERMAN MUSIC

ME: No and, if I die without having performed any of them, I won't mind. It's not that I think they're bad. It's that Schubert simply lacks Weber's instinct for the stage. He was a great lyric composer and one of history's great melodists. But he lacked the ability to cut, paste, edit and pace, which are essential skills when crafting the music according to the demands of the drama. All of his symphonies are worth hearing and the Fourth is particularly beautiful. He had something huge to say within limited means.

RH: While Mendelssohn made a huge impact on British cultural life, some 19th-century commentators felt that he was something of a musical lightweight when compared to Wagner. Do you share that view?

ME: Because of Wagner's personality, and what he wanted to express through his music, it's hard for anybody else *not* to seem lightweight by comparison. While he was interested in heroism, not every composer was. When I was 25 years old, I had no time for Mendelssohn and was much more interested in Wagner. Since those early years, I have conducted all of Mendelssohn's symphonies many times.

As his music must sound as if it's the simplest thing in the world to perform, it's not easy to conduct. The 'Italian' Symphony, for example, is an amazingly hard work to realise and always needs meticulous rehearsal. Mendelssohn lives in a childlike universe of sparkling transparency. While his skill at mixing the timbres of the various orchestral voices is astonishing, his orchestra is fundamentally Mozartian. That said, Mendelssohn's music must have space and must be able to breathe. You cannot conduct it successfully unless you breathe with the music.

RH: Let's turn to Wagner, and the much-discussed concept of *Gesamtkunstwerk*.

ME: First, what does *Gesamtkunstwerk* mean in reality? Surely, it means the balance of all the different elements of an opera. That being so, any self-respecting opera composer should be interested in *Gesamtkunstwerk*, as they will want all the component parts of their work to be balanced. Verdi was no less particular about this than Wagner. He, too, wanted control over the singers, lighting and scenery. The ways in which his operas were lit was of particular importance to him, as he felt that this had the biggest effect on how his music was perceived. Wagner's visions of what his pieces should be were somewhat more gargantuan, so he designed his opera house at Bayreuth to realise those visions. Those who have visited the theatre will know that you can't see the person sitting next to you when the lights go down. As the orchestra pit is covered, there is no visible light from it. The only light in the auditorium is the dimmest glow that reflects down onto the pit.

As the pit at the *Festspielhaus* is tiered, it creates a wonderfully balanced sound. And in order to preserve this miracle acoustic, nobody has ever dared touch any of the material that the theatre was originally constructed from. It's hard to make music there, as there is a time delay between the orchestra and the voices. The conductor has to be a little ahead of the singers, so that the sound reaches the audience together. The other reason that the pit remains covered is that Wagner wanted total concentration on the drama. He was keen that the audience should not be distracted in any way and that their line of concentration should be focussed totally on the stage.

Sadly, what has actually appeared on the Bayreuth stage over the last 40 or 50 years has become progressively more extreme and incomprehensible. Much of what is produced there today is only adored by

PART THREE: GERMAN MUSIC

a particular sort of intellectual. The current production of the *Ring* is one example. It would make a good Christmas quiz to cut out pictures of it without captions and say, 'Now guess the opera!' It's unbelievably ugly and vulgar. I haven't seen the performance but I *have* seen photographs of it. I see no interest in, or respect for, the music or for the sort of balance that the term *Gesamtkunstwerk* implies.

RH: Was Wagner as inadequate a librettist as some have made out?

ME: What ought to be kept in mind when discussing Wagner's theatrical path was that he was constantly searching for a new way to tell an old myth or legend. In the course of telling them, he wanted huge universal truths to be felt through his music. He was passionate about giving his people something that they could identify with as being purely German. Many other composers also wanted to do that for their countries; Smetana did it for the Czechs and Slovaks. Wagner did it on a grand scale, and his use of language is fabulous.

When you're working on his pieces, and you have that enormously rich wash of orchestral sound between the audience and the singers, the singers need diction that can stand on its own two feet in order to communicate with the public and complement the power of Wagner's imagination. His use of *Stabreim*, with its short rhymes and alliterations, is a clever way of moving the narrative forward. A century and a half later, his choice of language often seems remote to us as listeners. But it is precisely *because* he chose to use *Stabreim* that these great dramatic poems can be translated successfully by clever poets. And I'm absolutely sure that he would have loved these powerful translations.

Wagner's music works on so many levels. During his lifetime, one of the things that he was most noted for was the erotic quality of his music. As we are now surrounded by eroticism in so many different forms, it is almost second nature to us. But in the 1860s and the 1870s, the expectations of what was and wasn't acceptable were clearly delineated. Until that time, nobody had expressed the power of sexual love as he did with a modern symphony orchestra. *Tristan und Isolde* is the best-known example, but the power that draws two people together is found elsewhere in his *oeuvre*. The 'Winterstürme' in Act 1 of *Die Walküre* is the beginning of a most incredibly sensual love scene. Nobody had gone that far before.

His sensuality as a composer was also a reflection of his own personality and lifestyle. His favourite colour was pink and he had a pink dressing gown. People today might laugh but, until 1920, pink was regarded as a strong, masculine colour. That only changed after advertising agencies decided pink was for girls and blue was for boys. As Wagner's sensibilities were nothing short of hyper, he would hang roses in his room where he wrote his operas and had the walls covered with soft silks. Because he couldn't bear harsh fabrics next to his skin, he had his milliner in Vienna send him reams of soft silks and would have his shirts and underwear made from these fabrics. Even as he was dying, he was determined to put on his dressing gown, so that he could die in style. This was all part of his natural sensitivity. He must have been difficult to live with but, once you were accepted by him, you remained in his heart forever. He was a loyal man who suffered fools unwillingly. Although he had an iron self-discipline, he also had a huge sense of love for his fellow human beings.

That said, I'm not sure that I would have liked to have met Wagner. We should leave him on the page. Let's not worry too much about his antisemitism or some of the ridiculous things he wrote. They often get in the way of understanding his music. His works are incredible expressions of the human condition and, if you can bring that out with an orchestra and singers, it can be life-changing. Those who are

PART THREE: GERMAN MUSIC

resistant to the potential for that experience are often not prepared to give themselves whole-heartedly to his emotional message. You've got to give yourself over to him completely.

RH: What are your thoughts on performing Wagner in English?

ME: Wagner's mature works are founded on a uniquely expressive musical palette which is particularly evident in *Parsifal*. When I conducted that work at the Coliseum, I translated it with my friend Richard Stokes. He would produce a line of translation and I would alter the music to fit the line. Not one person noticed that I had made any alterations to the music at all. As they could understand it, they thought it was a good, strong translation. But to make the words lie well, so that they fall on the ear nicely, is the real problem. It can be done with Wagner, as you can just alter it by putting one syllable on two notes and nobody will be disquieted. If they can understand the piece, and if it's in their own language, they will like it. My experience in reading about composers, and talking to them, is that they all want their pieces to be understood.

    I know that some members of the audience don't really want to understand the libretto. For them, it's never worth understanding, as they consider it horrible poetry or a silly story. They will say, 'I just want to shut my eyes and listen to the music.' But if you are going to take opera seriously as drama and as theatre, and if you believe that theatre has a place in our lives, which it should, then understanding the text is crucial. If the purpose of the theatre is to help us to be richer human beings, to enable us to learn more about ourselves and to celebrate, suffer and rejoice, then the world of opera has to be taken seriously. I believe fully that Wagner in English before an English audience is a good thing. And the *Ring* translates pretty well into English, too!

RH: When I have discussed the role of Brünnhilde with some of her greatest interpreters, such as Dame Gwyneth Jones and Dame Anne Evans, they often talk about the *Ring*'s three Brünnhildes. Do you see the role as three distinct individuals or as one personality that evolves?

ME: What and how Brünnhilde sings throughout the last three nights of the *Ring* is defined by the action. Wagner composed, therefore, three different roles. It is thrilling when somebody can be found who can sing all three. When she appears for the first time in *Die Walküre*, she's young, full of vitality and exudes warlike confidence. But her tessitura is rather low, reflecting the darkness of what she has to express. Even though she starts with the war cry, 'Ho jo to ho!', which takes her up to top B and occasionally top C, she uses the middle of the voice when conveying her concern and love. It's a completely different technique on the part of the soprano to be able to sing those war cries and then to do the rest of the piece. Nevertheless, sopranos regard the part of Brünnhilde in *Die Walküre* as being on the low side.

Siegfried is the opposite. Awakened at the end of the work having been asleep on a rock, Brünnhilde sings with a radiance that reflects her new-found heroism. There isn't a phrase in *Siegfried* that corresponds with the music of *Die Walküre*. In *Siegfried*, she is full of joy, sings a great deal in C major and ends the whole opera with a terrific top C. As a result, sopranos tend to think of the *Siegfried* Brünnhilde as being 'the high one'. When it comes to *Götterdämmerung*, Brünnhilde's challenge is immense. As the work is extremely long, it is often hard for the singer to find her form. Brünnhilde's only top C in *Götterdämmerung* is at the end of the first scene when her voice is still fresh. It is extremely taxing for a soprano to sing all this material and her success is totally reliant on how she manages her technique. In the end, it's all about technique and self-knowledge.

PART THREE: GERMAN MUSIC

RH: George Bernard Shaw firmly believed that the *Ring* was a thinly veiled commentary on contemporary capitalism. Is it important to think in allegorical terms or should we take the work at face value?

ME: While the *Ring* might be viewed simply as a myth or legend, it is also part of the cultural legacy of northern Europe. Myths influence the way a society develops because they are shared by succeeding generations of people and operate on different layers of meaning. Wagner undoubtedly used these stories, and the profound truths they contain, to investigate the human condition. The *Ring* explores humanity's dark and light sides and examines how greed and love interact with each other. It is essential to grapple with its meaning, not just to take the music at face value. And, because there are so many different levels to understand in the *Ring*, there can never be one, single interpretation.

Many people talk about how unattractive Wagner was as a man and how his prose works were often contentious. These people are particularly concerned by his racism, his arrogance and his high-mindedness. I take a slightly different view. I think he needed to write those prose works in order to work out his own ideas and to clarify his artistic transition from *Tannhäuser* and *Lohengrin* to what we now know as music drama. He wanted to use the new form as an experimental tool that would bring together all the elements of opera into one balanced synthesis. By writing about his neuroses, problems and dreams before composing his mature works, he could achieve those artistic goals.

RH: Where does *Der fliegende Holländer* fit into this development of artistic maturity?

ME: When Wagner was young, his knowledge of opera was confined to the travelling Italian companies that toured northern Europe. As the concept of a Czech, Russian or German national opera had yet to be created, his operatic experiences were influenced enormously by the Italian style. So it was inevitable that when Wagner started to write his own operas, they would be covered in Italian fingerprints. And, as he was keen to write well for the voice, he used techniques that he heard when listening to these southern European singers.

In my view, *Der fliegende Holländer* is the last work in which he incorporated these Italian influences before he became more self-consciously and self-confidently German. The way in which he treats the voice is an extension of the way the Italians were writing for it in the early 19th century. The opera is a wonderfully enjoyable piece, particularly if you do it in one act: the three-act version makes it seem much longer and more disjointed. *Der fliegende Holländer* wasn't Wagner's first success; that honour goes to *Rienzi*, an enormous opera that was a particular favourite of Hitler's. But it can only be performed with cuts, as it is intolerable when given complete. So *Der fliegende Holländer* is Wagner's first attempt at setting a grand, northern European subject. Having composed it, he was ready to move on to *Tannhäuser* and *Lohengrin*.

RH: When Dame Anne Evans sang Isolde with Sir Charles Mackerras, he asked her to listen to Lillian Nordica's 1903 recording of the *Liebestod*. He felt that Nordica sang in an Italianate manner and was keen for Dame Anne to do the same.

ME: *Bel canto* is relevant to music from both sides of the Alps and it's essential for conductors to encourage singers of German music to think in those terms. While the German language is naturally different from the Italian, good singing remains good singing. In my opinion, it is possible to seek out *bel canto* in German music but it has to be practised and learned. The greatest Wagner singers are those who sing with a good understanding of line and phrasing but who still pronounce the words powerfully. Many German-trained singers are so concerned to make the words clear that they tend to put textual clarity above vocal finesse. This can also be true of English singers when working in their vernacular, as their language also has Anglo-Saxon roots. I am always keen for singers to balance a beautiful vocal line with a strong sense of text. One should not be achieved at the expense of the other, and this balance requires time and training. Even in the *Ring,* you're still dealing with an Italianate style of vocal writing that Wagner learned after hearing the works of the Italian masters in his youth. But he then made those techniques his own.

RH: Wagner stressed the need for *Melos* – a sense of line – when interpreting Beethoven and his other predecessors. Do you think his understanding of *Melos* derives from his interest in Italian music?

ME: All music has to have line. Stravinsky has to have line. But line can be expressed in so many different ways. Bellini's legacy to operatic literature was his endless melodies. These are melodies that went on for six to eight bars in one gesture, and he wrote them in a way that was uniquely his own, like a spider spinning melodic webs. Conversely, Verdi's melodies were fundamentally strong arches. But there is line in both Bellini and Verdi. The interpreter's challenge is to make the line apparent and moving. More importantly, the inherent emotion of the music must be portrayed by the singer and by the orchestra with complete commitment. The moment you fail to keep the *Melos* alive, the audience will feel it. They won't talk about it but they will be aware that the intensity of the performance has slipped. Line is the one aspect of a performance that is completely in the conductor's control. By the way in which the conductor works with the players and the singers, he or she can ensure a sense of line which brings a structural integrity to the performance.

RH: For Wagner, *Melos* was inextricably linked to tempo. He argued that conductors often lacked an understanding of *Melos* as they were frequently ignorant of singing. Do you also see a link between tempo, singing and good orchestral technique?

ME: Beautiful instrumental playing comes from imitating the greatest possible singing. That's what players should constantly strive to do. When a composer marks a passage *cantabile*, what he's really saying is, 'Please play this in a singing style.' But what does a singing style really mean? That can only be found by listening to the greatest singers, whose command of the music and the text is completely within their control. When Pavarotti was at his best in the early 1970s, he made some recordings that one could not stop listening to. His control of line was so beautiful and so thrilling that you wanted it to go on and on. Mirella Freni was another such singer.

When conducting you have to show how the line is shared between different parts of the orchestra. This can only be done through well-chosen gestures and by the way you relate both to the music and to the players. Such gestures are particularly important in Wagner, where his command of his enormous orchestra was so detailed and so full of variety. It can only be achieved when the orchestra becomes familiar with the idiom. It's like orienteering on a map and the conductor *must* chart the route.

RH: Bruno Walter frequently wrote '*espressivo*' into his scores. The term appears no fewer than 249 times in his annotation of Mozart's Symphony No. 36. Are such annotations a tangible manifestation of a conductor's search for line?

ME: What does *espressivo* mean? For Walter's generation, it would have been something different from what we understand it to mean in the 21st century. If I were to perform that symphony with the Hallé or with the OAE today, it wouldn't occur to me to write the word in the score, as the material that needs to be played expressively would automatically be played expressively. That said, you must be clear as to what you want expressed. By putting that word in his score, Walter might have been in search of a particular type of clarity related directly to the degree of vibrato used by the players. I would do the opposite. I would use either less or no vibrato and would only add it to a specific note to shape a particular part of the phrase.

Dolce was an instruction that Brahms applied both carefully and selectively. As *dolce* means gentle or sweet, his application of it implies a particular type of intimacy, tenderness and sensitivity. Conductors should consider why he wanted something different at that particular juncture. I have found that orchestras tend to make little, or no, difference in sound at such moments and think it is simply 'a nice bit'. But it's more than 'a nice bit': it must convey something deep, special and hallowed. This is true for both winds and strings. It should be remembered that the premiere of his Violin Concerto was given by Joseph Joachim, who played with almost no vibrato, and the sound-world at that first performance would have been completely different from that of today. Perhaps Brahms was indicating something quite specific by writing *dolce* over a particular bar or phrase, a meaning that since has been lost. This is one of the things that makes studying scores from the past so interesting.

Expressiveness is not restricted to vibrato but is also linked to tempo. When orchestras from the late 19th and early 20th centuries introduced a melody or a new section in a symphony or a symphonic poem, not only would they have played the passage more slowly but more flexibly. Even though works from this period can be full of energy and forward movement, I'm sure it was normal for that music to be performed slower than the marked tempo. This is especially true for some works by Mahler, where he clearly wants the conductor *not* to begin too fast but to move forward a little later on.

A more specific example of flexibility can be found in the first movement of Elgar's Second Symphony. This is an extremely difficult movement, full of notes but also full of feeling. Every time there's a new musical idea, he indicates a specific tempo. The movement should not be performed as if it is a long red carpet being rolled out in one tempo; rather, the conductor should use those tempo modifications as a means by which to clarify a series of contrasting musical ideas, so that the audience has a better understanding of the movement's overall structure. Even though much of this would have been taken for granted when the music was first performed, it is lost today. But this is also true for music composed nearer to our own time.

When studying works from the beginning of the 20th century, I find recordings from the period to be particularly informative. When you listen to Elgar conducting his own music, both as a younger man and towards the end of his life, there is a noticeable shift in orchestral technique. I often ask the string section to slide, to achieve a slight portamento by bringing their fingers lightly up the string. This was common practice at the beginning of the 20th century; nobody would have discussed it. As I understand it from conversations with people who remember that time, it was the next generation of musicians who wanted to 'clean up their act', so to speak. They applied a little musical detergent and began to play legato without portamento. Consequently, the orchestras that Elgar conducted towards the end of his life had a different, cleaner sound. Brahms, too, would linger occasionally and was keen for particular notes to blossom before moving on. Even though Brahms hardly wrote anything down, he obviously wanted his music to be flexible, to have give and take. Modern conductors need to be more aware of this and to be braver in how they allow the music to live and breathe.

RH: In 2013, you celebrated the bicentenary of Wagner's birth by performing Act 3 from *Die Meistersinger von Nürnberg* at the Bridgewater Hall. It was as if you had the complete musical resources of Manchester at your disposal and were trying to reflect the community spirit of that great city. Do you think that your approach that night reflected Wagner's vision of the work in general?

ME: Having fallen on hard times while writing the *Ring*, Wagner decided to write a powerful love story and a small comedy, both of which could be staged in any theatre in Europe and could accrue royalties quickly. So he wrote *Tristan und Isolde* and *Die Meistersinger von Nürnberg*. Even though Wagner intended *Die Meistersinger* to be short and accessible, it ended up being one of the longest operas ever written. Having become progressively interested in the central character, Hans Sachs, he poured himself into the work and left us with much more than a convenient comedy.

Die Meistersinger presents a community that respects its traditions and is serious about its artistic activities. It should continue to act as a wake-up call for presidents and prime ministers today. It leaves the listener in no doubt that, for a nation to be truly successful, it must be able to express itself artistically and creatively. No politician will admit to that, as there are no votes in it. Nevertheless, Wagner wanted to take a growing, industrious and aspirational community and to write a comedy about how everybody lived, loved and hated within it. He showed not only how difficult it is to accept change but how a community can only flourish *by* accepting change. Even though this enormous opera is so full of beautiful music, its true importance lies in its humanity and that is why I performed it in Manchester in 2013.

RH: This was a concert-hall performance, which presents quite different challenges and delights to a full staging.

ME: The idea of giving great operas in a good concert hall is an attractive one. Along with Act 3 of *Die Meistersinger*, we have given Act 1 of *Tristan und Isolde* and *Cavalleria rusticana* in Manchester. The *Ring* is being given over a ten-year period. Our audiences really enjoy these performances and I believe that one can engender an incredible sense of involvement between the public, singers and orchestra. This is particularly true if you not only get good voices but also the right sort of voices. It is also important that the orchestra makes the drama live.

Symphony orchestras don't get many opportunities to dig down into the operatic repertoire. And what better way to start than with Wagner? But the audience needs access to good subtitles. When we did *Die Walküre*, we had big, clear subtitles on the walls and the sides of the auditorium, rather than the usual surtitles which are often too small. But concert performances of opera require a great deal of rehearsal and considerable thought. In order to honour the drama as well as the music, the performers must not be glued to their scores.

PART THREE: GERMAN MUSIC

RH: Singers always tell me how difficult Wagner is for the voice. Do you think that is true?

ME: It's a question of technique and casting. If a singer has the right sound and the right technique, and is working with a conductor who is interested in what singers can and can't do, it is perfectly possible to sing Wagner. But even if those conditions are met, the singer must be fresh, fit and have enormous stamina. If that is not the case, they shouldn't perform his music. Conductors, producers and managers are notorious for asking a soprano to sing Sieglinde, for example, because she looks good or has a couple of lovely notes. But the danger is that she may not be ready for it and sings herself out by doing it. There have been so many examples of talented singers who have been destroyed by singing music they're not ready for.

A Wagner singer may rehearse a particular role for two months and give two performances a week in the space of 28 days, all the while competing with a large orchestra. They must be like a horse that is suitable for the *puissance*, not one that is simply capable of sprinting on the flat. If they know they can get over the jumps, they will live to fight another day.

A 'quick fix' will not do for Wagner. Unless the orchestra is practised at his music, and the singers have been performing it for years, it is impossible to bring off a wonderful performance. When preparing a Beethoven or a Dvořák symphony, it is possible to concentrate on the piece for several hours, do it the way the conductor wants and then present a lovely performance. When you're performing Wagner, the singers must have started two years earlier. I began to prepare *Götterdämmerung* in February for a May performance; not only because the work is long and the notes are difficult, but to allow the music to marinate. The material must sink in before you can actually realise it.

In England, we often say that we '*make* music'; an expression unknown in Germany. A performance of Wagner cannot be mounted quickly just because his music is so beautifully conceived. An orchestra needs to know the music well enough to play it quietly. And that is even truer of Richard Strauss, whose operas contain so many notes that they can overwhelm the singers unless the conductor is completely in charge of the music. The conductor must be calm and must not flail around, as the orchestra will simply play louder. The singers will then try to sing louder and that is a recipe for disaster. A young singer who comes with fresh vocal chords and starts to push his or her way into this music will have the most terrible wobble within two or three years. And once a wobble is there, you can't get rid of it. It's so important that young singers who love this music really pace themselves. By all means, learn some excerpts from these great works but not the whole thing. Unless a singer is very unusual, they should not expect to be cast in a Wagner role until they are at least 35 years old. If a singer has talent, they must look after it.

RH: While recording the *Ring* for Decca in 1964, Sir Georg Solti gave an interview in which he argued strongly that the Vienna Philharmonic was the ideal Wagner orchestra. Do you think there is such a thing as an ideal Wagner orchestra or an ideal Wagner sound?

ME: Given the context of the interview, Solti would say that, but surely his comment is only an expression of personal preference. There is also a conductor's 'Wagner sound'. We all conduct in our own ways and we all have different ways of communicating. In my view, Wagner's music needs an unforced quality of sound that is equivalent to large-scale chamber music. Even though there is no one way of doing it physically, the bigger you conduct in Wagner, the worse it sounds. The

PART THREE: GERMAN MUSIC

music has such intensity and is so wonderfully written for the players that big gestures are unnecessary. The players must listen to each other as if they were playing Beethoven's Septet or Schubert's String Quintet. They need to share it together and to judge how the harmonies progress. Particularly in Wagner's late operas, the conductor is there to manipulate the pulse, to determine how much space a particular moment needs and to ensure that the music doesn't drag. That way, each successive, important moment can be played and heard clearly. Only a conductor can do that and only a conductor can organise the tempo changes successfully.

The basis for this type of playing only comes after years of cultivation with a particular orchestra. That is why I've enjoyed the last 17 years in Manchester. I have been able to introduce the orchestra to Wagner and to get them accustomed to the length of his works. We did *Götterdämmerung* to begin with. The players were appalled when I first showed it to them and there was a good deal of talk: 'How many pages is your part? Mine is 187. Yours is 195. How are we going to get through it?' The length of these operas *is* a physical challenge. The players need stamina. They should know how to relax and to distinguish *when* to relax before entering the fray again. But all this only comes after learning how to make sense of the music. The conductor's role is to suggest and to allow the players time to absorb it.

The Orchestra of the Royal Opera plays Wagner fabulously. The musicians have a tremendous feeling for how it goes after years of experience under both distinguished and not-so-distinguished conductors, but they still need the conductor to decide how they're going to pace it. The business of organising the music is something that comes by doing it, listening to it, thinking about it and feeling it together.

Italian music is completely different. It needs to be illuminated and set on fire. In Italy, a conductor can't just say, 'Over to you,' or 'I'll let you do this bit.' You have to inseminate every gesture, rehearsal and performance. This is a direct reflection of the Italian personality and it stands in sharp contrast to that of the German. Italians live their life spontaneously; they will never be quiet as an audience. They want the opera to be beautiful but it also needs to be fresh and vibrant. And this applies to Puccini just as much as Rossini.

RH: How do you approach Brahms?

ME: We know from reports of Brahms conducting his own works that he, too, demanded space and time in his music. But the beginning of the First Symphony is marked *Un poco sostenuto*, an unusual instruction that is also found at the fascinating and volcanic opening of Beethoven's Seventh Symphony. There is clearly a link between the two works, but what does *Un poco sostenuto* mean? For me, the instruction is the composer's way of saying, 'Don't be too slow but don't be too fast.' He wants the music to have space but not *too* much. I conducted Brahms's First Symphony for the first time with the Britten Sinfonia in November 2017, an orchestra of modest proportions in keeping with Brahms's own vision of his music. He wanted the number of strings kept to a minimum so that the winds could be heard clearly. I am not the first conductor to approach Brahms in this way: Sir Charles Mackerras made wonderful recordings of the symphonies with the Scottish Chamber Orchestra. Using reduced forces entirely changes the way you perceive the score, and if *Un poco sostenuto* is all we have to go on, it makes me question what motivated many of my revered predecessors to approach this music so differently. The traditional, Germanic way to perform the opening was to conduct in six beats to

PART THREE: GERMAN MUSIC

the bar. Had Brahms wanted it that way, he would not have written the double-bass part with three notes to the bow. If there were no slurs, it would be clear that every note requires a different bow stroke, which was precisely what the older generation of Central European conductors did. Linking three notes to the bow here is crucial, as it indicates something quite specific. Once that is taken into consideration, and you realise that those notes need to be heard, both the tempo chosen and the music's meaning is affected. The absence of those slurs would suggest something different, something more monumental.

What does this all mean? If you take the information that the composer gives you in bar 1, and you have the bassists play three notes to the bow, there's a limit as to how slowly you can go. But you can't go at any old 'slowness'; the conductor needs to allow the strings to play loudly with the marked articulation. While Brahms was limited in the ways that he could pass on his intentions, *Un poco sostenuto* is a brilliant instruction, as it implies that the music must not be played too slowly. It must have '*Schwung*'.

RH: The First Symphony was premiered in Karlsruhe and the Fourth Symphony had its first performance in Meiningen. The orchestras used at those concerts were small, numbering only 49 players in Meiningen. Conversely, the Second and Third Symphonies were first heard with the Vienna Philharmonic, a considerably larger orchestra. Is your approach to the First Symphony also applicable to the Second and the Third?

ME: The four symphonies have such separate personalities, but it's a question of whether or not you think that monumentality is an essential quality in this music. As the orchestra increased in size, it got louder: bows became longer and heavier and brass instruments produced fatter sounds due to wider bores. Concurrent with those constructional changes, conductors adopted broader tempi and sought out greater orchestral power. As a result, these great, Romantic German symphonies became bigger, grander and more grandiose. For me, such an approach is not attractive. I believe we should try to reveal exactly what Brahms wrote, but also continue to experiment. That way, the music remains attractive and audiences continue to be engaged.

Many people want to hear canonical works in the way that they have always known them. This is also true of the theatre. When some people see a production of an opera that is different from what they are used to, they can't cope with it, as it stops them from enjoying the music that they love so much. Around the world, this is a constant problem and one that affects the central role that theatre plays in society as a whole.

But in the symphonies of Brahms, I am convinced we have missed out on great beauty by preferring monumentality to the printed score. In the last movement of the Second Symphony, for example, the second subject is not marked loud. When it returns in the home key of D major in the recapitulation, it is preceded by an increase in intensity: the strings come tumbling down the arpeggio and then the lovely tune appears again. As the tune is marked quieter than the material that directly precedes it, Brahms wants it to be more delicate and lyrical. But that rarely happens in performance: the strings take to their G strings and vibrate like mad. It's the musical equivalent of a huge American steak dinner.

It is far more exciting to find something that we never thought was there. This applies to all of the four symphonies, as the character, drama and the narrative of each is different. When I performed the Fourth Symphony with the Hallé, a wonderful thing happened. After one particular performance the orchestra was coming off the stage and were putting their instruments away when an old man came up the aisle and started shouting at the second violins. He said, 'There's a mistake in the second violin part in the first movement. It's still there and it's still wrong!' Naturally, they were taken aback. He went on to say, 'It's in the development of the first movement towards the end and here is the bar number.' He was absolutely correct: there was a mistake in the second violin part. At the next rehearsal, I asked for the parts to be put out on the players' stands and we re-checked them against my score. We may never know who the gentleman was but he was right and we corrected the mistake.

RH: Gustav Mahler once remarked to Jean Sibelius that a symphony should be like a world. Is that so?

ME: Mahler believed that his symphonies should contain the widest possible variety of musical ideas and that the heroism of one movement should be followed by something rough or mocking in the next. But imagine being present when Mahler met Sibelius. Sibelius said that he admired the strictness of symphonic style and its deep logic, which requires that all its motifs must be linked to each other. Whereas, according to Sibelius, Mahler disagreed: 'The symphony must be like the world. It must encompass everything.'

There is, for example, a great difference between Sibelius's First and Second Symphonies and his Sixth and Seventh. It is not simply to do with the fact that the last two works are shorter, but more to do with how rigorous Sibelius was in concentrating his musical ideas. Mahler was less interested in this kind of rigour and was more concerned with laying out a great panoply of contrasting events. One of his symphonies that I love most is the Third. While the

Second creates a fantastic impact in performance, the Third has more memorable material. It contains so many extraordinary contrasts and is something akin to a medieval pageant with its different characters and scales of invention. And the last movement is one of the most beautiful things he ever wrote.

In 2010 the Hallé shared a Mahler cycle with our colleagues in Manchester, the BBC Philharmonic. We did the symphonies in chronological order, preceding each of them with a world premiere. The context in which the audience listened to Mahler's music, which it may or may not have been familiar with, was always linked with something that it couldn't possibly have heard before. I did the Fifth Symphony, and in the first half we were joined by the amazing American jazz pianist and composer, Uri Caine. He wrote a piece inspired by the symphony, *Scenes from Childhood*, which we explained and talked about before we played the work itself. He's a brilliant magician with sound and hearing the opening of the Fifth after that was a fascinating and unexpected way into the work.

RH: And how do you feel about Mahler's Eighth Symphony?

ME: I know that many people who adore Mahler's music are dismissive of the Eighth Symphony. But I love it. It's a huge celebratory, moving and emotional work that appeals to the widest possible public. As he knew that his Seventh and Ninth Symphonies were never going to appeal to such a wide audience, he decided to write something that would bring people together and that would have an emotional impact on first hearing. While the end of the *Veni Creator Spiritus* is constructed both beautifully and marvellously, it is the second part that is the more demanding intellectually. Having conducted it some years ago, I found myself longing for him to have written an opera.

PART THREE: GERMAN MUSIC

RH: Richard Strauss has often been criticised for his *Weltanschauung*. As an atheist, family and nature were of the highest importance to him and were often the bases for his compositions. His orchestration vividly portrayed both family and nature. Yet such pictorial realisations have been used to reinforce an argument that his music lacks the substance of Mahler's works.

ME: Did Strauss write a single truly great work? Even though he was a brilliant purveyor of beautiful sounds, and dressed up his ideas with consummate skill, I think that his importance lies in a series of great moments rather than whole works. The ends of Acts 1 and 3 of *Der Rosenkavalier* are good examples of this. Elsewhere, I feel that Strauss manipulated his listeners with his skill. Conversely, Mahler tore musical ideas from his soul and tried to find the best way to put them down on paper. And while they were friends, there was always a certain tension between them as they *were* so different. Mahler constantly changed and improved his scores for future performance, whereas Strauss never altered a thing. He was like a head-waiter who knew how to serve with ease and panache. But orchestras love playing Strauss's music, as he not only writes marvellous parts for individual instruments but knows how to integrate them into the whole.

RH: You have recently conducted Alban Berg's *Wozzeck* at the Royal Opera in London. The *Sprechstimme* technique employed in the opera is, perhaps, not the least of its challenges.

ME: *Wozzeck* is a great work, but it's a hard opera to get to know because of its demanding idiom. Sometimes it is difficult to get to the heart of the work but it *is* a work of great heart. Preparing it with the singers is an extraordinary experience, as they often have difficulty with the notes. Even in the recordings of remarkable artists, such as Pierre Boulez and Claudio Abbado, their casts don't sing the right notes. So what does a conductor do if the singers have failed to master the printed page and the performance is two and a half weeks away? The singers can be asked to relearn the music completely. While some can manage that, others can't. Even if they correct the material for you in the rehearsal room, they'll just go back to singing it all a third too high the moment they stand on stage.

It's not through ill will that this happens but because of muscle memory. If a singer doesn't learn a score properly the first time, they will never get it. If it is in their system, it will never let them down. *Sprechstimme* is an important technique for singers to master but, when they come to rehearse with me, they sometimes have no idea what the notes might be. They see all the crosses on the notes and think that it doesn't really matter what they sing. But that's not good enough for Berg and Schoenberg. The notes for the *Sprechstimme* relate directly to what the orchestra plays. Some singers do find the essence of *Sprechstimme*. One of them is Karita Mattila, who sang Marie in the production you mentioned. She was particularly adept at the technique, and I admired her so much for that.

PART FOUR

ITALIAN MUSIC

RH: Let's travel back over the Alps and return to the topic of *bel canto*. Rossini argued that it was based on three principles: 'First, a naturally beautiful voice that is even in tone throughout its full range; second, careful training that encourages effortless delivery of highly florid music and, third, a mastery of style that cannot be taught but can only be assimilated from listening to the best Italian exponents.' Would you agree with his analysis?

ME: It could be argued that Rossini was at his best in 1820 when he had at his disposal the most brilliant orchestra that could play anything. It was full of fantastic virtuosos and by far the best ensemble on the Italian peninsula. He couldn't resist writing wonderful pieces for the orchestra to play. And the public complained. They said that the problem Rossini created was that the orchestra distracted them from understanding the poetry, and that the man who got it right was Bellini. Even though we all love Bellini's melodies, and the opportunities for great singing that they provide, his orchestral writing seems a little old-fashioned today. But Bellini was sainted for that during his lifetime, as the public could hear the rhythm and the pulse of the music. They could enjoy the quality of the vocal presentation and could listen to the poetry. We know that Bellini used to write his wonderful melodies by saying the poetry out loud. Apparently, deep into the night, he used to walk up and down his room reciting the text. He declaimed it in a public style until the melody was born naturally and until he could find the right rhythm and melodic contour. So, for me, Bellini was *the* great *bel canto* master. That being so, Rossini perhaps should have added a fourth principle to those you mentioned earlier: a powerful commitment to the declamation of the text.

Even though *bel canto* simply means beautiful song, all the main roles written by Bellini and others were for dramatic singers. They weren't written for operatic canaries who had no personality or theatrical energy. Compared to later operas, the dramaturgy in Bellini was much less demanding; the singer would take his or her place at the footlights, remain static and deliver important theatrical and musical material from that fixed position. This stood in sharp contrast to the elaborate production style that Mahler developed in Vienna some 60 years later. The greatest *bel canto* singers of the early 19th century were noted for what they did with their voices and how their vocal technique portrayed the drama. One tenor might be known as the tenor of the curse, while another singer might excel at jealous outbursts. There's a marvellous letter by Verdi about the possible casting of the soprano Eugenia Tadolini in the role of Lady Macbeth. He was absolutely clear in that letter that she was completely wrong for the part, even though she was a wonderful diva. Verdi was adamant that Lady Macbeth doesn't just sing but must shriek and growl. As Tadolini had such a beautiful voice, she would have been out of her depth in the part. We tend to forget that the 19th century was a period when dramatic and vocal skills were one and the same thing. And, for me, there's nothing more like purgatory than a bad performance of a *bel canto* opera. If I am stuck in the middle of a long row and can't get out, I feel wretched physically. I just want to run away.

RH: As part of your advocacy of Donizetti you have recorded many little known operas with Opera Rara.

ME: Opera Rara is an organisation of minuscule size. Yet in the 40 years of its existence, the company has done an incredible musicological and artistic job by finding material for operas that have sunk into oblivion. Curiously, their fall into obscurity was not because they were bad music but, simply, because the material wasn't available and it was hard to find singers who could do them justice. As Opera Rara receives no money from the Arts Council, and has to raise every penny that it needs, I've been trying to help keep it going in recent years by giving performances and making recordings with it.

Our aim is to bring to life scores that I believe have real drama and beauty. One such work is Donizetti's *Les martyrs*. Although it was originally written for Naples, it wasn't performed there; the king wouldn't allow it. He thought that it would be terrible to see Christians suffering on stage, so he banned it. Donizetti then changed, enlarged and enriched it for Paris. *Les martyrs* is often simply dismissed out of hand. But the truth is that nobody had heard a proper, complete edition of the work until we performed it. And it was a thrilling project. The singers were passionate about the work, the public came in large numbers to the Royal Festival Hall and we made a recording that has been well received.

Donizetti is as different from Bellini as Rossini is from Donizetti. Although Donizetti came from Bergamo in northern Italy, he was taught by the Bavarian composer, Simone Mayr. Mayr was at the forefront of new music at the beginning of the 19th century and was a composer with a Classical background but with a Romantic spirit. Donizetti was brought up, therefore, in the Italian tradition but with lashings of Bavarian extras. And it was Mayr who taught Donizetti that the most expressive woodwind instrument in the orchestra is the bassoon. He grasped that it could express both deep feeling and humour; it could sing in a way that no other woodwind instrument could. And that is why the aria 'Una furtiva lagrima' from *L'elisir d'amore* is introduced by the bassoon. If it were played on a cor anglais or a clarinet, it would sound completely different emotionally. The bassoon sounds like it's connected to Nemorino's soul; the soul of a man who is abused and teased by everybody. But, by incorporating the bassoon into the aria, Nemorino suddenly realises that it's going to be all right in the end. And Mayr taught Donizetti that; an unusual combination of scholarship and imagination.

Donizetti was also one of three composers who wrote at breakneck speed; the other two were Mozart and Shostakovich. As a result, Donizetti's manuscripts are extremely difficult to decipher. When we're preparing his works for Opera Rara, I spend a great deal of time with a professional copyist disentangling his intentions, which is a fascinating process in itself. And, as Donizetti's musical ideals and expressions are more Romantic than those of Bellini and Rossini, his music can be quite vulnerable. There are lovely touches in his orchestration and beautiful melodies which cannot be mistaken for either Bellini or Verdi. He contracted syphilis when he was a young man and it destroyed him much too early. But, by the end of his short life, he had written so many pieces for Italy and France that his success was prodigious. As his operas were being performed in different theatres in the French capital at the same time, his contemporaries in Paris

PART FOUR: ITALIAN MUSIC

were terrifically jealous of him. Even though he wrote to order, he was immensely successful because the Parisian public was enthralled by his music. If one performs his operas with singers who have not only beautiful voices but also panache, creativity and daring, it is both a rewarding and an enjoyable experience.

RH: You are closely associated with the music of Verdi. As a young man, who did you especially admire in this music?

ME: Carlo Maria Giulini particularly impressed me, though by the time I was old enough to pronounce his name, he'd stopped working in the theatre. He had become frustrated by the opera profession, but his work with the Royal Opera was legendary. He was a great leader and a great trainer of singers and orchestras. Towards the end of his life, he started to conduct and record operas again to please his wife, who had had a stroke. She meant an enormous amount to him and I think he wanted to do something to improve her spirits. I met him on the morning of his 60th birthday in a little flat in Mayfair and we talked about Verdi's *Don Carlos*. I was conducting the work at the time and he knew a great deal about it. What I admired about Giulini above all was his ability to make the drama apparent through the most beautiful music-making. He did this without any force and with great elegance. He also made Verdi's humanity speak. Anybody who's interested in Verdi's works should look for that in the music, even though some of the subject matter may seem so alien to us nowadays. While his works can be monumental, biblical and dramatic, he still has more to propose to the public than most creative artists. There are 12 operas by Verdi that are performed regularly all over the world, a figure unchallenged by any other composer. Operas by Puccini and Rossini are performed frequently, but the actual number of operas heard is less than that of Verdi. More importantly, Verdi has had an incredible impact on the way that we listen. I believe it's to do with the way that he depicts human contact and human passion through music. This quality has to be teased out and the orchestra needs to be made aware of it.

RH: The first opera that you conducted professionally was *Rigoletto*. Doubtless it occupies a special place in your affections. Do you think that it also holds a special place within Verdi's output?

ME: After the Second World War, when Europe was struggling to reconstruct itself, the heads of the Italian opera houses all came together to discuss how they could revive opera in their own country. They made a joint statement at the end of their meeting, before which they were asked, 'If, in the future, you could only have one opera by Verdi, which one would it be?' Both secretly and individually they all replied: '*Rigoletto*'. This was most fitting, as Verdi was asked some years after completing *Rigoletto* which opera he considered his best. He said, 'Speaking as a professional, *Rigoletto*, but speaking as an actor, *La traviata*.'

Rigoletto is a real challenge. No matter how many times ones sees it, it's still full of unexpected moments. It is a highly daring, original work and a powerful drama. The first time I conducted it in Melbourne was on April Fool's Day. It was a matinee performance, so I was just out of danger – or so I thought. *Rigoletto* starts very quietly with two instruments: a trumpet and a trombone. They play the tune that is associated with the curse and it soon fades away mysteriously. As I was so young and had no experience, I thought that all I had to do was to go and conduct. I did what I thought I was supposed to do and only the trombone came in; the trumpet remained silent. I remember thinking: 'You're in the wrong job. Give it up, do something else. If you can't get two instru-

PART FOUR: ITALIAN MUSIC

ments to come in together, what chance have you got when it's the whole lot?' It was a valuable lesson: it's always the conductor's fault!

RH: Even though that experience was challenging, would you recommend *Rigoletto* as an appropriate work for a young conductor to cut his operatic teeth on?

ME: Absolutely. First, because it's a masterpiece and, second, because it's so hard to conduct well. It teaches a young conductor when to lead the singers and when to accompany them. The year of my Melbourne debut, I gave 32 performances of *Rigoletto* and nothing else. It was a wonderful experience. By the time I had done those performances, I was ready for anything. If you can conduct 'Caro nome' with five different sopranos playing Gilda, all of whom breathe and are nervous in different places, then you're set for life! And Edward Downes gave me that opportunity.

I was preparing for those initial Australian performances of *Rigoletto* in Vienna, where I was working with Solti on his recording of *Parsifal*. In Verdi's opera, there is a bell that indicates the half hour: 11.30 pm and not midnight. I didn't know that when I was young, but I was in my little garret room, engrossed in the score, and at the moment that I looked at the 11.30 bell indication on the page, the bell outside started to ring. The timing was amazing. I thought, 'What's this other bell?' And it went ding, ding outside as I looked at it on the score. All of a sudden, I realised: that's what *that* bell is supposed to be! A little bell that has to be quite loud and clear for the half-hour chime.

RH: You have conducted a great deal of Verdi in English. What are the challenges of a local-language approach to an idiom in which melody is so closely wedded to text?

ME: Performing Verdi in English is highly challenging. His music uses particular forms that must be respected; they can't be treated arbitrarily just because it helps the translator. I can say honestly that I have spent more hours translating Italian operas into English than conducting them. The whole journey that one needs to make before a translation is remotely acceptable is enormous. There are very few people who are skilled at it. The music must never be changed and the words must fit it exactly. It must be done with great care.

RH: Where do you think Verdi stood in relation to his predecessors?

ME: The way that he reacted to his musical antecedents had a great deal to do with what was expected of him. Verdi's first *tutti* operas were not a success and he was eventually persuaded to write *Nabucco*. Everybody responded to the immediacy and the scale of the opera: it was his first great triumph at La Scala, though it is a bold and slightly crude work that contains a great many wonderful melodies. You could even call it a 'painting-by-numbers opera'. Right from the beginning, Verdi was known as the monumental composer; the composer with the loud orchestra. From the generation before him, Donizetti was a charmer, a great colleague and a man of infinite generosity. He encouraged Verdi, and Verdi learned an enormous amount from him. From Donizetti and his contemporaries, but mostly from Donizetti, Verdi worked out what was successful about their operas. He would go, listen and judge how the public responded to a particular trio, for example. He would analyse it and quickly grasp what worked and what didn't.

RH: Composers' lives are now often subdivided into early, middle and late periods. Does this affect how Verdi is perceived?

ME: Every time Verdi wrote a new opera towards the end of his life, the gaps between them became wider and wider. Although he was also accused of being a Wagnerian at that time, there is no doubt in my mind that the Beast of Bayreuth had no influence on him at all. Verdi was his own master, and he knew exactly what he wanted artistically. He just needed the right man to produce the right text. When he came to write *Falstaff* at the end of his life, he said, 'I want to write a comic opera. For 50 years, I've never been sent the right libretto. As I now have the libretto, the music will come.' Being old, he wrote it slowly and carefully. Consequently, it's one of the best things he ever did.

You *can* discuss his output as early, middle and late, but you mustn't do so if it means that you miss the line through his *oeuvre*. The better you know the earlier pieces through good performances and recordings, the easier it is to get a sense of Verdi's greatness. That said, his real greatness lies in *Rigoletto*, *Il trovatore* and *La traviata*. Those three middle-period operas were written close together and are a perfect balance of words and music. After these three remarkable works, Verdi embellished. Northern Europeans enjoy that; we appreciate the colour and virtuosity of the orchestra in *Falstaff* and *Otello*. But his greatness as a composer lies in his most-performed pieces, in the structural force and the dramatic originality of those three great middle-period operas.

RH: You conducted *Falstaff* with the Orchestra of the Age of Enlightenment at Glyndebourne.

ME: It's the most modern piece that I've done with the OAE. A few years earlier, we gave Verdi's Requiem. It was the best performance of that work that I have ever conducted. But it has as much to do with the way the members of the OAE think about making music as with the instruments themselves. The instruments that were used for *Falstaff* were all types or models in circulation before the opera was written. As the OAE can play with great bravura and attack, the experiment worked well. While the orchestra can be loud, it should always be clear and brilliant. *Falstaff* may require a fat sound, but only when the libretto demands it.

In Verdi's time, the sound-world would have been slimmer and the orchestra would have played with greater transparency. But it is also possible to play transparently with a modern symphony orchestra and it is part of a conductor's responsibility to search that out. Paavo Berglund was particularly good at it. He got orchestras to play Sibelius in a restrained and controlled manner that made the music clear and not coated with saccharine. It was still beautiful but he avoided warm, wide vibrato, so that the lines of the music came out.

This also applies to Wagner. I would love to work on his music with the OAE. I have never had the opportunity to do so, but I would love to perform *Tristan und Isolde* with that orchestra. It would shed new light on the work's sound-world.

RH: The battle lines in any discussion of Puccini are often very clear, marked out by critics such as Joseph Kerman, who dismissed *Tosca* as 'that shabby little shocker'. Why do you think Puccini remains so divisive?

ME: In my view, Puccini was certainly not a 'shocker' and he's only 'shabby' if we perform him shabbily. He was not a great composer, but does that matter? Of course it doesn't. If his music is performed at the highest level, you might well convince an audience that it is great. But, if it is performed shabbily and in a routine manner, the music will appear shabby and routine. The best of his operas are marvels of musical, theatrical and vocal joy.

As Puccini matured, he inserted more and more information into his scores. Aware that Italians can be ill-disciplined and in need of control, he decided to be prescriptive and to write all the details of how to perform his music in the score. But it is easy for the conductor to become confused by the sheer amount of information, to be indulgent and to exaggerate. His colleague Pietro Mascagni hardly wrote anything in his music, even though his compositions need incredible flexibility in performance. So you just have to love the music, get to know it and understand what the words mean.

I adore rehearsing and performing Puccini's music, as I am keen to make it as good as possible and to convince the musicians and the public that they are in the presence of a master. But the singers mustn't linger too long over a note or phrase. Sometimes they think that such indiscretions don't matter, as the opera that they are performing is so well known. I'm afraid that's completely unacceptable. Everybody must have one, single view of the work. For me, that is of the utmost importance and it is the conductor who must bring integrity to the performance.

Take *La bohème*, for example. It is an opera divided into four musical works, not a series of little musical gestures. Each act in *Bohème* is one piece of music. To start from the first bar of Act 1 and not stop or relax until you've finished the last note of that act is extremely difficult; there are so many little details. And all those involved in the performance must perform it with the same sense of organic continuity, regardless of those details.

As Puccini's personality was so sensitive, he was drawn naturally to the French style and what was happening culturally in Paris at the end of the 19th century. There is a perfume in Puccini that reminds me of Debussy and Ravel. His sense of colour and, above all, his sense of sensuousness was remarkable. His scores and texts are full of hidden dirty jokes and many of his contemporaries used to rush to the premieres of his operas to see how many they could notice in the text. The opening of *La bohème*, for example, is rambunctious, fast and noisy. The boys are joking with each other and saying how cold they are, even though the stove is burning a great deal of wood. Then, suddenly, the orchestra stops. Why? Why is it unaccompanied? Because it allows the text and the double meaning of the words to be clear to the audience. They will then remember what it was like to have been students, to have made jokes about their poverty, to have wondered where the next meal was coming from and to have been constantly freezing. But, if you've got a sense of humour, it'll see you through. Puccini was brilliant at depicting such moments. While he might not have been in the very front rank of creative artists, he was a great personality and a great operatic composer.

PART FIVE

BRITISH MUSIC

RH: Some commentators have argued that Sir Edward Elgar was the first great English composer. Can you quantify that greatness and say a little about why he means so much to you?

ME: Elgar was not the first great English composer, but the first since the death of Purcell. He was very aware of European traditions and practices from his youth onwards but quickly found his own compositional voice. Even in his earlier works there are fingerprints of a personal style that became more ubiquitous as time went by. His astonishing ability as a self-taught composer is one of his most outstanding qualities, and his thirst for musical knowledge was truly remarkable. As an outsider from Worcester, he used to get up before dawn and take the train to Paddington. From Paddington, he took another train to Upper Norwood, where he hoped to be in time for the last rehearsal for that day's concert at the Crystal Palace. After the performance, he would make his way back to Worcester, the culmination of a series of long and tiring journeys.

He was always keen to hear the new work on the programme and was terribly disappointed if he missed it. These trips were nothing short of pilgrimages, and he was always determined to hear the best orchestras in rehearsal and performance. He listened particularly to the way an orchestra sounded and how specific colours and effects were created. Being self-taught, he was constantly in search of his own poetic voice and one that represented the countryside in which he was born. He was once asked where the musical idea for the middle section of the second movement of the First Symphony came from. He replied simply that it was 'the sort of thing that one hears by the river'. What he meant was that many of his best ideas would come to him while meandering alone on his bike through the byways and highways of Worcestershire. As he said, the trees would sing to him. He was not from the musical or social establishment but became a member through his success, the intensity of his musical imagination and his ability to be a genuine populist.

RH: You are one of the few British conductors who has recorded Elgar's three great oratorios: *The Dream of Gerontius*, *The Apostles* and *The Kingdom*. For many modern listeners, these works are challenging, both religiously and culturally. Only *The Dream of Gerontius* is performed regularly, while *The Apostles* and *The Kingdom* have largely failed to ignite the public's interest. Why do you think that is?

ME: I remember one experienced British soprano saying to me that it was rare for her to be engaged to sing *The Kingdom* but that she would be booked for at least three performances of *The Apostles* each year. I would have thought that it would have been the other way around, as *The Apostles* is a much bigger work than *The Kingdom* and demands so much more money and time to rehearse and to perform successfully. Concerning the works' religiosity, *The Dream of Gerontius* upset the Anglicans because Cardinal Newman's text was so Roman. But once the work had been well prepared and well performed, unlike the disastrous first performance at Birmingham in 1900, it took on an incredible power that fired the listening public's imagination.

As the story of *Gerontius* is easily told, its simplicity also helped the oratorio to be accepted by audiences. Effectively, it is about a man who is at the point of death and is surrounded by well-wishers. After dying, Gerontius passes over to the other side and is supported by an angel before facing the Godhead. Elgar depicts this in music in a way that nobody else had done before.

The story of *The Apostles* is much harder to describe. When Elgar came to envisage this enormous work in three parts, he was so intent on surpassing *Gerontius*, and doing something that nobody had ever done before, that he ended up being late in fulfilling his contract. So he had to make compromises. He couldn't decide which passages from the Bible to use. He thought that if he chose sections that everybody recognised, and that were conspicuously Anglican in character, the work would be accepted more readily. Those choices influenced the compositional process of *The Apostles*. Originally, the work was going to be followed by two other parts and was to finish with the Last Judgement.

What later became *The Kingdom* was originally to be part of *The Apostles*. But, when he started to set the text, the notes poured from his pen. It was as if the music had been marinating for years. As he was so experienced at writing for voices and large orchestra by the time that he composed the works, he found that he had a great deal to say. He decided, therefore, to separate *The Kingdom* from *The Apostles* and to create two oratorios. It seems clear from his correspondence that the process of creating these two works prompted a nervous breakdown. He arrived at a crossroads in his career and it stopped him from writing for voices thereafter.

Elgar's three great oratorios require a great deal of time, both in their preparation and in their performance. Of the three, *Gerontius* is the most straightforward in the way that the music is laid out, as self-contained choruses often lead naturally to discrete solos. In *The Apostles*, the musical technique is more like a film, fading from one scene to the next without making it particularly clear what the next scene is. You simply have to know the work and be led by the words. Elgar would take one line from one section of the Bible and juxtapose it with another passage from elsewhere. By combining these materials, he attempted to create a narrative that depicted the point at which Jesus felt assured that he had a group of acolytes who would proselytise after his Ascension. It's about the founding of Christianity and how those who believed in Christ, through their humility and dedication, could prepare themselves and others for life eternal. Elgar was profoundly affected by the story and the music that he wrote for it is incomparably beautiful.

I have to admit that I didn't always think that. I found it difficult to decide whether to do *The Apostles* or *The Kingdom* first or, indeed, whether either was really worth the effort of studying and performing at all. Having now done them, I feel slightly ashamed of those concerns. But that is often the way with big pieces. Only by living with them, doing them and committing to them do I find a way into them. It is crucial not to be sanctimonious about them; they should not be treated as church music. They are spiritual pieces about religious topics that live in the concert hall. If they can be performed in an ecclesiastical building, all well and good, but don't halve the tempi just because you're in the presence of God!

PART FIVE: BRITISH MUSIC

RH: What kind of an impact do you think a voice such as that of Dame Clara Butt would have had on the performance of his works? It's a voice-type that has simply disappeared.

ME: When I was young there were two outstanding British contraltos: Helen Watts and Norma Procter. When either was needed for low parts, such as the Angel in *Gerontius*, you knew you had the real thing. The essence of such a tessitura is not to do with how high or low a singer can sing but where the colour of the voice sits naturally. Today, there are few singers who can tackle such low parts successfully: Patricia Bardon is one and Rebecca de Pont Davies is another. There were probably more when Elgar was writing and he composed the *Sea Pictures* with Clara Butt in mind. But she never performed the first and last of the cycle and only gave the much easier middle three. Even though Elgar knew her sound, I find it unacceptable, ugly and not at all interesting. Frankly, I am pleased that we don't have singers who sound like that anymore. It may be that her appeal was more than just her sound; perhaps it was the way her personality came across as she sang.

Another real contralto was Kathleen Ferrier, whose life and career were cut tragically short. She was a wonderful artist, natural and uninhibited, a real down-to-earth girl. And then there is Dame Janet Baker, a wonderful example of a great artist who has made the most of what God has given her. Unlike Butt, she sang the *Sea Pictures* complete and made a beautiful recording of them. It was difficult for her, but she is not alone in finding the *Sea Pictures* tricky: in my experience, all mezzo-sopranos and contraltos find them challenging.

But, to return to Elgar's oratorios, the central problem for me is that I have to select a singer who's free, whether it's to sing the Angel in *The Dream of Gerontius* or the contralto part in *The Apostles*, and simply make it work. To avoid her singing out of tune, I beg her not to shout and not to press on her voice, especially when it rises from the lower part of the register to the higher. It is also crucial that she should not be swamped by the orchestra and that I respect what she can do. There are always passages where the dynamics need to be changed. Some *crescendi* need to be less intense and some *forte* passages need to be played *piano*. If the singer has artistic credibility and has the right understanding of the material, I can make it work. But the orchestra has to shut up!

RH: A few years ago, you conducted a London orchestra in Elgar's First Symphony, and I brought a group of postgraduate conducting students from the Royal Academy of Music to a rehearsal. The orchestra had not performed the work for 15 years, and it was clear that a number of players were unfamiliar with the music in general and Elgar's string writing in particular. At the rehearsal break, you remarked to the students that this situation wouldn't have arisen 30 or 40 years ago, as the symphony would have been a standard part of any British orchestra's repertoire. Why is that no longer the case?

ME: The answer is quite simple. Orchestras only master these two huge symphonies if their principal conductors are interested in them. Otherwise they will be relegated to occasional works for occasional seasons. The BBC Symphony Orchestra performed Elgar's symphonies frequently in the era of Sir Adrian Boult. Sir Georg Solti also gave them regularly when he was Music Director of the London Philharmonic Orchestra. It's a reflection of the taste of the music director and not necessarily that of the public.

Elgar's two symphonies do not make easy listening, it must be said. Even if one has heard and played them often, they not only demand the ability to concentrate for up to 55 minutes but, also, the capacity to absorb Elgar's challenging aesthetic message. As they are enormously ambitious, they require repeated playing. A British orchestra shouldn't go for more than a year or two without performing one of them.

RH: Have you encountered resistance to Elgar's symphonies in the US or continental Europe?

ME: I gave the first performance of Elgar's Second Symphony in Atlanta, Georgia, and the orchestra was quite nervous about it. We did two performances between which there was a day off. On the morning of the second performance, they said, 'Maestro, it would be great if you could come down during intermission. We're having a bit of a party. We've got a surprise for you.' During the day off, someone in the orchestra had gone to a local patisserie and asked them to bake a sponge cake that was the size of a small table. They had it iced with a message: 'To the Atlanta Symphony Orchestra from Sir Edward Elgar: Bravo, chaps! Keep it up.'

Aside from such instances, Elgar doesn't travel well. There are a few pieces that American audiences like, such as the Cello Concerto, the 'Enigma' Variations and the 'Pomp and Circumstance' marches. But Vaughan Williams is a more popular composer. I think that this is based on prejudice. In America, choral societies adore *A Sea Symphony* and audiences love the *Tallis Fantasia* and *The Lark Ascending*.

However, I have conducted Delius and Bax with the Chicago Symphony Orchestra. In 2010 I did Bax's *Spring Fire* in Manchester. It's a wonderful piece and I find that the musicians are interested in it. All one can do is try.

I find talking to the audiences about these works is important, particularly if the piece is long, or if the audience has never heard it before. Some years ago, I went one Sunday afternoon with the London Philharmonic to the newly refurbished Dome in Brighton. After performing a Mozart concerto, we gave Mahler's Sixth Symphony. As it's more than an hour long, I thought that I'd better tell them something about it. I said, 'Ladies and gentlemen, the work we're going to play is one of the greatest Romantic symphonies and a wonderful testament to Mahler's personality. It contains autobiographical parts, is a very passionate work and is rather long. It's about an hour and a quarter.' Someone in the front row then shouted, 'Oh good! I've got a bus to catch.' I said, 'I particularly hope that the gentleman in the front row who says he has a bus to catch will be able to stay for the last movement. It's half an hour long and it's very dramatic and exciting.' The reply came, 'Anything for you, Mark.' There's a great public waiting for you, if you know how to prime them.

RH: Many British conductors have conducted one of Elgar's symphonies much more frequently than the other. Sir John Pritchard concentrated on the First, whereas Sir John Barbirolli conducted 103 performances of the Second Symphony and only 38 of the First. Do you have a preference?

ME: I like and perform them equally. Managements prefer the First because of its loud ending, but the Second is more mature and a greater piece overall. The challenge presented by the Second is how to bring off the long, quiet finish after the drama and brilliance of the preceding material. If audiences are unfamiliar with it, the end can be more downbeat than they were expecting. Another challenge for the conductor is Elgar's development passages. As they are often not the most distinguished parts of the symphonies, he actively encouraged conductors not to linger too long over them. Take the development section of the First Symphony's first movement: it is a little self-conscious, gauche and loud. It needs to be made less portentous and more vibrant and brilliant. It should never drag and should move on quickly to the following material.

Similar problems occur in the concert overture, *In the South*, which is more like a symphonic poem than an overture. Because of the character of the thematic material in the middle section, it is much better if the orchestra is made to play faster than it ever thought it could. Elgar does that on his own recording, which I find particularly inspirational. If this passage is performed too earnestly, attention is drawn to its inadequacies. But if the conductor moves it along, the audience will be impressed by the sheer volume of sound and will find relief in the lovely viola solo that follows.

RH: Elgar's younger contemporary was Ralph Vaughan Williams. For many listeners, their works are representative of British cultural life and are infused with a certain sense of Britishness. Is it possible to express such things in music?

ME: Is there such a thing as Britishness in British music? To answer that we must consider some of the influences that shaped British music-making. As I said, Elgar was aware of the Austro-German symphonic tradition and was equally aware of Wagner's impact on that tradition. Elgar made trips to Bayreuth to hear Wagner's works first-hand. He studied them in detail and composed his First Symphony in the key of *Parsifal*; A flat major, the only symphony by a significant composer written in that key.

Vaughan Williams took a completely different path. While he lacked Elgar's inner belief as a musician, he had greater conviction as a man. Elgar was nervousness, full of self-doubt and intolerable socially. As time went by, he became increasingly difficult and more unpredictable. Conversely, Vaughan Williams was grounded and the only thing that made him nervous was the possibility that he was not a good craftsman. Perhaps that is why he went to study orchestration with Maurice Ravel in his mid-30s. As a composer, Vaughan Williams was mystical in a way that Elgar was not. If there is anything English about Vaughan Williams's music – and I stress the word '*if*' – it's his use of folk song. And it is the beauty of those songs, combined with our love of country, which prompts us to believe that his works are English. But that doesn't mean that the music in which he imbeds them is of itself English.

After all, music as sound means nothing: a C major chord is just a C major chord. It is only through association and suggestion that it means whatever we want it to mean. Some years ago, I conducted a modern American piece that was inspired by the cliffs near San Diego, California. The sheer cliffs at Torrey Pines State Natural Reserve go down to the sea and waves break against them violently. To prepare the audience for the work, I explained its imagery to them. After the performance, a young man came up to me and said, 'I really enjoyed that modern piece but I didn't think it was about the cliffs at all. For me, it was about being in a cathedral when the summer sunlight pours in through the stained-glass windows and makes lovely colours on the floor. At that moment, you can see the little particles of dust dancing in the air. That's what the music said to me.' I was touched by his reaction. I said, 'That's fantastic. Hang on to that image, be proud of it and don't be embarrassed by it. The fact that you had such a strong reaction is the most important thing.'

Britons tend to be a bit uptight about Englishness in music. It is only natural that we want to have English music so that we can celebrate our love of country in sound. But I am convinced that Elgar

PART FIVE: BRITISH MUSIC

would have written music in the same way had he been born in Hagen, like Charles Hallé, rather than Worcester. While Elgar never used folk songs in the manner of Gustav Holst and Ralph Vaughan Williams, his works are covered with his musical fingerprints. Take, for example, his use of the seventh, a wide and expressive interval. When used in 'Nimrod', it builds intensity while creating a sense of yearning. On the other hand, triplet figures were one of Delius's most common musical traits. But, by employing such devices regularly, it doesn't make them English; it's simply part of who Elgar and Delius were as musicians.

When it comes to Vaughan Williams, I believe fully that he should be placed within a wider European context. It is a complete mistake to assume that an English symphony must be programmed with other English works. It is essential that the audience encounters different styles of music within a single concert. By juxtaposing Vaughan Williams with, say, Janáček, one can dispel the cosy notion of 'good old Vaughan Williams and his folk songs'. He was a modernist whose best pieces – and I consider all his symphonies among his best pieces – should be heard within as broad a context as possible.

I once conducted Ravel's Left-Hand Piano Concerto in the same concert as Vaughan Williams's Third Symphony. Arguably the composer's best symphony, it is a work of incredible beauty and profundity. Even though it was first published as 'A Pastoral Symphony', it has nothing to do with Gloucestershire. He originally gave the work this moniker to disguise its true meaning. Like Mahler in his Third Symphony, Vaughan Williams gave each movement a descriptive title which he later withdrew, allowing the music to speak for itself. It would have been better if he hadn't employed the 'Pastoral' sobriquet in the first place, as the piece is about the terrible rape of the Belgian and French landscape during the First World War and how that landscape was made a ghostly shadow of its former self. The music insinuates itself into our memories. It depicts the way in which the sun goes behind the clouds and casts a shroud of coldness over the land. Loneliness, emptiness and bleakness are ever present in the music. Sadly, commentators were disparaging about the symphony when it first appeared and deliberately misunderstood it. The wordless elegy sung by the off-stage soprano is particularly moving. The symphony is one of Vaughan Williams's greatest achievements and made still greater by being placed within a European context.

RH: Why does the music of Delius appeal to you so much? I know that you are particularly drawn to *Sea Drift*.

ME: While I find his music particularly beautiful, British orchestras generally loathe Delius. When his music appears on the stands of the Hallé in Manchester, there is always a sigh of despondency from the players. But, being British, the players' despondency is always tempered with wit and good humour. We were rehearsing the *Poème* by Chausson, for example, and I asked the players if they knew how the composer died. As the silence was deafening, I filled the void by explaining that it was terribly tragic. Chausson lived in the country and drew inspiration from going on bike-rides almost every day. He would cycle through the countryside using the same route, which he knew by heart and adored. But, on his last, fatal ride, his brakes failed on the way home. He careered down a hill, went straight into a brick wall and died instantly. One player snorted, 'Pity they didn't give a bike to Delius.'

When performing *Sea Drift*, the players say that they can't bear how the harmony slithers around like overcooked spaghetti. Even though they often temper their reaction by saying that they enjoy the work, they are not impressed by Delius's music in general. But I love his harmonic progressions and first got to know them when I was a student at Cambridge. I was fortunate to play bassoon in a performance of *Sea Drift* at the Snape Maltings under Sir David Willcocks with John Shirley-Quirk as soloist.

Sea Drift is about the pain of loss. The soloist describes how, as a boy, he watched birds mating. Having laid her eggs in the nest, the female bird flies off in search of food but never comes back. In the middle of the piece, the soloist becomes the remaining bird and sings an elegy for his lost love; a beautifully poetic idea. Delius was concerned with man's relationship with the wider world. He explored the power of nature, our reliance on it and its function as a model for good. He was deeply inspired by these concepts and developed them still further in *A Song of the High Hills*. This is one of his last pieces, written for a large, wordless chorus and orchestra. It expresses the ecstasy of being on top of a Norwegian mountain on a fine summer night and being able to see for miles. It explores how a big choir can convey a sense of space by singing very quietly. The orchestra gradually takes up the musical argument, reaches an incredible climax and then dies away. Commentators who say Delius doesn't travel well are wrong. In 2017 I conducted the Berlin premiere of *Sea Drift* with Roderick Williams and the Rundfunkchor Berlin. The choir's English was flawless and both choir and audience adored the work.

RH: A British composer who travels better than most is Benjamin Britten. That said, I recently attended a production of his *Albert Herring* at Munich's Residenztheater that completely misunderstood the work and was at odds with its Suffolk origins and setting. As Suffolk is so central to the opera's musical and dramatic narratives is there not a likelihood that it will always be misrepresented, misunderstood and considered somewhat parochial culturally by foreign audiences, performers and directors?

ME: If *Albert Herring* seems parochial, that is a great pity. But music isn't terribly successful at describing landscapes; it is ill-equipped to describe either the countryside or the city. It does, however, describe brilliantly our *responses* to urban and pastoral scenes, and neither *Albert Herring* nor *Peter Grimes* need be tied to Suffolk. In their failed attempts to be more place specific, some directors have even attempted productions using a Suffolk accent. But who can truly master such an accent? Not only do the singers hate it but it sounds horrible and unconvincing. A glass of lemonade is a glass of lemonade wherever you are. Aldeburgh beach is not the only pebbly beach in the world and Swan Vestas can be bought in towns other than Loxford.

It is perfectly possible to do works such as *Albert Herring* and *Peter Grimes* in different environments and in different cultural settings. I saw a fine performance of *Peter Grimes* in Berlin many years ago directed by Joachim Herz. He loved the piece and admired it enormously. To see an East German's view of this powerful Suffolk opera was fascinating. Herz extracted the essence of the story and showed that a myopic, bitchy, quarrelling village can exist in any country. He made clear that it was not necessary to set it where Crabbe had written the poem, and that it had more to do with human behaviour in general than Suffolk in particular.

RH: Did you ever see Britten conduct?

ME: Not only did I see him conduct, but I performed with him. While I was an undergraduate at Cambridge, I played the bassoon in a performance of the *Spring Symphony*. The concert had been prepared by Sir David Willcocks and Britten came to work with us on the day of the concert, the same concert at which I first played in Delius's *Sea*

PART FIVE: BRITISH MUSIC

Drift. He wore a tweed jacket, which remained buttoned, with the obligatory yellow leather pads on the elbows. He was extremely charming and calm. I remember him saying, 'I wonder whether or not you'd mind doing that little bit again for me, as I always find it rather hard.' What he was *actually* saying was, 'Let's do it again, as you couldn't get it right.' He was so generous in the way that he treated us and it was lovely to play for him, as he was so immediately communicative.

RH: Speaking of immediate communication, I would like to return to opera in the vernacular. You have strong views on Verdi and Wagner in English. How about Britten in Russian? If a conductor is going to perform a Britten opera in a non-English-speaking country, should he or she perform it in English?

ME: This depends entirely on the experience of the company, the linguistic skill of the local audience and the singers cast. Let me give you a slightly different example. If you cast a Janáček opera using only English-speaking singers, I see no reason to do it in Czech. If, on the other hand, you have four principal parts sung by leading Czech singers, then, by all means, do it in the original language. But, if that is the case, it is imperative that the rest of the cast is tireless in perfecting their Czech pronunciation. There was a company on the other side of the Atlantic which decided that if it staged a Janáček opera in translation it wouldn't be presenting the public with the real thing. For me, this kind of 'authenticity' is fake. It's the kind of snobbery in opera that we must guard against. It is a cause for concern when people think they are getting something provincial when hearing opera in translation. Whether it's provincial or not is decided solely by the quality of the performance. And there is something else to bear in mind: audiences today are multicultural and consist of many different nationalities. The purpose of having subtitles in a performance is not just for English-speaking members of the audience but for everybody who can manage English better than, say, German or Italian. While opera in the vernacular must always be viewed within a wider social context, the fact remains that opera should be communicated as far as possible in the language of the audience that's listening.

RH: Tell me about *Billy Budd*.

ME: It's Britten's greatest opera. Of course, I also love *Peter Grimes*, another masterpiece that received its premiere at an important moment in the musical life of our country. But I am fascinated by the action of *Billy Budd*, what motivates its characters and what their unspoken agendas are. The issues raised are extremely interesting and it is a marvellous project to work on. Britten had a remarkable ability to set words, and the text of *Budd* is brilliant. That's not something that can be said about all his operas. I love the music in *The Rape of Lucretia* but some of the words puzzle me. Britten's collaboration with E.M. Forster was extraordinary and, together, they created something truly remarkable. The concentration of the story, the depiction of life at sea and the way life in this tiny microcosm is developed help to produce a highly intense sound-world.

Britten created a particular sound-world for each opera. Verdi called it *'la tinta'*. He recognised that if he represented the libretto sufficiently cogently, the music would then be absolutely right for that particular libretto. That's also true for Wagner, particularly when you think of *Tannhäuser* and *Lohengrin*, two pieces I really enjoy. *Lohengrin* is the greatest German Romantic opera and a flawless piece. The sound-world at the opening of *Lohengrin* could not possibly be appropriate for *Tannhäuser*. In *Lohengrin*, the dove descending in the prelude and Lohengrin arriving are all in A major. In the *Ring*, there are only a few small passages in that key but nothing significant. In *Tannhäuser*, the use of key is also important, as keys really mattered to Wagner and were central to his *tinta*. Britten had that, too.

Britten's, Wagner's and Verdi's use of key are all distinctive and are a direct result of their involvements with the text. And that's the definition of a great opera composer. The sound-world of *The Turn of the Screw*, for example, could not possibly be confused with the sound-worlds of *Albert Herring*, *Peter Grimes* or *Billy Budd*. The music in *Budd* is lean; there is no fat. When you're at sea, and living that sort of life, it's very harsh. Consequently, when Billy eventually speaks from the heart, it is all the more moving and touching. But Britten's way of describing life on board, and the cruelty and brutality of that life, is distinguished by particularly fine musical and dramatic nuancing. The harsh, and rather unfair, beating of the young novice in Act 1 was deliberately and carefully placed by Britten. He was concerned that if he didn't engender sympathy for any of the other characters, the audience might be less inclined to be involved in the drama. So he invented this highly effective and beautifully written part for a young tenor. It always takes all the notices.

RH: Have you ever thought of doing *Budd* in the original four-act version?

ME: I would love to see the four-act version done once, as the great advantage of the original is that the characters have a scene earlier on the ship. When I conducted the opera at Glyndebourne, I considered the original but decided against it. The tightness of Britten's revision, from four acts to two, works to the opera's benefit.

RH: *The Rape of Lucretia*, *Albert Herring* and *The Turn of the Screw* were all written for small spaces but are now often performed in big theatres. How do you feel about that?

ME: The English National Opera staged *The Turn of the Screw* in my first year as Music Director. The sparseness in the writing and the mysterious atmosphere of the opera actually fitted the Coliseum rather well. The resonance of the space stretched the music and emphasised its beauty. That encouraged us to produce *The Rape of Lucretia*, which also benefitted from the extra space.

The Rape of Lucretia had its premiere at Glyndebourne in 1946, in a much smaller space than the present theatre. Being able to get a sense of the sound, and working out how to enrich that sound within the space while performing, was difficult. That said, the acoustic dryness of the old theatre was one of the reasons why it was so good for Mozart and Rossini, but quite difficult for anything bigger. The new house sits beautifully in terms of the repertoire that is performed there now, including large-scale works such as Verdi's *Otello* and *Simon Boccanegra*. I thought the second of these sounded less successful but I was pleased when we gave *Budd* there. Glyndebourne continues to perform smaller-scale operas and one shouldn't be too dogmatic about this. One should be prepared to try different things and to experiment with the spaces available.

PART SIX

FRENCH, SCANDINAVIAN, CZECH AND RUSSIAN MUSIC

RH: We've talked about the visceral relationship between Italian music and Italian audiences but do you think that kind of relationship also exists between the French and their music?

ME: While the French public is supportive of their music in general, it has never understood, nor fully appreciated, the compositions of Berlioz. At best, their praise of his works is half-hearted. I once conducted *Roméo et Juliette* in Lille. After rehearsing it for three days, one of the double-basses said, '*Ah ... Cette musique, ce n'est pas mal.*' So patronising, so dismissive. One of the reasons that the French have failed to grasp the importance of Berlioz is their system of music education. Young musicians go to the conservatoire to learn rules. Having learned the rules, they have to pass examinations to prove that they know them and to show that they take pride in being brought up properly as musicians. As Berlioz was the *enfant terrible* of French music, he was completely dismissive of such an approach and it took many years before he was accepted by Parisian society. He was a genius and a complete one-off.

But to answer your question more generally, the reason that the music of a particular country is reflective of that country's temperament is to do with speech. Music has to speak in much the same way as speech has to speak. Music, like speech, can't always be legato. Being continuously smooth and gorgeous is pointless unless it tells us something. The national quality of a certain country's music – and this has nothing to do with the Cotswolds, the Dordogne or Tuscany – has to do with the temperament of its creator and the context within which either he or she finds themselves. The French invented nouvelle cuisine, perfume and sensuality and are proud of their interest in the finer things of life. Their music reflects that pride in just the same way that their vowels reflect their attention to tiny linguistic inflections. The best French music, and here I include the works of Rameau, Debussy, Ravel, Messiaen and Dutilleux, is made up of details and perfumes. The way they write for the orchestra is full of musical *morceaux*. Everything is on the surface. This stands in sharp contrast to Italian music with its blood, thunder and guts. The attack and lack of inhibition found in Verdi's works reflect Italians as a nation and would never be found in French music.

RH: You once mentioned to me that Berlioz is one of the people with whom you would have most liked to have had dinner. What would you have liked to have asked him over that meal?

ME: In my imagination, our dinner would have taken place at the end of his life. I would have liked to have asked him about his life in general and why he thought that he would have ever been happy with an Irish actress when he couldn't speak any English and she couldn't speak any French. I would then like to know why he stopped writing operas and whether that was a result of *Benvenuto Cellini*'s reception. I would also be curious to learn whether his approach to dramatic subjects changed because he knew he couldn't get his pieces accepted by the Opéra or because he no longer believed in the genre. As *La damnation de Faust* and *Roméo et Juliette* are such daring alternatives to opera, the answer to the last question would have been of particular interest to me. I would also love to have asked him about his trips to Rome and to the mountains of the Abruzzo and what impacts they had on him. But I am sure that I would have been terrified by the prospect of our dinner, as my French wouldn't have been good enough and I can't imagine that his English would've been much better. So, we'd have had to have met *au milieu*. Nevertheless, I am sure that he would have been wonderful company.

RH: The English-speaking peoples have always been attracted to the music of Sibelius. Sir Henry Wood, Sir Thomas Beecham, Sir John Barbirolli, Sir Colin Davis, Leonard Bernstein and Lorin Maazel all gave complete cycles of his symphonies. Why do you think that Sibelius's music has such a special place in our affections?

ME: While this might seem facetious, I've always believed that the Germans don't take to Sibelius's music because they don't need him. As they have so many symphony composers of their own, they are not particularly interested in anyone else's. Theodor Adorno called it 'sauna Beethoven', a dreadful thing to say. As we have so few symphonists, perhaps we are more open to a broader symphonic landscape. The intellectual rigour that Sibelius's symphonies espouse touch a nerve within us and we welcome the journey he takes us on. Of course, his first two symphonies are full of big, broad, individual melodies but, from the Third onwards, there are comparatively few great tunes. But there *are* thematic ideas that are powerfully rendered. What Sibelius was trying to do was to prove that symphonic logic and symphonic thought did not necessarily mean gargantuan musical experiences. As he developed, his works became more disciplined, shorter and tougher. There is a sense of him stripping symphonic argument of its clothing, skin and flesh so that all that is left in the later works is muscle, sinew and bone.

This is particularly true of the Sixth Symphony, a work that I adore. At the time of its composition, he was studying the music of Palestrina. The rigour and discipline of Italian polyphony is completely in keeping with Sibelius's approach and, if one listens to the beginning of the symphony with that in mind, one can hear immediately the impact of the earlier composer. It is essential that the orchestra doesn't play too 'Hollywood' in this symphony. Rather, it must be objective and disciplined. For me, his music has an intellectual strength and maturity that is not easy to master and no less easy to absorb. But, once you have grasped his works, the experience is particularly rewarding.

Did you know that there was a questionnaire distributed to New York's listening public in the 1930s? It asked: 'Who is your favourite symphonist?' Perhaps surprisingly for the period, Sibelius came out above Beethoven. When Sibelius was young, he was very good-looking and had a mass of dark hair. He was a heavy drinker and regularly visited the brothels of Helsinki. Having completed his first two symphonies, Sibelius left the temptations of the Finnish capital behind him and moved to the country. His wife had had enough of his laddish behaviour and was determined that they should start a family. Surrounded by six daughters and a wife, Sibelius began to lose

PART SIX: FRENCH, SCANDINAVIAN, CZECH & RUSSIAN MUSIC

his hair in middle age. As its loss was more than he could bear, he decided to shave his head. As a result, all the iconography of him from middle age onwards depicts him with a huge, bald head. It was characteristic of him that he should act so impulsively and that he was neither concerned by nor neurotic about it. That was the kind of man he was: ruthless. And that's what attracts English-speaking audiences to his music.

RH: Towards the end of the 1970s, I attended a performance you gave of Dvořák's Sixth Symphony with the Royal Philharmonic Orchestra at the Fairfield Halls, Croydon. At the time, I was struck by the visceral nature of the performance and the difficulties of the score. What would your advice be to young conductors when tackling Dvořák's symphonies for the first time?

ME: Dvořák's greatest musical gift was his ability to express humanity naturally. And, as he was also a great craftsman, his music is always fun to conduct. But young conductors must never underestimate its difficulty when performing one of his more famous symphonies for the first time. His writing for the first violins is demanding. If the section hasn't played it before, or simply doesn't know it, it will sound shocking. It is essential that the conductor spends time with the players and allows them to absorb the material. As Dvořák's music is both irresistible and direct, what you see is what you get. There are no hidden agendas and nothing misleading intellectually. He was a wonderful family man, a deeply spiritual person and an open, honest and strong human being. And all those traits can be found in his music. While it is true that it might not be as great as that of Beethoven, it has a place in the musical firmament that is really important to me. Charm can be a difficult word nowadays and is particularly unfashionable in the theatre. But charm is something that Dvořák and Schubert share. And pain, of course. Both Dvořák's and Schubert's works have an underlying sense of pain.

But one of the reasons why orchestras find Dvořák's music such fun to play is that he was a viola player. By sitting in the middle of the ensemble, he learned how an orchestra should sound. As he was surrounded by the other strings, and was in close aural contact with the winds and brass, he experienced at first-hand how an orchestra functions, lives and breathes. And that is why a young conductor should be particularly alert when there is a lovely solo for the clarinet or the horn, as Dvořák might be keeping the second clarinet or the second horn on their toes by giving it to them rather than the principal player. By so doing, he allows the second player a moment to shine, a democratic sharing out of the jewels, so to speak, which is just marvellous. And, it goes without saying, that his melodies are some of the most memorable ever written.

Of the early symphonies, perhaps the Third is the best. Even though it has a weak last movement, the first two are really rather good. The Fifth Symphony is an excellent piece for a young conductor to perform. It's not particularly hard to conduct, is full of colour and is wonderfully effective. It is unlikely that the orchestra will know it and the players will enjoy the experience of being introduced to it. Being an immensely practical composer, Dvořák always exhibited great joy and skill when presenting his musical ideas. And that is why his music is so enjoyable to rehearse and to perform.

RH: Is Leoš Janáček the natural heir to Dvořák and Smetana?

ME: Janáček is not their natural heir and is as different from Dvořák and Smetana as Bohemia is from Moravia. Bohemia, where

PART SIX: FRENCH, SCANDINAVIAN, CZECH & RUSSIAN MUSIC

Dvořák came from, is a pastoral, rich and rolling land, while Moravia, the birthplace of Janáček, has sharp cliffs, gnarled trees and is more barren. The beauty and darkness of that Moravian landscape is reflected in the region's speech and music. What motivated Janáček was the idea of creating a national, Moravian musical style that his people would recognise. Unlike Bartók, who was interested in recording the musical content of his country's folk songs, Janáček documented local speech patterns. With notebook in hand, he would walk into town, stand and listen to his fellow Moravians as they strolled by. He would record the intonation of simple phrases and would write them down as if they were a musical line. Thus, the rhythms of the Moravian language permeated his approach as a composer. When writing operas, he inseminated his musical ideas with those speech rhythms. This means that his stage works are hard to perform in any language other than Czech.

One of the biggest problems a conductor faces in Janáček's music is the performance material itself. As his handwriting is particularly hard to decipher, it is often difficult to know whether or not the score in front of you contains the right notes and is the best possible edition. His habit of writing part of one work on one side of a page and a completely different work on the reverse makes his manuscripts a nightmare to interpret. Our great friend and colleague, Sir Charles Mackerras, worked tirelessly for many years on Janáček's autograph scores, sketches and fragments and we owe him an enormous debt of gratitude for all that he did on the composer's behalf.

While Janáček's works are exciting to do with an orchestra, they present certain practical problems. Unlike Dvořák, Janáček writes his music in small note values and is happiest when notating in quavers, semiquavers, demisemiquavers and hemidemisemiquavers. As these tiny note values are riddled with little tails, the music looks like something akin to an overgrown garden. I remember conducting the Australian premiere of *Kát'a Kabanová* in Sydney, and watching the musicians' faces as they opened their parts for the first time. As nobody could see the musical wood for the notational trees, there were frowns of disbelief. Chaos reigned. But they came to terms with its idiom once they had the music in their ears rather than their eyes. As Janáček constructed his music from tiny cells, there is an underlying nervousness about it. His music can't be rushed and requires time before it starts to sound beautiful.

RH: A composer about whom you feel deeply is Dmitri Shostakovich.

ME: Shostakovich suffered more than we can ever know. Having had such an auspicious and successful start, he lived for most of his long life under considerable duress. While there is a general reluctance to emphasise the impact of Joseph Stalin on him, my own view is that Shostakovich stopped writing operas because he was so humiliated by the dictator. Even though he was a natural composer for the theatre, he felt repressed and inhibited by the regime. Had Stalin not affected him so badly, we would have had five or six operas from him. I have always wondered what went through Shostakovich's mind when he found himself unable to write the operas that he thought he should have written. It's true that he continued to toy with the genre and even started *The Gambler*. While he went on to write some clever film scores and wonderful song cycles, it was the symphony and the string quartet that became his way of communicating.

With the fall of Soviet communism, we have been able to learn more about his circumstances and the impact of Soviet life on him. It has become increasingly clear that his music is full of games, tricks, quotations and themes constructed from people's names. These little

PART SIX: FRENCH, SCANDINAVIAN, CZECH & RUSSIAN MUSIC

gestures and messages help us to understand his music more fully. But, for those who never experienced the Soviet system, it is hard to get under the skin of his music and to understand how to perform it. As so much of it seems militaristic, it is often played too aggressively. No matter how loud it is, and Shostakovich's symphonies are some of the loudest in the repertoire, it is important that his music retains a lyrical quality. While it might be angry, pained or jealous, it must always remain expressive. And it is essential that the orchestra reflects the humanity and soul of the music. A work such as the 'Leningrad' Symphony requires the players to explore their own humanity if they are ever to understand, phrase and colour it successfully. Aside from the repetitive material in the first movement, it must never seem mechanical, cheap or kitschy. But even the relentless repetitive material presents challenges: the orchestra has to remain focussed and must never allow the tension to wane.

RH: Earlier, you said that when you are about to conduct Sibelius's First and Second Symphonies, you feel like you're about to embark on a journey. Do you have a similar sensation before performing a symphony by Shostakovich?

ME: I experience that sensation before conducting any large-scale work. The concept of music as narrative is something that is not discussed nearly enough. It implies a journey from one structural moment to the next within a unified whole. Many great works require that type of treatment and it is precisely the reason why conducting symphonies is so hard. It's about making the journey apparent to the musicians and the audience while not making the climaxes of the first movement more important than those of the last. Beethoven's Fifth Symphony is a wonderful case in point. The first movement is short, volcanic and constructed on one musical idea. The second is a series of variations of great power and beauty within a balanced whole. While the third is disturbed, soft and strange, it is also heroic and contains an uncertain coda that leads the listener inevitably to the finale. If handled correctly and sensitively, the music takes the listener on a journey from the dark, minor key at the opening to the triumphant and fulfilling major at the end.

Whenever one starts a symphony, one should always keep a journey such as that in mind. When I conduct Shostakovich's Fifth Symphony, I attempt to search out the music's personal message rather than any received wisdom about its composition. Shostakovich rarely wrote anything because it was required of him politically. No matter how weak his body eventually became, his musical mind remained as sharp as ever. Following the reception of the Fourth Symphony, he realised that he needed to write something more conventional. So, he wrote a symphony in a more traditional four-movement format, a structure that he considered foolproof. But the content of those four movements was nothing short of remarkable and what he expresses at the end is not victory but defiance. His music needs to be played by succeeding generations and I hope those who will grapple with his scores in the future will do their best to search out the music's true message. But, for each new generation, that message will mean something different. Personally, I have found a great deal in his works to satisfy, fulfil and intrigue me. He is a great composer and I'm always shocked and disheartened when I encounter fellow musicians who fail to acknowledge his importance.

RH: And what of your engagement with Prokofiev?

PART SIX: FRENCH, SCANDINAVIAN, CZECH & RUSSIAN MUSIC

ME: After immersing myself in the music of Shostakovich, Prokofiev's works became less important to me. During the early part of my career, Prokofiev's compositions were more central to my repertoire than they are now and, at the opening of the Sydney Opera House, I conducted *War and Peace*, an opera that I later performed in London and the US. But, as time passed, I almost invariably found Shostakovich's spirit and soul more engaging and more profound than that of Prokofiev. Now, however, I have time for both. Prokofiev's childlike quality, his naivety and his sense of orchestral colour are like no one else. I would love the opportunity to do more of his music. While I don't find him gifted as a creative artist, he is an important composer when discussing the cultural and political histories of Russia during the 20th century. He was an extraordinary man and had many talents apart from composition. The way he writes for the orchestra takes us into a fanciful world, whereas Shostakovich tackles life's big issues.

CODA

RH: As your remarkable career is now moving towards its fifth decade, what events or performances do you look back on fondly, and are there ambitions yet to be fulfilled?

ME: The night that the English National Opera performed in Moscow remains one of the most exciting events of my life. The whole of the ENO took part in the tour and we performed Verdi's *Macbeth* in the Bolshoi Theatre. With its then-new gold paint, the experience was rather overwhelming. It's a marvellous opera house in which to perform and the relationship between the pit and the stage is like no other. The audience had no idea who we were and had no clue what to expect. But they were quickly won over by the power of what we did. Our production really was very theatrical.

While that was a particularly exciting and unforgettable night, there were so many things at the ENO that were special. Our production of Shostakovich's *Lady Macbeth of Mtsensk* also comes to mind. We gave the English premiere of that original, great, magnificent, daring, wild and naughty piece. David Alden's production of Verdi's *Simon Boccanegra* was also a night that I shall never forget. Every time I looked at the stage, there was something that encouraged me to make the music still more powerful. It was a great production and an evening where booing and cheering were heard in equal measure.

Looking to the future, there are still a few operas that I am keen to explore. I would love to conduct Mozart's *Idomeneo*, Berlioz's *Les troyens*, Tchaikovsky's *Iolanta* and *The Enchantress*, Janáček's *The Excursions of Mr. Brouček* and *From the House of the Dead* and Strauss's *Die Frau ohne Schatten*. I am also looking forward to my future with my wonderful orchestra in Manchester. The Hallé continues to play with great passion and diligence and I really can't ask for anything more. But being able to continue to communicate with an audience is by far the most important thing for me as a performing musician. That's where my responsibility begins and ends. As a conductor, all I think of is empowering the players to communicate and to change hearts and lives. That means the bar has to be placed high but, unless the bar *is* high, there is little point to what we do.

INDEX

Abbado, Claudio, 116
Abruzzo, 155
Adorno, Theodor, 155
Albert Memorial, 88
Aldeburgh, 146
Alden, David, 166
America, United States of, 22, 35, 46–47, 50–51, 53, 54, 58, 65, 68, 69, 82, 87, 89, 112, 139, 142, 147, 156, 163
Arts Council England, 101 Atlanta (Georgia), 139
Atlanta Symphony Orchestra, 139
Australia, xi–xiii, 18, 39, 124, 125, 160, 163
Australian Opera, 11–12
Austria, 14, 40, 47, 87, 96, 120, 125

Bach, Johann Sebastian, 75, 82, 83, 84, 86–87; St John Passion, 86; Fantasia and Fugue in C minor (orch. Elgar), 87–88

Baker, Janet, 6–7, 137
Barbican (London), 92
Barbirolli, Evelyn, 28
Barbirolli, John, 25, 26, 27, 28, 38, 53, 64, 68–69, 71, 140, 155
Bardon, Patricia, 137
Bartók, Béla, 58–59, 159; Concerto for Orchestra, 58–59; *Bluebeard's Castle*, 58–59
Battle for Music, 53
Bax, Arnold, 139; *Spring Fire*, 139
Bayreuth, 94, 142
Bayreuth *Festspielhaus*, 94–95
BBC Philharmonic, 114
BBC Promenade Concerts (Proms), 34, 40, 46, 58
BBC Symphony Orchestra, 22, 58, 139
Beecham, Thomas, 53, 54, 85–86, 155
Beethoven, Ludwig van, 5, 15, 33, 59, 76–78, 80–81, 89–90, 101, 107, 108, 110, 155, 156, 161; Symphony No. 3

('Eroica'), 81; Symphony No. 4, 5
Symphony No. 5, 59, 161; Symphony
   No. 7, 33, 90, 91, 110; Symphony No. 8,
   90 Symphony No. 9 ('Choral'), 75;
   Fidelio, 15, 91; Septet, 109
Belgium, 143
Bellini, Vincenzo, 101, 119–120, 121, 122
Berg, Alban, 115–116; *Wozzeck*, 115–116
Bergamo, 121
Berglund, Paavo, 128
Berlin, 15–17, 37, 42, 145, 146
Berlin Philharmonic, 37, 71
Berlin Wall, 17
Berlioz, Hector, 36, 49, 60, 79, 153–154,
   135; *Rob Roy* Overture, 36; *Roméo et
   Juliette*, 153; *Benvenuto Cellini*, 154;
   La damnation de Faust, 154; *Les
   troyens*, 166
Bernstein, Leonard, 154
Birmingham, 135
Blumen, Alfred, 53
Bohemia, 158
Böhm, Karl, 88
Bologna, 15
Bolshoi Theatre (Moscow), 166
Boulez, Pierre, 70, 116
Boult, Adrian, 53, 138
Brahms, Johannes, 47, 78, 79, 84, 103,
   104, 110–112; Violin Concerto, 103;
   Symphony No. 1, 110–111; Symphony
   No. 2, 111–112; Symphony No. 3, 110;
   Symphony No. 4, 110, 111
Bridgewater Hall (Manchester), 38, 46,
   60, 65, 105
Brighton, 140
Brighton Dome, 140

British Broadcasting Corporation
   (BBC), 15
British National Opera Company, 64
Britten, Benjamin, 2–3, 145–150; *A
   Ceremony of Carols*, 2–3; 'In Freezing
   Winter Night' from *A Ceremony of
   Carols*, 2–3; *Albert Herring*, 145–146,
   149; *Peter Grimes*, 146, 148, 149;
   Spring Symphony, 146–147 *Billy
   Budd*, 148–149, 150; *The Rape of
   Lucretia*, 148, 149, 150; *The Turn of
   the Screw*, 149; as conductor,
   146–147
Britten Sinfonia, 110
Bryanston School, 3
Bülow, Hans von, 35, 41, 42
Busch, Fritz, 8, 87
Butt, Clara, 137

Caine, Uri, 114 *Scenes from Childhood*,
   114
California, 42
Cambridge, University of, 3–6, 72, 145,
   146
Cameron, Basil, 53
Canterbury Cathedral, 2–3
Canterbury Cathedral Chapter House,
   2–3
Cardiff, 83–84
Cavalli, Francesco, 7; *La calisto*, 7
Chausson, Ernest, 144–145; *Poème*, 144
Chicago Symphony Orchestra, 55, 58,
   83, 139
City of Birmingham Symphony
   Orchestra, 22
Clarke, Oz, 2
Cleveland Orchestra, The, 64

INDEX

Cologne, 23
Cotswolds, 154
Crabbe, George, 146
Croydon, 157
Crystal Palace, 133
Czech Philharmonic, 55
Czech Republic, 55, 158–159

Davis, Colin, 155
Debussy, Claude, 41, 130, 154; *La mer*, 41
Decca, 108
Delius, Frederick, 159, 143, 143–145, 147
  Sea Drift, 143, 145, 147 *A Song of the High Hills*, 145
deSingel (Antwerp), 38
Donizetti, Gaetano, 49, 121–123, 126
  Les martyrs, 121–122; 'Una furtiva lagrima' from *L'elisir d'amore*, 122
Dordogne, 154
Downes, Edward (Ted), 10, 13, 125
Downes, Joan, 10
Dresden, 52, 92
Düsseldorf, 87
Dutilleux, Henri, 154
Dvořák, Antonín, 41, 66, 107, 157–158
  Symphony No. 3, 158; Symphony No. 5, 158; Symphony No. 6, 157; Symphony No. 7, 66; Symphony No. 8, 66; Symphony No. 9 ('From the New World'), 66

Elder, Mark, singing as a child and activities as a chorister, 1–2, 7; recording debut as a chorister, 1–2; Bryanston School, 3–4; student at the University of Cambridge, 3–6, 72, 145, 146; choosing a conservatoire or university as an aspiring musician, 4; first attempts at conducting, 3–4; beating time with the left hand, 3–4; conducting an opera for the first time, 4; as a bassoonist, 4–5, 54, 55, 145, 146; as a pianist, 4; as a harpsichordist, 4; as an actor, 4–5; first experiences of opera, 5; interest in languages, 5; first concert as a conductor, 5; first paying engagement as a conductor, 6; acting as a super at Glyndebourne, 6; attending an opera for the first time, 7; early impressions of the art and craft of theatre, 7; thoughts on assisted suicide, 10–11; performing at the Sydney Opera House, 12–13; conducting an opera professionally for the first time, 11, 125; Music Director of the English National Opera, 12–13, 17–20, 149–150, 165; working in East Berlin, 14–16; encounters with Joachim Herz, 14–15 working in German for the first time, 15; the Berlin Wall, 15; life in East and West Berlin, 16; the opera house as a place for discussion and disagreement, 16–17; importance of theatre and music in society, 16–17, 22, 91, 97–99, 104–106, 124; English National Opera's financial difficulties, 18; restructuring the Orchestra of the English National Opera, 18–20; Music Director of the Rochester Philharmonic Orchestra, 20; music and education, 20–23;

music as entertainment, 20–23; Music Director of the Hallé, 26–28, 37–38, 46, 47–48, 55, 56, 57, 59–60, 65–66, 85–87, 111–112, 113–114, 144–145, 165–166 Hallé's financial difficulties, 26; Hallé audiences, 26, 36, 37–39 Hallé's record label, 26–27; young conductors, 39–40, 41–42, 46–47, 61, 63, 66–67, 68–71, 71–72, 81–82, 83–84, 124, 157–158 proposed new London concert hall, 39; Opera Rara, 121–123

Britishness and Englishness in music, 133, 141–144 response of foreign audiences and orchestras to British music, 88, 139–141, 145–146, 147; British music within a European context, 142–144, 145–146

On performance and conducting: thoughts on balance, 3, 8, 68, 78–79, 93, 94, 101–102, 127, 161–162 conductors and singing, 3; using a baton, 4, 45–46; importance of feeling at home on the podium as a young conductor, 5, 62; need for courage and strength of purpose as a young conductor, 5, 29, 62–64, 69–71, 71–72 studying scores, 5–6, 31, 32, 41–44, 66–68, 82, 105, 106, 107–108, 136 importance of Glyndebourne for young musicians, 6–9; Glyndebourne and tradition, 6, 9; importance of observing other conductors at work, 7–9, 60, 61, 70; the skill and importance of listening, 9, 23, 25, 31–34, 44, 46, 57–58, 69–70, 71, 102, 109, 110, 124–125; working with singers, 9–10, 44, 49–50, 98, 100–102, 106, 107–108, 115, 119–121, 125, 129–130, 127–128 need for detail, 9, 85–86, 102, 128–130, 153–154; opera in the vernacular, 13–14, 16, 97–98, 101, 125–127, 147–149, 158–159; opera in the United Kingdom, 13–14, 16, 18–19; responses of audiences, 14–15, 23, 25, 34, 36, 37–41, 46, 88, 90, 91–92, 94, 97, 101–102, 104, 105, 110, 112, 114, 128–129, 134, 139–144, 145–147, 124, 150, 157–158, 165–166; modern production style, 15–18, 94–95, 145–146 London Coliseum's acoustic qualities, 16 forms of beauty, 16, 47, 52, 5,5 78, 80, 85, 86 87–88, 112, 120–121, 141–142, 143, 149, 158, 162; importance of working abroad for young conductors, 17; orchestral players' deputy system, 19; young audiences, 22–23, 37–38; concert clothes, 37–38; talking to audiences, 25, 32–33, 46, 47, 139–140, 142; conducting and inspiration, 26, 28, 46; conducting technique, 26, 32–33, 44–47, 58–59, 60–63, 71, 82, 102, 108, 124–125; transforming the Hallé sound, 25–26, 48–49, 56; woodwind technique, 55–56, 122; string technique, 25, 55, 56–59, 85, 103–105, 110–111, 112–113, 138, 157–158; definition of a successful conductor, 31–35; essence of conducting, 31; impact and importance of reviews, 33; rehearsal technique, pacing and management, 33, 59–62; conducting and the solar

INDEX

plexus, 33; comparing the art and craft of conducting, 34, 45, 69–70; conductors and integrity, 34; symphonic music as narrative, 34, 155–156; conductors' critical, ethical, moral and political responsibilities, 34–35; programming, 36–39, 48, 50–51 66–68, 69–71, 157; new music, 35, 36, 114; budgeting, 37–41; performance spaces, 38, 39, 90, 150, 165–166; public subsidy of music and the arts, 40–41; conducting from memory, 41–44; prompting operas, 43–44; tempi in German operas, 44; conductors and multimedia, 46–47; performance practice, 47–57, 75–86, 88–90, 100–105, 110–113, 127–128; period performance and period performance orchestras, 47–50 60–61, 77–80 82–83, 85–87, 102–105, 127–128; sound-worlds of individual orchestras and players, 49–50 50–54, 55–57, 59–60, 75–77, 78 82–84, 89–90, 103–105, 127–128; vibrato and portamento, 48, 51, 55–56, 83, 103–104, 128; national styles of orchestral playing, 51–56, 59–60; working with America orchestras, 50–51; orchestral seating, disposition and size, 52–53, 90; placement of the piano for concertos, 53–54; rehearsal technique, 55–57; intonation, 57, 61; rhythmic control, 59; ability to be solitary as a conductor, 62–63; maximising orchestral players' potential, 64; the role of the music director, 65–67; challenges of conducting London's self-governing orchestras, 66; advice to young conductors when accepting an engagement, 66–70 157–158; working with stage directors, 68; conducting courses, 68–70; orchestral players and other jobbing musicians becoming conductors, 71–72; German opera-house system, 72; agents and managers, 72; conducting competitions, 72–73; content in German music, 75–77, 112–115; retouching orchestrations, 75–81; sound recordings and films as performance models, 81–82, 140–142; composer-conductors, 81–82; transcriptions, 85–86, 87–88; essence of operatic composition, 91, 92, 93; *bel canto*, 100–101, , 119–121; *Melos*, 101–102; *espressivo* and expressiveness, 103–105; *dolce*, 103–104; tempo flexibility and modification, 103–105, 109, 110, 111 128–130; concert performances of opera, 106–109; *Sprechstimme*, 115–116; music and language, 153–155, 158–160

On composers: Bach, 75, 82, 83, 84, 86–87; Bartók, 58–59, 159; Bax, 139; Beethoven, 5, 15, 33, 59, 76–78, 80–81, 89–90, 101, 107, 108, 110, 155, 156, 161; Bellini, 101, 119–120, 121, 122; Berg, 115–116; Berlioz, 36, 49, 60, 79, 153–154, 135; Brahms, 47, 78, 79, 84, 103, 104, 110–112; Britten, 2–3, 145–150; Caine, 114; Cavalli, 7; Chausson, 144–145; Debussy, 41,

130, 154; Delius, 159, 143, 143–145, 147; Donizetti, 49, 121–123, 126; Dutilleux, 154; Dvořák, 41, 66, 107, 157–158; Elgar, 27–28, 34–35, 41–42, 52, 53, 58–59, 85, 86–87, 104–105, 133–141, 142; Grieg, 53–54; Handel, 75, 85–86, 87; Haydn, 48, 84, 88–89; Holst, 143; Ives, 51; Janáček, 143, 147–148, 158–159, 166; Lloyd Webber, 2; Mahler, 5, 38, 52, 56, 104, 113–115, 120, 140, 143; Mascagni, 106, 129; Mendelssohn, 49, 79, 93; Messiaen, 154; Mozart, 8, 9, 11, 22, 37, 47–48, 70, 77, 83, 86–87, 88–89, 103, 122, 140, 150, 166; Palestrina, 156; Prokofiev, 11, 162–163; Puccini, 16–17, 110, 123, 128–130; Purcell, 133; Rachmaninov, 48, 53, 84; Rameau, 154; Ravel, 130, 142, 143, 154; Rossini, 43, 110, 119–123, 150; Scarlatti (Alessandro), 4; Schoenberg, 116; Schubert, 92–93, 109, 158; Schumann, 77–81, 84; Shostakovich, 35, 55, 122, 160–161, 162–163; Sibelius, 34, 41, 52, 113, 128, 155–156, 161; Smetana, 95, 158; Strauss, 8, 42, 44, 53, 54, 87–88, 108, 115, 166; Stravinsky, 48, 70, 81–82, 101; Tchaikovsky, 14, 54–55, 166; Vaughan Williams, 139, 141–144; Verdi, 11, 14, 15, 21, 41, 46, 49, 50, 91, 94, 101, 120, 122–128, 147, 148, 149, 150; Wagner, 12, 38, 77, 79, 91–102, 105–109, 127, 128, 141, 147, 148–149; Watkins, 36; Weber, 90–93

Elgar, Edward, 27–28, 34–35, 41–42, 52, 53, 58–59, 85, 86–87, 104–105, 133–141, 142; 'Pomp and Circumstance' Marches, 34–35, 58–59, 139–140; 'Pomp and Circumstance' March No. 1, 34–35, 58–59 'Enigma' Variations, 41–42, 139–140 Variation IX ('Nimrod') from 'Enigma' Variations, 143 *Sea Pictures*, 137 Cello Concerto, 139–140; *In the South*, 140–141 Symphony No. 1, 134, 138–139, 140, 141–142 Symphony No. 2, 104, 138–140, 140; *The Dream of Gerontius*, 85, 86–87, 134–137, 137, 138 *The Apostles*, 134–137, 138; *The Kingdom*, 134–137 religious content in sacred works, 134–138 impact of Wagner, 142

English National Opera (ENO), 13–15, 16–17, 20–22, 39–40, 61–62, 150, 165–166

English National Opera, Orchestra of the, 20–22, 61–62

Evans, Anne, 98, 100–101

Fairfield Halls (Croydon), 157–158
Ferrier, Kathleen, 137
Finland, 155–157
First World War, 143–144
Forster, Edward Morgan (E.M.), 148
France, 14, 121, 122, 129–130, 143–144, 153–154
Free Trade Hall (Manchester), 38–39
Freni, Mirella, 102
Friedrich, Götz, 15
Furtwängler, Wilhelm, 80, 89–90

Gardini, Ubaldo, 9
Garmisch-Partenkirchen, 44, 87–88

INDEX

Germany, 14, 15–18, 121, 23, 32, 37–38, 40, 41–42, 43–44, 52, 71–72, 86, 87, 91, 92, 93–94, 108, 112, 141, 142, 141, 142, 156–157
Giulini, Carlo Maria, 65, 123
Gloucestershire, 143
Glyndebourne Festival Opera, 6–9, 50, 87, 127–128, 149, 150
Glyndebourne Festival Opera Chorus, 6
Goossens, Eugene, 85
Great Britain, United Kingdom of, 9, 13, 14, 16, 19–27, 32, 33, 34, 35, 37–41, 43–47, 50, 51, 52, 53, 59, 60 64, 65, 69–73, 80–81 83–88, 91–92, 97–98, 108, 109, 114, 115, 121, 122, 127, 133, 132, 138, 139, 141–145, 146, 150, 153, 157–158, 163, 165
Grieg, Edvard, 53–54; Concerto for Piano and Orchestra, 53
Groves, Charles, 13, 39
Gui, Vittorio, 7
Gulf War (1990–1991), 34–35

Hagen, 143
Hallé, 5, 23–28, 46–48, 52, 55–58, 60, 65, 70, 71, 103–104, 109, 112–114, 143–144, 165–166
Hallé, Charles, 24, 143
Hallé Choir, 86
Handel, George Frideric, 75, 85–86, 87; *Messiah* (orch. Goossens), 85–86; *Messiah* (orch. Mozart), 86–87
Harewood, George (Earl of), 13
Harty, Hamilton, 38
Haydn, Joseph, 48, 84, 88–89; *Die Schöpfung*, 89; *Die Jahreszeiten*, 89

Helsinki, 156
Herz, Joachim, 15–17, 146
Hitler, Adolf, 100
Hofmannsthal, Hugo von, 44
Hollywood, 156
Holst, Gustav, 143
Hope, Bob, 23
Houston, 53
Hungary, 158–159

Italy, 14–15, 40–41, 75, 85, 110, 119–124, 126, 128–129, 153–157
Ives, Charles, 51

Janáček, Leoš, 143, 147–148, 158–159, 166; *Káťa Kabanová*, 160; *The Excursions of Mr. Brouček*, 166; *From the House of the Dead*, 166
Jesus Christ, 136
Joachim, Joseph, 103
Jonas, Peter, 18, 22
Jones, Gwyneth, 98
Joyce, Eileen, 53
Jurowski, Vladimir, 39

Karajan, Herbert von, 45, 47, 77, 80, 88
Karlsruhe, 111
Katchen, Julius, 53
Kerman, Joseph, 128
Kleiber, Carlos, 33, 42
Klemperer, Otto, 42, 80
Kobbé, Gustav, 87
Komische Oper (East Berlin), 15–18
Korchinska, Maria, 2

Lambert, Constant, 53
Lamoureux, Charles, 54

Leipzig, 37, 41–42
Leipzig Conservatoire, 41
Leipzig Gewandhaus Orchestra, 37
Leppard, Raymond, 7
Lille, 153
Lloyd Webber, Andrew, 2; *Evita*, 2
Loach, Ken, 35; *I, Daniel Blake*, 35
London, 10, 13–18, 18–21, 33, 34, 37–40, 43, 59, 60, 63–64, 65–66, 69–70, 92, 97–98, 109–110, 115–116, 121–123, 133, 138, 150, 163, 165
London Coliseum, 14, 15, 16, 18–21, 38, 39, 97, 150
London Mozart Players, 22
London Philharmonic Orchestra (LPO), 32, 39, 50, 53–54, 59, 138–139, 140
London Symphony Orchestra, 33, 66, 78
Los Angeles Philharmonic, 65

Maazel, Lorin, 43, 155
Mackerras, Charles, 55, 61, 71, 100, 110, 159
Mahler, Gustav, 5, 38, 52, 56, 104, 113–115, 120, 140, 143; *Lieder eines fahrenden Gesellen*, 5; Symphony No. 2 ('Resurrection'), 114; Symphony No. 3, 56, 114, 143; Symphony No. 5, 38, 114; Symphony No. 6, 140; Symphony No. 7, 114; Symphony No. 8 ('Symphony of a Thousand'), 114; Symphony No. 9, 114
Manchester, 23–24, 26–28, 36, 37–39, 44, 45, 51, 52, 53, 64, 70, 71, 86, 105, 106, 109, 114, 139, 144, 166

Mascagni, Pietro, 106, 129; *Cavalleria rusticana*, 106
Mattila, Karita, 116
Mayfair, 123
Mayr, Simone, 122
Meiningen, 111
Melbourne, 11, 124–125
Mendelssohn, Felix, 49, 79, 93; Symphony No. 4 ('Italian'), 93
Messel, Oliver, 7
Messiaen, Olivier, 154
Metro-Goldwyn-Mayer Studios Inc. (MGM), 22
Milan, 126
Moiseiwitsch, Benno, 53
Moravia, 158–159
Moscow, 165
Mozart, Wolfgang Amadeus, 8, 9, 11, 22, 37, 47–48, 70, 77, 83, 86–87, 88–89, 103, 122, 140, 150, 166; *Idomeneo*, 166; *Le nozze di Figaro*, 7, 47; *Don Giovanni*, 7; *Così fan tutte*, 87, 88; *Die Zauberflöte*, 11, 23; Requiem, 89; Symphony No. 36 ('Linz'), 103; Symphony No. 41 ('Jupiter'), 87
Mueller, Otto-Werner, 69
Munich, 21, 44, 145–146
Musicians' Union, 20
Muti, Riccardo, 88

Naples, 121
Newman, John Henry (Cardinal), 135
New South Wales government, 12
New York, 38, 51, 68, 69, 89, 156
New York Daily Telegraph, The, 87
New York Philharmonic Orchestra, 51, 87
Nikisch, Arthur, 37

INDEX

Nordica, Lillian, 100
Norway, 145

Opera Rara, 121–122
Orchestra of the Age of Enlightenment (OAE), 49–50, 60, 78–80, 103, 127–128

Paddington, 133
Palestrina, Giovanni Pierluigi de, 156
Paris, 14, 121, 122–123, 129, 154
Paris Opéra, 155
Pavarotti, Luciano, 102
Philadelphia Orchestra, The, 52
  'Philadelphia Sound', 52
Philharmonia Orchestra, 42
Pickett, Steve, 23
Pont, Rebecca de, 137
Pountney, David, 4, 18–19
Prague, 55
Premiere Ensemble, 70
Prinzregententheater (Munich), 44
Pritchard, John, 6–7, 71, 87, 140
Procter, Norma, 137
Prokofiev, Sergei, 11, 162–163; *War and Peace*, 11, 162–163
Puccini, Giacomo, 16–17, 110, 123, 128–130; *Madama Butterfly*, 16–17; *La bohème*, 31, 129; *Tosca*, 128
Purcell, Henry, 133

Queen's Hall (London), 40, 54
Queen's Hall Orchestra, 54

Rachmaninov, Sergei, 48, 53, 841; Symphony No. 3, 48; Concerto for Piano and Orchestra No. 2, 53

Rameau, Jean-Philippe, 154
Rattle, Simon, 49
Ravel, Maurice, 130, 142, 143, 154; Piano Concerto for the Left Hand, 143
Residenztheater (Munich), 145
Richter, Hans, 38, 70
Rochester, 22, 46, 50
Rochester Philharmonic Orchestra, 22, 46–47
Rome, 155
Rossini, Gioachino, 43, 110, 119–123, 150; *La cenerentola*, 7
Royal Academy of Music, 59–60, 64, 69–70, 138
Royal Albert Hall, 46, 53, 59, 88
Royal Festival Hall, 33, 34, 59–60, 121
Royal National Theatre, 19
Royal Northern College of Music, 37
Royal Opera House, Covent Garden, 10, 12, 13, 14, 38, 92, 115, 123
Royal Opera House, Covent Garden, Orchestra of the, 109
Royal Philharmonic Orchestra, 157
Rubinstein, Arthur, 53
Rundfunkchor Berlin, 145
Russia, 54, 55, 163

Sachs, Harvey, 59
Sadler's Wells Opera Company, 20
Sadler's Wells Opera Company, Orchestra of the, 20
Salzburg, 47, 88
Salzburg Festival, 47, 88
San Diego, 142
Sargent, Malcolm, 53
Sawallisch, Wolfgang, 45, 52, 80

175

Scarlatti, Alessandro, 4; *Il trionfo dell'onore*, 4
Schnabel, Artur, 86
Schoenberg, Arnold, 116
Schubert, Franz, 92–93, 109, 158; Symphony No. 4, 93; String Quintet, 109
Schumann, Robert, 77–81, 84, ; Symphony No. 2, 78; overture to *Genoveva*, 79; overture to *Manfred*, 79
Scottish Chamber Orchestra, 110
Second World War, 26, 36, 40, 80, 124
Shakespeare, William, 23; *Hamlet*, 23
Shaw, George Bernard, 99
Shirley-Quirk, John, 145
Shostakovich, Dmitri, 35, 55, 122, 160–161, 162–163; *The Gambler*, 160; Symphony No. 4, 162; Symphony No. 5, 162; Symphony No. 7 ('Leningrad'), 161; *Lady Macbeth of Mtsensk*, 165
Sibelius, Jean, 34, 41, 52, 113, 128, 155–156, 161; Symphony No. 1, 34, 41, 113, 161; Symphony No. 2, 34, 113, 161; Symphony No. 3, 156; Symphony No. 6, 113, 156; Symphony No. 7, 113
Smetana, Bedřich, 95, 158
Snape Maltings, 145
Solti, Georg, 44, 58–59, 108, 125, 138
Speakers' Corner, 35
Stalin, Joseph, 160
Steffens, Karl-Heinz, 71
Stokes, Richard, 97
Stokowski, Leopold, 52, 53, 54
Strasser, Jani, 9–10

Strauss, Richard, 8, 42, 44, 53, 54, 87–88, 108, 115, 166; *Burleske*, 53; *Salome*, 15; *Der Rosenkavalier*, 42–44, 115; *Die Frau ohne Schatten*, 166
Stravinsky, Igor, 48, 70, 81–82, 101; *Le sacre du printemps*, 38, 80
Suffolk, 145, 146
Sydney, 10–12, 18, 160, 163
Sydney Opera House, 10–12, 163
Szell, George, 64, 78

Tadolini, Eugenia, 120
Tchaikovsky, Pyotr Ilyich, 14, 54–55, 166; *Mazeppa*, 14; 'Hopak' from *Mazeppa*, 14; *Iolanta*, 166; *The Enchantress*, 166; Symphony No. 3, 54
Teatro alla Scala (Milan), 126
Tennstedt, Klaus, 32, 39
Torrey Pines State National Reserve, 142
Tuscany, 154

Union of Soviet Socialist Republics (USSR), 160–161
Upper Norwood, 133
Utzon, Jørn, 12

Vaughan Williams, Ralph, 139, 141–144; Symphony No. 1 ('A Sea Symphony'), 139; Symphony No. 3 ('A Pastoral Symphony'), 143; *Fantasia on a Theme by Thomas Tallis*, 139; *The Lark Ascending*, 139; use of folk songs, 141–144

INDEX

Verdi, Giuseppe, 11, 14, 15, 21, 41, 46, 49, 50, 91, 94, 101, 120, 122–128, 147, 148, 149, 150; *Nabucco*, 126; *Macbeth*, 120, 165; *Rigoletto*, 43, 124–125, 127; 'Caro nome' from *Rigoletto*, 125; *Il trovatore*, 127; *La traviata*, 15, 21, 124, 127; Prelude to Act 1 of *La traviata*, 15; *Simon Boccanegra*, 14, 150, 166; *Don Carlos*, 123; *Otello*, 127, 150; *Falstaff*, 50, 127–128; Requiem, 46, 127; in the vernacular, 125–126, 147
Vienna, 40, 96, 120, 125
Vienna Philharmonic, 108, 111
Vienna Staatsoper, 40

Wagner, Richard, 12, 38, 77, 79, 91–102, 105–109, 127, 128, 141, 147, 148–149; *Rienzi*, 100; *Der fliegende Holländer*, 99–100; *Tannhäuser*, 99, 100, 148; *Lohengrin*, 91, 100, 148–149; *Tristan und Isolde*, 96, 105, 106, 128; Act 1 of *Tristan und Isolde*, 106; 'Liebestod' from *Tristan und Isolde*, 100; *Die Meistersinger von Nürnberg*, 12, 105–106; Act 3 of *Die Meistersinger von Nürnberg*, 105–106; *Der Ring des Nibelungen*, 39, 95, 97–99, 101, 105, 106, 108, 149; *Das Rheingold*, 38, 45, 46; *Die Walküre*, 96, 98, 106; 'Wintersturme' from *Die Walküre*, 96; *Siegfried*, 98; *Götterdämmerung*, 35, 98, 107, 109; *Parsifal*, 46, 97, 125, 141 *Trauermusik nach Motiven von Euryanthe*, 91–92; *Gesamtkunstwerk*, 94–95; Wagner as librettist and use of *Stabreim*, 95–96; Wagner and eroticism, 96; personality, 96–97; in the vernacular, 97–98, 101, 147; performing Brünnhilde, 98; meaning of *Der Ring des Nibelungen*, 99; prose works, 99; Italian influences, 100–104; *Melos*, 101–102; difficulty for singers, 107–108; 'Wagner sound', 108–109
Walter, Bruno, 33, 41, 52, 62, 67, 78–79, 103; *Theme and Variations*, 62; *Of Music and Music-making*, 77
Washington, 52
Watkins, Huw, 36; Symphony, 36
Watts, Helen, 137
Weber, Carl Maria von, 90–93; *Der Freischütz*, 90–92; *Euryanthe*, 91–92; *Oberon*, 91–92
Weber, Max von, 92
Weingartner, Felix, 41
Wigglesworth, Mark, 69–70, 71
Willcocks, David, 145, 146
Williams, Roderick, 145
Wood, Henry, 25, 52, 53–54, 76, 155
Worcester, 133, 143
Worcestershire, 134
Yeomans, John, 12; *The Other Taj Mahal*, 12

177